# PREFACE

In dealing with the Septuagint in and for itself we feel that we are in a humble way acting as pioneers. For hitherto the Septuagint has been regarded only as an aid to the understanding of the Hebrew. We have reversed that procedure and have regarded the Hebrew only as an aid to the understanding of the Septuagint. This would be in a strict sense preposterous, were it not for the admitted fact that the Greek translation of the Old Testament has occasionally preserved traces of readings which are manifestly superior to those of the Massoretic text. That text, it should be remembered, was constituted centuries after the Septuagint was already in vogue in the Greek-speaking portion of the Jewish and Christian world.

For permission to use Dr. Swete's text we beg to offer our respectful thanks to the Syndics of the Cambridge Pitt Press and to Dr. Swete himself. To our own university also we owe a debt of gratitude. The Concordance to the Septuagint, edited by Dr. Hatch and Dr. Redpath, is a magnificent work worthy of a university press. Without this aid it would be impossible to speak, with the precision demanded by modern scholarship, about the usage of words in the Septuagint. It is greatly to be regretted that the list of contributors to this work should somehow have got lost owing to the lamented death of Dr. Edwin Hatch. The labour of many good men, such as the Rev. W. H. Seddon, now Vicar of Painswick, and the Rev. Osmond Archer, to name two who happen to fall under our own knowledge, has thus been left without acknowledgement. They toiled silently for the advancement of learning, like the coral insects who play their part beneath the waters in rearing a fair island for the abode of man.

No one can well touch on Old Testament studies without being indebted to Professor Driver, but our obligations in that and other directions have been acknowledged in the body of the work.

In composing the Grammar of Septuagint Greek we have had before us as a model Dr. Swete's short chapter on that subject in his Introduction to the Septuagint. Help has also been derived from the grammars of New Testament Greek by Winer and by Blass, and from the great historical grammar of the Greek language by Jannaris. But in the main our work in that department is the direct result of our own observation.

To come now to more personal debts, our common friend, Walter Scott, sometime Professor of Greek in the University of Sydney, not merely gave us the benefit of his critical judgement in the early stages of the work, but directly contributed to the subject-matter. We have accepted his aid as freely as it was offered. No Higher Critic is likely to trouble himself about disentangling the different strands of authorship in our Introductions and Notes. Still, if anyone should be tempted to exercise his wits in that direction by way of practice for the Pentateuch, we will give him one clue : If anything should strike him as being not merely sound but brilliant, he may confidently set it down to this third source.

To the Rev. Samuel Holmes, M.A., Kennicott Scholar in the University of Oxford, our thanks are due for guarding us against mistakes in relation to the Hebrew : but he is not to be held responsible for any weakness that may be detected in that direction.

It remains now only to express our sincere gratitude to Professor Thomas D. Seymour for his vigilant and scholarly care of our work during its passage through the press ; and to tender our thanks to Messrs. Ginn & Company for extending their patronage to a book produced in the old country. May the United Kingdom and the United States ever form a Republic of Letters one and indivisible !

OXFORD,
May 22, 1905.

# TABLE OF CONTENTS

# INTRODUCTION

The work of the Bible Society may be said to have been begun at Alexandria under the Ptolemies: for there the first translation of the Bible, so far as it then existed, was made.

Under the old kings of Egypt there was no city on the site of Alexandria, but only a coast-guard station for the exclusion of foreigners, and a few scattered huts of herdsmen. These monarchs had no enlightened appreciation of the benefits of commerce, and cherished a profound distrust of strangers, especially of Greeks, whom they regarded as land-grabbers.[1] But when the Greeks knocked at the doors of Egypt in a way that admitted of no refusal, the lonely coast-guard station saw a great change come over itself. Founded by Alexander the Great in B.C. 331, Alexandria became the capital of the new Greek kingdom of Egypt and took its place as a great centre both of commerce and of literature, the rival of Carthage in the one, of Athens in the other.

Alexander is credited with having perceived the advantages of situation which conferred upon Alexandria its rapid rise to prosperity. With the Mediterranean on the north and Lake Mareia or Mareotis on the south, it received the products of the inland, which came down the Nile and were conveyed into the lake by canal-boats, and then exported them from its harbours. Under the Romans it became of still greater commercial importance as the emporium of the trade then developed between the East and the West, of which it had a practical monopoly.

The vicinity of sea and lake had advantages also in the way of health: for in the summer the etesian winds set in from the north, and the lake, instead of stagnating, was kept full and sweet by the

---

[1] Strabo XVII § 6, p. 792 πορθηταὶ γὰρ ἦσαν καὶ ἐπιθυμηταὶ τῆς ἀλλοτρίας κατὰ σπάνιν γῆς.

1

rise of the Nile at that season. The kings too by their successive enclosures secured those breathing-places which are so necessary for the health of a great city. It is estimated by Strabo that a quarter, or even a third, of the whole area was occupied by parks and palaces.

Among the royal buildings was the famous Museum with its covered walk and arcades, and its hall for the "fellows" of the Museum, as Professor Mahaffy aptly calls them, to dine in.[1] This institution had endowments of its own, and was presided over by a priest, who was appointed by the King, and, at a later period, by the Emperor.

What relation, if any, the Alexandrian Library, which was the great glory of the Ptolemies, bore to the Museum, is not clear. The Museum stood there in Roman times, and became known as "the old Museum," when the emperor Claudius reared a new structure by its side, and ordained that his own immortal histories of the Etruscans and Carthaginians should be publicly read aloud once every year, one in the old building and the other in the new (Suet. *Claud.* 42). The library however is related to have been burnt during Cæsar's operations in Alexandria. Not a word is said on this subject by the historian of the Alexandrian War, but Seneca[2] incidentally refers to the loss of 400,000 volumes.

The inhabitants of Alexandria are described by Polybius, who visited the city under the reign of the second Euergetes, commonly known as Physcon (B.C. 146–117), as falling into three classes. There were first the native Egyptians, whom he describes as intelligent and civilised; secondly the mercenary soldiers, who were many and unmannerly; and thirdly the Alexandrian citizens, who were better behaved than the military element, for though of mixed origin they were mainly of Greek blood.[3]

Polybius makes no mention of Jews in Alexandria, but we know

---

[1] Strabo XVII § 8, p. 794 τῶν δὲ βασιλείων μέρος ἐστὶ καὶ τὸ Μουσεῖον, ἔχον περίπατον καὶ ἐξέδραν καὶ οἶκον μέγαν, ἐν ᾧ τὸ συσσίτιον τῶν μετεχόντων τοῦ Μουσείου φιλολόγων ἀνδρῶν.

[2] *De Tranq. An.* 9 — Quadringenta millia librorum Alexandriæ arserunt: pulcherrimum regiæ opulentiæ monumentum. According to Tertullian (*Apol.* 18) the MS. of the translators of the Old Testament was still to be seen in his day in the Serapeum along with the Hebrew original.

[3] Polyb. XXXIV 14, being a fragment quoted by Strabo XVII 1 § 12, p. 797.

from other sources that there was a large colony of that people there. Their presence in Egypt was partly compulsory and partly voluntary. The first Ptolemy, surnamed Soter, who had a long and prosperous reign (B.C. 323–285), had invaded Palestine and captured Jerusalem on the sabbath-day, on which the Jews offered no defence.[1] He carried away with him many captives from the hill-country of Judæa and from the parts about Jerusalem, and also from Samaria. These were all planted in Egypt, where they carried on their quarrel as to which was the true temple, whither yearly offerings should be sent — that at Jerusalem or the one on Gerizim. (Cp. Jn. 4[20].) Soter, recognising the fidelity of the Jew to his oath, employed many of these captives to garrison important posts, and gave them equal citizenship with the Macedonians. This liberal treatment of their countrymen induced many more Jews to immigrate voluntarily into Egypt, in spite of the prohibition in the Mosaic law — "Ye shall henceforth return no more that way" (Dt. 17[16]). There were also Jews in Egypt before this time, who came there under the Persian domination, and others before them who had been sent to fight with Psammetichus (B.C. 671–617) against the king of the Ethiopians (Aristeas § 13). Jeremiah, it will be remembered, was carried perforce by his countrymen into Egypt (Jer. 43[5-7], 44[1]), some of whom may have escaped the destruction which he prophesied against them (Jer. 42[16]). This was shortly after the reign of Psammetichus. Thus the return of the Jews to Egypt was no new thing, and there they again multiplied exceedingly, even as they are recorded to have done at the first. Philo, who was a contemporary of Jesus Christ, but lived into the reign of Claudius, declares that of the five districts of Alexandria, which were named according to the first five letters of the alphabet, two were especially known as Jewish quarters, and that the Jews were not confined to these (Lib. in Flac. § 8, II 525).

With this large Jewish population in Alexandria, whose native language was now Greek, and to whom Hebrew had ceased to be

---

[1] Josephus Ant. XII 1 confirms his statement of this fact by a quotation from Agatharchides of Cnidos, who wrote the history of the successors of Alexander —Ἔστιν ἔθνος Ἰουδαίων λεγόμενον, οἳ πόλιν ὀχυρὰν καὶ μεγάλην ἔχοντες Ἱεροσόλυμα, ταύτην ὑπερεῖδον ὑπὸ Πτολεμαίῳ γενομένην, ὅπλα λαβεῖν οὐ θελήσαντες, ἀλλὰ διὰ τὴν ἄκαιρον δεισιδαιμονίαν χαλεπὸν ὑπέμειναν ἔχειν δεσπότην.

intelligible, we see an obvious reason why the first translation of the Bible should have been made in that city. Arguing *a priori* we should certainly be inclined to assume that it was the necessities of the Alexandrian synagogue that brought about the translation. This however is not the account which has come down to us, and which worked its way into the fabric of Christian belief. That account represents the desire of the second Ptolemy for the completeness of his library, and Pagan curiosity about the sacred books of the Jews, as having been the motives which led to their translation into Greek. It is contained in a letter purporting to be written by one Aristeas to his brother Philocrates.

Aristeas, we gather, was a person of high account at the court of Ptolemy Philadelphus (B.C. 285–247), probably one of the three captains of the royal body-guard, Sosibius of Tarentum and Andreas (§§ 12, 40) being the other two.[1] He was a warm admirer of the Jewish religion, but not himself a Jew by race.[2] Rather we are invited to think of him as a philosophic Pagan interested in the national customs of the Jews (§ 306). On one occasion he was present when King Ptolemy addressed a question to his librarian, Demetrius of Phalerum, the Athenian statesman and philosopher, as to the progress of the library. Demetrius replied that it already contained more than 200,000 volumes, and that he hoped in a short time to bring the number up to 500,000; at the same time he mentioned that there were some books of the Jewish law which it would be worth while to have transcribed and placed in the library. 'Then why not have it done?' said the king. 'You have full powers in the matter.' Demetrius mentioned a difficulty about translation, and the king came to the conclusion that he must write to the High-priest of the Jews in order to have his purpose effected. Hereupon Aristeas seized an opportunity, for which he had long been waiting. He represented to the king that he could hardly with any grace ask a favour of the High-priest while so many of his countrymen were in bondage in Egypt. This suggestion being seconded by silent

---

[1] That Aristeas was himself captain of the body-guard is not stated in the letter, but it is not unnaturally inferred from it by Josephus.

[2] This again, while only implied in the letter, is explicitly stated by Josephus, who makes Aristeas say (*Ant.* XII 2 § 2) Ἴσθι μέντοι γε, ὦ βασιλεῦ, ὡς οὔτε γένει προσήκων αὐτοῖς, οὔτε ὁμόφυλος αὐτῶν ὢν ταῦτα περὶ αὐτῶν ἀξιῶ.

prayer on the part of Aristeas and by the concurrence of Sosibius and Andreas, the result was an immense act of emancipation, by which all the Jewish slaves in Egypt, amounting to over 100,000, regained their freedom, at a cost to the king of more than 660 talents. The way was now clear for the contemplated accession to the library. The king called upon the librarian to send in his report, which is quoted as from the royal archives. In it Demetrius recommended that the king should write to the High-priest at Jerusalem, asking him to send to Egypt six elders from each of the twelve tribes, men of approved life and well versed in their own law, in order that the exact meaning of it might be obtained from the agreement among the majority (§ 32). Not content with his munificence in the redemption of the slaves, the king further displayed his magnificence in the handsome presents he prepared for the Temple, consisting of a table inlaid with precious stones together with gold and silver vessels for the use of the sanctuary.[1] The conduct of the embassy was intrusted to Andreas and to Aristeas himself, who gives his brother an interesting account of the Temple and its services and the magnificent vestments of the High-priest, the conjoint effect of which he declares is enough to convert the heart of any man.[2] Notices are also given of the citadel and of the city and country — its cultivation, its commerce, its harbours, and its population — which in some respects show the temerity of the tourist, for the writer speaks of the Jordan as flowing 'at the country of the Ptolemæans' (§ 117) into another river, which in its turn empties itself into the sea.

The High-priest Eleazar, in compliance with the request of Philadelphus, selected seventy-two venerable elders, six from each tribe, whose names are given, men not only learned in the law, but also skilled in the language and literature of the Greeks,[3] who were to accompany the ambassadors to Egypt on the understanding that they were to be sent back when their work was done. Before their

---

[1] The description of these presents occupies a considerable portion of the letter, §§ 51–82.

[2] § 99 καὶ διαβεβαιοῦμαι πάντα ἄνθρωπον προσελθόντα τῇ θεωρίᾳ τῶν προειρημένων εἰς ἔκπληξιν ἥξειν καὶ θαυμασμὸν ἀδιήγητον, μετατραπέντα τῇ διανοίᾳ διὰ τὴν περὶ ἑκάστην ἁγίαν κατασκευήν.

[3] § 121: cp. Philo *Vita Mosis* II § 6, p. 139.

departure Eleazar held a conversation with his guests, in which he offered a defence of the ceremonial ordinances of the Jewish law, and expounded views on the symbolic meaning of clean and unclean animals, resembling those set forth in the Epistle which goes under the name of Barnabas.

When the deputation arrived in Egypt, the king waived the requirements of court ceremonial and received the elders in audience at once. He first paid reverence to the volume of the law written in letters of gold, which they carried with them, and then extended a welcome to its bearers. After this they were entertained for a week at banquets, at which everything was arranged by a special court functionary in accordance with their own customs, so that there might be nothing to offend their susceptibilities. Elisha, the eldest of the Seventy-two, was asked to say grace, the ordinary court-chaplains being superseded for the occasion. The grace he pronounced was as follows: 'May God almighty fill thee, O King, with all the good things which he hath created; and grant to thee and to thy wife and to thy children and to those who think with thee to have these things without fail all the days of thy life!' (§ 185). The delivery of this benediction was followed by a round of applause and clapping of hands.

The feast of reason was added to the enjoyment of the royal fare. For at a certain point in the proceedings the king addressed questions of a vaguely ethico-political character to the elders, which were answered by them to the admiration of all, especially of the philosophers who had been invited to meet them, among whom was Menedemus of Eretria.[1] Each evening for five days ten elders were interrogated, but on the sixth and seventh evenings eleven were taken, so as to complete the whole number. The questions were elaborated by the king beforehand, but the answers were given impromptu by the elders. The record of them occupies a considerable portion of the letter (§§ 187–294). The law of the answer, if we may so put it, seems to be that each should contain a reference to God and a compliment to the king. We are assured that we have them as they were taken down by the royal recorders.

At the close of this week's festivities an interval of three days

[1] Diog. Laert. II § 140 Ἐπρέσβευσε δὲ καὶ πρὸς Πτολεμαῖον (probably Soter) καὶ Λυσίμαχον.

was allowed, after which the elders were conducted by Demetrius to the island of Pharos, which was connected with the mainland by a dam nearly a mile long[1] and a bridge. At the north end of this island they were lodged in a building overlooking the sea, where they would enjoy absolute quiet. Demetrius then called upon them to perform their work of translation. We have particulars of their habit of life while it was going on. Early in the morning every day they presented themselves at court and, having paid their respects to the king, returned to their own quarters. Then they washed their hands in the sea, offered up a prayer to God, and betook themselves to the task of reading and translating. Their work was harmonized by collation, and the joint result was taken down by Demetrius (§ 302). After the ninth hour they were free to betake themselves to recreation. It so happened, we are told, that the work of transcription was accomplished in seventy-two days, just as though it had been done on purpose (§ 307).

When the whole was finished, Demetrius summoned all the Jews in Alexandria to the island of Pharos, and read the translation aloud to them all in the presence of the interpreters, after which a solemn curse was pronouncéd upon any one who altered it. Then the whole work was read over to the king, who expressed much admiration at the deep insight of the law-giver and asked how it was that historians and poets had combined to ignore his legislation. Demetrius of Phalerum replied that this was because of its sacred character. He had heard from Theopompus[2] that that historian had once wished to avail himself in his history of some inaccurate renderings from the Jewish law, and had suffered from mental disturbance for more than thirty days. In a lucid interval he prayed that it might be revealed to him why he was thus afflicted. Thereupon he was informed in a dream that it was because he had presumed to divulge divine things to 'common' men (§ 315: cp. Acts 10[15]). 'I have also,' added Demetrius, 'received information from Theodectes, the tragic poet,[3] that, when he wished to transfer some of the contents of the

---

[1] § 301 τὸ τῶν ἑπτὰ σταδίων ἀνάχωμα τῆς θαλάσσης: cp. Strabo XVII § 6, p. 792 τῷ ἑπτασταδίῳ καλουμένῳ χώματι.

[2] Theopompus came to Egypt during the reign of Ptolemy Soter.

[3] Theodectes died at the age of forty-one, about B.C. 334, i.e. at least half a century before the time of speaking: but the expression παρὰ Θεοδέκτου . . .

Bible into a play of his own, he found himself suffering from cataract on the eyes, from which he only recovered after a long time, when he had propitiated the god.' On hearing this the king paid reverence to the books, and ordered them to be kept with religious care.

The elders, having now accomplished the work for which they had come, were dismissed by the king with handsome presents both to themselves and to Eleazar, to whom Philadelphus at the same time wrote a letter begging that, if any of the elders purposed to come and see him again, the High-priest would not prevent it.

Such is the traditional account of the origin of the Septuagint, of which we have next to consider the value. But first there are a few points to be noted.

To begin with, we see the reason of the name. The Seventy (Lat. LXX: Gk. οἱ O′) is a round number for the Seventy-two. There were seventy-two interpreters, who took seventy-two days over their work.

Next we see that the name is a misnomer as applied to the Greek version of the Old Testament generally. There is no word in Aristeas as to a translation by the Elders of anything but the Law.[1] But the name, having once been applied to the Greek translation, was gradually extended, as the Prophets and the Books were added in a Greek dress to the Law.

Thirdly we have to notice that in the Letter of Aristeas no claim to inspiration is advanced on behalf of the translators.

That the Bible, as we have it in English, is inspired, has often been tacitly assumed, but seldom laid down as a doctrine. But the inspiration of the Greek version was a point of belief with those who used it, and presumably is so to the present day in the Greek church. Already in Philo we find this claim advanced. He says that the interpreters all agreed in employing exactly the same words, 'as though by the whispering of some unseen prompter'

---

μετέλαβον ἐγώ (§ 316), as contrasted with ἔφησεν ἀκηκοέναι Θεοπόμπου (§ 314), seems to imply that the communication was not direct.

[1] See §§ 30, 38, 309, 312 : Jos. *Ant.* Prooem. § 3 οὐδὲ γὰρ πᾶσαν ἐκεῖνος (sc. Ἐλεάζαρος) ἔφθη λαβεῖν τὴν ἀναγραφὴν, ἀλλ᾽ αὐτὰ μόνα τὰ τοῦ νόμου παρέδοσαν οἱ πεμφθέντες ἐπὶ τὴν ἐξήγησιν εἰς τὴν Ἀλεξάνδρειαν.

(*Vita Mosis* II § 7, II 140), and that a comparison of the original with the translation by those who are acquainted with both tongues will clearly show that they were not mere translators, but inspired hierophants and prophets.

Josephus (*Ant.* XII 2), presumably because he was not a Hellenist, and could read his Bible in the Hebrew, does not see the necessity for this doctrine of the inspiration of the Septuagint. He follows Aristeas closely, except at the end, where he actually turns the curse pronounced on alteration into an invitation to retrench superfluities or supply defects![1]

The early Christian Fathers gave play to their imagination over the story of the Septuagint. Justin Martyr (*Apol.* I 31 §§ 2–5) has a brief allusion to it, but the amount of credit which is due to him in this connexion may be judged from the fact that he makes Ptolemy send to King *Herod* for interpreters of the sacred books!

Irenæus about a quarter of a century later (A.D. 175) says that Ptolemy, being afraid lest the translators might combine to conceal the truth in some matter by their interpretation, had them isolated, and ordered each to translate the whole. When it was found that they all agreed word for word, then of a truth the Gentiles knew that the Scriptures were interpreted by inspiration of God. But this, he adds, was nothing surprising, seeing that, when the Scriptures had been lost during the captivity in Babylon, God inspired Ezra to rewrite them.[2]

Clement of Alexandria (about A.D. 190) follows to the same effect as to literal inspiration, and adds the prophetic writings to the work of the first interpreters (*Strom.* I § 148, p. 409 P).

Eusebius, with his exceptional regard for truth, is content to give us an epitome of Aristeas.[3]

Epiphanius however (died A.D. 402) is lavish of details. He tells us that the king had thirty-six houses constructed on the island of

---

[1] Cp. Aristeas § 211 with Jos. *Ant.* XII 2 § 13 *ad fin.*

[2] Irenæus quoted by Eus. *H.E.* V 8.

[3] *Præp. Ev.* VIII 2–5 and 9. Josephus, Tertullian, Eusebius, and most subsequent writers with the exception of St. Jerome call Aristeas Ἀρισταῖος. The two forms would appear not to have differed appreciably in pronunciation. In the names of two of the interpreters there is a similar variation, Βασέας and Βανέας appearing also as Βασαλας and Βαναλας, whence it is an easy step to the more familiar Greek termination -αῖος.

Pharos, in which he shut up the interpreters two together. In these houses, which had no windows in the wall, but only skylights, the interpreters worked from morning till evening under lock and key. In the evening they were taken over in thirty-six different boats to the palace of Ptolemy Philadelphus, to dine with him. Then they slept two together in thirty-six different bedrooms. All these precautions were taken to prevent communication between the pairs, and yet when the thirty-six copies of each book of the Bible were compared together, they were found to be identical. 'So manifestly were these men inspired by the Holy Ghost, and where there was an addition made to the original, it was made by all, and where there was something taken away, it was taken away by all; and what they took away is not needed, and what they added is needed.'

This explicit assertion of the plenary inspiration of the Septuagint is manifestly prompted by the craving for an infallible Bible, which was felt in ancient as in modern times. St. Jerome, who, unlike the bulk of the Christian Fathers, made himself acquainted with the text of the original, nailed this false coin to the counter;[1] nevertheless his younger[2] contemporary Augustine gave it full currency again, declaring that the same Spirit which spoke through the prophets spoke also through their interpreters, and that any diversities there may be between the translation and the original are due to 'prophetic depth.'[3]

These later embellishments of the story of the Septuagint may unhesitatingly be set aside as the outcome of pious imagination. But what of the original narrative which goes under the name of Aristeas? Is that to be regarded as fact or fiction?

At first sight we seem to have strong external evidence for its truth. There was an Alexandrian Jew named Aristobulus, who is

[1] *Preface to the Pentateuch* — et nescio quis primus auctor septuaginta cellulas Alexandriæ mendacio suo exstruxerit, quibus divisi eadem scriptitarint, cum Aristeas eiusdem Ptolemæi ὑπερασπιστὴς et multo post tempore Iosephus nihil tale retulerint, sed in una basilica congregatos contulisse scribant, non prophetasse.

[2] Jerome died A.D. 420, Augustine A.D. 430.

[3] Aug. *de Civ. Dei* XVIII 42 and 43.

mentioned at the beginning of Second Maccabees as 'the teacher of king Ptolemy' (1¹⁰). The Ptolemy in question was the sixth, surnamed Philometor (B.C. 180–145). Aristobulus, though a Jew, was also a Peripatetic philosopher, and anticipated Philo as an exponent of the allegorical method of interpreting Scripture. So at least we gather from Eusebius, who in his *Præparatio Evangelica* several times quotes a work on the 'Interpretation of the Holy Laws'[1] addressed by Aristobulus to Philometor. The interest of this work to us is that in it Aristobulus refers to the translation made in the reign of his majesty's ancestor Philadelphus under the superintendence of Demetrius Phalereus. This seems decisive in favour of the historic character of the main facts recorded in the Letter of Aristeas. And there is another piece of external evidence to be added. For Philo, who himself lived at Alexandria, tells us that a festival was held every year on the island of Pharos in honour of the place whence the blessing of the Greek Bible first shone forth (*Vita Mosis* II § 7, II 141).

The external evidence being thus favourable, let us now examine the internal.

Time is the great revealer of secrets, and it is also, in another sense, the great detector of forgeries. We have therefore first to inquire whether the document is consistent in point of chronology with its own claims. Who are the persons mentioned, and did they live together? With regard to what may be called the minor characters there is no difficulty. Aristeas himself, Andreas, and Sosibius are otherwise unknown, while in the case of Menedemus of Eretria, Theodectes, and Theopompus, we are not debarred by considerations of time from accepting what is said of them, though it would fit in better with the reign of the first than of the second Ptolemy. But the relations between Ptolemy Philadelphus and Demetrius of Phalerum, as represented in the Letter, are inconsistent with what we know from other sources. Demetrius was expelled from Athens in B.C. 307 by his namesake Demetrius the Besieger of Cities. Having subsequently found his way to Egypt, he became the chief friend of Ptolemy Soter, by whom he was even intrusted with legislation.[2] Unfortunately for himself he advised that monarch to leave the king-

---

[1] Eus. *Pr. Ev.* VII 13, 14 : VIII 9, 10 : IX 6 : XIII 11, 12.
[2] Ælian *V.H.* III 17 : Plut. *de Exsilio* p. 602.

dom to his children by his first wife Eurydice. Soter however left
it to Philadelphus, the son of Berenice, on whose accession Demetrius
was disgraced. He died soon after owing to a snake-bite received
during his sleep.[1] This account is given by Diogenes Laertius (V
§ 78) on the authority of Hermippus, whom Josephus[2] declares to
have been a very exact historian. If his authority is good in favour
of the Jews, it must be equally good against them.

It would seem then that, if Demetrius of Phalerum had anything
to do with the translation of the Jewish Scriptures, that translation
must have been made under the first Ptolemy. This is actually
asserted by Irenæus,[3] who seems here to have followed some account
independent of Aristeas. And in another respect this alternative
version of the facts is intrinsically more credible. For, whereas the
Letter of Aristeas represents Eleazar as an independent potentate,
Irenæus expressly says that the Jews were then subject to the
Macedonians, by whom he doubtless means Ptolemy Soter, who is
recorded to have subdued the country. But, if the Letter of Aristeas is wrong on so vital a point of chronology, it is plain that it
cannot have been written by its assumed author, who can hardly
be supposed to have been mistaken as to whose reign he was living
under. In that case its historical character is gone, and we are at
liberty to believe as much or as little of it as we please.

There are some minor points which have been urged as proofs of
historical inaccuracy in the Letter, which do not seem to us to have
any weight. One is connected with the letter of Eleazar, which begins thus (§ 41) — 'If thou thyself art well, and the queen Arsinoë,
thy sister, and the children, it will be well, and as we would have
it.' Now Philadelphus had two wives in succession, both named
Arsinoë. By the first, who was the daughter of Lysimachus, he had
three children, Ptolemy, Lysimachus, and Berenice; by the second,
who was his own sister, he had none. But then, as Eleazar was

---

[1] Cicero *pro Rab. Post.* § 23 implies that Demetrius was intentionally got rid
of in this way — Demetrium et ex republica, quam optime gesse-
rat, et ex doctrina nobilem et clarum, qui Phalereus vocitatus
est, in eodem isto Ægyptio regno aspide ad corpus admota
vita esse privatum.

[2] *Against Apion* I 22 — ἀνὴρ περὶ πᾶσαν ἱστορίαν ἐπιμελής.

[3] Quoted in Eusebius V 8.

addressing Ptolemy, who was aware of these facts, it would have been superfluous for him to guard himself against misconstruction (cp. § 45). Again (§ 180) Philadelphus is made to speak of his victory 'in the sea-fight against Antigonus.' It is asserted that Philadelphus was really defeated in this battle : but, if so, this falsification of fact is not inappropriate in the monarch's own mouth. Who does not know the elasticity of the term 'victory'?

More important than the preceding are two passages in which the author, despite his cleverness, seems to forget that he is Aristeas, and to speak from the standpoint of his own later age. For in § 28, in commenting on the systematic administration of the Ptolemies, he says 'for all things were done *by these kings* by means of decrees and in a very safe manner.' Now it is conceivable that Aristeas might say this with reference to Philadelphus and his father Soter, but it seems more like the expression of one who could already look back upon a dynasty. Again in § 182, in recording how the national customs of the Jews were complied with in the banquet, he says 'for it was so appointed by the king, as you can still see now.' This could hardly be said by a person writing in the reign of which he is speaking.

Our inquiries then seem to have landed us in this rather anomalous situation, that, while external evidence attests the genuineness of the Letter, internal evidence forbids us to accept it. But what if the chief witness be himself found to be an impostor? This is the view taken by those who are careful to speak of the pseudo-Aristobulus. Aristobulus, the teacher of Ptolemy, would be a tempting godfather to a Jewish author wishing to enforce his own opinions. One thing is certain, namely, that the Orphic verses quoted by Aristobulus (Eus. *Pr. Ev.* XIII 12) are not of Greek but of Jewish origin. This however does not prove much. For since they were employed by some Jew, why not by one as well as by another? The Jewish Sibylline verses also go back to the reign of Ptolemy Philometor. There is another thing which may be affirmed with safety, namely, that the closest parallel to the Greek of Aristeas is to be found in the Greek of Aristobulus. Indeed it might well be believed that both works were by the same hand. We incline therefore to think that whatever was the date of the 'Interpretation of the Holy Laws' was the date also of the Letter of Aristeas. If the former work is really by Aristobulus writing under Ptolemy Philometor, then we assign the Letter to the same period. But, if the Jewish love of pseudonymity deludes us here also, then we are unmoored from our anchorage, and can be certain of nothing except that the Letter was accepted as history by the time of Josephus, who paraphrases a great part of it, and mentions the name of the supposed author. Philo's evidence is not so clear. He agrees with the author of the Letter in making the translation take place under Philadelphus, but he diverges from him, as we have seen, in asserting its inspiration, nor does he anywhere refer to the writer as his authority in the way Josephus does.

The Teubner editor of the Letter, Paul Wendland, puts its composition later than the time of the Maccabees (say after B.C. 96) and before the invasion of Palestine by the Romans, B.C. 63. The earlier limit is determined by arguments from names, which might be disputed, and the later is taken for granted. We ourselves think that the work was composed before the Jews had any close acquaintance with the Romans: but there is a point which might be urged against this view. Among the questions asked by Philadelphus of the Elders there are two in immediate succession — (1) What kind of men ought to be appointed στρατηγοί? (2) What kind of men ought to be appointed 'commanders of the forces'? (§§ 280, 281). One or other of these questions seems superfluous until we inquire into the meaning of στρατηγοί in this context. The answer to the question in the text clearly shows that the word here stands for 'judges.' Now, if we remember that στρατηγός was the Greek equivalent for the Roman praetor, it might at first seem that it could only have been under the Romans that στρατηγός acquired the meaning of 'judge.' But this leaves out of sight the question how στρατηγός came to be selected as the equivalent of the Roman praetor. The word must already in Greek have connoted civil as well as military functions before it could have seemed to be a fit translation of praetor. And this we know to have been the case. The στρατηγοί at Athens were judges as well as generals. At Alexandria they seem to have become judges instead of generals.

Turning now from the date of the Letter of Aristeas to that of the Septuagint itself, we have already found that there were two forms of the tradition with regard to its origin, one putting it under the reign of the second, the other under that of the first Ptolemy. The latter comes to us through Irenæus and is compatible with the part assigned to Demetrius of Phalerum in getting the Law of Moses translated, whereas the former is not. Both versions of the story were known to Clement of Alexandria, who gives the preference to the former. They were combined by Anatolius (Eus. *H.E.* VII 32), who declares that Aristobulus himself was one of the Seventy, and addressed his books on the Interpretation of the Law of Moses to the first two Ptolemies. This however is out of keeping with the fragments of Aristobulus themselves.

From the Prologue to Ecclesiasticus we may fairly infer that 'the Law, the Prophecies, and the rest of the Books,' so far as the last were then written, already existed in Greek at the time of writing, and the text itself shows acquaintance with the phraseology of the Septuagint version of the Pentateuch. That Prologue cannot have been written later than 132 B.C., and may have been written as early as the reign of the first Euergetes, who succeeded Philadelphus (B.C. 247-222).[1]

Philo displays an acquaintance through the Greek with all the books of the Old Testament, except Esther, Ecclesiastes, the Song of Songs, and Daniel. But he quotes the Prophets and Psalms sparsely, and seems to regard them as inferior in authority to the Law.

The making of the Septuagint, as we have it, was not a single act, but a long process, extending perhaps from the reign of the first Ptolemy down to the second century after Christ: for the translation of Ecclesiastes looks as if it had been incorporated from the version of Aquila, of which we shall speak presently. Tradition is perhaps right in connecting the original translation of the Law with the desire of the early Ptolemies for the completeness of their library. Eusebius sees in this the hand of Providence preparing

---

[1] In that case the words 'In the eight and thirtieth year in the reign of Euergetes I came into Egypt' may mean simply 'When I was thirty-eight years old,' etc., which is the sense in which Professor Mahaffy takes them. Wendland has pointed out a resemblance of expression which might seem to imply that the writer of the Letter was acquainted with the Prologue to Ecclesiasticus. Cp. Aristeas § 7 with the words in the Prologue — καὶ ὡς οὐ μόνον . . . χρησίμους εἶναι.

the world for the coming of Christ by the diffusion of the Scriptures, a boon which could not otherwise have been wrung from Jewish exclusiveness (*Pr. Ev.* VIII 1).

We need not doubt Tertullian's word when he says that the Old Testament Scriptures in Greek were to be seen in the Serapeum in his own day along with their originals. But the question is how they got there. Were they really translated for the library? Or, having been translated by the Jews for their own use was a copy demanded for the library? On this question each must judge for himself. To us the story of the Seventy-two Interpreters carries no conviction. For why should the king send to Judæa for interpreters, when there was so large a Jewish population in his own kingdom? The seventy-two interpreters, six from each tribe, savour strongly of the same motive which dictated the subsequent embellishments of the story, namely, the desire to confer authority upon the Hellenist Scriptures. We lay no stress in this connexion on the loss of the ten tribes, which has been supposed to render the story impossible from the commencement. If it had been an utter impossibility to find six men from each tribe at Jerusalem, no Jew would have been likely to invent such a story. Moreover in New Testament times the ten tribes were not regarded as utterly lost (Acts 26[7], James 1[1]). Though they never came back as a body, probably many of them returned individually to Palestine; and the Jews were so careful of their genealogies that it would be known to what tribe they belonged. The wholesale emancipation of Jewish slaves by Philadelphus at his own cost is so noble an example to kings that it is a pity to attack its historicity: but it is necessary to point out that the price recorded to have been paid for each, namely twenty drachmas, is utterly below the market-value, so that the soldiers and subjects of Philadelphus would have had a right to complain of his being generous at their expense.[1] Josephus is so conscious of this flaw in the story, that in two places he quietly inserts 'a hundred' before the 'twenty drachmas,' notwithstanding that this sixfold, but still modest, price does not square with the total.

Of any attempt prior to the Septuagint to translate the Hebrew Scriptures we have no authentic information. It is true that the

---

[1] On the price of slaves see Xen. *Mem.* II 5 § 2 : Plato *Anterastæ* 135 C : Lucian *Vit. Auct.* 27.

writer of the Letter speaks of previous incorrect translations of the
Law (§ 314) as having been used by Theopompus: but his motive
seems to be a desire to exalt the correctness of what may be called
the authorised version. Similarly Aristobulus (Eus. *Pr. Ev.*
XIII 12) speaks of parts of the Pentateuch as having been translated ' before Demetrius of Phalerum ' and before 'the supremacy of
Alexander and the Persians.' But again there is a definite motive
to be found for this vague chronological statement in the attempt
which was made at Alexandria to show that Plato and before him
Pythagoras were deeply indebted to Moses.[1] For when the Alexandrian Jews paid Greek philosophy the compliment of finding that
in it lay the inner meaning of their own Scriptures, they endeavoured at the same time to redress the balance by proving that Greek
philosophy was originally derived from Jewish religion, so that, if
in Moses one should find Plato, that was only because Plato was
inspired by Moses. The motto of this school is conveyed in the
question of Numenius 'What is Plato but Moses Atticizing?' One
of its methods, we regret to add, was the fabrication of Orphic and
Sibylline verses, to which we have already had occasion to allude.
This industry was carried on by the Christians, and affords a reason
why in the vision of Hermas (Herm. *Past. Vis.* II 4 § 1) the Sibyl
could at first sight be confounded with the Church. In Lactantius
the Sibylline verses form one of the chief evidences of Christianity.

Of translations of the Old Testament subsequent to the Septuagint the three most famous are those of Aquila, Theodotion, and
Symmachus. Aquila, like his namesake, the husband of Priscilla,
was a native of Pontus, and though not a Jew by birth was a proselyte to the Jewish religion. His version is distinguished by the total
sacrifice of the Greek to the letter of the Hebrew text. So much is
this the case that a Hebrew prefix which is both a sign of the accusative and has also the meaning 'with' is represented, where it
occurs in the former sense, by σύν, so that we are presented with
the phenomenon of σύν with the accusative. This peculiarity pre-

---

[1] Aristobulus in Eus. *Pr. Ev.* XIII 12 § 1 — Φανερὸν ὅτι κατηκολούθησεν ὁ Πλά-
των τῇ καθ' ἡμᾶς νομοθεσίᾳ,.καὶ φανερός ἐστι περιειργασμένος ἕκαστα τῶν ἐν αὐτῇ.
Διερμήνευται γὰρ πρὸ Δημητρίου τοῦ Φαληρέως δι' ἑτέρων πρὸ τῆς 'Αλεξάνδρου .καὶ
Περσῶν ἐπικρατήσεως κτλ. . . . Γέγονε γὰρ πολυμαθὴς, καθὼς καὶ Πυθαγόρας πολλὰ
τῶν παρ' ἡμῖν μετενέγκας εἰς τὴν ἑαυτοῦ δογματοποιίαν κατεχώρισεν.

sents itself in the Greek version of Ecclesiastes [1] alone among the books of the Septuagint, so that the rendering of that late work may be conjectured to be due to Aquila. This translator lived during the reign of Hadrian (A.D. 117–138).

Theodotion of Ephesus is said to have lived towards the close of the same century, under Commodus (A.D. 180–192). He also was a Jewish proselyte. His work was rather a revision of the Septuagint than an independent translation. So far as the book of Daniel is concerned, it was accepted by the Christian Church, and the older Septuagint version was discarded.

Symmachus of Samaria, who, according to Eusebius (*H.E.* VI 17), was an Ebionite Christian, flourished in the next reign, that of Septimius Severus (A.D. 193–211). His version was more literary in form than that of Aquila.

The reader will observe that all three of these versions come from the side of Judaism. The Christian Church was content with the Septuagint, whereon to found its claim as to the witness of the Old Testament to Christ. Eusebius points to the providential nature of the fact that the prophecies which foretold his coming were stored in a public library under the auspices of a Pagan king centuries before his appearance, so that the coincidence between prediction and fulfilment could not be ascribed to any fraud on the part of the Christians. The Jews however were not so well satisfied with this aspect of things. The question of the Virgin birth divided the religious world then, as it does now. Aquila and Theodotion were at one in substituting νεᾶνις for παρθένος in Isaiah 7[14], and the Ebionites found support in this for their declaration that Jesus was the son of Joseph. There were writings of Symmachus still extant in the time of Eusebius, which were directed against the Gospel according to St. Matthew (*H.E.* VI 17).

Besides these well-known versions there were two other anonymous ones, which were brought to light through the industry and good fortune of Origen, the most scholarly of the Christian Fathers. One of these, which was called the Fifth Edition, was found hidden in an old wine-cask at Jericho in the reign of that Antoninus who is better known as Caracalla (A.D. 211–217); the other, which was called the Sixth Edition, was discovered in the subsequent reign of

[1] *E.g.* 2[17] καὶ ἐμίσησα σὺν τὴν ζωήν.

Alexander Severus (A.D. 222–235) concealed in a similar receptacle at Nicopolis in Epirus, where we may presume St. Paul to have spent his last winter (Tit. 3¹²). Who knows but that it may have been one of the books which he was so urgent upon Timothy to bring with him? We do not think the chances very strongly in favour of this hypothesis: but it would account for some things, if we knew St. Paul to have had access to another version besides the Septuagint.

The renderings of the four main versions were arranged by Origen in parallel columns along with the original both in Hebrew and Greek characters, in a work which was consequently known as the Hexapla. For the Psalms Eusebius tells us Origen employed 'not only a fifth, but also a sixth and seventh interpretation' (*H.E.* VI 16). There was another work published by Origen called the Tetrapla, which contained only the Septuagint along with the versions of Aquila, Symmachus, and Theodotion. What the 'seventh interpretation' spoken of by Eusebius was, it would be hard to say. What is called by Theodoret the Seventh Edition was the recension of Lucian, which was later than the work of Origen. Lucian was martyred under Diocletian (284–305 A.D.).

The work of Origen might enlighten the learned, but it did not affect the unique position held in the Christian Church by the Septuagint ever since it was taken over from the Hellenist Jews. We are familiar with the constant appeal made by the writers of the New Testament to 'Scripture,' an appeal couched in such words as 'It is written' or 'As the Scripture saith.' In the great majority of cases the Scripture thus appealed to is undoubtedly the Septuagint; seldom, if ever, is it the Hebrew original. We have seen how, even before the Christian era, the Septuagint had acquired for itself the position of an inspired book. Some four centuries after that era St. Augustine remarks that the Greek-speaking Christians for the most part did not even know whether there was any other word of God than the Septuagint (*C.D.* XVIII, 43). So when other nations became converted to Christianity and wanted the Scriptures in their own tongues, it was almost always the Septuagint which formed the basis of the translation. This was so in the case of the early Latin version, which was in use before the Vulgate; and it was so also in the case of the translations made into Coptic, Ethiopic, Armenian,

Georgian, Gothic, and other languages. The only exception to the
rule is the first Syriac version, which was made direct from the
Hebrew. When at the close of the fourth century St. Jerome had
recourse to the Hebrew original in revising the accepted Latin text,
the authority of the Septuagint stood in the way of the immediate
acceptance of his work. 'The Churches of Christ,' said St. Augustine, 'do not think that anyone is to be preferred to the authority
of so many men chosen out by the High-priest Eleazar for the
accomplishment of so great a work.'

Nevertheless Jerome's revision did triumph in the end, and under
the name of the Vulgate became the accepted text of the Western
Church. But the Vulgate itself is deeply tinctured by the Septuagint and has in its turn influenced our English Bible. Many of the
names of Scripture characters, e.g. Balaam and Samson, come to us
from the Septuagint, not from the Hebrew; our Bible often follows
the verse-division of the Septuagint as against that of the Hebrew;
the titles of the five books of Moses are derived from the Septuagint,
not from the Hebrew. Thus the Septuagint, while it still survives
in the East, continued its reign even in the West through the Vulgate; nor was it until the time of the Reformation that the Hebrew
Scriptures themselves began to be generally studied in Western
Europe.

Never surely has a translation of any book exercised so profound
an influence upon the world as the Septuagint version of the Old
Testament. This work has had more bearing upon ourselves than
we are perhaps inclined to think. For it was the first step towards
that fusion of the Hebraic with the Hellenic strain, which has
issued in the mind and heart of modern Christendom. Like the
opening of the Suez Canal, it let the waters of the East mingle
with those of the West, bearing with them many a freight of
precious merchandise. Without the Septuagint there could have
been, humanly speaking, no New Testament: for the former provided to the latter not only its vehicle of language, but to a great
extent also its moulds of thought. These last were of course ultimately Semitic, but when religious ideas had to be expressed in
Greek, it was difficult for them to escape change in the process.

So long as the New Testament is of interest to mankind, the
Septuagint must share that interest with it. The true meaning of

the former can only be arrived at by correct interpretation of the language, and such correct interpretation is well-nigh impossible to those who come to the Jewish Greek of the reign of Nero and later with notions derived from the age of Pericles. Not only had the literary language itself, even as used by the most correct writers, undergone great changes during the interval, but, further than this, the New Testament is not written in literary, but rather in colloquial Greek, and in the colloquial Greek of men whose original language and ways of thinking were Semitic, and whose expression was influenced at every turn by the phraseology of the Old Testament. If we wish then to understand the Greek of the New Testament, it is plain that we must compare it with the Greek of the Old, which belongs, like it, to post-classical times, is colloquial rather than literary, and is so deeply affected by Semitic influence as often to be hardly Greek at all, but rather Hebrew in disguise. That everything should be compared in the first instance with that to which it is most like is an obvious principle of scientific method, but one which hitherto can hardly be said to have been generally applied to the study of the New Testament. Now however there are manifold signs that scholars are beginning to realise the importance of the study of the Greek Old Testament in its bearing upon the interpretation of the New.

Attic Greek was like a vintage of rare flavour which would only grow on a circumscribed soil. When Greek became a world-language, as it did after the conquests of Alexander, it had to surrender much of its delicacy, but it still remained an effective instrument of thought and a fit vehicle for philosophy and history. The cosmopolitan form of literary Greek which then came into use among men of non-Attic, often of non-Hellenic origin, was known as the Common (κοινή, sc. διάλεκτος) or Hellenic dialect. Aristotle may be considered the first of the Hellenists, though, as a disciple of Plato, he is far nearer to Attic purity than the Stoics, Epicureans, and Academics who followed him.

Hellenistic Greek we may regard as the genus, of which Alexandrian Greek is a species. Now the language of the Septuagint is a variety of Alexandrian Greek, but a very peculiar variety. It is no fair specimen either of the colloquial or of the literary language of Alexandria.

The interesting light thrown upon the vocabulary of the Septuagint by the recent publication of Egyptian Papyri has led some writers to suppose that the language of the Septuagint has nothing to distinguish it from Greek as spoken daily in the kingdom of the Ptolemies. Hence some fine scorn has been wasted on the 'myth' of a 'Biblical' Greek. 'Biblical Greek' was a term aptly applied by the late Dr. Hatch to the language of the Septuagint and New Testament conjointly. It is a serviceable word, which it would be unwise to discard. For, viewed as Greek, these two books have features in common which are shared with them by no other documents. These features arise from the strong Semitic infusion that is contained in both. The Septuagint is, except on occasions, a literal translation from the Hebrew. Now a literal translation is only half a translation. It changes the vocabulary, while it leaves unchanged the syntax. But the life of a language lies rather in the syntax than in the vocabulary. So, while the vocabulary of the Septuagint is that of the market-place of Alexandria, the modes of thought are purely Hebraic. This is a rough statement concerning the Septuagint as a whole: but, as the whole is not homogeneous, it does not apply to all the parts. The Septuagint does contain writing, especially in the books of the Maccabees, which is Greek, not Hebrew, in spirit, and which may fairly be compared with the Alexandrian Greek of Philo.

The New Testament, having itself been written in Greek, is not so saturated with Hebrew as the Septuagint: still the resemblance in this respect is close enough to warrant the two being classed together under the title of Biblical Greek. Hence we must dissent from the language of Deissmann, when he says 'The linguistic unity of the Greek Bible appears only against the background of classical, not of contemporary "profane," Greek.' Biblical Greek does appear to us to have a linguistic unity, whether as compared with the current Alexandrian of the Papyri or with the literary language of such fairly contemporary authors as Aristeas, Aristobulus, and Philo, not to add others who might more justly be called 'profane.'

The language of the Septuagint, so far as it is Greek at all, is the colloquial Greek of Alexandria, but it is Biblical Greek, because it contains so large an element, which is not Hellenic, but Semitic.

Josephus, it has been asserted, employs only one Hebraism, namely, the use of προστίθεσθαι with another verb in the sense of 'doing something again' (see *Gram. of Sept. Gk.* § 113). For the accuracy of this statement it would be hazardous to vouch, but the possibility of its being made serves to show the broad difference that there is between Hellenistic Greek, even as employed by a Jew, who, we know, had to learn the language, and the Biblical Greek of the Septuagint.

The uncompromising Hebraism of the Septuagint is doubtless due in part to the reverence felt by the translators for the Sacred Text. It was their business to give the very words of the Hebrew Bible to the Greek world, or to those of their own countrymen who lived in it and used its speech; as to the genius of the Greek language, that was entirely ignored. Take for instance Numbers 9¹⁰ — Ἄνθρωπος ἄνθρωπος ὃς ἐὰν γένηται ἀκάθαρτος ἐπὶ ψυχῇ ἀνθρώπου, ἢ ἐν ὁδῷ μακρὰν ὑμῖν ἢ ἐν ταῖς γενεαῖς ὑμῶν, καὶ ποιήσει τὸ πάσχα Κυρίῳ. Does anyone suppose that stuff of that sort was ever spoken at Alexandria? It might as well be maintained that a schoolboy's translation of Euripides represents English as spoken in America.

One of our difficulties in explaining the meaning of the Greek in the Septuagint is that it is often doubtful whether the Greek *had* a meaning to those who wrote it. One often cannot be sure that they did not write down, without attaching any significance to them, the Greek words which seemed to be the nearest equivalents to the Hebrew before them. This is especially the case in the poetical passages, of which Deuteronomy 33¹⁰ ᵇ will serve for an instance — ἐπιθήσουσιν θυμίαμα ἐν ὀργῇ σου, διὰ παντὸς ἐπὶ τὸ θυσιαστήριόν σου. We can account for this by aid of the original: but what did it mean to the translator?

Another obvious cause of difference between Biblical and Alexandrian Greek is the necessity under which the translators found themselves of inventing terms to express ideas which were wholly foreign to the Greek mind.

The result of these various causes is often such as to cause disgust to the classical student. Indeed a learned Jesuit Father has confessed to us what a shock he received on first making acquaintance with the Greek of the Septuagint. But the fastidiousness of the classical scholar must not be nourished at the expense of narrowing the bounds of thought. The Greek language did not die with Plato; it is not dead yet; like the Roman Empire it is interesting in all stages of its growth and its decline. One important stage of its life-history is the ecclesiastical Greek, which followed the introduction of Christianity. This would never have been but for the New Testament. But neither, as we have said before, would the New Testament itself have been but for the Septuagint.

# GRAMMAR OF SEPTUAGINT GREEK

## ACCIDENCE

### NOUNS, 1-14

**1. Disuse of the Dual.** The Greek of the LXX has two numbers, the singular and the plural. The dual, which was already falling into disuse in the time of Homer, and which is seldom adhered to systematically in classical writers, has disappeared altogether.

Gen. 40² ἐπὶ τοῖς δυσὶν εὐνούχοις αὐτοῦ. Ex. 4⁹ τοῖς δυσὶ σημείοις τούτοις.

Contrast with the above —

Plat. *Rep.* 470 B ἐπὶ δυοῖν τινοῖν διαφοραῖν. Isocr. *Paneg.* 55 c περὶ τοῖν πολέοιν τούτοιν.

**2. Εἷς as Article.** Under the influence of Hebrew idiom we find the numeral εἷς turning into an indefinite pronoun in the Greek of the LXX, as in Gen. 42²⁷ λύσας δὲ εἷς τὸν μάρσιππον αὐτοῦ, and then subsiding into a mere article, as —

Jdg. 13² ἀνὴρ εἷς, 9⁵³ γυνὴ μία. ii K. 2¹⁸ ὡσεὶ μία δορκὰς ἐν ἀγρῷ. ii Esd. 4⁸ ἔγραψαν ἐπιστολὴν μίαν. Ezk. 4⁹ ἄγγος ἐν ὀστράκινον.

There are instances of the same usage in the two most Hebraistic books of the N.T.

Mt. 8¹⁹ εἷς γραμματεύς, 9¹⁸ ἄρχων εἷς, 21¹⁹ συκῆν μίαν, 26⁶⁹ μία παιδίσκη. Rev. 8¹³ ἑνὸς ἀετοῦ, 9¹³ φωνὴν μίαν, 18²¹ εἷς ἄγγελος, 19¹⁷ ἕνα ἄγγελον.

Our own indefinite article 'a' or 'an' (Scotch *ane*) is originally the same as 'one.' We can also see the beginning of the French article in the colloquial language of the Latin comedians.

Ter. *And.* 118 forte unam aspicio adulescentulam. Plaut. *Most.* 990 unum vidi mortuum efferri foras.

Apart from the influence of Hebrew, εἷς is occasionally found in good Greek on the way to becoming an article. See L. & S. under εἷς 4. In German the indefinite article and the first of the numerals coincide, and so a German, in beginning to speak English, frequently puts 'one' for 'a.' In the same way a Hebrew learning to speak Greek said εἷς ἀετός and so on.

**3. First Declension.** In classical Greek there is a tendency for proper names, especially those of foreign origin, which end in the nominative in -α preceded by a consonant other than ρ, to retain the α in the genitive, e.g. Λήδας, Ἀνδρομέδας, Κομπλέγας (name of a Spanish town, App. VI *De Reb. Hisp.* 43). In pursuance of this analogy we have such genitives as Βάλλας and Ζέλφας (Gen. 37²), Σουσάννας (Sus. O'³⁰).

On the other hand, nouns in -α pure, or -α preceded by ρ, are in a few instances found in the LXX to take the Ionic form of the genitive and dative in -ης and -ῃ.

Ex. 8²¹ κυνόμυιαν . . . κυνομυίης, 15⁹ and Gen. 27⁴⁰ τῇ μαχαίρῃ. i K. 25²⁰ αὐτῆς ἐπιβεβηκυίης ἐπὶ τὴν ὄνον. ii Mac. 8²³, 12²² σπείρης.

It is said that in the Papyri σπείρης is always used, never σπείρας. The plural of γῆ is found in the LXX.

Acc. γᾶς iv K. 18³⁵. Gen. γαιῶν iv K. 18³⁵: Ps. 48¹¹: Ezk. 36²⁴: ii Esd. 9¹ and three other passages. Dat. γαῖς iv K. 19¹¹. γαίαις Dan. O' 11⁴².

**4. Second Declension.** θεός has a vocative θεέ. Dt. 3²⁴: Jdg. 21³, 16²⁸: Wisd. 9¹. Usually, however, the nominative is employed for the vocative, as in —

Ps. 21¹ Ὁ Θεὸς ὁ Θεός μου πρόσχες μοι · ἰνατί ἐγκατέλιπές με ;

But in Matthew 27⁴⁶ this passage assumes the form —

Θεέ μου, Θεέ μου, ἰνατί με ἐγκατέλιπες ;

The Attic form of this declension is of rare occurrence in the LXX. λαός and ναός are the regular forms. λεώς does not occur at all, and νεώς only in Second Maccabees. ἅλως is common : but for that there is no non-Attic form, as it does not arise, like the others, on the principle of transposition of quantity.

**5. Third Declension.** The word σκνίψ (Ex. 8¹⁶) is interesting, as adding another instance of a noun-stem in -φ to the rare word κατῆλιψ and νίφα, which occurs only in the accusative in Hes. *Op.* 533. Σκνίψ is also found in the LXX with stem σκνιπ-.

**6. Absence of Contraction.** Many words are left uncontracted in the LXX which in Attic Greek would be contracted, e.g. —

Dt. 18¹¹ ἐπαείδων ἐπαοιδήν. Prov. 3⁸ ὀστέοις. Sir. 6³⁰ χρύσεος. Ps. 73¹⁷ ἔαρ.

The accusative plural of βοῦς is always βόας, e.g. Gen. 41⁴. Similarly the accusative plural of ἰχθύς is left uncontracted wherever it occurs. Gen. 9² : Nb. 11⁵ : Ps. 8⁸, 104²⁹ : Hbk. 1¹⁴ : Ezk. 29⁴. So also στάχυες, στάχυας, Gen. 41⁵,⁷.

**7. Feminine Forms of Movable Substantives.** The form βασίλισσα for βασίλεια was not approved by Atticists. It is common in the LXX, whereas βασίλεια does not occur. Cp. Acts 8²⁷. On the analogy of it we have Ἀράβισσα in Job 42¹⁷ ᶜ, φυλάκισσα in Song 1⁶. The following also may be noted : —

γενέτις Wisd. 7¹² A, τεχνῖτις 7²², μύστις 8⁴. ὑβρίστρια Jer. 27³¹.

**8. Heteroclite Nouns.**

αἰθάλη (Ex. 9⁸, ¹⁰) for αἴθαλος, which does not occur.

ἅλων (Hos. 9²), ἅλωνος (Jdg. 15⁵) for ἅλως, ἅλω. Cp. Mt. 3¹², Lk. 3¹⁷ τὴν ἅλωνα. In the LXX both ἅλων and ἅλως are of common gender. Thus Ruth 3² τὸν ἅλωνα, 3¹⁴ τὴν ἅλωνα : Jdg. 6³⁷ τῇ ἅλωνι : i Chr. 21¹⁵ ἐν τῷ ἅλῳ, 21²¹ ἐκ τῆς ἅλω. Josephus (Ant. V 9 § 3) has τῆς ἅλωος.

γήρους, γήρει for γήρως, γήρᾳ, but nominative always γῆρας. For γήρους see Gen. 37³ : Ps. 70⁹, ¹⁸ : but in Gen. 44²⁰ γήρως. For γήρει see Gen. 15¹⁵, Ps. 91¹⁵, Sir. 8⁶, Dan. O′ 6¹. When one form is used, the other generally occurs as a variant. In Clement i Cor. 63³ we have ἕως γήρους.

ἔλεος, τό for ἔλεος, ὁ. Plural τὰ ἐλέη (Ps. 16⁷). The masculine form occurs in some dozen and a half passages (e.g. Ps. 83¹¹ : Prov. 3¹⁶, 14²²). In N.T. also and in the Apostolic Fathers the neuter is the prevailing form, e.g. ii Tim. 1¹⁶, ¹⁸ : Tit. 3⁵ : Hb. 4¹⁶ : Herm. Past. Vis. II 2 § 3, III 9 § 1, Sim. IV § 2 : i Clem. 9¹, 14¹ : ii Clem. 3¹, 16² : Barn. Ep. 15². In Mt. 9¹³, 12⁷, 23²³ the masculine form occurs, the two former being quotations from Hos. 6⁶, where the LXX has the neuter.

ἔνεδρον (Jdg. 16²) for ἔνεδρα. The former is quite common, the latter occurs only in Josh. 8⁷,⁹, Ps. 9²⁸.

λύχνος, τό (Dan. O′ 5⁰).

νῖκος, τό (i Esd. 3⁹) for νίκη. Cp. i Cor. 15⁵⁵, ⁵⁷ : Herm. Past. Mdt. XII 2 § 5.

σκότος, τό for ὁ, occurs in the best Attic prose as well as in the LXX (e.g. Is. 42¹⁶) and in N.T. (e.g. i Thes. 5⁵). Cp. Barn. Ep. 14⁶, 18¹.

The N.T. and Apostolic Fathers afford other instances of heteroclites, which do not occur in the LXX. Thus —

ζῆλος, τό (Phil. 3⁶: i Clem. 4⁸, ¹¹, ¹³, 6¹, ², 9¹, 63², but in 5², ⁵ διὰ ζῆλον: Ignat. ad Tral. 4²).

πλοῦς declined like βοῦς (Acts 27⁹: Mart. S. Ign. III εἴχετο τοῦ πλοός).

πλοῦτος, τό (ii Cor. 8²: Eph. 1⁷, 2⁷, 3⁸, ¹⁶: Phil. 4¹⁹: Col. 1²⁷, 2²).

τῦφος, τό (i Clem. 13¹).

**9. Verbal Nouns in -μα.** a. The abundance of verbal nouns in -μα is characteristic of Hellenistic Greek from Aristotle onwards. The following instances from the LXX are taken at random —

ἀγνόημα Gen. 43¹² (6 times in all).

ἀνόμημα i K. 25²⁸ (17 times in all).

διχοτόμημα Gen. 15¹¹ (5 times in all).

κατάλειμμα Gen. 45⁷ (20 times in all).

ὕψωμα . . . γαυρίαμα . . . καύχημα Judith 15⁹.

b. A point better worth noting is the preference for the short radical vowel in their formation, e.g. —

ἀνάθεμα Lvt. 27²⁸ etc. So in N.T. Acts 23¹⁴: Rom. 9³: i Cor. 12³, 16²²: Gal. 1⁸, ⁹. In Judith 16¹⁹ we have the classical form ἀνάθημα. For the short vowel in the LXX, cp. θέμα, ἔκθεμα, ἐπίθεμα, παράθεμα, πρόσθεμα, σύνθεμα.

ἀφαίρεμα Ex. 29²⁷: Lvt. 7⁴, ²⁴ etc.

ἄφεμα i Mac. 9²⁸. So κάθεμα, Is. 3¹⁹, Ezk. 16¹¹.

δόμα Gen. 25⁶ etc. So in N.T.

εὕρεμα Sir. 20⁹, 29⁴.

ἔψεμα Gen. 25²⁹ etc.

σύστεμα Gen. 1¹⁰ etc. So ἀνάστεμα. In Judith 12⁸ ἀνάστημα.

χύμα (for χεῦμα) ii Mac. 2²⁴.

**10. Non-Attic Forms of Substantives.**

ἀλώπηκας accusative plural (Jdg. 15⁴) for ἀλώπεκας.

ἄρκος (i K. 17³⁴) for ἄρκτος, which does not occur. Cp. Rev. 13² ἄρκου.

δῖνα (Job 13¹¹, 28¹⁰) for δίνη.

ἔνυστρον (Dt. 18³) for ἤνυστρον. So in Jos. Ant. IV 4 § 4.

ACCIDENCE 29

ἐπαοιδός (Ex. 7¹¹) for ἐπῳδός, which does not occur.
κλίβανος (Ex. 7²⁸) for κρίβανος. So also in N.T.
μόλιβος (Ex. 15¹⁰), the Homeric form, for μόλυβδος.
ταμεῖον (Ex. 7²⁸ : Jdg. 3²⁴, 15¹, 16¹²) for ταμιεῖον, which also occurs
frequently. The shorter form is common in the Papyri.
ὑγεία (Tob. 8²¹) for ὑγίεια. In later Greek generally ὑγεία is usual,
but the fuller form prevails in the LXX.
χείμαρρος (i K. 17⁴⁰) for χειμάρρους.

**11. Non-Attic Forms of Adjectives.**

εὐθής, εὐθές for εὐθύς, εὐθεῖα, εὐθύ, which also occurs frequently.
ἥμισυς, -υ is an adjective of two terminations in the LXX. ἡμίσεια
does not occur. Cp. Nb. 34¹⁴ τὸ ἥμισυ φυλῆς Μανασσή with
Jos. Ant. IV 7 § 3 καὶ τῆς Μανασσίτιδος ἡμίσεια.
χάλκειος, -α, -ον, the Homeric form, occurs in Jdg. 16²¹, i Esd. 1³⁸,
5 times in Job, and in Sir. 28²⁰ for χαλκοῦς, χαλκῆ, χαλκοῦν,
which is very common.
ἀργυρικός i Esd. 8²⁴ only. Cp. Aristeas § 37, who has also ἐλαϊ-
κός, σιτικός, χαριστικός (§§ 112, 37, 227).
αἰσχυντηρός Sir. 26¹⁵, 35¹⁰, 42¹ only.
σιγηρός Prov. 18¹⁸, Sir. 26¹⁴ only.
κλεψιμαῖος Tob. 2¹³ only.
θνησιμαῖος often used in the neuter for 'a corpse,' e.g. iii K. 13²⁵.

**12. Comparison of Adjectives.**

ἀγαθώτερος (Jdg. 11²⁵, 15²) is perhaps an instance of that tendency to regularisation in the later stages of a language,
which results from its being spoken by foreigners.
αἰσχρότερος (Gen. 41¹⁹) is good Greek, though not Attic. Αἰσχίων
does not seem to occur in the LXX.
ἐγγίων and ἔγγιστος are usual in the LXX, e.g. Ruth 3¹², iii K. 20²,
Ἐγγύτερος does not seem to occur at all, and ἐγγύτατος only in
Job 6¹⁵, 19¹⁴.
πλησιέστερον adv. for πλησιαίτερον (iv Mac. 12³).

**13. Pronouns.** a. Classical Greek has no equivalent for our unemphatic pronoun 'he.' One cannot say exactly 'he said' in the Attic
idiom. Αὐτὸς ἔφη is something more, and ἔφη something less, for it may
equally mean 'she said.' The Greek of the LXX gets over this difficulty by the use of αὐτός as an unemphatic pronoun of the 3d person.
i K. 17⁴² καὶ εἶδεν Γολιὰδ τὸν Δαυεὶδ καὶ ἠτίμασεν αὐτόν, ὅτι αὐτὸς ἦν
παιδάριον καὶ αὐτὸς πυρράκης μετὰ κάλλους ὀφθαλμῶν.

In the above the repeated αὐτός is simply the nominative of the αὐτόν preceding. In a classical writer αὐτός so used would necessarily refer to Goliath himself. For other instances see Gen. 3[15, 16], 39[23]: Nb. 17[5], 22[22]: Jdg. 13[5, 16], 14[4, 17]: i K. 17[2], 18[16]. Winer denied that this use of αὐτός is to be found in the N.T. But here we must dissent from his authority. See Mt. 5[5] and following: Lk. 6[20]: i Cor. 7[12].

b. As usual in later Greek the compound reflexive pronoun of the 3d person is used for those of the 1st and 2d.

Gen. 43[22] καὶ ἀργύριον ἕτερον ἠνέγκαμεν μεθ᾿ ἑαυτῶν. Dt. 3[7] καὶ τὰ σκῦλα τῶν πόλεων ἐπρονομεύσαμεν ἑαυτοῖς. i K. 17[8] ἐκλέξασθε ἑαυτοῖς ἄνδρα.

So also in Aristeas §§ 3, 213, 217, 228 (ἑαυτόν = σεαυτόν), 248. This usage had already begun in the best Attic. Take for instance —

Plat. Phœdo 91 C ὅπως μὴ ἐγώ . . . ἅμα ἑαυτόν τε καὶ ὑμᾶς ἐξαπατήσας, 78 B δεῖ ἡμᾶς ἐρέσθαι ἑαυτούς, 101 D σὺ δὲ δεδιὼς ἄν . . . τὴν ἑαυτοῦ σκιάν.

Instances abound in N.T.

Acts 23[14] ἀνεθεματίσαμεν ἑαυτούς, 5[35] προσέχετε ἑαυτοῖς.

c. A feature more peculiar to LXX Greek is the use of the personal pronoun along with the reflexive, like the English 'me myself,' 'you yourselves,' etc.

Ex. 6[7] καὶ λήμψομαι ἐμαυτῷ ὑμᾶς λαὸν ἐμοί, 20[23] οὐ ποιήσετε ὑμῖν ἑαυτοῖς.

So also Dt. 4[16, 23]: Josh. 22[16].

As there is nothing in the Hebrew to warrant this duplication of the pronoun, it may be set down as a piece of colloquial Greek.

d. The use of ἴδιος as a mere possessive pronoun is common to the LXX with the N.T. e.g. —

Job 7[10] οὐδ᾿ οὐ μὴ ἐπιστρέψῃ εἰς τὸν ἴδιον οἶκον. Mt. 22[5] ἀπῆλθον, ὁ μὲν εἰς τὸν ἴδιον ἀγρόν, ὁ δὲ ἐπὶ τὴν ἐμπορίαν αὐτοῦ.

**14. Numerals.** a. δυσί(ν) is the regular form for the dative of δύο. So also in N.T. e.g. Mt. 6[24], 22[40]: Lk. 16[13]: Acts 12[6].

δυεῖν occurs in Job 13[20], δυοῖν in iv Mac. 1[28], 15[2]. Sometimes δύο is indeclinable, e.g. Jdg. 16[28] τῶν δύο ὀφθαλμῶν.

b. The following forms of numerals differ from those in classical use: —

δέκα δύο Ex. 28[21]: Josh. 21[40], 18[24]: i Chr. 6[23], 15[10], 25[10 ff.]. So in N.T. Acts 19[7], 24[11]. Cp. Aristeas § 97.

δέκα τρεῖς Gen. 17²⁵: Josh. 19⁶.

δέκα τέσσαρες Josh. 15³⁶: Tob. 8²⁰.   So in N.T. ii Cor. 12², Gal. 2¹.
Cp. Diog. Laert. VII § 55.

δέκα πέντε Ex. 27¹⁵: Jdg. 8¹⁰: ii K. 19¹⁷.   So in N.T. Gal. 1¹⁸.

δέκα ἕξ Gen. 46¹⁸: Ex. 26²⁵: Josh. 15⁴¹.

δέκα ἑπτά Gen. 37², 47²⁸.

δέκα ὀκτώ Gen. 46²²: Josh. 24³³ ᵇ: Jdg. 3¹⁴, 10⁸, 20⁴⁴: i Chr. 12³¹:
ii Chr. 11²¹.

The above numerals occur also in the regular forms —

δώδεκα Gen. 5⁸.

τρεῖς καὶ δέκα, τρισκαίδεκα Nb. 29¹³, ¹⁴.

τέσσαρες καὶ δέκα Nb. 16⁴⁹.

πέντε καὶ δέκα Lvt. 27⁷: ii K. 9¹⁰.

ἑκκαίδεκα, ἑξ καὶ δέκα Nb. 31⁴⁰, ⁴⁶, ⁵².

ἑπτὰ καὶ δέκα Jer. 39⁹.

ὀκτὼ καὶ δέκα ii K. 8¹³.

ἐννέα καὶ δέκα ii K. 2³⁰ only.

c. The forms just given may be written separately or as one word.
This led to the τέσσαρες in τεσσαρεσκαίδεκα becoming indeclinable, e.g. —
ii Chr. 25⁵ υἱους τεσσαρεσκαίδεκα.

The same license is extended in the LXX to δέκα τέσσαρες.

Nb. 29²⁹ ἀμνοὺς ἐνιαυσίους δέκα τέσσαρες ἀμώμους.

The indeclinable use of τεσσαρεσκαίδεκα is not peculiar to the LXX.
Hdt. VII 36 τεσσαρεσκαίδεκα (τριήρεας).   Epict. Ench. 40 ἀπὸ
τεσσαρεσκαίδεκα ἐτῶν.   Strabo p. 177, IV 1 § 1 προσέθηκε δὲ
τεσσαρεσκαίδεκα ἔθνη, 189, IV 2 § 1 ἐθνῶν τεσσαρεσκαίδεκα.

d. The alternative expressions ὁ εἷς καὶ εἰκοστός (ii Chr. 24¹⁷) and
ὁ εἰκοστὸς πρῶτος (ii Chr. 25²⁸) are quite classical: but the following
way of expressing days of the month may be noted —
Haggai 2¹ μιᾷ καὶ εἰκάδι τοῦ μηνός.   i Mac. 1⁵⁹ πέμπτῃ καὶ εἰκάδι
τοῦ μηνός.   Cp. 4⁵⁹.   ii Mac. 10⁵ τῇ πέμπτῃ καὶ εἰκάδι τοῦ αὐτοῦ
μηνός.

## VERBS, 15–33

**15. The Verb Εἶναι.**   ἤμην the 1st person singular of the imperfect,
which is condemned by Phrynichus, occurs frequently in the LXX.
It is found also in the N.T.—i Cor. 13¹¹: Gal. 1¹⁰, ²²: Acts 10³⁰, 11⁵, ¹⁷,

$22^{19, \, 20}$: Mt. $25^{35}$: Jn. $11^{15}$. According to the text of Dindorf it occurs even in Eur. *Hel.* 931. It is a familiar feature of Hellenistic Greek, being common in Philo and Josephus, also in the *Pastor* of Hermas, and occurring moreover in such authors as Epictetus (*Diss.* I 16 § 19), Plutarch (*Pomp.* 74), Diogenes Laertius (VI § 56), Lucian (*Asinus* 46).

ἧς for ἦσθα, which is condemned by the same authority, occurs in Jdg. $11^{35}$: Ruth $3^2$: Job $38^4$: Obd. $1^{11}$. *Cp.* Epict. *Diss.* IV 1 § 132.

ἔστωσαν is the only form for the 3d person plural imperative, neither ἔστων nor ὄντων being used. This form is found in Plato (*Meno* 92 D). See § 16 d.

ἤτω for ἔστω occurs in Ps. $103^{31}$: i Mac. $10^{31}$, $16^3$. So in N.T. i Cor. $16^{22}$: James $5^{12}$. *Cp.* Herm. *Past. Vis.* III 3 § 4: i Clem. $48^5$, where it occurs four times.

ἤμεθα for ἦμεν occurs in i K. $25^{16}$: Baruch $1^{19}$. This form appears in the Revisers' text in Eph. $2^3$.

**16. The Termination -σαν.** *a.* Probably the thing which will first arrest the attention of the student who is new to the Greek of the LXX is the termination in -σαν of the 3d person plural of the historical tenses of the active voice other than the pluperfect.

There are in Greek two terminations of the 3d person plural of the historic tenses — (1) in -ν, (2) in -σαν. Thus in Homer we have ἔβαν and also ἔβησαν. In Attic Greek the rule is that thematic aorists (*i.e.* those which have a connecting vowel between the stem and the termination) and imperfects take ν, *e.g.* —

ἔ-λυσ-α-ν,    ἔ-λαβ-ο-ν,    ἐ-λάμβαν-ο-ν,

while non-thematic tenses and the pluperfect take -σαν, *e.g.* —

ἔ-δο-σαν,    ἐ-τί-θε-σαν,    ἐ-λε-λύκ-ε-σαν.

In the Greek of the LXX, which in this point represents the Alexandrian vernacular, thematic 2d aorists and imperfects may equally take -σαν.

Of 2d aorists we may take the following examples —

εἴδοσαν or ἴδοσαν, εἴποσαν, ἐκρίνοσαν, ἐλάβοσαν, ἐπίοσαν, εὕροσαν, ἐφέροσαν (= 2d aor.), ἐφάγοσαν, ἐφύγοσαν, ἤλθοσαν, ἡμάρτοσαν, ἤροσαν (Josh. $3^{14}$).

Compounds of these and others abound, *e.g.* —

ἀπήλθοσαν, διήλθοσαν, εἰσήλθοσαν, ἐξήλθοσαν, παρήλθοσαν, περιήλθοσαν, προσήλθοσαν, συνήλθοσαν, ἐνεβάλοσαν, παρενεβάλοσαν, ἐξελίποσαν, κατελίποσαν, ἀπεθάνοσαν, εἰσηγάγοσαν.

*b.* Instances of imperfects, which, for our present purpose, mean historic tenses formed from a strengthened present stem, do not come so readily to hand. But here are two —

ἐλαμβάνοσαν Ezk. 22¹². ἐφαίνοσαν i Mac. 4⁵⁰.

These seem to be more common in the case of contracted vowel verbs —

| | |
|---|---|
| ἐγεννῶσαν Gen. 6⁴ | εὐθηνοῦσαν Lam. 1⁵. |
| ἐπηξονοῦσαν Nb. 1¹⁸. | ἠνομοῦσαν Ezk. 22¹¹. |
| ἐποιοῦσαν Job 1⁴. | κατενοοῦσαν Ex. 33⁸. |
| ἐταπεινοῦσαν Judith 4⁹. | οἰκοδομοῦσαν ii Esd. 14¹⁸. |
| εὐλογοῦσαν Ps. 61⁵. | παρετηροῦσαν Sus. Θ¹². |
| ἐδολιοῦσαν Ps. 5⁹, 13³. | |

*Cp.* Herm. *Past. Sim.* VI 2 § 7 εὐσταθοῦσαν, IX 9 § 5 ἐδοκοῦσαν.

Such forms occur plentifully in Mss. of the N.T., but the Revisers' text has only ἐδολιοῦσαν in Romans 3¹³ (a quotation from Ps. 13³) and παρελάβοσαν in ii Thes. 3⁶.

*c.* The same termination -σαν sometimes takes the place of -εν in the 3d person plural of the optative.

| | |
|---|---|
| αἰνέσαισαν Gen. 49⁸. | θηρεύσαισαν Job 18⁷. |
| εἴποισαν Ps. 34²⁵. | ἴδοισαν Job 21²⁰. |
| ἐκκόψαισαν Prov. 24⁵². | καταφάγοισαν Prov. 30¹⁷. |
| ἐκλείποισαν Ps. 103³⁵. | ὀλέσαισαν Job 18¹¹, 20¹⁰. |
| ἔλθοισαν Dt. 33¹⁶ : Job 18⁹,¹¹. | περιπατήσαισαν Job 20²⁶. |
| ἐνέγκαισαν Is. 66²⁰. | ποιήσαισαν Dt. 1⁴⁴. |
| εὐλογήσαισαν Ps. 34²⁵. | πυρσεύσαισαν Job 20¹⁰. |
| εὕροισαν Sir. 33⁹. | ψηλαφήσαισαν Job 5¹⁴, 12²⁵. |

*d.* In Hellenistic Greek generally -σαν is also the termination of the 3d person plural of the imperative in all voices, *e.g.* —

i K. 30²² ἀπαγέσθωσαν καὶ ἀποστρεφέτωσαν.

For instances in N.T. see i Cor. 7⁹, ³⁶ : i Tim. 5⁴ : Tit. 3¹⁴ : Acts 24²⁰, 25⁵.

**17. Termination of the 2d Person Singular of Primary Tenses Middle and Passive.** In the LXX, as in Attic, the 2d person singular of the present and futures, middle and passive, ends in -η, *e.g.* ἄρξη, φάγη, λυπηθήση. The only exceptions to this rule in Attic are βούλει, οἴει, ὄψει, and ἔσει, of which the last is only used occasionally. In the LXX we have ὄψει in Nb. 23¹³.

The full termination-of the 2d person singular of primary tenses middle and passive (-σαι), which in Attic Greek appears only in the perfect of all verbs and in the present of -μι verbs, as λέ-λυ-σαι, δί-δο-σαι, is occasionally to be found in the LXX in other cases.

ἀπεξενοῦσαι iii K. 14⁶.

κοιμᾶσαι Dt. 31¹⁶ (A).

κτᾶσαι Sir. 6⁷.

πίεσαι Dt. 28³⁹: Ruth 2⁹, ¹⁴: iii K. 17⁴: Ps. 127²: Jer. 29¹³ (A): Ezk. 4¹¹, 12¹⁸, 23³², ³⁴.

φάγεσαι Ruth 2¹⁴: Ezk. 12¹⁸.

So in N.T. —

καυχᾶσαι Rom. 2¹⁷, ²³: i Cor. 4⁷.

κατακαυχᾶσαι Rom. 9¹⁸.

ὀδυνᾶσαι Lk. 16²⁵.

φάγεσαι καὶ πίεσαι σύ Lk. 17⁸.

The *Pastor* of Hermas yields us ἐπισπᾶσαι, πλανᾶσαι, χρᾶσαι. Such forms are still used in Modern Greek.

In theory -σαι is the termination of every 2d person singular in the middle and passive voices, as in δί-δο-σαι, λέ-λυ-σαι, so that πί-ε-σαι is a perfectly regular formation. But in Attic Greek the σ has dropped out wherever there is a connecting vowel, and then contraction has ensued. Thus πίεσαι becomes first πίεαι, and finally πίῃ. Confirmation of this theory is to be found in Homer, where there are many examples of the intermediate form, e.g. ἀναίρεαι, δευήσεαι, ἔρχεαι, εὔχεαι, ἴδηαι, κέλεαι, λέξεαι, λιλαίεαι, μαίνεαι, νέμεαι, ὀδύρεαι, πώλεαι. It is an interesting question whether πίεσαι and φάγεσαι are survivals in the popular speech of pre-Homeric forms, or rather revivals, as Jannaris and others think, on the analogy of the perfect middle and passive of all verbs and of the present middle and passive of -μι verbs.

In καυχᾶσαι and the like, contraction has taken place in the vowels preceding the σ (καυχάεσαι = καυχᾶσαι). ἀπεξενοῦσαι (iii K. 14⁶) looks like a barbarism for ἀπεξένωσαι.

As against these fuller forms, we sometimes find contracted forms in the LXX, where the -σαι is usual in Attic.

δύνῃ for δύνασαι. Dan. O' 5¹⁶. So in N.T. Lk. 16²: Rev. 2². In Eur. *Hec.* 253 Porson substituted δύνᾳ for δύνῃ, as being more Attic. δύνασαι itself occurs in Job 10¹³, 35⁶, ¹⁴, 42²: Wisd. 11²³: Dan. Θ 2²⁶, 4¹⁵, 5¹⁶: Bel Θ²⁴.

ἐπίστῃ for ἐπίστασαι. Nb. 20¹⁴: Dt. 22²: Josh. 14⁶: Job 38⁴: Jer. 17¹⁶: Ezk. 37⁴.

**18. Aorist in -α.** *a.* Another inflexional form for the frequency of which the classical student will hardly be prepared is the aorist in -α in other than semivowel verbs. Attic Greek offers some rare instances of this formation, as εἶπ-α, ἤνεγκ-α, ἔχε-α, and in Homer we have such stray forms as κήαντες (*Od.* IX 231), ἀλέασθαι (*Od.* IX 274), σεῦα (*Il.* XX 189). Nevertheless this is the type which has prevailed in the modern language.

*b.* In Attic the aorist εἶπα occurs more frequently in the other moods than in the indicative (*e.g.* Plat. *Soph.* 240 D εἴπαιμεν, *Prot.* 353 A εἴπατον imperative, *Phileb.* 60 D εἰπάτω, *Meno* 71 D εἶπον imperative).

In the LXX this aorist is equally common in the indicative.

εἶπα Dt. 1²⁰ : Ps. 40⁵.

εἶπας Gen. 44²³ : Judith 16¹⁴.   *Cp.* Hom. *Il.* I 106, 108.

εἴπαμεν Gen. 42³¹, 44²², ²⁶.

εἴπατε Gen. 43²⁹, 44²⁸, 45⁹.

εἶπαν Jdg. 14¹⁵, ¹⁸ : i K. 10¹⁴ : ii K. 17²⁰, 19⁴² : iv K. 1⁶ : Tob. 7⁵ : Jer. 49².

εἰπόν Gen. 45¹⁷ : Dan. Ο' 2⁷.

εἰπάτω Dan. Θ 2⁷.

εἴπατε (imperative) Gen. 50⁷.   *Cp.* Hom. *Od.* III 427.

εἶπας Gen. 46².

*c.* While the classical aorist ἦλθον is common in the LXX, the form with -α also occurs, especially in the plural.

ἤλθαμεν Nb. 13²⁸.

ἤλθατε Gen. 26²⁷, 42¹² : Dt. 1²⁰ : Jdg. 11⁷.

ἦλθαν Gen. 47¹⁸ : Jdg. 12¹ : ii K. 17²⁰, 24⁷ : ii Chr. 25¹⁸ : Dan. Θ 2².

ἐλθάτω Esther 5⁴, ⁸ : Is. 5¹⁹ : Jer. 17¹⁵.

ἔλθατε Prov. 9⁵.

εἰσελθάτωσαν Ex. 14⁶.

This aorist is common in Mss. of the N.T., but has not been admitted into the Revisers' text.   *Cp.* Herm. *Past. Vis.* I 4 § 1 ἦλθαν, § 3 ἀπῆλθαν : i Clem. 38³ εἰσήλθαμεν.

*d.* By the side of εἶδον we have an aorist in -α, especially in the 3d person plural, where its advantage is obvious.   (See *h* below.)

εἴδαμεν i K. 10¹⁴.

εἶδαν Jdg. 6²⁸, 16²⁴ : i K. 6¹⁹ : ii K. 10¹⁴, ¹⁹.

*e.* Similarly by the side of εἷλον we have parts formed as though from εἷλα.

καθεῖλαν Gen. 44¹¹ : iii K. 19¹⁴.
εἵλατο Dt. 26¹⁸.
ἀνείλατο Ex. 2⁵.
ἀφείλατο i K. 30¹⁸.
διείλαντο Josh. 22⁸.
ἐξειλάμην i K. 10¹⁸.
ἐξείλατο Ex. 18⁴, ⁸ : Josh. 24¹⁰ : i K. 12¹¹, 17³⁷, 30¹⁸.
παρείλατο Nb. 11²⁵.

*f.* The aorist ἔπεσα occurs frequently in the 3d person plural, but is rare in other parts.

ἔπεσα Dan. O' 8¹⁷.               πεσάτω Jer. 44²⁰ (AS), 49² (AS).
ἔπεσας ii K. 3³⁴.               πέσατε Hos. 10⁸.

Among compounds we find ἀποπεσάτωσαν, διέπεσαν, ἐνέπεσαν, ἐπέπεσαν. So in N.T. —

ἔπεσα Rev. 1¹⁷.
ἔπεσαν Rev. 5¹⁴, 6¹³, 11¹⁶, 17¹⁰ : Hb. 11³⁰.
ἐξεπέσατε Gal. 5⁴.

*Cp.* Polyb. III 19 § 5 ἀντέπεσαν.

*g.* Other aorists of the same type are —

ἀπέθαναν Tob. 3⁹.               ἔλαβαν ii K. 23¹⁶.
ἐγκατέλιπαν ii Chr. 29⁶.        ἐφάγαμεν ii K. 19⁴².
ἔβαλαν iii K. 6³.               ἔφυγαν Jdg. 7²¹.
ἐμβάλατε Gen. 44¹.

*h.* The frequency of the 3d person plural in this form is no doubt due to a desire to differentiate the 3d person plural from the 1st person singular, which are confounded in the historic tenses ending in -ον. It also secured uniformity of ending with the aorist in -σα. In ii K. 10¹⁴ we have this collocation —

εἶδαν . . . ἔφυγαν . . . εἰσῆλθαν . . . ἀνέστρεψαν.

In Jdg. 6³ we find the anomalous form ἀνέβαιναν followed by συνανέβαινον.

**19. Augment.** *a.* The augment with the pluperfect is at times omitted by Plato and the best Attic writers. Instances in the LXX are —

βεβρώκει i K. 30¹².             ἐνδεδύκει Lvt. 16²³.
δεδώκειν ii K. 18¹¹.            ἐπιβεβήκει Nb. 22²².
δεδώκει iii K. 10¹³.            πεπώκει i K. 30¹².
ἐνδεδύκειν Job 29¹⁴.

So in N.T. —

δεδώκει Mk. 14⁴⁴.　　　　　　　μεμενήκεισαν i Jn. 2¹⁹.

δεδώκεισαν Jn. 11⁵⁷: cp. Mk. 15¹⁰.　πεπιστεύκεισαν Acts 14²³.

ἐκβεβλήκει Mk. 16⁹.　　　　　　πεποιήκεισαν Mk. 15⁷.

κεκρίκει Acts 20¹⁶.

But in the LXX we occasionally find other historic tenses without the augment, e.g. ii Esd. 14¹⁸ οἰκοδομοῦσαν. This is especially the case with εἶδον.

ἴδες Lam. 3⁵⁹.　　　　　　　　ἴδον Gen. 37²⁵, 40⁵.

ἴδεν Gen. 37⁹, 40⁶.　　　　　　πρόιδον Gen. 37¹⁸

b. In Attic Greek, when a preposition had lost its force and was felt as part of the verb, the augment was placed before, instead of after, it, as ἐκάθευδον, ἐκάθιζον, ἐκαθήμην.

The same law holds in the Greek of the LXX, but is naturally extended to fresh cases, e.g. to προνομεύειν, which in the Alexandrian dialect seems to have been the common word for 'to ravage.'

ἐπρονομεύσαμεν Dt. 2³⁵, 3⁷.　　ἠνεχύρασαν Job 24³.

ἐπρονόμευσαν Nb. 31⁹.

c. The aorist ἤνοιξα is already found in Xenophon. In the LXX it is common, though by no means to the exclusion of the form with internal augment. Besides ἤνοιξα itself, which is conjugated throughout the singular and plural, we have also the following —

ἠνοίχθη Nb. 16³²: Ps. 105¹⁷, 108¹.　ἤνοιγον i Mac. 11².

ἠνοίχθησαν Ezk. 1¹.　　　　　　ἠνοίγετο iii K. 7²¹.

ἠνοιγμένα Is. 42²⁰.

So also in N.T. —

ἤνοιξε Acts 12¹⁴, 14²⁷: Rev. 8¹.　διηνοιγμένους Acts 7⁵⁶.

διήνοιξε Acts 16¹⁴.　　　　　　ἠνοίγη Rev. 11¹⁹.

Besides the Attic form with double internal augment, ἀνέῳξα, the LXX has also forms which augment the initial vowel of this, and so display a triple augment —

ἠνέῳξε Gen. 8⁶: iii Mac. 6¹⁸.

ἠνεῴχθησαν Gen. 7¹¹: Sir. 43¹⁴: Dan. 7¹⁰.

ἠνεῳγμένους iii K. 8²⁹: ii Chr. 6²⁰, ⁴⁰, 7¹⁵: Neh. 1⁶.

ἠνεῳγμένα iii K. 8⁵².

So in N.T. —

ἠνεῳγμένον Rev. 10⁸.

*d.* In προφητεύειν the internal augment is wrong, since the verb is formed on the noun προφήτης. In the LXX προεφήτευσεν occurs only in i K. 18¹⁰ (A) and Sir. 46²⁰. Nevertheless this is the form which has been everywhere preferred in the Revisers' text of the N.T.

προεφήτευον Acts 19⁶.
προεφήτευσε Mt. 15⁷: Mk. 7⁶: Lk. 1⁶⁷: Jn. 11⁵¹: Jude¹⁴.
προεφητεύσαμεν Mt. 7²².
προεφήτευσαν Mt. 11¹⁸.

*e.* Instances of double augment in the LXX are —

ἀπεκατέστη Ex. 15²⁷.
ἀπεκατέστησεν i Esd. 1³³.
ἠνωχλήθην i K. 30¹³. *Cp.* Dan. 3⁵⁰: Dan. O' 6¹⁸.

**20. Reduplication.** *a.* In verbs compounded with a preposition reduplication is sometimes applied to the preposition.

κεκαταραμένος Dt. 21²³: Sir. 3¹⁶. *Cp.* Enoch 27².
πεπρονομευμένος Is. 42². *Cp.* § 19 *b.*

*b.* In the form κεκατήρανται (Nb. 22⁶, 24⁹. *Cp.* Enoch 27¹˒².) we have what may be called double reduplication.

*c.* With ῥεριμμένος (Jdg. 4²²) and ἐκρεριμμένην (Jdg. 15¹⁵) may be compared Homer's ῥερυπωμένα (*Od.* VI 59). ῥερίφθαι [ῥερῖφθαι] is cited from Pindar by Chœroboscus.

*d.* The reduplicated present ἐκδιδύσκειν occurs in four passages — i K. 31⁸: ii K. 23¹⁰: Neh. 4²³: Hos. 7¹. It is used also by Josephus. Κιχρᾶν, 'to lend,' occurs in three passages — i K. 1²⁸: Prov. 13¹¹: Ps. 111⁵. κίχρημι is used in this sense by Demosthenes.

*e.* The verb κράζειν has a reduplicated weak aorist, ἐκέκραξα, which is very common, especially in the Psalms; also a reduplicated strong aorist, though this is very rare.

ἐκέκραγεν Is. 6³.      ἐκέκραγον Is. 6⁴.

**21. Attic Future.** *a.* What is called the Attic future, *i.e.* the future out of which σ has dropped, is more common in the LXX than in Attic Greek. Thus the future of ἐλπίζειν, so far as it appears in Attic authors at all, is ἐλπίσω: but in the LXX it is always ἐλπιῶ. Among verbs in -ιζω which take this form of future are —

| | | | |
|---|---|---|---|
| αἰχμαλωτίζειν | ἐγγίζειν | κερατίζειν | οἰωνίζειν |
| ἀποσκορακίζειν | ἐπιστηρίζειν | κομίζειν | σαββατίζειν |
| ἀφαγνίζειν | εὐαγγελίζειν | μελίζειν | συλλογίζειν |
| ἀφανίζειν | καθαρίζειν | μερίζειν | συνετίζειν |
| ἀφορίζειν | καθίζειν | | |

There is no apparent reason for the contraction in the future of verbs in -ίζειν. The retention of σ in the future of such verbs is quite exceptional, as in Eccl. 11⁴ θερίσει (mid.), Lvt. 25⁵ ἐκθερίσεις. Of the two versions of Daniel O' has in 4²⁹ ψωμίσουσι, while Θ has ψωμιοῦσιν. Μηνίειν has a future in the LXX of the same sort as verbs in -ίζειν.

μηνιῶ Jer. 3¹².                          μηνιεῖς Lvt. 19¹⁸.
μηνιεῖ Ps. 102⁹.

*b.* In Attic Greek there are a few instances of verbs in -άζειν dropping the σ and contracting in the future. Thus βιβάζειν, ἐξετάζειν have the futures βιβῶ, ἐξετῶ in addition to the full forms. In the LXX the former of these sometimes retains the σ in the future (Dt. 6⁷: Ps. 31⁸: Is. 40¹³: Wisd. 6³: Sir. 13¹¹), the latter always: but the tendency which they exemplify is carried out in the case of other verbs in -άζειν. Hence we meet with the following futures —

ἁρπᾷ Lvt. 19¹³.
ἁρπῶμαι Hos. 5¹⁴.
ἐκδικᾶται Lvt. 19¹⁸: Dt. 32⁴³: Judith 11¹⁰.
ἐργᾷ Gen. 4¹², 29²⁷: Ex. 20⁹, 34²¹: Lvt. 25⁴⁰: Dt. 5¹³,15¹⁹: ii K. 9¹⁰.
ἐργᾶται Lvt. 25⁴⁰: Job 33²⁹.
ἐργῶνται Is. 5¹⁰: Jer. 37⁸,⁹, 22¹³, 41¹⁴: Ezk. 48¹⁹.
κατεργᾷ Dt. 28³⁹.
κοιμᾷ Dt. 31¹⁶.
κοιμᾶται Job 8¹⁷.

*c.* Both in the LXX and in the N.T. semivowel verbs, *i.e.* those with λ, ρ, μ, ν, have a contracted future, as in Attic, *e.g.* ψαλῶ, σπερεῖς, τεμεῖς, ῥανεῖ.

*d.* In Attic Greek the future of χέω is still χέω and indistinguishable from the present. In the LXX the future is distinguished by being treated as a contracted tense. Thus we have —

ἐκχεῶ,    ἐκχεεῖς,    ἐκχεεῖ,
ἐκχεεῖτε,    ἐκχεοῦσι.

The 1st person plural does not seem to occur.

*e.* To the contracted futures the LXX adds the post-classical ἐλῶ, from the same stem as εἶλον. This future occurs both in the active and the middle voices, *e.g.* ἀφελῶ (Nb. 11¹⁷), ἐξελεῖσθε (Josh. 2¹³).

So in N.T. —

ἀνελεῖ ii Th. 2⁸.

*f.* In Attic τελεῖν and καλεῖν are in the future indistinguishable from the present. In the later Greek of the LXX this ambiguity is avoided by the retention of the full form of the future. Thus we have—

|  | | |
|---|---|---|
| συντελέσω, | συντελέσεις, | συντελέσει, |
| | συντελέσετε, | συντελέσουσιν, |

and

|  | | |
|---|---|---|
| καλέσω, | καλέσεις, | καλέσει, |
| | καλέσετε, | καλέσουσιν. |

*g.* The future ὀλέσω, which is common in Homer but rare in Attic, does not occur in the LXX, which has only the contracted forms —

ὀλεῖ Prov. 1[32].
ὀλεῖται Job 8[13].

ὀλοῦνται Prov. 2[22], 13[2], 15[5], 16[33], 25[19].

*h.* On the other hand, ἐλάσεις in Ex. 25[11] is the only instance of the future of ἐλαύνω in the LXX.

*i.* In Attic σκεδάννυμι has future σκεδῶ, but in the LXX it retains the σ, *e.g.* διασκεδάσω Jdg. 2[1].

**22. Retention of Short Vowel in the Future.** As a rule in Greek α and ε verbs lengthen the vowel in forming the future. Exceptions are σπάω and χαλάω among α verbs, and among ε verbs αἰνέω, καλέω, τελέω. When the vowel is short in the future, it is also short in the 1st aorist.

To the ε verbs which have the vowel short in the future and 1st aorist we may add from the LXX πονεῖν, φθονεῖν, φορεῖν.

So in N.T.—

ἐφορέσαμεν . . . φορέσομεν i Cor. 15[49].

*Cp.* Herm. *Past. Sim.* IX 13 § 3, 15 § 6 ἐφόρεσαν.

**23. Aorist of Semivowel Verbs.** In Attic Greek semivowel verbs with ᾰ in their stem lengthen the ᾰ into η in forming the 1st aorist (as φαν-, ἔφηνα), except after ι or ρ, when they lengthen into ᾱ (as μιαν-, ἐμίανα, περαν-, ἐπέρανα). See G. § 672.

In the LXX many such verbs lengthen into ᾱ when the ᾰ of the stem is preceded by a consonant. Hence we meet with such forms as ἐγλύκανας, ἐκκάθαρον, ἐξεκάθαρα, ἐπέχαρας, ἐπίφανον, ἐποίμανεν, ἐσήμα-νεν, σημάνῃ, ὑφᾶναι, ὕφανεν, ὑφάνῃς, ψάλατε. In Amos 5[2] ἔσφαλεν is ambiguous, as it might be 2d aorist.

The form καθάρῃς is read in Dindorf's text of Xen. *Œc.* 18 § 8, and in Hermann's text of Plato *Laws* 735 we have καθάρῃ in B followed by καθήρειεν in D. The aorist ἐσήμανα is found as early as Xenophon. *Cp.* Aristeas §§ 16, 33. Ἐκέρδανα was always regarded as good Attic.

Such forms are also to be found in the N.T., *e.g.* —

ἐβάσκανεν Gal. 3¹.        ἐσήμανεν Rev. 1¹.

**24. The Strong Tenses of the Passive.** The Greek of the LXX displays a preference for the strong over the weak tenses of the passive, *i.e.* for the tenses which are formed directly from the verbal stem, namely, the 2d aorist and the 2d future. Thus ἠγγέλην, which is not to be found in classical authors, except in a disputed reading of Eur. *I. T.* 932, occurs frequently (in compounds) in the LXX, and the future passive, when employed, is the corresponding form in -ήσομαι, *e.g.* Ps. 21⁸¹ ἀναγγελήσεται, Ps. 58¹³ διαγγελήσονται.

So again from ῥίπτω we find only the 2d aorist and 2d future passive, *e.g.* Ezk. 19¹² ἐρρίφη, ii K. 20²¹ ῥιφήσεται.

The following are other instances of the same formation: —

βραχήσεται (βρέχω) Is. 34³.
γραφήσονται Ezk. 13⁹.    *Cp.* Aristeas § 32.
διεθρύβησαν Nahum 1⁶.
ἐκλεγῆναι Dan. O' 11³⁵.
ἐλιγήσεται Is. 34⁴.
ἐνεφράγη Ps. 62¹².
ἐξαλιφῆναι i Chr. 29⁴.    *Cp.* Plat. *Phœdr.* 258 B.
ἐπεσκέπησαν i Chr. 26³¹.
ἠκαταστάτησαν Tobit 1¹⁵.
ὀρυγῇ Ps. 93¹⁸.
περιεπλάκησαν Ps. 118⁶¹.
συνεφρύγησαν Ps. 101⁴.
ὑπετάγησαν Ps. 59¹⁰.

**25. The Verbs πεινᾶν and διψᾶν.** In Attic Greek these two verbs contract into η instead of ᾱ. In the LXX they contract into ᾱ, and πεινάω further forms its future and aorist in ᾱ instead of η.

ἐὰν πεινᾷ . . . ἐὰν διψᾷ Prov. 25²¹.    ἐπείνας Dt. 25¹⁸.
διψᾷ (ind.) Is. 29⁸.

The parts of πεινᾶν which occur in the future and aorist are πεινάσει, πεινάσετε, πεινάσουσι, ἐπείνασεν, ἐπείνασαν, πεινάσω (subj.), πεινάσωμεν, πεινάσητε.

So also in N.T. —

πεινᾶν Phil. 4¹².

πεινᾷ (ind.) i Cor. 11²¹.

πεινᾷ . . . διψᾷ (subj.) Rom. 12²⁰ (quoted from Prov. 25²¹).

ἐάν τις διψᾷ Jn. 7³⁷.

For the future and aorist of πεινᾶν in N.T. see Mt. 12¹ˌ³, 25³⁵:
Lk. 4²: Jn. 6³⁵: Rev. 7¹⁶.

**26. The Perfect of ἥκειν.** Ἥκειν in the LXX has a perfect ἧκα,
which occurs however only in the plural.

ἥκαμεν Gen. 47⁴: Josh. 9¹².

ἥκατε Gen. 42⁷ˌ⁹: Dt. 12⁹: i Chr. 12¹⁷.

ἥκασι(ν) 18 times.

This form occurs once in the N.T. —

ἥκασι Mk. 8³.

*Cp.* i Clem. 12² in a quotation from Josh. 2³.

The aorist ἧξα, which is found in late authors, is not used in the
LXX.

Wherever the form ἧκε occurs, it is either imperative, as in ii K.
14³², or imperfect, as in ii Mac. 4³¹, 8³⁵, 14⁴ˌ²⁶.

**27. Presents formed from Perfects.**    *a.* From the perfect ἕστηκα there
was formed a new present στήκω, which occurs in two or three passages of the LXX.

στήκει Jdg. 16²⁶.                στήκειν iii K. 8¹¹.

στήκετε (imper.) Ex. 14¹³ (A).

So in N.T. —

στήκει Rom. 14⁴.

στήκετε (ind.) Phil. 1²⁷.

στήκετε (imper.) i Cor. 16¹³: Gal. 5¹: Phil. 4¹: ii Thes. 2¹⁵.

στήκητε i Th. 3⁸: Mk. 11²⁵.

*b.* Similar to this is the verb γρηγορεῖν, formed from ἐγρήγορα. We
may conjecture that the pluperfect ἐγρηγόρει came to be regarded as
a contracted imperfect, and so gave rise to γρηγορῶ.

ἐγρηγόρουν Jer. 38²⁸.

γρηγορεῖν i Mac. 12²⁷.

γρηγορούντων Neh. 7³.

γρηγορήσω Jer. 38²⁸ː

ἐγρηγόρησε(ν) Jer. 5⁶: Bar. 2⁹: Dan. Θ 9¹⁴.

ἐγρηγορήθη Lam. 1¹⁴.

From this verb in its turn was formed a new verbal noun γρηγόρη-
σις Dan. Θ 5¹¹,¹⁴.   Cp. also the proper name Γρηγόριος.
So in N.T. —

γρηγορῶμεν i Th. 5⁶. .
γρηγορεῖτε (imper.) i Cor. 16¹³ : Mk. 13³⁷.
γρηγορήσατε i Pet. 5⁸.

c. Of like origin is the aorist ἐπεποίθησα, which occurs in Job 31²⁴.
From πεποιθεῖν again we have the noun πεποίθησις iv K. 18¹⁹.

d. The tendency to form new presents from perfects is already
exhibited in Homer.   Thus we have ἀνώγει (Od. V 139 etc.) formed
from ἄνωγα, and γεγωνεῖν (Il. XII 337) from γέγωνα; also the imperfect ἐμέμηκον (Od. IX 439) from μέμηκα.

**28. The Verb ἱστάναι and its Cognates.**   By the side of the forms in
-μι there existed from Homer downwards alternative forms in -ω.
Some of these present themselves in the LXX.   Thus we have the
following parts of the transitive verb ἱστάω.

ἱστῶσιν i Mac. 8¹.
ἱστῶν ii K. 22³⁴ : Job 6² : Ps. 17³³ : Sir. 27²⁶ : Is. 44²⁶ : i Mac. 2²⁷.
Among its compounds we may notice the following —
καθιστῶν Dt. 17¹⁵ : Dan. O' 4³⁴.   Cp. Aristeas § 228.
καθιστᾷ . . . μεθιστᾷ Dan. Θ 2²¹.
μεθιστῶν . . . καθιστῶν Dan. O' 2²¹.
μεθιστῶσι i Mac. 8¹³.
μεθιστᾶν iii Mac. 6²⁴.
So in N.T. —

| | |
|---|---|
| ἱστῶμεν Rom. 3³¹. | συνιστῶν ii Cor. 10¹⁸. |
| ἀποκαθιστᾷ Mk. 9¹². | συνιστῶντες ii Cor. 4², 6⁴. |

The form ἱστάνειν, also transitive, occurs in Ezk. 17¹⁴.   Cp. Aristeas §§ 280, 281 καθιστάνειν.
So in N.T. —

μεθιστάνειν i Cor. 13².       συνιστάνειν ii Cor. 3¹.   Cp. 5¹², 10¹².

Cp. Herm. Past. Vis. I 3 § 4 μεθιστάνει.

Later Greek has a transitive perfect ἕστᾰκα, which is implied by
the rare, though classical, perfect passive ἕσταμαι (Plat. Tim. 81 D).
Thus in [Plato] Axiochus 370 D we find περιέστακας.

ἑστάκαμεν i Mac. 11³⁴.
ἀφέστακα Jer. 16⁵.
καθέστακα Jer. 1¹⁰, 6¹⁷.
καθεστάκαμεν i Mac. 10²⁰.   Cp. Aristeas § 37.

So in N.T. —

ἐξεστακέναι Acts 8¹¹.

In Josh. 10¹⁹ there occurs the irregular perfect imperative ἐστήκατε with connecting vowel α instead of ε. With this form may be compared πεποίθατε Ps. 145³ : Is. 50¹⁰ : Jer. 9⁴.

**29. The Verb τιθέναι and its Cognates.** This verb does not offer much scope for remark. The imperfect is formed, so far as it occurs, from the alternative form τιθέω.

ἐτίθεις Ps. 49¹⁸,²⁰. ἐτίθει Prov. 8²⁸.

This is in accordance with classical usage, which however has ἐτίθην in the 1st person. Ἐτίθη is read by A in Esther 4⁴.

The strong and weak aorists active seem to be about equally frequent. The only person of the latter that is missing is the 2d person plural. Ἐθήκαμεν is found (ii Esd. 15¹⁰ : Is. 28¹⁵) and ἔθηκαν is common.

The 2d person singular of the strong aorist middle is always ἔθου, as in Attic.

In i Esd. 4³⁰ we find ἐπιτιθοῦσαν formed from the thematic τιθέω.

**30. The Verb διδόναι and its Cognates.** The present tense runs thus —

δίδωμι, δίδως, δίδωσι,
διδόασιν.

In Ps. 36²¹ we find 3d person singular διδοῖ from the cognate διδόω. The imperfect runs thus —

ἐδίδουν, ἐδίδους, ἐδίδου,
ἐδίδουν or ἐδίδοσαν.

Ἐδίδουν as 3d person plural occurs in ii Chr. 27⁵ : iii Mac. 3³⁰; ἐδίδοσαν in Judith 7²¹ : Jer. 44²¹ : Ezk. 23⁴² : iii Mac. 2³¹.

The imperative active δίδου is found in Tobit 4¹⁶ : Prov. 9⁹, 22²⁶. The 1st aorist is common in the singular and in the 3d person plural of the indicative, ἔδωκαν.

The 2d aorist subjunctive runs thus —

δῶ, δῷς, δῷ,
δῶτε, δῶσι.

Of the above forms only διδοῖ, 3d person plural ἐδίδουν, and ἔδωκαν are non-Attic.

The optative of the 2d aorist has the stem vowel long —

δῴης Ps. 84[7], 120[3].

δῴη 29 times. In Job 6[8], 19[23]: Sir. 45[26] δοίη occurs as a variant. Cp. Aristeas § 185 δῴη.

So in N.T. —

δῴη ii Th. 3[16]: Rom. 15[5]: Eph. 1[17]: ii Tim. 1[16, 18], 2[25].

**31. The Verb ἰέναι and its Cognates.** *a.* The simple verb ἰέναι does not occur in the LXX. It has therefore to be studied in its compounds. The regular inflexion of the imperfect in Attic is supposed to be ἴην, ἴεις, ἴει, though in Plat. *Euthyd.* 293 A we have 1st person singular ᾔειν. Ἡφίεις therefore (Sus. O[′53]) may be considered classical.

*b.* The following two passages will set before us the points that have to be noticed with regard to ἀφιέναι —

Ex. 32[32] εἰ μὲν ἀφεῖς . . . ἄφες.     i Esd. 4[7] εἶπεν ἀφεῖναι, ἀφίουσιν.

In the former of these ἀφεῖς must be from ἀφέω, a cognate thematic form to ἀφίημι, but without the reduplication.

In the latter we have a new formation which treats the reduplication as though it were itself the stem. Of this new verb we have the following parts —

ἀφίω Eccl. 2[18].     ἀφίουσι i Esd. 4[50].
ἀφίων Eccl. 5[11].

In the N.T. also we find ἀφεῖς (Rev. 2[20]) and ἤφιε(ν) (Mk. 1[34], 11[16]) the imperfect of ἀφίω. Cp. Herm. *Past. Vis.* III 7 § 1 ἀφίουσιν.

The weak aorist occurs in the singular and in the 3d person plural ἀφῆκαν, *e.g.* Jdg. 1[34].

*c.* A thematic verb συνιεῖν existed in classical Greek. Theognis 565 has the infinitive συνιεῖν: Plat. *Soph.* 238 E uses ξυνιεῖς. Of this verb we find the following parts in the LXX, if we may trust the accentuation —

συνιεῖν iii K. 3[9, 11].     συνιοῦσιν (dat. pl.) Prov. 8[9].
συνιῶν ii Chr. 34[12].

So also in N.T. —

ὁ συνιῶν Rom. 3[11].   In Mt. 13[23] the R.V. text has συνιών.
συνιοῦσι (3d pl.) Mt. 13[13]: ii Cor. 10[12].

*d.* In addition to this we find a verb of new formation like
ἀφίω —

συνίεις Tob. 3⁸ ; Job 15⁹, 36⁴.
συνίει Prov. 21¹²,²⁹ : Wisd. 9¹¹.
συνίων Dan. Θ 8⁵,²³,²⁷ and *passim.*
συνιόντων (gen. pl.) ii Chr. 30²².

In ii Chr. 26⁵ συνιόντος and ii Esd. 8¹⁶ συνιόντας the accent seems
to be misplaced.

The new participle συνίων has not entirely ousted the -μι form in
the LXX. We have συνιείς Ps. 32¹⁵ : οἱ συνιέντες Dan. 12³ : συνιέντας
Dan. Θ 1:4 τῶν συνιέντων Dan. 11³⁵.

*e.* The 3d person plural of the 1st aorist ἧκαν, which occurs in
Xen. *Anab.* IV 5 § 18, is used in the LXX in its compound
ἀφῆκαν.

*f.* The verb συνίειν is to be met with also in the Apostolic
Fathers —

συνίω Herm. *Past. Mdt.* IV 2 § 1, X 1 § 3.
συνίει IV 2 § 2.
συνίουσιν X 1 § 6.
σύνιε VI 2 §§ 3, 6 : *Sim.* IX 12 § 1.
συνίων Barn. *Ep.* 12¹⁰.

*g.* The 2d person singular present middle προίῃ in Job 7¹⁹ is doubtless formed on the analogy of λύῃ, but might be reached from προίεσαι
by loss of σ and contraction.

**32. The Imperatives ἀνάστα and ἀπόστα, etc.** It is the by-forms in
-ω which account for these imperatives (ἀνάστα = ἀνάστα-ε). Ἀνάστα
in the LXX is used interchangeably with ἀνάστηθι. Thus in Dan. 7⁵
O' has ἀνάστα, while Θ has ἀνάστηθι. But the same writer even will
go from one to the other. Thus in iii K. 19 we have ἀνάστηθι in
v. 5 and ἀνάστα in v. 7, and again in iii K. 20 ἀνάστα in v. 15 and ἀνάστηθι in v. 18. So also Ps. 43²⁴,²⁷ ἀνάστηθι . . . ἀνάστα. Ἀπόστα occurs
in Job 7¹⁶, 14⁶, 21¹⁴.

So in N.T., where we find in addition the 3d person singular and
the 2d person plural.

ἀνάστα Acts 12⁷ : Eph. 5¹⁴.          καταβάτω Mt. 27⁴².
ἀνάβα Rev. 4¹.                       ἀναβάτε Rev. 11¹².

*Cp.* Herm. *Past. Mdt.* VI 2 §§ 6, 7 ἀπόστα . . . ἀπόστηθι, *Vis.* 2 § 8
ἀντίστα.

Similar forms are to be found even in the Attic drama and earlier.

ἔμβα Eur. *Elec.* 113 : Ar. *Ran.* 377.

ἐπίβα Theognis 845.

ἔσβα Eur. *Phœn.* 193.

κατάβα Ar. *Ran.* 35, *Vesp.* 979.

πρόβα Eur. *Alc.* 872 : Ar. *Ach.* 262.

### 33. Special Forms of Verbs.

αἱρετίζειν denominative from αἱρετός.

ἀμφιάζειν iv K. 17⁹ : Job 29¹⁴, 31¹⁹ (in 40⁵ ἀμφίεσαι) = ἀμφιεννύναι.

ἀποκτέννειν Ex. 4²³ : ii K. 4¹² : iv K. 17²⁵ : Ps. 77³⁴, 100⁸ : Wisd. 16¹⁴ : Hab. 1¹⁷ : Is. 66³ : Dan. Θ 2¹³ : iii Mac. 7¹⁴.

ἀποτιννύειν Gen. 31³⁹ : Ps. 68⁵ : Sir. 20¹².

ἐλεᾶν for ἐλεεῖν. Ps. 36²⁶, 114⁶ : Prov. 13⁹, 14²¹, ³¹, 21²⁶, 28⁸ : Sir. 18¹⁴ : Tobit 13² : iv Mac. 6¹², 9³. So in N.T., Jude²², ²³. *Cp.* i Clem. 13² : Barn. Ep. 20².

ἐλούσθης Ezk. 16⁴.

ἑόρακας ii K. 18¹¹. Maintained by some to be the true Attic form.

ἐρρηγώς for ἐρρωγώς. Job 32¹⁹.

ἔσθειν for ἐσθίειν. Lvt. 7¹⁵, 11³⁴, 17¹⁰, 19⁸, ²⁶ : Sir. 20¹⁶. Old poetic form. Hom. *Il.* XXIV 415 : *Od.* IX 479, X 273.

κάθου for κάθησο. Gen. 38¹¹ : Jdg. 17¹⁰ : Ruth 3¹⁸ : i K. 1²³, 22⁵, ²³ : iv K. 2², ⁴, ⁶ : Ps. 109¹ : Sir. 9⁷. Formed on the analogy of λύου. Κάθησο itself occurs in ii Chr. 25¹⁹. In Ezk. 23⁴¹ we have imperfect ἐκάθου. So in N.T., Mt. 22⁴⁴ : Mk. 12³⁶ : Lk. 20⁴² : Acts 2³⁴ : Hb. 1¹³ (all quotations from Ps. 109¹) : James 2³.

μαιμάσσειν Jer. 4¹⁹.

οἶσθας Dt. 9². Cp. Eur. *Ion* 999 (Dindorf).

πιάζειν for πιέζειν. Song 2¹⁵ : Sir. 23²¹. Πιέζειν occurs only in Micah 6¹⁵ in the original sense of ' to press.'

ῥάσσειν Jer. 23³⁹ and eight other passages.

### 34. Adverbs.

Hellenistic Greek supplied the missing adverb to ἀγαθός. Ἀγαθῶς occurs in Aristotle *Rh.* II 11 § 1. In the LXX it is found in i K. 20⁷ : iv K. 11¹⁸ : Tob. 13¹⁰.

Among adverbs of time we may notice ἐκ πρωίθεν and ἀπὸ πρωίθεν as peculiar to the LXX. For the former see ii K. 2²⁷ : iii K. 18²⁶ : i Mac. 10⁸⁰ ; for the latter Ex. 18¹³, ¹⁴ : Ruth 2⁷ : Job 4²⁰ : Sir. 18²⁶ : i Mac. 9¹³. Similar to these among adverbs of place is ἀπὸ μακρόθεν, Ps. 138². Such expressions remind us of our own double form ' from whence,' which purists condemn.

In the Greek of the LXX ποῦ is used for ποῖ, just as we commonly say 'where' for 'whither.'

Jdg. 19¹⁷ Ποῦ πορεύῃ, καὶ πόθεν ἔρχῃ;

Cp. Gen. 37³¹: Josh. 2⁵, 8¹⁰: Jdg. 19¹⁷: i K. 10¹⁴: Zech. 2².

Ποῖ occurs only in a doubtful reading in Jer. 2²⁸, and has there the sense of ποῦ.

Similarly οὗ is used for οἷ, which is not found at all.

Jer. 51²³ οὗ ἐὰν βαδίσῃς ἐκεῖ.

Cp. Gen. 40³: Ex. 21¹³: iii K. 18¹⁰: Ezk. 12¹⁶.

So in N.T. —

ποῦ = ποῖ i Jn. 2¹¹, 3⁸: Jn. 8¹⁴: Hb. 11⁸.

ὅπου = ὅποι James 3⁴.

ὅποι does not occur in Biblical Greek.

**35. Homerisms.** The Ionic infusion which is observable in the Greek of the LXX may possibly be due to the use of Homer as a schoolbook in Alexandria. This would be a *vera causa* in accounting for such stray Ionisms as κυνομυίης, μαχαίρῃ, ἐπιβεβηκυίης, and the use of σπείρης in the Papyri; possibly also for γαιῶν, γαίαις. Such forms also as ἐπαοιδός, ἔσθειν, ἐτάνυσαν (Sir. 43¹²), μόλιβος, χάλκειος, χείμαρρος, πολεμιστής, have an Homeric ring about them.

**36. Movable Consonants.** ν ἐφελκυστικόν is freely employed before consonants, as in Gen. 31¹⁵, 41⁵⁵: Dt. 19¹: Ruth 2³: Jdg. 16¹¹.

To ἄχρι and μέχρι ς is sometimes appended before a vowel and sometimes not.

| | |
|---|---|
| Jdg. 11³³ ἄχρις Ἄρνων. | Josh. 4²³ μέχρις οὗ. |
| Job 32¹¹ ἄχρι οὗ. | i Esd. 1⁵⁴ μέχρι οὗ. |
| ii Mac. 14¹⁵ ἄχρι αἰῶνος. | Job 32¹² μέχρι ὑμῶν. |

Ἀντικρύ and ἀντίκρυς differ from one another by more than the σ. The former does not occur at all in the LXX, the latter in Swete's text only once, iii Mac. 5¹⁶ ἀντικρυς ἀνακλιθῆναι αὐτοῦ.

In the Revisers' text of the N.T. we find ἄχρι before a consonant in Gal. 4²; ἄχρις οὗ i Cor. 11²⁶, 15²⁵: Gal. 3¹⁹, 4¹⁹: Hb. 3¹³; μέχρις οὗ Mk. 13³⁰; μέχρις αἵματος Hb. 12⁴; ἀντικρὺ Χίου Acts 20¹⁵.

**37. Spelling.** In matters of spelling Dr. Swete's text appears to reflect variations in the Mss.

*a.* The diphthong ει is often replaced by ι, as in i Esd. 1¹¹ χαλκίοις compared with ii Chr. 35¹³ χαλκείοις. This is especially the case with feminine nouns in -εία, as

ἀπωλία, δουλία, λατρία, πλινθία, συγγενία, ὑγία, φαρμακία.

Neuters plural in -εῖα also sometimes end in -ια with recession of accent, as —

ἄγγια Gen. 42²⁵.            πόρια Gen. 45¹⁷.

In the pluperfect of ἵστημι again we sometimes find ι for ει —

ἱστήκει Jdg. 16²⁹.          ἐφιστήκει Nb. 23⁶,¹⁷.

παριστήκει Gen. 45¹.

So also in the future and 1st aorist of λείχω, as —

ἐκλίξει, ἐκλίξαι, ἔλιξαν, λίξουσιν.

On the other hand εἰδέαι for ἰδέαι (nom. pl. of ἰδέα) occurs in Dan. ℧ 1¹³.

*b.* ν in composition is sometimes changed into μ before a labial and sometimes not, as —

συμβιβάσω Ex. 4¹².         συνβιβασάτω Jdg. 13⁸.

Before a guttural or π, ν is often retained, instead of being turned into γ, as —

ἐνκάθηται, ἐνκρατεῖς, ἐνκρούσῃς, ἐνκρυφίας, ἐνποίῃ, ἐνχωρίῳ.

But on the other hand —

σύγκρισις, συγγενία.

*c.* In the spelling of λαμβάνειν μ appears in parts not formed from the present stem, as —

λήμψομαι, λήμψῃ, λήμψεσθε, ἐλήμφθη, καταλήμψῃ.

This may indicate that the syllable in which the μ occurs was pronounced with β. In modern Greek μπ stands for *b*, and we seem to find this usage as early as Hermas (*Vis.* III 1 § 4), who represents the Latin *subsellium* by συμψέλιον. *Cp.* Ἀμβακούμ for *Habakkuk*.

*d.* The doubling of ρ in the augment of verbs is often neglected, as —

ἐξερίφησαν, ἔρανεν, ἐράπιζον, ἔριψεν.

*e.* The following also may be noticed—

ἐραυνᾶν for ἐρευνᾶν Dt. 13¹⁴.

μιερός, μιεροφαγία, μιεροφαγεῖν, μιεροφονία all in Maccabees only.

τεσσεράκοντα Dt. 9⁹,¹¹: Josh. 14⁷.

# SYNTAX

**38. The Construction of the LXX not Greek.** In treating of Accidence we have been concerned only with dialectical varieties within the Greek language, but in turning to syntax we come unavoidably upon what is not Greek. For the LXX is on the whole a literal translation, that is to say, it is only half a translation — the vocabulary has been changed, but seldom the construction. We have therefore to deal with a work of which the vocabulary is Greek and the syntax Hebrew.

**39. Absence of μέν and δέ.** How little we are concerned with a piece of Greek diction is brought home to us by the fact that the balance of clauses by the particles μέν and δέ, so familiar a feature of Greek style, is rare in the LXX, except in the books of Wisdom and Maccabees. It does not occur once in all the books between Deuteronomy and Proverbs nor in Ecclesiastes, the Song, the bulk of the Minor Prophets, Jeremiah, and Ezekiel; and in each of the following books it occurs once only — Leviticus ($27^7$), Numbers ($22^{33}$), Tobit ($14^{10}$), Haggai ($1^4$), Zechariah ($1^{15}$), Isaiah ($6^2$). Where the antithesis is employed, it is often not managed with propriety, *e.g.* in Job $32^6$. As instances of the non-occurrence of one or both of the particles where their presence is obviously required we may take —

Gen. $27^{22}$ Ἡ φωνὴ φωνὴ Ἰακώβ, αἱ δὲ χεῖρες χεῖρες Ἡσαύ. Jdg. $16^{29}$ καὶ ἐκράτησεν ἕνα τῇ δεξίᾳ αὐτοῦ καὶ ἕνα τῇ ἀριστερᾷ αὐτοῦ. ii K. $11^{25}$ ποτὲ μὲν οὕτως καὶ ποτὲ οὕτως. iii K. $18^6$ μιᾷ . . . ἄλλῃ.

**40. Paratactical Construction of the LXX.** Roughly speaking, it is true to say that in the Greek of the LXX there is no syntax, only parataxis. The whole is one great scheme of clauses connected by καί, and we have to trust to the sense to tell us which is to be so emphasized as to make it into the apodosis. It may therefore be laid down as a general rule that in the LXX the apodosis is introduced

50

by καί. This is a recurrence to an earlier stage of language than that which Greek itself had reached long before the LXX was written, but we find occasional survivals of it in classical writers, *e.g.* Xen. *Cyrop.* I 4 § 28 .καὶ ὁδόν τε οὔπω πολλὴν διηνύσθαι αὐτοῖς καὶ τὸν Μῆδον ἥκειν. Here it is convenient to translate καί 'when,' but the construction is really paratactical. So again Xen. *Anab.* IV 2 § 12 Καὶ τοῦτόν τε παρεληλύθεσαν οἱ Ἕλληνες, καὶ ἕτερον ὁρῶσιν ἔμπροσθεν λόφον κατεχόμενον. *Cp. Anab.* I 8 § 8, II 1 § 7, IV 6 § 2; also Verg. *Æn.* II 692 —

> Vix ea fatus erat senior, subitoque fragore
> intonuit laevom.

In the above instances the two clauses are coördinate. But in the LXX, even when the former clause is introduced by a subordinative conjunction, καί still follows in the latter, *e.g.* —

> Gen. 44²⁹ ἐὰν οὖν λάβητε . . . καὶ κατάξετε κτλ. Ex. 13¹⁴ ἐὰν δὲ ἐρωτήσῃ . . . καὶ ἐρεῖς κτλ. *Cp.* 7⁹. Josh. 4¹ καὶ ἐπεὶ συνετέλεσεν πᾶς ὁ λαὸς διαβαίνων τὸν Ἰορδάνην, καὶ εἶπεν Κύριος.

Sometimes a preposition with a verbal noun takes the place of the protasis, *e.g.* —

> Ex. 3¹² ἐν τῷ ἐξαγαγεῖν . . . καὶ λατρεύσετε.

In Homer also καί is used in the apodosis after ἐπεί (*Od.* V 96), ἦμος (*Il.* I 477 : *Od.* X 188), or ὅτε (*Od.* V 391, 401 : X 145, 157, 250). The difficulty which sometimes arises in the LXX in determining which is the apodosis amid a labyrinth of καί clauses, *e.g.* in Gen. 4¹⁴, 39¹⁰, may be paralleled by the difficulty which sometimes presents itself in Homer with regard to a series of clauses introduced by δέ, *e.g. Od.* X 112, 113; XI 34–6.

**41. Introduction of the Sentence by a Verb of Being.** Very often in imitation of Hebrew idiom the whole sentence is introduced by ἐγένετο or ἔσται.

> Gen. 39¹⁹ ἐγένετο δὲ ὡς ἤκουσεν . . . καὶ ἐθυμώθη ὀργῇ. *Cp.* vs. 5, 7, 13. iii K. 18¹² καὶ ἔσται ἐὰν ἐγὼ ἀπέλθω ἀπὸ σοῦ, καὶ πνεῦμα Κυρίου ἀρεῖ σε εἰς τὴν γῆν ἣν οὐκ οἶδας.

In such cases in accordance with western ideas of what a sentence ought to be, we say that καί introduces the apodosis, but it may be that, in its original conception at least, the whole construction was paratactical. It is easy to see this in a single instance like —

> Gen. 41⁸ ἐγένετο δὲ πρωὶ καὶ ἐταράχθη ἡ ψυχὴ αὐτοῦ,

but the same explanation may be applied to more complex cases, *e.g.* —

Nb. 21⁹ καὶ ἐγένετο ὅταν ἔδακνεν ὄφις ἄνθρωπον, καὶ ἐπέβλεψεν ἐπὶ τὸν ὄφιν τὸν χαλκοῦν, καὶ ἔζη. And *there was* when a serpent bit a man, and he looked on the brazen serpent, and lived. *Cp.* Gen. 42³⁵, 43², ²¹ : Jdg. 14¹¹.

**42. Apposition of Verbs.** Sometimes the καί does not appear after ἐγένετο, ἐγενήθη, or ἔσται, thus presenting a construction which we may denote by the phrase Apposition of Verbs.

Jdg. 19³⁰ καὶ ἐγένετο πᾶς ὁ βλέπων ἔλεγεν . . .      i K. 31⁸ καὶ ἐγενήθη τῇ ἐπαύριον, ἔρχονται οἱ ἀλλόφυλοι.      Gen. 44³¹ καὶ ἔσται ἐν τῷ ἰδεῖν αὐτὸν μὴ ὂν τὸ παιδάριον μεθ᾽ ἡμῶν, τελευτήσει.

In two versions of the same Hebrew we find one translator using the καί and the other not.

iv K. 19¹ καὶ ἐγένετο ὡς ἤκουσεν βασιλεὺς Ἐζεκίας, καὶ διέρρηξεν τὰ ἱμάτια ἑαυτοῦ.      Is. 37¹ καὶ ἐγένετο ἐν τῷ ἀκοῦσαι τὸν βασιλέα Ἐζεκίαν, ἔσχισεν τὰ ἱμάτια.

**43. Δέ in the Apodosis.** The use of δέ to mark the apodosis, which is found occasionally in classical authors from Homer downwards, is rare in the LXX.

Josh. 2⁸ καὶ ἐγένετο ὡς ἐξήλθοσαν . . . αὕτη δὲ ἀνέβη.

## THE ARTICLE, 44, 45

**44. Generic Use of the Article.** This is due to following the Hebrew.

i K. 17³⁴ ὁ λέων καὶ ἡ ἄρκος = ' a lion or a bear,' 17³⁶ καὶ τὴν ἄρκον ἔτυπτεν ὁ δοῦλός σου καὶ τὸν λέοντα.      Amos 5¹⁹ ὃν τρόπον ἐὰν φύγῃ ἄνθρωπος ἐκ προσώπου τοῦ λέοντος, καὶ ἐμπέσῃ αὐτῷ ἡ ἄρκος. Is. 7¹⁴ ἰδοὺ ἡ παρθένος ἐν γαστρὶ λήμψεται.

**45. Elliptical Use of the Feminine Article.** The use of the feminine article with some case of χώρα or γῆ understood is not due to the influence of the Hebrew.

ἡ ὑπ᾽ οὐρανόν Job 18⁴.

τὴν ὑπ᾽ οὐρανόν Job 1⁷, 2², 5¹⁰, 9⁶, 28²⁴, 34¹³, 38²⁴.

τῆς ὑπὸ τὸν οὐρανόν Ex. 17⁴ : Prov. 8²⁸ : ii Mac. 2¹⁸.

τῆς ὑπ᾽ οὐρανόν Job 38¹⁸.

τῇ ὑπ᾽ οὐρανόν Esther 4¹⁷ : Baruch 5³.

So in N.T. —

Lk. 17²⁴ ἡ ἀστραπὴ ἀστράπτουσα ἐκ τῆς ὑπὸ τὸν οὐρανὸν εἰς τὴν ὑπ᾽ οὐρανόν λάμπει.

## GENDER, 46, 47

**46. Elliptical Use of the Feminine Adjective.** There is nothing about the feminine gender which should make ellipse more frequent with it than with the masculine or neuter. Only it happens that some of the words which can be most easily supplied are feminine. This elliptical use of the feminine adjective (or of adv. = adj.) is a feature of Greek generally. It is not very common in the LXX. Instances are —

ἐπ᾽ εὐθείας (ὁδοῦ) Josh. 8¹⁴.

ἐν τῇ εὐθείᾳ Ps. 142¹⁰.

τῆς πλατείας Esther 4¹.

τὴν σύμπασαν (γῆν) Job 2², 25².

ἕως τῆς σήμερον (ἡμέρας) ii Chr. 35²⁵.

τὴν αὔριον iii Mac. 5³⁸.

ἐβόησεν μεγάλῃ (τῇ φωνῇ) iv K. 18²⁸.

εἰς τὴν ὑψηλήν (χώραν) ii Chr. 1³.

In the N.T. this idiom occurs much more frequently. Take for instance Lk. 12⁴⁷, ⁴⁸ δαρήσεται πολλάς . . . ὀλίγας (πληγάς).

*Cp.* also —

τὴν πρὸς θάνατον (ὁδόν) Eus. *H.E.* II 23.

οὐκ εἰς μακράν Philo *Leg. ad C.* § 4.

ἐπ᾽ εὐθείας Philo *Q.O.P.L.* § 1.

ἐπὶ ξένης (χώρας or γῆς) Philo *Leg. ad C.* § 3.

πεδιάς τε καὶ ὀρεινή *ibid.* § 7.

τῇ πατρίῳ (γλώσσῃ) Jos. *B. J. Prooem.* 1.

τὰς περιοίκους (πόλεις) *ibid.* 8.

**47. Feminine for Neuter.** The use of the feminine for the neuter is a pure Hebraism, which occurs principally in the Psalms.

Jdg. 15⁷ ἐὰν ποιήσητε οὕτως ταύτην, 21³ εἰς τί . . . ἐγενήθη αὕτη; i K. 4⁷ οὐ γέγονεν τοιαύτη ἐχθὲς καὶ τρίτην. Ps. 26³ ἐν ταύτῃ ἐγὼ ἐλπίζω, 26⁴ μίαν ᾐτησάμην . . . ταύτην ἐκζητήσω, 31⁶ ὑπὲρ ταύτης προσεύξεται πᾶς ὅσιος, 117²³ παρὰ Κυρίου ἐγένετο αὕτη, 118⁵⁰ αὕτη με παρεκάλεσεν, 118⁵⁶ αὕτη ἐγενήθη μοι.

In the N.T. this license only occurs in Mk. 12¹¹, Mt. 21⁴² in a quotation from Ps. 117²³.

**48. Singular for Plural.** Sometimes in imitation of Hebrew idiom
we find the singular used in the sense of the plural. When the
article is employed along with a singular noun, we have the Generic
Use of the Article (§ 44), but the presence of the article is not
necessary.

Ex. 8⁶ ἀνεβιβάσθη ὁ βάτραχος (= frogs), 8¹⁸ ἐξαγαγεῖν τὸν σκνῖφα,
10¹³ καὶ ὁ ἄνεμος ὁ νότος ἀνέλαβεν τὴν ἀκρίδα, 10¹⁴ οὐ γέγονεν τοιαύτη
ἀκρίς.     Jdg. 7¹² ὡσεὶ ἀκρὶς εἰς πλῆθος (cp. Judith 2²⁰ ὡς ἀκρίς),
21¹⁶ ἠφανίσθη ἀπὸ Βενιαμεὶν γυνή.     iv K. 2¹² ἄρμα Ἰσραὴλ καὶ
ἱππεὺς αὐτοῦ.   Ezk. 47⁹ ἔσται ἐκεῖ ἰχθὺς πολὺς σφόδρα.

This throws light on an otherwise startling piece of grammar —
Jdg. 15¹⁰ εἶπαν ἀνὴρ Ἰούδα.

**49. Singular Verb with more than One Subject.** In accordance with
Hebrew idiom a singular verb often introduces a plurality of subjects, e.g. —

iv K. 18²⁶ καὶ εἶπεν Ἐλιακεὶμ . . . καὶ Σόμνας καὶ Ἰώας, 18³⁷ καὶ εἰσῆλθεν Ἐλιακεὶμ κτλ.

This may happen also in Greek apart from Hebrew.

Xen. Anab. II 4 § 16 Ἔπεμψέ με Ἀριαῖος καὶ Ἀρτάοζος.

CASE, 50–61

**50. Nominative for Vocative.** a. The use of the nominative for the
vocative was a colloquialism in classical Greek. It occurs in Plato,
and is common in Aristophanes and Lucian. When so employed,
the nominative usually has the article. As in Hebrew the vocative
is regularly expressed by the nominative with the article, it is not
surprising that the LXX translators should often avail themselves
of this turn of speech.

iii K. 17¹⁸ τί ἐμοὶ καὶ σοί, ὁ ἄνθρωπος τοῦ Θεοῦ; 18²⁶ ἐπάκουσον ἡμῶν,
ὁ Βάαλ.   Cp. iii K. 20²⁰: Ps. 21¹, 42².

For an instance of the nominative without the article standing
for the vocative take —

Baruch 4⁵ θαρσεῖτε, λαός μου.

The nominative, when thus employed, is often put in apposition
with a vocative, as —

iii K. 17²⁰ Κύριε, ὁ μάρτυς τῆς χήρας, 17²¹ Κύριε, ὁ Θεός μου.

*b.* In the N.T. also the nominative with the article is often put for the vocative.

Mt. 11²⁶ ναί, ὁ πατήρ. Lk. 8⁵⁴ ἡ παῖς, ἐγείρου. Mk. 9²⁵ τὸ πνεῦμα τὸ ἄλαλον . . . ἔξελθε. Lk. 6²⁵ οὐαὶ ὑμῖν, οἱ ἐμπεπλησμένοι νῦν. Col. 3¹⁸ αἱ γυναῖκες, ὑποτάσσεσθε. Eph. 6¹, Col. 3²⁰ τὰ τέκνα, ὑπακούετε.

The use of the nominative without the article for the vocative is rare in the N.T., as it is also in the LXX. In Lk. 12²⁰ and i Cor. 15³⁶ we find ἄφρων put for ἄφρον, and in Acts 7⁴² οἶκος Ἰσραήλ does duty as vocative.

As instances of apposition of nominative with vocative we may take —

Rom. 2¹ ὦ ἄνθρωπε πᾶς ὁ κρίνων.  Rev. 15³ Κύριε ὁ Θεός, ὁ παντο-κράτωρ.

In Rev. 18²⁰ we have vocative and nominative conjoined —

οὐρανέ, καὶ οἱ ἅγιοι.

**51. Nominative Absolute.** Occasionally we get a construction in the LXX, which can be described only by this name.

Nb. 22²⁴ καὶ ἔστη ὁ ἄγγελος τοῦ θεοῦ ἐν ταῖς αὔλαξιν τῶν ἀμπέλων, φραγμὸς ἐντεῦθεν καὶ φραγμὸς ἐντεῦθεν.  Nb. 24⁴ ὅστις ὅρασιν θεοῦ εἶδεν, ἐν ὕπνῳ, ἀποκεκαλυμμένοι οἱ ὀφθαλμοὶ αὐτοῦ.

As this construction arises out of a literal following of the Hebrew, it would be superfluous to adduce Greek parallels. Like effects might be found, but the cause would be different.

**52. Nominative of Reference.** What is meant by this term will be best understood from the examples —

Job 28⁷ τρίβος, οὐκ ἔγνω αὐτὴν πετεινόν.  Ps. 102¹⁵ ἄνθρωπος, ὡσεὶ χόρτος αἱ ἡμέραι αὐτοῦ.

To throw out the subject of discourse first, and then proceed to speak about it, is a Hebraism, but at the same time it is a common resource of language generally.

So in N.T. —

Acts 7⁴⁰ ὁ γὰρ Μωσῆς οὗτος . . . οὐκ οἴδαμεν τί ἐγένετο αὐτῷ.  Rev. 3¹² ὁ νικῶν, ποιήσω αὐτὸν στῦλον ἐν τῷ ναῷ τοῦ Θεοῦ μου.

**53. Nominativus Pendens.** The nominative which is left without a verb owing to a sudden change of construction is a familiar feature in classical Greek, especially if this be at all colloquial.   It is not however very common in the LXX.

Dan. O' 7¹⁵ καὶ ἀκηδιάσας ἐγὼ . . . ἐτάρασσόν με.

Such cases can generally be explained on the principle of construction according to the sense.

It is seldom that we meet with so violent an anacoluthon as the following in the N.T. —

Mk. 9²⁰ καὶ ἰδὼν αὐτόν, τὸ πνεῦμα εὐθὺς συνεσπάραξεν αὐτόν.

**54. Accusative for Vocative.**   The accusative for vocative might seem an impossibility, yet here is an instance of it.

Ps. 51⁶ ἠγάπησας πάντα τὰ ῥήματα καταποντίσμου, γλῶσσαν δολίαν.

**55. Accusative of Time When.**   In connexion with classical Greek we think of Time When as being expressed by the genitive or dative, rather than by the accusative, though the latter also is used.   The employment of the accusative became more frequent after the classical period, and alone survives in the modern language.

Gen. 43¹⁶ μετ᾽ ἐμοῦ γὰρ φάγονται οἱ ἄνθρωποι ἄρτους τὴν μεσημβρίαν.

Ex. 9¹⁸ ἰδοὺ ἐγὼ ὕω ταύτην τὴν ὥραν αὔριον χάλαζαν.

Dan. Θ 9²¹ ὡσεὶ ὥραν θυσίας ἑσπερινῆς (O' has ἐν ὥρᾳ).

So also sometimes in N.T. —

Jn. 4⁵² χθὲς ὥραν ἑβδόμην ἀφῆκεν αὐτὸν ὁ πυρετός.     Rev. 3³ καὶ οὐ μὴ γνῷς ποίαν ὥραν ἥξω ἐπί σε.

**56. Cognate Accusative.**   *a.* By a Cognate Accusative is here meant that particular form of the *Figura Etymologica* in which a verb is followed by an accusative of kindred derivation with itself, irrespective of the question whether it be an accusative of the external or of the internal object.   We have both kinds of accusative together in the following verse, where θήραν = venison.

Gen. 27³ ἐξέστη δὲ Ἰσαὰκ ἔκστασιν μεγάλην σφόδρα καὶ εἶπεν "Τίς οὖν ὁ θηρεύσας μοι θήραν; "

*b.* The great frequency of the cognate accusative in the LXX is due to the fact that here the genius of the Hebrew and of the Greek language coincides.   Besides being a legitimate Greek usage, this construction is also one of the means employed for translating a constantly recurring Hebrew formula.   Sometimes the appended accusative merely supplies an object to the verb, as in such phrases as δάνιον δανείζειν, διαθέσθαι διαθήκην, διηγεῖσθαι διήγημα, ἐνύπνιον ἐνυπνιάζεσθαι, ἐπιθυμεῖν ἐπιθυμίαν, θύειν θυσίαν, νηστεύειν νηστείαν, ὁρισμὸν ὁρίζεσθαι, πλημμελεῖν πλημμέλησιν or πλημμελίαν, προφασίζεσθαι προφάσεις. At other times it is accompanied by some specification, as —

Nb. 18⁶ λειτουργεῖν τὰς λειτουργίας τῆς σκηνῆς τοῦ μαρτυρίου. Dan. 11² πλουτήσει πλοῦτον μέγαν. i Mac. 2⁵⁸ ἐν τῷ ζηλῶσαι ζῆλον νόμου.

c. Sometimes the cognate accusative is conveyed in a relative clause, as —

Ex. 3⁹ τὸν θλιμμὸν ὃν οἱ Αἰγύπτιοι θλίβουσιν αὐτούς. Nb. 1⁴⁴ ἡ ἐπίσκεψις ἣν ἐπεσκέψαντο. i K. 2²³ ἡ ἀκοὴ ἣν ἐγὼ ἀκούω.

d. By other changes of construction we have still the *figura etymologica*, but no longer a cognate accusative. Thus, starting from the common phrase δοῦναι δόμα, we have δεδομένοι δόμα (Nb. 3⁹) and δόμα δεδομένον (Nb. 18⁶).

e. In one instance the cognate accusative is reinforced by a still further application of the etymological figure —

Gen. 47²² ἐν δόσει γὰρ ἔδωκεν δόμα τοῖς ἱερεῦσιν.

This is not due to the Hebrew.

f. In a wider sense the term 'cognate accusative' includes an accusative of kindred meaning, though not of kindred derivation, as —

Jdg. 15⁸ ἐπάταξεν . . . πληγὴν μεγάλην.

g. Instances of cognate accusative are common enough in the N.T., e.g. —

i Jn. 5¹⁶ ἁμαρτάνοντα ἁμαρτίαν μὴ πρὸς θάνατον. Mt. 2¹⁰ ἐχάρησαν χαρὰν μεγάλην σφόδρα. Jn. 7²⁴ τὴν δικαίαν κρίσιν κρίνατε.

There also it occurs sometimes in a relative clause —

Mk. 10³⁸ τὸ βάπτισμα ὃ ἐγὼ βαπτίζομαι. Jn. 17²⁶ ἡ ἀγάπη ἣν ἠγάπηκάς με. Eph. 4¹ τῆς κλήσεως ἧς ἐκλήθητε.

h. We have a triple use of the etymological figure in —

Lk. 8⁵ ἐξῆλθεν ὁ σπείρων τοῦ σπεῖραι τὸν σπόρον αὐτοῦ.

i. That the playing with paronymous terms is in accordance with the spirit of the Greek language may be seen from the frequent employment of the device by Plato, e.g. —

Prot. 326 D ὥσπερ οἱ γραμματισταὶ τοῖς μήπω δεινοῖς γράφειν τῶν παίδων ὑπογράψαντες γραμμὰς τῇ γραφίδι οὕτω τὸ γραμματεῖον δι-

δόασι.    *Hip. Maj.* 296 C Ἄλλα μέντοι δυνάμει γε δύνανται οἱ
δυνάμενοι· οὐ γάρ που ἀδυναμίᾳ γε.

**57. Accusative in Apposition to Indeclinable Noun.** In the LXX an
indeclinable noun is sometimes followed by an accusative in apposition to it, even though by the rules of grammar it is itself in some
other case, *e.g.* —

Is. 37[38] ἐν τῷ οἴκῳ Νασαρὰχ τὸν πάτραρχον αὐτοῦ.    iv K. 1[2] ἐν τῷ
Βάαλ μυῖαν θεὸν ᾿Ακκαρών.

Perhaps it would be more satisfactory if this and § 54 were thrown
together under a head of Bad Grammar, a category which the reader
might be inclined to enlarge.

**58. Genitive Absolute.** Strictly speaking, a Genitive Absolute is
a clause in the genitive which does not affect the general construction. It ought not therefore to refer either to the subject or the
object of the sentence. Even in classical authors however the so-
called genitive absolute is sometimes not employed with the precision which grammarians might desire, *e.g.* —

Plat. *Rep.* 547 B βιαζομένων δὲ καὶ ἀντιτεινόντων ἀλλήλοις . . . ὡμο-
λόγησαν.    Xen. *Cyrop.* I 4 § 2 καὶ γὰρ ἀσθενήσαντος αὐτοῦ οὐδέποτε ἀπέλειπε τὸν πάππον.    Xen. *Anab.* I 2 § 17 θᾶσσον προϊόν-
των . . . δρόμος ἐγένετο τοῖς στρατιώταις.

The genitive absolute is often employed in the same loose way
in the LXX.

Tob. 4[1] ὅτε ἤμην ἐν τῇ χώρᾳ μου . . . νεωτέρου μου ὄντος.
Dt. 15[10] οὐ λυπηθήσῃ τῇ καρδίᾳ σου διδόντος σου αὐτῷ.
Ex. 2[10] ἀδρυνθέντος δὲ τοῦ παιδίου, εἰσήγαγεν αὐτό.
Ex. 5[20] συνήντησαν δὲ . . . ἐρχομένοις . . . ἐκπορευομένων αὐτῶν.

So in N.T. —

Mt. 1[18] μνηστευθείσης τῆς μητρὸς . . . εὑρέθη.    Acts 21[17] γενομέ-
νων δὲ ἡμῶν εἰς Ἱεροσόλυμα ἀσμένως ἀπεδέξαντο ἡμᾶς οἱ ἀδελφοί.
ii Cor. 4[18] κατεργάζεται ἡμῖν, μὴ σκοπούντων ἡμῶν.

**59. The Genitive Infinitive of Purpose.** The genitive of the verbal
noun formed by prefixing the article to the infinitive, which we may
call for convenience the Genitive Infinitive, is one of the regular
ways of expressing purpose in Biblical Greek, corresponding to our
use of 'to.' The construction is not entirely unknown to classical
authors (*e.g.* Plat. *Gorg.* 457 E τοῦ καταφανὲς γενέσθαι) and is especially

favoured by Thucydides. There is nothing in the Hebrew to suggest it. The following will serve as examples —

Jdg. 16⁵ καὶ δήσομεν αὐτὸν τοῦ ταπεινῶσαι αὐτόν. Ps. 9³⁰ ἐνεδρεύει τοῦ ἁρπάσαι πτωχόν. Job 1¹⁹ ἦλθον τοῦ ἀπαγγεῖλαί σοι.

So also frequently in N.T., e.g. —

Mt. 13³ ἐξῆλθεν ὁ σπείρων τοῦ σπείρειν. James 5¹⁷ προσηύξατο τοῦ μὴ βρέξαι.

**60. Other Uses of the Genitive Infinitive.** *a.* The genitive infinitive of purpose is only one use out of many to which this syntactical device is applied. Take for instance —

Ex. 14⁵ Τί τοῦτο ἐποιήσαμεν τοῦ ἐξαποστεῖλαι τοὺς υἱοὺς Ἰσραὴλ τοῦ μὴ δουλεύειν ἡμῖν (= ὥστε μὴ δουλεύειν);

Purpose is not expressed in either of these cases. In the former we have what may be called the Explanatory Use of the Genitive Infinitive; in the latter we have something which represents 'from serving us' in the original, but which we shall nevertheless class as a Genitive Infinitive of Consequence, since it is only thus that the Greek can be explained.

*b.* The Explanatory Use of the Genitive Infinitive is common in the LXX, e.g. —

Gen. 3²² Ἰδοὺ Ἀδὰμ γέγονεν ὡς εἷς ἐξ ἡμῶν, τοῦ γιγνώσκειν καλὸν καὶ πονηρόν. Ex. 8²⁹ μὴ προσθῇς ἔτι, Φαραώ, ἐξαπατῆσαι τοῦ μὴ ἐξαποστεῖλαι τὸν λαόν. Ps. 26⁴ ταύτην (§ 47) ἐκζητήσω· τοῦ κατοικεῖν με κτλ.

So in N.T. —

Acts 7¹⁹ ἐκάκωσε τοὺς πατέρας ἡμῶν, τοῦ ποιεῖν ἔκθετα τὰ βρέφη αὐτῶν. Gal. 3¹⁰ ὃς οὐκ ἐμμένει ἐν πᾶσι τοῖς γεγραμμένοις . . . τοῦ ποιῆσαι αὐτά.

*c.* As an instance of the Genitive Infinitive of Consequence we may take —

Ex. 7¹⁴ βεβάρηται ἡ καρδία Φαραὼ τοῦ μὴ ἐξαποστεῖλαι τὸν λαόν.

So in N.T. —

Hb. 11⁵ Ἐνὼχ μετετέθη τοῦ μὴ ἰδεῖν θάνατον.

*d.* What is called in Latin Grammar the 'prolative infinitive' after 'extensible' verbs, or more simply, the latter of two verbs, is also commonly expressed in the LXX by the genitive infinitive, e.g. —

Ps. 39¹³ οὐκ ἠδυνάσθην τοῦ βλέπειν. ii Chr. 3¹ ἤρξατο τοῦ οἰκοδομεῖν. Gen. 18⁷ ἐτάχυνεν τοῦ ποιῆσαι αὐτό.

So in N.T. —

Acts 3¹² ὡς . . . πεποιηκόσι τοῦ περιπατεῖν αὐτόν, 15²⁰ ἐπιστεῖλαι . . . τοῦ ἀπέχεσθαι, 27¹ ἐκρίθη τοῦ ἀποπλεῖν.

**61. Cognate Dative.** *a.* Another form of the *figura etymologica* which abounds in the LXX may be called Cognate Dative. As in the case of the cognate accusative its frequency is in great measure due to the coincidence of idiom in this particular between Greek and Hebrew. Let us first show by a few examples from Plato that this construction is in accordance with the genius of the Greek language.

*Crat.* 385 B λόγῳ λέγειν? *Phdr.* 265 C παιδίᾳ πεπαῖσθαι. *Symp.* 195 B φεύγων φυγῇ τὸ γῆρας. *Crat.* 383 A φύσει . . . πεφυκυῖαν. *Cp.* 389 C, D. *Phileb.* 14 C φύσει . . . πεφυκότα.

*b.* But while we have to search for this idiom in classical Greek, it thrusts itself upon us at every turn in the Greek of the LXX, owing to its aptness for rendering a mode of expression familiar in the original.

*c.* Corresponding to the cognate dative in Greek, we find in Latin also a cognate ablative as a rare phenomenon, *e.g.* —

curriculo percurre Ter. *Heaut.* 733. *Cp.* Plaut. *Most.* 349
qui non curro curriculo domum.
occidione occisum Cic. *Fam.* XV 4 § 7. *Cp.* Liv. II 51 § 9.

*d.* The instances of cognate dative of most frequent occurrence in the LXX are ἀκοῇ ἀκούειν, ζωῇ ζῆν, θανάτῳ ἀποθανεῖν, θανάτῳ θανατοῦσθαι, σάλπιγγι σαλπίζειν. But besides these there are many others, as —

| | |
|---|---|
| ἀγαπήσει ἀγαπᾶσθαι | ἐκλείψει ἐκλείπειν |
| ἀλαλαγμῷ ἀλαλάζειν | ἐκτριβῇ ἐκτριβῆναι |
| ἀλοιφῇ ἐξαλείφειν | ἐκτρίψει ἐκτριβῆναι |
| ἀπωλίᾳ ἀπολλύναι | ἐξεραυνᾶν ἐξεραυνήσει |
| ἀφανισμῷ ἀφανίζειν | ἐξουδενώσει ἐξουδενοῦν |
| βδελύγματι βδελύσσειν | ἐπιθυμίᾳ ἐπιθυμεῖν |
| δεσμῷ δεῖν | ἐπισκοπῇ ἐπισκέπτεσθαι |
| διαλύσει διαλύειν | θελήσει θέλειν |
| διαμαρτυρίᾳ διαμαρτυρεῖν | καθαιρέσει καθαίρειν |
| διαφθείρειν φθορᾷ | καθαρισμῷ καθαρίζειν |
| δίκῃ ἐκδικεῖν | κακίᾳ κακοποιεῖν |
| ἐκβάλλειν ἐκβολῇ | κακίᾳ κακοῦν |
| ἐκθλίβειν ἐκθλιβῇ | κατάραις καταρᾶσθαι |

SYNTAX 61

| | |
|---|---|
| κλαυθμῷ κλαίειν | πλημμελίᾳ πλημμελεῖν |
| λήθῃ λαθεῖν | προνομῇ προνομευθῆναι |
| λίθοις λιθοβολεῖν | προσοχθίσματι προσοχθίζειν |
| λύτροις λυτροῦν | πτώσει πίπτειν |
| μνείᾳ μνησθῆναι | ταλαιπωρίᾳ ταλαιπωρεῖν |
| οἰωνισμῷ οἰωνίζεσθαι | ταραχῇ ταράσσειν |
| ὀργίζεσθαι ὀργῇ | ὑπεροράσει ὑπεριδεῖν |
| ὅρκῳ ὁρκίζειν | φερνῇ φερνίζειν |
| παραδόσει παραδοθῆναι | φθορᾷ φθαρῆναι |
| περιπίπτειν περιπτώματι | χαίρειν χαρᾷ |

*e.* From the foregoing instances it is an easy step to others in which the substantive is of kindred meaning, though not of kindred derivation with the verb.

Gen. 1¹⁶ βρώσει φαγῇ, 31¹⁵ κατέφαγεν καταβρώσει.    Ex. 19¹², 21¹⁶,¹⁷ θανάτῳ τελευτᾶν.    Ex. 22²⁰ θανάτῳ ὀλεθρευθήσεται.    Nb. 11¹⁵ ἀπόκτεινόν με ἀναίρεσει, 35²⁶ ἐξόδῳ ἐξέλθῃ.    Ezk. 33²⁷ θανάτῳ ἀποκτενῶ.

*f.* Instances of the cognate dative are to be found also in the N.T., though not with anything like the frequency with which they occur in the LXX.

Jn. 3²⁹·χαρᾷ χαίρει.    Lk. 22¹⁵ ἐπιθυμίᾳ ἐπεθύμησα.    Acts 4¹⁷ ἀπειλῇ (margin) ἀπειλησώμεθα, 5²⁸ παραγγελίᾳ παρηγγείλαμεν, 23¹⁴ ἀναθέματι ἀναθεματίσαμεν.    James 5¹⁷ προσευχῇ προσηύξατο.    Gal. 5¹ τῇ ἐλευθερίᾳ ἡμᾶς Χριστὸς ἠλευθέρωσε.

*g.* The expression in ii Pet. 3³ ἐν ἐμπαιγμονῇ ἐμπαῖκται, while not exactly parallel with the foregoing, belongs to the same range of idiom; so also Rev. 2²³ ἀποκτενῶ ἐν θανάτῳ.

### ADJECTIVES, 62–65

**62. ἥμισυς.** In Attic Greek ἥμισυς, like some other adjectives, mostly of quantity, has a peculiar construction. It governs a noun in the genitive, but agrees with it in gender. Thus —

Plat. *Phœdo* 104 A ὁ ἥμισυς τοῦ ἀριθμοῦ ἅπας.    Thuc. V 31 § 2 ἐπὶ τῇ ἡμισείᾳ τῆς γῆς.    Demosth. p. 44, iv 16 τοῖς ἡμίσεσι τῶν ἱππέων.

This idiom is kept up by Hellenistic writers, such as Philo, Strabo, and the translator of Josephus' *Jewish War*.    It is however very rare in the LXX, occurring only in the following passages —

iii K. 16⁹ ὁ ἄρχων τῆς ἡμίσους (§ 11) τῆς ἵππου.  Josh. 4¹², i Chr. 5²³ οἱ ἡμίσεις φυλῆς Μανασσή.  Tob. 10¹⁰ τὰ ἥμισυ (sic) τῶν ὑπαρχόντων.  Ezk. 16⁵¹ τὰς ἡμίσεις τῶν ἁμαρτιῶν.  i Mac. 3³⁴, ³⁷ τὰς ἡμίσεις τῶν δυνάμεων.

Elsewhere instead of the Attic idiom we find τὸ ἥμισυ or ἥμισυ, irrespective of the gender and number of the noun which follows, e.g. —

τὸ ἥμισυ τοῦ σίκλου Ex. 39².    ἥμισυ ἀρχόντων ii Esd. 4¹⁶.
τὸ ἥμισυ αὐτῆς Lvt. 6²⁰.    ἐν ἡμίσει ἡμερῶν Ps. 101²⁵.
τὸ ἥμισυ τοῦ αἵματος Ex. 24⁶.    τὸ ἥμισυ τῶν ὑπαρχόντων Tob. 8²¹.

**63. πᾶς.**  a. In classical Greek the rule for πᾶς in the singular is that with the article it is collective, without the article it is distributive —

πᾶσα ἡ πόλις = all the city.
πᾶσα πόλις  = every city.

πᾶς differs from ordinary adjectives in taking the predicative position in an attributive sense.  Thus while ἀγαθὴ ἡ πόλις means 'the city is good,' πᾶσα ἡ πόλις means 'all the city.'  πᾶς may however also take the attributive position, like any other adjective.  When it does so, the collective force is intensified —

πᾶσα ἡ πόλις = all the city.
ἡ πᾶσα πόλις = the whole city.

Thus Plato's expression (Apol. 40 E) ὁ πᾶς χρόνος is rendered by Cicero (T.D. I § 97) perpetuitas omnis consequentis temporis.  For other instances of this use in classical authors we may take —

Hdt. VII 46 ὁ πᾶς ἀνθρώπινος βίος.    Plat. Rep. 618 B ὁ πᾶς κίνδυνος, Phileb. 67 B οἱ πάντες βόες = all the oxen in the world.  Xen. Anab. V 6 § 5 οἱ πάντες ἄνθρωποι.

In such cases there is an additional stress gained by the unusual position assigned to πᾶς.

b. In the LXX the same distinction seems to be maintained.  It is true a writer will go from one to the other, e.g. —

Jdg. 16¹⁷, ¹⁸ καὶ ἀνήγγειλαν αὐτῇ τὴν πᾶσαν καρδίαν αὐτοῦ . . . καὶ εἶδ‧ν Δαλειδὰ ὅτι ἀπήγγειλεν αὐτῇ πᾶσαν τὴν καρδίαν αὐτοῦ—

but so in English we might first say *he told her his whole heart*, and then add *and she saw that he had told her all his heart*.

Other instances of the strongly collective force of πᾶς in the attributive position are —

Gen. 45²⁰ τὰ γὰρ πάντα ἀγαθὰ Αἰγύπτου ὑμῖν ἔσται. Josh. 4¹⁴ ἐναντίον τοῦ παντὸς γένους Ἰσραήλ. Wisd. 7⁹ ὁ πᾶς χρυσός. ii Mac. 8⁹ τὸ πᾶν τῆς Ἰουδαίας . . . γένος.

Still there is a tendency in the LXX to assimilate πᾶς to adjectives generally and to employ it in the attributive position without any special emphasis.

c. Neither is the rule that πᾶς without the article is distributive at all closely adhered to, e.g. —

Ex. 8¹⁶ ἐν πάσῃ γῇ Αἰγύπτου, 16⁶ πρὸς πᾶσαν συναγωγὴν υἱῶν Ἰσραήλ. i K. 7² πᾶς οἶκος Ἰσραήλ.

d. In the plural οἱ πάντες is rare, but may be found —

Jdg. 20⁴⁶ οἱ πάντες οὗτοι. i Mac. 2³⁷ Ἀποθάνωμεν οἱ πάντες ἐν τῇ ἁπλότητι ἡμῶν. ii Mac. 12⁴⁰ τοῖς δὲ πᾶσι σαφὲς ἐγένετο. *Cp.* Aristeas § 36 τοῖς πᾶσι . . . πολίταις.

Αἱ πᾶσαι is still rarer, but see —

iii Mac. 1¹ παραγγείλας ταῖς πάσαις δυνάμεσιν.

Τὰ πάντα is comparatively common, occurring, e.g., in Gen. 1³¹, 9³: Ex. 29²⁴: Lvt. 19¹³: ii Mac. 10²³, 12²²: iii Mac. 2³.

e. In the N.T. the collective use of πᾶς followed by the article is clearly marked in many passages, e.g. —

Gal. 5¹⁴ ὁ . . . πᾶς νόμος. Mt. 8³⁴ πᾶσα ἡ πόλις ἐξῆλθεν.

Also the distributive use of πᾶς without the article, as in i Cor. 11⁴, ⁵ πᾶς ἀνήρ . . . πᾶσα δὲ γυνή. In Rom. 3¹⁹ we have the two usages brought into contrast — ἵνα πᾶν στόμα φραγῇ, καὶ ὑπόδικος γένηται πᾶς ὁ κόσμος τῷ Θεῷ.

On the other hand there are also instances of πᾶς in the singular and without the article being used collectively, e.g. —

Eph. 2²¹ πᾶσα οἰκοδομή. Mt. 2³ πᾶσα Ἱεροσόλυμα. Acts 2³⁶ πᾶς οἶκος Ἰσραήλ.

f. In the plural οἱ πάντες is more common in St. Paul than in the LXX. Take for instance —

Phil. 2²¹ οἱ πάντες γὰρ τὰ ἑαυτῶν ζητοῦσι. *Cp.* ii Cor. 5¹⁴. i Cor. 10¹⁷ οἱ γὰρ πάντες ἐκ τοῦ ἑνὸς ἄρτου μετέχομεν. *Cp.* Eph. 4¹³.

64     GRAMMAR OF SEPTUAGINT GREEK

Rom. 11³² συνέκλεισε γὰρ ὁ Θεὸς τοὺς πάντας εἰς ἀπείθειαν.   ii Cor.
5¹⁰ τοὺς γὰρ πάντας ἡμᾶς κτλ.     i Cor. 9²² τοῖς πᾶσι γέγονα πάντα.

In Acts 19⁷ we have οἱ πάντες ἄνδρες.
Τὰ πάντα occurs in Rom. 8³², 11³⁶: i Cor. 15²⁷, 12⁶,¹⁹: Eph. 5¹³: Acts
17²⁵: Mk. 4¹¹ and perhaps in other passages.

**64. Comparison of Adjectives.** Owing to the peculiarity of Hebrew
syntax the treatment of this subject mostly falls under the head of
Prepositions.   We need only notice here that the positive may be
put for the comparative, and μᾶλλον omitted at will or inserted even
after a comparative.

Gen. 49¹² λευκοὶ οἱ ὀδόντες αὐτοῦ ἢ γάλα.     Dt. 7¹⁷ πολὺ τὸ ἔθνος
τοῦτο ἢ ἐγώ, 9¹ ἔθνη μεγάλα καὶ ἰσχυρότερα μᾶλλον ἢ ὑμεῖς.

So in N.T. —
Mt. 18⁸,⁹ καλόν σοι ἐστὶν εἰσελθεῖν . . . ἢ . . . βληθῆναι.   Cp.
Mk. 9⁴³,⁴⁵.

**65. Omission of μᾶλλον.** The comparison of attributes may be
effected by the use of verbs as well as of adjectives.   In such cases
the omission of μᾶλλον is common in the LXX.

Nb. 22⁶ ἰσχύει οὗτος ἢ ἡμεῖς, 24⁷ ὑψωθήσεται ἢ Γὼγ βασιλεία.   Hos.
7⁶ ἔλεος θέλω ἢ θυσίαν.     ii Mac. 7² ἕτοιμοι γὰρ ἀποθνήσκειν
ἐσμὲν ἢ πατρῴους νόμους παραβαίνειν.

Cp. Aristeas § 322 τέρπειν γὰρ οἴομαί σε ταῦτα ἢ τὰ τῶν μυθολόγων βιβλία.

PRONOUNS, 66–71

**66. Superfluous Use of Pronoun.** A pronoun is sometimes employed
superfluously after the object, direct or indirect, has been already
expressed, e.g. —

Ex. 12⁴⁴ καὶ πᾶν (sic) οἰκέτην ἢ ἀργυρώνητον περιτεμεῖς αὐτόν.
Nb. 26³⁷ καὶ τῷ Σαλπαὰδ υἱῷ Ὀφερ οὐκ ἐγένοντο αὐτῷ υἱοί.

The above may be considered as deflexions of the Nominative of
Reference (§ 52) into an oblique case by Attraction.
So in N.T. —

ii Cor. 12¹⁷ μή τινα ὧν ἀπέσταλκα πρὸς ὑμᾶς, δι᾽ αὐτοῦ ἐπλεονέκτησα
ὑμᾶς ;   Mt. 25²⁹ τοῦ δὲ μὴ ἔχοντος, καὶ ὃ ἔχει ἀρθήσεται ἀπ᾽ αὐτοῦ.
Rev. 2⁷,¹⁷ τῷ νικῶντι δώσω αὐτῷ.   Cp. 6⁴.

SYNTAX 65

In Josh. 24²² — ὑμεῖς ἐξελέξασθε Κυρίῳ λατρεύειν αὐτῷ — Κυρίῳ should be τὸν Κύριον (which A has). Then λατρεύειν αὐτῷ would be an explanatory clause added after the usual manner.

**67. Frequent Use of Pronouns.** Apart from any Semitic influence there is also a tendency in later Greek to a much more lavish use of pronouns than was thought necessary by classical authors. We have seen already (§ 13) that the missing pronoun of the 3d person was supplied. The possessive use of the article moreover was no longer thought sufficient, and a possessive genitive was added, e.g. —

Gen. 38²⁷ καὶ τῇδε ἦν δίδυμα ἐν τῇ κοιλίᾳ αὐτῆς.

So in N.T. —

Mt. 19⁹ ὃς ἂν ἀπολύσῃ τὴν γυναῖκα αὐτοῦ.     i Pet. 2²⁴ αὐτὸς ἀνήνεγκεν ἐν τῷ σώματι αὐτοῦ.

**68. Ἀδελφός as a Reciprocal Pronoun.** The use of ἀδελφός as a reciprocal pronoun is a sheer Hebraism, e.g. —

Ex. 10²³ καὶ οὐκ εἶδεν οὐδεὶς τὸν ἀδελφὸν αὐτοῦ = they saw not one another.

**69. Hebrew Syntax of the Relative.** a. One of the most salient characteristics of LXX Greek is the repetition of the pronoun after the relative, as though in English, instead of saying 'the land which they possessed,' we were to say habitually 'the land which they possessed it,' and so in all similar cases. This anomaly is due to the literal following of the Hebrew text. Now in Hebrew the relative is indeclinable. Its meaning therefore is not complete until a pronoun has been added to determine it. But the relative in Greek being declinable, the translator was forced to assign to it gender, number, and case, which rendered the addition of the pronoun after it unnecessary. Nevertheless the pronoun was retained out of regard for the sacred text. As instances of the simplest kind we may take the following —

Nb. 35²⁵ ὃν ἔχρισαν αὐτόν, 13³³ τῆς γῆς ἣν κατεσκέψαντο αὐτήν.     Is. 62² ὃ ὁ κύριος ὀνομάσει αὐτό.     Gen. 1¹¹ οὗ τὸ σπέρμα αὐτοῦ ἐν αὐτῷ.     Dt. 4⁷ ᾧ ἐστιν αὐτῷ.     Ps. 18⁴ ὧν οὐχὶ ἀκούονται αἱ φωναὶ αὐτῶν.     Ex. 6²⁶ οἷς εἶπεν αὐτοῖς.

b. Where the relative is followed by ἐάν the same construction is employed, e.g. —

Nb. 17⁵ ὁ ἄνθρωπος ὃν ἐὰν ἐκλέξωμαι αὐτόν, 19²² παντὸς οὗ ἐὰν ἅψηται αὐτοῦ ὁ ἀκάθαρτος.

*c.* Sometimes a demonstrative takes the place of the personal pronoun —

Gen. 3¹¹ οὗ ἐνετειλάμην σοι τούτου μόνου μὴ φαγεῖν.

*d.* In all the foregoing instances the appended pronoun is in the same case as the relative, but this is not necessary.

Nb. 3³ οὓς ἐτελείωσεν τὰς χεῖρας αὐτῶν ἱερατεύειν.

The construction here, though determined by the Hebrew, happens to agree with the Greek Accusative of the Part Affected.

*e.* Very often there is the same preposition both before the relative and before the appended pronoun —

Ex. 34¹² εἰς ἣν εἰσπορεύῃ εἰς αὐτήν.    Nb. 11²¹ ἐν οἷς εἰμι ἐν αὐτοῖς.
Gen. 28¹³ ἡ γῆ ἐφ᾽ ἧς σὺ καθεύδεις ἐπ᾽ αὐτῆς.

*f.* Occasionally the preposition is the same, but the case it governs is different, *e.g.* —

Jdg. 16²⁶ ἐφ᾽ οἷς ὁ οἶκος στήκει ἐπ᾽ αὐτούς.    Josh. 24¹³ γῆν ἐφ᾽ ἣν οὐκ ἐκοπιάσατε ἐπ᾽ αὐτῆς.

*g.* Sometimes the preposition is confined to the appended pronoun. Then the problem arises, Into what case is the relative to be put? — a problem which is solved differently in different passages. In some the case chosen coincides with that of the pronoun following, *e.g.* —

Gen. 24⁴² τὴν ὁδόν μου, ἣν νῦν ἐγὼ πορεύομαι ἐπ᾽ αὐτήν.    Ex. 25²⁸ τοὺς κυάθους, οἷς σπείσεις ἐν αὐτοῖς.    Gen. 21²³ τῇ γῇ ᾗ σὺ παρῴ-κησας ἐν αὐτῇ.

In others it does not —

Nb. 14³¹ τὴν γῆν ἣν ὑμεῖς ἀπέστητε ἀπ᾽ αὐτῆς, 19² ᾗ οὐκ ἐπεβλήθη ἐπ᾽ αὐτὴν ζυγός.    iii K. 17¹ ᾧ παρέστην ἐνώπιον αὐτοῦ.

*h.* Sometimes the relative has a different preposition from the pronoun following —

Nb. 13²⁰ τίς ἡ γῆ εἰς ἣν οὗτοι ἐνκάθηνται ἐπ᾽ αὐτῆς . . . τίνες αἱ πόλεις εἰς ἃς οὗτοι κατοικοῦσιν ἐν αὐταῖς.    For other instances see Ex. 6⁴: Nb. 15³⁹: Dt. 1²², 1³³, 28⁴⁹.

*i.* Sometimes the preposition is the same, but instead of a mere pronoun we have a phrase, *e.g.* —

Gen. 24³⁸ ἐν οἷς ἐγὼ παροικῶ ἐν τῇ γῇ αὐτῶν.

*j.* The construction of which we have been speaking is not confined to the simple relative, *e.g.* —

Gen. 41¹⁹ οἵας οὐκ εἶδον τοιαύτας. Ex. 9¹⁸, ²⁴, 11⁶ ἥτις τοιαύτη οὐ γέγονεν.

*k.* The habitual repetition of the pronoun in the LXX is a mere Hebraism, though a search among Greek writers might reveal traces of a somewhat similar usage arising independently. Here are a few instances —

Plat. *Tim.* 28 A ὅτου μὲν οὖν ἂν ὁ δημιουργός . . . τὴν ἰδέαν καὶ δύναμιν αὐτοῦ ἀπεργάζηται, *Parm.* 130 E ὧν τάδε τὰ ἀλλὰ μεταλαμβάνοντα τὰς ἐπωνυμίας αὐτῶν ἴσχειν. Arist. *Cat.* 5 § 38 οἷον ἐπὶ μὲν τῶν ἄλλων οὐκ ἂν ἔχοι τις τὸ τοιοῦτο προενεγκεῖν.

*l.* In the N.T. this Hebrew syntax of the relative occurs not infrequently.

Philemon¹² ὃν ἀνέπεμψά σοι αὐτόν. Gal. 2¹⁰ ὃ καὶ ἐσπούδασα αὐτὸ τοῦτο ποιῆσαι. Acts 15¹⁷ ἐφ' οὓς ἐπικέκληται τὸ ὄνομά μου ἐπ' αὐτούς. Mk. 7²⁵ ἧς εἶχε τὸ θυγάτριον αὐτῆς πνεῦμα ἀκάθαρτον. *Cp.* Mk. 1⁷: Lk. 3¹⁶: also Mk. 13¹⁹, 9³.

Instances are most frequent in the very Hebraistic book of Revelation. See Rev. 3⁸, 7³, ⁹, 13⁸, 20⁸. *Cp.* i Clem. 21⁹ οὗ ἡ πνοὴ αὐτοῦ ἐν ἡμῖν ἐστίν.

**70. ἀνήρ = ἕκαστος.** The use of ἀνήρ as a distributive pronoun is a pure Hebraism.

iv K. 18³¹ πίεται ἀνὴρ τὴν ἄμπελον αὐτοῦ, καὶ ἀνὴρ τὴν συκῆν αὐτοῦ φάγεται. Jdg. 16⁵ ἡμεῖς δώσομέν σοι ἀνὴρ χιλίους καὶ ἑκατὸν ἀργυρίου.

**71. ὅστις for ὅς.** Except in the neuter singular ὅ τι, as in Josh. 24²⁷, and in the expression ἕως ὅτου, as in i K. 22³, or μέχρι ὅτου, which is found only in the *Codex Sinaiticus* version of Tob. 5⁷, ὅστις occurs in Swete's text only in the nominative, singular or plural. In meaning it is often indistinguishable from ὅς.

Ex. 20² Ἐγώ εἰμι Κύριος . . . ὅστις ἐξήγαγόν σε. *Cp.* Dan. ⊙ 6²⁷. Ps. 89⁴ ἡ ἡμέρα ἡ ἐχθὲς ἥτις διῆλθεν. *Cp.* Nb. 14⁸. i K. 30¹⁰ διακόσιοι ἄνδρες οἵτινες ἐκάθισαν πέραν τοῦ χειμάρρου. *Cp.* Ex. 32⁴, ⁹: Nb. 1⁵: i Mac. 13⁴⁸. Jdg. 21¹² τετρακοσίας νεάνιδας παρθένους, αἵτινες οὐκ ἔγνωσαν ἄνδρα.

Οἵτινες = οἵ occurs several times in Aristeas — §§ 102, 121, 138, 200, 308.

The same use of ὅστις for the simple relative is found in the N.T., e.g. —

Col. 3⁵ τὴν πλεονεξίαν, ἥτις ἐστὶν εἰδωλολατρεία.     Acts 8¹⁵ τὸν Πέ-
τρον καὶ Ἰωάννην· οἵτινες καταβάντες κτλ.     i Tim. 6⁹ ἐπιθυμίας
. . . αἵτινες βυθίζουσι τοὺς ἀνθρώπους.     Gal. 4²⁴ ἅτινά ἐστιν ἀλλη-
γορούμενα.

## VERBS, 72–84

**72. Analytic Tenses.** By an Analytic Tense is meant one which
is formed with an auxiliary instead of by an inflexion, as in English
'is coming' for 'comes.' No reader of the LXX can fail to be struck
by the frequency of such forms. It results from the fact that both
languages combine to produce them. They are suggested by the
great use made of the participle in Hebrew, while at the same time
there was a strong tendency towards the employment of such forms
within the Greek language itself. They are to be found in the best
writers, both in prose and poetry, from Homer downwards. Plato
often has recourse to them, partly for the sake of philosophical precision, and partly, it must be confessed, because in his later style he
preferred two words to one. In the *Laws* πρέπον ἐστί almost altogether displaces πρέπει.

### Present

| | |
|---|---|
| iii K. 20⁵ | οὐκ εἶ σὺ ἐσθίων ἄρτον; *Cp.* Is. 10⁸: Ezk. 36¹³. |
| iii K. 18¹² | ἐστὶν φοβούμενος. |
| Nb. 14⁸ | ἐστὶν ῥέουσα. *Cp.* iii K. 20¹⁵: Dan. 2²⁸. |
| ii Esd. 23²⁴ | οὐκ εἰσὶν ἐπιγινώσκοντες. |
| Prov. 3⁵ | ἴσθι πεποιθώς. |
| Jdg. 11¹⁰ | ἔστω ἀκούων. |
| Dan. O′ 6²⁶ | ἔστωσαν προσκυνοῦντες. |
| ii Chr. 15¹⁶ | εἶναι . . . λειτουργοῦσαν. |

### Future Simple

| | |
|---|---|
| Gen. 4¹⁴ | ἔσομαι στένων καὶ τρέμων. *Cp.* Dan. O′ 6²⁷. |
| Is. 47⁷ | ἔσομαι ἄρχουσα. |
| Gen. 4¹² | στένων καὶ τρέμων ἔσῃ. *Cp.* Ex. 22²⁵: Dt. 28²⁹. |
| Dt. 28²⁹ | ἔσῃ . . . ἀδικούμενος. |
| Nb. 8¹⁹ | ἔσται . . . προσεγγίζων. *Cp.* Gen. 18¹⁸. |
| Mal. 3³ | ἔσονται . . . προσάγοντες. |
| Is. 22²⁴ | ἔσονται ἐπικρεμάμενοι. |
| Ezk. 34²⁹ | ἔσονται ἀπολλύμενοι. *Cp.* Dt. 14³³. |

PERFECT

| | |
|---|---|
| Is. 8¹⁴ | πεποιθὼς ἦς. |
| Is. 10²⁰, 17⁸ | πεποιθότες ὦμεν. |
| Nb. 22¹² | ἔστιν γὰρ εὐλογημένος. |

FUTURE PERFECT

| | |
|---|---|
| Gen. 43⁹, 44³² | ἡμαρτηκὼς ἔσομαι. |
| ii K. 22³: Is. 12², 8¹⁷ | πεποιθὼς ἔσομαι (fut. simp. in force). |
| Sir. 7²⁵ | ἔσῃ τετελεκώς. |
| Is. 58¹⁴ | ἔσῃ πεποιθώς. |
| Is. 17⁷, 22²⁴ | πεποιθὼς ἔσται. |
| Ex. 12⁶ | ἔσται ὑμῖν διατετηρημένον. |
| Is. 32³ | ἔσονται πεποιθότες. |
| Gen. 41³⁶ | ἔσται . . . πεφυλαγμένα. |

IMPERFECT

| | |
|---|---|
| Dan. 10² | ἤμην πενθῶν. |
| Dan. O′ 7¹¹ | θεωρῶν ἤμην. |
| Gen. 40¹³ | ἦσθα οἰνοχοῶν. |
| Gen. 37²: Ex. 3¹ | ἦν ποιμαίνων.   Cp. Gen. 39²³, 42⁶: Nb. 11¹: Jdg. 16²¹: Jonah 1¹⁰: Sus.¹: i Mac. 6⁴³. |
| i K. 17³⁴ | ποιμαίνων ἦν. |
| Jer. 4²⁴ | ἦν τρέμοντα (sc. τὰ ὄρη). |
| iii K. 18³ | ἦν φοβούμενος.   Cp. Dan. O′ 6¹⁸. |
| Dan. O′ 1¹⁶ | ἦν . . . ἀναιρούμενος. |
| Baruch 1¹⁹ | ἤμεθα ἀπειθοῦντες. |
| Dt. 9²⁴ | ἀπειθοῦντες ἦτε.   Cp. Dt. 9²², 31²⁷. |
| Jdg. 1⁷ | ἦσαν συλλέγοντες.   Cp. Josh. 10²⁶: i Mac. 11⁴¹ |

PLUPERFECT

| | |
|---|---|
| Dan. O′ 10⁹ | ἤμην πεπτωκώς. |
| Dan. Θ 10⁹ | ἤμην κατανενυγμένος. |
| ii Chr. 18³⁴ | ἦν ἑστηκώς. |
| i K. 4¹³ | ἦν . . . ἐξεστηκυῖα. |
| Jdg. 8¹¹: Sus. Θ³⁵ | ἦν πεποιθυῖα. |
| Josh. 7²² | ἦν ἐνκεκρυμμένα. |
| ii Chr. 5⁸ | ἦν διαπεπετακότα. |
| Tob. 6¹⁸ | ἡτοιμασμένη ἦν. |
| Is. 20⁶ | ἦμεν πεποιθότες. |
| Ex. 39²³ | ἦσαν πεποιηκότες αὐτά. |

*b.* Γίγνεσθαι may be used as an auxiliary instead of εἶναι.

Ps. 72¹⁴ ἐγενόμην μεμαστιγωμένος.　Is. 30¹² πεποιθὼς ἐγένου.
Nb. 10³⁴ ἐγένετο σκιάζουσα.　Ps. 125³ ἐγενήθημεν εὐφραινόμενοι.
Ex. 17¹² ἐγένοντο . . . ἐστηριγμέναι.　Sir. 13⁹ ὑποχωρῶν γίνου,
18³³ μὴ γίνου . . . συμβολοκοπῶν.

*c.* Sometimes the verbal adjective is used in place of the participle.

Is. 18³ ἀκουστὸν ἔσται.　　Dt. 4³⁶ ἀκουστὴ ἐγένετο.　　Gen. 45²:
Is. 48³ ἀκουστὸν ἐγένετο.　　Is. 23⁵ ὅταν δὲ ἀκουστὸν γένηται.
Dt. 30⁵ πλεοναστόν σε ποιήσει.

*d.* When a causative form is wanted corresponding to ἀκουστὸν γενέσθαι recourse is had to ἀκουστὸν ποιεῖν, *e.g.* —

Sir. 46¹⁷ ἀκουστὴν ἐποίησεν τὴν φωνὴν αὐτοῦ.　*Cp.* Ps. 105², 142⁸:
Jer. 27², 38⁷: Is. 30³⁰, 45²¹, 48⁵, ⁶, ¹⁰, 52⁷, 62¹¹.

*e.* In the N.T. these analytic tenses are relatively even commoner than in the LXX.

#### PRESENT

| | |
|---|---|
| Col. 3² | ἐστιν . . . καθήμενος. |
| ii Cor. 9¹² | ἐστὶ προσαναπληροῦσα. |
| Col. 1⁶ | ἐστὶ καρποφορούμενον καὶ αὐξανόμενον. |
| Col. 2²³ | ἐστι . . . ἔχοντα. |
| ii Cor. 2¹⁷ | ἐσμὲν . . . καπηλεύοντες. |
| Acts 5²⁵ | εἰσὶν . . . ἐστῶτες καὶ διδάσκοντες. |
| Mt. 5²⁵ | ἴσθι εὐνοῶν. |

#### FUTURE SIMPLE

| | |
|---|---|
| Lk. 5¹¹ | ἀνθρώπους ἔσῃ ζωγρῶν. |
| Acts 7⁶ | ἔσται . . . πάροικον. |
| i Cor. 14¹⁰ | ἔσεσθε . . . λαλοῦντες. |

#### PERFECT

| | |
|---|---|
| Acts 25¹⁰ | ἐστώς εἰμι (present in meaning). |
| Acts 21³³ | ἐστὶ πεποιηκώς. |
| i Cor. 15⁹ | ἠλπικότες ἐσμέν. |
| Hb. 7²¹, ²³ | εἰσὶ γεγονότες. |
| James 5¹⁶ | ἦ πεποιηκώς. |
| ii Cor. 1¹⁹ | πεποιθότες ὦμεν. |
| Hb. 4² | ἐσμὲν εὐηγγελισμένοι. |
| Hb. 10¹⁰ | ἡγιασμένοι ἐσμέν. |
| Acts 2¹³ | μεμεστωμένοι εἰσί. |

FUTURE PERFECT

Hb. 2¹³      ἔσομαι πεποιθώς (from Is. 12² and perfect only in form).

IMPERFECT

Acts 10³⁰, 11⁵    ἤμην προσευχόμενος.    Cp. 22¹⁹, ²⁰ : Gal. 1²².

Lk. 4⁴⁴           ἦν κηρύσσων.    Cp. Lk. 5¹⁶, 23⁸ : Acts 7⁶⁰, 8¹³, ²⁸, 9²⁸, 10²⁴, 12²⁰ : Phil. 2²⁶.

Acts 12⁵       ἦν γινομένη.

Acts 21³       ἦν . . . ἀποφορτιζόμενον.

Acts 16¹²     ἦμεν . . . διατρίβοντες.

Gal. 1²³       ἀκούοντες ἦσαν.    Cp. Acts 1¹⁰.

Acts 1¹³       ἦσαν καταμένοντες.    Cp. Acts 1¹⁴, 2², ⁵, ¹², ⁴² : Mk. 2¹⁸.

*f.* Besides εἶναι other auxiliaries are used in the N.T. —

ii Cor. 6¹⁴ μὴ γίνεσθε ἑτεροζυγοῦντες.     Col. 1¹⁸ ἵνα γένηται . . . πρω-
τεύων.    Rev. 3² γίνου γρηγορῶν.    Acts 8¹⁶ βεβαπτισμένοι ὑπῆρ-
χον.

With the last example *cp.* Aristeas § 193 εἰ μὴ πεποιθὼς ὑπάρχοι. The same author has κεχαρισμένος ἔσῃ in § 40 and ἰσχύόν ἐστι in 241.

*g.* Instances of analytic tenses occur here and there in Josephus, *e.g.* —

    *B.J.* I 31 § 1 καὶ τοῦτο ἦν μάλιστα τάρασσον Ἀντίπατρον.

    *Ant.* II 6 § 7 τί παρόντες εἴημεν.

*h.* Also in the Apostolic Fathers —

ii Clem. 17⁷ ἔσονται δόξαν δόντες.     Barn. *Ep.* 19⁴ ἔσῃ τρέμων,
19⁶ οὐ μὴ γίνῃ ἐπιθυμῶν.    *Cp.* 19⁹.     Herm. *Past. Vis.* III 4
§ 2 ὑπερέχοντες αὐτούς εἰσιν, *Sim.* V 4 § 2 ἔσομαι ἑωρακώς . . .
ἀκηκοώς, IX 13 § 2 ἔσῃ . . . φορῶν, *Mdt.* V 2 § 8 ἔσῃ εὑρισκόμε-
νος, *Sim.* IX 1 § 8 εὐθηνοῦν ἦν, IX 4 § 1 ὑποδεδυκυῖαι ἦσαν . . .
ὑποδεδύκεισαν.

**73. Deliberative Use of the Present Indicative.** The deliberative use of the present indicative is not unknown in Latin, especially in Ter-ence, *e.g. Phorm.* 447 quid ago?    *Cp. Heaut.* 343 : *Eun.* 811 : *Ad.* 538.    It occurs also in the Greek of the LXX.

    Gen. 37³⁰ ἐγὼ δὲ ποῦ πορεύομαι ἔτι;

So in N.T. —

    Jn. 11⁴⁷ τί ποιοῦμεν; *What is our course ?*

**74. The Jussive Future.** *a.* The Jussive Future is rare in Attic Greek, and, when it does occur, is regarded as a weak form of imperative. In the LXX, on the other hand, it is very common, and is employed in the most solemn language of legislation. From the nature of the case it is not used in the first person. It may be employed in command or in prohibition. As instances of the former we may take —

Lvt. 19[18] ἀγαπήσεις τὸν πλησίον σου ὡς σεαυτόν. *Cp.* Ex. 34[18, 20]: iii K. 17[11]. Lvt. 19[19] τὸν νόμον μου φυλάξεσθε. *Cp.* Lvt. 11[44]. Lvt. 19[22] καὶ ἐξιλάσεται ὁ ἱερεύς. *Cp.* Lvt. 19[20, 21].

*b.* Very often the jussive future follows an imperative.

Gen. 40[14] μνήσθητί μου . . . καὶ ποιήσεις. *Cp.* Gen. 44[4]: Ex. 7[26], 9[1, 13]: Nb. 15[2, 17]: iii K. 17[13]. Josh. 8[4] μὴ μακρὰν γίνεσθε . . . καὶ ἔσεσθε πάντες ἕτοιμοι. *Cp.* Nb. 13[18].

*c.* Of the use of the jussive future in prohibition we have a conspicuous example in the Ten Commandments (Ex. 20[13-17]: Dt. 5[17-21]) — Οὐ μοιχεύσεις, Οὐ κλέψεις κτλ. So also —

Dt. 6[16] οὐκ ἐκπειράσεις Κύριον τὸν θεόν σου. *Cp.* Nb. 22[12]: Ex. 22[28]: Lvt. 19[12-19].

*d.* In the case of the jussive future we have οὐ in prohibition, because the formula was originally one of prediction.

*e.* Occasionally there is a transition from the jussive future to οὐ μή with subjunctive —

Nb. 23[25] οὔτε κατάραις καταράσῃ μοι αὐτόν, οὔτε εὐλογῶν μὴ εὐλογήσῃς αὐτόν.

*f.* In the N.T. the jussive future is often used in passages quoted from the LXX. In Matthew it is employed independently.

Mt. 5[48] ἔσεσθε οὖν ὑμεῖς τέλειοι, 6[45] οὐκ ἔσεσθε ὡς οἱ ὑποκριταί, 20[26-28] οὐχ οὕτως ἔσται ἐν ὑμῖν . . . ἔσται ὑμῶν δοῦλος, 21[3] καὶ ἐάν τις ὑμῖν εἴπῃ τι, ἐρεῖτε κτλ.

**75. The Optative.** *a.* The pure optative, *i.e.* the optative as employed to express a wish, is of frequent occurrence in the LXX, as might be expected from the character of the contents, so much of which is in the form either of aspiration or of imprecation. But the use of the optative where in Latin we should have the historic tenses of the subjunctive is hardly to be found outside of Maccabees.

ii Mac. 3³⁷ τοῦ δὲ βασιλέως ἐπερωτήσαντος τὸν Ἡλιόδωρον, ποῖός τις εἴη ἐπιτήδειος. iv Mac. 17¹ ἔλεγον δὲ καὶ τῶν δορυφόρων τινὲς ὡς ... ἵνα μὴ ψαύσειέν τι τοῦ σώματος αὐτῆς, ἑαυτὴν ἔρριψεν κατὰ τῆς πυρᾶς.

The established practice is for the subjunctive to follow the historic tenses in a final clause —

Ex. 1¹¹ ἐπέστησεν . . . ἵνα κακώσωσιν, 9¹⁶ διετηρήθης ἵνα ἐνδείξωμαι. Wisd. 16¹¹ διεσώζοντο, ἵνα μὴ . . . γένωνται. Cp. 16¹⁸.

Cp. Aristeas §§ 11, 18, 19, 26, 29, 42, 45, 111, 175, 193.

b. In the N.T. also the subjunctive is regularly employed in final clauses after an historic tense, e.g. —

Tit. 1⁵ τούτου χάριν ἀπέλιπον σε ἐν Κρήτῃ, ἵνα τὰ λείποντα ἐπιδιορθώσῃ.

c. The pure optative is said to occur 35 times in the N.T., always, except in Philemon²⁰, in the 3d person.

In Luke-Acts the optative is commonly employed in dependent questions, e.g. —

Luke 18³⁶ ἐπυνθάνετο τί εἴη τοῦτο,

with which contrast

Mk. 14¹¹ ἐζήτει πῶς εὐκαίρως αὐτὸν παραδῷ.

Outside of Acts the optative with εἰ is found only in four passages — i Cor. 14¹⁰, 15³⁷ (εἰ τύχοι) : i Pet. 3¹⁴, ¹⁷.

**76. Conditional without ἄν.** Occasionally we find the apodosis in a conditional sentence devoid of ἄν.

Nb. 22³³ καὶ εἰ μὴ ἐξέκλινεν, νῦν οὖν σὲ μὲν ἀπέκτεινα, ἐκείνην δὲ περιεποιησάμην. Contrast 22²⁹ and compare ii K. 2²⁷.

**77. Infinitive of Purpose.** The use of the infinitive to express purpose, as in English, is common to all stages of the Greek language, but abounds more in the LXX than in classical Greek.

Gen. 37²⁵ ἐκάθισαν δὲ φαγεῖν ἄρτον. Cp. 39¹⁴, 42⁷, ²⁷, 43²²: Ex. 14¹¹: Nb. 22²⁰ : Job 2¹.

Of the use of the infinitive with the article to express purpose we have had occasion to speak already (§ 59).

**78. Infinitive of Consequence.** This construction is of doubtful propriety in Attic Greek. In the LXX it is much less common than the Infinitive of Purpose.

Ex. 11¹ καὶ οὐκ εἰσήκουσεν ἐξαποστεῖλαι τοὺς υἱοὺς Ἰσραήλ.

**79. Paucity of Participles.** The small use made of participles in
the LXX, as compared with classical Greek, is a natural result of
the paratactical construction which reigns throughout. The same
is the case, though to a less extent, in the N.T. Take for instance —

Mk. 14¹⁶ καὶ ἐξῆλθον οἱ μαθηταί, καὶ ἦλθον εἰς τὴν πόλιν, καὶ εὗρεν
καθὼς εἶπεν αὐτοῖς· καὶ ἡτοίμασαν τὸ πάσχα.

The participle has disappeared in the modern language. Doubtless
the influence of Biblical Greek was among the causes of its decline.

**80. Misuse of the Participle.** The misuse of the participle marks
a stage of its decline. We find this tendency already manifesting
itself in the LXX. Such an anacoluthon indeed as the following —

Ex. 8¹⁵, 9⁷ ἰδὼν δὲ Φαραώ . . . ἐβαρύνθη ἡ καρδία αὐτοῦ

may be passed over, as it might easily be paralleled from the most
strictly classical writers. But we find sentences in the LXX in
which a participle is the only verb. Sometimes this arises from
following the Hebrew as in —

Jdg. 13¹⁹, ²⁰ καὶ Μανῶε καὶ ἡ γυνὴ αὐτοῦ βλέποντες, 14⁴ καὶ ἐν τῷ καιρῷ
ἐκείνῳ οἱ ἀλλόφυλοι κυριεύοντες ἐν Ἰσραήλ.

More often it does not, as in —

Ex. 12³⁷ ἀπάραντες δὲ οἱ υἱοὶ Ἰσραήλ, 15¹⁸ κύριος βασιλεύων τὸν αἰῶνα.
Jdg. 4¹⁶ καὶ Βαρὰκ διώκων.

Moreover we find a participle coupled with a finite verb by καί.
When the subject of the two is the same, it is open to us to say that
it is not copulative, but merely emphasizes the verb, as in —

Nb. 21¹¹ καὶ ἐξάραντες (Hb. impf.) ἐξ Ὠβώθ, καὶ παρενέβαλον ἐν Χαλ-
γαεί, 22²³ καὶ ἰδοῦσα ἡ ὄνος . . . καὶ ἐξέκλινεν.

Hardly so however when the subject is different.

Ex. 12³⁰ καὶ ἀναστὰς Φαραώ . . . καὶ ἐγενήθη κραυγή.     Nb. 22²³
καὶ ἰδὼν Βαλάκ . . . καὶ ἐφοβήθη Μωάβ.

**81. The Intensive Participle.** On the other hand there is a cause
in operation in the LXX tending to an unnecessary use of participles.
For in place of a cognate dative we often find the participle used
along with a finite form of the same verb, to convey the intensive
force that is accomplished in Hebrew by the addition of the infinitive to the finite verb, e.g. —

Gen. 22¹⁷ εἰ μὴν εὐλογῶν εὐλογήσω σε, καὶ πληθύνων πληθυνῶ τὸ σπέρμα σου.    Jdg. 11²⁵ μὴ μαχόμενος ἐμαχέσατο μετὰ Ἰσραὴλ ἢ πολεμῶν ἐπολέμησεν αὐτόν;

We might fill pages with instances of this idiom, but a statement of its frequency must suffice. This emphatic use of the participle is a more unmitigated Hebraism than the other forms of the etymological figure. The cognate accusative is quite Greek and the cognate dative is to be found in pure Greek, but we should search in vain among classical authors for the intensive use of the participle. There is a clear instance indeed in Lucian (*Dialogi Marini* IV 3 ἰδὼν εἶδον), but it is interesting to remember that Lucian himself came from the banks of the Euphrates. In Hdt. V 95 αὐτὸς μὲν φεύγων ἐκφεύγει there is a difference of meaning between the participle and the finite verb — *he himself escapes by flight*.

In the N.T. we have one instance, other than a quotation, of this Hebraism, namely —

Eph. 5⁵ ἴστε γινώσκοντες,

but both the reading and the interpretation of this passage are disputed.

**82. Other Varieties of the Etymological Figure.** In Josh. 17¹³ ἐξολεθρεῦσαι δὲ αὐτοὺς οὐκ ἐξωλέθρευσαν the infinitive absolute of the Hebrew is represented in Greek by the infinitive, instead of by a participle or a cognate dative, so that sheer nonsense is made of the translation.

In another passage, where the Greek departs from our Hebrew, an adjective takes the place of the participle —

Jdg. 5³⁰ οἰκτείρμων οἰκτειρήσει.

Sometimes we find an adverb in place of the participle —

Ex. 15¹ ἐνδόξως γὰρ δεδόξασται.    Nb. 22¹⁷ ἐντίμως γὰρ τιμήσω σε. Prov. 23¹ νοητῶς νόει, 27²³ γνωστῶς ἐπιγνώσῃ.

The following turns of expression may also be noticed —

Jdg. 11²⁵ ἐν ἀγαθῷ ἀγαθώτερος.    Dt. 18⁸ μερίδα μεμερισμένην. i K. 1¹¹ δώσω αὐτὸν ἐνώπιόν σου δοτόν.

**83. Middle and Passive Voices.** In later Greek the boundary lines between the middle and passive voices are not clearly demarcated. Even in classical authors we find the future middle used in a passive sense, as it is also in —

Ex. 12¹⁰ οὐκ ἀπολείψεται ἀπ᾽ αὐτοῦ ἕως πρωί, καὶ ὀστοῦν οὐ συντρίψεται ἀπ᾽ αὐτοῦ.

The same seems to be the case with ξυρήσωμαι and ἐξυρήσατο in Jdg. 16¹⁷, ²².
So in N.T. —

i Cor. 6¹¹ ἀλλὰ ἀπελούσασθε, ἀλλὰ ἡγιάσθητε, ἀλλ᾽ ἐδικαιώθητε, 10² καὶ πάντες εἰς τὸν Μωσῆν ἐβαπτίσαντο,

though here Riddell's semi-middle sense of the verb might plausibly be brought in by way of explanation.

Instances of passive form with middle meaning are common in the LXX —

Nb. 22³⁴ ἀποστραφήσομαι *I will get me back again.*    Jdg. 15⁹ ἐξερίφησαν *spread themselves,* 16²⁰ ἐκτιναχθήσομαι *shake myself,* 16²⁶ ἐπιστηριχθήσομαι *support myself.*    iii K. 17³ κρύβηθι *hide thyself,* 18¹ πορεύθητι καὶ ὄφθητι τῷ ᾽Αχαάβ *go and shew thyself,* 20²⁵ ἐπράθη *sold himself.*

So in N.T. in Luke 11³⁸ ἐβαπτίσθη is used for ἐβαπτίσατο.

**84. Causative Use of the Verb.** *a.* The causative use of the verb which is found in the LXX may be set down with confidence as a Hebrarism. Βασιλεύειν according to the Greek language means ' to be king,' but it is frequently employed in the LXX in the sense of ' to make king,' *e.g.* —

Jdg. 9⁶ ἐβασίλευσαν τὸν ᾽Αβειμέλεχ.    i K. 8²² βασίλευσον αὐτοῖς βασιλέα, 15¹¹ ἐβασίλευσα τὸν Σαοὺλ εἰς βασιλέα.

There are all together thirty-six occurrences of the word in this causative sense.

*b.* Classical Greek again knows βδελύσσεσθαι in the sense of ' to loathe ' or ' abominate,' but not βδελύσσειν in the sense of ' to make abominable,' as in —

Ex. 5²¹ ἐβδελύξατε τὴν ὀσμὴν ἡμῶν ἐναντίον Φαραώ.    Lvt. 11⁴³ καὶ οὐ μὴ βδελύξητε τὰς ψυχὰς ὑμῶν.    Cp. Lvt. 20²⁵ : i Mac. 1⁴⁸.

*c.* Still more strange to classical Greek is the sense of ' to make to sin ' often imposed upon ἐξαμαρτάνειν, *e.g.* —

iv K. 17²¹ καὶ ἐξήμαρτεν αὐτοὺς ἁμαρτίαν μεγάλην.

This is the prevailing sense of the word in the LXX, which is found all together twenty-eight times, mostly in the phrase ὃς ἐξήμαρτεν τὸν ᾽Ισραήλ.

*d.* In this causative use of the verb is to be found the explanation

of Ex. 14²⁵ καὶ ἤγαγεν αὐτοὺς μετὰ βίας, where the R.V. margin has
'made them to drive.' Other similar instances are —

Ex. 13¹⁸ ἐκύκλωσεν = he led round. i K. 4³ κατὰ τί ἔπταισεν ἡμᾶς
κύριος σήμερον; Ps. 142¹¹ ζήσεις με.

## 85. Reduplication of Words. In Greek we are accustomed to re-
duplication of syllables, but not to reduplication of words. This
primitive device of language is resorted to in the LXX, in imitation
of the Hebrew, for at least three different purposes —

(1) intensification,<br>
(2) distribution,<br>
(3) universalisation.

(1) The intensifying use.

σφόδρα σφόδρα Gen. 30⁴³ : Ex. 1⁷⁽¹² : Nb. 14⁷ : Ezk. 9⁹ : Judith 4².
σφόδρα σφοδρῶς Gen. 7¹⁹ : Josh. 3¹⁶.

To the same head may be assigned —

Ex. 8¹⁴ συνήγαγον αὐτοὺς θιμωνιὰς θιμωνιάς. Dt. 28⁴³ ὁ προσήλυτος
ὁ ἐν σοὶ ἀναβήσεται ἄνω ἄνω, σὺ δὲ καταβήσῃ κάτω κάτω.

In all the above instances perhaps the kind of intensification
involved is that of a repeated process.

(2) The distributive use.

εἷς εἷς i Chr. 24⁶.
δύο δύο Gen. 6¹⁹, 7³ : Sir. 36¹⁵.
ἑπτὰ ἑπτά Gen. 7³.
χιλίους ἐκ φυλῆς, χιλίους ἐκ φυλῆς Nb. 31⁶.
τὸ πρωὶ πρωί i Chr. 9²⁷.
ἐργασίᾳ καὶ ἐργασίᾳ ii Chr. 34¹³.

In pure Greek such ideas would be expressed by the use of ἀνά
or κατά. Sometimes we find κατά employed in the LXX along with
the reduplication, as in —

Dt. 7²² κατὰ μικρὸν μικρόν. Zech. 12¹² κατὰ φυλὰς φυλάς.

The idea 'year by year' is expressed in many different ways —

ἐνιαυτὸν κατ' ἐνιαυτόν Dt. 14²¹ : i K. 1⁷ : ii Chr. 24⁵.
κατ' ἐνιαυτὸν ἐνιαυτόν i K. 7¹⁶.
ἐνιαυτὸν ἐξ ἐνιαυτοῦ Dt. 15²⁰.
τὸ κατ' ἐνιαυτὸν ἐνιαυτῷ iii K. 10²⁸.
τὸ κατ' ἐνιαυτὸν ἐνιαυτόν ii Chr. 9²⁴.

(3) The universalising use.

ἄνθρωπος ἄνθρωπος = whatsoever man Lvt. 17³, ⁸, ¹⁰, ¹³, 18⁶, 20⁹, 22¹⁸:
Ezk. 14⁴, ⁷.

ἀνδρὶ ἀνδρί Lvt. 15³.

Of the above three uses the distributive is the only one which is to be found in the N.T.

Mk. 6⁷ δύο δύο, 6³⁹ συμπόσια συμπόσια, 6⁴⁰ πρασιαὶ πρασιαί.

So also in the *Pastor* of Hermas —

Sim. VIII 2 § 8 ἦλθον τάγματα τάγματα, 4 § 2 ἔστησαν τάγματα τάγματα.

**86. Expressions of Time.** *a.* 'Year after year' is expressed in ii K. 21¹ by a nominative absolute ἐνιαυτὸς ἐχόμενος ἐνιαυτοῦ without any pretence of grammar.

*b.* The use of the word 'day' in vague expressions of time is a Hebraism, *e.g.* —

Gen. 40⁴ ἡμέρας = for some time.   *Cp.* Dan. O' 11⁹.     Jdg. 15¹ μεθ' ἡμέρας = after some time.   *Cp.* iii K. 17⁷.     iii K. 18¹ μεθ' ἡμέρας πολλάς = after a long time.

*c.* 'Day by day' (Hb. *day, day*) is expressed in Gen. 39¹⁰ by ἡμέραν ἐξ ἡμέρας (*cp.* Lat. diem ex die).   In Esther 3⁴ καθ' ἑκάστην ἡμέραν is correctly used as the Greek equivalent for the phrase *day and day*, which St. Paul (ii Cor. 4¹⁶) has reproduced word for word in the form ἡμέρᾳ καὶ ἡμέρᾳ.

*d.* The use of 'yesterday and the day before' as a general expression for past time = *heretofore* is a Hebraism which presents itself in the LXX under a variety of slight modifications.

ἐχθὲς καὶ τρίτην i K. 4⁷, 10¹¹: ii K. 3¹⁷, 5²: i Chr. 11².
ἐχθὲς καὶ τρίτην ἡμέραν Gen. 31²,⁵: Ex. 5⁷,¹⁴: Josh. 4¹⁸: i K. 14²¹, 19⁷, 21⁵: i Mac. 9⁴⁴.
ἐχθὲς καὶ τρίτης Ruth 2¹¹: iv K. 13⁵: Sus. Θ¹⁵.
ἀπ' ἐχθὲς κὶ τρίτης ἡμέρας Josh. 3⁴.
πρὸ τῆς ἐχθὲς καὶ τρίτης Dt. 19⁴.
πρὸ τῆς ἐχθὲς καὶ πρὸ τῆς τρίτης Ex. 21²⁹.
πρὸ τῆς ἐχθὲς καὶ πρὸ τῆς τρίτης ἡμέρας Ex. 21³⁶.
πρὸ τῆς ἐχθὲς οὐδὲ πρὸ τῆς τρίτης Dt. 4⁴², 19⁶. ˙
πρὸ τῆς ἐχθὲς οὐδὲ πρὸ τῆς τρίτης ἡμέρας Ex. 4¹⁰.

In Joshua 20⁵, which occurs only in the *Codex Alexandrinus*, we have ἀπ' ἐχθὲς καὶ τρίτην, where ἐχθὲς-καὶ-τρίτην is treated as a single indeclinable noun.

*e.* 'Just at that time' is expressed variously as follows —

αὐθωρί Dan. O' 3¹⁵.

αὐτῇ τῇ ὥρᾳ i Esd. 8⁶⁵: Dan. 3⁵, Θ 3¹⁵.   *Cp.* Acts 22¹³.

ἐν αὐτῇ τῇ ὥρᾳ Dan. Θ 5⁵.   *Cp.* Lk. 12¹², 13³¹, 20¹⁹.

ἐν αὐτῇ τῇ ὥρᾳ ἐκείνῃ Dan. O' 5⁵.

ἐν αὐτῷ τῷ καιρῷ Tob. 3¹⁷.   *Cp.* Lk. 13¹.

**87. Pleonastic Use of ἐκεῖ and ἐκεῖθεν.** Just as a personal pronoun is supplied after the relative (§ 69), so a demonstrative adverb of place is supplied after a relative adverb or after some phrase equivalent to one.

Gen. 33¹⁹ οὗ ἔστησεν ἐκεῖ τὴν σκηνὴν αὐτοῦ.   *Cp.* 39²⁰, 40³: Ex. 21¹³. Ex. 20²⁴ οὗ ἐὰν ἐπονομάσω τὸ ὄνομά μου ἐκεῖ.   Dan. Θ 9⁷ οὗ διέσπειρας αὐτοὺς ἐκεῖ.   iii K. 17¹⁹ ἐν ᾧ αὐτὸς ἐκάθητο ἐκεῖ.   *Cp.* Gen. 39²⁰: Ex. 12¹³.   Gen. 31¹³ ἐν τῷ τόπῳ ᾧ ἤλειψάς μοι ἐκεῖ στήλην.   Nb. 14²⁴ εἰς ἣν εἰσῆλθεν ἐκεῖ.   *Cp.* 15¹⁸, 35²⁶: Dt. 4²⁷. Ex. 8²² ἐφ' ἧς οὐκ ἔσται ἐκεῖ.   iv K. 1⁴ ἡ κλίνη ἐφ' ἧς ἀνέβης ἐκεῖ.   Dt. 9²⁸ ὅθεν ἐξήγαγες ἡμᾶς ἐκεῖθεν.   Nb. 23¹³ ἐξ ὧν οὐκ ὄψῃ αὐτὸν ἐκεῖθεν.   Dan. O' 9⁷ εἰς ἃς διεσκόρπισας αὐτοὺς ἐκεῖ.

This idiom, which is thoroughly Hebrew, is to be explained on the same principle as in § 69. In the N.T. it is found only in Revelation —

Rev. 12⁶ ὅπου ἔχει ἐκεῖ τόπον, 12¹⁴ ὅπου τρέφεται ἐκεῖ, 17⁹ ὅπου ἡ γυνὴ κάθηται ἐπ' αὐτῶν (= ἐκεῖ).

**88. πᾶς with οὐ and μή.** *a.* The use of πᾶς with a negative particle, where in classical Greek οὐδείς or μηδείς would be employed, is a Hebraism, even though in certain cases the resulting expression may be paralleled from pure Greek usage.

The πᾶς may either precede or follow the negative (οὐ, μή, μηδέ, οὐ μή) without difference of meaning.

*b.* We will first take instances from the LXX where the πᾶς precedes the negative.

Ex. 12⁴³ πᾶς ἀλλογενὴς οὐκ ἔδεται ἀπ' αὐτοῦ.   *Cp.* 12⁴⁸: Ezek. 44⁹. Dan. O' 5⁹ πᾶς ἄνθρωπος οὐ δύναται.   *Cp.* Dan. O' 2¹⁰.   Hbk. 2¹⁹ πᾶν πνεῦμα οὐκ ἔστιν ἐν αὐτῷ.   i Mac. 2⁶¹ πάντες . . . οὐκ ἀσθενήσουσιν.   Ex. 22²² πᾶσαν χήραν καὶ ὀρφανὸν οὐ κακώσετε. Jer. 17²² πᾶν ἔργον οὐ ποιήσετε.   *Cp.* Ex. 12¹⁶, ²⁰: Nb. 28¹⁸: Jdg. 13¹⁴.

So in N.T. —

Rom. 10¹² πᾶς ὁ πιστεύων ἐπ' αὐτῷ οὐ καταισχυνθήσεται. *Cp.* Eph.
4²⁹, 5⁵. Rev. 18²² πᾶς τεχνίτης . . . οὐ μὴ εὑρεθῇ ἐν σοὶ ἔτι.
ii Pet. 1²⁰ πᾶσα προφητεία γραφῆς ἰδίας ἐπιλύσεως οὐ γίνεται.
i Jn. 2²¹ πᾶν ψεῦδος ἐκ τῆς ἀληθείας οὐκ ἔστι. *Cp.* i Jn. 3⁶, ¹⁰, ¹⁵,
4³, 5¹⁸ : Rev. 22³.

*c.* In the following passages of the LXX the πᾶς follows the
negative —

Ps. 142² οὐ δικαιωθήσεται ἐνώπιόν σου πᾶς ζῶν. Eccl. 1⁹ οὐκ ἔστιν
πᾶν πρόσφατον ὑπὸ τὸν ἥλιον. Ex. 20¹⁰ : Dt. 5¹⁴ οὐ ποιήσετε ἐν
αὐτῇ πᾶν ἔργον. *Cp.* Ex. 20¹⁶. ii K. 15¹¹ οὐκ ἔγνωσαν πᾶν
ῥῆμα. Tob. 12¹¹ οὐ μὴ κρύψω ἀφ' ὑμῶν πᾶν ῥῆμα. Ps. 33¹¹
οὐκ ἐλαττωθήσονται παντὸς ἀγαθοῦ. Jdg. 13⁴ μὴ φάγῃς πᾶν ἀκάθαρτον. Tob. 4⁷ μὴ ἀποστρέψῃς τὸ πρόσωπόν σου ἀπὸ παντὸς
πτωχοῦ.

So in N.T. —

Rom. 3²⁰ ἐξ ἔργων νόμου οὐ δικαιωθήσεται πᾶσα σάρξ. *Cp.* Gal. 2¹⁶ :
Mt. 24²². Lk. 1³⁷ οὐκ ἀδυνατήσει παρὰ τοῦ Θεοῦ πᾶν ῥῆμα.
Acts 10¹⁴ οὐδέποτε ἔφαγον πᾶν κοινόν. i Cor. 1²⁹ ὅπως μὴ καυχή-
σηται πᾶσα σάρξ. Rev. 21²⁷ οὐ μὴ εἰσέλθῃ εἰς αὐτὴν πᾶν κοινόν.

## PREPOSITIONS, 89–98

**89. Prominence of Prepositions.** The prominence of prepositions in
the LXX is partly a characteristic of later Greek generally and partly
due to the careful following of the Hebrew. But while prepositions
are employed to express relations for which in classical Greek cases
would have been thought sufficient, there is at the same time a tendency to blur some of the nice distinctions between the uses of the
same preposition with different cases.

**90. εἰς.** *a.* εἰς in classical Greek denotes motion or direction : in
Biblical Greek it denotes equally rest or position, and may be translated by ' at ' or ' in ' as well as by ' to,' *e.g.* —

Gen. 37¹⁷ πορευθῶμεν εἰς Δωθάειμ . . . καὶ εὗρεν αὐτοὺς εἰς Δωθάειμ.
Josh. 7²² ἔδραμον εἰς τὴν σκηνὴν . . . καὶ ταῦτα ἦν ἐνκεκρυμμένα εἰς
τὴν σκηνήν. Jdg. 14¹ καὶ κατέβη Σαμψὼν εἰς Θαμνάθα, καὶ εἶδεν
γυναῖκα εἰς Θαμνάθα.

For examples of the former meaning only we may take —

Gen. 42³² ὁ δὲ μικρότερος . . . εἰς γῆν Χανάαν.    Nb. 25³³ τὴν γῆν
εἰς ἣν ὑμεῖς κατοικεῖτε.    Judith 16²³ ἀπέθανεν εἰς Βαιτυλουά.

b. In the N.T. εἰς denoting rest or position is very common.

Mk. 2¹ εἰς οἶκον = at home.    Cp. Lk. 9⁶¹: Mk. 10¹⁰.    Mk. 13³ καθημένου αὐτοῦ εἰς τὸ ὄρος τῶν ἐλαιῶν.    Jn. 1¹⁸ ὁ ὢν εἰς τὸν κόλπον
τοῦ πα. ός.    Acts 21¹³ ἀποθανεῖν εἰς Ἰερουσαλήμ.

Cp. also Eph. 3¹⁶: i Pet. 3²⁰, 5¹²: Mk. 1⁹, ³⁹, 13⁹: Lk. 4²³, 11⁷: Jn. 9⁷,
20⁷: Acts 7⁴, 8⁴⁰, 25⁴.

The obliteration of the distinction between rest and motion is
one of the marks of declining Greek.    In the modern language εἰς
has usurped the functions both of ἐν and πρός.

c. The use of εἰς with the accusative after εἶναι and γενέσθαι as
practically equivalent to the nominative may safely be regarded
as a Hebraism.

d. i Chr. 11²¹ ἦν αὐτοῖς εἰς ἄρχοντα, 17⁷ εἶναι εἰς ἡγούμενον.    iii K.
20² ἔσται μοι εἰς κῆπον λαχάνων.    Cp. Gen. 48¹⁹: i Chr. 11⁶.    i K.
17⁹ ἐσόμεθα ὑμῖν εἰς δούλους.    Jer. 38³³ ἔσομαι αὐτοῖς εἰς θεὸν, καὶ
αὐτοὶ ἔσονταί μοι εἰς λαόν.    Cp. Jer. 38¹: Gen. 48¹⁹: ii K. 7¹⁴.
Gen. 2⁷ ἐγένετο ὁ ἄνθρωπος εἰς ψυχὴν ζῶσαν.    Ex. 2¹⁰ ἐγενήθη
αὐτῇ εἰς υἱόν.    i K. 4⁹ γένεσθε εἰς ἄνδρας.

πρός in one passage takes the place of εἰς.

Sir. 46⁴ μία ἡμέρα ἐγενήθη πρὸς δύο.

e. In the New Testament this idiom occurs both in quotations
from the Old and otherwise.

i Jn. 5⁸ καὶ οἱ τρεῖς εἰς τὸ ἕν εἰσιν.    Lk. 3⁵ ἔσται τὰ σκολιὰ εἰς
εὐθείας (Is. 40⁴).    ii Cor. 6¹⁸ ἔσεσθέ μοι εἰς υἱούς καὶ θυγατέρας (ii K. 7⁸: Is. 43⁶).    Mt. 19⁵ ἔσονται οἱ δύο εἰς σάρκα
μίαν (Gen. 2²⁴).    Mt. 21⁴² ἐγενήθη εἰς κεφαλὴν γωνίας (Ps. 117²²).
Lk. 13¹⁹ ἐγένετο εἰς δένδρον.    Cp. Rev. 8¹¹.    Jn. 16²⁰ ἡ λύπη
ὑμῶν εἰς χαρὰν γενήσεται.

The same usage is to be found also in the Apostolic Fathers —

Herm. Past. Sim. IX 13 § 5 ἔσονται εἰς ἕν πνεῦμα, εἰς ἕν σῶμα.
i Clem. 11² εἰς κρίμα καὶ εἰς σημείωσιν . . . γίνονται.    Ign. Eph.
11¹ ἵνα μὴ ἡμῖν εἰς κρίμα γένηται.

f. The employment of εἰς to express the object or destination of a
thing might easily be paralleled from classical Greek, but its fre-

quent use in the LXX is due to its convenience as a translation of the corresponding Hebrew.

Gen. 34¹² καὶ δώσετέ μοι τὴν παῖδα ταύτην εἰς γυναῖκα.  Ps. 104¹⁷ εἰς δοῦλον ἐπράθη ᾿Ιωσήφ.  iii K. 19¹⁵ χρίσεις τὸν ᾿Αζαὴλ εἰς βασιλέα. Gen. 12² ποιήσω σε εἰς ἔθνος μέγα.

When the verb is active and transitive, as in all but the second of the above instances, εἰς might be dispensed with as far as Greek is concerned.  When a verb of being is employed, this use runs into the preceding —

Gen. 1²⁹ ὑμῖν ἔσται εἰς βρῶσιν, 1¹⁴ ἔστωσαν εἰς σημεῖα.

g. The use of εἰς with the accusative, where classical Greek would simply have employed a dative, is shown by the Papyri to have been a feature of the vernacular Greek of Alexandria.

Ex. 9²¹ ὃς δὲ μὴ προσέσχεν τῇ διανοίᾳ εἰς τὸ ῥῆμα κυρίου κτλ.

So in N.T. —

i Cor. 16¹ τῆς λογίας τῆς εἰς τοὺς ἁγίους (the collection for the saints).

**91. ἐν.**  a. Although ἐν was destined ultimately to disappear before εἰς, yet in Biblical Greek we find it in the plenitude of its power, as expressing innumerable relations, some of which seem to the classical student to be quite beyond its proper sphere.  One principal use may be summed up under the title of "The ἐν of Accompanying Circumstances."  This includes the instrumental use, but goes far beyond it.  Under this aspect ἐν invades the domain of μετά and σύν. In most cases it may be rendered by the English 'with.'

Hos. 1⁷ σώσω αὐτοὺς ἐν κυρίῳ θεῷ αὐτῶν, καὶ οὐ σώσω αὐτοὺς ἐν τόξῳ οὐδὲ ἐν ῥομφαίᾳ οὐδὲ ἐν πολέμῳ οὐδὲ ἐν ἵπποις οὐδὲ ἐν ἱππεῦσιν. Cp. i K. 17⁴⁵, ⁴⁷: i Mac. 3¹². Ex. 6¹ ἐν γὰρ χειρὶ κραταιᾷ κτλ. (But in Ex. 3¹⁹ we have ἐὰν μὴ μετὰ χειρὸς κραταιᾶς.) Cp. Ex. 3²⁰: Jdg. 15¹⁵, ¹⁶. Jdg. 14¹⁸ εἰ μὴ ἠροτριάσατε ἐν τῇ δαμάλει μου. Cp. iii K. 19¹⁹. iv K. 18¹⁷ ἐν δυνάμει βαρείᾳ. In the parallel passage Is. 36² μετὰ δυνάμεως πολλῆς. i Mac. 4⁶ ὤφθη ᾿Ιούδας . . . ἐν τρισχιλίοις ἀνδράσιν.

So in N.T. —

i Cor. 4²¹ ἐν ῥάβδῳ ἔλθω πρὸς ὑμᾶς; Cp. i K. 17⁴³: Ps. 2⁹. Eph. 6² ἐντολὴ πρώτη ἐν ἐπαγγελίᾳ. ii Pet. 3¹⁶ ἐν ἀνθρώπου φωνῇ. Mt. 9³⁴ ἐν τῷ ἄρχοντι τῶν δαιμονίων ἐκβάλλει τὰ δαιμόνια. Cp. Mt. 12²⁴, 25¹⁶. Mt. 26⁵² ἐν μαχαίρᾳ ἀπολοῦνται.

*b.* The ἐν of accompanying circumstances is not wholly foreign to classical Greek, though the extended use made of it in Biblical diction is.

Eur. *Tro.* 817 ὦ χρυσέαις ἐν οἰνοχόαις ἁβρὰ βαίνων.

*c.* In another of its Biblical uses ἐν becomes indistinguishable from εἰς, as in —

Ex. 4²¹ πάντα τὰ τέρατα ἃ ἔδωκα ἐν ταῖς χερσίν σου.   Jdg. 13¹ παρέδωκεν αὐτοὺς Κύριος ἐν χειρὶ Φυλιστιείμ.   *Cp.* Jdg. 15¹²⸴ ¹³, 16²³⸴ ²⁴. Is. 37¹⁰ οὐ μὴ παραδοθῇ Ἱερουσαλὴμ ἐν χειρὶ βασιλέως, while the parallel passage in iv K. 19¹⁰ has εἰς χεῖρας βασιλέως.   Tob. 5⁵ πορευθῆναι ἐν Ῥάγοις.   *Cp.* Tob. 6⁶, 9².

So in N.T. —

ii Cor. 8¹⁶ χάρις δὲ τῷ Θεῷ τῷ διδόντι τὴν αὐτὴν σπουδὴν ὑπὲρ ὑμῶν ἐν τῇ καρδίᾳ Τίτου.   Mt. 14³ ἔθετο ἐν φυλακῇ.   Jn. 3³⁵ πάντα δίδωκεν ἐν τῇ χειρὶ αὐτοῦ.   Rev. 11¹¹ πνεῦμα ζωῆς ἐκ τοῦ Θεοῦ εἰσῆλθεν ἐν αὐτοῖς.

**92. ἀπό.** *a.* ἀπό in the LXX is often little more than a sign of the genitive, like our English 'of,' provided that the genitive be partitive.

Ex. 12⁴⁶ καὶ ὀστοῦν οὐ συντρίψετε ἀπ' αὐτοῦ.   Josh. 9⁸ οὐκ ἦν ῥῆμα ἀπὸ πάντων ὧν ἐνετείλατο Μωυσῆς τῷ Ἰησοῖ ὃ οὐκ ἀνέγνω Ἰησοῦς. iii K. 18¹³ ἔκρυψα ἀπὸ τῶν προφητῶν Κυρίου ἑκατὸν ἄνδρας.   Joel 2²⁸ ἐκχεῶ ἀπὸ τοῦ πνεύματός μου.   ii Esd. 11² εἷς ἀπὸ ἀδελφῶν μου.

So in N.T. —

Lk. 6¹³ ἐκλεξάμενος ἀπ' αὐτῶν δώδεκα.   Jn. 21¹⁰ ἐνέγκατε ἀπὸ τῶν ὀψαρίων ὧν ἐπιάσατε νῦν.

*b.* ἀπό = 'by reason of' is another unclassical use which occurs in the LXX.

Gen. 41³¹ καὶ οὐκ ἐπιγνωσθήσεται ἡ εὐθηνία ἐπὶ τῆς γῆς ἀπὸ τοῦ λιμοῦ. Ex. 2²³ καὶ κατεστέναξαν οἱ υἱοὶ Ἰσραὴλ ἀπὸ τῶν ἔργων, 3⁷ καὶ τῆς κραυγῆς αὐτῶν ἀκήκοα ἀπὸ τῶν ἐργοδιωκτῶν.   Ps. 11⁶ ἀπὸ τῆς ταλαιπωρίας τῶν πτωχῶν . . . ἀναστήσομαι.   Sir. 20⁶ ἔστιν μισητὸς ἀπὸ πολλῆς λαλιᾶς.   Nahum 1⁶ αἱ πέτραι διεθρύβησαν ἀπ' αὐτοῦ.

In this way ἀπό becomes = ὑπό, as in Dan. O' 1¹⁸.

So in N.T. —

Hb. 5⁷ εἰσακουσθεὶς ἀπὸ τῆς εὐλαβείας.     Lk. 19³ οὐκ ἠδύνατο ἀπὸ τοῦ ὄχλου, 24⁴¹ ἀπιστούντων αὐτῶν ἀπὸ τῆς χαρᾶς.     Cp. Acts 12¹⁴, 22¹¹.     Jn. 21⁶ οὐκέτι αὐτὸ ἑλκύσαι ἴσχυον ἀπὸ τοῦ πλήθους τῶν ἰχθύων.

Of ἀπό = ὑπό see instances in Lk. 9²², 17²⁵: Acts 20⁹.

c. The combination ἀπό . . . ἕως is a Hebraism.  It may be rendered "from . . . unto," as in —

Dt. 8³⁵ ἀπὸ ἴχνους τῶν ποδῶν σου ἕως τῆς κορυφῆς σου,

or "both . . . and," as in —

Ex. 9²⁵ ἀπὸ ἀνθρώπου . . . ἕως κτήνους.

Sometimes καί precedes the ἕως —

Jdg. 15⁵ ἀπὸ . . . καὶ ἕως . . . καὶ ἕως both . . . and . . . and.
Cp. Sir. 40³: Jer. 27³.

**93. μετά.**  μετά with genitive = 'in dealing with' is a Hebraism.

Jdg. 15³ ὅτι ποιῶ ἐγὼ μετ' αὐτῶν πονηρίαν.

So in N.T. —

Lk. 10³⁷ ὁ ποιήσας τὸ ἔλεος μετ' αὐτοῦ: Acts 14²⁷.    Cp. Herm. Past. Sim. v 1 § 1: i Clem. 61³.

**94. ὑπέρ.**  a. The frequent use of ὑπέρ in the LXX to express comparison is due to the fact that the Hebrew language has no special form for the comparative degree.  We therefore sometimes find the LXX representing the original by the positive with ὑπέρ.

Ruth 4¹⁵ ἥ ἐστιν ἀγαθή σοι ὑπὲρ ἑπτὰ υἱούς.  Cp. i K. 1⁸, 15²⁸: iii K. 20²: ii Chr. 21¹⁴.    i K. 9² ὑψηλὸς ὑπὲρ πᾶσαν τὴν γῆν.    i Chr. 4⁹ ἔνδοξος ὑπὲρ τοὺς ἀδελφοὺς αὐτοῦ.    Sir. 24²⁰ ὑπὲρ μέλι γλυκύ. Ezk. 5¹ ῥομφαίαν ὀξεῖαν ὑπὲρ ξυρὸν κουρέως.

b. More often however the comparative is used, but the construction with ὑπέρ still retained.

Jdg. 15² ἀγαθωτέρα ὑπὲρ αὐτήν.  Cp. Jdg. 11²⁵.    Jdg. 18²⁶ δυνατώτεροι εἰσιν ὑπὲρ αὐτόν.    Ruth 3¹² ἐγγίων ὑπὲρ ἐμέ.    iii K. 19⁴ κρείσσων . . . ὑπὲρ τοὺς πατέρας.  Cp. Sir. 30¹⁷.    Hbk. 1⁸ ὀξύτεροι ὑπὲρ λύκους.    Dan. O' 1²⁰ σοφωτέρους δεκαπλασίως ὑπὲρ τοὺς σοφιστάς.

*c.* ὑπέρ is employed in the same way after verbs —

Ex. 1⁹ ἰσχύει ὑπὲρ ἡμᾶς.  i K. 1⁵ τὴν Ἄνναν ἠγάπα Ἑλκανὰ ὑπὲρ ταύτην.  Ps. 39¹³ ἐπληθύνθησαν ὑπὲρ τὰς τρίχας τῆς κεφαλῆς μου. i Chr. 19¹² ἐὰν κρατήσῃ ὑπὲρ ἐμὲ Σύρος.  Jer. 5³ ἐστερέωσαν . . . ὑπὲρ πέτραν, 16¹² ὑμεῖς ἐπονηρεύσασθε ὑπὲρ τοὺς πατέρας ὑμῶν.  Cp. 17²³.  Jer. 26²³ πληθύνει ὑπὲρ ἀκρίδα.  Dan. Ο′ 3²² ἡ κάμινος ἐξεκαύθη ὑπὲρ τὸ πρότερον ἑπταπλασίως.

*d.* So in N.T. —
after a comparative —

Lk. 16⁸ φρονιμώτεροι ὑπὲρ τοὺς υἱοὺς τοῦ φωτός.  Hb. 4¹² τομώτερος ὑπὲρ πᾶσαν μάχαιραν.

after a verb —
Gal. 1¹⁴ προέκοπτον . . . ὑπὲρ πολλούς.  Mt. 10³⁷ ὁ φιλῶν πατέρα ἢ μητέρα ὑπὲρ ἐμέ.
*Cp.* Herm. *Past. Mdt.* V 1 § 6 ἡ μακροθυμία γλυκυτάτη ἐστὶν ὑπὲρ τὸ μέλι.  *Mart. Polyc.* 18 δοκιμώτερα ὑπὲρ χρυσίον ὀστᾶ αὐτοῦ.

**95.** ἐπί. *a.* ἐπί with the accusative is used of rest as well as of motion.

Gen. 41¹⁷ ἑστάναι ἐπὶ τὸ χεῖλος τοῦ ποταμοῦ.  Ex. 10¹⁴ καὶ ἀνήγαγεν αὐτὴν (τὴν ἀκρίδα) ἐπὶ πᾶσαν γῆν Αἰγύπτου, καὶ κατέπαυσεν ἐπὶ πάντα τὰ ὅρια Αἰγύπτου πολλὴ σφόδρα.  Jdg. 16²⁷ ἐπὶ τὸ δῶμα = upon the roof.

*b.* ἐπί is sometimes used to reinforce an accusative of duration of time.

Jdg. 14¹⁷ καὶ ἔκλαυσεν πρὸς αὐτὸν ἐπὶ τὰς ἑπτὰ ἡμέρας ἃς ἦν αὐτοῖς ὁ πότος.

*c.* In Josh. 25¹⁰ we find μέγαν ἐπὶ τοῦ ἰδεῖν where in classical Greek we should have only μέγαν ἰδεῖν.

*d.* In the N.T. also ἐπί with the accusative is used of rest or position —

ii Cor. 3¹⁵ κάλυμμα ἐπὶ τὴν καρδίαν αὐτῶν κεῖται.  Mk. 2¹⁴ καθήμενον ἐπὶ τὸ τελώνιον.  *Cp.* Lk. 5²⁷.  Mk. 4³⁸ ἐπὶ τὸ προσκεφάλαιον καθεύδων.  Mt. 14²⁸ περιπατῶν ἐπὶ τὴν θάλασσαν (in Jn. 6¹⁹ περιπατοῦντα ἐπὶ τῆς θαλάσσης).  Lk. 2²⁵ πνεῦμα ἅγιον ἦν ἐπ᾽ αὐτόν.  *Cp.* Lk. 2⁴⁰.  Jn. 1³² ἔμεινεν ἐπ᾽ αὐτόν.

**96.** παρά. *a.* παρά naturally lends itself to the expression of comparison, and is so used occasionally in the best Greek, *e.g.* Thuc. I 23

§ 4 : Xen. *Mem.* I 4 § 14: Hdt. VII 103.   It is therefore not surprising that it should have been employed by the translators in the same way as ὑπέρ.

Ex. 18¹¹ μέγας Κύριος παρὰ πάντας τοὺς θεούς.   *Cp.* Ps. 134⁵: Dan. Ο′ 11¹². Nb. 12³ καὶ ὁ ἄνθρωπος Μωυσῆς πραῢς σφόδρα παρὰ πάντας τοὺς ἀνθρώπους.    Dan. Ο′ 1¹⁰ ἀσθενῆ παρὰ τοὺς συντρεφομένους ὑμῖν (Θ has σκυθρωπὰ παρὰ τὰ παιδάρια τὰ συνήλικα ὑμῖν). *Cp.* Ο′ 1¹³.    Dan. Θ 7⁷ διάφορον περισσῶς παρὰ πάντα τὰ θηρία. i Esd. 4³⁵ ἰσχυροτέρα παρὰ πάντα.    Dan. Ο′ 11¹³ μείζονα παρὰ τὴν πρώτην (Θ has πολὺν ὑπὲρ τὸν πρότερον).    Dt. 7⁷ ὑμεῖς γάρ ἐστε ὀλιγοστοὶ παρὰ πάντα τὰ ἔθνη.    Gen. 43³⁴ ἐμεγαλύνθη δὲ ἡ μερὶς Βενιαμεὶν παρὰ τὰς μερίδας πάντων.    Ps. 8⁶ ἠλάττωσας αὐτὸν βραχύ τι παρ᾽ ἀγγέλους.

b. In the N.T. παρά after a comparative is abundant in Hebrews — 1⁴, 3³, 9²³, 11⁴, 12²⁴.

We find it after a positive and after a comparative in Luke —

Lk. 13² ἁμαρτωλοὶ παρὰ πάντας τοὺς Γαλιλαίους, 3¹³ μηδὲν πλέον παρὰ τὸ διατεταγμένον ὑμῖν πράσσετε,

and after verbs in —

Rom. 14⁵ ὃς μὲν κρίνει ἡμέραν παρ᾽ ἡμέραν.      Hb. 1⁹ ἔχρισέ σε ὁ Θεός . . . παρὰ τοὺς μετόχους σου.

c. In the Apostolic Fathers *cp.* —

Herm. *Past. Vis.* III 12 § 1 ἱλαρωτέραν παρὰ τὸ πρότερον, *Sim.* IX 18 § 2 πλείονα . . . παρά.      Barn. *Ep.* 4⁵ (in a quotation from Daniel which is neither Ο′ nor Θ) χαλεπώτερον παρὰ πάντα τὰ θηρία.

**97. New Forms of Preposition.**   *a.* Besides the more liberal use made of the prepositions already current in classical Greek, we meet also in the LXX with new forms of preposition.

*b.* ἀπάνωθεν occurs in Swete's text in Jdg. 16²⁰: ii K. 11²⁰, ²⁴, 20²¹: iii K. 1⁵³: iv K. 2³.   It not unnaturally gets confused in some places with the classical ἐπάνωθεν, which is very common in the LXX, having been found a convenient rendering of certain compound prepositions in the Hebrew.

*c.* ὑποκάτωθεν, which is only used as an adverb in classical Greek, assumes in the LXX the function of a preposition, *e.g.* —

Dt. 9¹⁴ ἐξαλείψω τὸ ὄνομα αὐτῶν ὑποκάτωθεν τοῦ οὐρανοῦ.

The corresponding form ὑπεράνωθεν occurs in the LXX only twice, once as an adverb in Ps. 77²³ and once as a preposition in — Ezk. 1²⁵ ὑπεράνωθεν τοῦ στερεώματος.

*d.* ἔναντι, ἀπέναντι, and κατέναντι are prepositions unknown to classical authors, though ὑπέναντι is to be found in Polybius.

ἔναντι in many passages of the LXX has been replaced in Swete's text by ἐναντίον, but there are still numerous instances of it left, *e.g.* Ex. 28¹², ²³, ³⁴, 29¹⁰, ²³, ²⁴, ²⁵, ²⁶, ⁴². In N.T. it occurs in Lk. 1⁸, Acts 8²¹.

ἀπέναντι is also common, *e.g.* Gen. 3²⁴, 21²⁶, 23¹⁹, 25⁹, 49³⁰. In the N.T. it occurs in the sense of 'contrary to' in Acts 17⁷.

κατέναντι is specially frequent in the book of Sirach.

*e.* ἐνώπιον is another preposition unknown to classical authors, but extremely common in Biblical Greek, as being an apt equivalent for certain Hebrew forms of expression. Deissmann gives instances of its adverbial use in the Papyri, so that we need not suppose it to have been invented by the translators of the O.T. In the N.T. it occurs frequently in Luke-Acts, Paul, and Revelation, but is not used in Matthew or Mark.

κατενώπιον occurs in the LXX in Lvt. 4¹⁷: Josh. 1⁵, 3⁷, 21⁴⁴, 23⁹: Esther 5¹: Dan. Θ 5²². In N.T. in Eph. 1⁴: Col. 1²²: Jude²⁴.

*f.* ὀπίσω as a preposition is unclassical, but extremely common in the LXX.

In the N.T. it occurs in i Tim. 5¹⁵: Acts 5³⁷, 20³⁰: Mt. 4¹⁹, 10³⁸, 16²⁴: Lk. 14²⁷: Jn. 12¹⁹: Rev. 13³.

*g.* κατόπισθε(ν) is construed with a genitive in Hom. *Od.* XII 148, but its classical use is almost wholly adverbial, whereas in the LXX, in which it occurs twenty-four times in all, it is mainly prepositional. In ii Chr. 34³⁸ we have ἀπὸ ὄπισθεν Κυρίου. *Cp.* Eccl. 1¹⁰ ἀπὸ ἔμπροσθεν ἡμῶν.

*h.* κυκλόθεν occurs in the LXX as a preposition in iii K. 18³²: Sir. 50¹² A: Jer. 17²⁶, 31¹⁷: i Mac. 14¹⁷.

In N.T. only in Rev. 4³, 5¹¹ κυκλόθεν τοῦ θρόνου.

κύκλῳ is sometimes used in the same way, as in iii K. 18³⁵: Sir. 23¹⁸: Is. 6²: Jer. 39⁴⁴.

*Cp.* Strabo XVII 6, p. 792 τὰ δὲ κύκλῳ τῆς κώμης.

*i.* Other prepositions that may be briefly noticed are ἐχόμενα πέτρας Ps. 140⁶, ἐσώτερον τῆς κολυμβήθρας Is. 22¹¹.

In Sir. 29²⁵ we have the combination καὶ πρὸς ἐπὶ τούτοις.

**98. Prepositions after Verbs.** The great use made of prepositions after verbs is one of the main characteristics of Biblical Greek. It

is partly a feature of later Greek generally, but to a still greater
extent it is due to the influence of the Hebrew.   In the following
list of instances perhaps the last only is irreproachable as Greek: —

ἀδυνατεῖν ἀπό Dt. 17⁸.

ἀθετεῖν ἐν iv K. 1¹, 3⁵,⁷, 18⁷, 24¹,²⁰ : ii Chr. 10¹⁹.

αἱρετίζειν ἐν i Chr. 29¹: ii Chr. 29¹¹.

βδελύσσεσθαι ἀπό Ex. 1¹².

βοᾶν ἐν iii K. 18²⁴.

ἐκδικεῖν ἐκ Dt. 18¹⁹.

ἐκλέγειν ἐν i Chr. 28⁵.

ἐλπίζειν ἐπί with accusative Ps. 4⁶, 5¹², 9¹¹, 40¹⁰.

ἐλπίζειν ἐπί with dative Ps. 7¹.

ἐνεδρεύειν ἐπί Jdg. 16².

ἐντρέπεσθαι ἀπό ii Chr. 36¹²: i Esd. 1⁴⁵.

ἐπικαλεῖσθαι ἐν iii K. 18²⁵,²⁶.

ἐσθίειν ἀπό Lvt. 22⁶: Jdg. 13¹⁶.

εὐδοκεῖν ἐν Ps. 146¹⁰.

θέλειν ἐν i K. 18²²: i Chr. 28⁴: Ps. 146¹⁰.

θεωρεῖν ἐν Jdg. 16²⁷.

καταφρονεῖν ἐπί Tobit 4¹⁸.

λογίζεσθαι εἰς i K. 1¹³.

μυκτηρίζειν ἐν i Esd. 1⁵¹.

πατάσσειν ἐν ii. Chr. 28⁵,¹⁷.

ποιεῖν ἔλεος ἐν Josh. 2¹².

ποιεῖν ἔλεος μετά Jdg. 8³⁵.

πολεμεῖν ἐν i K. 28¹⁵.

προσέχειν εἰς Ex. 9²¹.

προσοχθίζειν ἀπό Nb. 22³.

συνιέναι εἰς Ps. 27⁵.

ὑπερηφανεύεσθαι ἀπό Tobit 4¹⁴.

φείδεσθαι ἐπί Dt. 7¹⁶.

φοβεῖσθαι ἀπό Dt. 1²⁹, 7²⁹: Josh. 11⁶: iv K. 1¹⁵: Ps. 3⁷.

φυλάσσεσθαι ἀπό Jdg. 13¹⁴.    Cp. Xen. Cyrop. II 3 § 9, Hell. VII
     2 § 10.


## CONJUNCTIONS, 99–111

**99. εἰ with the Subjunctive.**  a.  In Homer εἰ, or its equivalent αἰ, is
common with the subjunctive, especially when accompanied by κε(ν),
e.g. Il. I 80, IV 249, VII 375, VIII 282, XI 791, XV 403, XVI 861,
XVIII 601 : Od. IV 35, V 471, 472, XVI 98, XXII 7.

In classical authors instances of εἰ with the subjunctive (without ἄν) are rare rather than absent. Some of them may have been improved out of existence, owing to a desire for uniformity.

Plato *Laws* 761 C εἴ τί που ἄλσος . . . ἀνειμένον ᾖ. Xen. *Anab.* III 2 § 22 οἱ πόταμοι, εἰ καὶ πρόσω τῶν πηγῶν ἄποροι ὦσι. Soph. *Ant.* 710 κεἴ τις ᾖ σοφός. See GMT. 454.

*b.* In Hellenistic Greek the use of εἰ with the subjunctive becomes common, *e.g.* —

Arist. *E.E.* II 1 § 17 εἰ ᾖ ἄνθρωπος, 8 § 9 εἴ τις προσθῇ, 18 εἰ γὰρ . . . ἀποκτείνῃ, 10 § 21 εἰ πολεμῶσιν. Philo II 19, *De Abr.* § 25 εἰ ἔμμισθος ᾖ. Jos. *B.J.* I 31 § 1 εἰ . . . ἀσθενήσῃ, *Ant.* I 2 § 3 εἰ καὶ συμβῇ.

We should therefore antecedently expect to find this construction in the LXX, and yet it is seldom found. It occurs in Jdg. 11⁹, where an indicative and subjunctive are both made dependent on εἰ — εἰ ἐπιστρέφετέ με ὑμεῖς παρατάξασθαι ἐν υἱοῖς 'Αμμὼν καὶ παραδῷ Κύριος αὐτοὺς ἐνώπιον ἐμοῦ. In Dt. 8⁵ Swete's text has παιδεῦσαι in place of παιδεύσῃ. In i K. 14³⁷ εἰ καταβῶ ὀπίσω τῶν ἀλλοφύλων is so punctuated as to become an instance of εἰ interrogative (§ 100). In Sirach 22²⁶ εἰ κακά μοι συμβῇ, the συμβῇ has given place to συμβήσεται.

In the N.T. there are a few instances of εἰ with the subjunctive — Rom. 11¹⁴ εἴ πως παραζηλώσω. Phil. 3¹¹ εἴ πως καταντήσω εἰς τὴν ἐξανάστασιν, 3¹² εἰ καὶ καταλάβω.

**100. εἰ Interrogative.** *a.* In classical Greek εἰ is often used in indirect questions, *e.g.* —

Thuc. I 5 § 2 ἐρωτῶντες εἰ λῃσταί εἰσιν. Plat. *Apol.* 21 D ἤρετο γὰρ δή, εἴ τις ἐμοῦ εἴη σοφώτερος. Xen. *Anab.* I 10 § 5 ἐβουλεύετο . . . εἰ πέμποιέν τινας ἢ πάντες ἴοιεν.

*b.* In Biblical Greek εἰ has become a direct interrogative particle. This transition seems so natural as to make us doubt the statement of Jannaris (*Hist. Gk. Gr.* § 2055) that εἰ is in all these cases 'nothing but an itacistic misspelling for the colloquial ἦ.' In

Gen. 43⁷ λέγων Εἰ ἔτι ὁ πατὴρ ὑμῶν ζῇ; εἰ ἔστιν ὑμῖν ἀδελφός; . . . μὴ ᾔδειμεν εἰ ἐρεῖ ἡμῖν κτλ.

we have first the direct and then the indirect use of εἰ as an interrogative particle. For other instances of the former take —

i K. 15³² καὶ εἶπεν 'Αγάγ Εἰ οὕτως πικρὸς ὁ θάνατος; ii K. 20¹⁷ καὶ εἶπεν ἡ γυνή Εἰ σὺ εἶ 'Ιωάβ; iii K. 20²⁰ καὶ εἶπεν 'Αχαὰβ πρὸς

Ἠλειού Εἰ εὕρηκάς με, ὁ ἐχθρός μου; Cp. also Gen. 17¹⁷, 39⁸, 43²⁷:
Ex. 2¹⁴: Jdg. 13¹¹: i K. 9¹¹, 10²², ²⁴, 14³⁷, ⁴⁵, 15²²: iii K. 13¹⁴, 18¹⁷:
iv K. 1³: Tob. 5⁵: Jonah 4⁴, ⁹: Joel 1²: Dan. 6²⁰.

c. The interrogative εἰ is sometimes followed by the deliberative
conjunctive, e.g. —

Jdg. 20²⁸ Εἰ προσθῶμεν ἔτι ἐξελθεῖν; ii K. 2¹ Εἰ ἀναβῶ εἰς μίαν
τῶν πόλεων Ἰούδα; i Chr. 14¹⁰ Εἰ ἀναβῶ ἐπὶ τοὺς ἀλλοφύλους;

d. In the N.T. εἰ interrogative is of common occurrence —

Mk. 8²³ ἐπηρώτα αὐτόν, Εἴ τι βλέπεις; Cp. Mk. 10², where the
question may be either direct or indirect. Mt. 12¹⁰ ἐπηρώ-
τησαν αὐτὸν λέγοντες, Εἰ ἔξεστι τοῖς σάββασι θεραπεύειν; Cp. Mt.
19³. Lk. 13²³ Κύριε, εἰ ὀλίγοι οἱ σωζόμενοι; Cp. Lk. 22⁴⁹.
Acts 1⁶ Κύριε, εἰ ἐν τῷ χρόνῳ τούτῳ κτλ. Cp. Acts 7¹, 19², 21³⁷,
22²⁵, 23⁹.

**101. εἰ in Oaths.** a. εἰ is often found in the LXX after an oath in
a sense practically equivalent to a negative, e.g. —

Ps. 94¹¹ ὡς ὤμοσα ἐν τῇ ὀργῇ μου Εἰ ἐλεύσονται εἰς τὴν κατάπουσίν μου.

This use of εἰ is a sheer Hebraism. The negative force imported
into εἰ is due to a suppression of the apodosis, which the reader may
supply as his own sense of reverence suggests. Other instances will
be found in Gen. 14²³: Nb. 32¹⁰, ¹¹: Dt. 1³⁴, ³⁵: i K. 3¹⁴, 14⁴⁵, 17⁵⁵,
19⁶, 28¹⁰: ii K. 19³⁵: iii K. 1⁵², 2⁸, 17¹, ¹², 18¹⁰: iv K. 2²: Ps. 131²⁻⁴:
Jer. 45¹⁶.

b. When an affirmative asseveration is conveyed by the oath, it is
introduced by ὅτι, not by εἰ, as in —

i K. 29⁶ ζῇ Κύριος, ὅτι εὐθὴς σὺ καὶ ἀγαθὸς ἐν ὀφθαλμοῖς μου.
iii K. 18¹⁵ ζῇ Κύριος . . . ὅτι σήμερον ὀφθήσομαί σοι,

or else is devoid of a conjunction, as in —

i K. 1²⁶ ζῇ ἡ ψυχή σου, ἐγὼ ἡ γυνὴ κτλ. Jdg. 8¹⁹ ζῇ Κύριος, εἰ
ἐζωογονήκειτε αὐτούς, οὐκ ἂν ἀπέκτεινα ὑμᾶς.

c. In iv K. 3¹⁴ ὅτι εἰ μή is merely a strengthened form of εἰ μή, so
that the ἦ by which it is followed in Swete's text, instead of εἰ, seems
to destroy the sense.

d. In the N.T. we have the jurative use of εἰ in —

Mk. 8¹² ἀμὴν λέγω ὑμῖν, εἰ δοθήσεται τῇ γενεᾷ ταύτῃ σημεῖον.

Also in Hb. 3¹¹, 4³ in quotations from Ps. 94¹¹.

**102. εἰ μή in Oaths.** As εἰ assumes a negative force in oaths and asseverations, so on the same principle εἰ μή becomes positive. Instances are—

Nb. 14³⁵ ἐγὼ Κύριος ἐλάλησα, εἰ μὴ οὕτως ποιήσω (= I will do so). Is. 45²³ κατ᾽ ἐμαυτοῦ ὀμνύω, εἰ μὴ ἐξελεύσεται ἐκ τοῦ στόματός μου δικαιοσύνη (= righteousness shall go forth from my mouth).

In iii K. 21²³ ἐὰν δὲ πολεμήσομεν αὐτοὺς κατ᾽ εὐθύ, εἰ μὴ κραταιώσομεν ὑπὲρ αὐτούς the oath itself is suppressed as well as the apodosis.

**103. εἰ μήν.** εἰ μήν as a formula of asseveration has been supposed to be a blend between the Hebraistic εἰ μή (§ 102) and the Greek ἦ μήν. It is however not confined to Biblical Greek, but occurs also on the Papyri. We treat it under the head of Conjunctions because of the lack of accent. It would perhaps be more correct to write it εἰ μήν and regard it as an Interjection. The following are all the passages in which it occurs in the LXX—

Gen. 22¹⁷ εἰ μὴν εὐλογῶν εὐλογήσω σε, 42¹⁵ νὴ τὴν ὑγίαν Φαραώ, εἰ μὴν κατάσκοποί ἐστε. Nb. 14²³, ²⁸: Jdg. 15⁷: Job 1¹¹, 2⁵, 27³: Judith 1¹²: Baruch 2²⁹: Ezk. 33²⁷, 34⁸, 36⁵, 38¹⁹.

In ii K. 19³⁵ what we have is εἰ interrogative (§ 100) followed by μήν.

In the N.T. εἰ μήν occurs only in Hb. 6¹⁴ in a quotation from Gen. 22¹⁷:

**104. ἐάν, etc., with the Indicative.** *a.* As in Hellenistic Greek εἰ may take the subjunctive, so on the other hand ἐάν, ὅταν and the like are found with the indicative.

Instances of ἐάν with the indicative in the LXX are—

Gen. 44³⁰ ἐὰν εἰσπορεύομαι. Jdg. 6³ ἐὰν ἔσπειραν. iii K. 21²³ ἐὰν δὲ πολεμήσομεν αὐτοὺς κατ᾽ εὐθύ. Job 22³ ἐὰν σὺ ἦσθα.

So in N.T.—

i Jn. 5¹⁵ ἐὰν οἴδαμεν. Acts 7⁷ τὸ ἔθνος, ᾧ ἐὰν δουλεύσουσι. Cp. Herm. *Past. Vis.* III 12 § 3 ἐὰν . . . εἰρηνεύετε, I 3 § 2 ἐὰν . . . μετανοήσουσιν.

*b.* Instances of ὅταν with the indicative in the LXX are—

Gen. 38⁹ ὅταν εἰσήρχετο. Ex. 17¹¹ ὅταν ἐπῆρεν Μωυσῆς τὰς χείρας. Nb. 11⁹ καὶ ὅταν κατέβη ἡ δρόσος, 21⁹ ὅταν ἔδακνεν ὄφις ἄνθρωπον. i K. 17³⁴ ὅταν ἤρχετο ὁ λέων καὶ ἡ ἄρκος. Ps. 119⁷ ὅταν ἐλάλουν αὐτοῖς.

c. So in N.T. —

Mk. 3¹¹ καὶ τὰ πνεύματα τὰ ἀκάθαρτα, ὅταν αὐτὸν ἐθεώρει, προσέπιπτεν αὐτῷ, 11¹⁹ ὅταν ὀψὲ ἐγένετο.  Rev. 8¹ ὅταν ἤνοιξε.

Cp. Barn. Ep. 4¹⁴ ὅταν βλέπετε, 15⁵ ὅταν . . . καταργήσει.  Ign. Eph. 8¹ ὅταν γὰρ μηδεμία ἔρις ἐνήρεισται ἐν ὑμῖν.  Herm. Past. Sim. IX 1 § 6 ὅταν ὁ ἥλιος ἐπικεκαύκει, ξηραὶ ἐγίνοντο, 4 § 5 ὅταν . . . ἐτέθησαν.  Cp. 17 § 3.  6 § 4 ὅταν ἐπάτασσεν.

d. Under the same head come the following —

Ex. 33⁸, 34³⁴ ἡνίκα δ᾽ ἂν εἰσεπορεύετο Μωσῆς, 40³⁰ ἡνίκα δ᾽ ἂν ἀνέβη ἀπὸ τῆς σκηνῆς ἡ νεφέλη.  Tobit 7¹¹ ὁπότε ἐὰν εἰσεπορεύοντο. Cp. Barn. Ep. 12³ ὁπόταν καθεῖλεν.

**105. ἐάν after a Relative.** a. ἐάν for ἄν after a relative seems to occur occasionally in Mss. of Attic authors, especially of Xenophon, but to have been expunged by editors.  It is proved by the Papyri to have been in common use in Egypt during the first two centuries B.C. Biblical Greek is so full of this usage that it is superfluous to collect examples.  Besides the simple relative in its various cases we have —

ὅσα ἐάν Gen. 44¹: Ex. 13¹².     ἡνίκα ἐάν Gen. 24⁴¹: Ex. 13⁵.
οὗ ἐάν Ex. 20²⁴.               καθὼς ἐάν Sir. 14¹¹: Dan. O′ 1¹³.
ὅθεν ἐάν Ex. 5¹¹.

As a rule the subjunctive follows, but not always.

Gen. 2¹⁹ πᾶν ὃ ἐὰν ἐκάλεσεν.

b. The use of ἄν in such cases is not quite excluded, e.g. Ex. 12¹⁵, ¹⁹: Nb. 22²⁰.

c. In the N.T. also it is easier to find ἐάν in this connexion than ἄν, e.g. —

ὃς ἐάν Mt. 5¹⁹, 10¹⁴, ⁴²: Lk. 17³³.
ᾧ ἐάν Mt. 11²⁷: Lk. 10²².
οὓς ἐάν i Cor. 16³.
ὃ ἐάν i Cor. 6¹⁸: Gal. 6⁷: Col. 3²³: Eph. 6⁸: Jn. 15⁷: i Jn. 3²²: iii Jn.⁵
καθὸ ἐάν ii Cor. 8¹².
ὅπου ἐάν Mt. 8¹⁹.
ὅ τι ἐάν i Jn. 3¹⁹.

For instances of ἄν take i Jn. 3¹⁷: Mt. 10¹¹: Lk. 10⁵, ⁸, ¹⁰, ³⁵.

*d.* In the Apostolic Fathers also we find the same use of ἐάν after relatives —

Barn. *Ep.* 7¹¹ ὃς ἐὰν θέλῃ, 11⁸ πᾶν ῥῆμα ὃ ἐὰν ἐξελεύσεται.    Herm. *Past. Vis.* III 2 § 1 ὃς ἐὰν πάθῃ, *Sim.* VII 7 ὅσοι [ἐὰν] ἐν ταῖς ἐντολαῖς μου ταύταις πορευθῶσιν, IX 2 § 7 ὅσα ἐάν σοι δείξω.

**106. ἵνα with the Indicative.** *a.* In the vast majority of places in which ἵνα occurs in the LXX it governs the subjunctive. The optative, as we have seen, has practically vanished from dependent clauses. But there are a few passages in Swete's text, and perhaps Ms. authority for more, in which ἵνα after a primary tense or the imperative mood takes a future indicative.

Gen. 16² εἴσελθε . . . ἵνα τεκνοποιήσεις.    iii K. 2⁸ φυλάξεις . . . ἵνα ποιήσεις.    Sus. O′²⁸ ἐνεδρεύοντες ἵνα θανατώσουσιν αὐτήν. Dan. O′ 3⁹⁶ ἐγὼ κρίνω ἵνα πᾶν ἔθνος . . . διαμελισθήσεται.

*b.* The 1st person singular of the 1st aorist subjunctive may possibly have served as a stepping-stone to this use. Take for instance —

ii K. 19²² ἀπόστηθι . . . ἵνα μὴ πατάξω σε.

This might easily lead by false analogy to —

ἀπελεύσομαι, ἵνα μὴ πατάξεις με.

This theory however fails to account for the following —

i Esd. 4⁵⁰ ἵνα ἀφίουσι.    Tob. 14⁹ σὺ δὲ τήρησον τὸν νόμον . . . ἵνα σοι καλῶς ᾖν.

The last can only be regarded as a monstrosity.

*c.* In the N.T. ἵνα with the future indicative occurs occasionally and is common in Revelation —

i Cor. 9¹⁸ ἵνα . . . θήσω.    Gal. 2⁴ ἵνα ἡμᾶς καταδουλώσουσιν. i Pet. 3¹ ἵνα . . . κερδηθήσονται.    Rev. 3⁹, 6⁴, 8³, 9²⁰, 14¹³, 22²⁴ ἵνα ἔσται . . . καὶ . . . εἰσελθωσιν.

The last instance shows that even in the debased Greek of this book the subjunctive still claimed its rights on occasions.

*d.* There are two apparent instances in St. Paul's writings of ἵνα with a present indicative —

i Cor. 4⁶ ἵνα μὴ . . . φυσιοῦσθε.    Gal. 1¹⁷ ἵνα αὐτοὺς ζηλοῦτε.

With regard to these Winer came to the conclusion that 'ἵνα with the indicative present is to be regarded as an impropriety of later

Greek.' Perhaps however in these cases it is the accidence, not the syntax, that is astray, φυσιοῦσθε and ζηλοῦτε being meant for the subjunctive. Winer closes his discussion of the subject by saying, 'It is worthy of remark, however the case may be, that in both instances the verb ends in οω.' Here the true explanation seems to lie. The hypothesis of an irregular contraction is not in itself a violent one, and it is confirmed by a passage of the LXX —

Ex. 1¹⁶ ὅταν μαιοῦσθε τὰς Ἑβραίας καὶ ὦσιν πρὸς τῷ τίκτειν.

**107. Ellipse before ὅτι.** By the suppression of an imperative of a verb of knowing ὅτι acquires the sense of ' know that.'

Ex. 3¹² λέγων Ὅτι ἔσομαι μετὰ σοῦ.    Jdg. 15⁷ εἶπεν . . . Σαμψών
. . . ὅτι εἰ μὴν ἐκδικήσω ἐν ὑμῖν.    iii K. 19² εἶπεν . . . ὅτι ταύτην τὴν ὥραν κτλ.

This usage originates in the Hebrew, but has a parallel in Greek in the similar ellipse before ὡς, which is common in Euripides, e.g. Med. 609 : Alc. 1094 : Phœn. 720, 1664 : Ion 935, 1404 : Hel. 126, 831 : Hec. 346, 400. Cp. Soph. Aj. 39.

**108. ἀλλ' ἤ.** a. The combination of particles ἀλλ' ἤ occurs in Swete's text 114 times at least. In most of these passages ἀλλ' ἤ is simply a strengthened form of ἀλλά. If it differs at all from it, it is in the same way as ' but only' in English differs from the simple 'but.' In the remainder of the 114 passages ἀλλ' ἤ has the same force as the English 'but' in the sense of 'except' after a negative expressed or implied. It is thus an equivalent for the classical εἰ μή. But even this latter meaning can be borne by the simple ἀλλά, if we may trust the reading of —

Gen. 21²⁶ οὐδὲ ἐγὼ ἤκουσα ἀλλὰ σήμερον.

b. The idea has been entertained that ἀλλ' ἤ is not for ἀλλὰ ἤ, as the accentuation assumes, but for ἄλλο ἤ. This view would suit very well with such passages as Gen. 28¹⁷, 47¹⁸ : Dt. 10¹² : ii K. 12³ : Sir. 22¹⁴, where it happens that a neuter singular precedes, but it seems to have nothing else to recommend it.

Where ἀλλ' ἤ follows ἄλλος or ἕτερος, as in iv K. 5¹⁷ : Dan. 3⁹⁵, Θ 2¹¹ : i Mac. 10³⁸, the ἀλλά would be superfluous in classical Greek, so that in these cases it might be thought that the ἤ was strengthened by the ἀλλά, and not vice versa : but if we accept the use in Gen. 21²⁶, it follows that even here it is the ἀλλά which is strengthened.

c. In contrast with the abundance of instances in the O.T. and in

Hellenistic Greek generally, *e.g.* in Aristotle, it is strange how rare this combination is in the N.T. In the Revisers' text it occurs only twice—

Lk. 12⁵¹ οὐχί, λέγω ὑμῖν, ἀλλ᾽ ἢ διαμερισμόν. ii Cor. 1¹³ οὐ γὰρ ἄλλα γράφομεν ὑμῖν, ἀλλ᾽ ἢ ἃ ἀναγινώσκετε.

**109. ὅτι ἀλλ᾽ ἤ.** This combination of particles occurs in the following passages of the LXX — Jdg. 15¹³ : i K. 2³⁰, 21⁴, 21⁶, 30¹⁷, 30²² : ii K. 13³³, 21² : iii K. 18¹⁸ : iv K. 4², 5¹⁵, 10²³, 14⁶, 17³⁵, ³⁶, 23²³ : ii Chr. 2⁶.

An examination of these instances will show that they all fall under the same two heads as ἀλλ᾽ ἤ. In the bulk of them ὅτι ἀλλ᾽ ἤ is simply a strongly adversative particle (= but); in the remainder it is like our ' but ' = ' except ' after a negative expressed or implied. The reader will observe that the range of literature, within which this combination of particles is found, is very limited, being almost confined to the four books of Kingdoms. It looks therefore as if we had here a mere device of translation, not any recognised usage of later Greek. In all but the first two instances the underlying Hebrew is the same, consisting of two particles; in the first two there is only the particle corresponding to ὅτι, and these passages seem really to fall under § 107.

There is one place in which we find this combination of particles still more complicated by the use of διότι in place of ὅτι.

iii K. 22¹⁸ Οὐκ εἶπα πρὸς σέ Οὐ προφητεύει οὗτός μοι καλά, διότι ἀλλ᾽ ἢ κακά;

**110. ὅτι εἰ μή.** This combination occurs in the following passages —

ii K. 2²⁷ Ζῇ Κύριος, ὅτι εἰ μὴ ἐλάλησας, διότι τότε ἐκ πρωίθεν ἀνέβη ὁ λαός. iii K. 17¹ Ζῇ Κύριος . . . εἰ ἔσται . . . ὑετός· ὅτι εἰ μὴ διὰ στόματος λόγου μου. iv K. 3¹⁴ Ζῇ Κύριος . . . ὅτι εἰ μὴ πρόσωπον Ἰωσαφὰθ . . . ἐγὼ λαμβάνω, εἰ (A) ἐπέβλεψα πρὸς σέ.

In the first of the above passages ' unless,' in the second ' except,' in the third ' only that ' seem to give the exact shade of meaning. In all of them the ὅτι might be dispensed with, and owes its presence to the Hebrew.

**111. ἀλλ᾽ ἢ ὅτι.** There are four passages in which this combination occurs —

Nb. 13²⁹ ἀλλ᾽ ἢ ὅτι θρασὺ τὸ ἔθνος. i K. 10¹⁹ Οὐχί, ἀλλ᾽ ἢ ὅτι βασιλέα στήσεις ἐφ᾽ ἡμῶν, 12¹² Οὐχί, ἀλλ᾽ ἢ ὅτι βασιλεὺς βασιλεύσει ἐφ᾽ ἡμῶν. ii K. 19²⁸ ὅτι οὐκ ἦν πᾶς ὁ οἶκος τοῦ πατρός μου ἀλλ᾽ ἢ ὅτι ἄνδρες θανάτου.

No one meaning suits all the above passages. In the first of them the Hebrew which corresponds to ἀλλ' ἢ ὅτι is rendered in the R.V. 'howbeit.' In the next two ἀλλ' ἢ ὅτι might just as well have been ὅτι ἀλλ' ἤ (= Lat. *sed*), as in Jdg. 15³ (§ 109). In the fourth also ὅτι ἀλλ' ἤ might have been used in the sense of 'but' in 'nothing but,' *etc.*, as in i K. 21⁶, 30¹⁷: iv K. 4², 5¹⁵: ii Chr. 2⁶.

**112. λέγων, etc., for the Hebrew Gerund.** *a.* A special cause of irregularity in LXX Greek is the treatment of the Hebrew gerund of the verb 'to say' (= Lat. *dicendo*), which is constantly used to introduce speeches. As the Greek language has no gerund, this is rendered in the LXX by a participle. But the form being fixed in the Hebrew, the tendency is to keep it so in the Greek also. Hence it is quite the exception to find the participle agreeing with its subject, as in —

i K. 19² ἀπήγγειλεν . . . λέγων, 19¹¹ ἀπήγγειλε . . . λέγουσα.

*b.* If the subject is neuter or feminine, the participle may still be masculine —

Gen. 15¹: i K. 15¹⁰ ἐγενήθη ῥῆμα Κυρίου . . . λέγων.    iv K. 18³⁶ ὅτι ἐντολὴ τοῦ βασιλέως λέγων.

Also, if the sentence is impersonal —

iii K. 20⁹ ἐγέγραπτο . . λέγων.    ii Chr. 21¹² ἦλθεν . . . ἐν γραφῇ . . . λέγων.    Jonah 3⁷ ἐρρέθη . . . λέγων.

*c.* But the participle may even refer to another subject, as —

iv K. 19⁹ ἤκουσεν . . . λέγων = he heard say.

*d.* It is rare for the Greek to fare so well as in —

Dt. 13¹² ἐὰν δὲ ἀκούσῃς . . . λεγόντων.

And here the genitive is probably not governed by ἀκούειν, but used absolutely. *Cp.* —

i K. 24² ἀπηγγέλη αὐτῷ λεγόντων.

*e.* A very common case is to have the verb in the passive, either impersonally or personally, and the participle in the nominative plural masculine, thus —

ἀπηγγέλη . . . λέγοντες Gen. 38²⁴, 48²: Josh. 2², 10¹⁷: i K. 14³³, 15¹², 19¹⁹, 23¹.
ἀνηγγέλη . . . λέγοντες Jdg. 16²: Gen. 22²⁰.
διεβοήθη ἡ φωνὴ . . . λέγοντες Gen. 45¹⁶.
εὐλογηθήσεται Ἰσραὴλ λέγοντες Gen. 48²⁰.

An adjacent case is —

Ezk. 12²² Τίς ἡ παραβολὴ ὑμῖν . . . λέγοντες;

*f.* When the verb is active and finite, the construction presents itself as good Greek, as in —

iii K. 12¹⁰ ἐλάλησαν . . . λέγοντες,

but this is little better than an accident, for what immediately follows is —

Τάδε λαλήσεις τῷ λαῷ τούτῳ τοῖς λαλήσασι πρὸς σὲ λέγοντες κτλ.

In Dt. 18¹⁶ we have even ἠτήσω . . . λέγοντες.

*g.* Where the principal verb is not one of saying, the divorce between it and the participle is complete, both in sense and grammar —

Ex. 5¹⁴ ἐμαστιγώθησαν . . . λέγοντες, 5¹⁹ ἑώρων . . . λέγοντες,

where the 'being beaten' and the 'seeing' are predicated of one set of persons and the 'saying' of another. *Cp.* the complex case in i Mac. 13¹⁷, ¹⁸.

*h.* In the N.T. this Hebraism occurs only once —

Rev. 11¹⁵ φωναὶ . . . λέγοντες.

**113. Idiomatic Use of προστιθέναι.** *a.* Another very common Hebraism is the use of προστιθέναι with the infinitive of another verb in the sense of doing a thing more or again, *e.g.* —

Gen. 37⁸ προσέθεντο ἔτι μισεῖν = they hated still more. *Cp.* Gen. 4², ¹², 8²¹, 44²³. Ex. 8²⁹ μὴ προσθῇς ἔτι . . . ἐξαπατῆσαι. *Cp* Ex. 9²⁸, 10²⁸, 14¹³. Nb. 22¹⁵, ¹⁹, ²⁵: Dt. 3²⁶, 5²⁵: Josh. 7¹²: Jdg. 8²⁸, 10⁶, 13¹, ²¹: i Mac. 9¹.

*b.* Sometimes τοῦ precedes the infinitive, as —

Ex. 9³⁴ προσέθετο τοῦ ἁμαρτάνειν. Josh. 23¹³ οὐ μὴ προσθῇ Κύριος τοῦ ἐξολεθρεῦσαι. Jdg. 2²¹ οὐ προσθήσω τοῦ ἐξᾶραι. *Cp.* Jdg. 9³⁷, 10¹³.

*c.* The same construction may be used impersonally in the passive —

Ex. 5⁷ οὐκέτι προστεθήσεται διδόναι ἄχυρον τῷ λαῷ.

*d.* Sometimes the dependent verb is dropped after the middle or passive —

Nb. 22²⁶ καὶ προσέθετο ὁ ἄγγελος τοῦ θεοῦ καὶ ἀπελθὼν ὑπέστη. *Cp.* iv K. 1¹¹. Ex. 11⁶ ἥτις τοιαύτη οὐ γέγονεν καὶ τοιαύτη οὐκέτι προστεθήσεται.

# Selections from the Septuagint

# INTRODUCTION TO THE STORY OF JOSEPH

THE story of Joseph, whatever else it may be, is one of the best novels ever written. The interest inspired by the youthful hero, the play of human passion, the variety of incident, the simplicity of the language, all combine to confer upon it a peculiar charm. We may gauge the dramatic effectiveness of a tale with which use has rendered us familiar, by comparing it with the plot of one of the plays of Terence or Plautus, which represent to us those of Menander and his fellow-writers. Few will contest the superior power of the tale of Joseph from the point of view of the requirements of fiction. We have first the pathetic affection of the widowed father for the son of his favourite wife, and the consequent jealousy of the elder brothers, goaded to fury by the boy's naïve recital of the dreams which foreshadow his future greatness. Then we have the brothers unwittingly bringing about the exaltation of the object of their envy by their own wicked act; the vain attempt of one better than the rest to save him; the youth's fidelity to his master in rejecting the advances of his mistress; the false charge and undeserved imprisonment; the diverse fates of the chief butler and the chief baker; the release of the hero through the accident of Pharaoh's dream; his successful interpretation of it and sudden rise to fortune. The dramatic interest culminates in Joseph's brethren being led by the most elementary of human needs to prostrate themselves before the dispenser of corn in Egypt, and thus fulfil the dreams which had so enraged them. Joseph recognises them, though they do not recognise him, and he takes upon them no ungenerous revenge before the full 'recognition' (ἀναγνώρισις) is allowed to come about. Then he sends for his aged father, whose heart had been sore tried by the steps which Joseph had taken to punish his brothers, but who is now comforted and utters the pathetic words 'It is enough; Joseph my son is yet alive: I will go and see him before I die.' This seemed to be the most fitting conclusion to the narrative, when

101

being treated, as it is treated here, solely from the point of view of dramatic effect. For at this point the valedictory formula of old-world story may well come in — 'And so they lived happily ever afterwards.'

The rest of the narrative rather represents Joseph as an eminent Hebrew statesman with all the financial capacity of his race. If we were dealing with the tale as history, it might be worth while to point out that the fiscal policy of Joseph, however satisfactory to the Pharaohs, could hardly have been equally so to their subjects, and that the heavy impost of twenty per cent on agricultural produce, which has been, it is said, the land-tax of Egypt down to within quite recent times, may well have had something to do with the unpopularity of the Jews in Egypt.

In the dream-interpretation there is just that touch of the supernatural which is still thought not inappropriate to a good novel. But in the treatment of the tender passion this Hebrew romance stands in marked contrast with a good deal of modern fiction. There is not the slightest attempt made to render the would-be adulteress interesting or to dally with unlawful passion. Joseph knows that the proposal which she makes to him in such direct language involves ingratitude to his master and sin against God, and on those grounds refuses to comply. 'How can I do this great wickedness and sin against God?' These words contain the secret of the high standard of morality in sexual matters, to which the Jews attained. Chastity with them was a question not merely of duty towards one's neighbour, but still more of duty towards God. In this way all the awful sanctities of the unseen world were called in to the aid in the struggle against passion.

Among the Greek moralists the tendency was to regard love as a disease from which the sage would not suffer. In the early Greek drama the delineation of this feeling was thought to be below the dignity of tragedy, and Euripides was regarded by the older school as having degraded the stage by depicting the passion of Phædra for Hippolytus. This story naturally occurs to one's mind as a classical analogue to the story of Joseph. But it would be injustice to Phædra to put her on the same level as the wife of Potiphar. She has indeed all the vindictive injustice of the Egyptian matron, and is more successful in wreaking vengeance on her victim, yet she is not the willing slave of passion, and shame in her heart struggles successfully against unlawful love, at least as the story is told by Euripides.

A closer parallel in Greek mythology is afforded by the legend of Antæa and Bellerophontes, which forms part of the episode of Glaucus and Diomede in the sixth book of the *Iliad* (119–236). There the unfaithful wife of Prœtus, king of Argos, foiled of her purpose by the virtuous youth, appeals to her husband to slay him for having made dishonourable proposals to her; but the youth escapes all dangers and comes to honour, like Joseph, though, such is the waywardness of human fate, of which the Greek mind was acutely conscious, he dies at last of melancholy madness —

ὃν θυμὸν κατέδων, πάτον ἀνθρώπων ἀλεείνων.

The Egyptian tale of Anpu and Bata opens with a situation resembling that of Joseph and Potiphar's wife. Bata is a peasant-lad devoted to his elder brother Anpu, who is to him as a father. The youth grows to be so excellent a worker that 'there was not his equal in the whole land; behold, the spirit of a god was in him.' One day, when he was alone with his brother's wife, 'her heart knew him with the knowledge of youth. And she arose and came to him, and conversed with him, saying, " Come, stay with me, and it shall be well for thee, and I will make for thee beautiful garments." Then the youth became like a panther of the south with fury at the evil speech which she had made to him; and she feared greatly.' To save herself she plays the same part as Antæa, as Phædra, and as Potiphar's wife. If all the story had the beautiful simplicity of the opening, it might bear away the palm both from Greek and Hebrew fiction: but, unfortunately, it soon degenerates into a tissue of meaningless marvels. The papyrus which contains the tale is said to be of the XIXth Dynasty and to have been the property of Sety II when crown prince; but Professor Flinders Petrie thinks that the earlier part of the tale may belong to the XVIIIth Dynasty, which would bring it back close to the time when Joseph is supposed to have lived. This is a curious coincidence, but there is no reason to think it anything more.

In view of the literary merit of the story of Joseph it seems a pity that criticism should lay its cold touch upon it. To do so is like treating a beautiful body as a subject for dissection rather than as a model for the painter. But the science of anatomy has its claims upon us as well as the art of painting. Artistic effect is one thing and historic fact another. To the latter domain belongs the question how the story, as we have it, came into being. Was it written as one or put together from different sources.? Taking the story as one and indivisible, there are certain difficulties which must not be ignored.

(1) As Reuben in 37$^{22}$ has already persuaded his brothers not to shed the blood of Joseph, why does Judah in v. 26 say — 'What profit is it if we slay our brother and conceal his blood?'

(2) In v. 25 we are told 'a travelling company of Ishmaelites came from Gilead.' In v. 28 we have the parallel statement ' And there passed by Midianites, merchantmen,' but in the same verse we are given to understand that his brethren 'sold Joseph to the Ishmaelites.' Now Midianites were not Ishmaelites any more than Irishmen are Welshmen or the Dutch Germans. Both were Abrahamic peoples, but Ishmael was the son of Abraham by Hagar (Gen. 25$^{12}$) and Midian by Keturah (Gen. 25$^2$).

(3) Why does Reuben in v. 29 expect to find Joseph in the pit, when he had just been taken up and sold to the Ishmaelites ?

Now let us appeal to the critics to see whether they help us at all out of our difficulties. On a great variety of grounds they have arrived at the general conclusion that the Hexateuch (*i.e.* the five books of Moses and that of Joshua) was put together from the following pre-existing materials —

(1) A primitive historical work, in which the sacred name, of which the consonants are JHVH, is habitually employed, and which is believed to have emanated from the Kingdom of Judah. This is commonly called J, and its author is known as the Jahvist (=Jehovist).

(2) Another very similar work, in which the Hebrew word for God (Elohim) is usually employed in place of the sacred name, and which is ascribed to the Kingdom of Israel. This is denoted by the symbol E, and its author is known as the Elohist.

(3) The bulk of Deuteronomy, which is designated as D.

(4) A later priestly document known as P.

The hand of the editor is to be detected here and there, reconciling his materials, when they are discrepant, after the manner of a Gospel-harmonizer.

In telling the story of Joseph we are to suppose that the editor had before him J and E, containing the same tradition in slightly different forms.

In J it is Judah who intervenes to save Joseph. He persuades his brothers not to kill the lad, but to sell him to some Ishmaelites, who are passing by. In this version of the story there is no mention of a pit. It is drawn upon by the editor in $37^{25-27, 28b, 31-35}$.

'And they sat down . . . hearkened unto him, and sold Joseph to the Ishmaelites for twenty pieces of silver.

'And they took . . . wept for him.'

The words in $45^{4}$, 'I am Joseph your brother whom ye sold into Egypt,' are a reference to this account of the matter.

In E it is Reuben, the first-born, and so a fit representative of the Northern Kingdom, who plays the better part. He persuades his brothers not to kill the lad, but to put him alive into a pit, his intention being to come and take him out again. When he and his brothers however have left the place, some Midianites come by and kidnap Joseph. Reuben, returning to the pit, finds Joseph gone, a fact of which he informs his brothers. This form of the legend is drawn upon in $37^{21-24, 28a, 28c-30, 36}$.

'And Reuben . . . water in it. And there passed by Midianites, merchantmen; and they drew, and lifted up Joseph out of the pit. And they brought Joseph into Egypt . . . whither shall I go? And the Midianites sold him into Egypt unto Potiphar, an officer of Pharaoh's, the captain of the guard.'[1]

The words in $40^{15}$, 'for indeed I was stolen away out of the land of the Hebrews,' refer to this account of the matter.

With regard to Potiphar it must be admitted that there is some confusion in the narrative as we have it. For we are told in $37^{36}$ that 'the Midianites sold Joseph to Potiphar, an officer of Pharaoh's, the captain of the guard.' Potiphar then is Joseph's master, as we are told again in $39^{1}$. Now Joseph's master 'put him into the prison, the place where the king's prisoners were bound' ($39^{21}$), where Joseph found favour with the 'keeper of the prison.' But 'the keeper of the

[1] See Driver *Introduction to the Literature of the Old Testament* 7th edit. p. 17.

prison' was presumably Potiphar himself, for the prison was 'in the
house of the captain of the guard' (40³), and 'the captain of the
guard' was Potiphar? How are we to get out of this circle? Let
us again have recourse to the hypothesis of a mixture of documents.

The E version of the story goes on to tell that the Midianites,
having taken Joseph out of the pit, brought him to Egypt and there
sold him to Potiphar (37³⁶), who was a eunuch and captain of the
guard, and himself the keeper of the prison, but naturally not a
married man. Joseph, being found faithful by him, is given charge
over the prisoners, not being himself a prisoner, but 'servant to the
captain of the guard' (41¹²).

In the J version on the other hand Joseph is sold by the Ishmaelites to 'an Egyptian,' whose name is not mentioned; for the theory
requires us to suppose that the words in 39¹ — 'Potiphar, an officer
of Pharaoh's, the captain of the guard' — are inserted there from
37³⁶. This 'Egyptian' (39¹, ², ⁵) has a wife, who brings a false
charge against Joseph, whereupon his master consigns him to the
king's prison (39¹⁻²⁰). If this hypothesis be accepted, we must give
up 'Potiphar's wife' as a person who has no just claim to existence
even in fiction: for it is only by the amalgamation of 'the Egyptian'
with Potiphar that she comes into being. If this should appear a
loss, it may on the other hand be deemed a gain not to have to regard
the lady's husband as a eunuch, which seems to be the real meaning
of the word 'officer' (37³⁶, 39¹).

Chapter 40 is supposed to belong as a whole to E: but, if so, it
must have been adjusted in places to the story of the false charge,
which has been incorporated from J. We see this in vv. 3, 7, 15.
In chapter 41 again, which is referred as a whole to the same source,
we have to suppose the words in v. 14, 'and they brought him hastily
out of the dungeon,' to come from the reconciling hand of the editor.

Further on in the story there are duplications and inconsistencies
which, it may be claimed, find their easiest explanation in the hypothesis of 'contamination,' to borrow the term applied to a Latin
play made up from different Greek originals. Thus in 42²⁷, ²⁸ it is
at the lodging-place on the way home that one of the brothers finds
his money in his sack, whereas in v. 36 of the same chapter they all
find their money in their sacks after their return to their father.
Again in chapter 42 the brothers, when taxed by Joseph with being

spies, volunteer the information that they have a younger brother living (v. 13), and so report the matter to their father (v. 32); whereas in the following chapters Judah assures his father that this information was imparted only in reply to a question from Joseph (43[7]), and so recounts the matter to Joseph himself (44[19, 20]). Further, in 42[37] Reuben goes surety to his father for the safe return of Benjamin, whereas in 43[9] it is Judah who does this.

The story of Joseph is as good an illustration as could be chosen of the service rendered by modern criticism to the intelligent study of the Bible. If we take the narrative as it stands, it perplexes us with contradictions, and we have to suppose that the writer could not tell a story properly: but on the hypothesis that he had before him two documents, resembling each other in the main, but differing in details, we can understand how reverence for his authorities would lead him into inconsistencies which he would not have committed in a story invented by himself. Without then pledging ourselves to particular hypotheses we may surely say after Plato— ‘The truth in these matters God knows: but that what the Higher Critics say is like the truth — this we would venture to affirm.’

# I. THE STORY OF JOSEPH

$^1$Κατῴκει δὲ Ἰακὼβ ἐν τῇ γῇ οὗ παρῴκησεν ὁ πατὴρ αὐτοῦ, ἐν γῇ Χανάαν. $^2$αὗται δὲ αἱ γενέσεις Ἰακώβ. Ἰωσὴφ δέκα ἑπτὰ ἐτῶν ἦν ποιμαίνων μετὰ τῶν ἀδελφῶν αὐτοῦ τὰ πρόβατα, ὢν νέος, μετὰ τῶν υἱῶν Βάλλας καὶ μετὰ τῶν υἱῶν Ζέλφας τῶν γυναικῶν τοῦ πατρὸς αὐτοῦ· κατή-

1. **Κατῴκει ... παρῴκησεν**: κατοικεῖν here signifies a more permanent residence than παροικεῖν. Jacob dwelt where Abraham only sojourned. Abraham was a pure nomad, whereas Jacob combined agriculture (v. 7) with pasture (v. 12). In classical Greek παροικεῖν means ' to dwell near.' For the sense of ' dwelling as a stranger in ' cp. Lk. 24$^{18}$ Σὺ μόνος παροικεῖς Ἰερουσαλήμ ; From meaning a settlement of Jews in a foreign country (Sirach, Prologue) παροικία in the mouths of the Christians came to be used for an ecclesiastical district or diocese, as the παροικία of Alexandria, Ephesus, etc. Through the Latin form parœcia it is the origin of the French word paroisse and of our parish.

2. **αὗται ... Ἰακώβ**: part of the framework of P (see Introd. to the Story of Joseph). The preceding chapter dealt with the descendants of Esau. Here the writer turns to Jacob, but the detailed list of his descendants does not come till ch. 46. — **δέκα ἑπτά**: similar forms of numeral occur in Latin in good writers, as Cæsar B.G. I 8 § 1 decem novem : Livy XXVIII 38 § 5 decem quatuor. § 14. — **ἦν ποιμαίνων**: the analytic form of the imperfect = ἐποίμαινε. Cp. Ex. 3$^1$. Such forms occur in all stages of the language, e.g. Soph. Trach. 22 ἦν θακῶν : Plato Polit. 273 B. They are especially common in the N.T. § 72. The Hebrew idiom in this passage coincides with the Greek, so that this is an instance of a usage already current in Greek, which was intensified by its adaptation to the Hebrew. — **ὢν νέος**: while yet a lad, Spurrell. Had the translators here used παῖς, it would have reflected better the ambiguity of the original, which may mean that Joseph was serving as a shepherd-lad with his brethren. — **Βάλλας**: of Bilhah. For the form of the genitive see § 3. The sons of Bilhah were Dan and Naphtali ; Gen. 46$^{23-25}$. — **Ζέλφας**: of Zilpah. The sons of Zilpah were Gad and Asher; Gen. 46$^{16-18}$. Only the sons of Jacob's concubines are here mentioned, but afterwards Reuben and Judah are named, who were sons of Leah. Perhaps the actual work of tending the flock was done by the sons of the concubines, who would be in an inferior

Genesis XXXVII 7

νεγκαν δὲ Ἰωσὴφ ψόγον πονηρὸν πρὸς Ἰσραὴλ τὸν πατέρα
αὐτῶν. ³Ἰακὼβ δὲ ἠγάπα τὸν Ἰωσὴφ παρὰ πάντας τοὺς
υἱοὺς αὐτοῦ, ὅτι υἱὸς γήρους ἦν αὐτῷ· ἐποίησεν δὲ αὐτῷ
χιτῶνα ποικίλον. ⁴ἰδόντες δὲ οἱ ἀδελφοὶ αὐτοῦ ὅτι αὐτὸν
ἐφίλει ὁ πατὴρ αὐτοῦ ἐκ πάντων τῶν υἱῶν αὐτοῦ, ἐμίσησαν
αὐτόν, καὶ οὐκ ἐδύναντο λαλεῖν αὐτῷ οὐδὲν εἰρηνικόν.
⁵ἐνυπνιασθεὶς δὲ Ἰωσὴφ ἐνύπνιον ἀπήγγειλεν αὐτὸ τοῖς
ἀδελφοῖς αὐτοῦ, ⁶καὶ εἶπεν αὐτοῖς "Ἀκούσατε τοῦ ἐνυπνίου
τούτου οὗ ἐνυπνιάσθην. ⁷ᾤμην ὑμᾶς δεσμεύειν δράγματα
ἐν μέσῳ τῷ πεδίῳ· καὶ ἀνέστη τὸ ἐμὸν δράγμα καὶ ὠρθώθη·
περιστραφέντα δὲ τὰ δράγματα ὑμῶν προσεκύνησαν τὸ

position to those of the legitimate wives.
Joseph was the son of Rachel, but he
may have been called upon to ' bear the
yoke in his youth.' — κατήνεγκαν δὲ
κτλ.: *and they brought against Joseph
an evil report to Israel their father.*
Here the sense of the LXX differs from
that of the Hebrew, and saves us from
regarding Joseph as a tell-tale.

3. παρὰ πάντας : *more than all.* Cp.
Dt. 7⁶,⁷. The Hebrew is more exactly
represented by ἐκ πάντων in v. 4. παρά
first signifies comparison and then
superiority. Xen. *Mem.* I 4 § 14 παρὰ
τὰ ἀλλὰ ζῶα (*as compared with the lower
animals*) ὥσπερ θεοὶ ἄνθρωποι βιοτεύουσι.
In Biblical Greek it is constantly employed after a comparative adjective.
We may see this use beginning in classical writers, *e.g.* Hdt. VII 103 παρὰ τὴν
ἑαυτῶν φύσιν ἀμείνονες ? § 96. — γήρους :
for the form see § 8. — χιτῶνα ποικίλον :
χιτών here represents the Hebrew word
*kᵉthôneth*, with which it is perhaps connected. The language spoken by the
Phœnicians was almost the same as
Hebrew, and the Greeks may have

borrowed this word from Phœnician
traders. The same Hebrew phrase
which is used here of Joseph's coat is
applied in ii S. 13¹⁸ to the garment worn
by Tamar to denote her rank as a
princess. The LXX rendering however is there (ii K. 13¹⁸) χιτὼν καρ-
πωτός = a garment with sleeves.

4. ἐκ πάντων : *out of* and so *above
all.* ἐκ πάντων = παρὰ πάντας in v. 3,
being a different rendering of the same
original. The Hebrew language has no
special forms for comparative and
superlative.

5. ἐνυπνιασθεὶς . . . ἐνύπνιον : § 56.
The active verb ἐνυπνιάζω has here
become a deponent passive. Cp. 41⁵,
Nb. 23²⁴ γαυριωθήσεται.

6. οὗ ἐνυπνιάσθην : the attraction
of the relative into the case of the
antecedent is the prevailing idiom in
Biblical as in classical Greek. Cp. Gen.
39⁶ : Ex. 3²⁰, 5⁸ : Dt. 8¹⁰ : i Cor. 6¹⁹.

7. δράγμα : literally *a handful* =
*manipulus.* For the meaning 'sheaf'
cp. Ruth 2⁷ and Jos. *Ant.* II 2 § 2 in
this context. — προσεκύνησαν : literally

ἐμὸν δράγμα." ⁸εἶπαν δὲ αὐτῷ οἱ ἀδελφοί " Μὴ βασιλεύων βασιλεύσεις ἐφ' ἡμᾶς, ἢ κυριεύων κυριεύσεις ἡμῶν ; " καὶ προσέθεντο ἔτι μισεῖν αὐτὸν ἕνεκεν τῶν ἐνυπνίων αὐτοῦ καὶ ἕνεκεν τῶν ῥημάτων αὐτοῦ. ⁹ἶδεν δὲ ἐνύπνιον ἕτερον, καὶ διηγήσατο αὐτὸ τῷ πατρὶ αὐτοῦ καὶ τοῖς ἀδελφοῖς αὐτοῦ, καὶ εἶπεν " Ἰδοὺ ἐνυπνιάσθην ἐνύπνιον ἕτερον· ὥσπερ ὁ ἥλιος καὶ ἡ σελήνη καὶ ἕνδεκα ἀστέρες προσεκύνουν με." ¹⁰καὶ ἐπετίμησεν αὐτῷ ὁ πατὴρ αὐτοῦ καὶ εἶπεν " Τί τὸ ἐνύπνιον τοῦτο ὃ ἐνυπνιάσθης ; ἀρά γε ἐλθόντες ἐλευσόμεθα ἐγώ τε καὶ ἡ μήτηρ σου καὶ οἱ ἀδελφοί σου προσκυνῆσαί σοι ἐπὶ τὴν γῆν ; " ¹¹ἐζήλωσαν δὲ αὐτὸν οἱ ἀδελφοὶ αὐτοῦ· ὁ δὲ πατὴρ αὐτοῦ διετήρησεν τὸ ῥῆμα. ¹²Ἐπορεύθησαν δὲ οἱ ἀδελφοὶ αὐτοῦ βόσκειν τὰ πρόβατα τοῦ πατρὸς αὐτῶν εἰς Συχέμ. ¹³καὶ εἶπεν Ἰσραὴλ πρὸς Ἰωσήφ " Οὐχ οἱ ἀδελφοί σου ποιμαίνουσιν ἐν Συχέμ ; δεῦρο ἀποστείλω σε πρὸς αὐτούς." εἶπεν

*kissed* (? *the ground*) *before.* The Greek word for the Oriental prostration. In classical writers it governs an accusative, as here and in v. 9 and in Jos. *Ant.* II 2 § 2: but in the N.T. (Mt. 2², ¹¹: Jn. 4²³) we find it with a dative, as in v. 10. In Aristeas (§§ 135, 137) both constructions are employed. In their version of the LXX the ancient Armenians regularly render προσκυνεῖν as above.

**8. βασιλεύων βασιλεύσεις:** § 81. — **προσέθεντο ἔτι μισεῖν:** literally *they added yet to hate* = 'they hated still more,' a Hebraism very common in the LXX. Josephus has here (*Ant.* II 2 § 2) καὶ πρὸς αὐτὸν ἔτι μᾶλλον ἀπεχθῶς ἔχοντες διετέλουν. § 113.

**9. ἶδεν:** § 19. — **ὁ ἥλιος καὶ ἡ σελήνη:** Josephus (*Ant.* II 2 § 3) explains that the moon stood for the mother, owing to the power of the moon in

nourishing all things and making them grow, and the sun for the father, because that imparted to things their shape and strength. — **ἕνδεκα ἀστέρες:** Josephus (*Ant.* II 2 § 3) says τοὺς δ' ἀστέρας τοῖς ἀδελφοῖς (εἰκάζων), καὶ γὰρ τούτους ἕνδεκα εἶναι καθάπερ καὶ τοὺς ἀστέρας. But on what system were the stars reckoned as eleven ?

**10. ἐλθόντες ἐλευσόμεθα:** § 81. — **προσκυνῆσαί σοι:** 7 n. προσεκύνησαν.

**11. ὁ δὲ πατὴρ κτλ.:** Lk. 2¹⁹, ⁵¹ are evidently modelled on this verse. *Cp.* also Dan. O' 4²⁵ τοὺς λόγους ἐν τῇ καρδίᾳ συνετήρησε.

**12. εἰς Συχέμ:** *at Shechem,* to be taken with βόσκειν, not with ἐπορεύθησαν. § 90. Josephus (*Ant.* II 2 § 4) represents the brethren as removing to Shechem after the harvest without their father's knowledge.

Genesis XXXVII 22

δὲ αὐτῷ " Ἰδοὺ ἐγώ." ¹⁴ εἶπεν δὲ αὐτῷ Ἰσραήλ " Πορευθεὶς
ἴδε εἰ ὑγιαίνουσιν οἱ ἀδελφοί σου καὶ τὰ πρόβατα, καὶ ἀνάγγειλόν μοι." καὶ ἀπέστειλεν αὐτὸν ἐκ τῆς κοιλάδος τῆς
Χεβρών· καὶ ἦλθεν εἰς Συχέμ. ¹⁵ καὶ εὗρεν αὐτὸν ἄνθρωπος
πλανώμενον ἐν τῷ πεδίῳ· ἠρώτησεν δὲ αὐτὸν ὁ ἄνθρωπος
λέγων " Τί ζητεῖς ; " ¹⁶ ὁ δὲ εἶπεν " Τοὺς ἀδελφούς μου ζητῶ·
ἀπάγγειλόν μοι ποῦ βόσκουσιν." ¹⁷ εἶπεν δὲ αὐτῷ ὁ ἄνθρωπος " Ἀπήρκασιν ἐντεῦθεν· ἤκουσα γὰρ αὐτῶν λεγόντων
' Πορευθῶμεν εἰς Δωθάειμ.' " καὶ ἐπορεύθη Ἰωσὴφ κατόπι-
σθεν τῶν ἀδελφῶν αὐτοῦ, καὶ εὗρεν αὐτοὺς εἰς Δωθάειμ.
¹⁸ πρόιδον δὲ αὐτὸν μακρόθεν πρὸ τοῦ ἐγγίσαι αὐτὸν πρὸς
αὐτούς· καὶ ἐπορεύοντο ἀποκτεῖναι αὐτόν. ¹⁹ εἶπαν δὲ ἕκαστος
πρὸς τὸν ἀδελφὸν αὐτοῦ " Ἰδοὺ ὁ ἐνυπνιαστὴς ἐκεῖνος ἔρχεται·
²⁰ νῦν οὖν δεῦτε ἀποκτείνωμεν αὐτόν, καὶ ῥίψομεν αὐτὸν εἰς
ἕνα τῶν λάκκων, καὶ ἐροῦμεν ' Θηρίον πονηρὸν κατέφαγεν
αὐτόν·' καὶ ὀψόμεθα τί ἔστιν τὰ ἐνύπνια αὐτοῦ." ²¹ ἀκούσας
δὲ Ῥουβὴν ἐξείλατο αὐτὸν ἐκ τῶν χειρῶν αὐτῶν, καὶ εἶπεν
" Οὐ πατάξομεν αὐτὸν εἰς ψυχήν." ²² εἶπεν δὲ αὐτοῖς Ῥουβήν

**14. κοιλάδος :** κοιλάς is very common in the LXX for *vale, e.g.* Gen. 14⁸ ἐν τῇ κοιλάδι τῇ ἀλυκῇ, which in v. 3 of the same is called τὴν φάραγγα τὴν ἀλυκήν. The word occurs in the sense of 'a hollow' in some verses ascribed to Plato (*Anth. P.* vi. 43).

**17. ἀπήρκασιν :** *they have departed.* This intransitive use of ἀπαίρειν, which is common in the best authors, originated in an ellipse of ναῦς (acc. pl.) or στρατόν. The word is an apt equivalent for the Hebrew, which means literally 'tear up,' and refers to the pulling up of the tent-pegs previous to resuming a march. *Cp.* ἐξῆρεν Ex. 14¹⁹. — **κατό-πισθεν τῶν ἀδελφῶν :** this use of κατόπισθε with genitive in the sense of μετά

with accusative is unclassical. § 97. — **εἰς Δωθάειμ :** *at Dothan. Cp.* 42³². § 90.

**18. πρόιδον :** § 19. — **ἐπορεύοντο :** *they went about.*

**20. λάκκων :** λάκκος 'a pit' is connected with Latin *lacus* and *lacuna*. It is used in Xen. *Anab.* IV 2 § 22 for large tanks in which wine was kept — καὶ γὰρ οἶνος πολὺς ἦν, ὥστε ἐν λάκκοις κονιατοῖς (*plastered*) εἶχον. The λάκκος in this instance was a dry reservoir. See v. 24. The word is used in 40¹⁵ of the dungeon into which Joseph was cast. *Cp.* also Ex. 12²⁹ : iv K. 18³¹.

**21. Ῥουβήν :** Josephus calls him Ῥούβηλος. — **εἰς ψυχήν :** *so as to slay him.* A Hebraism.

" Μὴ ἐκχέητε αἷμα· ἐμβάλετε δὲ αὐτὸν εἰς ἕνα τῶν λάκκων τῶν ἐν τῇ ἐρήμῳ, χεῖρα δὲ μὴ ἐπενέγκητε αὐτῷ· " ὅπως ἐξέληται αὐτὸν ἐκ τῶν χειρῶν αὐτῶν καὶ ἀποδῷ αὐτὸν τῷ πατρὶ αὐτοῦ. ²³ ἐγένετο δὲ ἡνίκα ἦλθεν Ἰωσὴφ πρὸς τοὺς ἀδελφοὺς αὐτοῦ, ἐξέδυσαν τὸν Ἰωσὴφ τὸν χιτῶνα τὸν ποικίλον τὸν περὶ αὐτόν, ²⁴ καὶ λαβόντες αὐτὸν ἔρριψαν εἰς τὸν λάκκον· ὁ δὲ λάκκος ἐκεῖνος ὕδωρ οὐκ εἶχεν. ²⁵ ἐκάθισαν δὲ φαγεῖν ἄρτον· καὶ ἀναβλέψαντες τοῖς ὀφθαλμοῖς ἴδον, καὶ ἰδοὺ ὁδοιπόροι Ἰσμαηλεῖται ἤρχοντο ἐκ Γαλαάδ, καὶ οἱ κάμηλοι αὐτῶν ἔγεμον θυμιαμάτων καὶ ῥιτίνης καὶ στακτῆς· ἐπορεύοντο δὲ καταγαγεῖν εἰς Αἴγυπτον. ²⁶ εἶπεν δὲ Ἰούδας πρὸς τοὺς ἀδελφοὺς αὐτοῦ " Τί χρήσιμον ἐὰν ἀποκτείνωμεν τὸν ἀδελφὸν ἡμῶν καὶ κρύψωμεν τὸ αἷμα αὐτοῦ ; ²⁷ δεῦτε ἀποδώμεθα αὐτὸν τοῖς Ἰσμαηλίταις τούτοις· αἱ δὲ χεῖρες ἡμῶν μὴ ἔστωσαν ἐπ' αὐτόν, ὅτι ἀδελφὸς ἡμῶν καὶ σὰρξ ἡμῶν ἐστίν." ἤκουσαν δὲ οἱ ἀδελφοὶ αὐτοῦ. ²⁸ καὶ παρε-

---

**22.** ὅπως ἐξέληται αὐτόν: so that he may deliver him. The primary sequence after an historic tense was sometimes used in classical Greek to present the intention of the speaker with greater vividness. In Biblical Greek it supplants the optative altogether. § 75. Josephus (Ant. II 3 § 2) represents Reuben as lowering Joseph by a rope into the pit, and then going off in search of pasture.

**25.** φαγεῖν ἄρτον: § 77. — Ἰσμαηλεῖται: Josephus (Ant. II 3 § 3) Ἄραβας τοῦ Ἰσμαηλιτῶν γένους. He has no mention of Midianites. — ἔγεμον: γέμειν, which is properly used of a ship, is here transferred to 'the ship of the desert.' — ῥιτίνης: ῥιτίνη, commonly spelt ῥητίνη, Latin resīna = the resin of the terebinth or the pine. Theoph. H.P. IX 12 § 1 τῆς δὲ τερμίνθου καὶ τῆς

πεύκης καὶ ἔκ τινων ἄλλων ῥητίνη γίνεται μετὰ τὴν βλάστησιν. Ῥητίνη is mentioned again in 43¹¹ as a special product of Palestine, and here it is being brought from Gilead. It is therefore presumably the famous 'balm of Gilead' (Jer. 8²², 28⁸, 46¹¹). The word occurs six times in the LXX always as a translation of the Hebrew word which our version renders 'balm.' — στακτῆς: cp. 43¹¹. στακτή is spoken of as a kind of myrrh. Theoph. H.P. IX 4 ad fin. τῆς σμύρνης δὲ ἡ μὲν στακτὴ, ἡ δὲ πλαστή. Josephus (Ant. II 3 § 3) is vague in his language — ἀρώματα καὶ Σύρα φορτία κομίζοντας Αἰγυπτίοις ἐκ τῆς Γαλαδηνῆς.

**27.** ἔστωσαν: § 16. — ἤκουσαν: not only 'heard,' but 'obeyed.' ὑπακούειν has this double meaning in classical Greek, like the English 'hearken.'

Genesis XXXVII 32

πορεύοντο οἱ ἄνθρωποι οἱ Μαδιηναῖοι οἱ ἔμποροι, καὶ ἐξεῖλκυσαν καὶ ἀνεβίβασαν τὸν Ἰωσὴφ ἐκ τοῦ λάκκου· καὶ
ἀπέδοντο τὸν Ἰωσὴφ τοῖς Ἰσμαηλίταις εἴκοσι χρυσῶν·
καὶ κατήγαγον τὸν Ἰωσὴφ εἰς Αἴγυπτον. ²⁹ ἀνέστρεψεν
δὲ Ῥουβὴν ἐπὶ τὸν λάκκον, καὶ οὐχ ὁρᾷ τὸν Ἰωσὴφ ἐν τῷ
λάκκῳ· καὶ διέρρηξεν τὰ ἱμάτια αὐτοῦ. ³⁰ καὶ ἀνέστρεψεν πρὸς τοὺς ἀδελφοὺς αὐτοῦ καὶ εἶπεν "Τὸ παιδάριον
οὐκ ἔστιν· ἐγὼ δὲ ποῦ πορεύομαι ἔτι ;" ³¹ λαβόντες δὲ
τὸν χιτῶνα τοῦ Ἰωσὴφ ἔσφαξαν ἔριφον αἰγῶν, καὶ ἐμόλυ-
ναν τὸν χιτῶνα αἵματι. ³² καὶ ἀπέστειλαν τὸν χιτῶνα τὸν

So has *auscultare* in Latin with its French equivalent *écouter*. Cic. *Div.* I § 131 magis audiendum quam auscultandum.

**28.** παρεπορεύοντο: *were coming by*, they having before been seen only in the distance. But see Introd. — οἱ ἄνθρωποι ... οἱ Μ. ... οἱ ἔμποροι: the use here of the article, which is not in the Hebrew, serves to identify the Midianites with the Ishmaelites of v. 25 and hides the difficulty which otherwise presents itself as to the introduction of a caravan at this point as a fresh fact unknown before. — οἱ Μαδιηναῖοι: *the Midianites*, here regarded as a species of Ishmaelites, in defence of which might be quoted Jdg. 8²², ²⁴. Some of them dwelt in the south-east of the Peninsula of Sinai, along the Gulf of Elath (Akaba). Ex. 2¹⁵, 3¹. But their chief home was in the north of Arabia east of the Gulf of Akabah. — ἐξεῖλκυσαν: here the subject changes to Joseph's brethren. — χρυσῶν: Hebrew, 'silver'; Vulg. viginti argenteis; Josephus μνῶν εἴκοσιν. In Ex. 21³² the normal value of a slave is estimated at 30 shekels. The translator

seems to have taken the word 'silver' in the general sense of 'money' (*cp.* Fr. *argent*), and so made of it 20 gold pieces, the money to which he was accustomed at Alexandria. Coined money is not supposed to have been used among the Jews until the time of Darius Hystaspes, B.C. 521–486. The silver with which Abraham bought the cave of Machpelah was paid by weight (Gen. 23¹⁶). In Amos 8⁵ (about 800 B.C.) the Israelite corn-dealers are described as 'making the ephah small, and the shekel great, and dealing falsely with balances of deceit,' *i. e.* having one weight for the corn which they sold and another for the silver which they received. There would be no meaning in this, if the customers paid in coin.

**30.** ποῦ: § 34. — πορεύομαι: *am I to go?* § 73.

**31.** ἔριφον αἰγῶν: *a kid of the goats.* Cp. Jdg. 6¹⁹, 13¹⁵, ¹⁹: i K. 16²⁰. So χίμαρον ἐξ αἰγῶν Nb. 7¹⁶, ²², 15²⁴, 28¹⁵ : Dt. 14⁴ : i K. 16²⁰ — τράγος αἰγῶν Dan. 10⁵ — δάμαλιν ἐκ βοῶν Dt. 21³ — μόσχον ἕνα ἐκ βοῶν Nb. 7¹⁵, ²¹, etc. — ἐρίφους ἀπὸ τῶν τέκνων τῶν αἰγῶν ii Chr. 35⁷ — κριὸν προβάτων Tob. 7⁹.

ποικίλον καὶ εἰσήνεγκαν τῷ πατρὶ αὐτῶν, καὶ εἶπαν " Τοῦτον
εὕρομεν· ἐπίγνωθι εἰ χιτὼν τοῦ υἱοῦ σού ἐστιν ἢ οὔ."  ³³καὶ
ἐπέγνω αὐτὸν καὶ εἶπεν " Χιτὼν τοῦ υἱοῦ μού ἐστιν· θηρίον
πονηρὸν κατέφαγεν αὐτόν, θηρίον ἥρπασεν τὸν Ἰωσήφ."
³⁴διέρρηξεν δὲ Ἰακὼβ τὰ ἱμάτια αὐτοῦ, καὶ ἐπέθετο σάκκον
ἐπὶ τὴν ὀσφὺν αὐτοῦ, καὶ ἐπένθει τὸν υἱὸν αὐτοῦ ἡμέρας
τινάς.  ³⁵συνήχθησαν δὲ πάντες οἱ υἱοὶ αὐτοῦ καὶ αἱ θυγατέρες, καὶ ἦλθον παρακαλέσαι αὐτόν· καὶ οὐκ ἤθελεν παρα-
καλεῖσθαι, λέγων ὅτι " Καταβήσομαι πρὸς τὸν υἱόν μου πεν-
θῶν εἰς ᾅδου·" καὶ ἔκλαυσεν αὐτὸν ὁ πατὴρ αὐτοῦ.  ³⁶οἱ δὲ
Μαδιηναῖοι ἀπέδοντο τὸν Ἰωσὴφ εἰς Αἴγυπτον τῷ Πετρεφῇ
τῷ σπάδοντι Φαραὼ ἀρχιμαγείρῳ.

**35.** λέγων ὅτι : this use of ὅτι with the direct oration is found in the best writers, e.g. Plat. Apol. 21 C, 34 D λέγων ὅτι ἐμοί, ὦ ἄριστε κτλ. It is as common in the LXX as elsewhere in Greek, e.g. 45²⁶, 48¹: Ex. 4¹.

**36.** Μαδιηναῖοι : not the same word in the Hebrew as in v. 28, being here equivalent to Medanites, there to Midianites. From Gen. 24¹ we learn that Medan was brother of Midian. — σπάδοντι : σπάδων is a eunuch, Lat. spädo. The genitive in Greek is in -ωνος or -οντος. The only other passage in the LXX in which the word occurs is Is. 39⁷ ποιήσουσιν σπάδοντας ἐν τῷ οἴκῳ τοῦ βασιλέως. The same Hebrew original is in Gen. 39¹, 40²,⁷ translated εὐνοῦχος. The English rendering 'officer' is no doubt affected by the fact that Potiphar figures in the story as a married man. On this point see Introd. — ἀρχιμαγείρῳ : not 'chief cook.' Even as a matter of derivation it may equally mean 'chief butcher' or 'slaughterer,'

which brings us round to the Hebrew 'chief of the executioners.' The English rendering is 'captain of the guard.' In use the term signifies a high officer, something like the praefectus praetorio at Rome, who combined the functions of commander of the body-guard and chief of police. It is applied to Potiphar (Gen. 37³⁶, 39¹, 41¹²), to Nebuzaradan (iv K. 25⁸ : Jer. 40¹, etc.), and to Arioch (Dan. 2¹⁴). The last-named is described by Josephus (Ant. X 10 § 3) as having the command over the king's body-guard. The word ἀρχιμάγειρος is used also by Philo (I 604, De Mut. Nom. § 32) καταστήσας εἰρκτοφύλακα, ὥς φησι τὸ λόγιον, Πεντεφρὴ τὸν σπάδοντα καὶ ἀρχιμάγειρον and again in I 662, De Somn. § 2, and II 63, De Jos. § 26, where his allegorical treatment shows that he took the word to mean 'chief cook.' Josephus (Ant. II 4 § 2) seems to have fallen into the same error — Πετεφρής, ἀνὴρ Αἰγύπτιος ἐπὶ τῶν Φαραώθου μαγείρων τοῦ βασιλέως.

Genesis XXXIX 7

$^1$Ἰωσὴφ δὲ κατήχθη εἰς Αἴγυπτον· καὶ ἐκτήσατο αὐτὸν Πετεφρῆς ὁ εὐνοῦχος Φαραὼ ὁ ἀρχιμάγειρος, ἀνὴρ Αἰγύπτιος, ἐκ χειρῶν Ἰσμαηλειτῶν, οἳ κατήγαγον αὐτὸν ἐκεῖ. $^2$καὶ ἦν Κύριος μετὰ Ἰωσήφ, καὶ ἦν ἀνὴρ ἐπιτυγχάνων· καὶ ἐγένετο ἐν τῷ οἴκῳ παρὰ τῷ κυρίῳ τῷ Αἰγυπτίῳ. $^3$ᾔδει δὲ ὁ κύριος αὐτοῦ ὅτι Κύριος μετ᾽ αὐτοῦ, καὶ ὅσα ἂν ποιῇ, Κύριος εὐοδοῖ ἐν ταῖς χερσὶν αὐτοῦ. $^4$καὶ εὗρεν Ἰωσὴφ χάριν ἐναντίον τοῦ κυρίου αὐτοῦ, εὐηρέστει δὲ αὐτῷ· καὶ κατέστησεν αὐτὸν ἐπὶ τοῦ οἴκου αὐτοῦ, καὶ πάντα ὅσα ἦν αὐτῷ ἔδωκεν διὰ χειρὸς Ἰωσήφ. $^5$ἐγένετο δὲ μετὰ τὸ κατασταθῆναι αὐτὸν ἐπὶ τοῦ οἴκου αὐτοῦ καὶ ἐπὶ πάντα ὅσα ἦν αὐτῷ, καὶ ηὐλόγησεν Κύριος τὸν οἶκον τοῦ Αἰγυπτίου διὰ Ἰωσήφ· καὶ ἐγενήθη εὐλογία Κυρίου ἐπὶ πᾶσιν τοῖς ὑπάρχουσιν αὐτῷ ἐν τῷ οἴκῳ καὶ ἐν τῷ ἀγρῷ. $^6$καὶ ἐπέστρεψεν πάντα ὅσα ἦν αὐτῷ εἰς χεῖρας Ἰωσήφ, καὶ οὐκ ᾔδει τῶν καθ᾽ ἑαυτὸν οὐδὲν πλὴν τοῦ ἄρτου οὗ ἤσθιεν αὐτός. καὶ ἦν Ἰωσὴφ καλὸς τῷ εἴδει καὶ ὡραῖος τῇ ὄψει σφόδρα. $^7$καὶ

2. **ἦν ἀνὴρ ἐπιτυγχάνων**: *he was a man who succeeded*, literally 'who hit the mark.'

3. **εὐοδοῖ**: *makes to prosper*. Cp. v. 23. We have the passive of this verb in Rom. 1$^{10}$ εὐοδωθήσομαι in the literal sense of being vouchsafed a good journey. The force of the ὅτι here extends to εὐοδοῖ, which is indicative, not optative, as it would be in classical Greek.

4. **εὐηρέστει**: *was well-pleasing.* The Greek here departs from the Hebrew. — **ἔδωκεν διὰ χειρός**: *he put into the hand of.* Cp. v. 22. Διδόναι in the LXX often means 'to put' or 'set' as well as 'to give.' Cp. Dt. 28$^1$: iii K. 20$^{22}$: iv K. 19$^{7,18}$.

5. **ἐγένετο . . . καί**: *it came to pass*

that. § 41. — **ἐπὶ τοῦ οἴκου . . . ἐπὶ πάντα**: here the use of the word πάντα in the latter clause makes the accusative natural as implying that Joseph's rule extended over all that his master had, but this distinction would perhaps be an over-refinement. See 41$^{17}$ n. — **ἐγενήθη**: in Biblical Greek the 1st aorist passive of γίγνομαι is used in the same sense as the 2d aorist middle. In the earlier editions of his N.T. Dean Alford tried to establish a difference between the two forms, but retracted in the later. See his note on i Thes. 1$^5$.

6. **ἐπέστρεψεν**: *turned over.* The reading ἐπέτρεψεν *entrusted* would be more in accordance with classical usage. — **οὗ ἤσθιεν**: 37$^6$ n.

ἐγένετο μετὰ τὰ ῥήματα ταῦτα καὶ ἐπέβαλεν ἡ γυνὴ τοῦ
κυρίου αὐτοῦ τοὺς ὀφθαλμοὺς αὐτῆς ἐπὶ Ἰωσήφ, καὶ εἶπεν
" Κοιμήθητι μετ᾽ ἐμοῦ." ⁸ὁ δὲ οὐκ ἤθελεν, εἶπεν δὲ τῇ γυναικὶ τοῦ κυρίου αὐτοῦ " Εἰ ὁ κύριός μου οὐ γινώσκει δι᾽ ἐμὲ
οὐδὲν ἐν τῷ οἴκῳ αὐτοῦ, καὶ πάντα ὅσα ἐστὶν αὐτῷ ἔδωκεν εἰς
τὰς χεῖράς μου, ⁹ καὶ οὐχ ὑπερέχει ἐν τῇ οἰκίᾳ αὐτοῦ οὐθὲν ἐμοῦ
οὐδὲ ὑπεξῄρηται ἀπ᾽ ἐμοῦ οὐδὲν πλὴν σοῦ, διὰ τὸ σὲ γυναῖκα
αὐτοῦ εἶναι· καὶ πῶς ποιήσω τὸ ῥῆμα τὸ πονηρὸν τοῦτο καὶ
ἁμαρτήσομαι ἐναντίον τοῦ θεοῦ ; " ¹⁰ἡνίκα δὲ ἐλάλει Ἰωσὴφ
ἡμέραν ἐξ ἡμέρας, καὶ οὐχ ὑπήκουεν αὐτῇ καθεύδειν μετ᾽
αὐτῆς τοῦ συγγενέσθαι αὐτῇ. ¹¹ἐγένετο δὲ τοιαύτη τις
ἡμέρα· εἰσῆλθεν Ἰωσὴφ εἰς τὴν οἰκίαν τοῦ ποιεῖν τὰ ἔργα

8. Εἰ ὁ κύριός μου κτλ.: *Does
my master know nothing in his house
owing to his trust in me ?* § 100.
The Hebrew word corresponding to
εἰ is 'behold,' but in Aramaic the
same word means 'if.' The translator has here given an Aramaic
sense to a Hebrew word.— δι᾽ ἐμέ:
cp. v. 23 δι᾽ αὐτόν. Δι᾽ ἐμέ here does
not represent the Hebrew, which
means *with me.* The R.V. margin
gives the exact rendering — *knoweth
not with me what is in the house*
(= οὐ σύνοιδεν ἐμοί). This seems to
give the most satisfactory sense. The
master's confidence in Joseph was so
complete that he did not even seek
to share his knowledge of household
matters.

9. καὶ οὐχ ὑπερέχει: *and has no
superiority in his house over me.* Cp.
R.V. margin. — καὶ πῶς ποιήσω: the
καί here marks an impassioned question. — ῥῆμα: cp. 40¹, 44⁷: Ex. 2¹⁴.
Ῥῆμα in the LXX means 'the thing
spoken of' (Gen. 41²⁸), and so simply

'thing'; then even 'act.' This is
evidently the meaning that the word
has in Lk. 2¹⁵. It is therefore fair to
argue that this is the meaning also in
Lk. 1³⁷, which was rendered in the old
version *for with God nothing shall be
impossible.* The Revisers seem here
to have missed the sense by translating
*for no word from God shall be void of
power.* In the same way the word
λόγος has in the LXX (*e.g.* iii K. 12³⁰,
14²⁹: i Mac. 16²³) accomplished that
transition from 'word' to 'deed,'
which Dr. Faust, when the Devil was
entering into him, is represented by
Goethe as devising for it. Ῥητόν is
also used, like ῥῆμα, for 'thing.' Ex.
9⁴. For λόγος = *thing* see Dan. Oʹ
2⁴, ¹¹.

10. Ἰωσήφ: dative — ἡμέραν ἐξ
ἡμέρας: cp. Esther 3⁷ ἡμέραν ἐξ ἡμέρας
καὶ μῆνα ἐκ μηνός. § 86. — καὶ οὐχ ὑπήκουεν: the καί here introduces the
apod. in the same way as after ἐγένετο.
§ 41. On ὑπήκουεν see 37²⁷ n.

11. τοῦ ποιεῖν: the Genitive Infini-

Genesis XXXIX 20

αὐτοῦ, καὶ οὐθεὶς ἦν ἐν τῇ οἰκίᾳ ἔσω· ¹²καὶ ἐπεσπάσατο
αὐτὸν τῶν ἱματίων αὐτοῦ λέγουσα "Κοιμήθητι μετ᾽ ἐμοῦ."
καὶ καταλείπων τὰ ἱμάτια αὐτοῦ ἔφυγεν καὶ ἐξῆλθεν ἔξω.
¹³καὶ ἐγένετο ὡς εἶδεν ὅτι κατέλειπεν τὰ ἱμάτια αὐτοῦ ἐν ταῖς
χερσὶν αὐτῆς καὶ ἔφυγεν καὶ ἐξῆλθεν ἔξω, ¹⁴καὶ ἐκάλεσεν
τοὺς ὄντας ἐν τῇ οἰκίᾳ καὶ εἶπεν αὐτοῖς λέγουσα "Ἴδετε,
εἰσήγαγεν ἡμῖν παῖδα Ἑβραῖον ἐμπαίζειν ἡμῖν· εἰσῆλθεν
πρὸς μὲ λέγων ' Κοιμήθητι μετ᾽ ἐμοῦ·' καὶ ἐβόησα φωνῇ
μεγάλῃ. ¹⁵ἐν δὲ τῷ ἀκοῦσαι αὐτὸν ὅτι ὕψωσα τὴν φωνήν
μου καὶ ἐβόησα, καταλείπων τὰ ἱμάτια αὐτοῦ παρ᾽ ἐμοὶ
ἔφυγεν καὶ ἐξῆλθεν ἔξω." ¹⁶καὶ καταλιμπάνει τὰ ἱμάτια
παρ᾽ ἑαυτῇ ἕως ἦλθεν ὁ κύριος εἰς τὸν οἶκον αὐτοῦ. ¹⁷καὶ
ἐλάλησεν αὐτῷ κατὰ τὰ ῥήματα ταῦτα λέγουσα "Εἰσῆλθεν
πρὸς μὲ ὁ παῖς ὁ Ἑβραῖος, ὃν εἰσήγαγες πρὸς ἡμᾶς, ἐμπαῖξαί
μοι, καὶ εἶπέν μοι ' Κοιμήθητι μετ᾽ ἐμοῦ.' ¹⁸ὡς δὲ ἤκουσεν
ὅτι ὕψωσα τὴν φωνήν μου καὶ ἐβόησα, κατέλειπεν τὰ ἱμάτια
αὐτοῦ παρ᾽ ἐμοὶ καὶ ἔφυγεν καὶ ἐξῆλθεν ἔξω." ¹⁹ἐγένετο δὲ
ὡς ἤκουσεν ὁ κύριος τὰ ῥήματα τῆς γυναικὸς αὐτοῦ, ὅσα
ἐλάλησεν πρὸς αὐτὸν λέγουσα "Οὕτως ἐποίησέν μοι ὁ παῖς
σου," καὶ ἐθυμώθη ὀργῇ. ²⁰καὶ ἔλαβεν ὁ κύριος Ἰωσὴφ
καὶ ἐνέβαλεν αὐτὸν εἰς τὸ ὀχύρωμα, εἰς τὸν τόπον ἐν ᾧ οἱ

tive of Purpose. § 59.— ἐν τῇ οἰκίᾳ
ἔσω: Hebrew, 'there in the house.'

12. καταλείπων: there is another
reading καταλιπών. Jos. Ant. II 4 § 5
προσκαταλιπὼν καὶ τὸ ἱμάτιον.

14. καὶ ἐκάλεσεν: this goes closely
with καὶ ἐγένετο in v. 13. § 41. — εἰσήγαγεν: sc. ὁ κύριος or αὐτός (= ipse the
master: cp. 'himself' in the mouth
of an Irish peasant-wife). — ἐμπαίζειν
ἡμῖν: § 77.

16. καταλιμπάνει: a strengthened
present from stem λιπ-, of the type of

λαμβάνω, λανθάνω κτλ. It occurs only
in three passages of the LXX — Gen.
39¹⁶, ii K. 5²¹, iii K. 18¹⁸: but is found
in good authors, e.g. Thuc. viii 17 § 1 :
Plat. Epist. 358 B. Cp. διελίμπανεν
Tob. 10⁷, ἐκλιμπάνον Zech. 11¹⁶.

20. ὀχύρωμα: stronghold. This
word occurs in the Fayûm papyri
(Swete Introd. p. 292). — εἰς τὸν τόπον
κτλ.: an extraordinary piece of tautology — He threw him into the stronghold, into the place in which the king's
prisoners are kept there in the strong-

Genesis XXXIX 21

δεσμῶται τοῦ βασιλέως κατέχονται ἐκεῖ ἐν τῷ ὀχυρώματι.
²¹ καὶ ἦν Κύριος μετὰ Ἰωσὴφ καὶ κατέχεεν αὐτοῦ ἔλεος, καὶ
ἔδωκεν αὐτῷ χάριν ἐναντίον τοῦ ἀρχιδεσμοφύλακος.    ²² καὶ
ἔδωκεν ὁ ἀρχιδεσμοφύλαξ τὸ δεσμωτήριον διὰ χειρὸς Ἰωσὴφ
καὶ πάντας τοὺς ἀπηγμένους ὅσοι ἐν τῷ δεσμωτηρίῳ, καὶ
πάντα ὅσα ποιοῦσιν ἐκεῖ.    ²³ οὐκ ἦν ὁ ἀρχιδεσμοφύλαξ
γινώσκων δι᾽ αὐτὸν οὐθέν· πάντα γὰρ ἦν διὰ χειρὸς Ἰωσήφ,
διὰ τὸ τὸν κύριον μετ᾽ αὐτοῦ εἶναι· καὶ ὅσα αὐτὸς ἐποίει,
Κύριος εὐοδοῖ ἐν ταῖς χερσὶν αὐτοῦ.

¹ Ἐγένετο δὲ μετὰ τὰ ῥήματα ταῦτα ἥμαρτεν ὁ ἀρχιοινοχόος τοῦ βασιλέως Αἰγύπτου καὶ ὁ ἀρχισιτοποιὸς τῷ κυρίῳ
αὐτῶν βασιλεῖ Αἰγύπτου.    ² καὶ ὠργίσθη Φαραὼ ἐπὶ τοῖς
δυσὶν εὐνούχοις αὐτοῦ, ἐπὶ τῷ ἀρχιοινοχόῳ καὶ ἐπὶ τῷ ἀρχι-
σιτοποιῷ·    ³ καὶ ἔθετο αὐτοὺς ἐν φυλακῇ παρὰ τῷ ἀρχι-
δεσμοφύλακι εἰς τὸ δεσμωτήριον, εἰς τὸν τόπον οὗ Ἰωσὴφ
ἀπῆκτο ἐκεῖ.    ⁴ καὶ συνέστησεν ὁ ἀρχιδεσμώτης τῷ Ἰωσὴφ

hold = He threw him into the stronghold in which the king's prisoners are
kept. The addition of 'there' after
'in which' is normal in the LXX.
See § 69. But the further addition
of 'in the stronghold' seems to arise
from a misreading of the Hebrew
text.

**21.** ἔλεος : § 8.

**22.** ἀρχιδεσμοφύλαξ : Gen. 39²¹,²²,²³,
40³, 41¹⁰. Cp. 40⁴ ἀρχιδεσμώτης. Neither word is known elsewhere. — ἔδωκεν . . . διὰ χειρός: 4 n. — τοὺς ἀπηγμένους: the prisoners. Ἀπάγειν is the
regular word used of leading off to
prison. Cp. 42¹⁶ : Plat. Men. 80 B ὡς
γόης ἀπαχθείης. Sometimes it implies
execution as in Acts 12¹⁹.

**23.** ἦν . . . γινώσκων: analytic
form of imperfect. § 72. — δι᾽ αὐτόν:
cp. 8 δι᾽ ἐμέ. Here again δι᾽ αὐτόν has

nothing to correspond to it in the
Hebrew, in which the sentence is also
divided differently from the way in
which it is in the Greek. — αὐτός : § 13.

**1.** ῥήματα : things. Cp. 39⁹ n.
This use is very common. — ἥμαρτεν :
§ 42. — ἀρχιοινοχόος . . . . ἀρχισιτο-
ποιός : used also by Philo I 662, De
Somn. § 2 : II 63, De Jos. § 26. The
functions of the king's cup-bearer at
the Persian court are described in Xen.
Cyrop. I 3 §§ 8, 9.

**2.** δυσίν : § 14.

**3.** εἰς τὸν τόπον οὗ . . . ἐκεῖ : literally in the place where Joseph had been
led off there. § 69. οὗ here stands
for οἷ. § 34.

**4.** συνέστησεν : put them under the
charge of. This word is often used in
classical authors of putting a pupil under a master or introducing a person

Genesis XL 13

αὐτούς, καὶ παρέστη αὐτοῖς· ἦσαν δὲ ἡμέρας ἐν τῇ φυλακῇ. ⁵καὶ ἴδον ἀμφότεροι ἐνύπνιον, ἑκάτερος ἐνύπνιον ἐν μιᾷ νυκτί, ὅρασις τοῦ ἐνυπνίου αὐτοῦ, ὁ ἀρχιοινοχόος καὶ ὁ ἀρχισιτοποιὸς οἳ ἦσαν τῷ βασιλεῖ Αἰγύπτου, οἱ ὄντες ἐν τῷ δεσμωτηρίῳ. ⁶εἰσῆλθεν δὲ πρὸς αὐτοὺς τὸ πρωὶ Ἰωσήφ, καὶ ἴδεν αὐτοὺς καὶ ἦσαν τεταραγμένοι. ⁷καὶ ἠρώτα τοὺς εὐνούχους Φαραώ, οἳ ἦσαν μετ' αὐτοῦ ἐν τῇ φυλακῇ παρὰ τῷ κυρίῳ αὐτοῦ, λέγων " Τί ὅτι τὰ πρόσωπα ὑμῶν σκυθρωπὰ σήμερον; " ⁸οἱ δὲ εἶπαν αὐτῷ " Ἐνύπνιον ἴδομεν, καὶ ὁ συγκρίνων αὐτὸ οὐκ ἔστιν." εἶπεν δὲ αὐτοῖς Ἰωσήφ " Οὐχὶ διὰ τοῦ θεοῦ ἡ διασάφησις αὐτῶν ἐστίν; διηγήσασθε οὖν μοι." ⁹καὶ διηγήσατο ὁ ἀρχιοινοχόος τὸ ἐνύπνιον αὐτοῦ τῷ Ἰωσὴφ καὶ εἶπεν " Ἐν τῷ ὕπνῳ μου ἦν ἄμπελος ἐναντίον μου· ¹⁰ἐν δὲ τῇ ἀμπέλῳ τρεῖς πυθμένες, καὶ αὐτὴ θάλλουσα ἀνενηνοχυῖα βλαστούς· πέπειροι οἱ βότρυες σταφυλῆς. ¹¹καὶ τὸ ποτήριον Φαραὼ ἐν τῇ χειρί μου· καὶ ἔλαβον τὴν σταφυλὴν καὶ ἐξέθλιψα αὐτὴν εἰς τὸ ποτήριον, καὶ ἔδωκα τὸ ποτήριον εἰς τὰς χεῖρας Φαραώ." ¹²καὶ εἶπεν αὐτῷ Ἰωσήφ " Τοῦτο ἡ σύγκρισις αὐτοῦ. οἱ τρεῖς πυθμένες τρεῖς ἡμέραι εἰσίν· ¹⁸ἔτι τρεῖς ἡμέραι καὶ μνησθήσεται Φαραὼ τῆς ἀρχῆς σου, καὶ ἀποκαταστήσει σε ἐπὶ τὴν ἀρχιοινοχοίαν σου, καὶ

to a patron. —παρέστη: like Latin *aderat*. The subject is Joseph. — ἡμέρας: *for some time.* A Hebraism. § 86.

5. ὅρασις τοῦ ἐνυπνίου αὐτοῦ: these words have no construction and add nothing to the meaning. Let us call them ' nominative in apposition to the sentence.'

6. τὸ πρωί: *in the morning.* Such adverbial expressions are common in the LXX.

8. ὁ συγκρίνων: *to interpret. Cp.*

Dan. Oʹ 5⁷ τὸ σύγκριμα τῆς γραφῆς, 17 ἡ σύγκρισις αὐτῶν. Συγκρίνειν also means ' to compare.' In i Cor. 2¹³ πνευματικοῖς πνευματικὰ συγκρίνοντες the meaning perhaps is ' expounding spiritual things to the spiritual.' — διασάφησις: ≐ σύγκρισις. In LXX only in Gen. 40⁸: ii Esdr. 5⁶, 7¹¹.

10. πυθμένες: *stems.*

12. Τοῦτο ἡ σύγκρισις: in Attic Greek attraction is usual in such cases, as in 18 Αὕτη ἡ σύγκρισις.

13. ἀρχιοινοχοίαν: ἅπαξ εἰρημένον.

δώσεις τὸ ποτήριον Φαραὼ εἰς τὴν χεῖρα αὐτοῦ κατὰ τὴν ἀρχήν σου τὴν προτέραν, ὡς ἦσθα οἰνοχοῶν. ¹⁴ἀλλὰ μνήσθητί μου διὰ σεαυτοῦ ὅταν εὖ σοι γένηται, καὶ ποιήσεις ἐν ἐμοὶ ἔλεος, καὶ μνησθήσῃ περὶ ἐμοῦ Φαραώ, καὶ ἐξάξεις με ἐκ τοῦ ὀχυρώματος τούτου · ¹⁵ὅτι κλοπῇ ἐκλάπην ἐκ γῆς Ἑβραίων, καὶ ὧδε οὐκ ἐποίησα οὐδέν, ἀλλ᾽ ἐνέβαλόν με εἰς τὸν λάκκον τοῦτον." ¹⁶καὶ ἴδεν ὁ ἀρχισιτοποιὸς ὅτι ὀρθῶς συνέκρινεν, καὶ εἶπεν τῷ Ἰωσήφ "Κἀγὼ ἴδον ἐνύπνιον, καὶ ᾤμην τρία κανᾶ χονδριτῶν αἴρειν ἐπὶ τῆς κεφαλῆς μου · ¹⁷ἐν δὲ τῷ κανῷ τῷ ἐπάνω ἀπὸ πάντων τῶν γενημάτων ὧν ὁ βασιλεὺς Φαραὼ ἐσθίει, ἔργον σιτοποιοῦ · καὶ τὰ πετεινὰ τοῦ οὐρανοῦ κατήσθιεν αὐτὰ ἀπὸ τοῦ κανοῦ τοῦ ἐπάνω τῆς κεφαλῆς μου." ¹⁸ἀποκριθεὶς δὲ Ἰωσὴφ εἶπεν αὐτῷ "Αὕτη ἡ σύγκρισις αὐτοῦ. τὰ τρία κανᾶ τρεῖς ἡμέραι εἰσίν · ¹⁹ἔτι τριῶν ἡμερῶν ἀφελεῖ Φαραὼ τὴν κεφαλήν σου ἀπὸ σοῦ, καὶ κρεμάσει σε ἐπὶ ξύλου, καὶ φάγεται τὰ ὄρνεα τοῦ οὐρανοῦ τὰς σάρκας σου ἀπὸ σοῦ." ²⁰ἐγένετο δὲ ἐν τῇ ἡμέρᾳ τῇ τρίτῃ ἡμέρα γενέσεως ἦν Φαραώ, καὶ ἐποίει πότον πᾶσι

—ἀρχήν: perhaps τιμήν would be used here in classical Greek. —ἦσθα οἰνοχοῶν: analytic imperfect. § 72.

14. διὰ σεαυτοῦ: in thyself. —ποιήσεις . . . ἔλεος: § 74.

15. κλοπῇ ἐκλάπην: § 61. —λάκκον: 37²⁾ n.

16. κανᾶ: κανοῦν, a basket of reed (κάννα), is used specially for a bread-basket (Lat. canistrum). —χονδριτῶν: in Athen. 109 c χονδρίτης is enumerated among the species of bread, and it is further explained that it was made of ζειαί. Barley (κριθή), it is added, does not make groats (χόνδρος). By Hdt. II 36 ζειαί is identified with ὄλυραι, which is supposed to be rye.

The Egyptians, he says, do not live on wheat or barley, like the rest of the world, ἀλλὰ ἀπὸ ὀλυρέων ποιεῦνται σιτία, τὰς ζειὰς μετεξέτεροι καλέουσι. In another passage Herodotus gives us the Egyptian name for these loaves, II 77 ἀρτοφαγέουσι δὲ ἐκ τῶν ὀλυρέων ποιεῦντες ἄρτους, τοὺς ἐκεῖνοι κυλλήστις ὀνομάζουσι. Cp. iii K. 19⁶ ἐνκρυφίας ὀλυρείτης.

17. γενημάτων: = γεννημάτων, products.

20. ἡμέρα γενέσεως: an obvious way of expressing 'birthday,' but not employed by classical writers. The idea is generally conveyed by τὰ γενέθλια, the birthday feast. Xen. Cyrop. I 3 § 10 ὅτε εἱστίασας σὺ τοὺς φίλους ἐν

Genesis XLI 8

τοῖς παισὶν αὐτοῦ· καὶ ἐμνήσθη τῆς ἀρχῆς τοῦ ἀρχιοινο-
χόου καὶ τῆς ἀρχῆς τοῦ ἀρχισιτοποιοῦ ἐν μέσῳ τῶν παίδων
αὐτοῦ. ²¹καὶ ἀπεκατέστησεν τὸν ἀρχιοινοχόον ἐπὶ τὴν
ἀρχὴν αὐτοῦ, καὶ ἔδωκεν τὸ ποτήριον εἰς τὴν χεῖρα Φαραώ·
²²τὸν δὲ ἀρχισιτοποιὸν ἐκρέμασεν, καθὰ συνέκρινεν αὐτοῖς
Ἰωσήφ. ²³οὐκ ἐμνήσθη δὲ ὁ ἀρχιοινοχόος τοῦ Ἰωσήφ,
ἀλλὰ ἐπελάθετο αὐτοῦ.

¹Ἐγένετο δὲ μετὰ δύο ἔτη ἡμερῶν Φαραὼ ἴδεν ἐνύπνιον.
ᾤετο ἑστάναι ἐπὶ τοῦ ποταμοῦ, ²καὶ ἰδοὺ ὥσπερ ἐκ τοῦ
ποταμοῦ ἀνέβαινον ἑπτὰ βόες καλαὶ τῷ εἴδει καὶ ἐκλεκταὶ
ταῖς σαρξίν, καὶ ἐβόσκοντο ἐν τῷ ἄχει· ³ἄλλαι δὲ ἑπτὰ
βόες ἀνέβαινον μετὰ ταύτας ἐκ τοῦ ποταμοῦ, αἰσχραὶ τῷ
εἴδει καὶ λεπταὶ ταῖς σαρξίν, καὶ ἐνέμοντο αἱ βόες παρὰ τὸ
χεῖλος τοῦ ποταμοῦ ἐν τῷ ἄχει· ⁴καὶ κατέφαγον αἱ ἑπτὰ
βόες αἱ αἰσχραὶ καὶ λεπταὶ ταῖς σαρξὶν τὰς ἑπτὰ βόας τὰς
καλὰς τῷ εἴδει καὶ τὰς ἐκλεκτάς. ἠγέρθη δὲ Φαραώ. ⁵καὶ
ἐνυπνιάσθη τὸ δεύτερον· καὶ ἰδοὺ ἑπτὰ στάχυες ἀνέβαινον
ἐν πυθμένι ἑνί, ἐκλεκτοὶ καὶ καλοί· ⁶ἄλλοι δὲ ἑπτὰ στάχυες
λεπτοὶ καὶ ἀνεμόφθοροι ἀνεφύοντο μετ' αὐτούς· ⁷καὶ κατέπιον οἱ ἑπτὰ στάχυες οἱ λεπτοὶ καὶ ἀνεμόφθοροι τοὺς ἑπτὰ
στάχυας τοὺς ἐκλεκτοὺς καὶ τοὺς πλήρεις. ἠγέρθη δὲ
Φαραώ, καὶ ἦν ἐνύπνιον. ⁸ἐγένετο δὲ πρωὶ καὶ ἐταράχθη
ἡ ψυχὴ αὐτοῦ· καὶ ἀποστείλας ἐκάλεσεν πάντας τοὺς ἐξη-

τοῖς γενεθλίοις. — **παισίν**: *servants.* So
frequently. The usage is common also
in classical Greek, *e.g.* Ar. *Ran.* 40.
Similarly in France a 'garçon' may
be a greybeard. In 43²⁸ Joseph's father
is called his παῖς. — **ἐμνήσθη τῆς ἀρχῆς**:
divergent from the Hebrew.

21. **ἔδωκεν**: *sc.* ὁ ἀρχιοινοχόος.

1. **ἔτη ἡμερῶν**: the addition of
ἡμερῶν is a Hebraism. *Cp.* i Mac. 1²⁹.
—**Ἐγένετο . . . ἴδεν**: § 42.

2. **τῷ ἄχει**: Hebrew *aḥu*. This is
perhaps the Egyptian name for the
reed-grass of the Nile. The word is
indeclinable. Sir. 40¹⁶ ἄχει ἐπὶ παντὸς
ὕδατος καὶ χείλους ποταμοῦ. In Is. 19⁷
the spelling is τὸ ἄχι.

4. **βόας**: § 5, 6.

6. **ἀνεμόφθοροι**: *blasted by the
wind.* *Cp.* Prov. 10⁵: Hos. 8⁷: Is. 19⁷:
Philo II 431, *De Exsecr.* § 4.

8. **ἐγένετο . . . καί**: § 41. —

γητὰς Αἰγύπτου καὶ πάντας τοὺς σοφοὺς αὐτῆς, καὶ διηγήσατο αὐτοῖς Φαραὼ τὸ ἐνύπνιον· καὶ οὐκ ἦν ὁ ἀπαγγελλων
αὐτὸ τῷ Φαραώ. ⁹καὶ ἐλάλησεν ὁ ἀρχιοινοχόος πρὸς
Φαραὼ λέγων "Τὴν ἁμαρτίαν μου ἀναμιμνήσκω σήμερον.
¹⁰Φαραὼ ὠργίσθη τοῖς παισὶν αὐτοῦ, καὶ ἔθετο ἡμᾶς ἐν
φυλακῇ ἐν τῷ οἴκῳ τοῦ ἀρχιδεσμοφύλακος, ἐμέ τε καὶ τὸν
ἀρχισιτοποιόν· ¹¹καὶ ἴδομεν ἐνύπνιον ἐν νυκτὶ μιᾷ, ἐγὼ
καὶ αὐτός· ἕκαστος κατὰ τὸ αὐτοῦ ἐνύπνιον ἴδομεν. ¹²ἦν
δὲ ἐκεῖ μεθ᾽ ἡμῶν νεανίσκος παῖς Ἑβραῖος τοῦ ἀρχιμαγείρου,
καὶ διηγησάμεθα αὐτῷ, καὶ συνέκρινεν ἡμῖν. ¹³ἐγενήθη
δὲ καθὼς συνέκρινεν ἡμῖν, οὕτως καὶ συνέβη, ἐμέ τε ἀπο-
κατασταθῆναι ἐπὶ τὴν ἀρχήν μου, ἐκεῖνον δὲ κρεμασθῆ-
ναι." ¹⁴Ἀποστείλας δὲ Φαραὼ ἐκάλεσεν τὸν Ἰωσήφ, καὶ
ἐξήγαγεν αὐτὸν ἐκ τοῦ ὀχυρώματος. καὶ ἐξύρησαν αὐτὸν
καὶ ἤλλαξαν τὴν στολὴν αὐτοῦ· καὶ ἦλθεν πρὸς Φαραώ.
¹⁵εἶπεν δὲ Φαραὼ τῷ Ἰωσήφ "Ἐνύπνιον ἑώρακα, καὶ ὁ συγκρίνων αὐτὸ οὐκ ἔστιν· ἐγὼ δὲ ἀκήκοα περὶ σοῦ λεγόντων,
ἀκούσαντά σε ἐνύπνια συγκρῖναι αὐτά." ¹⁶ἀποκριθεὶς δὲ
Ἰωσὴφ τῷ Φαραὼ εἶπεν "Ἄνευ τοῦ θεοῦ οὐκ ἀποκριθήσεται
τὸ σωτήριον Φαραώ." ¹⁷ἐλάλησεν δὲ Φαραὼ τῷ Ἰωσὴφ
λέγων "Ἐν τῷ ὕπνῳ μου ᾤμην ἑστάναι ἐπὶ τὸ χεῖλος τοῦ
ποταμοῦ· ¹⁸καὶ ὥσπερ ἐκ τοῦ ποταμοῦ ἀνέβαινον ἑπτὰ βόες
καλαὶ τῷ εἴδει καὶ ἐκλεκταὶ ταῖς σαρξίν, καὶ ἐνέμοντο ἐν

---

ὁ ἀπαγγέλλων: cp. 40⁸ ὁ συγκρίνων.
In classical Greek a future participle
would be used in such cases.

13. ἐγενήθη . . . συνέβη : § 42.

14. ἐξήγαγεν: Hebrew, 'they
brought him hastily.' — ἐξύρησαν :
Hebrew, 'he shaved himself.'

16. ἄνευ τοῦ θεοῦ κτλ. : without
God there shall not be given the answer of safety to Pharaoh. The word
which in the R.V. is translated 'It

is not in me' has here been taken
as a preposition governing 'God,'
and a negative has somehow got in
after it.

17. ἐπὶ τὸ χεῖλος : in v. 2 we had
ἑστάναι ἐπὶ τοῦ ποταμοῦ, which is better
Greek. In a classical writer we might
explain the accusative here as a pregnant construction, meaning 'to go to
the bank of the river and stand there.'
But see § 95.

Genesis XLI 29

τῷ ἄχει· ¹⁹καὶ ἰδοὺ ἑπτὰ βόες ἕτεραι ἀνέβαινον ὀπίσω
αὐτῶν ἐκ τοῦ ποταμοῦ, πονηραὶ καὶ αἰσχραὶ τῷ εἴδει καὶ
λεπταὶ ταῖς σαρξίν, καὶ ἐνέμοντο ἐν τῷ ἄχει· οἵας οὐκ
εἶδον τοιαύτας ἐν ὅλῃ Αἰγύπτῳ αἰσχροτέρας· ²⁰καὶ κατέφαγον αἱ ἑπτὰ βόες αἱ αἰσχραὶ καὶ λεπταὶ τὰς ἑπτὰ βόας
τὰς πρώτας τὰς καλὰς καὶ ἐκλεκτάς, ²¹καὶ εἰσῆλθον εἰς τὰς
κοιλίας αὐτῶν· καὶ οὐ διάδηλοι ἐγένοντο ὅτι εἰσῆλθον εἰς
τὰς κοιλίας αὐτῶν, καὶ αἱ ὄψεις αὐτῶν αἰσχραὶ καθὰ καὶ τὴν
ἀρχήν. ἐξεγερθεὶς δὲ ἐκοιμήθην. ²²καὶ ἴδον πάλιν ἐν τῷ
ὕπνῳ μου, καὶ ὥσπερ ἑπτὰ στάχυες ἀνέβαινον ἐν πυθμένι ἑνὶ
πλήρεις καὶ καλοί· ²³ἄλλοι δὲ ἑπτὰ στάχυες λεπτοὶ καὶ
ἀνεμόφθοροι ἀνεφύοντο ἐχόμενοι αὐτῶν· ²⁴καὶ κατέπιον οἱ
ἑπτὰ στάχυες οἱ λεπτοὶ καὶ ἀνεμόφθοροι τοὺς ἑπτὰ στάχυας
τοὺς καλοὺς καὶ τοὺς πλήρεις. εἶπα οὖν τοῖς ἐξηγηταῖς, καὶ
οὐκ ἦν ὁ ἀπαγγέλλων μοι." ²⁵καὶ εἶπεν Ἰωσὴφ τῷ Φαραώ
" Τὸ ἐνύπνιον Φαραὼ ἕν ἐστιν· ὅσα ὁ θεὸς ποιεῖ, ἔδειξεν τῷ
Φαραώ. ²⁶αἱ ἑπτὰ βόες αἱ καλαὶ ἑπτὰ ἔτη ἐστίν, καὶ οἱ
ἑπτὰ στάχυες οἱ καλοὶ ἑπτὰ ἔτη ἐστίν· τὸ ἐνύπνιον Φαραὼ
ἕν ἐστιν. ²⁷καὶ αἱ ἑπτὰ βόες αἱ λεπταὶ αἱ ἀναβαίνουσαι
ὀπίσω αὐτῶν ἑπτὰ ἔτη ἐστίν, καὶ οἱ ἑπτὰ στάχυες οἱ λεπτοὶ
καὶ ἀνεμόφθοροι ἔσονται ἑπτὰ ἔτη λιμοῦ. ²⁸τὸ δὲ ῥῆμα ὃ
εἴρηκα Φαραώ· ὅσα ὁ θεὸς ποιεῖ ἔδειξεν τῷ Φαραώ. ²⁹ἰδοὺ
ἑπτὰ ἔτη ἔρχεται εὐθηνία πολλὴ ἐν πάσῃ γῇ Αἰγύπτῳ·

19. οἵας ... τοιαύτας: literally
such as I never saw the like in all Egypt
more ill-favoured. A mixture of two
constructions. The first is an instance
of that insertion of a demonstrative
after the relative which is a mark of
Biblical Greek (§ 69) ; the second is
οἵων αἰσχροτέρας. — αἰσχροτέρας : § 12.
21. διάδηλοι ἐγένοντο: sc. αἱ ἑπτὰ
βόες αἱ αἰσχραὶ καὶ λεπταί. — καθά :
adverb meaning ' as,' originally καθ' ἅ.

Common in the LXX and in Hellenistic Greek generally. — τὴν ἀρχήν:
adverbial accusative, at the beginning.
23. ἐχόμενοι αὐτῶν : close after
them.
28. τὸ δὲ ῥῆμα κτλ. : but as for
the thing which I said unto Pharaoh,
with reference to v. 25. This is a good
instance to show how ῥῆμα passes from
' word ' to ' thing.' See 39⁹ n.
29. εὐθηνία : the verb εὐθηνεῖν is

<sup>30</sup>ἥξει δὲ ἑπτὰ ἔτη λιμοῦ μετὰ ταῦτα, καὶ ἐπιλησθήσονται
τῆς πλησμονῆς ἐν ὅλῃ τῇ γῇ Αἰγύπτῳ, καὶ ἀναλώσει ὁ
λιμὸς τὴν γῆν· <sup>31</sup>καὶ οὐκ ἐπιγνωσθήσεται ἡ εὐθηνία ἐπὶ τῆς
γῆς ἀπὸ τοῦ λιμοῦ τοῦ ἐσομένου μετὰ ταῦτα, ἰσχυρὸς γὰρ
ἔσται σφόδρα.    <sup>32</sup>περὶ δὲ τοῦ δευτερῶσαι τὸ ἐνύπνιον
Φαραὼ δίς, ὅτι ἀληθὲς ἔσται τὸ ῥῆμα τὸ παρὰ τοῦ θεοῦ, καὶ
ταχυνεῖ ὁ θεὸς τοῦ ποιῆσαι αὐτό.    <sup>33</sup>νῦν οὖν σκέψαι ἄνθρωπον φρόνιμον καὶ συνετόν, καὶ κατάστησον αὐτὸν ἐπὶ τῆς γῆς
Αἰγύπτου· <sup>34</sup>καὶ ποιησάτω Φαραὼ καὶ καταστησάτω τοπάρχας ἐπὶ τῆς γῆς, καὶ ἀποπεμπτωσάτωσαν πάντα τὰ γενή-
ματα τῆς γῆς Αἰγύπτου τῶν ἑπτὰ ἐτῶν τῆς εὐθηνίας, <sup>35</sup>καὶ
συναγαγέτωσαν πάντα τὰ βρώματα τῶν ἑπτὰ ἐτῶν τῶν ἐρχο-
μένων τῶν καλῶν τούτων· καὶ συναχθήτω ὁ σῖτος ὑπὸ χεῖρα
Φαραώ, βρώματα ἐν ταῖς πόλεσιν συναχθήτω.    <sup>36</sup>καὶ ἔσται
τὰ βρώματα πεφυλαγμένα τῇ γῇ εἰς τὰ ἑπτὰ ἔτη τοῦ λιμοῦ
ἃ ἔσονται ἐν γῇ Αἰγύπτῳ, καὶ οὐκ ἐκτριβήσεται ἡ γῆ ἐν τῷ

used in Arist. *E.N.* I 9 § 11 for the
external side of happiness, and εὐθηνία
itself occurs in *Rhet.* I 5 § 3 in the
same connexion.  *Cp.* Philo I 438, *De
Migr. Abr.* § 3 τὴν σωματικὴν εὐθηνίαν
καὶ τὰς τῶν ἐκτὸς ἀφθόνους περιουσίας.
Josephus (*Ant.* II 5 § 7) has in this
context εὐετηρία.  *Cp.* Arist. *E.N.* I 8
§ 6, VIII 1 § 1.

**31.** ἀπὸ τοῦ λιμοῦ: *by reason of
the famine.*  An unclassical use of the
preposition § 92.

**32.** δευτερῶσαι . . . δίς: the same
kind of pleonasm is used in English, —
'the repeating twice.'  For δευτεροῦν
*cp.* i K. 26<sup>8</sup>: iii K. 18<sup>34</sup>.  It occurs 13
times in the LXX.—ὅτι: (*the reason
is*) *that.* — τοῦ ποιῆσαι αὐτό: in Biblical Greek the latter of two verbs is
often put into the genitive infinitive.
§ 60.

**34.** καὶ ποιησάτω: a literal following of the Hebrew. — τοπάρχας:
*prefects.*  For the form *cp.* κωμάρχης
Esther 2<sup>3</sup>: Xen. *Anab.* IV 5 §§ 10, 24:
γενεσιάρχης Wisd. 13<sup>3</sup>.  The word τοπάρχης occurs 17 times in the LXX and
was probably a technical term of administration in Egypt under the Ptolemies.  *Cp.* iv K. 18<sup>24</sup>.  Strabo (XVII
§ 3, p. 787) mentions that most of the
νομοί in Egypt were divided into το-
παρχίαι. — ἀποπεμπτωσάτωσαν: *take
the fifth part of.*  *Cp.* 47<sup>24</sup>: Philo I 469,
*De Migr. Abr.* § 37 τὸν γὰρ σῖτον ἀπο-
πεμπτοῦν κελεύει.

**36.** ἔσται . . . πεφυλαγμένα: analytic form of future perfect = πεφυλά-
ξεται.  § 72. — ἃ ἔσονται: the stress laid
on the plurality of the years might
justify the use of the plural verb here
even in classical Greek.  In Hellenistic

Genesis XLI 45

λιμῷ." ³⁷Ἤρεσεν δὲ τὰ ῥήματα ἐναντίον Φαραὼ καὶ ἐναντίον πάντων τῶν παίδων αὐτοῦ· ³⁸καὶ εἶπεν Φαραὼ πᾶσιν τοῖς παισὶν αὐτοῦ " Μὴ εὑρήσομεν ἄνθρωπον τοιοῦτον, ὃς ἔχει πνεῦμα θεοῦ ἐν αὐτῷ;" ³⁹εἶπεν δὲ Φαραὼ τῷ Ἰωσήφ "Ἐπειδὴ ἔδειξεν ὁ θεός σοι πάντα ταῦτα, οὐκ ἔστιν ἄνθρωπος φρονιμώτερός σου καὶ συνετώτερος. ⁴⁰σὺ ἔσῃ ἐπὶ τῷ οἴκῳ μου, καὶ ἐπὶ τῷ στόματί σου ὑπακούσεται πᾶς ὁ λαός μου· πλὴν τὸν θρόνον ὑπερέξω σου ἐγώ." ⁴¹εἶπεν δὲ Φαραὼ τῷ Ἰωσήφ " Ἰδοὺ καθίστημί σε σήμερον ἐπὶ πάσης γῆς Αἰγύπτου." ⁴²καὶ περιελόμενος Φαραὼ τὸν δακτύλιον ἀπὸ τῆς χειρὸς αὐτοῦ περιέθηκεν αὐτὸν ἐπὶ τὴν χεῖρα Ἰωσήφ, καὶ ἐνέδυσεν αὐτὸν στολὴν βυσσίνην, καὶ περιέθηκεν κλοιὸν χρυσοῦν περὶ τὸν τράχηλον αὐτοῦ· ⁴³καὶ ἀνεβίβασεν αὐτὸν ἐπὶ τὸ ἅρμα τὸ δεύτερον τῶν αὐτοῦ, καὶ ἐκήρυξεν ἔμπροσθεν αὐτοῦ κήρυξ· καὶ κατέστησεν αὐτὸν ἐφ' ὅλης τῆς γῆς Αἰγύπτου. ⁴⁴εἶπεν δὲ Φαραὼ τῷ Ἰωσήφ "Ἐγὼ Φαραώ· ἄνευ σοῦ οὐκ ἐξαρεῖ οὐθεὶς τὴν χεῖρα αὐτοῦ ἐπὶ πάσῃ γῇ Αἰγύπτου." ⁴⁵καὶ ἐκάλεσεν Φαραὼ τὸ ὄνομα Ἰωσὴφ Ψονθομφανήχ· καὶ

Greek, however, the observation of the rule of syntax about the neuter plural is capricious. We have the plural again in 53 and 54 and in 42²⁰. *Cp.* Ps. 17²³, ³⁷.

**40.** πλήν : *only.* Cp. Jdg. 14¹⁶. — τὸν θρόνον : probably accusative of respect and ὑπερέξω intransitive.

**42.** βυσσίνην : *of fine linen.* Hdt. II 86 speaks of the Egyptian mummies as being wrapt in σίνδων βυσσίνη. — κλοιόν : from κλείω. Properly *a dog-collar.*

**43.** ἐκήρυξεν κτλ.: in the Hebrew the verb is in the plural and the sentence runs thus — *and they cried before him* ' *abrekh,*' the last word being supposed to be Egyptian. If so, the Alexandrian

translator ought to have known what it meant. The Vulgate has here — c l a - m a n t e   p r æ c o n e   u t   o m n e s   c o r a m eo genu flecterent. — κῆρυξ : this accentuation is correct in principle, since the υ is naturally long, but the word is generally written κήρυξ, like φοῖνιξ.

**44.** Ἐγὼ Φαραώ : *So sure as I am Pharaoh.*

**45.** Ψονθομφανήχ : Jos. *Ant.* II 6 § 1 προσηγόρευσεν αὐτὸν Ψοθομφάνηχον . . . σημαίνει γὰρ τὸ ὄνομα κρυπτῶν εὑρετήν (*finder of hidden things*). The Vulgate here has — V e r t i t q u e   n o m e n eius, et vocavit eum lingua Ægyptiaca, Salvatorem mundi. Crum in Hastings' *Dict. of the Bible*

ἔδωκεν αὐτῷ τὴν 'Ασεννὲθ θυγατέρα Πετρεφῆ ἱερέως 'Ηλίου
πόλεως αὐτῷ εἰς γυναῖκα.   ⁴⁶'Ιωσὴφ δὲ ἦν ἐτῶν τριάκοντα ὅτε ἔστη ἐναντίον Φαραὼ βασιλέως Αἰγύπτου. ἐξῆλθεν
δὲ 'Ιωσὴφ ἐκ προσώπου Φαραώ, καὶ διῆλθεν πᾶσαν γῆν
Αἰγύπτου.   ⁴⁷καὶ ἐποίησεν ἡ γῆ ἐν τοῖς ἑπτὰ ἔτεσιν τῆς εὐθηνίας δράγματα·  ⁴⁸καὶ συνήγαγεν πάντα τὰ βρώματα τῶν ἑπτὰ
ἐτῶν ἐν οἷς ἦν ἡ εὐθηνία ἐν γῇ Αἰγύπτου, καὶ ἔθηκεν τὰ βρώματα ἐν ταῖς πόλεσιν· βρώματα τῶν πεδίων τῆς πόλεως τῶν
κύκλῳ αὐτῆς *Ων ἔθηκεν ἐν αὐτῇ.   ⁴⁹καὶ συνήγαγεν 'Ιωσὴφ
σῖτον ὡσεὶ τὴν ἄμμον τῆς θαλάσσης πολὺν σφόδρα, ἕως
οὐκ ἠδύνατο ἀριθμῆσαι· οὐ γὰρ ἦν ἀριθμός.   ⁵⁰τῷ δὲ
'Ιωσὴφ ἐγένοντο υἱοὶ δύο πρὸ τοῦ ἐλθεῖν τὰ ἑπτὰ ἔτη τοῦ
λιμοῦ, οὓς ἔτεκεν αὐτῷ 'Ασεννὲθ θυγάτηρ Πετρεφῆ ἱερέως
'Ηλίου πόλεως.   ⁵¹ἐκάλεσεν δὲ 'Ιωσὴφ τὸ ὄνομα τοῦ πρωτοτόκου Μαννασσῆ λέγων " Ὅτι ἐπιλαθέσθαι με ἐποίησεν ὁ
θεὸς πάντων τῶν πόνων μου καὶ πάντων τῶν τοῦ πατρός μου · "

explains the word from the Egyptian,
as meaning 'God speaks (and) he
lives.' —'Ασεννέθ: Jos. *Ant.* II 6 § 1
'Ασανέθη: Hebrew *Asenath:* Vulgate
*Aseneth.* The name is said to mean
'dedicated to Neith.' — Πετρεφῆ :
Hebrew *Poti-phera'.* The Greek name
is identical, and the Hebrew very
nearly so, with that of the captain of
the guard. It is explained to mean
'gift of the Sun-god' = Greek Heli-
odorus. —'Ηλίου πόλεως: Heliopolis,
the Hebrew Ôn and Egyptian An,
lies about 10 miles to the north-east
of Cairo. It was the site of a great
temple of the Sun. An obelisk dedicated to this god is still standing on
the site of the temple of Ra (*i.e.* the
Sun) at Heliopolis. *Cp.* Ex. 1¹¹ "Ων,
ἥ ἐστιν 'Ηλίου πόλις. For the form of

the proper name *cp.* Gen. 46²⁸ 'Ηρώων
πόλιν.

**47.** δράγματα: *handfuls,* indicating plenty. 37⁷ n.

**48.** ἐν οἷς ἦν ἡ εὐθηνία: perhaps
this points to a better reading than
that of our present Hebrew text.—βρώματα: the omission of the article is
only due to its absence from the Hebrew. The Greek, as it stands, must
be construed thus — *the food of the
city-plains that are round about Ôn itself did he put therein.* But there is
no mention here of Ôn in the Hebrew.

**51.** Μαννασσῆ: *making to forget.*
Jos. *Ant.* II 6 § 8 σημαίνει δ' ἐπιλῆθον.
—πάντων τῶν τοῦ πατρός μου: *all my
father's house,* or possibly neuter, as
in Lk. 2⁴⁹, *all my father's affairs.*

Genesis XLII 5

⁵²τὸ δὲ ὄνομα τοῦ δευτέρου ἐκάλεσεν Ἐφράιμ, "Ὅτι ὕψωσέν με ὁ θεὸς ἐν γῇ ταπεινώσεώς μου." ⁵³Παρῆλθον δὲ τὰ ἑπτὰ ἔτη τῆς εὐθηνίας ἃ ἐγένετο ἐν γῇ Αἰγύπτῳ, ⁵⁴καὶ ἤρξαντο τὰ ἑπτὰ ἔτη τοῦ λιμοῦ ἔρχεσθαι, καθὰ εἶπεν Ἰωσήφ. καὶ ἐγένετο λιμὸς ἐν πάσῃ τῇ γῇ· ἐν δὲ πάσῃ γῇ Αἰγύπτου οὐκ ἦσαν ἄρτοι. ⁵⁵καὶ ἐπείνασεν πᾶσα ἡ γῆ Αἰγύπτου· ἐκέκραξεν δὲ πᾶς ὁ λαὸς πρὸς Φαραὼ περὶ ἄρτων· εἶπεν δὲ Φαραὼ πᾶσι τοῖς Αἰγυπτίοις "Πορεύεσθε πρὸς Ἰωσήφ, καὶ ὃ ἐὰν εἴπῃ ὑμῖν ποιήσατε." ⁵⁶καὶ ὁ λιμὸς ἦν ἐπὶ προσώπου πάσης τῆς γῆς· ἀνέῳξεν δὲ Ἰωσὴφ πάντας τοὺς σιτοβολῶνας, καὶ ἐπώλει πᾶσι τοῖς Αἰγυπτίοις. ⁵⁷καὶ πᾶσαι αἱ χῶραι ἦλθον εἰς Αἴγυπτον ἀγοράζειν πρὸς Ἰωσήφ· ἐπεκράτησεν γὰρ ὁ λιμὸς ἐν πάσῃ τῇ γῇ.

¹Ἰδὼν δὲ Ἰακὼβ ὅτι ἐστὶν πρᾶσις ἐν Αἰγύπτῳ εἶπεν τοῖς υἱοῖς αὐτοῦ "Ἵνα τί ῥαθυμεῖτε; ²ἰδοὺ ἀκήκοα ὅτι ἐστὶν σῖτος ἐν Αἰγύπτῳ· κατάβητε ἐκεῖ καὶ πρίασθε ἡμῖν μικρὰ βρώματα, ἵνα ζῶμεν καὶ μὴ ἀποθάνωμεν." ³κατέβησαν δὲ οἱ ἀδελφοὶ Ἰωσὴφ οἱ δέκα πρίασθαι σῖτον ἐξ Αἰγύπτου· ⁴τὸν δὲ Βενιαμεὶν τὸν ἀδελφὸν Ἰωσὴφ οὐκ ἀπέστειλεν μετὰ τῶν ἀδελφῶν αὐτοῦ· εἶπεν γάρ "Μή ποτε συμβῇ αὐτῷ μαλακία." ⁵ἦλθον δὲ οἱ υἱοὶ Ἰσραὴλ ἀγοράζειν μετὰ τῶν ἐρχο-

52. Ἐφράιμ: explained differently in the Hebrew, 'for God hath made me fruitful.' Jos. Ant. II 6 § 1 has another interpretation — ὁ δὲ νεώτερος Ἐφραίμης· ἀποδιδοὺς δὲ τοῦτο σημαίνει, διὰ τὸ ἀποδοθῆναι αὐτὸν τῇ ἐλευθερίᾳ τῶν προγόνων.

55. ἐπείνασεν: § 25. — ἐκέκραξεν: reduplicated 1st aorist. § 20.

56. ἐπὶ προσώπου: a Hebraism. — σιτοβολῶνας: granaries. From σῖτος and βάλλω. Only here in LXX.

1. πρᾶσις: a market, Latin annona. In the Hebrew the word is the same as that which in the next verse is translated σῖτος. — ἵνα τί: sometimes written as one word ἱνατί. This way of expressing 'why' is common in Biblical Greek (e.g. Gen. 44⁴,⁷, 47¹⁵: Ex. 5⁴,¹⁵,²²: Mt. 27⁴⁶: Acts 7²⁶), from which it is imitated by St. Augustine in the Latin formula ut quid (e.g. C.D. IV 18). It is not unknown to classical writers. Plat. Apol. 26 C ἵνα τί ταῦτα λέγεις; Symp. 205 A.

4. μαλακία: cp..v. 38 μαλακισθῆναι, 44²⁹ for the meaning of 'harm.'

μένων· ἦν γὰρ ὁ λιμὸς ἐν γῇ Χανάαν.  ⁶Ἰωσὴφ δὲ ἦν
ἄρχων τῆς γῆς, οὗτος ἐπώλει παντὶ τῷ λαῷ τῆς γῆς· ἐλθόντες δὲ οἱ ἀδελφοὶ Ἰωσὴφ προσεκύνησαν αὐτῷ ἐπὶ πρόσωπον
ἐπὶ τὴν γῆν.  ⁷ἰδὼν δὲ Ἰωσὴφ τοὺς ἀδελφοὺς αὐτοῦ ἐπέγνω,
καὶ ἠλλοτριοῦτο ἀπ᾽ αὐτῶν καὶ ἐλάλησεν αὐτοῖς σκληρά, καὶ
εἶπεν αὐτοῖς " Πόθεν ἥκατε ;"  οἱ δὲ εἶπαν "Ἐκ γῆς Χανάαν,
ἀγοράσαι βρώματα."  ⁸ἐπέγνω δὲ Ἰωσὴφ τοὺς ἀδελφοὺς
αὐτοῦ, αὐτοὶ δὲ οὐκ ἐπέγνωσαν αὐτόν·  ⁹καὶ ἐμνήσθη Ἰωσὴφ
τῶν ἐνυπνίων ὧν ἴδεν αὐτός.  καὶ εἶπεν αὐτοῖς " Κατάσκοποί
ἐστε, κατανοῆσαι τὰ ἴχνη τῆς χώρας ἥκατε."  ¹⁰οἱ δὲ εἶπαν
"Οὐχί, κύριε·  οἱ παῖδές σου ἤλθομεν πριάσασθαι βρώματα·
¹¹πάντες ἐσμὲν υἱοὶ ἑνὸς ἀνθρώπου, εἰρηνικοί ἐσμεν· οὐκ εἰσὶν
οἱ παῖδές σου κατάσκοποι."  ¹²εἶπεν δὲ αὐτοῖς "Οὐχί, ἀλλὰ
τὰ ἴχνη τῆς γῆς ἤλθατε ἰδεῖν."  ¹³οἱ δὲ εἶπαν " Δώδεκά
ἐσμεν οἱ παῖδές σου ἀδελφοὶ ἐν γῇ Χανάαν·  καὶ ἰδοὺ ὁ νεώτερος μετὰ τοῦ πατρὸς ἡμῶν σήμερον, ὁ δὲ ἕτερος οὐχ ὑπάρχει."  ¹⁴εἶπεν δὲ αὐτοῖς Ἰωσήφ "Τοῦτό ἐστιν ὃ εἴρηκα
ὑμῖν, λέγων ὅτι κατάσκοποί ἐστε·  ¹⁵ἐν τούτῳ φανεῖσθε· νὴ
τὴν ὑγίαν Φαραώ, οὐ μὴ ἐξέλθητε ἐντεῦθεν ἐὰν μὴ ὁ ἀδελφὸς
ὑμῶν ὁ νεώτερος ἔλθῃ ὧδε.  ¹⁶ἀποστείλατε ἐξ ὑμῶν ἕνα,
καὶ λάβετε τὸν ἀδελφὸν ὑμῶν·  ὑμεῖς δὲ ἀπάχθητε ἕως τοῦ
φανερὰ γενέσθαι τὰ ῥήματα ὑμῶν, εἰ ἀληθεύετε ἢ οὔ· εἰ δὲ
μή, νὴ τὴν ὑγίαν Φαραώ, εἰ μὴν κατάσκοποί ἐστε."  ¹⁷καὶ

---

7. **ἥκατε**: perfect of **ἥκω**, used only
in the plural.  § 26.— **ἀγοράσαι βρώματα**: § 77.

9. **τὰ ἴχνη**: R.V. 'the naked-
ness.'

11. **εἰρηνικοί**: R.V. 'true men.'

12. **ἤλθατε**: § 18.

15. **νὴ τὴν ὑγίαν**: so in v. 16.
**νή** occurs nowhere else in the
LXX.  **ὑγίεια** commonly appears in

late Greek as **ὑγιεία**, here as **ὑγία**.
§ 10.

16. **ἀπάχθητε**: be ye sent to prison.
1st aorist imperfect passive.  39²² n. —
**ἢ οὔ**: in the second alternative of a
dependent disjunctive question either
οὔ or μή may be used.  Cp. Plat. Rep.
451 D καὶ σκοπῶμεν, εἰ ἡμῖν πρέπει ἢ οὔ
with 339 A εἰ δὲ ἀληθὲς ἢ μή, πειράσομαι
μαθεῖν.— **εἰ μήν**: verily = ἦ μήν.  § 103.

Genesis XLII 27

ἔθετο αὐτοὺς ἐν φυλακῇ ἡμέρας τρεῖς · ¹⁸εἶπεν δὲ αὐτοῖς τῇ ἡμέρᾳ τῇ τρίτῃ "Τοῦτο ποιήσατε, καὶ ζήσεσθε · τὸν θεὸν γὰρ ἐγὼ φοβοῦμαι. ¹⁹εἰ εἰρηνικοί ἐστε, ἀδελφὸς ὑμῶν εἷς κατασχεθήτω ἐν τῇ φυλακῇ · αὐτοὶ δὲ βαδίσατε καὶ ἀπαγάγετε τὸν ἀγορασμὸν τῆς σιτοδοσίας ὑμῶν, ²⁰καὶ τὸν ἀδελφὸν ὑμῶν τὸν νεώτερον καταγάγετε πρὸς μέ, καὶ πιστευθήσονται τὰ ῥήματα ὑμῶν · εἰ δὲ μή, ἀποθανεῖσθε." ἐποίησαν δὲ οὕτως. ²¹καὶ εἶπεν ἕκαστος πρὸς τὸν ἀδελφὸν αὐτοῦ "Ναί, ἐν ἁμαρτίᾳ γάρ ἐσμεν περὶ τοῦ ἀδελφοῦ ἡμῶν, ὅτι ὑπερίδομεν τὴν θλίψιν τῆς ψυχῆς αὐτοῦ ὅτε κατεδέετο ἡμῶν καὶ οὐκ εἰσηκούσαμεν αὐτοῦ · ἕνεκεν τούτου ἐπῆλθεν ἐφ' ἡμᾶς ἡ θλίψις αὕτη." ²²ἀποκριθεὶς δὲ Ῥουβὴν εἶπεν αὐτοῖς "Οὐκ ἐλάλησα ὑμῖν λέγων 'Μὴ ἀδικήσητε τὸ παιδάριον'; καὶ οὐκ εἰσηκούσατέ μου · καὶ ἰδοὺ τὸ αἷμα αὐτοῦ ἐκζητεῖται." ²³αὐτοὶ δὲ οὐκ ᾔδεισαν ὅτι ἀκούει Ἰωσήφ, ὁ γὰρ ἑρμηνευτὴς ἀνὰ μέσον αὐτῶν ἦν · ²⁴ἀποστραφεὶς δὲ ἀπ' αὐτῶν ἔκλαυσεν Ἰωσήφ. καὶ πάλιν προσῆλθεν πρὸς αὐτοὺς καὶ εἶπεν αὐτοῖς · καὶ ἔλαβεν τὸν Συμεὼν ἀπ' αὐτῶν, καὶ ἔδησεν αὐτὸν ἐναντίον αὐτῶν. ²⁵ἐνετείλατο δὲ Ἰωσὴφ ἐμπλῆσαι τὰ ἄγγια αὐτῶν σίτου, καὶ ἀποδοῦναι τὸ ἀργύριον ἑκάστου εἰς τὸν σάκκον αὐτοῦ, καὶ δοῦναι αὐτοῖς ἐπισιτισμὸν εἰς τὴν ὁδόν. καὶ ἐγενήθη αὐτοῖς οὕτως. ²⁶καὶ ἐπιθέντες τὸν σῖτον ἐπὶ τοὺς ὄνους αὐτῶν ἀπῆλθον ἐκεῖθεν. ²⁷λύσας δὲ εἷς τὸν μάρσιππον αὐτοῦ, δοῦναι χορτάσματα τοῖς ὄνοις αὐτοῦ οὗ

19. ἀδελφὸς ὑμῶν εἷς: the genitive is shown by the Hebrew to be possessive, not partitive — *one of your brethren*, not *one of you brothers*. — τὸν ἀγορασμὸν τῆς σιτοδοσίας ὑμῶν: *the corn you have purchased*. Σιτοδοσία is properly 'a gratuitous distribution of corn.' Cp. *frumentatio*, Suet. *Aug.* 40, 42.

20. πιστευθήσονται τὰ ῥήματα ὑμῶν: cp. 41³⁶ ἃ ἔσονται. — ἐποίησαν δὲ

οὕτως: these words are also in the Hebrew, but they seem to be misplaced in this context.

22. Ῥουβήν: 37²².

23. ἀνὰ μέσον: common in LXX, e.g. Gen. 49¹⁴: Nb. 26⁵⁶, 30¹⁷. Cp. i Cor. 6⁵.

25. ἄγγια: = ἀγγεῖα. § 37.

27. εἷς: § 2. — μάρσιππον: Hebrew *saq* whence, through the Greek

κατέλυσαν, ἴδεν τὸν δεσμὸν τοῦ ἀργυρίου αὐτοῦ, καὶ ἦν
ἐπάνω τοῦ στόματος τοῦ μαρσίππου· ²⁸καὶ εἶπεν τοῖς ἀδελφοῖς αὐτοῦ " Ἀπεδόθη μοι τὸ ἀργύριον, καὶ ἰδοὺ τοῦτο ἐν τῷ
μαρσίππῳ μου." καὶ ἐξέστη ἡ καρδία αὐτῶν, καὶ ἐταράχθησαν πρὸς ἀλλήλους λέγοντες "Τί τοῦτο ἐποίησεν ὁ θεὸς ἡμῖν;"
²⁹ἦλθον δὲ πρὸς Ἰακὼβ τὸν πατέρα αὐτῶν εἰς γῆν Χανάαν,
καὶ ἀπήγγειλαν αὐτῷ πάντα τὰ συμβεβηκότα αὐτοῖς λέγοντες ³⁰ " Λελάληκεν ὁ ἄνθρωπος ὁ κύριος τῆς γῆς πρὸς ἡμᾶς
σκληρά, καὶ ἔθετο ἡμᾶς ἐν φυλακῇ ὡς κατασκοπεύοντας τὴν
γῆν. ³¹εἴπαμεν δὲ αὐτῷ ʻΕἰρηνικοί ἐσμεν, οὐκ ἐσμὲν κατάσκο-
ποι· ³²δώδεκα ἀδελφοί ἐσμεν, υἱοὶ τοῦ πατρὸς ἡμῶν· ὁ εἷς οὐχ
ὑπάρχει, ὁ δὲ μικρότερος μετὰ τοῦ πατρὸς ἡμῶν σήμερον εἰς
γῆν Χανάαν.' ³³εἶπεν δὲ ἡμῖν ὁ ἄνθρωπος ὁ κύριος τῆς γῆς
ʻ Ἐν τούτῳ γνωσόμεθα ὅτι εἰρηνικοί ἐστε· ἀδελφὸν ἕνα ἄφετε
ὧδε μετʼ ἐμοῦ, τὸν δὲ ἀγορασμὸν τῆς σιτοδοσίας ὑμῶν
λαβόντες ἀπέλθατε· ³⁴καὶ ἀγάγετε πρὸς μὲ τὸν ἀδελφὸν
ὑμῶν τὸν νεώτερον, καὶ γνώσομαι ὅτι οὐ κατάσκοποί ἐστε,
ἀλλʼ ὅτι εἰρηνικοί ἐστε· καὶ τὸν ἀδελφὸν ὑμῶν ἀποδώσω
ὑμῖν, καὶ τῇ γῇ ἐμπορεύεσθε.' " ³⁵ἐγένετο δὲ ἐν τῷ κατακε-

and Latin, our ʻ sack.' Here the bag
containing the asses' provender. In
Xen. *Anab.* iv 3 § 11 it is used of a
clothes-bag, and spelt μάρσιπος. The
word has a diminutive, which occurs
in the forms μαρσίπιον, μαρσίππιον (Sir.
18³³), μαρσύπειον, and μαρσύπιον; Latin
*marsupium*, whence ʻ marsupial ' of an
animal with a pouch. — τὸν δεσμὸν τοῦ
ἀργυρίου αὐτοῦ: *the tying up of his
money*, i.e. *his money tied up.* See
the plural of this expression in v. 35.
In classical Greek δεσμοί often means
ʻ imprisonment,' *e.g.* Plat. *Rep.* 378 D,
*Symp.* 195 C, whereas δεσμά means
ʻ chains,' *e.g.* Plat. *Euthph.* 9 A, Acts

20²³, Luc. *Prom.* 1. The use of δεσμοί
in v. 35 is in accordance with the
implied principle that, when δεσμός
is an abstract noun, its plural is
δεσμοί. In Jdg. 15¹⁴ however we
have δεσμοί = δεσμά. — ἐπάνω τοῦ
στόματος: a pleonasm for *at the
mouth of.*

**32.** μικρότερος: = νεώτερος in v. 13.
— εἰς γῆν Χανάαν: § 90.

**33.** ἀπέλθατε: § 18.

**34.** τῇ γῇ ἐμπορεύεσθε: imperative.

**35.** κατακενοῦν: this word occurs
again in the LXX in ii K. 13⁹; otherwise it does not appear to be known.

Genesis XLIII 5

νοῦν αὐτοὺς τοὺς σάκκους αὐτῶν, καὶ ἦν ἑκάστου ὁ δεσμὸς
τοῦ ἀργυρίου ἐν τῷ σάκκῳ αὐτῶν· καὶ ἴδον τοὺς δεσμοὺς
τοῦ ἀργυρίου αὐτῶν αὐτοὶ καὶ ὁ πατὴρ αὐτῶν, καὶ ἐφοβήθησαν. ³⁶εἶπεν δὲ αὐτοῖς Ἰακὼβ ὁ πατὴρ αὐτῶν " Ἐμὲ ἠτεκ-
νώσατε· Ἰωσὴφ οὐκ ἔστιν, Συμεὼν οὐκ ἔστιν, καὶ τὸν Βενιαμεὶν λήμψεσθε· ἐπ' ἐμὲ ἐγένετο πάντα ταῦτα." ³⁷εἶπεν
δὲ Ῥουβὴν τῷ πατρὶ αὐτοῦ λέγων " Τοὺς δύο υἱούς μου ἀπό-
κτεινον, ἐὰν μὴ ἀγάγω αὐτὸν πρὸς σέ· δὸς αὐτὸν εἰς τὴν
χεῖρά μου, κἀγὼ ἀνάξω αὐτὸν πρὸς σέ." ³⁸ὁ δὲ εἶπεν " Οὐ
καταβήσεται ὁ υἱός μου μεθ' ὑμῶν, ὅτι ὁ ἀδελφὸς αὐτοῦ ἀπέθανεν, καὶ αὐτὸς μόνος καταλέλειπται· καὶ συμβήσεται
αὐτὸν μαλακισθῆναι ἐν τῇ ὁδῷ ᾗ ἂν πορεύεσθε, καὶ κατάξετέ μου τὸ γῆρας μετὰ λύπης εἰς ᾄδου."
¹Ὁ δὲ λιμὸς ἐνίσχυσεν ἐπὶ τῆς γῆς. ²ἐγένετο δὲ ἡνίκα
συνετέλεσαν καταφαγεῖν τὸν σῖτον ὃν ἤνεγκαν ἐξ Αἰγύπτου,
καὶ εἶπεν αὐτοῖς ὁ πατὴρ αὐτῶν " Πάλιν πορευθέντες πρίασθε ἡμῖν μικρὰ βρώματα." ³εἶπεν δὲ αὐτῷ Ἰούδας λέγων
" Διαμαρτυρίᾳ διαμεμαρτύρηται ἡμῖν ὁ ἄνθρωπος λέγων ' Οὐκ
ὄψεσθε τὸ πρόσωπόν μου ἐὰν μὴ ὁ ἀδελφὸς ὑμῶν ὁ νεώτερος
καταβῇ πρὸς μέ.' ⁴εἰ μὲν οὖν ἀποστέλλεις τὸν ἀδελφὸν
ἡμῶν μεθ' ἡμῶν, καταβησόμεθα καὶ ἀγοράσωμέν σοι βρώ-
ματα· ⁵εἰ δὲ μὴ ἀποστέλλεις τὸν ἀδελφὸν ἡμῶν μεθ' ἡμῶν,
οὐ πορευσόμεθα· ὁ γὰρ ἄνθρωπος εἶπεν ἡμῖν λέγων ' Οὐκ
ὄψεσθέ μου τὸ πρόσωπον ἐὰν μὴ ὁ ἀδελφὸς ὑμῶν ὁ νεώτερος

—σάκκους: the Hebrew word is the
same for which μάρσιππος was used
in v. 27.
  36. ἠτεκνώσατε: cp. 43¹⁴ : i K. 15³³
καθότι ἠτέκνωσεν γυναῖκας ἡ ῥομφαία
σου, οὕτως ἀτεκνωθήσεται ἐκ γυναικῶν
ἡ μήτηρ σου. — λήμψεσθε : § 37. —
ἐπ' ἐμὲ ἐγένετο : have come upon
me.

  38. μαλακισθῆναι: 4 n.
  3. Διαμαρτυρίᾳ διαμεμαρτύρηται:
cognate dative § 61.
  4. καταβησόμεθα καὶ ἀγοράσωμεν:
this combination of the future with
the aorist subjunctive recurs in Ex.
8⁸. It is more intelligible when the
sentence is interrogative, as in Gen.
44¹⁶.

μεθ᾽ ὑμῶν ᾖ.᾽ ” ⁶εἶπεν δὲ Ἰσραήλ “ Τί ἐκακοποιήσατέ μοι,
ἀναγγείλαντες τῷ ἀνθρώπῳ εἰ ἔστιν ὑμῖν ἀδελφός ; ” ⁷οἱ δὲ
εἶπαν “ Ἐρωτῶν ἐπηρώτησεν ἡμᾶς ὁ ἄνθρωπος καὶ τὴν γενεὰν
ἡμῶν, λέγων ‘ Εἰ ἔτι ὁ πατὴρ ὑμῶν ζῇ ; εἰ ἔστιν ὑμῖν ἀδελφός ;᾽
καὶ ἀπηγγείλαμεν αὐτῷ κατὰ τὴν ἐπερώτησιν αὐτοῦ. μὴ
ᾔδειμεν εἰ ἐρεῖ ἡμῖν ‘ Ἀγάγετε τὸν ἀδελφὸν ὑμῶν᾽ ;” ⁸εἶπεν δὲ
Ἰούδας πρὸς Ἰσραὴλ τὸν πατέρα αὐτοῦ “ Ἀπόστειλον τὸ
παιδάριον μετ᾽ ἐμοῦ, καὶ ἀναστάντες πορευσόμεθα, ἵνα ζῶμεν
καὶ μὴ ἀποθάνωμεν καὶ ἡμεῖς καὶ σὺ καὶ ἡ ἀποσκευὴ ἡμῶν.
⁹ἐγὼ δὲ ἐκδέχομαι αὐτόν, ἐκ χειρός μου ζήτησον αὐτόν· ἐὰν
μὴ ἀγάγω αὐτὸν πρὸς σὲ καὶ στήσω αὐτὸν ἐναντίον σου,
ἡμαρτηκὼς ἔσομαι πρὸς σὲ πάσας τὰς ἡμέρας. ¹⁰εἰ μὴ
γὰρ ἐβραδύναμεν, ἤδη ἂν ὑπεστρέψαμεν δίς.” ¹¹εἶπεν δὲ
αὐτοῖς Ἰσραὴλ ὁ πατὴρ αὐτῶν “ Εἰ οὕτως ἐστίν, τοῦτο ποιή-
σατε· λάβετε ἀπὸ τῶν καρπῶν τῆς γῆς ἐν τοῖς ἀγγίοις ὑμῶν,
καὶ καταγάγετε τῷ ἀνθρώπῳ δῶρα τῆς ῥιτίνης καὶ τοῦ μέλιτος, θυμίαμα καὶ στακτὴν καὶ τερέμινθον καὶ κάρυα. ¹²καὶ

**6.** Τί ἐκακοποιήσατέ κτλ. : *Why did ye do me so ill a turn as to . . . ?*

**7.** ἐπη ᾽ότησεν ἡμᾶς: *asked about us.* The construction is good Greek. *Cp.* Hdt. vii 100 — παρέπλεε παρὰ τὰς πρώρας τῶν νεῶν, ἐπειρωτέων τε ἑκάστας ὁμοίως καὶ τὸν πεζὸν καὶ ἀπογραφόμενος. — εἰ ἔτι: § 100.

**8.** ἀποσκευή: the Hebrew word here used is translated ‘ little ones ’ in Gen. 34²⁹, 43⁸, 46⁵: Ex. 10¹⁰, ²⁴, 12³⁷: Nb. 16²⁷, 31⁹, 32¹⁶, ¹⁷, ²⁴, ²⁶: Dt. 20¹⁴. Ἀπο-σκευή is a word of vague meaning, something like our ‘ gear ’ or ‘ belongings,’ or the Latin *impedimenta.* See Ex. 10¹⁰ n., and *cp.* i Chr. 5²¹ : ii Mac. 12²¹.

**9.** ἐκδέχομαι: the Hebrew word which is here represented by ἐκδέχομαι is formed from the same Semitic root as ἀρραβών, ‘ pledge,’ which was borrowed

by the Greeks from Semitic traders. Perhaps ἐκδέχομαι αὐτόν may be rendered ‘ I undertake him.’ — ἡμαρτηκὼς ἔσομαι: literally *I shall be having sinned.* Analytic form of future perfect. § 72.

**11.** ῥιτίνης: 37²⁵ n. Josephus (*Ant.* II 6 § 5) has here τό τε τῆς βαλάνου μύρον καὶ στάκτην, τερέβινθόν τε καὶ μέλι. — θυμίαμα: instead of continuing the partitive genitive the construction reverts to an accusative after καταγάγετε. — στακτήν: 37²⁵ n. — τερέμινθον: τέρμινθος, τερέμινθος, τερέβινθος (Is. 1³⁰, 6¹³) are different forms of the name of the tree which is known in botany as pistacia terebinthus. τέρμινθος does not occur in Swete’s text, in which τερέμινθος is the prevailing form. Pistachio-nuts are here

Genesis XLIII 18

τὸ ἀργύριον δισσὸν λάβετε ἐν ταῖς χερσὶν ὑμῶν· τὸ ἀργύριον τὸ ἀποστραφὲν ἐν τοῖς μαρσίπποις ὑμῶν ἀποστρέψατε
μεθ᾽ ὑμῶν· μή ποτε ἀγνόημά ἐστιν. ¹⁸ καὶ τὸν ἀδελφὸν
ὑμῶν λάβετε, καὶ ἀναστάντες κατάβητε πρὸς τὸν ἄνθρωπον.
¹⁴ ὁ δὲ θεός μου δῴη ὑμῖν χάριν ἐναντίον τοῦ ἀνθρώπου, καὶ
ἀποστεῖλαι τὸν ἀδελφὸν ὑμῶν τὸν ἕνα καὶ τὸν Βενιαμείν·
ἐγὼ μὲν γὰρ καθὰ ἠτέκνωμαι, ἠτέκνωμαι." ¹⁵ Λαβόντες
δὲ οἱ ἄνδρες τὰ δῶρα ταῦτα καὶ τὸ ἀργύριον διπλοῦν ἔλαβον
ἐν ταῖς χερσὶν αὐτῶν, καὶ τὸν Βενιαμείν· καὶ ἀναστάντες
κατέβησαν εἰς Αἴγυπτον, καὶ ἔστησαν ἐναντίον Ἰωσήφ.
¹⁶ ἴδεν δὲ Ἰωσὴφ αὐτοὺς καὶ τὸν Βενιαμεὶν τὸν ἀδελφὸν αὐτοῦ
τὸν ὁμομήτριον, καὶ ἐνετείλατο τῷ ἐπὶ τῆς οἰκίας αὐτοῦ εἰσαγαγεῖν τοὺς ἀνθρώπους εἰς τὴν οἰκίαν " Καὶ σφάξον θύματα
καὶ ἑτοίμασον· μετ᾽ ἐμοῦ γὰρ φάγονται οἱ ἄνθρωποι ἄρτους
τὴν μεσημβρίαν." ¹⁷ ἐποίησεν δὲ ὁ ἄνθρωπος καθὰ εἶπεν
Ἰωσήφ, καὶ εἰσήγαγεν τοὺς ἀνθρώπους εἰς τὴν οἰκίαν
Ἰωσήφ. ¹⁸ ἰδόντες δὲ οἱ ἄνθρωποι ὅτι εἰσηνέχθησαν εἰς τὸν
οἶκον Ἰωσὴφ εἶπαν " Διὰ τὸ ἀργύριον τὸ ἀποστραφὲν ἐν τοῖς
μαρσίπποις ἡμῶν τὴν ἀρχὴν ἡμεῖς εἰσαγόμεθα, τοῦ συκο-

---

meant by τερέμινθος. — κάρυα : a general name for nuts. Here rendered
'almonds' in the R.V., as in Nb. 17⁸.

**12. δισσόν**: δισσός and τρισσός are
good Greek for 'double,' 'treble.' This
series of multiplicatives never got any
further. For δισσός cp. 45²². It occurs
eight times in the LXX. — ἀποστρέψατε : bring back. Unclassical. Cp.
v. 21, 44⁸ : Ex. 10⁸. Often intransitive
go back, as in Ex. 13¹⁷. — μή ποτε . . .
ἐστιν: μή ποτε = haply. The expression perhaps originated in an ellipse
of some word like ὅρα. Cp. Jdg. 3²⁴ :
iii K. 18²⁷. This is more evident
when the verb is in the subjunctive,

as in Ex. 13¹⁷ μή ποτε μεταμελήσῃ τῷ
λαῷ.

**14. δῴη**: § 30. — τὸν ἕνα : we
should say 'your other brother,' and
so does the Hebrew. The Greek reading
may be due merely to a confusion between two letters in the Hebrew. The
reference is to Simeon 42²⁴. — ἐγὼ μέν :
the μέν here serves merely to empha-
sise the ἐγώ or else contrasts it with
the ὑμῖν which has gone before, invert-
ing the usual order. § 39.

**16. ὁμομήτριον**: Gen. 46¹⁹. — τὴν
μεσημβρίαν: § 55.

**18. τοῦ συκοφαντῆσαι ... τοῦ λα-
βεῖν**: § 59.

φαντῆσαι ἡμᾶς καὶ ἐπιθέσθαι ἡμῖν, τοῦ λαβεῖν ἡμᾶς εἰς παῖδας καὶ τοὺς ὄνους ἡμῶν." ¹⁹προσελθόντες δὲ πρὸς τὸν ἄνθρωπον τὸν ἐπὶ τοῦ οἴκου Ἰωσὴφ ἐλάλησαν αὐτῷ ἐν τῷ πυλῶνι τοῦ οἴκου ²⁰λέγοντες " Δεόμεθα, κύριε· κατέβημεν τὴν ἀρχὴν πρίασθαι βρώματα · ²¹καὶ ἐγένετο ἡνίκα ἤλθομεν εἰς τὸ καταλῦσαι καὶ ἠνοίξαμεν τοὺς μαρσίππους ἡμῶν, καὶ τόδε τὸ ἀργύριον ἑκάστου ἐν τῷ μαρσίππῳ αὐτοῦ. τὸ ἀργύριον ἡμῶν ἐν σταθμῷ ἀπεστρέψαμεν νῦν ἐν τοῖς μαρσίπποις ἡμῶν, ²²καὶ ἀργύριον ἕτερον ἠνέγκαμεν μεθ' ἑαυτῶν ἀγοράσαι βρώματα· οὐκ οἴδαμεν τίς ἐνέβαλεν τὸ ἀργύριον εἰς τοὺς μαρσίππους ἡμῶν." ²³εἶπεν δὲ αὐτοῖς ὁ ἄνθρωπος " Ἵλεως ὑμῖν, μὴ φοβεῖσθε· ὁ θεὸς ὑμῶν καὶ ὁ θεὸς τῶν πατέρων ὑμῶν ἔδωκεν ὑμῖν θησαυροὺς ἐν τοῖς μαρσίπποις ὑμῶν· τὸ δὲ ἀργύριον ὑμῶν εὐδοκιμοῦν ἀπέχω." καὶ ἐξήγαγεν πρὸς αὐτοὺς Συμεών, ²⁴καὶ ἤνεγκεν ὕδωρ νίψαι τοὺς πόδας αὐτῶν, καὶ ἤνεγκεν χορτάσματα τοῖς ὄνοις αὐτῶν. ²⁵ἡτοίμασαν δὲ τὰ δῶρα ἕως τοῦ ἐλθεῖν Ἰωσὴφ μεσημβρίᾳ· ἤκουσαν γὰρ ὅτι ἐκεῖ μέλλει ἀριστᾶν. ²⁶εἰσῆλθεν δὲ Ἰωσὴφ εἰς τὴν οἰκίαν, καὶ προσήνεγκαν αὐτῷ τὰ δῶρα ἃ εἶχον ἐν ταῖς χερσὶν αὐτῶν εἰς τὸν οἶκον, καὶ προσεκύνησαν αὐτῷ ἐπὶ πρόσωπον ἐπὶ τὴν γῆν. ²⁷ἠρώτησεν δὲ αὐτούς " Πῶς ἔχετε ; " καὶ εἶπεν αὐτοῖς " Εἰ ὑγιαίνει ὁ πατὴρ ὑμῶν ὁ πρεσβύτερος ὃν

---

**20. κατέβημεν** : for καταβάντες κατέβημεν, the Hebrew idiom being for once neglected where it seems to have no particular force.

**21. εἰς τὸ καταλῦσαι** : the Hebrew word rendered 'lodging-place' in the R.V. seems to have been understood by the Greek translator of the process of putting up for the night. Josephus (Ant. II 6 § 6) has here κατ᾽ οἶκον. — **καὶ τόδε** : this second καί marks the

apodosis. § 40.— **ἐν σταθμῷ** : in full weight.

**23. Ἵλεως ὑμῖν** : sc. εἴη ὁ Θεός. Cp. i Chr. 11¹⁹ ἵλεώς μοι ὁ θεὸς τοῦ ποιῆσαι τὸ ῥῆμα τοῦτο : Mt. 16²². R.V. ' Peace be to you.' The Hebrew word here used is connected with the Arabic salaam. — **εὐδοκιμοῦν ἀπέχω** : I have to my full satisfaction. Cp. Mt. 6² ἀπέχουσι τὸν μισθὸν αὐτῶν. The Hebrew is simply ' Your money came to me.'

Genesis XLIII 34

εἴπατε; ἔτι ζῇ;" ²⁸ οἱ δὲ εἶπαν " Ὑγιαίνει ὁ παῖς σου ὁ πατὴρ ἡμῶν, ἔτι ζῇ." καὶ εἶπεν " Εὐλογητὸς ὁ ἄνθρωπος ἐκεῖνος τῷ θεῷ." καὶ κύψαντες προσεκύνησαν. ²⁹ ἀναβλέψας δὲ τοῖς ὀφθαλμοῖς Ἰωσὴφ ἴδεν Βενιαμεὶν τὸν ἀδελφὸν αὐτοῦ τὸν ὁμομήτριον, καὶ εἶπεν αὐτοῖς " Οὗτός ἐστιν ὁ ἀδελφὸς ὑμῶν ὁ νεώτερος, ὃν εἴπατε πρὸς μὲ ἀγαγεῖν;" καὶ εἶπεν " Ὁ θεὸς ἐλεήσαι σε, τέκνον." ³⁰ ἐταράχθη δὲ Ἰωσήφ· συνεστρέφετο γὰρ τὰ ἔντερα αὐτοῦ ἐπὶ τῷ ἀδελφῷ αὐτοῦ, καὶ ἐζήτει κλαῦσαι· εἰσελθὼν δὲ εἰς τὸ ταμιεῖον ἔκλαυσεν ἐκεῖ. ³¹ καὶ νιψάμενος τὸ πρόσωπον ἐξελθὼν ἐνεκρατεύσατο, καὶ εἶπεν " Παράθετε ἄρτους." ³² καὶ παρέθηκαν αὐτῷ μόνῳ, καὶ αὐτοῖς καθ' ἑαυτούς, καὶ τοῖς Αἰγυπτίοις τοῖς συνδειπνοῦσιν μετ' αὐτοῦ καθ' ἑαυτούς· οὐ γὰρ ἐδύναντο οἱ Αἰγύπτιοι συνεσθίειν μετὰ τῶν Ἑβραίων ἄρτους, βδέλυγμα γάρ ἐστιν τοῖς Αἰγυπτίοις πᾶς ποιμὴν προβάτων. ³³ ἐκάθισαν δὲ ἐναντίον αὐτοῦ, ὁ πρωτότοκος κατὰ τὰ πρεσβεῖα αὐτοῦ καὶ ὁ νεώτερος κατὰ τὴν νεότητα αὐτοῦ· ἐξίσταντο δὲ οἱ ἄνθρωποι ἕκαστος πρὸς τὸν ἀδελφὸν αὐτοῦ. ³⁴ ἦραν δὲ μερίδα παρ' αὐτοῦ πρὸς αὐτούς· ἐμεγαλύνθη δὲ ἡ μερὶς Βενιαμεὶν παρὰ τὰς μερίδας πάντων πενταπλασίως πρὸς τὰς ἐκείνων. ἔπιον δὲ καὶ ἐμεθύσθησαν μετ' αὐτοῦ.

28. ὁ παῖς σου: thy servant. See 40²⁰ n. — καὶ εἶπεν . . . τῷ θεῷ: not in the Hebrew.

29. εἴπατε: = ye promised.

30. συνεστρέφετο κτλ. : = ' his heart yearned over his brother.' — ταμιεῖον: cp. Mt. 6⁶ for this use of ταμιεῖον as a private chamber. § 10.

31. ἐνεκρατεύσατο: he controlled himself.

32. βδέλυγμα . . . πᾶς ποιμὴν προβάτων: cp. 46³⁴. Nothing further is known on this subject.

33. ἐξίσταντο: the word which commonly expresses the feeling of surprise is here used for the expression of that feeling. — ἕκαστος πρὸς τὸν ἀδελφὸν αὐτοῦ: each to his brother = to one another. The Hebrew is ' each to his neighbour.'

34. ἦραν: sc. οἱ παῖδες. — ἐμεγαλύνθη . . . παρά: 37³ n. The general statement ' was larger than ' is further specified by πενταπλασίως πρὸς τὰς ἐκείνων. For another illustration of the principle of helping one ' as you love

Genesis XLIV 1

¹Καὶ ἐνετείλατο Ἰωσὴφ τῷ ὄντι ἐπὶ τῆς οἰκίας αὐτοῦ λέγων
" Πλήσατε τοὺς μαρσίππους τῶν ἀνθρώπων βρωμάτων ὅσα
ἐὰν δύνωνται ἆραι, καὶ ἐμβάλατε ἑκάστου τὸ ἀργύριον ἐπὶ τοῦ
στόματος τοῦ μαρσίππου αὐτοῦ · ²καὶ τὸ κόνδυ μου τὸ ἀργυροῦν ἐμβάλατε εἰς τὸν μάρσιππον τοῦ νεωτέρου, καὶ τὴν
τιμὴν τοῦ σίτου αὐτοῦ." ἐγενήθη δὲ κατὰ τὸ ῥῆμα Ἰωσὴφ
καθὼς εἶπεν. ³τὸ πρωὶ διέφαυσεν καὶ οἱ ἄνθρωποι ἀπε-
στάλησαν, αὐτοὶ καὶ οἱ ὄνοι αὐτῶν. ⁴ἐξελθόντων δὲ αὐτῶν
τὴν πόλιν οὐκ ἀπέσχον μακράν, καὶ Ἰωσὴφ εἶπεν τῷ ἐπὶ τῆς
οἰκίας αὐτοῦ λέγων " Ἀναστὰς ἐπιδίωξον ὀπίσω τῶν ἀνθρώπων καὶ καταλήμψῃ αὐτούς, καὶ ἐρεῖς αὐτοῖς ' Τί ὅτι ἀνταπε-
δώκατέ μοι πονηρὰ ἀντὶ καλῶν ; ἵνα τί ἐκλέψατέ μου τὸ
κόνδυ τὸ ἀργυροῦν ; ⁵οὐ τοῦτό ἐστιν ἐν ᾧ πίνει ὁ κύριός
μου ; αὐτὸς δὲ οἰωνισμῷ οἰωνίζεται ἐν αὐτῷ· πονηρὰ συντε-
τέλεσθε ἃ πεποιήκατε.'" ⁶εὑρὼν δὲ αὐτοὺς εἶπεν αὐτοῖς κατὰ
τὰ ῥήματα ταῦτα. ⁷οἱ δὲ εἶπον αὐτῷ " Ἵνα τί λαλεῖ ὁ κύριος

him' see Xen. *Cyrop.* I 3 § 6, where
Astyages helps Cyrus so largely to
meat that the boy has to distribute it
among the servants. Josephus (*Ant.*
II 6 § 6) softens down πενταπλασίως
into διπλασίοισι μοίραις. The importance here assigned to Benjamin
has been used as an argument
that this legend took shape in the
time of Saul, who belonged to that
tribe.

**1.** ὅσα ἐάν : § 105. — ἐμβάλατε :
imperative from aorist ἐνέβαλα. § 18.

**2.** κόνδυ : *drinking-cup.* Outside
this chapter the word occurs in the
LXX only in Is. 51¹⁷, ²². A plural κόνδυα
is used in a letter of Alexander the
Great to the satraps of Asia quoted
by Athen. 784 a. Hence it has been
inferred that the word is Persian.

Josephus (*Ant.* II 6 § 7) has here
σκύφος.

**3.** τὸ πρωὶ διέφαυσεν : τὸ πρωί is
adverbial (40⁶ n.) and διέφαυσεν intransitive.

**4.** ἐξελθόντων . . . ἀπέσχον : § 58.
— καὶ Ἰωσήφ : in such paratactical
constructions καί may be rendered in
English by 'when.' This use of καί is
found in classical authors, *e.g.* Plat.
*Euthd.* 273 A, 277 B. *Cp.* Verg. *Æn.*:
nec longum tempus et ingens
exiit ad cælum ramis felicibus
arbos.
— ὀπίσω τῶν ἀνθρώπων : unclassical
substitute for μετὰ τοὺς ἀνθρώπους. § 97.
— καταλήμψῃ . . . ἐρεῖς : jussive futures. § 74.

**5.** οἰωνισμῷ οἰωνίζεται : cognate
dative. *Cp.* 15. § 61.

Genesis XLIV 18

κατὰ τὰ ῥήματα ταῦτα; μὴ γένοιτο τοῖς παισίν σου ποιῆσαι τὸ ῥῆμα τοῦτο. ⁸εἰ τὸ μὲν ἀργύριον ὃ εὕραμεν ἐν τοῖς μαρσίπποις ἡμῶν ἀπεστρέψαμεν πρὸς σὲ ἐκ γῆς Χανάαν, πῶς ἂν κλέψαιμεν ἐκ τοῦ οἴκου τοῦ κυρίου σου ἀργύριον ἢ χρυσίον; ⁹παρ᾽ ᾧ ἂν εὑρεθῇ τὸ κόνδυ τῶν παίδων σου, ἀποθνησκέτω· καὶ ἡμεῖς δὲ ἐσόμεθα παῖδες τῷ κυρίῳ ἡμῶν." ¹⁰ὁ δὲ εἶπεν "Καὶ νῦν ὡς λέγετε, οὕτως ἔσται· ὁ ἄνθρωπος παρ᾽ ᾧ ἂν εὑρεθῇ τὸ κόνδυ, αὐτὸς ἔσται μου παῖς, ὑμεῖς δὲ ἔσεσθε καθαροί." ¹¹καὶ ἔσπευσαν καὶ καθεῖλαν ἕκαστος τὸν μάρσιππον αὐτοῦ ἐπὶ τὴν γῆν, καὶ ἤνοιξεν ἕκαστος τὸν μάρσιππον αὐτοῦ. ¹²ἠρεύνα δὲ ἀπὸ τοῦ πρεσβυτέρου ἀρξάμενος ἕως ἦλθεν ἐπὶ τὸν νεώτερον, καὶ εὗρεν τὸ κόνδυ ἐν τῷ μαρσίππῳ τῷ Βενιαμείν. ¹³καὶ διέρρηξαν τὰ ἱμάτια αὐτῶν, καὶ ἐπέθηκαν ἕκαστος τὸν μάρσιππον αὐτοῦ ἐπὶ τὸν ὄνον αὐτοῦ, καὶ ἐπέστρεψαν εἰς τὴν πόλιν. ¹⁴εἰσῆλθεν δὲ Ἰούδας καὶ οἱ ἀδελφοὶ αὐτοῦ πρὸς Ἰωσήφ, ἔτι αὐτοῦ ὄντος ἐκεῖ· καὶ ἔπεσον ἐναντίον αὐτοῦ ἐπὶ τὴν γῆν. ¹⁵εἶπεν δὲ αὐτοῖς Ἰωσήφ "Τί τὸ πρᾶγμα τοῦτο ἐποιήσατε; οὐκ οἴδατε ὅτι οἰωνισμῷ οἰωνιεῖται ἄνθρωπος οἷος ἐγώ;" ¹⁶εἶπεν δὲ Ἰούδας "Τί ἀντεροῦμεν τῷ κυρίῳ ἢ τί λαλήσωμεν ἢ τί δικαιωθῶμεν; ὁ δὲ θεὸς εὗρεν τὴν ἀδικίαν τῶν παίδων σου· ἰδού ἐσμεν οἰκέται τῷ κυρίῳ ἡμῶν, καὶ ἡμεῖς καὶ παρ᾽ ᾧ εὑρέθη τὸ κόνδυ." ¹⁷εἶπεν δὲ Ἰωσήφ "Μή μοι γένοιτο ποιῆσαι τὸ ῥῆμα τοῦτο· ὁ ἄνθρωπος παρ᾽ ᾧ εὑρέθη τὸ κόνδυ, αὐτὸς ἔσται μου παῖς· ὑμεῖς δὲ ἀνάβητε μετὰ σωτηρίας πρὸς τὸν πατέρα ὑμῶν." ¹⁸Ἐγγίσας δὲ αὐτῷ Ἰούδας εἶπεν "Δέομαι, κύριε·

---

7. **τὸ ῥῆμα τοῦτο**: cp. 17. See 39⁹ n.

8. **εὕραμεν**: § 18. — **ἀργύριον ἢ χρυσίον**: for the concurrence of the two diminutives cp. Ar. Eq. 472: καὶ ταῦτα μ᾽ οὔτ᾽ ἀργύριον οὔτε χρυσίον διδοὺς ἀναπείσεις.

11. **καθεῖλαν**: § 18.

13. **ἐπέστρεψαν**: returned. The intransitive use of this verb is very common in the LXX. Cp. Mt. 12⁴⁴ ἐπιστρέψω εἰς τὸν οἶκόν μου.

16. **ἀντεροῦμεν, λαλήσωμεν**: 43¹ n.

Genesis XLIV 19

λαλησάτω ὁ παῖς σου ῥῆμα ἐναντίον σου, καὶ μὴ θυμωθῇς τῷ παιδί σου, ὅτι σὺ εἶ μετὰ Φαραώ. ¹⁹κύριε, σὺ ἠρώτησας τοὺς παῖδάς σου λέγων ' Εἰ ἔχετε πατέρα ἢ ἀδελφόν ; ' ²⁰καὶ εἴπαμεν τῷ κυρίῳ ' Ἔστιν ἡμῖν πατὴρ πρεσβύτερος, καὶ παιδίον νεώτερον γήρως αὐτῷ, καὶ ὁ ἀδελφὸς αὐτοῦ ἀπέθανεν, αὐτὸς δὲ μόνος ὑπελείφθη τῷ πατρὶ αὐτοῦ, ὁ δὲ πατὴρ αὐτὸν ἠγάπησεν.' ²¹εἶπας δὲ τοῖς παισίν σου ὅτι ' Καταγάγετε αὐτὸν πρός μέ, καὶ ἐπιμελοῦμαι αὐτοῦ.' ²²καὶ εἴπαμεν τῷ κυρίῳ ' Οὐ δυνήσεται τὸ παιδίον καταλιπεῖν τὸν πατέρα· ἐὰν δὲ καταλείπῃ τὸν πατέρα, ἀποθανεῖται.' ²³σὺ δὲ εἶπας τοῖς παισίν σου ' 'Εὰν μὴ καταβῇ ὁ ἀδελφὸς ὑμῶν ὁ νεώτερος μεθ' ὑμῶν, οὐ προσθήσεσθε ἔτι ἰδεῖν τὸ πρόσωπόν μου.' ²⁴ἐγένετο δὲ ἡνίκα ἀνέβημεν πρὸς τὸν παῖδά σου πατέρα δὲ ἡμῶν, ἀπηγγείλαμεν αὐτῷ τὰ ῥήματα τοῦ κυρίου. ²⁵εἶπεν δὲ ἡμῖν ὁ πατὴρ ἡμῶν ' Βαδίσατε πάλιν, ἀγοράσατε ἡμῖν μικρὰ βρώματα.' ²⁶ἡμεῖς δὲ εἴπαμεν ' Οὐ δυνησόμεθα καταβῆναι· ἀλλ' εἰ μὲν ὁ ἀδελφὸς ἡμῶν ὁ νεώτερος καταβαίνει μεθ' ἡμῶν, καταβησόμεθα· οὐ γὰρ δυνησόμεθα ἰδεῖν τὸ πρόσωπον τοῦ ἀνθρώπου, τοῦ ἀδελφοῦ τοῦ νεωτέρου μὴ ὄντος μεθ' ἡμῶν.' ²⁷εἶπεν δὲ ὁ παῖς σου ὁ πατὴρ ἡμῶν πρὸς ἡμᾶς ' Ὑμεῖς γινώσκετε ὅτι δύο ἔτεκέν μοι ἡ γυνή · ²⁸καὶ ἐξῆλθεν ὁ εἷς ἀπ' ἐμοῦ, καὶ εἴπατε " Θηριόβρωτος γέγονεν," καὶ οὐκ ἴδον αὐτὸν ἔτι. ²⁹ἐὰν οὖν λάβητε καὶ τοῦτον ἐκ προσώπου μου καὶ συμβῇ αὐτῷ μαλακία ἐν τῇ ὁδῷ, καὶ κατάξετέ μου τὸ γῆρας μετὰ λύπης εἰς ᾅδου.' ³⁰νῦν οὖν ἐὰν εἰσπορεύομαι πρὸς τὸν παῖδά σου πατέρα δὲ ἡμῶν, καὶ τὸ παιδάριον μὴ ᾖ μεθ' ἡμῶν, ἡ δὲ ψυχὴ αὐτοῦ ἐκκρέμαται ἐκ τῆς τούτου ψυχῆς·

---

**18.** μετὰ Φαραώ : μετά here means *on a level with*.

**21.** ὅτι : 37³⁵ n.

**23.** προσθήσεσθε ἔτι ἰδεῖν : § 113.

**29.** μαλακία : 42⁴ n. — καὶ κατά-

ξετε : the καί introduces the apodosis. § 40.

**30.** ἐὰν εἰσπορεύομαι : § 104. — ἡ δὲ ψυχὴ κτλ. : this clause is thrown in parenthetically as a reason for the

Genesis XLV 7

³¹ καὶ ἔσται ἐν τῷ ἰδεῖν αὐτὸν μὴ ὂν τὸ παιδάριον μεθ᾽ ἡμῶν, τελευτήσει, καὶ κατάξουσιν οἱ παῖδές σου τὸ γῆρας τοῦ παιδός σου πατρὸς δὲ ἡμῶν μετ᾽ ὀδύνης εἰς ᾅδου. ³² ὁ γὰρ παῖς σου ἐκδέδεκται τὸ παιδίον παρὰ τοῦ πατρὸς λέγων ʿ Ἐὰν μὴ ἀγάγω αὐτὸν πρὸς σὲ καὶ στήσω αὐτὸν ἐναντίον σου, ἡμαρτηκὼς ἔσομαι πρὸς τὸν πατέρα πάσας τὰς ἡμέρας.᾽ ³³ νῦν οὖν παραμενῶ σοι παῖς ἀντὶ τοῦ παιδίου, οἰκέτης τοῦ κυρίου· τὸ δὲ παιδίον ἀναβήτω μετὰ τῶν ἀδελφῶν. ³⁴ πῶς γὰρ ἀναβήσομαι πρὸς τὸν πατέρα, τοῦ παιδίου μὴ ὄντος μεθ᾽ ἡμῶν; ἵνα μὴ ἴδω τὰ κακὰ ἃ εὑρήσει τὸν πατέρα μου."

¹ Καὶ οὐκ ἠδύνατο Ἰωσὴφ ἀνέχεσθαι πάντων τῶν παρεστηκότων αὐτῷ, ἀλλ᾽ εἶπεν " Ἐξαποστείλατε πάντας ἀπ᾽ ἐμοῦ·" καὶ οὐ παριστήκει οὐδεὶς ἔτι τῷ Ἰωσὴφ ἡνίκα ἀνεγνωρίζετο Ἰωσὴφ τοῖς ἀδελφοῖς αὐτοῦ. ² καὶ ἀφῆκεν φωνὴν μετὰ κλαυθμοῦ· ἤκουσαν δὲ πάντες οἱ Αἰγύπτιοι, καὶ ἀκουστὸν ἐγένετο εἰς τὸν οἶκον Φαραώ. ³ εἶπεν δὲ Ἰωσὴφ πρὸς τοὺς ἀδελφοὺς αὐτοῦ " Ἐγώ εἰμι Ἰωσὴφ ὁ ἀδελφὸς ὑμῶν, ὃν ἀπέδοσθε εἰς Αἴγυπτον· ἔτι ὁ πατήρ μου ζῇ;" καὶ οὐκ ἐδύναντο οἱ ἀδελφοὶ ἀποκριθῆναι αὐτῷ· ἐταράχθησαν γάρ. ⁴ καὶ εἶπεν " Ἐγώ εἰμι Ἰωσὴφ ὁ ἀδελφὸς ὑμῶν, ὃν ἀπέδοσθε εἰς Αἴγυπτον. ⁵ νῦν οὖν μὴ λυπεῖσθε, μηδὲ σκληρὸν ὑμῖν φανήτω ὅτι ἀπέδοσθέ με ὧδε· εἰς γὰρ ζωὴν ἀπέστειλέν με ὁ θεὸς ἔμπροσθεν ὑμῶν. ⁶ τοῦτο γὰρ δεύτερον ἔτος λιμὸς ἐπὶ τῆς γῆς, καὶ ἔτι λοιπὰ πέντε ἔτη ἐν οἷς οὐκ ἔσται ἀροτρίασις οὐδὲ ἄμητος· ⁷ ἀπέστειλεν γάρ με ὁ θεὸς ἔμπροσθεν ὑμῶν,

apodosis, which begins at καὶ ἔσται in v. 31.

**32. ἐκδέδεκται**: 43⁹ n.
**34. εὑρήσει**: shall find, i.e. come upon.
**1. ἀνέχεσθαι**: endure. R.V. 'refrain himself before.' — **παριστήκει**: = παρειστήκει. § 37.

**2. ἀκουστὸν ἐγένετο**: a substitute for ἠκούσθη — it was heard. § 72.
**6. ἀροτρίασις**: ploughing. Only here in LXX. From the simple verb ἀρόω is formed ἄροτρον denoting the instrument; from ἄροτρον again is formed a verb ἀροτριάω (Jdg. 14¹⁸), and from this we have the abstract noun ἀροτρίασις.

ὑπολείπεσθαι ὑμῶν κατάλειμμα ἐπὶ τῆς γῆς καὶ ἐκθρέψαι ὑμῶν κατάλειψιν μεγάλην. ⁸νῦν οὖν οὐχ ὑμεῖς με ἀπεστάλκατε ὧδε, ἀλλ' ἢ ὁ θεός · καὶ ἐποίησέν με ὡς πατέρα Φαραὼ καὶ κύριον παντὸς τοῦ οἴκου αὐτοῦ καὶ ἄρχοντα πάσης γῆς Αἰγύπτου. ⁹σπεύσαντες οὖν ἀνάβητε πρὸς τὸν πατέρα μου καὶ εἴπατε αὐτῷ 'Τάδε λέγει ὁ υἱός σου Ἰωσήφ "Ἐποίησέν με ὁ θεὸς κύριον πάσης γῆς Αἰγύπτου · κατάβηθι οὖν πρὸς μέ, καὶ μὴ μείνῃς · ¹⁰καὶ κατοικήσεις ἐν γῇ Γέσεμ Ἀραβίας, καὶ ἔσῃ ἐγγύς μου σὺ καὶ οἱ υἱοί σου καὶ οἱ υἱοὶ τῶν υἱῶν σου, τὰ πρόβατά σου καὶ αἱ βόες σου καὶ ὅσα σοὶ ἐκεῖ · ¹¹καὶ ἐκθρέψω σε ἐκεῖ, ἔτι γὰρ πέντε ἔτη λιμός · ἵνα μὴ ἐκτριβῇς σὺ καὶ οἱ υἱοί σου καὶ πάντα τὰ ὑπάρχοντά σου." ' ¹²ἰδοὺ οἱ ὀφθαλμοὶ ὑμῶν βλέπουσιν καὶ οἱ ὀφθαλμοὶ Βενιαμεὶν τοῦ ἀδελφοῦ μου ὅτι τὸ στόμα μου τὸ λαλοῦν πρὸς ὑμᾶς. ¹³ἀπαγγείλατε οὖν τῷ πατρί μου πᾶσαν τὴν δόξαν μου τὴν ἐν Αἰγύπτῳ καὶ ὅσα ἴδετε, καὶ ταχύναντες καταγάγετε τὸν πατέρα μου ὧδε." ¹⁴ καὶ ἐπιπεσὼν ἐπὶ τὸν τράχηλον Βενιαμεὶν τοῦ ἀδελφοῦ αὐτοῦ ἐπέπεσεν ἐπ' αὐτῷ, καὶ Βενιαμεὶν ἔκλαυσεν ἐπὶ τῷ τραχήλῳ αὐτοῦ. ¹⁵καὶ καταφιλήσας πάντας τοὺς ἀδελφοὺς αὐτοῦ ἔκλαυσεν ἐπ' αὐτοῖς, καὶ μετὰ ταῦτα ἐλάλησαν οἱ ἀδελφοὶ αὐτοῦ πρὸς αὐτόν. ¹⁶Καὶ διε-

---

7. καὶ ἐκθρέψαι κτλ. : *and to rear up from you a great leaving* (= *posterity*). Κατάλειψις seems to be used for variety in the same sense as κατάλειμμα.

8. ἀλλ' ἢ ὁ θεός : § 108. — ὡς πατέρα Φαραώ : the same expression is used in the Egyptian tales of a trusted officer.

10. Γέσεμ Ἀραβίας : *Goshen in Arabia.* Ἀραβίας is an addition of the LXX, which causes a verbal contradiction between this passage and 47²⁷; but 'Arabia' is here supposed to be the name of a 'nome' in Egypt. Goshen seems to have been the district watered by the Sweet Water Canal, lying to the east of the Delta, and bounded on the east by the Arabian Desert. — ὅσα σοὶ ἐκεῖ : ἐκεῖ must be taken with ἔσῃ ἐγγύς μου at the beginning of the verse. There is another reading ἐστί, which is more probable, as there is nothing corresponding to ἐκεῖ in the Hebrew.

14. ἐπιπεσών . . . ἐπέπεσεν : intensive participle. § 81.

Genesis XLV 23

βοήθη ἡ φωνὴ εἰς τὸν οἶκον Φαραὼ λέγοντες "Ἥκασιν οἱ
ἀδελφοὶ Ἰωσήφ·" ἐχάρη δὲ Φαραὼ καὶ ἡ θεραπεία αὐτοῦ.
¹⁷εἶπεν δὲ Φαραὼ πρὸς Ἰωσήφ "Εἰπὸν τοῖς ἀδελφοῖς σου
'Τοῦτο ποιήσατε· γεμίσατε τὰ πόρια ὑμῶν καὶ ἀπέλθατε εἰς
γῆν Χανάαν, ¹⁸καὶ παραλαβόντες τὸν πατέρα ὑμῶν καὶ τὰ
ὑπάρχοντα ὑμῶν ἥκετε πρὸς μέ· καὶ δώσω ὑμῖν πάντων τῶν
ἀγαθῶν Αἰγύπτου, καὶ φάγεσθε τὸν μυελὸν τῆς γῆς.' ¹⁹σὺ
δὲ ἔντειλαι ταῦτα, λαβεῖν αὐτοῖς 'ἁμάξας ἐκ γῆς Αἰγύπτου
τοῖς παιδίοις ὑμῶν καὶ ταῖς γυναιξίν, καὶ ἀναλαβόντες τὸν
πατέρα ὑμῶν παραγίνεσθε· ²⁰καὶ μὴ φείσησθε τοῖς ὀφθαλμοῖς ὑμῶν τῶν σκευῶν, τὰ γὰρ πάντα ἀγαθὰ Αἰγύπτου ὑμῖν
ἔσται.'" ²¹ἐποίησαν δὲ οὕτως οἱ υἱοὶ Ἰσραήλ· ἔδωκεν δὲ
Ἰωσὴφ αὐτοῖς ἁμάξας κατὰ τὰ εἰρημένα ὑπὸ Φαραὼ τοῦ
βασιλέως, καὶ ἔδωκεν αὐτοῖς ἐπισιτισμὸν εἰς τὴν ὁδόν·
²²καὶ πᾶσιν ἔδωκεν δισσὰς στολάς, καὶ τῷ Βενιαμεὶν ἔδωκεν
τριακοσίους χρυσοῦς καὶ πέντε ἀλλασσούσας στολάς· ²³καὶ
τῷ πατρὶ αὐτοῦ ἀπέστειλεν κατὰ τὰ αὐτά, καὶ δέκα ὄνους
αἴροντας ἀπὸ πάντων τῶν ἀγαθῶν Αἰγύπτου, καὶ δέκα ἡμιό-

16. λέγοντες: we may say that this participle agrees with the vague plural implied in διεβοήθη ἡ φωνή. § 112. —Ἥκασιν: 42⁷ n. — ἡ θεραπεία αὐτοῦ: = his court.

17. πόρια: =πορεῖα, means of transport. § 37. Here, no doubt, camels and asses. The Hebrew word means 'cattle.'

18. ἥκετε: imperative of ἥκω.

19. σὺ δὲ ἔντειλαι κτλ.: and do thou give this command, that they should take to them waggons from the land of Egypt for your children and women, and take ye your father and come. There is a sudden change of construction from the oblique to the direct oration. To substitute λάβετε ἑαυτοῖς for λαβεῖν αὐτοῖς makes the Greek run smoothly enough, but there is perhaps something amiss with the Hebrew at the beginning of the verse.

20. καὶ μὴ φείσησθε κτλ.: and spare not your goods with your eyes, i.e. regard not the loss of them, a common Hebrew phrase.—τὰ . . . πάντα ἀγαθά: the whole goods. § 63.

22. δισσάς: 43¹² n. — τριακοσίους χρυσοῦς: sc. στατῆρας. The Hebrew is 'three hundred (shekels) of silver.' Cp. 37²⁸ n. — ἀλλασσούσας στολάς: changes of raiment. Cp. Jdg. 14¹⁸ τριάκοντα ἀλλασσομένας στολὰς ἱματίων.

23. αἴροντας, αἰρούσας: the common meaning of αἴρειν in the LXX is 'to carry.' Cp. 46⁵: i K. 16²¹, 17⁷. — ἡμιόνους: Hebrew, 'she-asses.'

νους αἰρούσας ἄρτους τῷ πατρὶ αὐτοῦ εἰς ὁδόν.  ²⁴ἐξαπέστει-
λεν δὲ τοὺς ἀδελφοὺς αὐτοῦ καὶ ἐπορεύθησαν· καὶ εἶπεν
αὐτοῖς " Μὴ ὀργίζεσθε ἐν τῇ ὁδῷ."    ²⁵καὶ ἀνέβησαν ἐξ Αἰγύπτου, καὶ ἦλθον εἰς γῆν Χανάαν πρὸς Ἰακὼβ τὸν πατέρα
αὐτῶν, ²⁶καὶ ἀνήγγειλαν αὐτῷ λέγοντες ὅτι " Ὁ υἱός σου
Ἰωσὴφ ζῇ, καὶ οὗτος ἄρχει πάσης τῆς γῆς Αἰγύπτου."    καὶ
ἐξέστη ἡ διάνοια Ἰακώβ, οὐ γὰρ ἐπίστευσεν αὐτοῖς.    ²⁷ἐλά-
λησαν δὲ αὐτῷ πάντα τὰ ῥηθέντα ὑπὸ Ἰωσήφ, ὅσα εἶπεν
αὐτοῖς· ἰδὼν δὲ τὰς ἁμάξας ἃς ἀπέστειλεν Ἰωσὴφ ὥστε ἀνα-
λαβεῖν αὐτόν, ἀνεζωπύρησεν τὸ πνεῦμα Ἰακὼβ τοῦ πατρὸς
αὐτῶν.    ²⁸εἶπεν δὲ Ἰσραήλ " Μέγα μοί ἐστιν εἰ ἔτι ὁ
υἱός μου Ἰωσὴφ ζῇ· πορευθεὶς ὄψομαι αὐτὸν πρὸ τοῦ
ἀποθανεῖν με."

24. Μὴ ὀργίζεσθε : the Greek translators are at one with the English
here : but a reminder not to quarrel is
hardly in keeping with the magnanim-
ity hitherto displayed by Joseph.  The
Hebrew word is wider than the Greek,
and covers any form of mental disturbance.  Perhaps Joseph is merely wishing his brothers a safe and comfortable
journey.
    27. ἀνεζωπύρησεν : here intransi-
tive ; *revived*.

# INTRODUCTION TO THE STORY OF THE EXODUS

IF the story of Joseph may be viewed as a novel, the story of the
Exodus belongs rather to the romance of history. Both narratives
indeed have their national side. For the story of Joseph accounts
for the Israelites coming into Egypt, while that of the Exodus
accounts for their going out of it. And both also have their personal side. For the story of the Exodus begins with the birth and
upbringing of Moses and in its initial stages pursues merely his
individual adventures. On the picturesqueness of the whole tale it
is needless to dilate. Like Ulysses in beggar's rags, its majesty
shines even through the garb of a literal translation into Alexandrian Greek. Subsequent Jewish imagination has enriched the life
of Moses with additional details tending to the glorification of the
national hero. Thus Josephus (*Ant.* II 9 § 2) introduces a story
similar to that of the Magi and Herod in the First Gospel — how
one of the sacred scribes of the Egyptians had prophesied to Pharaoh
that a child was about to be born among the Hebrews who should
humble the pride of Egypt, and how Pharaoh in consequence issued
the edict that all male children should be put to death. But Moses,
as Livy would say, was 'due to the Fates,' and, though set adrift on
the Nile in his paper-boat, even as Romulus and Remus in their
'floating hull'[1] on the Tiber floods, he could not perish: for he
carried with him the destinies, not so much of a nation as of a religion. Help came to him in the form, not of a she-wolf and of a
shepherd, but of the princess of the land and the daughter of the
oppressor of his people. By her he was educated to become the
saviour of his race.

The name of Pharaoh's daughter, according to Josephus, was
Thermuthis. Her first care was to provide a nurse for the child,
and she tried with him one Egyptian woman after another, but he
rejected the alien milk. Then Miriam, who was standing by, as

---

[1] Liv. I 1 § 6 fluitantem alveum, quo expositi erant pueri.

though a disinterested spectator, made the happy suggestion that the child might perhaps not refuse the breasts of one of his countrywomen, and was accordingly allowed to fetch his mother.

Thermuthis was rewarded for her womanly compassion by the extraordinary beauty and intelligence developed in the child as he grew. People would turn round on the road and even leave their work to look at him. His stature too at the age of three was remarkable. Of all this we know nothing from the Old Testament beyond the hint in Exodus $2^2$, that Moses was a goodly child. But the New Testament tells us that he was ' divinely fair,' adding that he ' was instructed in all the wisdom of the Egyptians ' and that ' he was mighty in his words and works ' (Acts $7^{20, 22}$).

One day Thermuthis in the pride of her heart presented the child to her father, and even asked that he might be appointed heir to the throne. Pharaoh, willing to gratify her, took the infant in his arms and placed the royal crown upon his head, with the result that it was dashed to the ground and trampled under foot by the babe. Then the sacred scribe, horror-stricken at the sight, exclaimed that this was the very child against whom he had already warned the king and insisted that he should be got rid of. But Pharaoh's daughter hurried the boy out of the royal presence, so that he lived to be the hope of the Hebrews.

That Moses when grown up should have commenced his career by manslaughter and have fled in fear of Pharaoh's vengeance was more than Josephus could bring himself to relate to a Gentile audience. So he quietly suppresses this part of the narrative and substitutes an account more gratifying to Jewish feeling.

Egypt was being overrun by an invasion of Ethiopians and was in danger of utter destruction, when the Egyptians in their distress asked advice from God. They were told to call in the aid of 'the Hebrew.' Thereupon Pharaoh asked Thermuthis to let her son act as general. This she did after extracting an oath from the king that he would do no harm to the youth. Moses accordingly assumed the command and at once exhibited his superior intelligence. Had he taken his troops up the river, the enemy would have had notice of his approach; so he marched them overland through a country infested by dangerous reptiles and by those flying serpents, which we know from Herodotus also (II 75, 76) to have been among the marvels of Egypt. Their wings, he says, were like those of bats. Moses however had provided himself with hutches full of ibises, which he opened on reaching the dangerous part of his route; and these pioneers easily cleared a way for his army. Then, falling suddenly upon the Ethiopians, he cooped them up into the royal city of Saba, which Cambyses afterwards called Meroe, after the name of his sister. Built on an island, this city was impregnable owing to its fortifications and dams. But what the war-god could not do was accomplished by the love-goddess. Tharbis, the daughter of the king of the Ethiopians, played the part of Tarpeia.[1] Smitten with passion for the beautiful and brave youth who was attacking her country, she sent secret emissaries to arrange for the betrayal of the city, if only he would promise to marry her. This Moses consented to do and, after destroying the Ethiopians, returned in triumph to Egypt, only however to find that his life was in danger owing to the envy aroused by his success. That was why he had to fly from Egypt, not because, as in the Bible story, his spirit had been roused to wrath at the sight of the oppression of his countrymen.

Josephus however does not fail to record the gallantry with which Moses rescued the distressed maidens at the well, and how he was in consequence rewarded by the priest of Midian with the hand of one of his daughters.

It will now be instructive to take a glance at the history of Moses as presented from an alien, though not hostile, source. Artapanus, whose name suggests a Persian origin, though his ideas are Greek, was used by Alexander Polyhistor, a contemporary of Sulla, as one of his authorities on the history of the Jews. According to this author, Merrhis, the daughter of King Palmanothes, being wedded by her father to Chenephres, king of the part of Egypt above Memphis (for at that time there were several kingdoms in Egypt), but having no children by him, adopted as her son a Jewish infant, to whom she gave the name Moÿsos. This was he, who, when he grew to man's estate, was known to the Greeks as Musæus, the teacher of Orpheus, while among the Egyptians themselves he was called Hermes, because he taught the priests the sacred writing. He was the author of many inventions both for the benefit of Egypt and for

---

[1] Is the resemblance of name more than accidental?

the behoof of mankind, and it was he who sanctified cats and dogs and ibises.   He was animated by a single-hearted desire to secure Chenephres on his throne, which was then exposed to mob-violence. Nevertheless his adoptive father looked upon him with suspicion and availed himself of an Ethiopic invasion as a seemly pretext for getting rid of him.   He therefore put Moÿsos at the head of a rustic army of some 100,000 of his countrymen, acting apparently on the Roman principle with regard to the Jews that, if they perished, it was vile damnum.   Moÿsos however and his followers carried on the war successfully for ten years, during which they had time to build the city of Hermopolis, where they consecrated the ibis; and Moÿsos himself so won the esteem even of his enemies, the Ethiopians, that they adopted from him the practice of circumcision.   When the war at last came to a close, Moÿsos received but a cold welcome from Chenephres.   His troops were partly despatched to the Egyptian frontier to keep guard and partly employed in replacing a brick temple in Diospolis by one of stone.   As for Moÿsos himself, Chenephres charged one Chanethoth with the task of getting rid of him. To this end, when Merrhis died, Chanethoth was sent along with Moÿsos to bury her beyond the borders of Egypt.   Being warned however of the plot against his life, Moÿsos contrived to bury Merrhis safely in an island-city, to which he gave the name of Meroe.   Then by the advice of his brother Aaron he fled to Arabia, managing on the way to kill Chanethoth, who had laid an ambush against him.   In Arabia he married the daughter of Raguel, the king of those parts.   His father-in-law wished to march against Egypt and secure the crown for his daughter and her husband : but Moÿsos dissuaded him from this purpose out of regard for his countrymen, who were in Pharaoh's power.

Shortly after this King Chenephres died of elephantiasis, being the first to be smitten with this disease, which was a judgement upon him owing to his having compelled the Jews to distinguish themselves by wearing muslin instead of woollen garments.   Moÿsos prayed to God that the oppression of his people might cease, whereupon a mysterious fire was seen burning from the ground, though there was no bush or timber of any sort in the place.   Fleeing at first in alarm, Moÿsos was arrested by a divine voice which bade him march against Egypt and conduct his people to their ancient fatherland. Encouraged hereby Moÿsos resolved to fulfil the divine command. First however he went to Egypt to see his brother Aaron, whereupon the new king of Egypt asked him his business and, on receiving the reply that the Lord of the World had sent him to release the Jews, promptly put him into prison. But at night all the doors of the prison-house opened of their own accord; some of the guards died, others were overmastered by sleep, while the weapons of all were broken. Then Moÿsos went forth to the palace, where he found the gates open and the guards disabled, so that he could go in and waken the king, who asked him the name of the God on whose service he came. Into the ear of the still jeering monarch Moÿsos whispered the awful syllables, on hearing which the king fell speechless to the ground, and so remained until Moÿsos himself recalled him to life. So powerful was this name that a priest, who spoke slightingly of a tablet on which Moÿsos had written it, died immediately of convulsions. In spite of his recent experience the king still asked for a sign. Then Moÿsos flung down his rod, which turned into a serpent, and, as all shrank back from the hissing reptile, he took hold of it by the tail, when it again became a rod. Next he smote the Nile with his rod, whereupon it turned all colours [1] and overflowed the whole of Egypt. Then, as it went down, its waters stank, the fishes died, and the people were perishing of thirst, when the king promised to let the Israelites go in a month, if Moÿsos would restore the river to its natural condition. Moÿsos, agreeing, struck the water with his rod and all was well. Then the king summoned the priests from beyond Memphis, threatening them with death and their temples with destruction, if they could not muster magic enough to cope with Moÿsos. Under this stimulus the priests succeeded in producing a serpent and changing the colour of the river, which so elated the king that he redoubled his oppression of the Jews. Then followed plague on plague. A blow of Moÿsos' rod upon the earth brought forth winged creatures that hurt the Egyptians, so that their bodies were a mass of ulcers; then came frogs, locusts, and sand-flies. As the king had not yet learnt wisdom, Moÿsos brought on hail and earthquakes during the night, so that those who escaped the earthquakes perished by the hail, while those who avoided the hail were destroyed by the earth-

[1] Reading conjecturally πολύχρουν for πολύχουν.

quakes. At that time all the houses and most of the temples collapsed. This last lesson was effectual. The king let the people go; and they, having borrowed cups and raiment and all kinds of treasure, crossed the rivers on the side towards Arabia and came in three days to the Red Sea. There, so said the people of Memphis, Moÿsos, being acquainted with the country, waited for the ebb-tide and brought the multitude across on dry land. But the Heliopolitans add to the story that the king with a great force, accompanied by the sacred animals, came in pursuit of the Israelites, because they were carrying away the property of the Egyptians. Then a divine voice told Moÿsos to strike the sea with his rod, which being done, the floods parted, and the force went over on dry land. The Egyptians, having plunged in after it, were met by a flashing fire in front, while behind them the sea closed over their road, so that they all perished. The Jews, thus miraculously released from danger, spent thirty years in the wilderness, during which they were fed on a kind of meal resembling millet and in colour as white as snow, which God rained on them from heaven.

Artapanus adds a description of Moÿsos as being tall and of a ruddy hue, with long grey hair and a dignified appearance. The above exploits, he adds, were accomplished by Moÿsos when he was about eighty-nine years old.

The preceding narrative, which has been preserved by Eusebius (*Præparatio Evangelica* IX 27), is interesting both in its resemblance to and its difference from the Bible story. It seems hardly to have received as much attention as it deserves. Among other things it shows that Josephus' story of the war between Moses and the Ethiopians was at all events not invented by himself. The Heliopolitan tradition too about the destruction of Pharaoh's host is in accordance with Manetho's statement that Moses was a priest of Heliopolis. This brings us from Jewish or neutral sources to the representations of declared enemies.

Manetho, the historian of Egypt, gives the current tradition of the Egyptians with regard to the Exodus as follows.

An Egyptian king, named Amenophis, was desirous of seeing the Gods, as his predecessor Orus had done. So he consulted with a prophet who was a namesake of his own, Amenophis, the son of

Papis,[1] and was told that he would be able to see the Gods, if he cleared the land of lepers and other polluted persons. The king went gladly about the task and had soon a collection of 80,000 physically undesirable individuals, whom he sent to work in the quarries to the east of the Nile. Unfortunately there were among them some learned priests who suffered from leprosy. The prophet hereupon feared the vengeance of the Gods upon himself and the king: but, not daring to tell the king so by word of mouth, he wrote a prophecy that the polluted ones would get help from somewhere and be masters of Egypt for thirteen years; which done, he put an end to himself, leaving the king in great despondency. After some time the king, in answer to a petition from the polluted ones, granted them the city of Avaris, which had been left empty by the Shepherds, who had been driven out of Egypt more than five centuries before. Here they established themselves under the leadership of Osarsiph, a priest of Heliopolis, who now changed his name to Moses, and taught them to contravene the religion of Egypt, to sacrifice sacred animals, and forswear communion with strangers. This Moses sent an embassy to the Shepherds, who, after being driven out of Egypt, had established themselves in Jerusalem, promising to restore to them their ancestral city of Avaris and help them in regaining possession of Egypt. Two hundred thousand of them came at his summons, and Amenophis, fearing to fight against God, took refuge in Ethiopia, whose king was friendly to him, where he stayed during the thirteen years of his predestined banishment; after which he and his son Sethon or Ramesses, now grown to manhood, returned and expelled the invaders and the polluted ones, who are described as having used the images of the Gods for fuel to roast the sacred animals, which they compelled the priests and prophets to slaughter. This last touch is so like what the Jews would have been glad to do, that, if not true, it is well invented. (Josephus *Against Apion* I 26–31.)

Manetho was a writer of great authority who lived under the first Ptolemy. A later writer of Egyptian history, Chæremon, who lived in the early years of the Christian era, tells the tale somewhat differently. King Amenophis was frightened by the appearance of

---

[1] On the Egyptian monuments there is mention of a king Amen-hetep III, and of a priest of the same name, the son of Ḥāp. Budge, Vol. IV, p. 110.

Isis to him in a dream, and a sacred scribe Phritiphantes told him
that, if he purged Egypt of polluted persons, he would no longer be
liable to perturbation.   Accordingly he expelled no less than a quarter of a million of people.   These, under the leadership of Moses
and Joseph, whose names in Egyptian were Tisithen and Peteseph,
came to Pelusium, where they met a body of 380,000, who had been
left there for some unexplained reason by Amenophis.   Making
common cause with one another, the two hosts invaded Egypt.
Amenophis fled to Ethiopia in such a hurry that he left his wife
behind him.   She gave birth in a cave to a son named Ramesses,[1]
who, when grown up, chased 'the Jews' into Syria and restored his
father Amenophis.

Another Greek author, named Lysimachus, departs more widely
from Manetho.   He puts the date much earlier under a king named
Bocchoris.   The land at that time was suffering from sterility, and
the king, on consulting the oracle of Ammon, was told that he must
clear the country of the impure and impious beggars known as the
people of the Jews, who clustered round the temples seeking food;
those that suffered from leprosy and scab were to be drowned and
the rest to be driven into the desert; then, when the temples had
been purified, the land would bring forth its fruits.   The command
of the oracle was obeyed.   The leprous and scabby mendicants had
sheets of lead attached to them and were consigned to the depths of
the sea; the rest were left to perish in the desert.   To them, thus
abandoned by gods and men, one Moses offered the following advice
— to march straight on at all hazards till they came to an inhabited
country, to show no kindness to any man, nor give good advice to
others, but only bad, and to overthrow the temples and altars of the
gods wherever they came across them.   Adhering faithfully to these
principles the refuse of Egypt established themselves in Palestine,
where they called their city Ἱερόσυλα (Sacrilege), but afterwards
changed it into Ἱεροσόλυμα.   (Josephus Against Apion I § 34, p. 466.)
Josephus, who had the advantage of having learnt another language
than his own, is easily able to dispose of this piece of popular ety-
mology, as well as of another for which Apion is responsible,
namely, that the Egyptian exiles, having reached Judæa in six days,

[1] The Tauchnitz text has here (Against Apion I 32) Μεσσήνην, but, as the
son has already been called Ramesses, the error is obvious.

were laid up with buboes on the seventh, whence it was called the sabbath, because *sabbo* was the Egyptian for a bubo. (Josephus *Against Apion* II § 2, p. 470.)

The account of the Exodus given by Tacitus is an echo of the hatred of the Alexandrian Greek for the Jew. Lysimachus is the author whom the Roman historian is following, as will be plain to the student who compares V 3 and 4 of the *Histories* with the account from Lysimachus above given. Tacitus adds that the way in which Moses discovered water for his thirsty host was by following a herd of wild asses.

Justinus, or rather the Augustan writer Trogus Pompeius, whom he is epitomising, is not quite so one-sided. He shows an acquaintance with the story of Joseph and with the tradition of the beauty of Moses, whom he represents as the son of Joseph. But he agrees with the Egyptian version in saying that, when those who were suffering from scab and tetter were expelled from Egypt in compliance with an oracle, Moses was expelled with them and became their leader. He adds that Moses stole the sacred things of the Egyptians and that the Egyptians, who endeavoured to recover them by arms, were forced back by storms. The geography of this author however is perplexing. Moses, he says, after seven days' march without food through the desert, having reached Damascena, the home of his fathers, where Abrahames and Israhel had been kings, occupied Mount Sina, and there dedicated the Sabbath as a fast for all time. The exclusive habits of the Jews he explains as due to their having been originally shunned as plague-stricken (XXXVI 2).

The merely literary point of view from which we are treating the Septuagint relieves us from any obligation to speculate on the amount of historic truth underlying the story of the Exodus. We could wish that it exempted us also from the task of examining the internal consistency of the tale. But a few words must be said on this subject before we close.

To begin with, how could two midwives (Ex. 1$^{15}$) suffice for a population in which the males alone numbered over half a million (Ex. 12$^{37}$: Jos. *Ant.* II 9 § 3)?

Again, where did the Israelites live? Was it apart in Goshen? Or mixed up with their oppressors in Egypt? The narrative, as we have it, sometimes puts the matter one way and sometimes

another.   Ex. 8$^{22}$ and 9$^{26}$, for instance, tell us that in the land of
Goshen, where the children of Israel were, there were no flies and
no hail; but on the other hand the marking of the houses of the
Israelites with blood (Ex. 12$^{22, 23}$) and their borrowing jewels of
their neighbours (Ex. 12$^{35}$) implies that they were living in the
midst of the Egyptians.

Thirdly, how is it that after Moses has solemnly told Pharaoh 'I
will see thy face again no more' (10$^{29}$), he does see him again in the
next chapter (11$^{8}$)?

These and the like difficulties seem to find their easiest solution
in the assumption of a mixture of sources.   The theory is that E
represents the Israelites as a comparatively small body of people
living in Egypt itself, while J represents them as very numerous and
dwelling apart in Goshen.   The account of the institution of the
Passover is referred to the priestly document P.

The supernatural elements in the Story of the Exodus centre
round the rod of Moses.   We are reminded of this magic rod, which
earth and sea obey, when we read in the Egyptian tale of 'The Taking of Joppa' of 'the great cane of King Men-kheper-ra . . . to
whom Amen his father gives power and strength.'   Just as the
New Testament knows more about the childhood of Moses than the
Old, so it knows more about Pharaoh's sorcerers.   We learn from
ii Tim. 3$^{8}$ that their names were Jannes and Jambres.   This
information is confirmed by a Neo-Platonist philosopher named
Numenius, who is supposed to have lived in the age of the Antonines.
He says that these were the names of the sacred scribes who were
put forward by the Egyptian people to oppose Musæus, the leader of
the Jews, 'a man who was most powerful in prayer to God,' and
that they were able to dispel some of the most grievous of the calam-
ities which he was bringing upon Egypt (Eus. *Pr. Ev.* IX 8).   The
name of one of these sorcerers was known to the Pagan world still
earlier: for Pliny the elder speaks of a school of magic many thou-
sands of years after Zoroaster, which depended on Moses and Jannes
and Lotapes and the Jews.[1]

Josephus tells the story of the passage of the Red Sea, but hardly

---

[1] Est et alia magices factio a Mose et Janne et Lotape ac Ju-
daeis pendens, sed multis millibus annorum post Zoroastrem.
Plin. *N.H.* XXX 11, Detlefsen.

expects it to be believed by his Pagan readers.  He cites the account, agreed upon, he assures us, by all the historians of Alexander, of how the Pamphylian Sea made way for the march of that monarch, when it was the will of God that he should destroy the Empire of Persia.  It is worth noticing in this connexion that the Euphrates is recorded to have yielded a passage on foot to the army of the younger Cyrus, when it was not the will of God that he should possess himself of the Persian throne (Xen. *Anab.* I 4 § 18).

In Roman history too there is an incident which reminds us of the passage of the Red Sea.  For Livy (XXVI 47) records how the elder Africanus was enabled to take New Carthage owing to the combination of a low tide with a strong north wind, and how he encouraged his soldiers on that occasion by an appeal to their religious feelings — 'Neptune was opening a new way to the armies of the Roman people : let them follow the God ! '

## II. THE STORY OF THE EXODUS

8Ἀνέστη δὲ βασιλεὺς ἕτερος ἐπ᾽ Αἴγυπτον, ὃς οὐκ ᾔδει τὸν Ἰωσήφ. 9εἶπεν δὲ τῷ ἔθνει αὐτοῦ " Ἰδοὺ τὸ γένος τῶν υἱῶν Ἰσραὴλ μέγα πλῆθος, καὶ ἰσχύει ὑπὲρ ἡμᾶς · 10δεῦτε οὖν κατασοφισώμεθα αὐτούς, μή ποτε πληθυνθῇ, καὶ ἡνίκα ἂν συμβῇ ἡμῖν πόλεμος προστεθήσονται καὶ οὗτοι πρὸς τοὺς ὑπεναντίους, καὶ ἐκπολεμήσαντες ἡμᾶς ἐξελεύσονται ἐκ τῆς γῆς." 11καὶ ἐπέστησεν αὐτοῖς ἐπιστάτας τῶν ἔργων, ἵνα κακώσωσιν αὐτοὺς ἐν τοῖς ἔργοις · καὶ ᾠκοδόμησαν πόλεις ὀχυρὰς τῷ Φαραώ, τήν τε Πειθὼ καὶ Ῥαμεσσὴ καὶ Ὤν, ἥ ἐστιν Ἡλίου πόλις. 12καθότι δὲ αὐτοὺς ἐταπείνουν, τοσούτῳ πλείους ἐγίνοντο, καὶ ἴσχυον σφόδρα σφόδρα · καὶ ἐβδελύσσοντο οἱ Αἰγύπτιοι ἀπὸ τῶν υἱῶν Ἰσραήλ. 13καὶ κατεδυνάστευον οἱ Αἰγύπτιοι τοὺς υἱοὺς Ἰσραὴλ βίᾳ, 14καὶ κατωδύνων αὐτῶν τὴν ζωὴν ἐν τοῖς ἔργοις τοῖς σκληροῖς, τῷ πηλῷ καὶ

8. βασιλεὺς ἕτερος : generally identified with Rameses II on the evidence óf v. 11.

9. ὑπὲρ ἡμᾶς : § 94.

10. κατασοφισώμεθα αὐτούς : *let us outwit them* (since we cannot overcome them by strength). *Cp.* Judith 5¹¹, 10¹⁹ : Acts 7¹⁹. — πληθυνθῇ : sc. τὸ γένος : but in the next verb the plural subject is resumed. — προστεθήσονται : the indicative expresses the certainty of the consequence in the assumed case.

11. ἐπέστησεν . . . ἵνα κακώσωσιν :. § 75. The verb corresponding to ἐπέστησεν in our Hebrew text has the plural affix ; in that of the LXX we may in-

fer that it had not. — Πειθὼ καὶ Ῥαμεσσή : Pithom and Raamses. — καὶ Ὤν κτλ. : an addition of the LXX. In Gen. 41⁴⁵, ⁴⁸ we find Heliopolis already in existence. Indeed according to Budge (*History of Egypt* II 67) there is evidence that this ' City of the Sun-God ' was in existence as early as the Vth Dynasty of Egyptian kings, *i.e.* about B.C. 3500.

12. σφόδρα σφόδρα : § 85 — ἐβδελύσσοντο . . . ἀπό : § 98.

14. κατωδύνων : imperfect of κατοδυνᾶν, *to afflict grievously*. The passive of the same verb is used in Ezk. 9⁴ and in Tobit. — πηλῷ : *mortar. Cp.* Gen.

Exodus I 20

τῇ πλινθίᾳ καὶ πᾶσι τοῖς ἔργοις τοῖς ἐν τοῖς πεδίοις, κατὰ πάντα τὰ ἔργα ὧν κατεδουλοῦντο αὐτοὺς μετὰ βίας. ¹⁵Καὶ εἶπεν ὁ βασιλεὺς τῶν Αἰγυπτίων ταῖς μαίαις τῶν Ἑβραίων, τῇ μιᾷ αὐτῶν ᾗ ὄνομα Σεπφωρά, καὶ τὸ ὄνομα τῆς δευτέρας Φουά · ¹⁶καὶ εἶπεν "Ὅταν μαιοῦσθε τὰς Ἑβραίας καὶ ὦσιν πρὸς τῷ τίκτειν, ἐὰν μὲν ἄρσεν ᾖ, ἀποκτείνατε αὐτό · ἐὰν δὲ θῆλυ, περιποιεῖσθε αὐτό." ¹⁷ἐφοβήθησαν δὲ αἱ μαῖαι τὸν θεόν, καὶ οὐκ ἐποίησαν καθότι συνέταξεν αὐταῖς ὁ βασιλεὺς Αἰγύπτου, καὶ ἐζωογόνουν τὰ ἄρσενα. ¹⁸ἐκάλεσεν δὲ ὁ βασιλεὺς Αἰγύπτου τὰς μαίας καὶ εἶπεν αὐταῖς "Τί ὅτι ἐποιήσατε τὸ πρᾶγμα τοῦτο καὶ ἐζωογονεῖτε τὰ ἄρσενα;" ¹⁹εἶπαν δὲ αἱ μαῖαι τῷ Φαραώ "Οὐχ ὡς γυναῖκες Αἰγύπτου αἱ Ἑβραῖαι, τίκτουσιν γὰρ πρὶν ἢ εἰσελθεῖν πρὸς αὐτὰς τὰς μαίας, καὶ ἔτικτον." ²⁰εὖ δὲ ἐποίει ὁ θεὸς ταῖς μαίαις, καὶ

11³.—πλινθίᾳ : = πλινθεία, brick-making. § 37. — ὧν κατεδουλοῦντο : to which they enslaved them.

15. μαίαις : in LXX only in this chapter and in Gen. 35¹⁷, 38²⁸. It is used in Eur. Alc. 393 as a child's word for 'mother.' In Plat. Theæt. 149 A it is used as here for a midwife. Does μαῖα stand to the μη- in μήτηρ as γαῖα to γῆ? — Σεπφωρά : the LXX makes the name of this midwife the same as that of the wife of Moses (2²¹), but in the Hebrew they are different. — καὶ τὸ ὄνομα κτλ. : had the construction been continued regularly, this would have been καὶ τῇ δευτέρᾳ ᾗ ὄνομα Φουά.

16. μαιοῦσθε : § 106. — Ἑβραίας : apparently 'Hebrews' was the name by which Jews were known to foreigners, and 'children of Israel' that by which they called themselves at home. Hence the name Hebrews

comes to the front in the account of their relations with the Egyptians. — ἐὰν μέν . . . ἐὰν δέ : § 39.

17. ἐζωογόνουν : preserved alive. Cp. Jdg. 8¹⁹ : i K. 2⁶ Κύριος θανατοῖ καὶ ζωογονεῖ, 27⁹, ¹¹ : iii K. 21³¹ : iv K. 7⁴. So in N.T. Lk. 17³³, Acts 7¹⁹, i Tim. 6¹³. The word appears to be used in its natural sense of producing young alive in Lev. 11⁴⁷. Cp. the use of ζωοποιεῖν in Jdg. 21¹⁴.

19. καὶ ἔτικτον : these words seem to arise out of a misapprehension of the Hebrew text, which, as we have it, runs literally thus — 'for they are lively ; not yet came the midwife to them and they brought forth.' The word rendered 'they are lively' having been taken by the Greek translator as a verb (τίκτουσιν), no meaning was left for the verb at the end.

20. ταῖς μαίαις : in Attic Greek this

ἐπλήθυνεν ὁ λαὸς καὶ ἴσχυεν σφόδρα. ²¹ἐπειδὴ ἐφοβοῦντο αἱ μαῖαι τὸν θεόν, ἐποίησαν ἑαυταῖς οἰκίας· ²²Συνέταξεν δὲ Φαραὼ παντὶ τῷ λαῷ αὐτοῦ λέγων "Πᾶν ἄρσεν ὃ ἐὰν τεχθῇ τοῖς Ἑβραίοις εἰς τὸν ποταμὸν ῥίψατε, καὶ πᾶν θῆλυ, ζωογονεῖτε αὐτό."

¹ʼΗν δέ τις ἐκ τῆς φυλῆς Λευεὶ ὃς ἔλαβεν τῶν θυγατέρων Λευεί. ²καὶ ἐν γαστρὶ ἔλαβεν καὶ ἔτεκεν ἄρσεν· ἰδόντες δὲ αὐτὸ ἀστεῖον ἐσκέπασαν αὐτὸ μῆνας τρεῖς. ³ἐπεὶ δὲ οὐκ ἠδύναντο αὐτὸ ἔτι κρύπτειν, ἔλαβεν αὐτῷ ἡ μήτηρ αὐτοῦ θῖβιν καὶ κα-έχρισεν αὐτὴν ἀσφαλτοπίσσῃ καὶ ἐνέβαλεν τὸ παιδίον εἰς αὐτήν, καὶ ἔθηκεν αὐτὴν εἰς τὸ ἕλος παρὰ τὸν ποταμόν. ⁴καὶ κατεσκόπευεν ἡ ἀδελφὴ αὐτοῦ μακρόθεν μαθεῖν τί τὸ ἀποβησόμενον αὐτῷ. ⁵κατέβη δὲ ἡ θυγάτηρ Φαραὼ λούσασθαι ἐπὶ τὸν ποταμόν, καὶ αἱ ἅβραι αὐτῆς

---

would be τὰς μαίας.— ἐπλήθυνεν : intransitive = ἐπλήθυνεν.

**21. ἐποίησαν ἑαυταῖς οἰκίας :** the Hebrew is 'He made for them houses,' *i.e.* gave them descendants. Does this imply that in the time of the writer there were Jews who claimed to be descended from these two midwives? If so, the fact had been forgotten later, for Josephus (*Ant.* II 9 § 2) expressly says that the midwives were Egyptians.

**2. ἰδόντες, ἐσκέπασαν :** Hebrew, 'she saw, she hid.' — ἀστεῖον : *a pretty child.* Cp. Acts 7²⁰ : Judith 11²³ Ἀστεία εἶ σὺ ἐν τῷ εἴδει σου : Sus. Ο′ 7. Ἀστεῖος (*urbanus*) with its opposite ἄγροικος (*agrestis*) recalls the contempt of the town for the country. The meaning of the word was deepened by the Stoics, who used it in the same sense as Aristotle uses σπουδαῖος. In Jdg. 3¹⁷ ἀστεῖος is used where the

Hebrew has 'fat' : Nb. 22³² οὐκ ἀστεία ἡ ὁδός σου : ii Mac. 6²³ ὁ δὲ λογισμὸν ἀστεῖον ἀναλαβών. In ii Mac. 12⁴³ we have the adverb ἀστείως. These are all the occurrences of the word in the LXX.

**3. οὐκ ἠδύναντο :** Hebrew, 'she could not.' — θῖβιν : the Hebrew word, which is here transliterated by θῖβιν, is the same which is used of Noah's ark in Gen. 6¹⁴ and which is there rendered κιβωτός. Jos. *Ant.* II 9 § 4 μηχανῶνται πλέγμα τι βύβλινον ἐμφερὲς τῇ κατασκευῇ κοιτίδι (*made like a cradle*).

**4. ἡ ἀδελφή :** Jos. *Ant.* II 9 § 4 Μαριάμμη.

**5. ἅβραι :** *maidens.* Cp. Gen. 24⁶¹. The word occurs also in the LXX, in Judith and Esther, and is found in the fragments of Menander. The accent is against supposing a connexion with ἁβρός, and the word seems to be an importation into Greek perhaps

παρεπορεύοντο παρὰ τὸν ποταμόν · καὶ ἰδοῦσα τὴν θῖβιν ἐν τῷ ἕλει, ἀποστείλασα τὴν ἅβραν ἀνείλατο αὐτήν. ⁶ἀνοίξασα δὲ ὁρᾷ παιδίον κλαῖον ἐν τῇ θίβει · καὶ ἐφείσατο αὐτοῦ ἡ θυγάτηρ Φαραώ, καὶ ἔφη " Ἀπὸ τῶν παιδίων τῶν Ἑβραίων τοῦτο." ⁷καὶ εἶπεν ἡ ἀδελφὴ αὐτοῦ τῇ θυγατρὶ Φαραώ " Θέλεις καλέσω σοι γυναῖκα τροφεύουσαν ἐκ τῶν Ἑβραίων, καὶ θηλάσει σοι τὸ παιδίον ;" ⁸ἡ δὲ εἶπεν ἡ θυγάτηρ Φαραώ " Πορεύου." ἐλθοῦσα δὲ ἡ νεᾶνις ἐκάλεσεν τὴν μητέρα τοῦ παιδίου. ⁹εἶπεν δὲ πρὸς αὐτὴν ἡ θυγάτηρ Φαραώ " Διατήρησόν μοι τὸ παιδίον τοῦτο καὶ θήλασόν μοι αὐτό, ἐγὼ δὲ δώσω σοι τὸν μισθόν." ἔλαβεν δὲ ἡ γυνὴ τὸ παιδίον καὶ ἐθήλαζεν αὐτό. ¹⁰ἁδρυνθέντος δὲ τοῦ παιδίου, εἰσήγαγεν αὐτὸ πρὸς τὴν θυγατέρα Φαραώ, καὶ ἐγενήθη αὐτῇ εἰς υἱόν · ἐπωνόμασεν δὲ τὸ ὄνομα αὐτοῦ Μωυσῆν λέγουσα " Ἐκ τοῦ

from a Chaldee word meaning ' female companion.' The Hebrew word which ἅβραι here represents means 'young women,' and is supposed to have given rise to the name Neæra, but that which underlies ἅβραν at the end of the verse is different. — ἀνείλατο : cp. 10. Ἀναιρεῖν like *tollere* means both ' to take up ' and ' to destroy.' Here it has the former and original sense.

6. ἐφείσατο αὐτοῦ : literally *spared him.* Here *pitied him.*

7. γυναῖκα τροφεύουσαν : a *wet-nurse.* Philo II 83, *Vit. Mos.* § 4 προφάσει τοῦ ἐπὶ μισθῷ τροφεύσειν.

8. ἡ δὲ . . . ἡ θυγάτηρ Φαραώ : the construction seems modelled on such phrases as ἦ δ᾽ ὃς ὁ Γλαύκων. It is not warranted by the Hebrew. — νεᾶνις : in classical writers mostly poetic, as Soph. *Ant.* 784.

10. ἁδρυνθέντος : cp. Jdg. 13²⁴. The word occurs eight times in the LXX,

always in connexion with the growth of children, except in Ps. 143¹¹, where it refers, directly at least, to plants. On the construction see § 58. — ἐγενήθη αὐτῇ εἰς υἱόν : Hebraism, § 90. — Μωυσῆν λέγουσα κτλ. : the derivation here suggested is based on a superficial resemblance of the Hebrew name *Mosheh* to the verb *mashah, to draw out.* Josephus makes the name Egyptian, which is more consistent with its being given by Pharaoh's daughter — *Ant.* II 9 § 6 τὸ γὰρ ὕδωρ μῶ οἱ Αἰγύπτιοι καλοῦσιν, ὑσῆς δὲ τοὺς ἐξ ὕδατος σωθέντας : in another passage (*Against Apion* I 31) he tells us — τὸ γὰρ ὕδωρ οἱ Αἰγύπτιοι μῶ καλοῦσιν. Renan (*Hist. Peuple d'Israel* I 159) agrees with Josephus in regarding the word as Egyptian, but thinks that it contains the syllable *mos* ( = son) found in such forms as *Thoutmos* ( = son of Tehuti or Θώθ), Amenmos, *etc.*

ὕδατος αὐτὸν ἀνειλόμην." ¹¹Ἐγένετο δὲ ἐν ταῖς ἡμέραις
ταῖς πολλαῖς ἐκείναις μέγας γενόμενος Μωυσῆς ἐξῆλθεν
πρὸς τοὺς ἀδελφοὺς αὐτοῦ τοὺς υἱοὺς Ἰσραήλ. κατανοήσας
δὲ τὸν πόνον αὐτῶν ὁρᾷ ἄνθρωπον Αἰγύπτιον τύπτοντά τινα
Ἐβραῖον τῶν ἑαυτοῦ ἀδελφῶν τῶν υἱῶν Ἰσραήλ · ¹²περιβλε-
ψάμενος δὲ ὧδε καὶ ὧδε οὐχ ὁρᾷ οὐδένα, καὶ πατάξας τὸν Αἰγύπτιον ἔκρυψεν αὐτὸν ἐν τῇ ἄμμῳ. ¹³ἐξελθὼν δὲ τῇ ἡμέρᾳ
τῇ δευτέρᾳ ὁρᾷ δύο ἄνδρας Ἐβραίους διαπληκτιζομένους,
καὶ λέγει τῷ ἀδικοῦντι " Διὰ τί σὺ τύπτεις τὸν πλησίον; "
¹⁴ὁ δὲ εἶπεν " Τίς σε κατέστησεν ἄρχοντα καὶ δικαστὴν ἐφ'
ἡμῶν ; μὴ ἀνελεῖν με σὺ θέλεις ὃν τρόπον ἀνεῖλες ἐχθὲς
τὸν Αἰγύπτιον; " ἐφοβήθη δὲ Μωυσῆς καὶ εἶπεν " Εἰ οὕτως
ἐμφανὲς γέγονεν τὸ ῥῆμα τοῦτο; " ¹⁵ἤκουσεν δὲ Φαραὼ τὸ
ῥῆμα τοῦτο, καὶ ἐζήτει ἀνελεῖν Μωυσῆν · ἀνεχώρησεν δὲ
Μωυσῆς ἀπὸ προσώπου Φαραὼ καὶ ᾤκησεν ἐν γῇ Μαδιάμ ·
ἐλθὼν δὲ εἰς γῆς Μαδιὰμ ἐκάθισεν ἐπὶ τοῦ φρέατος. ¹⁶τῷ
δὲ ἱερεῖ Μαδιὰμ ἦσαν ἑπτὰ θυγατέρες, ποιμαίνουσαι τὰ
πρόβατα τοῦ πατρὸς αὐτῶν Ἰοθόρ · παραγενόμεναι δὲ
ἤντλουν ἕως ἔπλησαν τὰς δεξαμενάς, ποτίσαι τὰ πρόβατα

11. ἐν ταῖς ἡμέραις ταῖς πολλαῖς
ἐκείναις : "a long time after that."
Cp. 23, 4¹⁸. The Hebrew here has only
'in those days.' Acts 7²³ ὡς δὲ ἐπλη-
ροῦτο αὐτῷ τεσσαρακονταέτης χρόνος.
12. ὧδε καὶ ὧδε : this way and that.
13. διαπληκτιζομένους : only here
in LXX.
14. Εἰ οὕτως κτλ. : Has this thing
become thus known? Hebrew, 'Certainly the thing is known.' On εἰ interrogative see § 100, and on ῥῆμα
39⁹ n.
15. ἐν γῇ Μαδιάμ : Gen. 37²⁸ n.
Josephus calls the country ἡ Τρωγλοδῦτις
(Ant. II 9 § 3) and the inhabitants οἱ
Τρωγλοδύται (II 11 § 2). The Midian-

ites were the descendants of Abraham
by Keturah.
16. ποιμαίνουσαι ... Ἰοθόρ : added
in LXX, as is also the name Ἰοθόρ
(= Jethro) at the end of the verse.
The name Jethro (Hb. Yithro) does
not occur in the Hebrew until 3¹, where
the LXX again has Ἰοθόρ. The form
Jethro comes from the Vulgate. —
δεξαμενάς : cisterns. Plat. Crit. 117 A :
Philo I 647, De Somn. I § 29. The
accent shows that it is not used as a
participle. But Plat. Tim. 57 C uses ἡ
δεχομένη convertibly with ἡ δεξαμένη
(53 A) for 'a receptacle.' There is a
Nereid called Δεξαμένη mentioned in
Hom. Il. XVIII 44.

τοῦ πατρὸς αὐτῶν Ἰοθόρ. ¹⁷παραγενόμενοι δὲ οἱ ποιμένες ἐξέβαλλον αὐτάς· ἀναστὰς δὲ Μωυσῆς ἐρρύσατο αὐτάς, καὶ ἤντλησεν αὐταῖς καὶ ἐπότισεν τὰ πρόβατα αὐτῶν. ¹⁸παρεγένοντο δὲ πρὸς Ῥαγουὴλ τὸν πατέρα αὐτῶν· ὁ δὲ εἶπεν αὐταῖς "Διὰ τί ἐταχύνατε τοῦ παραγενέσθαι σήμερον;" ¹⁹αἱ δὲ εἶπαν "Ἄνθρωπος Αἰγύπτιος ἐρρύσατο ἡμᾶς ἀπὸ τῶν ποιμένων, καὶ ἤντλησεν ἡμῖν καὶ ἐπότισεν τὰ πρόβατα ἡμῶν." ²⁰ὁ δὲ εἶπεν ταῖς θυγατράσιν αὐτοῦ "Καὶ ποῦ ἐστι; καὶ ἵνα τί καταλελοίπατε τὸν ἄνθρωπον; καλέσατε οὖν αὐτὸν ὅπως φάγῃ ἄρτον." ²¹κατῳκίσθη δὲ Μωυσῆς παρὰ τῷ ἀνθρώπῳ· καὶ ἐξέδοτο Σεπφώραν τὴν θυγατέρα αὐτοῦ Μωυσῇ γυναῖκα. ²²ἐν γαστρὶ δὲ λαβοῦσα ἡ γυνὴ ἔτεκεν υἱόν· καὶ ἐπωνόμασεν Μωυσῆς τὸ ὄνομα αὐτοῦ Γηρσάμ, λέγων "Ὅτι πάροικός εἰμι ἐν γῇ ἀλλοτρίᾳ."

²³Μετὰ δὲ τὰς ἡμέρας τὰς πολλὰς ἐκείνας ἐτελεύτησεν ὁ βασιλεὺς Αἰγύπτου· καὶ κατεστέναξαν οἱ υἱοὶ Ἰσραὴλ ἀπὸ τῶν ἔργων καὶ ἀνεβόησαν, καὶ ἀνέβη ἡ βοὴ αὐτῶν πρὸς τὸν θεὸν ἀπὸ τῶν ἔργων. ²⁴καὶ εἰσήκουσεν ὁ θεὸς τὸν στεναγμὸν αὐτῶν, καὶ ἐμνήσθη ὁ θεὸς τῆς διαθήκης αὐτοῦ τῆς πρὸς Ἀβραὰμ καὶ Ἰσαὰκ καὶ Ἰακώβ. ²⁵καὶ ἔπιδεν ὁ θεὸς τοὺς υἱοὺς Ἰσραήλ, καὶ ἐγνώσθη αὐτοῖς.

---

18. Ῥαγουήλ : the father-in-law of Moses is called by many names : Hebrew Reʻuel, LXX Ῥαγουήλ, Jos. (*Ant.* II 11 § 2) Ῥαγούηλος, Vulgate Raguel, English Reuel (Ex. 2¹⁸, Nb. 10²⁹); Hebrew Yithrô (Ex. 3¹, 18¹, ²), LXX Ἰοθόρ (Ex. 2¹⁶ : Jdg. 1¹⁶); Hebrew Yether (Ex. 4¹⁸), Jos. (*Ant.* II 12 § 1) Ἰεθέγλαιος ; Hebrew Ḥobab, LXX Ὀβάβ (Nb. 10²⁹), Ἰωβάβ (Jdg. 4¹¹), Vulgate Hobab. — ἐταχύνατε τοῦ παραγενέσθαι : Gen. 41³² n.

21. Σεπφώραν : Jos. *Ant.* II 13 § 1 Σαπφώραν. 1¹⁵ n.
22. Γηρσάμ : Hebrew Gershom. Jos. *Ant.* II 13 § 1 Γηρσὸς μὲν σημαίνει κατὰ Ἑβραίων διάλεκτον, ὅτι εἰς ξένην ἦν γῆν.
23. ἀπὸ τῶν ἔργων : *by reason of their toils.* So perhaps in the next clause. § 92.
25. ἐγνώσθη αὐτοῖς : R.V. 'God took knowledge of them.' The Hebrew for αὐτοῖς, omitting vowel points, differs from that for 'God' only by a 'jot.'

Exodus III 1

¹Καὶ Μωυσῆς ἦν ποιμαίνων τὰ πρόβατα Ἰοθὸρ τοῦ γαμβροῦ αὐτοῦ τοῦ ἱερέως Μαδιάμ, καὶ ἤγαγεν τὰ πρόβατα ὑπὸ
τὴν ἔρημον καὶ ἦλθεν εἰς τὸ ὄρος Χωρήβ. ²ὤφθη δὲ αὐτῷ
ἄγγελος Κυρίου ἐν πυρὶ φλογὸς ἐκ τοῦ βάτου· καὶ ὁρᾷ ὅτι ὁ
βάτος καίεται πυρί, ὁ δὲ βάτος οὐ κατεκαίετο. ³εἶπεν δὲ
Μωυσῆς "Παρελθὼν ὄψομαι τὸ ὅραμα τὸ μέγα τοῦτο, ὅτι οὐ
κατακαίεται ὁ βάτος." ⁴ὡς δὲ ἴδεν Κύριος ὅτι προσάγει
ἰδεῖν, ἐκάλεσεν αὐτὸν Κύριος ἐκ τοῦ βάτου λέγων "Μωυσῆ
Μωυσῆ." ὁ δὲ εἶπεν "Τί ἐστιν;" ⁵ὁ δὲ εἶπεν "Μὴ ἐγγίσῃς
ὧδε· λῦσαι τὸ ὑπόδημα ἐκ τῶν ποδῶν σου, ὁ γὰρ τόπος ἐν ᾧ
σὺ ἔστηκας γῆ ἁγία ἐστίν." ⁶καὶ εἶπεν "Ἐγώ εἰμι ὁ θεὸς
τοῦ πατρός σου, θεὸς Ἀβραὰμ καὶ θεὸς Ἰσαὰκ καὶ θεὸς Ἰακώβ." ἀπέστρεψεν δὲ Μωυσῆς τὸ πρόσωπον αὐτοῦ· εὐλαβεῖτο γὰρ κατεμβλέψαι ἐνώπιον τοῦ θεοῦ. ⁷εἶπεν δὲ Κύριος
πρὸς Μωυσῆν "Ἰδὼν ἴδον τὴν κάκωσιν τοῦ λαοῦ μου τοῦ ἐν
Αἰγύπτῳ, καὶ τῆς κραυγῆς αὐτῶν ἀκήκοα ἀπὸ τῶν ἐργοδιω-

---

**1.** ἦν ποιμαίνων : § 72.— γαμβροῦ :
γαμβρός is a vague word for a male
connexion by marriage, Lat. *affinis*.
It is sometimes used by classical
authors in the sense of πενθερός, as
here, but it generally means the cor-
relative ' son-in-law.' In Jdg. 1¹⁶ Ἰοθὸρ
. . . τοῦ γαμβροῦ Μωυσέως, the Hebrew
has not the proper name, and γαμβροῦ
is rendered in the R.V. ' brother-in-
law.'— ὑπὸ τὴν ἔρημον : Hebrew, ' behind the wilderness.' The meaning
seems to be "deep into the wilderness." — εἰς τὸ ὄρος Χωρήβ: Hebrew,
'to the mountain of God, to Horeb.'
Jos. *Ant.* II 12 § 1 ἐπὶ τὸ Σιναῖον καλούμενον ὄρος. The use of the two names
Horeb and Sinai is supposed to indicate
different documents. Josephus says
that the place already had the reputa-
tion of being the abode of God, and

that therefore no shepherds had ever
ventured to drive their flocks there.

**2.** ἄγγελος Κυρίου: in v. 4 Κύριος. So in 14¹⁹, ²⁴ we have first ὁ ἄγγελος τοῦ θεοῦ and then Κύριος. *Cp.* Jdg.
13²². — τοῦ βάτου : *the bush*. The Hebrew also has the article here. This
seems to show that the story was
already well known by the time this
account was written. Outside this
chapter βάτος = *rubus* occurs in LXX
only in Dt. 33¹⁶ : Job 31⁴⁰. It is masculine in the LXX but feminine in Mk.
12²⁶ : Lk. 20³⁷. In classical authors
there is the same variation of gender.

**6.** εὐλαβεῖτο : a word specially used
of pious fear. Hence ἀνὴρ εὐλαβής.
*Cp.* Lk. 2²⁵ : Acts 2⁵, 8², 22¹².

**7.** Ἰδὼν ἴδον : § 81. — ἀπὸ τῶν
ἐργοδιωκτῶν : § 92. *Cp.* 5⁶, ¹⁰, ¹³ : i Chr.
23⁴ : ii Chr. 2¹⁸, 8¹⁰ ἐργοδιωκτοῦντες :

Exodus III 13

κτῶν· οἶδα γὰρ τὴν ὀδύνην αὐτῶν, ⁸καὶ κατέβην ἐξελέσθαι
αὐτοὺς ἐκ χειρὸς Αἰγυπτίων καὶ ἐξαγαγεῖν αὐτοὺς ἐκ τῆς γῆς
ἐκείνης, καὶ εἰσαγαγεῖν αὐτοὺς εἰς γῆν ἀγαθὴν καὶ πολλήν,
εἰς γῆν ῥέουσαν γάλα καὶ μέλι, εἰς τὸν τόπον τῶν Χαναναίων καὶ Χετταίων καὶ Ἀμορραίων καὶ Φερεζαίων καὶ Γεργεσαίων καὶ Εὐαίων καὶ Ἰεβουσαίων. ⁹καὶ νῦν ἰδοὺ κραυγὴ
τῶν υἱῶν Ἰσραὴλ ἥκει πρός μέ, κἀγὼ ἑώρακα τὸν θλιμμὸν ὃν
οἱ Αἰγύπτιοι θλίβουσιν αὐτούς. ¹⁰καὶ νῦν δεῦρο ἀποστείλω
σε πρὸς Φαραὼ βασιλέα Αἰγύπτου, καὶ ἐξάξεις τὸν λαόν
μου τοὺς υἱοὺς Ἰσραὴλ ἐκ γῆς Αἰγύπτου." ¹¹Καὶ εἶπεν
Μωυσῆς πρὸς τὸν θεόν " Τίς εἰμι ἐγὼ ὅτι πορεύσομαι πρὸς
Φαραὼ βασιλέα Αἰγύπτου, καὶ ὅτι ἐξάξω τοὺς υἱοὺς Ἰσραὴλ
ἐκ γῆς Αἰγύπτου;" ¹²εἶπεν δὲ ὁ θεὸς Μωυσεῖ λέγων "Ὅτι
ἔσομαι μετὰ σοῦ· καὶ τοῦτό σοι τὸ σημεῖον ὅτι ἐγώ σε
ἐξαποστελῶ· ἐν τῷ ἐξαγαγεῖν σε τὸν λαόν μου ἐξ Αἰγύπτου,
καὶ λατρεύσετε τῷ θεῷ ἐν τῷ ὄρει τούτῳ." ¹³καὶ εἶπέν
Μωυσῆς πρὸς τὸν θεόν "Ἰδοὺ ἐγὼ ἐξελεύσομαι πρὸς τοὺς
υἱοὺς Ἰσραὴλ καὶ ἐρῶ πρὸς αὐτούς 'Ὁ θεὸς τῶν πατέρων
ἡμῶν ἀπέσταλκέν με πρὸς ὑμᾶς·' ἐρωτήσουσίν με 'Τί ὄνομα

i Esd. 5⁵⁶. Ἐργοδιώκτής was the current word at Alexandria for a superin-
tendent of works (it is contrasted in
ii Chr. 2¹⁸ B with νωτοφόρος), as is
shown by its use in the Fayûm Papyri ;
Philo II 86, Vit. Mos. I § 7 also employs it. Cp. ἐργοπαρέκτης i Clem. 34¹.
8. ῥέουσαν γάλα καὶ μέλι : cognate
accusative in a loose sense of that term.
In the next verse we have the same
construction in its more precise form.
— Γεργεσαίων : added in the LXX.
9. θλιμμόν . . . θλίβουσιν : § 56.
θλιμμός (= θλῖψις) occurs in the LXX
only here and in Dt. 26⁷.
12. Ὅτι ἔσομαι : the use of ὅτι here

is due to the presence in the original
of a particle to which it corresponds.
Both in the Greek and Hebrew perhaps
the construction may be explained by
an ellipse — (Know) that I will be with
thee. § 107. — καὶ λατρεύσετε : the καί
here has nothing in the Hebrew to
correspond to it. Translate — When
thou leadest out my people from Egypt,
ye shall also sacrifice to God on this
mountain. This sacrifice was to be a
public recognition of the fact that the
exodus was under the auspices of
Jehovah. Perhaps then the σημεῖον
referred to above is not one given by
Jehovah but expected by him.

αὐτῷ;' τί ἐρῶ πρὸς αὐτούς;" ¹⁴καὶ εἶπεν ὁ θεὸς πρὸς Μωυσῆν λέγων "'Εγώ εἰμι ὁ ὤν·" καὶ εἶπεν "Οὕτως ἐρεῖς τοῖς υἱοῖς 'Ισραήλ 'Ο ὢν ἀπέσταλκέν με πρὸς ὑμᾶς.'" ¹⁵καὶ εἶπεν ὁ θεὸς πάλιν πρὸς Μωυσῆν "Οὕτως ἐρεῖς τοῖς υἱοῖς 'Ισραήλ 'Κύριος ὁ θεὸς τῶν πατέρων ὑμῶν, θεὸς 'Αβραὰμ καὶ θεὸς 'Ισαὰκ καὶ θεὸς 'Ιακώβ, ἀπέσταλκέν με πρὸς ὑμᾶς·' τοῦτό μού ἐστιν ὄνομα αἰώνιον καὶ μνημόσυνον γενεῶν γενεαῖς. ¹⁶ἐλθὼν οὖν συνάγαγε τὴν γερουσίαν τῶν υἱῶν 'Ισραὴλ καὶ ἐρεῖς πρὸς αὐτούς 'Κύριος ὁ θεὸς τῶν πατέρων ὑμῶν ὦπταί μοι, θεὸς 'Αβραὰμ καὶ θεὸς 'Ισαὰκ καὶ θεὸς 'Ιακώβ, λέγων "'Επισκοπῇ ἐπέσκεμμαι ὑμᾶς καὶ ὅσα συμβέβηκεν ὑμῖν ἐν Αἰγύπτῳ·" ¹⁷καὶ εἶπεν "'Αναβιβάσω ὑμᾶς ἐκ τῆς κακώσεως τῶν Αἰγυπτίων εἰς τὴν γῆν τῶν Χαναναίων καὶ Χετταίων καὶ 'Αμορραίων καὶ Φερεζαίων καὶ Γεργεσαίων καὶ Εὐαίων καὶ 'Ιεβουσαίων, εἰς γῆν ῥέουσαν γάλα καὶ μέλι."' ¹⁸καὶ εἰσακούσονταί σου τῆς φωνῆς· καὶ εἰσελεύσῃ σὺ καὶ ἡ γερουσία

---

**14.** ὁ ὤν: the difference of gender between this expression and the Greek τὸ ὄν marks the difference between Hebrew religion and Greek philosophy in the conception of the Deity. To the one God was a person, to the other a principle. Jos. Ant. II 12 § 4 says καὶ ὁ θεὸς αὐτῷ σημαίνει τὴν ἑαυτοῦ προσηγορίαν, οὐ πρότερον εἰς ἀνθρώπους παρελθοῦσαν· περὶ ἧς οὐ μοί θέμις εἰπεῖν.

**15.** Κύριος ὁ θεός: the Hebrew word corresponding to Κύριος here, as usually in the LXX, is JHVH, the name which had just been revealed to Moses and explained as meaning ὁ ὤν. The Jews considered this name too holy to be lightly pronounced, and therefore in reading the sacred text aloud, substituted for Jahveh, wherever it occurred,

the word Adonai (= Lord). The fact that the Seventy thus translated Jahveh by Κύριος seems to show that this practice of substitution was already established in the third century B.C. The English version regularly represents the word Jahveh by LORD. The form Jehovah has arisen from the practice of disguising the sacred name even in the text by putting under it the vowel-points of Adonai. When Κύριος stands in the LXX for the proper name Jahveh, it is used, like any other proper name, without the article. — γενεῶν γενεαῖς: a Hebraism.

**16.** τὴν γερουσίαν: *the body of elders.* We hear of elders also in connexion with other Semitic peoples, such as Moab and Midian. Cp. Nb. 22⁷. — 'Επισκοπῇ ἐπέσκεμμαι: § 61.

Exodus IV 6

Ἰσραὴλ πρὸς Φαραὼ βασιλέα Αἰγύπτου, καὶ ἐρεῖς πρὸς αὐτόν
'Ὁ θεὸς τῶν Ἑβραίων προσκέκληται ἡμᾶς· πορευσώμεθα οὖν
ὁδὸν τριῶν ἡμερῶν εἰς τὴν ἔρημον, ἵνα θύσωμεν τῷ θεῷ ἡμῶν.'
¹⁹ἐγὼ δὲ οἶδα ὅτι οὐ προήσεται ὑμᾶς Φαραὼ βασιλεὺς Αἰγύπτου πορευθῆναι, ἐὰν μὴ μετὰ χειρὸς κραταιᾶς · ²⁰καὶ ἐκτείνας
τὴν χεῖρα πατάξω τοὺς Αἰγυπτίους ἐν πᾶσι τοῖς θαυμασίοις
μου οἷς ποιήσω ἐν αὐτοῖς, καὶ μετὰ ταῦτα ἐξαποστελεῖ ὑμᾶς.
²¹καὶ δώσω χάριν τῷ λαῷ τούτῳ ἐναντίον τῶν Αἰγυπτίων ·
ὅταν δὲ ἀποτρέχητε, οὐκ ἀπελεύσεσθε κενοί · ²²αἰτήσει γυνὴ
παρὰ γείτονος καὶ συσκήνου αὐτῆς σκεύη ἀργυρᾶ καὶ
χρυσᾶ καὶ ἱματισμόν, καὶ ἐπιθήσετε ἐπὶ τοὺς υἱοὺς ὑμῶν
καὶ ἐπὶ τὰς θυγατέρας ὑμῶν · καὶ σκυλεύσατε τοὺς Αἰγυπτίους." ¹Ἀπεκρίθη δὲ Μωυσῆς καὶ εἶπεν " Ἐὰν μὴ πιστεύσωσίν μοι μηδὲ εἰσακούσωσιν τῆς φωνῆς μου, ἐροῦσιν
γὰρ ὅτι 'Οὐκ ὦπταί σοι ὁ θεός,' τί ἐρῶ πρὸς αὐτούς ; " ²εἶπεν
δὲ αὐτῷ Κύριος " Τί τοῦτό ἐστιν τὸ ἐν τῇ χειρί σου ; " ὁ δὲ
εἶπεν " Ῥάβδος." ³καὶ εἶπεν " Ῥίψον αὐτὴν ἐπὶ τὴν γῆν."
καὶ ἔρριψεν αὐτὴν ἐπὶ τὴν γῆν, καὶ ἐγένετο ὄφις · καὶ ἔφυγεν
Μωυσῆς ἀπ' αὐτοῦ. ⁴καὶ εἶπεν Κύριος πρὸς Μωυσῆν " Ἔκτεινον τὴν χεῖρα καὶ ἐπιλαβοῦ τῆς κέρκου · " ἐκτείνας οὖν
τὴν χεῖρα ἐπελάβετο τῆς κέρκου, καὶ ἐγένετο ῥάβδος ἐν τῇ
χειρὶ αὐτοῦ · ⁵" ἵνα πιστεύσωσίν σοι ὅτι ὦπταί σοι ὁ θεὸς
τῶν πατέρων αὐτῶν, θεὸς Ἀβραὰμ καὶ θεὸς Ἰσαὰκ καὶ θεὸς
Ἰακώβ." ⁶εἶπεν δὲ αὐτῷ Κύριος πάλιν " Εἰσένεγκον τὴν
χεῖρά σου εἰς τὸν κόλπον σου." καὶ εἰσήνεγκεν τὴν χεῖρα
αὐτοῦ εἰς τὸν κόλπον αὐτοῦ · καὶ ἐξήνεγκεν τὴν χεῖρα αὐτοῦ

---

**20.** ἐν πᾶσι τοῖς θαυμασίοις μου : with all my wonders. § 91.

**21.** ἀποτρέχητε : Nb. 24¹⁴ n.

**22.** συσκήνου : originally a military term = Latin contubernalis. The Hebrew word means a female so-journer without any reference to a tent. — σκυλεύσατε : do ye spoil. Hebrew, ' ye shall spoil.'

**5.** ἵνα πιστεύσωσιν : referring back to ἐπιλαβοῦ τῆς κέρκου, the intermediate words being parenthetical.

Exodus IV 7

ἐκ τοῦ κόλπου αὐτοῦ, καὶ ἐγενήθη ἡ χεὶρ αὐτοῦ ὡσεὶ χιών. ⁷καὶ εἶπεν πάλιν " Εἰσένεγκον τὴν χεῖρά σου εἰς τὸν κόλπον σου· " καὶ εἰσήνεγκεν τὴν χεῖρα εἰς τὸν κόλπον αὐτοῦ· καὶ ἐξήνεγκεν αὐτὴν ἐκ τοῦ κόλπου αὐτοῦ, καὶ πάλιν ἀπεκατέστη εἰς τὴν χρόαν τῆς σαρκὸς αὐτῆς· ⁸" ἐὰν δὲ μὴ πιστεύσωσίν σοι μηδὲ εἰσακούσωσιν τῆς φωνῆς τοῦ σημείου τοῦ πρώτου, πιστεύσουσίν σοι τῆς φωνῆς τοῦ σημείου τοῦ ἐσχάτου. ⁹καὶ ἔσται ἐὰν μὴ πιστεύσωσίν σοι τοῖς δυσὶ σημείοις τούτοις μηδὲ εἰσακούσωσιν τῆς φωνῆς σου, λήμψῃ ἀπὸ τοῦ ὕδατος τοῦ ποταμοῦ καὶ ἐκχεεῖς ἐπὶ τὸ ξηρόν, καὶ ἔσται τὸ ὕδωρ ὃ ἐὰν λάβῃς ἀπὸ τοῦ ποταμοῦ αἷμα ἐπὶ τοῦ ξηροῦ." ¹⁰Εἶπεν δὲ Μωυσῆς πρὸς Κύριον " Δέομαι, Κύριε, οὐχ ἱκανός εἰμι πρὸ τῆς ἐχθὲς οὐδὲ πρὸ τῆς τρίτης ἡμέρας οὐδὲ ἀφ' οὗ ἤρξω λαλεῖν τῷ θεράποντί σου· ἰσχνόφωνος καὶ βραδύγλωσσος

**6.** ὡσεὶ χιών : Jos. *Ant.* II 12 § 3 Ὑπακούσας δὲ λευκὴν καὶ τιτάνῳ (chalk) ὁμοίαν προεκόμισεν.
**9.** τοῖς δυσὶ σημείοις : § 1. Josephus makes the third sign of turning water into blood to be actually performed at the burning bush. — λήμψῃ : § 37. — ἐκχεεῖς : the accentuation seems due to false analogy from vowel verbs. § 21. — ὃ ἐάν : = ὃ ἄν. § 105.
**10.** πρὸ τῆς ἐχθὲς κτλ. : a literal translation of the Hebrew phrase, which is condensed into 'heretofore' in R.V. *Yesterday and the day before* is meant to cover all past time. The meaning of πρὸ τῆς ἐχθές must not be pressed : its form is assimilated to that of πρὸ τῆς τρίτης, Ex. 21²⁹ : Dt. 4⁴². This use of πρό in expressions of time became common in later Greek, owing apparently to its coincidence with Latin idiom. Jos. *Ant.* XIII 9 § 2 πρὸ ὀκτω εἰδῶν Φεβρουαρίων : Plut. *Cæs.* 63

πρὸ μιᾶς ἡμέρας = ante unum diem; *Sulla* 27 πρὸ μιᾶς νωνῶν Κυντιλίων, 37 πρὸ δυεῖν ἡμερῶν ἢ ἐτελεύτα. Here we cannot suspect any Roman influence to have been at work, and the occurrence in Herodotus of the phrase πρὸ πολλοῦ in the sense of 'long before' indicates a tendency to this use of the preposition in pure Greek. We find πρὸ μικροῦ χρόνου in ii Mac. 10⁶. — ἰσχνόφωνος : cp. 6³⁰, where the Hebrew is different. This word, which naturally means 'thin-voiced,' is used as though it were ἰσχόφωνος of a person with an impediment in his speech. Aristotle (*Probl.* XI 35) says that the ἰσχνόφωνοι are incapable of speaking low because of the effort that is required to overcome the obstruction to their voice. In *Probl.* XI 30 ἰσχνοφωνία is distinguished from τραυλότης and ψελλότης. A person is τραυλός who is unable to pronounce some par-

Exodus IV 17

ἐγώ εἰμι." ¹¹ εἶπεν δὲ Κύριος πρὸς Μωυσῆν "Τίς ἔδωκεν στόμα ἀνθρώπῳ, καὶ τίς ἐποίησεν δύσκωφον καὶ κωφόν, βλέποντα καὶ τυφλόν ; οὐκ ἐγὼ ὁ θεός ; ¹² καὶ νῦν πορεύου καὶ ἐγὼ ἀνοίξω τὸ στόμα σου, καὶ συμβιβάσω σε ὃ μέλλεις λαλῆσαι." ¹³ καὶ εἶπεν Μωυσῆς " Δέομαι, Κύριε, προχείρισαι δυνάμενον ἄλλον ὃν ἀποστελεῖς." ¹⁴ καὶ θυμωθεὶς ὀργῇ Κύριος ἐπὶ Μωυσῆν εἶπεν " Οὐκ ἰδοὺ 'Ααρὼν ὁ ἀδελφός σου ὁ Λευείτης ; ἐπίσταμαι ὅτι λαλῶν λαλήσει αὐτός σοι· καὶ ἰδοὺ αὐτὸς ἐξελεύσεται εἰς συνάντησίν σοι, καὶ ἰδών σε χαρήσεται ἐν ἑαυτῷ. ¹⁵ καὶ ἐρεῖς πρὸς αὐτὸν καὶ δώσεις τὰ ῥήματά μου εἰς τὸ στόμα αὐτοῦ· καὶ ἐγὼ ἀνοίξω τὸ στόμα σου καὶ τὸ στόμα αὐτοῦ, καὶ συμβιβάσω ὑμᾶς ἃ ποιήσετε. ¹⁶ καὶ αὐτός σοι λαλήσει πρὸς τὸν λαόν, καὶ αὐτὸς ἔσται σου στόμα· σὺ δὲ αὐτῷ ἔσῃ τὰ πρὸς τὸν θεόν. ¹⁷ καὶ τὴν

ticular letter, whereas the ψελλός exaggerates some letter or syllable, but ἰσχνοφωνία consists in an inability to attach one syllable quickly to another. Herodotus (IV 155) seems to use the words synonymously — πάϊς ἰσχνόφωνος καὶ τραυλὸς, τῷ οὔνομα ἐτέθη Βάττος.

11. δύσκωφον: used by Aristotle in the sense of 'stone-deaf.' Here however it is used for 'dumb,' while κωφός (which in itself may mean either 'deaf' or 'dumb') is here reserved for 'deaf.'

12. συμβιβάσω σε: I will instruct thee. Cp. v. 15, 18¹³ : Jdg. 13⁸ : Is. 40¹³ : i Cor. 2¹⁶. Also προβιβάσεις Dt. 6⁷. Προσβιβάζειν is used by classical writers in a somewhat similar sense. Plat. Men. 74 B, Phdr. 229 E : Xen. Mem. I 2 § 17.

14. 'Ααρών: as Aaron was three years older than Moses (7⁷), we may suppose that the order for the destruction of male infants was subsequent to his birth. — ὁ Λευείτης : Moses was as much a Levite as Aaron (Ex. 6²) : but to the mind of the writer the word probably signified function rather than descent, so that its use here involves an anachronism. — σοί : added in the LXX, the meaning no doubt being "for thee."

16. τὰ πρὸς τὸν θεόν: the Greek translator has substituted this abstract expression for the blunter 'for God' of the original. Aaron, instead of taking his instructions directly from God (as Moses does), is to take them from Moses. Τὰ πρὸς τὸν θεόν (= his relations with God) may therefore be taken to mean "his medium of communication with God." This seems to typify the relation of the priest to the prophet under the ideal Hebrew theocracy.

Exodus IV 18

ῥάβδον ταύτην τὴν στραφεῖσαν εἰς ὄφιν λήμψῃ ἐν τῇ χειρί σου, ἐν ᾗ ποιήσεις ἐν αὐτῇ τὰ σημεῖα."

¹⁸ Ἐπορεύθη δὲ Μωυσῆς καὶ ἀπέστρεψεν πρὸς Ἰοθὸρ τὸν γαμβρὸν αὐτοῦ καὶ λέγει " Πορεύσομαι καὶ ἀποστρέψω πρὸς τοὺς ἀδελφούς μου τοὺς ἐν Αἰγύπτῳ, καὶ ὄψομαι εἰ ἔτι ζῶσιν." καὶ εἶπεν Ἰοθὸρ Μωυσῇ " Βάδιζε ὑγιαίνων." μετὰ δὲ τὰς ἡμέρας τὰς πολλὰς ἐκείνας ἐτελεύτησεν ὁ βασιλεὺς Αἰγύπτου. ¹⁹ εἶπεν δὲ Κύριος πρὸς Μωυσῆν ἐν Μαδιάμ " Βάδιζε ἄπελθε εἰς Αἴγυπτον· τεθνήκασιν γὰρ πάντες οἱ ζητοῦντές σου τὴν ψυχήν." ²⁰ ἀναλαβὼν δὲ Μωυσῆς τὴν γυναῖκα καὶ τὰ παιδία ἀνεβίβασεν αὐτὰ ἐπὶ τὰ ὑποζύγια, καὶ ἐπέστρεψεν εἰς Αἴγυπτον· ἔλαβεν δὲ Μωυσῆς τὴν ῥάβδον τὴν παρὰ τοῦ θεοῦ ἐν τῇ χειρὶ αὐτοῦ. ²¹ εἶπεν δὲ Κύριος πρὸς Μωυσῆν " Πορευομένου σου καὶ ἀποστρέφοντος εἰς Αἴγυπτον, ὅρα πάντα τὰ τέρατα ἃ ἔδωκα ἐν ταῖς χερσίν σου, ποιήσεις αὐτὰ ἐναντίον Φαραώ· ἐγὼ δὲ σκληρυνῶ τὴν καρδίαν αὐτοῦ, καὶ οὐ μὴ ἐξαποστείλῃ τὸν λαόν. ²² σὺ δὲ ἐρεῖς τῷ Φαραώ ʻ Τάδε λέγει Κύριος " Υἱὸς πρωτότοκός μου Ἰσραήλ· ²³ εἶπα δέ σοι ʻ Ἐξαπόστειλον τὸν λαόν μου ἵνα μοι λατρεύσῃ· εἰ μὲν οὖν μὴ βούλει ἐξαποστεῖλαι αὐτούς, ὅρα οὖν, ἐγὼ ἀποκτέννω τὸν υἱόν σου τὸν πρωτότοκον.' "

²⁷ Εἶπεν δὲ Κύριος πρὸς Ἀαρών " Πορεύθητι εἰς συνάντησιν Μωσεῖ εἰς τὴν ἔρημον· " καὶ ἐπορεύθη καὶ συνήντησεν αὐτῷ

---

17. **τὴν στραφεῖσαν εἰς ὄφιν**: added in the LXX Στρέφειν = classical τρέπειν. — **ἐν ᾗ** . . . **ἐν αὐτῇ**: § 69.
18. **Βάδιζε ὑγιαίνων**: Ὑγίαινε corresponds to the Latin *vale* as a formula of leave-taking. — **μετὰ δὲ** . . . **Αἰγύπτου**: these words are repeated from 2²³. They are not in the Hebrew and do not suit the context. On the form of expression see 2¹¹ n.

19. **Βάδιζε ἄπελθε**: a literal translation from the Hebrew. *Cp.* βάσκ᾽ ἴθι in Homer and v a d e a g e in Vergil.
20. **τὰ παιδία**: for the names of Moses' sons see 18³, ⁴.
21. **Πορευομένου σου . . . ὅρα**: § 58. — **ἔδωκα ἐν ταῖς χερσίν σου**: § 91.
23. **ἀποκτέννω**: the present of stem κτεν- is here strengthened by nasalisation instead of by inserting ι.

Exodus V 5

ἐν τῷ ὄρει τοῦ θεοῦ, καὶ κατεφίλησαν ἀλλήλους. ²⁸καὶ
ἀνήγγειλεν Μωυσῆς τῷ Ἀαρὼν πάντας τοὺς λόγους Κυρίου
οὓς ἀπέστειλεν καὶ πάντα τὰ ῥήματα ἃ ἐνετείλατο αὐτῷ.
²⁹ἐπορεύθη δὲ Μωυσῆς καὶ Ἀαρών, καὶ συνήγαγον τὴν
γερουσίαν τῶν υἱῶν Ἰσραήλ. ³⁰καὶ ἐλάλησεν Ἀαρὼν
πάντα τὰ ῥήματα ταῦτα ἃ ἐλάλησεν ὁ θεὸς πρὸς Μωυσῆν,
καὶ ἐποίησεν τὰ σημεῖα ἐναντίον τοῦ λαοῦ. ³¹καὶ ἐπίστευσεν ὁ λαός, καὶ ἐχάρη ὅτι ἐπεσκέψατο ὁ θεὸς τοὺς υἱοὺς
Ἰσραὴλ καὶ ὅτι εἶδεν αὐτῶν τὴν θλίψιν· κύψας δὲ ὁ λαὸς
προσεκύνησεν. ¹Καὶ μετὰ ταῦτα εἰσῆλθεν Μωυσῆς καὶ
Ἀαρὼν πρὸς Φαραὼ καὶ εἶπαν αὐτῷ " Τάδε λέγει Κύριος ὁ
θεὸς Ἰσραὴλ 'Ἐξαπόστειλον τὸν λαόν μου, ἵνα μοι ἑορτάσω-
σιν ἐν τῇ ἐρήμῳ.'" ²καὶ εἶπεν Φαραώ " Τίς ἐστιν οὗ εἰσα-
κούσομαι τῆς φωνῆς αὐτοῦ ὥστε ἐξαποστεῖλαι τοὺς υἱοὺς
Ἰσραήλ; οὐκ οἶδα τὸν κύριον, καὶ τὸν Ἰσραὴλ οὐκ ἐξαποστέλλω." ³καὶ λέγουσιν αὐτῷ "Ὁ θεὸς τῶν Ἑβραίων
προσκέκληται ἡμᾶς· πορευσόμεθα οὖν ὁδὸν τριῶν ἡμερῶν
εἰς τὴν ἔρημον, ὅπως θύσωμεν τῷ θεῷ ἡμῶν, μή ποτε συναν-
τήσῃ ἡμῖν θάνατος ἢ φόνος." ⁴καὶ εἶπεν αὐτοῖς ὁ βασιλεὺς
Αἰγύπτου "Ἵνα τί, Μωυσῆ καὶ Ἀαρών, διαστρέφετε τὸν λαόν
μου ἀπὸ τῶν ἔργων; ἀπέλθατε ἕκαστος ὑμῶν πρὸς τὰ ἔργα
αὐτοῦ." ⁵καὶ εἶπεν Φαραώ "Ἰδοὺ νῦν πολυπληθεῖ ὁ λαός·

27. τῷ ὄρει τοῦ θεοῦ : iii K.
19⁸ n.
28. οὓς ἀπέστειλεν: *wherewith he
had sent him.* An irregular attraction of the relative. *Cp.* 6⁵ ὃν . . . καταδουλοῦνται.
29. ἐπορεύθη . . . συνήγαγον: in
this change from singular to plural the
Greek exactly follows the Hebrew. Συ-
νάγειν is the verb to which συναγωγή
(12³) belongs. Josephus (*Ant.* II 13
§ 1) makes the elders go out to meet

Moses and Aaron, having heard of
their coming.
1. Τάδε λέγει Κύριος : instead of
these words Josephus here makes
Moses recount to the new Pharaoh his
services against the Ethiopians.
2. οὗ . . . αὐτοῦ: § 69.
5. πολυπληθεῖ : *is numerous.* The
word occurs in the LXX only here,
in Lev. 11⁴² ὃ πολυπληθεῖ ποσίν, and
Dt. 7⁷ πολυπληθεῖτε παρὰ πάντα τὰ
ἔθνη.

μὴ οὖν καταπαύσωμεν αὐτοὺς ἀπὸ τῶν ἔργων."  ⁶συνέταξεν
δὲ Φαραὼ τοῖς ἐργοδιώκταις τοῦ λαοῦ καὶ τοῖς γραμματεῦσιν
λέγων ⁷"Οὐκέτι προστεθήσεται διδόναι ἄχυρον τῷ λαῷ εἰς
τὴν πλινθουργίαν καθάπερ ἐχθὲς καὶ τρίτην ἡμέραν· αὐτοὶ
πορευέσθωσαν καὶ συναγαγέτωσαν ἑαυτοῖς ἄχυρα.   ⁸καὶ
τὴν σύνταξιν τῆς πλινθίας ἧς αὐτοὶ ποιοῦσιν καθ᾽ ἑκάστην
ἡμέραν ἐπιβαλεῖς αὐτοῖς, οὐκ ἀφελεῖς οὐδέν· σχολάζουσιν
γάρ, διὰ τοῦτο κεκράγασιν λέγοντες ᾽Εγερθῶμεν καὶ θύσωμεν τῷ θεῷ ἡμῶν.᾽   ⁹βαρυνέσθω τὰ ἔργα τῶν ἀνθρώπων
τούτων, καὶ μεριμνάτωσαν ταῦτα, καὶ μὴ μεριμνάτωσαν ἐν
λόγοις κενοῖς."   ¹⁰κατέσπευδον δὲ αὐτοὺς οἱ ἐργοδιῶκται
καὶ οἱ γραμματεῖς, καὶ ἔλεγον πρὸς τὸν λαὸν λέγοντες "Τάδε
λέγει Φαραώ ᾽Οὐκέτι δίδωμι ὑμῖν ἄχυρα·  ¹¹αὐτοὶ πορευόμενοι
συλλέγετε ἑαυτοῖς ἄχυρα ὅθεν ἐὰν εὕρητε, οὐ γὰρ ἀφαιρεῖται
ἀπὸ τῆς συντάξεως ὑμῶν οὐθέν.'"   ¹²καὶ διεσπάρη ὁ λαὸς ἐν
ὅλῃ γῇ Αἰγύπτῳ συναγαγεῖν καλάμην εἰς ἄχυρα·  ¹³οἱ δὲ
ἐργοδιῶκται κατέσπευδον αὐτοὺς λέγοντες "Συντελεῖτε τὰ
ἔργα τὰ καθήκοντα καθ᾽ ἡμέραν καθάπερ καὶ ὅτε τὸ ἄχυρον
ἐδίδοτο ὑμῖν."   ¹⁴καὶ ἐμαστιγώθησαν οἱ γραμματεῖς τοῦ
γένους τῶν υἱῶν Ἰσραὴλ οἱ κατασταθέντες ἐπ᾽ αὐτοὺς ὑπὸ
τῶν ἐπιστατῶν τοῦ Φαραώ, λέγοντες "Διὰ τί οὐ συνετελέσατε

---

**6.** συνέταξεν : *gave orders to.* Cp.
6¹³, 12³⁵ : Nb. 1¹⁸. Used absolutely in
Ex. 9¹². — γραμματεῦσιν : these were
Hebrew, not Egyptian, officers. Cp.
vs. 14, 19.

**7.** προστεθήσεται διδόναι : *shall it
be added to give.* The impersonal form
of a common construction in Biblical
Greek : Gen. 37⁸ n. On the use of straw
for bricks Swete (*Introd.* p. 293) compares Flinders Petrie *Papyri* II xiv 2
ἐς τὰ ἄχυρα πρὸς τὴν πλίνθον. — πλινθουργίαν : in Swete's text only here in
LXX. Josephus uses πλινθεία. — ἐχθὲς

καὶ τρίτην ἡμέραν : a general expression for past time. See 4¹⁰ n. § 86.

**8.** σύνταξιν : used by Demosthenes
(*e.g.* pp. 60, 95) of the contributions
which Athens levied from her allies.
The 'tale' of the bricks in our version
= the 'count' of the bricks, *i.e.* the
fixed number which the Israelites were
expected to provide. — κεκράγασιν :
perfect used as present ; found also in
good authors, as Soph. *Aj.* 1236.

**14.** λέγοντες : here we have a participle which has nothing to agree with
except the agent implied in the passive

Exodus V 23

τὰς συντάξεις ὑμῶν τῆς πλινθίας καθάπερ ἐχθὲς καὶ τρίτην ἡμέραν καὶ τὸ τῆς σήμερον;" ¹⁵εἰσελθόντες δὲ οἱ γραμματεῖς τῶν υἱῶν Ἰσραὴλ κατεβόησαν πρὸς Φαραὼ λέγοντες "Ἵνα τί οὕτως ποιεῖς τοῖς σοῖς οἰκέταις; ¹⁶ἄχυρον οὐ δίδοται τοῖς οἰκέταις σου, καὶ τὴν πλίνθον ἡμῖν λέγουσιν ποιεῖν, καὶ ἰδοὺ οἱ παῖδές σου μεμαστίγωνται· ἀδικήσεις οὖν τὸν λαόν σου." ¹⁷καὶ εἶπεν αὐτοῖς "Σχολάζετε, σχολασταί ἐστε· διὰ τοῦτο λέγετε 'Πορευθῶμεν θύσωμεν τῷ θεῷ ἡμῶν.' ¹⁸νῦν οὖν πορευθέντες ἐργάζεσθε· τὸ γὰρ ἄχυρον οὐ δοθήσεται ὑμῖν, καὶ τὴν σύνταξιν τῆς πλινθίας ἀποδώσετε." ¹⁹ἑώρων δὲ οἱ γραμματεῖς τῶν υἱῶν Ἰσραὴλ ἑαυτοὺς ἐν κακοῖς λέγοντες "Οὐκ ἀπολείψετε τῆς πλινθίας τὸ καθῆκον τῇ ἡμέρᾳ." ²⁰συνήντησαν δὲ Μωυσῇ καὶ Ἀαρὼν ἐρχομένοις εἰς συνάντησιν αὐτοῖς, ἐκπορευομένων αὐτῶν ἀπὸ Φαραώ, ²¹καὶ εἶπαν αὐτοῖς "Ἴδοι ὁ θεὸς ὑμᾶς καὶ κρίναι, ὅτι ἐβδελύξατε τὴν ὀσμὴν ἡμῶν ἐναντίον Φαραὼ καὶ ἐναντίον τῶν θεραπόντων αὐτοῦ, δοῦναι ῥομφαίαν εἰς τὰς χεῖρας αὐτοῦ ἀποκτεῖναι ἡμᾶς." ²²Ἐπέστρεψεν δὲ Μωυσῆς πρὸς Κύριον καὶ εἶπεν "Δέομαι, Κύριε, τί ἐκάκωσας τὸν λαὸν τοῦτον; καὶ ἵνα τί ἀπέσταλκάς με; ²³καὶ ἀφ' οὗ πεπόρευμαι πρὸς Φαραὼ

verb ἐμαστιγώθησαν. This is even more unreasonable than when the construction which precedes is impersonal, as in Gen. 45¹⁶. § 112.—καθάπερ . . . σήμερον: to-day also as heretofore. Τὸ τῆς σήμερον (ἡμέρας) is a periphrasis for σήμερον. Cp. ἐν τῇ σήμερον Ex. 13⁴, Dt. 4⁴: ἐν τῇ σήμερον ἡμέρᾳ Josh. 5⁸ (cp. 22²⁹). The phrase ἕως τῆς σήμερον ἡμέρας occurs in the Hexateuch in Gen. 19³⁸, 26³³, 35⁴: Nb. 22³⁰: Dt. 11⁴: and frequently in Joshua. Epict. Diss. I 11 § 38 ἀπὸ τῆς σήμερον τοίνυν ἡμέρας. See i K. 17¹⁰ n.

16. ἀδικήσεις κτλ.: R.V. 'But the fault is in thine own people.' The original is here obscure.

17. σχολασταί ἐστε: more expressive than σχολάζετε. This is a kind of analytic form. Σχολαστής occurs only here in LXX.

19. λέγοντες: here, as in 14, there is a subject γραμματεῖς, with which the participle appears to agree, but does not. § 112.

21. ἐβδελύξατε: Ye have made . . . to be abhorred. § 84.—ῥομφαίαν: the usual word for a sword in Hellenistic Greek. Cp. Nb. 22²³: Lk. 2³⁵.

Exodus VI 1

λαλῆσαι ἐπὶ τῷ σῷ ὀνόματι, ἐκάκωσεν τὸν λαὸν τοῦτον, καὶ οὐκ ἐρρύσω τὸν λαόν σου." ¹καὶ εἶπεν Κύριος πρὸς Μωυσῆν "Ἤδη ὄψει ἃ ποιήσω τῷ Φαραώ· ἐν γὰρ χειρὶ κραταιᾷ ἐξαποστελεῖ αὐτούς, καὶ ἐν βραχίονι ὑψηλῷ ἐκβαλεῖ αὐτοὺς ἐκ τῆς γῆς αὐτοῦ."

²Ἐλάλησεν δὲ ὁ θεὸς πρὸς Μωυσῆν καὶ εἶπεν πρὸς αὐτόν "Ἐγὼ Κύριος· ³καὶ ὤφθην πρὸς Ἀβραὰμ καὶ Ἰσαὰκ καὶ Ἰακώβ, θεὸς ὢν αὐτῶν, καὶ τὸ ὄνομά μου Κύριος οὐκ ἐδήλωσα αὐτοῖς· ⁴καὶ ἔστησα τὴν διαθήκην μου πρὸς αὐτοὺς ὥστε δοῦναι αὐτοῖς τὴν γῆν τῶν Χαναναίων, τὴν γῆν ἣν παρῳκήκασιν, ἐν ᾗ καὶ παρῴκησαν ἐπ' αὐτῆς. ⁵καὶ ἐγὼ εἰσήκουσα τὸν στεναγμὸν τῶν υἱῶν Ἰσραήλ, ὃν οἱ Αἰγύπτιοι καταδουλοῦνται αὐτούς, καὶ ἐμνήσθην τῆς διαθήκης ὑμῶν. ⁶βάδιζε εἰπὸν τοῖς υἱοῖς Ἰσραὴλ λέγων 'Ἐγὼ Κύριος, καὶ ἐξάξω ὑμᾶς ἀπὸ τῆς δυναστείας τῶν Αἰγυπτίων, καὶ ῥύσομαι ὑμᾶς ἐκ τῆς δουλίας, καὶ λυτρώσομαι ὑμᾶς ἐν βραχίονι ὑψηλῷ καὶ κρίσει μεγάλῃ· ⁷καὶ λήμψομαι ἐμαυτῷ ὑμᾶς λαὸν ἐμοί, καὶ ἔσομαι ὑμῶν θεός, καὶ γνώσεσθε ὅτι ἐγὼ Κύριος ὁ θεὸς ὑμῶν ὁ ἐξαγαγὼν ὑμᾶς ἐκ τῆς καταδυναστείας

---

**1. ἐν γὰρ χειρί ... καὶ ἐν κτλ.** : the second clause nearly repeats the first, but the Greek translator has varied the phraseology to avoid monotony. The ἐν denotes the accompanying circumstances. § 91. But on whose part was the strong hand to be? The words might be taken to mean that Pharaoh would be so glad to get rid of the Israelites that he would not only *permit* but *force* them to go, and 11¹, 12³³ might be quoted in favour of this view. A comparison however with v. 6 of this chapter and other passages, such as 14⁸, seems to show that the 'strong hand' here spoken of was to

be on the part of Jehovah. It is evidently so understood by the Deuteronomist (Dt. 26⁸) and in Jeremiah (39²¹).

**4. τὴν γῆν ἥν ... ἐπ' αὐτῆς** : literally *the land which they sojourned, in which they also sojourned upon it.* This bit of tautology represents five words in the original — 'the land of-their-sojournings which-they-sojourned in-it.'

**5. ὅν ... καταδουλοῦνται** : 4¹⁸ n.

**6. δουλίας** : = δουλείας. § 37.

**7. ἐμαυτῷ ... ἐμοί** : § 13. — **καταδυναστείας** : *oppression.* The word occurs five times in the LXX, but apparently not elsewhere.

Exodus VI 30

τῶν Αἰγυπτίων· ⁸καὶ ἐξάξω ὑμᾶς εἰς τὴν γῆν εἰς ἣν ἐξέτεινα
τὴν χεῖρά μου δοῦναι αὐτὴν τῷ Ἀβραὰμ καὶ Ἰσαὰκ καὶ
Ἰακώβ, καὶ δώσω ὑμῖν αὐτὴν ἐν κλήρῳ· ἐγὼ Κύριος.' "
⁹ἐλάλησεν δὲ Μωυσῆς οὕτως τοῖς υἱοῖς Ἰσραήλ· καὶ οὐκ
εἰσήκουσαν Μωυσῇ ἀπὸ τῆς ὀλιγοψυχίας καὶ ἀπὸ τῶν ἔργων
τῶν σκληρῶν.

¹⁰Εἶπεν δὲ Κύριος πρὸς Μωυσῆν λέγων ¹¹" Εἴσελθε λάλησον Φαραὼ βασιλεῖ Αἰγύπτου ἵνα ἐξαποστείλῃ τοὺς υἱοὺς
Ἰσραὴλ ἐκ τῆς γῆς αὐτοῦ." ¹²ἐλάλησεν δὲ Μωυσῆς ἔναντι
Κυρίου λέγων " Ἰδοὺ οἱ υἱοὶ Ἰσραὴλ οὐκ εἰσήκουσάν μου, καὶ
πῶς εἰσακούσεταί μου Φαραώ; ἐγὼ δὲ ἄλογός εἰμι." ¹³εἶπεν
δὲ Κύριος πρὸς Μωυσῆν καὶ Ἀαρών, καὶ συνέταξεν αὐτοῖς
πρὸς Φαραὼ βασιλέα Αἰγύπτου ὥστε ἐξαποστεῖλαι τοὺς
υἱοὺς Ἰσραὴλ ἐκ γῆς Αἰγύπτου.

²⁸ᵉῌ ἡμέρᾳ ἐλάλησεν Κύριος Μωυσῇ ἐν γῇ Αἰγύπτῳ
²⁹καὶ ἐλάλησεν Κύριος πρὸς Μωυσῆν λέγων " Ἐγὼ Κύριος·
λάλησον πρὸς Φαραὼ βασιλέα Αἰγύπτου, καὶ ἐγὼ λέγω
πρὸς σέ." ³⁰καὶ εἶπεν Μωυσῆς ἐναντίον Κυρίου " Ἰδοὺ
ἐγὼ ἰσχνόφωνός εἰμι, καὶ πῶς εἰσακούσεταί μου Φαραώ; "

9. εἰσήκουσαν Μωυσῇ: so in Herodotus εἰσακούειν = ' obey ' takes a
dative. In v. 12 below it has a genitive.

12. ἔναντι: § 97. — ἄλογος: desti-
tute, not of the inner, but of the outer,
λόγος, or, as it was sometimes called,
the λόγος προφορικός. This is a bold
rendering of the Hebrew, which means
' of uncircumcised lips.' The same
original is rendered in 30 by ἰσχνόφωνος.

13. συνέταξεν αὐτοῖς πρός: gave
them a commission to. Cp. 5⁶. —
πρὸς Φαραώ: before this the Hebrew
has the words ' unto the children of

Israel and,' which are not in the
LXX.

28. Ἧ ἡμέρᾳ . . . καὶ ἐλάλησεν: to
supply before this καὶ ἐγένετο to which
the Hebrew points, would make the
passage more in accordance with LXX
grammar, but it would not relieve it of
its tautology, which may be surmised to
arise from a mixture of documents.

29. καὶ ἐγὼ λέγω: the sense requires ἅ to be supplied before this.

30. καὶ εἶπεν Μωυσῆς: 6³⁰-7² is a
repetition with variations of 4¹⁰⁻¹⁶.
Here the communication made by the
Lord to Moses is in Egypt instead of
in the land of Midian.

¹καὶ εἶπεν Κύριος πρὸς Μωυσῆν λέγων " Ἰδοὺ δέδωκά σε
θεὸν Φαραώ, καὶ Ἀαρὼν ὁ ἀδελφός σου ἔσται σου προφήτης · ²σὺ δὲ λαλήσεις αὐτῷ πάντα ὅσα σοι ἐντέλλομαι, ὁ δὲ
Ἀαρὼν ὁ ἀδελφός σου λαλήσει πρὸς Φαραὼ ὥστε ἐξαποστεῖλαι τοὺς υἱοὺς Ἰσραὴλ ἐκ τῆς γῆς αὐτοῦ.    ³ἐγὼ δὲ σκληρυνῶ τὴν καρδίαν Φαραώ, καὶ πληθυνῶ τὰ σημεῖά μου καὶ
τὰ τέρατα ἐν γῇ Αἰγύπτῳ · ⁴καὶ οὐκ εἰσακούσεται ὑμῶν
Φαραώ.    καὶ ἐπιβαλῶ τὴν χεῖρά μου ἐπ' Αἴγυπτον, καὶ
ἐξάξω σὺν δυνάμει μου τὸν λαόν μου τοὺς υἱοὺς Ἰσραὴλ ἐκ
γῆς Αἰγύπτου σὺν ἐκδικήσει μεγάλῃ · ⁵καὶ γνώσονται πάντες οἱ Αἰγύπτιοι ὅτι ἐγώ εἰμι Κύριος, ἐκτείνων τὴν χεῖρα ἐπ'
Αἴγυπτον · καὶ ἐξάξω τοὺς υἱοὺς Ἰσραὴλ ἐκ μέσου αὐτῶν."
⁶ἐποίησεν δὲ Μωυσῆς καὶ Ἀαρὼν καθάπερ ἐνετείλατο αὐτοῖς
Κύριος, οὕτως ἐποίησαν.    ⁷Μωυσῆς δὲ ἦν ἐτῶν ὀγδοήκοντα,
Ἀαρὼν δὲ ὁ ἀδελφὸς αὐτοῦ ἐτῶν ὀγδοήκοντα τριῶν, ἡνίκα
ἐλάλησεν πρὸς Φαραώ.

⁸Καὶ εἶπεν Κύριος πρὸς Μωυσῆν καὶ Ἀαρὼν λέγων ⁹" Καὶ
ἐὰν λαλήσῃ πρὸς ὑμᾶς Φαραὼ λέγων ' Δότε ἡμῖν σημεῖον
ἢ τέρας,' καὶ ἐρεῖς Ἀαρὼν τῷ ἀδελφῷ σου ' Λάβε τὴν
ῥάβδον καὶ ῥίψον ἐπὶ τὴν γῆν ἐναντίον Φαραὼ καὶ ἐναντίον
τῶν θεραπόντων αὐτοῦ, καὶ ἔσται δράκων.' "    ¹⁰εἰσῆλθεν
δὲ Μωυσῆς καὶ Ἀαρὼν ἐναντίον Φαραὼ καὶ τῶν θεραπόντων αὐτοῦ, καὶ ἐποίησαν οὕτως καθάπερ ἐνετείλατο αὐτοῖς Κύριος · καὶ ἔριψεν Ἀαρὼν τὴν ῥάβδον ἐναντίον Φαραὼ
καὶ ἐναντίον τῶν θεραπόντων αὐτοῦ, καὶ ἐγένετο δράκων.
¹¹συνεκάλεσεν δὲ Φαραὼ τοὺς σοφιστὰς Αἰγύπτου καὶ τοὺς

1. **Φαραώ**: dative. — **προφήτης**: in
its primary meaning of ' forth-teller,'
' spokesman.'

3. **σημεῖα** . . . **καὶ τέρατα**: this is
the first instance of this combination
so common afterwards both in the Old
and New Testament ; *e.g.* Dt. 4³⁴, 6²²,

7¹⁹ : Dan. Οʹ 4³⁴ : Mt. 24²⁴.  *Cp.* Jos.
*B. J. Præm.* § 11 καὶ τὰ πρὸ ταύτης
(the capture of Jerusalem) σημεῖα καὶ
τέρατα.

10. **ἔριψεν**: = ἔρριψεν.    § 37.

11. **σοφιστάς**: in LXX only here
and in Daniel, where Theodotion has

φαρμακούς· καὶ ἐποίησαν καὶ οἱ ἐπαοιδοὶ τῶν Αἰγυπτίων ταῖς φαρμακίαις αὐτῶν ὡσαύτως, ¹²καὶ ἔρριψαν ἕκαστος τὴν ῥάβδον αὐτῶν, καὶ ἐγένοντο δράκοντες· καὶ κατέπιεν ἡ ῥάβδος ἡ Ἀαρὼν τὰς ἐκείνων ῥάβδους. ¹³καὶ κατίσχυσεν ἡ καρδία Φαραώ, καὶ οὐκ εἰσήκουσεν αὐτῶν, καθάπερ ἐνετείλατο αὐτοῖς Κύριος. ¹⁴Εἶπεν δὲ Κύριος πρὸς Μωυσῆν " Βεβάρηται ἡ καρδία Φαραὼ τοῦ μὴ ἐξαποστεῖλαι τὸν λαόν. ¹⁵βάδισον πρὸς Φαραὼ τὸ πρωί· ἰδοὺ αὐτὸς ἐκπορεύεται ἐπὶ τὸ ὕδωρ, καὶ ἔσῃ συναντῶν αὐτῷ ἐπὶ τὸ χεῖλος τοῦ ποταμοῦ· καὶ τὴν ῥάβδον τὴν στραφεῖσαν εἰς ὄφιν λήμψῃ ἐν τῇ χειρί σου, ¹⁶καὶ ἐρεῖς πρὸς αὐτόν ' Κύριος ὁ θεὸς τῶν Ἑβραίων ἀπέσταλκέν με πρὸς σὲ λέγων " Ἐξαπόστειλον τὸν λαόν μου ἵνα μοι λατρεύσῃ ἐν τῇ ἐρήμῳ·" καὶ ἰδοὺ οὐκ εἰσήκουσας ἕως τούτου. ¹⁷τάδε λέγει Κύριος " Ἐν τούτῳ γνώσῃ ὅτι ἐγὼ Κύριος·" ἰδοὺ ἐγὼ τύπτω τῇ ῥάβδῳ τῇ ἐν τῇ χειρί μου ἐπὶ τὸ ὕδωρ τὸ ἐν τῷ ποταμῷ, καὶ μεταβαλεῖ εἰς αἷμα· ¹⁸καὶ οἱ ἰχθύες οἱ ἐν τῷ ποταμῷ τελευτήσουσιν, καὶ ἐποζέσει ὁ ποταμός, καὶ οὐ δυνήσονται οἱ Αἰγύπτιοι πιεῖν ὕδωρ ἀπὸ τοῦ ποταμοῦ.'" ¹⁹εἶπεν δὲ Κύριος πρὸς Μωυσῆν " Εἰπὸν Ἀαρὼν τῷ ἀδελφῷ σου 'Λάβε τὴν ῥάβδον σου ἐν τῇ χειρί σου, καὶ ἔκτεινον τὴν χεῖρά

σοφοί and in one passage (1²⁰) ἐπαοιδοί.
— φαρμακούς : cp. 9¹¹, 22¹⁸ φαρμακοὺς οὐ περιποιήσετε. The use of φαρμακός for a ' medicine-man ' or ' sorcerer ' seems to be peculiar to Biblical Greek Dan. O' 2², ²⁷, 5⁷, ⁸. — ἐπαοιδοί : = ἐπῳδοί, enchanters. Cp. 22, 8⁷, ¹⁸, ¹⁹ : i K. 6² : Dan. O' 2², ²⁷ etc. The contracted form does not occur in the LXX.—
φαρμακίαις : = φαρμακείαις. § 37.
13. κατίσχυσεν : intransitive, was strong. Cp. 17.
14. βεβάρηται : a Hebraism, for which cp. 8¹⁵, ³², 9⁷, ³⁴. The form βαρεῖν

occurs in the LXX only here and in ii Mac. 13⁹ βεβαρημένος. Βαρύνειν is common.
15. ἔσῃ συναντῶν : analytic form of the future. § 72. — ἐπὶ τὸ χεῖλος τοῦ ποταμοῦ : § 95.
17. τύπτω . . . ἐπὶ τὸ ὕδωρ : as in English, ' smite upon the water.'
18. ἐποζέσει : future of ἐπόζειν. We have the aorist in 21 and in 16²⁰, ²⁴. These are all the occurrences in the LXX.
19. εἶπεν δὲ κτλ. : this verse is inconsistent with 15–18 and contradicts

σου ἐπὶ τὰ ὕδατα Αἰγύπτου καὶ ἐπὶ τοὺς ποταμοὺς αὐτῶν καὶ
ἐπὶ τὰς διώρυγας αὐτῶν καὶ ἐπὶ τὰ ἕλη αὐτῶν καὶ ἐπὶ πᾶν
συνεστηκὸς ὕδωρ αὐτῶν, καὶ ἔσται αἷμα·'" καὶ ἐγένετο αἷμα
ἐν πάσῃ γῇ Αἰγύπτου, ἔν τε τοῖς ξύλοις καὶ ἐν τοῖς λίθοις.
²⁰ καὶ ἐποίησαν οὕτως Μωυσῆς καὶ Ἀαρὼν καθάπερ ἐνετείλατο αὐτοῖς Κύριος· καὶ ἐπάρας τῇ ῥάβδῳ αὐτοῦ ἐπάταξεν
τὸ ὕδωρ τὸ ἐν τῷ ποταμῷ ἐναντίον Φαραὼ καὶ ἐναντίον τῶν
θεραπόντων αὐτοῦ, καὶ μετέβαλεν πᾶν τὸ ὕδωρ τὸ ἐν τῷ
ποταμῷ εἰς αἷμα. ²¹ καὶ οἱ ἰχθύες οἱ ἐν τῷ ποταμῷ ἐτελεύτησαν, καὶ ἐπώζεσεν ὁ ποταμός, καὶ οὐκ ἠδύναντο οἱ Αἰγύπτιοι πιεῖν ὕδωρ ἐκ τοῦ ποταμοῦ, καὶ ἦν τὸ αἷμα ἐν πάσῃ γῇ
Αἰγύπτου. ²² ἐποίησαν δὲ ὡσαύτως καὶ οἱ ἐπαοιδοὶ τῶν
Αἰγυπτίων ταῖς φαρμακίαις αὐτῶν· καὶ ἐσκλήρυνεν ἡ καρδία
Φαραώ, καὶ οὐκ εἰσήκουσεν αὐτῶν, καθάπερ εἶπεν Κύριος.
²³ ἐπιστραφεὶς δὲ Φαραὼ εἰσῆλθεν εἰς τὸν οἶκον αὐτοῦ, καὶ
οὐκ ἐπέστησεν τὸν νοῦν αὐτοῦ οὐδὲ ἐπὶ τούτῳ. ²⁴ ὤρυξαν
δὲ πάντες οἱ Αἰγύπτιοι κύκλῳ τοῦ ποταμοῦ ὥστε πιεῖν ὕδωρ
ἀπὸ τοῦ ποταμοῦ, καὶ οὐκ ἠδύναντο πιεῖν ὕδωρ ἀπὸ τοῦ
ποταμοῦ· ²⁵ καὶ ἀνεπληρώθησαν ἑπτὰ ἡμέραι μετὰ τὸ
πατάξαι Κύριον τὸν ποταμόν.

24. It is assigned to P.—διώρυγας:
canals. Cp. Hdt. vii 23 : Strab. IV 1 § 8.
—συνεστηκὸς ὕδωρ: like our *standing
water.*—ἔν τε τοῖς ξύλοις καὶ ἐν τοῖς
λίθοις: R.V. 'both in vessels of wood
and in vessels of stone,' which is no
doubt the meaning intended here.
20. ἐπάρας τῇ ῥάβδῳ αὐτοῦ: cp.
14¹⁶.
22. ἐποίησαν δὲ ὡσαύτως: these
words are more consistent with the
miracle promised in 4⁹ than with that
which has been related.—ἐσκλήρυνεν:
here intransitive. Cp. 7²², 13¹⁵. It is
generally transitive as in 4²¹, 7³, 9¹²,

10¹, ²⁰, ²⁷, 11¹⁰, 14⁴, ⁸, ¹⁷. Cp. Rom. 9¹⁸,
Hb. 3⁸.
23. ἐπέστησεν τὸν νοῦν: this explains the elliptical use of ἐφιστάναι
which meets us in Greek authors in the
sense of 'dwelling' on a subject, e.g.
Arist. E.N. VI 12 § 8, Pol. VII 17 § 12
ὕστερον δ' ἐπιστήσαντες δεῖ διορίσαι μᾶλλον.
24. πάντες οἱ Αἰγύπτιοι: What
then did the Israelites do for drink?
If this statement belongs to the narrative which puts the Israelites away in
Goshen, the difficulty is removed.
Josephus's explanation (*Ant.* II 14 § 1)

Exodus VIII 8

¹Εἶπεν δὲ Κύριος πρὸς Μωυσῆν " Εἴσελθε πρὸς Φαραὼ καὶ ἐρεῖς πρὸς αὐτόν ' Τάδε λέγει Κύριος Ἐξαπόστειλον τὸν λαόν μου ἵνα μοι λατρεύσωσιν · ²εἰ δὲ μὴ βούλει σὺ ἐξαποστεῖλαι, ἰδοὺ ἐγὼ τύπτω πάντα τὰ ὅριά σου τοῖς βατράχοις. ³καὶ ἐξερεύξεται ὁ ποταμὸς βατράχους · καὶ ἀναβάντες εἰσελεύσονται εἰς τοὺς οἴκους σου καὶ εἰς τὰ ταμεῖα τῶν κοιτώνων σου καὶ ἐπὶ τῶν κλινῶν σου, καὶ ἐπὶ τοὺς οἴκους τῶν θεραπόντων σου καὶ τοῦ λαοῦ σου, καὶ ἐν τοῖς φυράμασίν σου καὶ ἐν τοῖς κλιβάνοις σου · ⁴καὶ ἐπὶ σὲ καὶ ἐπὶ τοὺς θεράποντάς σου καὶ ἐπὶ τὸν λαόν σου ἀναβήσονται οἱ βάτραχοι.' " ⁵εἶπεν δὲ Κύριος πρὸς Μωυσῆν " Εἰπὸν Ἀαρὼν τῷ ἀδελφῷ σου ' Ἔκτεινον τῇ χειρὶ τὴν ῥάβδον σου ἐπὶ τοὺς ποταμοὺς καὶ ἐπὶ τὰς διώρυγας καὶ ἐπὶ τὰ ἕλη, καὶ ἀνάγαγε τοὺς βατράχους.' " ⁶καὶ ἐξέτεινεν Ἀαρὼν τὴν χεῖρα ἐπὶ τὰ ὕδατα Αἰγύπτου, καὶ ἀνήγαγεν τοὺς βατράχους · καὶ ἀνεβιβάσθη ὁ βάτραχος, καὶ ἐκάλυψεν τὴν γῆν Αἰγύπτου. ⁷ἐποίησαν δὲ ὡσαύτως καὶ οἱ ἐπαοιδοὶ τῶν Αἰγυπτίων ταῖς φαρμακίαις αὐτῶν, καὶ ἀνήγαγον τοὺς βατράχους ἐπὶ γῆν Αἰγύπτου. ⁸καὶ ἐκάλεσεν Φαραὼ Μωυσῆν καὶ Ἀαρὼν καὶ εἶπεν " Εὔξασθε περὶ ἐμοῦ πρὸς Κύριον, καὶ περιελέτω τοὺς βατράχους ἀπ' ἐμοῦ καὶ ἀπὸ τοῦ ἐμοῦ λαοῦ, καὶ ἐξαποστελῶ αὐτοὺς καὶ

is that the same Nile water which was foul and deadly to the Egyptians was pure and sweet to the Hebrews. — οὐκ ἠδύναντο πιεῖν: Josephus (*Ant.* II 14 § 1) says that the water caused 'pains and sharp anguish to those who did try to drink of it.'

1. Εἴσελθε . . . καὶ ἐρεῖς: § 74. Vs. 1–4 end chapter 7 in the Hebrew, but begin chapter 8 in the English.

3. τὰ ταμεῖα τῶν κοιτώνων: *bedchambers.* § 10. — φυράμασιν: *lumps of dough.* The word occurs again in

12³⁴ and in Nb. 15²⁰, ²¹. *Cp.* Rom. 9²¹ : i Cor. 5⁶, ⁷ : Gal. 5⁹. Jos. *Ant.* II 14 § 2 τάς τε κατ' οἶκον αὐτῶν διαίτας ἠφάνιζον ἐν βοτοῖς (*eatables*) εὑρισκόμενοι καὶ ποτοῖς. — κλιβάνοις : κλίβανος = Attic κρίβανος an *oven* or rather *baking-pot.*

6. ὁ βάτραχος : collective use of the singular, as in the Hebrew. *Cp.* 18 τὸν σκνῖφα, 10¹³ τὴν ἀκρίδα, 10¹⁴ τοιαύτη ἀκρίς § 48.

8. ἐξαποστελῶ . . . καὶ θύσωσιν : 43⁴ n.

θύσωσιν τῷ κυρίῳ." ⁹εἶπεν δὲ Μωυσῆς πρὸς Φαραώ "Τάξαι πρὸς μὲ πότε εὔξωμαι περὶ σοῦ καὶ περὶ τῶν θεραπόντων
σου καὶ περὶ τοῦ λαοῦ σου, ἀφανίσαι τοὺς βατράχους ἀπὸ
σοῦ καὶ ἀπὸ τοῦ λαοῦ σου καὶ ἐκ τῶν οἰκιῶν ὑμῶν· πλὴν ἐν
τῷ ποταμῷ ὑπολειφθήσονται." ¹⁰ὁ δὲ εἶπεν "Εἰς αὔριον."
εἶπεν οὖν "'Ως εἴρηκας· ἵνα ἴδῃς ὅτι οὐκ ἔστιν ἄλλος πλὴν
Κυρίου· ¹¹καὶ περιαιρεθήσονται οἱ βάτραχοι ἀπὸ σοῦ καὶ
ἐκ τῶν οἰκιῶν ὑμῶν καὶ ἐκ τῶν ἐπαύλεων καὶ ἀπὸ τῶν θεραπόντων σου καὶ ἀπὸ τοῦ λαοῦ σου· πλὴν ἐν τῷ ποταμῷ
ὑπολειφθήσονται." ¹²ἐξῆλθεν δὲ Μωυσῆς καὶ 'Ααρὼν ἀπὸ
Φαραώ· καὶ ἐβόησεν Μωυσῆς πρὸς Κύριον περὶ τοῦ ὁρισμοῦ τῶν βατράχων, ὡς ἐτάξατο Φαραώ. ¹³ἐποίησεν δὲ
Κύριος καθάπερ εἶπεν Μωυσῆς, καὶ ἐτελεύτησαν οἱ βάτραχοι
ἐκ τῶν οἰκιῶν καὶ ἐκ τῶν ἐπαύλεων καὶ ἐκ τῶν ἀγρῶν·
¹⁴καὶ συνήγαγον αὐτοὺς θιμωνιὰς θιμωνιάς, καὶ ὤζεσεν ἡ
γῆ. ¹⁵ἰδὼν δὲ Φαραὼ ὅτι γέγονεν ἀνάψυξις, ἐβαρύνθη ἡ
καρδία αὐτοῦ καὶ οὐκ εἰσήκουσεν αὐτῶν, καθάπερ ἐλάλησεν
Κύριος.

9. Τάξαι πρὸς μὲ κτλ.: *Arrange
with me when I am to pray.* The Hebrew differs here. See R.V.

10. οὐκ ἔστιν ἄλλος πλὴν Κυρίου:
again a slight difference from the Hebrew. See R.V.

11. ἐπαύλεων: genitive plural of
ἔπαυλις, a word which bears different
meanings, one of which is 'cattle-
shed,' as in Nb. 32¹⁶, ²⁴, ³⁶, another
'village,' as in i Chr. 4³², ³³. In the
Hebrew there is nothing to correspond
to the word in this passage, though
there is in v. 13.

12. ὁρισμοῦ: Hebrew, 'about the
matter of the frogs.' The Greek rendering is a curious one. Can it mean
*about the limitation of the frogs (to the*

*river*), with reference to v. 5 ? — Φαραώ :
dative, as appears from the Hebrew.

14. θιμωνιὰς θιμωνιάς: *heaps upon
heaps.* A Hebraism. § 85. Θιμωνιά
= θημωνιά is a longer form of θημών a
*heap*, connected with τίθημι. For the
word *cp.* i Mac. 11⁴. It occurs seven
times in the LXX.

15. ἰδὼν δὲ Φαραώ . . . ἐβαρύνθη ἡ
καρδία αὐτοῦ: *nominativus pendens,*
of which there are plenty of instances
in classical Greek. There is nothing
to suggest this license in the Hebrew,
which runs literally thus — 'And
Pharaoh saw . . . and he made heavy
his heart.' § 80. — ἀνάψυξις: literally
*a cooling.* Here *a respite.* The word
occurs only here in the LXX.

II. THE STORY OF THE EXODUS   177

¹⁶Εἶπεν δὲ Κύριος πρὸς Μωυσῆν " Εἰπὸν ᾿Ααρών '῎Εκτει-
νον τῇ χειρὶ τὴν ῥάβδον σου καὶ πάταξον τὸ χῶμα τῆς γῆς,
καὶ ἔσονται σκνῖφες ἔν τε τοῖς ἀνθρώποις καὶ ἐν τοῖς τετράποσιν καὶ ἐν πάσῃ γῇ Αἰγύπτου.'" ¹⁷ἐξέτεινεν οὖν ᾿Ααρὼν
τῇ χειρὶ τὴν ῥάβδον καὶ ἐπάταξεν τὸ χῶμα τῆς γῆς, καὶ
ἐγένοντο οἱ σκνῖφες ἐν τοῖς ἀνθρώποις καὶ ἐν τοῖς τετρά-
ποσιν· καὶ ἐν παντὶ χώματι τῆς γῆς ἐγένοντο οἱ σκνῖφες.
¹⁸ἐποίησαν δὲ ὡσαύτως καὶ οἱ ἐπαοιδοὶ ταῖς φαρμακίαις αὐτῶν
ἐξαγαγεῖν τὸν σκνῖφα, καὶ οὐκ ἠδύναντο· καὶ ἐγένοντο οἱ
σκνῖφες ἐν τοῖς ἀνθρώποις καὶ ἐν τοῖς τετράποσιν.   ¹⁹εἶπαν
οὖν οἱ ἐπαοιδοὶ τῷ Φαραώ " Δάκτυλος θεοῦ ἐστὶν τοῦτο·"
καὶ ἐσκληρύνθη ἡ καρδία Φαραώ, καὶ οὐκ εἰσήκουσεν
αὐτῶν, καθάπερ ἐλάλησεν Κύριος.

²⁰Εἶπεν δὲ Κύριος πρὸς Μωυσῆν "῎Ορθρισον τὸ πρωὶ καὶ
στῆθι ἐναντίον Φαραώ· καὶ ἰδοὺ αὐτὸς ἐξελεύσεται ἐπὶ τὸ
ὕδωρ, καὶ ἐρεῖς πρὸς αὐτόν ' Τάδε λέγει Κύριος " Ἐξαπόστειλον τὸν λαόν μου ἵνα μοι λατρεύσωσιν ἐν τῇ ἐρήμῳ·   ²¹ἐὰν δὲ
μὴ βούλῃ ἐξαποστεῖλαι τὸν λαόν μου, ἰδοὺ ἐγὼ ἐπαποστέλλω
ἐπὶ σὲ καὶ ἐπὶ τοὺς θεράποντάς σου καὶ ἐπὶ τὸν λαόν σου
καὶ ἐπὶ τοὺς οἴκους ὑμῶν κυνόμυιαν, καὶ πλησθήσονται αἱ

---

**16. τὸ χῶμα τῆς γῆς :** cp. Job 14¹⁹.
χῶμα is properly *earth thrown up* (*by
the spade*), the result of the process
signified by χώννυμι or χόω. From this
general sense we have χῶμα = Latin
*agger*, while here the word signifies
*loose earth*, answering to the Hebrew
word which is rendered *dust.* — σκνῖφες : nominative singular σκνίψ. In
Ps. 104³¹ σκνῖπες : Wisd. 19¹⁰ σκνῖπα.
§ 5. Josephus (*Ant.* II 14 § 3) has
φθεῖρες and the R.V. 'lice.' Josephus
comments on the shamefulness to the
Egyptians of this plague. *Cp.* what
Herodotus (II 37) says of the careful-

ness of the Egyptian priests about
avoiding lice on their persons.— ἐν
πάσῃ γῇ : § 63.
**20.** ῎Ορθρισον : ὀρθρίζειν is Biblical
Greek for ὀρθρεύειν, which occurs only
in Tob. 9³, whereas ὀρθρίζειν is very
common in the LXX. *Cp.* Lk. 21³⁸.
**21.** κυνόμυιαν : *cp.* Ps. 77⁴⁵, 104³¹.
The common house-fly in Egypt has a
poisonous bite, as it has sometimes in
England in a very hot summer. As
soon as one arrives in the harbour of
Alexandria, one has experience of this
Egyptian plague. Josephus (*Ant.* II
14 § 3) seems to give the rein to his

οἰκίαι τῶν Αἰγυπτίων τῆς κυνομυίης, καὶ εἰς τὴν γῆν ἐφ᾽ ἧς εἰσὶν ἐπ᾽ αὐτῆς. ²²καὶ παραδοξάσω ἐν τῇ ἡμέρᾳ ἐκείνῃ τὴν γῆν Γέσεμ, ἐφ᾽ ἧς ὁ λαός μου ἔπεστιν ἐπ᾽ αὐτῆς, ἐφ᾽ ἧς οὐκ ἔσται ἐκεῖ ἡ κυνόμυια· ἵνα εἰδῇς ὅτι ἐγώ εἰμι Κύριος ὁ κύριος πάσης τῆς γῆς. ²³καὶ δώσω διαστολὴν ἀνὰ μέσον τοῦ ἐμοῦ λαοῦ καὶ ἀνὰ μέσον τοῦ σοῦ λαοῦ· ἐν δὲ τῇ αὔριον ἔσται τοῦτο ἐπὶ τῆς γῆς.""" ²⁴ἐποίησεν δὲ Κύριος οὕτως, καὶ παρεγένετο ἡ κυνόμυια πλῆθος εἰς τοὺς οἴκους Φαραὼ καὶ εἰς τοὺς οἴκους τῶν θεραπόντων αὐτοῦ καὶ εἰς πᾶσαν τὴν γῆν Αἰγύπτου· καὶ ἐξωλεθρεύθη ἡ γῆ ἀπὸ τῆς κυνομυίης. ²⁵ἐκάλεσεν δὲ Φαραὼ Μωυσῆν καὶ Ἀαρὼν λέγων "Ἐλθόντες θύσατε τῷ θεῷ ὑμῶν ἐν τῇ γῇ." ²⁶καὶ εἶπεν Μωυσῆς "Οὐ δυνατὸν γενέσθαι οὕτως τὸ ῥῆμα τοῦτο, τὰ γὰρ βδελύγματα τῶν Αἰγυπτίων θύσομεν Κυρίῳ τῷ θεῷ ἡμῶν· ἐὰν γὰρ θύσωμεν τὰ βδελύγματα τῶν Αἰγυπτίων ἐναντίον αὐτῶν, λιθοβοληθησόμεθα. ²⁷ὁδὸν τριῶν ἡμερῶν πορευσόμεθα εἰς τὴν ἔρημον, καὶ θύσομεν τῷ θεῷ ἡμῶν καθάπερ εἶπεν Κύριος ἡμῖν." ²⁸καὶ εἶπεν Φαραώ "Ἐγὼ ἀποστέλλω ὑμᾶς, καὶ

fancy here— Θηρίων γὰρ παντοίων καὶ πολυτρόπων, ὧν εἰς ὄψιν οὐδεὶς ἀπηντήκει πρότερον, τὴν χώραν αὐτῶν ἐγέμισεν, ὑφ᾽ ὧν αὐτοί τε ἀπώλλυντο, καὶ ἡ γῆ τῆς ἐπιμελείας τῆς παρὰ τῶν γεωργῶν ἀπεστέρητο.

**22. παραδοξάσω**: *make remarkable* and so *distinguish*. *Cp.* the two uses of 'distinguished' in English. The word occurs also in 9⁴, 11⁷: Dt. 28⁵⁹: Sir. 10¹³: ii Mac. 3³⁰: iii Mac. 2⁹.

**23. δώσω διαστολήν**: *make a separation*. The phrase in this sense occurs only here. In i Mac. 8⁷ the meaning is different. —**ἀνὰ μέσον . . . καὶ ἀνὰ μέσον**: a common Hebraism.

**24. πλῆθος**: adverb, *in abundance*.

The Hebrew runs literally thus — 'and fly came heavy to the house of Pharaoh.' —**ἐξωλεθρεύθη**: from ἐξολεθρεύω. The right form, according to L. & S. is ἐξολοθρεύω, which occurs in iii K. 18⁵ and is adopted by the Revisers in the N.T. (Acts 3²³).

**26. τὰ γὰρ βδελύγματα κτλ.**: this looks as if it referred to sheep or oxen (*cp.* Gen. 46³⁴), but the Hebrew has the word for 'abomination' in the singular, which may be taken as a cognate accusative after 'sacrifice,' so that the words may mean merely *our sacrifice will be an abomination to the Egyptians*, i.e. the sight of a foreign ritual will be hateful to them. — **λιθοβοληθησόμεθα**: λιθοβολεῖν is common in

Exodus IX 4

θύσατε τῷ θεῷ ὑμῶν ἐν τῇ ἐρήμῳ, ἀλλ' οὐ μακρὰν ἀποτενεῖτε πορευθῆναι· εὔξασθε οὖν περὶ ἐμοῦ πρὸς Κύριον."
²⁹ εἶπεν δὲ Μωυσῆς "Ὅδε ἐγὼ ἐξελεύσομαι ἀπὸ σοῦ καὶ εὔξο-
μαι πρὸς τὸν θεόν, καὶ ἀπελεύσεται ἀπὸ σοῦ ἡ κυνόμυια καὶ
ἀπὸ τῶν θεραπόντων σου καὶ τοῦ λαοῦ σου αὔριον· μὴ προσθῇς ἔτι, Φαραώ, ἐξαπατῆσαι τοῦ μὴ ἐξαποστεῖλαι τὸν λαὸν
θῦσαι Κυρίῳ."    ³⁰ ἐξῆλθεν δὲ Μωυσῆς ἀπὸ Φαραὼ καὶ
ηὔξατο πρὸς τὸν θεόν·    ³¹ ἐποίησεν δὲ Κύριος καθάπερ εἶπεν
Μωυσῆς, καὶ περιεῖλεν τὴν κυνόμυιαν ἀπὸ Φαραὼ καὶ τῶν
θεραπόντων αὐτοῦ καὶ τοῦ λαοῦ αὐτοῦ, καὶ οὐ κατελείφθη
οὐδεμία.    ³² καὶ ἐβάρυνεν Φαραὼ τὴν καρδίαν αὐτοῦ καὶ
ἐπὶ τοῦ καιροῦ τούτου, καὶ οὐκ ἠθέλησεν ἐξαποστεῖλαι
τὸν λαόν.

¹ Εἶπεν δὲ Κύριος πρὸς Μωυσῆν " Εἴσελθε πρὸς Φαραὼ
καὶ ἐρεῖς αὐτῷ ' Τάδε λέγει Κύριος ὁ θεὸς τῶν Ἑβραίων " Ἐξαπόστειλον τὸν λαόν μου ἵνα μοι λατρεύσωσιν·    ² εἰ μὲν οὖν μὴ
βούλει ἐξαποστεῖλαι τὸν λαόν μου ἀλλ' ἔτι ἐνκρατεῖς αὐτοῦ,
³ ἰδοὺ χεὶρ Κυρίου ἐπέσται ἐν τοῖς κτήνεσίν σου τοῖς ἐν τοῖς
πεδίοις, ἔν τε τοῖς ἵπποις καὶ ἐν τοῖς ὑποζυγίοις καὶ ταῖς
καμήλοις καὶ βουσὶν καὶ προβάτοις θάνατος μέγας σφόδρα.
⁴ καὶ παραδοξάσω ἐγὼ ἐν τῷ καιρῷ ἐκείνῳ ἀνὰ μέσον τῶν

Biblical Greek, but rare outside of
it.
**28.** οὐ μακρὰν ἀποτενεῖτε πορευθῆναι : Hebrew, 'going-to-a-distance ye
shall not go-to-a-distance for-going.'
R.V. 'ye shall not go very far away.'
**29.** Ὅδε ἐγώ : R.V. 'Behold I go
out from thee.' The Greek translator
seems to have taken the first two words
together in the sense of Ecce ego!
In the rest of the verse the Greek
has the 2d person, while the Hebrew
has the 3d. — τοῦ μὴ ἐξαποστεῖλαι :
§ 78.

**2.** εἰ μὲν οὖν : there is no clause
with εἰ δὲ μή to balance this, such as
one would expect in classical Greek.
§ 39. — ἐνκρατεῖς : § 37.
**3.** ὑποζυγίοις : Hebrew, 'asses.' —
ταῖς καμήλοις : The feminine is the
prevailing gender of κάμηλος in the
LXX. It is masculine only in Lev.
11⁴ : Dt. 14⁷ : Jdg. 6⁵ : i Esd. 5⁴³. —
προβάτοις : Hebrew, 'flocks.' It would
seem that the Egyptians kept sheep,
notwithstanding their abomination of
shepherds.
**4.** παραδοξάσω : 8²² n. — ἀνὰ μέσον

Exodus IX 5

κτηνῶν τῶν Αἰγυπτίων καὶ ἀνὰ μέσον τῶν κτηνῶν τῶν υἱῶν
Ἰσραήλ· οὐ τελευτήσει ἀπὸ πάντων τῶν τοῦ Ἰσραὴλ υἱῶν
ῥητόν." ' " ⁵καὶ ἔδωκεν ὁ θεὸς ὅρον λέγων " Ἐν τῇ αὔριον
ποιήσει Κύριος τὸ ῥῆμα τοῦτο ἐπὶ τῆς γῆς." ⁶καὶ ἐποίησεν
Κύριος τὸ ῥῆμα τοῦτο· τῇ ἐπαύριον, καὶ ἐτελεύτησεν πάντα
τὰ κτήνη τῶν Αἰγυπτίων· ἀπὸ δὲ τῶν κτηνῶν τῶν υἱῶν
Ἰσραὴλ οὐκ ἐτελεύτησεν οὐδέν. ⁷ἰδὼν δὲ Φαραὼ ὅτι οὐκ
ἐτελεύτησεν ἀπὸ πάντων τῶν κτηνῶν τῶν υἱῶν Ἰσραὴλ οὐδέν,
ἐβαρύνθη ἡ καρδία Φαραώ, καὶ οὐκ ἐξαπέστειλεν τὸν λαόν.

⁸Εἶπεν δὲ Κύριος πρὸς Μωυσῆν καὶ Ἀαρὼν λέγων "Λάβετε
ὑμεῖς πλήρεις τὰς χεῖρας αἰθάλης καμιναίας, καὶ πασάτω
Μωυσῆς εἰς τὸν οὐρανὸν ἐναντίον Φαραὼ καὶ ἐναντίον τῶν
θεραπόντων αὐτοῦ, ⁹καὶ γενηθήτω κονιορτὸς ἐπὶ πᾶσαν τὴν
γῆν Αἰγύπτου· καὶ ἔσται ἐπὶ τοὺς ἀνθρώπους καὶ ἐπὶ τὰ
τετράποδα ἕλκη, φλυκτίδες ἀναζέουσαι, ἔν τε τοῖς ἀνθρώποις
καὶ ἐν τοῖς τετράποσιν καὶ πάσῃ γῇ Αἰγύπτου." ¹⁰καὶ ἔλαβεν τὴν αἰθάλην τῆς καμιναίας ἐναντίον Φαραὼ καὶ ἔπασεν
αὐτὴν Μωυσῆς εἰς τὸν οὐρανόν, καὶ ἐγένετο ἕλκη, φλυκτίδες
ἀναζέουσαι, ἐν τοῖς ἀνθρώποις καὶ ἐν τοῖς τετράποσιν.
¹¹καὶ οὐκ ἠδύναντο οἱ φαρμακοὶ στῆναι ἐναντίον Μωυσῆ διὰ
τὰ ἕλκη· ἐγένετο γὰρ τὰ ἕλκη ἐν τοῖς φαρμακοῖς καὶ ἐν
πάσῃ γῇ Αἰγύπτου. ¹²ἐσκλήρυνεν δὲ Κύριος τὴν καρδίαν
Φαραώ, καὶ οὐκ εἰσήκουσεν αὐτῶν, καθὰ συνέταξεν Κύριος.

¹³Εἶπεν δὲ Κύριος πρὸς Μωυσῆν "*Ὄρθρισον τὸ πρωὶ
καὶ στῆθι ἐναντίον Φαραώ, καὶ ἐρεῖς πρὸς αὐτόν ' Τάδε λέγει

---

. . . καὶ ἀνὰ μέσον: 8²³ n. — ῥητόν :
= ῥῆμα, a thing. Gen. 39⁹ n.

7. ἰδὼν δὲ Φαραώ . . . ἐβαρύνθη ἡ
καρδία : 8¹⁵ n.

8. αἰθάλης καμιναίας :·soot from the
furnace. From 10 it appears that
καμιναίας is a substantive depending on

αἰθάλης. Καμιναῖα does not seem to be
so used anywhere else. On the form
αἰθάλη see § 8. — πασάτω : imperative
of ἔπασα, 1st aorist of πάσσω.

9. φλυκτίδες : φλυκτίς = φλύκταινα
a blister (Ar. Ran. 236) occurs only
here in LXX.

Exodus IX 23

Κύριος ὁ θεὸς τῶν Ἑβραίων " Ἐξαπόστειλον τὸν λαόν μου ἵνα λατρεύσωσίν μοι. ¹⁴ἐν τῷ γὰρ νῦν καιρῷ ἐγὼ ἐξαποστέλλω πάντα τὰ συναντήματά μου εἰς τὴν καρδίαν σου καὶ τῶν θεραπόντων σου καὶ τοῦ λαοῦ σου, ἵν᾽ εἰδῇς ὅτι οὐκ ἔστιν ὡς ἐγὼ ἄλλος ἐν πάσῃ τῇ γῇ. ¹⁵νῦν γὰρ ἀποστείλας τὴν χεῖρα πατάξω σε, καὶ τὸν λαόν σου θανατώσω, καὶ ἐκτριβήσῃ ἀπὸ τῆς γῆς · ¹⁶καὶ ἕνεκεν τούτου διετηρήθης ἵνα ἐνδείξωμαι ἐν σοὶ τὴν ἰσχύν μου, καὶ ὅπως διαγγελῇ τὸ ὄνομά μου ἐν πάσῃ τῇ γῇ. ¹⁷ἔτι οὖν σὺ ἐνποιῇ τοῦ λαοῦ μου τοῦ μὴ ἐξαποστεῖλαι αὐτούς ; ¹⁸ἰδοὺ ἐγὼ ὕω ταύτην τὴν ὥραν αὔριον χάλαζαν πολλὴν σφόδρα, ἥτις τοιαύτη οὐ γέγονεν ἐν Αἰγύπτῳ ἀφ᾽ ἧς ἡμέρας ἔκτισται ἕως τῆς ἡμέρας ταύτης. ¹⁹νῦν οὖν κατάσπευσον συναγαγεῖν τὰ κτήνη σου καὶ ὅσα σοί ἐστιν ἐν τῷ πεδίῳ · πάντες γὰρ οἱ ἄνθρωποι καὶ τὰ κτήνη ὅσα σοί ἐστιν ἐν τῷ πεδίῳ καὶ μὴ εἰσέλθῃ εἰς οἰκίαν, πέσῃ δὲ ἐπ᾽ αὐτὰ ἡ χάλαζα, τελευτήσει." " ²⁰ὁ φοβούμενος τὸ ῥῆμα Κυρίου τῶν θεραπόντων Φαραὼ συνήγαγεν τὰ κτήνη αὐτοῦ εἰς τοὺς οἴκους · ²¹ὃς δὲ μὴ προσέσχεν τῇ διανοίᾳ εἰς τὸ ῥῆμα Κυρίου, ἀφῆκεν τὰ κτήνη ἐν τοῖς πεδίοις. ²²Εἶπεν δὲ Κύριος πρὸς Μωυσῆν " Ἔκτεινον τὴν χεῖρά σου εἰς τὸν οὐρανόν, καὶ ἔσται χάλαζα ἐπὶ πᾶσαν γῆν Αἰγύπτου, ἐπί τε τοὺς ἀνθρώπους καὶ τὰ κτήνη καὶ ἐπὶ πᾶσαν βοτάνην τὴν ἐπὶ τῆς γῆς." ²³ἐξέτεινεν δὲ Μωυσῆς τὴν χεῖρα εἰς τὸν οὐρανόν, καὶ Κύριος ἔδωκεν φωνὰς καὶ χάλαζαν, καὶ διέτρε-

---

**14.** συναντήματα : literally *occurrences*, but used here with a sinister meaning to represent the Hebrew word for 'plagues.' *Cp.* iii K. 8³⁷. So in classical Greek τύχαι in the plural commonly means 'misfortunes.'

**16.** διαγγελῇ: § 24.

**17.** ἐνποιῇ : § 37.

**18.** ταύτην τὴν ὥραν : accusative of point of time. § 55. — ἥτις τοιαύτη : = classical οἵα. A Hebraism, which recurs in v. 24 and 11⁶. *Cp.* Ezk. 5⁹ ὅ ... ὅμοια αὐτοῖς. § 69.

**21.** προσέσχεν . . . εἰς: § 90.

**23.** φωνάς : *voices.* A literal translation of the Hebrew word. But thunder was habitually spoken of as

Exodus IX 24

χεν τὸ πῦρ ἐπὶ τῆς γῆς· καὶ ἔβρεξεν Κύριος χάλαζαν ἐπὶ
πᾶσαν γῆν Αἰγύπτου. ²⁴ἦν δὲ ἡ χάλαζα καὶ τὸ πῦρ φλογί-
ζον ἐν τῇ χαλάζῃ· ἡ δὲ χάλαζα πολλὴ σφόδρα, ἥτις τοιαύτη
οὐ γέγονεν ἐν Αἰγύπτῳ ἀφ᾽ ἧς ἡμέρας γεγένηται ἐπ᾽ αὐτῆς
ἔθνος. ²⁵ἐπάταξεν δὲ ἡ χάλαζα ἐν πάσῃ γῇ Αἰγύπτου ἀπὸ
ἀνθρώπου ἕως κτήνους, καὶ πᾶσαν βοτάνην τὴν ἐν τῷ πεδίῳ
ἐπάταξεν ἡ χάλαζα, καὶ πάντα τὰ ξύλα τὰ ἐν τοῖς πεδίοις
συνέτριψεν ἡ χάλαζα· ²⁶πλὴν ἐν γῇ Γέσεμ, οὗ ἦσαν οἱ υἱοὶ
Ἰσραήλ, οὐκ ἐγένετο ἡ χάλαζα. ²⁷ἀποστείλας δὲ Φαραὼ
ἐκάλεσεν Μωυσῆν καὶ Ἀαρὼν καὶ εἶπεν αὐτοῖς "Ἡμάρτηκα
τὸ νῦν· ὁ κύριος δίκαιος, ἐγὼ δὲ καὶ ὁ λαός μου ἀσεβεῖς.
²⁸εὔξασθε οὖν περὶ ἐμοῦ πρὸς Κύριον, καὶ παυσάσθω τοῦ
γενηθῆναι φωνὰς θεοῦ καὶ χάλαζαν καὶ πῦρ· καὶ ἐξαποστελῶ ὑμᾶς, καὶ οὐκέτι προστεθήσεσθε μένειν." ²⁹εἶπεν δὲ
αὐτῷ Μωυσῆς "Ὡς ἂν ἐξέλθω τὴν πόλιν, ἐκπετάσω τὰς χεῖράς μου, καὶ αἱ φωναὶ παύσονται, καὶ ἡ χάλαζα καὶ ὁ ὑετὸς
οὐκ ἔσται ἔτι· ἵνα γνῷς ὅτι τοῦ κυρίου ἡ γῆ. ³⁰καὶ σὺ καὶ οἱ
θεράποντές σου ἐπίσταμαι ὅτι οὐδέπω πεφόβησθε τὸν θεόν."
³¹τὸ δὲ λίνον καὶ ἡ κριθὴ ἐπλήγη· ἡ γὰρ κριθὴ παρεστη-

---

'the voice of God.' *Cp.* 48: i K. 12¹⁷.
—**ἔβρεξεν**: this use of βρέχειν for 'to
rain' is common in Biblical Greek, *e.g.*
Gen. 2⁵, 19²⁴: Mt. 4⁴⁵: Lk. 17²⁹. It is
condemned by Phrynichus as non-
Attic (Swete *Introd.* p. 296).
**25. ἀπό . . . ἕως**: Hebraism.
§ 92.
**29. ὡς ἂν**: *as soon as.* *Cp.* Ceb.
*Tab.* IV ὡς ἂν εἰσέλθωσιν εἰς τὸν βίον, IX
ὡς ἂν παρέλθῃς: in N.T. Phil. 2²³ ὡς ἂν
ἀπίδω τὰ περὶ ἐμέ. —**ἐξέλθω τὴν πόλιν**:
*cp.* 12²² οὐκ ἐξελεύσεσθε ἕκαστος τὴν
θύραν. This transitive use of ἐξέρ-
χεσθαι, like Latin *egredi*, is not unknown to classical writers, but it is

here used because it exactly reflects
the original.
**30. πεφόβησθε**: for the perfect
used as present *cp.* Soph. *Aj.* 139 —
μέγαν ὄκνον ἔχω καὶ πεφόβημαι. The
R.V. has here 'ye will not fear.' The
vagueness of the Hebrew tense-system
renders such variations possible without any difference of reading. —**τὸν**
**θεόν**: Hebrew, 'JHVH God.'
**31. παρεστηκυῖα**: supply ἦν — *had
come*, *i.e.* the ears had formed themselves. Similarly dairy-maids talk of
butter 'coming' in the churn. The
Hebrew word here is Abib, which is
also the name of the month in which

Exodus X 3

κυΐα, τὸ δὲ λίνον σπερματίζον · ³²ὁ δὲ πυρὸς καὶ ἡ ὄλυρα οὐκ
ἐπλήγησαν, ὄψιμα γὰρ ἦν. ³³ἐξῆλθεν δὲ Μωυσῆς ἀπὸ
Φαραὼ ἐκτὸς τῆς πόλεως καὶ ἐξέτεινεν τὰς χεῖρας πρὸς
Κύριον · καὶ αἱ φωναὶ ἐπαύσαντο, καὶ ἡ χάλαζα καὶ ὁ ὑετὸς
οὐκ ἔσταξεν οὐκέτι ἐπὶ τὴν γῆν. ³⁴ἰδὼν δὲ Φαραὼ ὅτι
πέπαυται ὁ ὑετὸς καὶ ἡ χάλαζα καὶ αἱ φωναί, προσέθετο τοῦ
ἁμαρτάνειν, καὶ ἐβάρυνεν αὐτοῦ τὴν καρδίαν καὶ τῶν θεραπόντων αὐτοῦ. ³⁵καὶ ἐσκληρύνθη ἡ καρδία Φαραώ, καὶ οὐκ
ἐξαπέστειλεν τοὺς υἱοὺς Ἰσραήλ, καθάπερ ἐλάλησεν Κύριος
τῷ Μωυσῇ.

¹Εἶπεν δὲ Κύριος πρὸς Μωυσῆν λέγων " Εἴσελθε πρὸς
Φαραώ · ἐγὼ γὰρ ἐσκλήρυνα αὐτοῦ τὴν καρδίαν καὶ τῶν
θεραπόντων αὐτοῦ, ἵνα ἑξῆς ἐπέλθῃ τὰ σημεῖα ταῦτα ἐπ᾽
αὐτούς · ²ὅπως διηγήσησθε εἰς τὰ ὦτα τῶν τέκνων ὑμῶν καὶ
τοῖς τέκνοις τῶν τέκνων ὑμῶν ὅσα ἐμπέπαιχα τοῖς Αἰγυπτίοις,
καὶ τὰ σημεῖά μου ἃ ἐποίησα ἐν αὐτοῖς, καὶ γνώσεσθε ὅτι
ἐγὼ Κύριος." ³εἰσῆλθεν δὲ Μωυσῆς καὶ Ἀαρὼν ἐναντίον
Φαραὼ καὶ εἶπαν αὐτῷ " Τάδε λέγει Κύριος ὁ θεὸς τῶν
Ἑβραίων ' Ἕως τίνος οὐ βούλει ἐντραπῆναί με; ἐξαπόστειλον

the buds spring. — σπερματίζον : was
in seed. The word occurs in the LXX
only here and in Lvt. 12².

**32.** ὄλυρα : Gen. 40¹⁶ n. — ὄψιμα :
late crops, as compared with the barley
and flax. The Hebrew word corresponding to ὄψιμα is of doubtful meaning. R.V. ' not grown up.' For ὄψιμος
cp. Xen. Œc. XVII 4 and in N.T. St.
James 5⁷.

**1.** ἐγὼ γὰρ ἐσκλήρυνα κτλ. : cp. the
Greek conception of Atè as exemplified
by the tragedians, e.g. Soph. Ant. 621–
4 : also the Prophets, as Is. 6⁹,¹⁰. Here
the final cause of hardening Pharaoh's
heart is explained to be that God might
exhibit his power as a deliverer of

Israel. — ἵνα ἑξῆς ἐπέλθῃ κτλ. : the
Greek here differs slightly from the
Hebrew. See R.V.

**2.** ἐμπέπαιχα : cp. Nb. 22²⁹. This
form of the perfect of ἐμπαίζω is quoted
by Veitch from Plutarch Demosth. 9.
The earlier form is ἐμπέπαικα as from
a dental stem.

**3.** ἐντραπῆναί με : reverence me.
The verb in this sense with a genitive is common in classical Greek
from Homer downwards, but with
accusative it is post-classical. From
the meaning of ' reverence ' it
is an easy step to that of ' be
ashamed,' as in Ps. 34⁴ : ii Thes.
3¹⁴ : Tit. 2⁸.

Exodus X 4

τὸν λαόν μου ἵνα λατρεύσωσίν μοι.  ⁴ἐὰν δὲ μὴ θέλῃς σὺ
ἐξαποστεῖλαι τὸν λαόν μου, ἰδοὺ ἐγὼ ἐπάγω ταύτην τὴν ὥραν
αὔριον ἀκρίδα πολλὴν ἐπὶ πάντα τὰ ὅριά σου· ⁵καὶ καλύψει
τὴν ὄψιν τῆς γῆς, καὶ οὐ δυνήσῃ κατιδεῖν τὴν γῆν· καὶ κατέδεται πᾶν τὸ περισσὸν τῆς γῆς τὸ καταλειφθέν, ὃ κατέλιπεν
ὑμῖν ἡ χάλαζα, καὶ κατέδεται πᾶν ξύλον τὸ φυόμενον ὑμῖν
ἐπὶ τῆς γῆς· ⁶καὶ πλησθήσονταί σου αἱ οἰκίαι καὶ αἱ οἰκίαι
τῶν θεραπόντων σου καὶ πᾶσαι αἱ οἰκίαι ἐν πάσῃ γῇ τῶν
Αἰγυπτίων, ἃ οὐδέποτε ἑωράκασιν οἱ πατέρες σου οὐδὲ οἱ
πρόπαπποι αὐτῶν, ἀφ᾽ ἧς ἡμέρας γεγόνασιν ἐπὶ τῆς γῆς ἕως
τῆς ἡμέρας ταύτης.'" καὶ ἐκκλίνας Μωυσῆς ἐξῆλθεν ἀπὸ
Φαραώ. ⁷καὶ λέγουσιν οἱ θεράποντες Φαραὼ πρὸς αὐτόν
"Ἕως τίνος ἔσται τοῦτο ἡμῖν σκῶλον; ἐξαπόστειλον τοὺς
ἀνθρώπους ὅπως λατρεύσωσιν τῷ θεῷ αὐτῶν· ἢ εἰδέναι
βούλει ὅτι ἀπόλωλεν Αἴγυπτος;" ⁸καὶ ἀπέστρεψαν τόν τε
Μωυσῆν καὶ Ἀαρὼν πρὸς Φαραώ, καὶ εἶπεν αὐτοῖς "Πορεύεσθε καὶ λατρεύσατε τῷ θεῷ ὑμῶν· τίνες δὲ καὶ τίνες εἰσὶν οἱ
πορευόμενοι;" ⁹καὶ λέγει Μωυσῆς "Σὺν τοῖς νεανίσκοις καὶ
πρεσβυτέροις πορευσόμεθα, σὺν τοῖς υἱοῖς καὶ θυγατράσιν
καὶ προβάτοις καὶ βουσὶν ἡμῶν· ἔστιν γὰρ ἑορτὴ Κυρίου."
¹⁰καὶ εἶπεν πρὸς αὐτούς "Ἔστω οὕτως, Κύριος μεθ᾽ ὑμῶν·

---

5. τὴν ὄψιν τῆς γῆς : literally *the eye
of the earth.* A Hebraism. *Cp.* Nb.
22⁵, ¹¹.— οὐ δυνήσῃ : a fair equivalent
for the vague use of the 3d person in
the Hebrew.

6. πρόπαπποι : *great-grandfathers,*
Latin *proavi.* Only here in LXX.
The Hebrew means only 'grand-
fathers.'

7. τοῦτο : R.V. ' this man,' a meaning of which the Greek also admits by
attraction — σκῶλον : *a stumbling-
block,* like σκάνδαλον. Dt. 7¹⁶ : Jdg.
8²⁷, 11³⁵ (A) : ii Chr. 28²³ : Is. 57¹⁴.

Σκῶλος is used by Hom. *Il.* XIII 564 in
the same sense as σκόλοψ, a stake.—
εἰδέναι βούλει : Hebrew, 'Dost thou
not yet know?'

8. καὶ ἀπέστρεψαν : *and they
brought back,* just as in the Hebrew.
In the R.V. the sentence is turned
into the passive. — τίνες δὲ καὶ τίνες : a
literal translation from the Hebrew.
The form of the question seems to imply that a detailed answer is expected
— ' These and those shall go.'

10. Ἔστω οὕτως κτλ. : the passage
ought perhaps to be punctuated as

Exodus X 17

καθότι ἀποστέλλω ὑμᾶς, μὴ καὶ τὴν ἀποσκευὴν ὑμῶν ; ἴδετε, ὅτι πονηρία πρόσκειται ὑμῖν. ¹¹μὴ οὕτως· πορευέσθωσαν δὲ οἱ ἄνδρες καὶ λατρευσάτωσαν τῷ θεῷ· τοῦτο γὰρ αὐτοὶ ἐζητεῖτε." ἐξέβαλον δὲ αὐτοὺς ἀπὸ προσώπου Φαραώ. ¹²Εἶπεν δὲ Κύριος πρὸς Μωυσῆν "Ἔκτεινον τὴν χεῖρα ἐπὶ γῆν Αἰγύπτου, καὶ ἀναβήτω ἀκρὶς ἐπὶ τὴν γῆν, καὶ κατέδεται πᾶσαν βοτάνην τῆς γῆς καὶ πάντα τὸν καρπὸν τῶν ξύλων ὃν ὑπελίπετο ἡ χάλαζα." ¹³καὶ ἐπῆρεν Μωυσῆς τὴν ῥάβδον εἰς τὸν οὐρανόν, καὶ ἐπήγαγεν ἄνεμον νότον ἐπὶ τὴν γῆν ὅλην τὴν ἡμέραν ἐκείνην καὶ ὅλην τὴν νύκτα· τὸ πρωὶ ἐγενήθη, καὶ ὁ ἄνεμος ὁ νότος ἀνέλαβεν τὴν ἀκρίδα ¹⁴καὶ ἀνήγαγεν αὐτὴν ἐπὶ πᾶσαν γῆν Αἰγύπτου, καὶ κατέπαυσεν ἐπὶ πάντα τὰ ὅρια Αἰγύπτου πολλὴ σφόδρα· προτέρα αὐτῆς οὐ γέγονεν τοιαύτη ἀκρὶς καὶ μετὰ ταῦτα οὐκ ἔσται οὕτως. ¹⁵καὶ ἐκάλυψεν τὴν ὄψιν τῆς γῆς, καὶ ἐφθάρη ἡ γῆ· καὶ κατέφαγεν πᾶσαν βοτάνην τῆς γῆς καὶ πάντα τὸν καρπὸν τῶν ξύλων ὃς ὑπελείφθη ἀπὸ τῆς χαλάζης· οὐχ ὑπελείφθη χλωρὸν οὐδὲν ἐν τοῖς ξύλοις καὶ ἐν πάσῃ βοτάνῃ πεδίου ἐν γῇ Αἰγύπτου. ¹⁶κατέσπευδεν δὲ Φαραὼ καλέσαι Μωυσῆν καὶ Ἀαρὼν λέγων " Ἡμάρτηκα ἐναντίον Κυρίου τοῦ θεοῦ ὑμῶν καὶ εἰς ὑμᾶς· ¹⁷προσδέξασθε οὖν μου τὴν ἁμαρ-

follows—Ἔστω οὕτως Κύριος μεθ᾽ ὑμῶν, καθότι ἀποστέλλω ὑμᾶς. μὴ καὶ τὴν ἀποσκευὴν ὑμῶν; *So be the LORD with you, as I let you go* (i.e. *not at all*)! (*Am I to let go*) *your belongings also?* *Look out, for mischief is upon you.* Without the μή the passage would run as in the Hebrew and there would be no question-mark after ὑμῶν. For the threat with which Pharaoh closes his speech, *cp.* v. 28. — ἀποσκευήν : a word of vague meaning, as we have seen already. Gen. 43⁸ n. Here it includes the women and children : *cp.*

v. 24, 12³⁷. In Dt. 20¹⁴ the women are excluded.

**11.** ἐξέβαλον : the verb in the Hebrew is singular, but means 'one drove,' so that ἐξέβαλον correctly represents it. R.V. 'they were driven.'

**13.** ἐπήγαγεν : Hebrew, 'the LORD brought.' —ἀνέλαβεν : took up in the sense of *brought.*

**14.** καὶ ἀνήγαγεν αὐτήν : Hebrew, ' and the locust went up.'—ἀκρίς : collective for a locust-swarm. *Cp.* Jdg. 7¹² ὡσεὶ ἀκρὶς εἰς πλῆθος : Nahum 3¹⁷ § 48.

**17.** προσδέξασθε : from ' accepting '

τίαν ἔτι νῦν, καὶ προσεύξασθε πρὸς Κύριον τὸν θεὸν ὑμῶν, καὶ περιελέτω ἀπ᾽ ἐμοῦ τὸν θάνατον τοῦτον." ¹⁸ἐξῆλθεν δὲ Μωυσῆς ἀπὸ Φαραὼ καὶ ηὔξατο πρὸς τὸν θεόν. ¹⁹καὶ μετέβαλεν Κύριος ἄνεμον ἀπὸ θαλάσσης σφοδρόν, καὶ ἀνέλαβεν τὴν ἀκρίδα καὶ ἔβαλεν αὐτὴν εἰς τὴν ἐρυθρὰν θάλασσαν · καὶ οὐχ ὑπελείφθη ἀκρὶς μία ἐν πάσῃ γῇ Αἰγύπτου. ²⁰καὶ ἐσκλήρυνεν Κύριος τὴν καρδίαν Φαραώ, καὶ οὐκ ἐξαπέστειλεν τοὺς υἱοὺς Ἰσραήλ.

²¹Εἶπεν δὲ Κύριος πρὸς Μωυσῆν "Ἔκτεινον τὴν χεῖρά σου εἰς τὸν οὐρανόν, καὶ γενηθήτω σκότος ἐπὶ γῆν Αἰγύπτου, ψηλαφητὸν σκότος." ²²ἐξέτεινεν δὲ Μωυσῆς τὴν χεῖρα εἰς τὸν οὐρανόν, καὶ ἐγένετο σκότος γνόφος θύελλα ἐπὶ πᾶσαν γῆν Αἰγύπτου τρεῖς ἡμέρας · ²³καὶ οὐκ εἶδεν οὐδεὶς τὸν ἀδελφὸν αὐτοῦ τρεῖς ἡμέρας, καὶ οὐκ ἐξανέστη οὐδεὶς ἐκ τῆς κοίτης αὐτοῦ τρεῖς ἡμέρας · πᾶσι δὲ τοῖς υἱοῖς Ἰσραὴλ φῶς ἦν ἐν πᾶσιν οἷς κατεγίνοντο. ²⁴καὶ ἐκάλεσεν Φαραὼ Μωυσῆν καὶ Ἀαρὼν λέγων "Βαδίζετε λατρεύσατε Κυρίῳ τῷ θεῷ ὑμῶν · πλὴν τῶν προβάτων καὶ τῶν βοῶν ὑπολίπεσθε, καὶ ἡ ἀποσκευὴ ὑμῶν ἀποτρεχέτω μεθ᾽ ὑμῶν." ²⁵καὶ εἶπεν Μωυσῆς "Ἀλλὰ καὶ σὺ δώσεις ἡμῖν ὁλοκαυτώματα καὶ θυσίας ἃ ποιήσομεν Κυρίῳ τῷ θεῷ ἡμῶν, ²⁶καὶ τὰ κτήνη ἡμῶν πορεύ-

atonement for sin, προσδέχεσθαι here passes into the meaning of 'to forgive.'
—τὸν θάνατον τοῦτον : Hebrew, 'only this death.'

21. ψηλαφητὸν σκότος : the neuter σκότος occurs in good writers, but the masculine is more common.

22. σκότος γνόφος θύελλα : Hebrew, 'a thick darkness.' Cp. 14²⁰ καὶ ἐγένετο σκότος καὶ γνόφος, 20²¹ εἰς τὸν γνόφον : Dt. 4¹¹, 6²² σκότος γνόφος θύελλα. γνόφος = δνόφος. For the asyndeton cp. 15⁴.

23. οὐδεὶς τὸν ἀδελφὸν αὐτοῦ : § 68.
—ἐν πᾶσιν οἷς κατεγίνοντο : in all the

places in which they dwelt. Καταγίνεσθαι occurs also in Nb. 5³ : Dt. 9⁹ : Bel. O' ²¹.

24. πλὴν . . . ὑπολίπεσθε : R.V. 'Only let your flocks and your herds be stayed' (i.e. left where they are). The meaning intended by the Greek is perhaps Only leave yourselves without your flocks and your herds. Or has πλήν drawn τὰ πρόβατα κτλ. into the genitive ?

25. ὁλοκαυτώματα : iii Κ. 18²⁹ n.—
ἃ ποιήσομεν : which we shall offer. In classical Greek ποιεῖν and ῥέζειν are the

Exodus XI 5

σεται μεθ᾽ ἡμῶν, καὶ οὐχ ὑπολειφθησόμεθα ὁπλήν· ἀπ᾽ αὐτῶν γὰρ λημψόμεθα λατρεῦσαι Κυρίῳ τῷ θεῷ ἡμῶν· ἡμεῖς δὲ οὐκ οἴδαμεν τί λατρεύσωμεν Κυρίῳ τῷ θεῷ ἡμῶν ἕως τοῦ ἐλθεῖν ἡμᾶς ἐκεῖ." ²⁷ ἐσκλήρυνεν δὲ Κύριος τὴν καρδίαν Φαραώ, καὶ οὐκ ἐβουλήθη ἐξαποστεῖλαι αὐτούς. ²⁸ καὶ λέγει Φαραώ "Ἄπελθε ἀπ᾽ ἐμοῦ, πρόσεχε σεαυτῷ ἔτι προσθεῖναι ἰδεῖν μου τὸ πρόσωπον· ᾗ δ᾽ ἂν ἡμέρᾳ ὀφθῇς μοι, ἀποθανῇ." ²⁹ λέγει δὲ Μωσῆς " Εἴρηκας· οὐκέτι ὀφθήσομαί σοι εἰς πρόσωπον."

¹ Εἶπεν δὲ Κύριος πρὸς Μωυσῆν "Ἔτι μίαν πληγὴν ἐπάξω ἐπὶ Φαραὼ καὶ ἐπ᾽ Αἴγυπτον, καὶ μετὰ ταῦτα ἐξαποστελεῖ ὑμᾶς ἐντεῦθεν· ὅταν δὲ ἐξαποστέλλῃ ὑμᾶς, σὺν παντὶ ἐκβαλεῖ ὑμᾶς ἐκβολῇ. ² λάλησον οὖν κρυφῇ εἰς τὰ ὦτα τοῦ λαοῦ, καὶ αἰτησάτω ἕκαστος παρὰ τοῦ πλησίον σκεύη ἀργυρᾶ καὶ χρυσᾶ καὶ ἱματισμόν." ³ Κύριος δὲ ἔδωκεν τὴν χάριν τῷ λαῷ αὐτοῦ ἐναντίον τῶν Αἰγυπτίων, καὶ ἔχρησαν αὐτοῖς· καὶ ὁ ἄνθρωπος Μωσῆς μέγας ἐγενήθη σφόδρα ἐναντίον τῶν Αἰγυπτίων καὶ ἐναντίον Φαραὼ καὶ ἐναντίον πάντων τῶν θεραπόντων αὐτοῦ. ⁴ Καὶ εἶπεν Μωσῆς "Τάδε λέγει Κύριος 'Περὶ μέσας νύκτας ἐγὼ εἰσπορεύομαι εἰς μέσον Αἰγύπτου, ⁵ καὶ τελευτήσει πᾶν πρωτότοκον ἐν γῇ

regular words for 'doing sacrifice,' like *facere* and *operari* in Latin : but ποιεῖν does not seem to be constructed with an accusative of the victim, whereas ῥέζειν is. Verg. *Ecl.* III 77 cum faciam vitula ·pro frugibus.

**26.** τί λατρεύσωμεν : cognate accusative — *what service we are to perform.*

**28.** πρόσεχε . . . ἰδεῖν : literally *take heed to thyself about seeing me again.*

**29.** Εἴρηκας : Hebrew, 'Thus hast thou spoken.'

**1.** σὺν παντί : like our 'bag and baggage.' — ἐκβαλεῖ . . . ἐκβολῇ : cognate dative § 61. See 6¹ n.

**3.** καὶ ἔχρησαν αὐτοῖς : these words are not in the Hebrew here and seem to be imported from 12³⁶, but they serve to bring out the meaning. Here, as in 3²¹, ²², the Israelites are regarded as dwelling in the midst of the Egyptians.

**4.** Περὶ μέσας νύκτας : the use of the plural is classical. See for instance Xen. *Anab.* II 2 § 8, III 1 § 33: Plat. *Phileb.* 50 D, *Rep.* 621 B.

Exodus XI 6

Αἰγύπτῳ, ἀπὸ πρωτοτόκου Φαραὼ ὃς κάθηται ἐπὶ τοῦ θρόνου, καὶ ἕως πρωτοτόκου τῆς θεραπαίνης τῆς παρὰ τὸν μύλον
καὶ ἕως πρωτοτόκου παντὸς κτήνους· ⁶ καὶ ἔσται κραυγὴ
μεγάλη κατὰ πᾶσαν γῆν Αἰγύπτου, ἥτις τοιαύτη οὐ γέγονεν
καὶ τοιαύτη οὐκέτι προστεθήσεται. ⁷ καὶ ἐν πᾶσι τοῖς
υἱοῖς Ἰσραὴλ οὐ γρύξει κύων τῇ γλώσσῃ αὐτοῦ, οὐδὲ ἀπὸ
ἀνθρώπου ἕως κτήνους· ὅπως ἴδῃς ὅσα παραδοξάζει Κύριος
ἀνὰ μέσον τῶν Αἰγυπτίων καὶ τοῦ Ἰσραήλ.' ⁸ καὶ καταβή-
σονται πάντες οἱ παῖδές σου οὗτοι πρὸς μὲ καὶ προσκυνή-
σουσίν με λέγοντες '"Εξελθε σὺ καὶ πᾶς ὁ λαός σου οὗ σὺ
ἀφηγῇ·' καὶ μετὰ ταῦτα ἐξελεύσομαι." ἐξῆλθεν δὲ Μωυσῆς ἀπὸ Φαραὼ μετὰ θυμοῦ. ⁹ Εἶπεν δὲ Κύριος πρὸς
Μωυσῆν "Οὐκ εἰσακούσεται ὑμῶν Φαραώ, ἵνα πληθύνων
πληθύνω μου τὰ σημεῖα καὶ τὰ τέρατα ἐν γῇ Αἰγύπτῳ."
¹⁰ Μωσῆς δὲ καὶ Ἀαρὼν ἐποίησαν πάντα τὰ σημεῖα καὶ τὰ
τέρατα ταῦτα ἐν γῇ Αἰγύπτῳ ἐναντίον Φαραώ· ἐσκλήρυνεν
δὲ Κύριος τὴν καρδίαν Φαραώ, καὶ οὐκ εἰσήκουσεν ἐξαποστεῖλαι τοὺς υἱοὺς Ἰσραὴλ ἐκ γῆς Αἰγύπτου.

²⁹ Ἐγενήθη δὲ μεσούσης τῆς νυκτὸς καὶ Κύριος ἐπάταξεν
πᾶν πρωτότοκον ἐν γῇ Αἰγύπτῳ, ἀπὸ πρωτοτόκου Φαραὼ

---

**6.** ἥτις τοιαύτη : 9¹⁸ n. — οὐκέτι
προστεθήσεται : § 112.

**7.** οὐ γρύξει κύων : shall not a dog
growl. Demosthenes (p. 353, xix 39)
has οὐδὲ γρῦ in the sense of ' not a mut-
ter.' In the mind of the Greek translator a contrast seems to be here intended between the stillness among the
Jews (ἐν is an insertion of the LXX)
and the 'great cry' among the Egyptians. But this way of taking the
passage leaves no meaning to the
words οὐδὲ ἀπὸ ἀνθρώπου ἕως κτήνους. For γρύζειν cp. Josh. 10²¹ : Judith 11¹⁹ καὶ οὐ γρύξει κύων τῇ γλώσσῃ

αὐτοῦ ἀπέναντί σου. — παραδοξάζει :
8²² n.

**8.** ἐξῆλθεν δὲ Μωυσῆς : these words
form a natural sequel to Εἴρηκας κτλ.
at the end of chapter 10. From Josephus we might gather that in his copy
11⁸ followed immediately upon 10²⁹
(*Ant.* II 14 § 5).

**10.** ἐξαποστεῖλαι : infinitive of consequence. § 78. The short summary
of events given in this and the preceding verse seems to belong to the same
priestly document from which the Institution of the Passover (12¹⁻²⁸) is
taken. 12²⁹ follows very well on 11⁸.

Exodus XII 37

τοῦ καθημένου ἐπὶ τοῦ θρόνου ἕως πρωτοτόκου τῆς αἰχμα-
λωτίδος τῆς ἐν τῷ λάκκῳ, καὶ ἕως πρωτοτόκου παντὸς κτήνους.　³⁰ καὶ ἀναστὰς Φαραὼ νυκτὸς καὶ οἱ θεράποντες
αὐτοῦ καὶ πάντες οἱ Αἰγύπτιοι, καὶ ἐγενήθη κραυγὴ μεγάλη
ἐν πάσῃ γῇ Αἰγύπτῳ· οὐ γὰρ ἦν οἰκία ἐν ᾗ οὐκ ἦν ἐν αὐτῇ
τεθνηκώς.　³¹ καὶ ἐκάλεσεν Φαραὼ Μωυσῆν καὶ Ἀαρὼν
νυκτὸς καὶ εἶπεν αὐτοῖς "Ἀνάστητε καὶ ἐξέλθατε ἐκ τοῦ
λαοῦ μου, καὶ ὑμεῖς καὶ οἱ υἱοὶ Ἰσραήλ· βαδίζετε καὶ
λατρεύσατε Κυρίῳ τῷ θεῷ ὑμῶν καθὰ λέγετε·　³² καὶ τὰ
πρόβατα καὶ τοὺς βόας ὑμῶν ἀναλαβόντες πορεύεσθε, εὐ-
λογήσατε δὴ κἀμέ."　³³ καὶ κατεβιάζοντο οἱ Αἰγύπτιοι τὸν
λαὸν σπουδῇ ἐκβαλεῖν αὐτοὺς ἐκ τῆς γῆς· εἶπαν γὰρ ὅτι
"Πάντες ἡμεῖς ἀποθνήσκομεν."　³⁴ ἀνέλαβεν δὲ ὁ λαὸς τὸ
σταῖς πρὸ τοῦ ζυμωθῆναι, τὰ φυράματα αὐτῶν ἐνδεδεμένα
ἐν τοῖς ἱματίοις αὐτῶν ἐπὶ τῶν ὤμων.　³⁵ οἱ δὲ υἱοὶ Ἰσραὴλ
ἐποίησαν καθὰ συνέταξεν αὐτοῖς Μωυσῆς, καὶ ᾔτησαν
παρὰ τῶν Αἰγυπτίων σκεύη ἀργυρᾶ καὶ χρυσᾶ καὶ ἱματισμόν.　³⁶ καὶ ἔδωκεν Κύριος τὴν χάριν τῷ λαῷ αὐτοῦ
ἐναντίον τῶν Αἰγυπτίων, καὶ ἔχρησαν αὐτοῖς· καὶ ἐσκύ-
λευσαν τοὺς Αἰγυπτίους.

³⁷ Ἀπάραντες δὲ οἱ υἱοὶ Ἰσραὴλ ἐκ Ῥαμεσσὴ εἰς Σοκχώθα
εἰς ἑξακοσίας χιλιάδας πεζῶν οἱ ἄνδρες, πλὴν τῆς ἀπο-

29. λάκκῳ: *dungeon.* It is the
word used in Daniel for the den of
lions. See Gen. 37²⁰ n.

30. καὶ ἀναστάς: participle for
finite verb. § 80.

31. καὶ ἐκάλεσεν κτλ.: inconsistent
with 10²⁸, ²⁹ and seeming to point to a
mixture of sources in the story.

33. κατεβιάζοντο: 6¹ n.

34. σταῖς: *dough.* Herodotus (II
36), in speaking of the queer customs
of the Egyptians, says φυρῶσί τὸ μὲν

σταῖς τοῖσι ποσί, τὸν δὲ πηλὸν τῇσι
χερσί.

35, 36. *Cp.* 11², ³.

37. Ἀπάραντες: § 80. —Σοκχώθα:
= Σοκχώθ in 13²⁰, with the Hebrew
suffix denoting motion to a place
left clinging to it. *Cp.* Nb. 22⁵:
Jdg. 14¹, ². — ἑξακοσίας χιλιάδας:
600,000 adult males to represent the
'75 souls of the house of Jacob' mentioned in Gen. 46²⁷. — τῆς ἀποσκευῆς:
10¹⁰ n.

Exodus XII 38

σκευῆς· ³⁸καὶ ἐπίμικτος πολὺς συνανέβη αὐτοῖς, καὶ πρόβατα καὶ βόες καὶ κτήνη πολλὰ σφόδρα. ³⁹καὶ ἔπεψαν
τὸ σταῖς ὃ ἐξήνεγκαν ἐξ Αἰγύπτου ἐνκρυφίας ἀζύμους, οὐ
γὰρ ἐζυμώθη· ἐξέβαλον γὰρ αὐτοὺς οἱ Αἰγύπτιοι, καὶ οὐκ
ἠδυνήθησαν ἐπιμεῖναι, οὐδὲ ἐπισιτισμὸν ἐποίησαν ἑαυτοῖς
εἰς τὴν ὁδόν.

¹⁷Ὡς δὲ ἐξαπέστειλεν Φαραὼ τὸν λαόν, οὐχ ὡδήγησεν
αὐτοὺς ὁ θεὸς ὁδὸν γῆς Φυλιστιείμ, ὅτι ἐγγὺς ἦν· εἶπεν
γὰρ ὁ θεός "Μή ποτε μεταμελήσῃ τῷ λαῷ ἰδόντι πόλεμον,
καὶ ἀποστρέψῃ εἰς Αἴγυπτον." ¹⁸καὶ ἐκύκλωσεν ὁ θεὸς τὸν
λαὸν ὁδὸν τὴν εἰς τὴν ἔρημον, εἰς τὴν ἐρυθρὰν θάλασσαν·
πέμπτῃ δὲ γενεᾷ ἀνέβησαν οἱ υἱοὶ Ἰσραὴλ ἐκ γῆς Αἰγύπτου. ¹⁹Καὶ ἔλαβεν Μωυσῆς τὰ ὀστᾶ Ἰωσὴφ μεθ᾽
ἑαυτοῦ· ὅρκῳ γὰρ ὥρκισεν τοὺς υἱοὺς Ἰσραὴλ λέγων "Ἐπι-
σκοπῇ ἐπισκέψεται ὑμᾶς Κύριος, καὶ συνανοίσετέ μου τὰ
ὀστᾶ ἐντεῦθεν μεθ᾽ ὑμῶν." ²⁰Ἐξάραντες δὲ οἱ υἱοὶ
Ἰσραὴλ ἐκ Σοκχὼθ ἐστρατοπέδευσαν ἐν Ὀθὸμ παρὰ τὴν
ἔρημον. ²¹ὁ δὲ θεὸς ἡγεῖτο αὐτῶν, ἡμέρας μὲν ἐν στύλῳ

38. ἐπίμικτος πολύς : sc. ὄχλος. It
would appear from this that the Hebrew nation was only in part descended
from Jacob.

39. ἐνκρυφίας : ἐγκρυφίας (ἄρτος)
was a loaf baked in the ashes. Lucian
Dial. Mort. XX 4 ὁ δὲ σποδοῦ πλέως,
ὥσπερ ἐγκρυφίας ἄρτος. Cp. Gen. 18⁶ :
Nb. 11⁸ : iii K. 17¹², 19⁶. The accusative here is due to the fact that ἔπεψεν
= 'made into.'

17. ὅτι ἐγγὺς ἦν : R.V. 'although
that was near.' This sense may be
got out of the Greek by taking the
words closely with οὐχ ὡδήγησεν αὐτούς — "he did not make the near-
ness of the land of the Philistines
a reason for leading them that

way." — Μή ποτε μεταμελήσῃ : Gen.
43¹² n.

18. ἐκύκλωσεν : led round. Κυ-
κλοῦν generally means 'to go round,'
as in Gen. 2¹¹ : Dt. 2¹. § 84.

20. Ὀθόμ : Etham. Called Βουθάν
in Nb. 33⁶,⁷. — παρὰ τὴν ἔρημον : on
the edge of the wilderness. The first
two stages of their journey then, from
Rameses to Succoth (12³⁷) and from
Succoth to Etham (13²⁰), were not
through the wilderness. Succoth =
Thuket = Pithom on the Sweet Water
Canal, a little west of Ismailia.

21. ἡμέρας μὲν κτλ. : A pillar of
cloud by day and a pillar of fire by
night is just the appearance presented
by a volcano.

Exodus XIV 8

νεφέλης δεῖξαι αὐτοῖς τὴν ὁδόν, τὴν δὲ νύκτα ἐν στύλῳ πυρός· ²²οὐκ ἐξέλιπεν δὲ ὁ στύλος τῆς νεφέλης ἡμέρας καὶ ὁ στύλος τοῦ πυρὸς νυκτὸς ἐναντίον τοῦ λαοῦ παντός.

¹Καὶ ἐλάλησεν Κύριος πρὸς Μωυσῆν λέγων ²" Λάλησον τοῖς υἱοῖς Ἰσραήλ, καὶ ἀποστρέψαντες στρατοπεδευσάτωσαν ἀπέναντι τῆς ἐπαύλεως, ἀνὰ μέσον Μαγδώλου καὶ ἀνὰ μέσον τῆς θαλάσσης, ἐξ ἐναντίας Βεελσεπφών· ἐνώπιον αὐτῶν στρατοπεδεύσεις ἐπὶ τῆς θαλάσσης. ³καὶ ἐρεῖ Φαραὼ τῷ λαῷ αὐτοῦ ' Οἱ υἱοὶ Ἰσραὴλ πλανῶνται οὗτοι ἐν τῇ γῇ· συνκέκλεικεν γὰρ αὐτοὺς ἡ ἔρημος.' ⁴ἐγὼ δὲ σκληρυνῶ τὴν καρδίαν Φαραώ, καὶ καταδιώξεται ὀπίσω αὐτῶν· καὶ ἐνδοξασθήσομαι ἐν Φαραὼ καὶ ἐν πάσῃ τῇ στρατιᾷ αὐτοῦ, καὶ γνώσονται πάντες οἱ Αἰγύπτιοι ὅτι ἐγώ εἰμι Κύριος." καὶ ἐποίησαν οὕτως. ⁵καὶ ἀνηγγέλη τῷ βασιλεῖ τῶν Αἰγυπτίων ὅτι " πέφευγεν ὁ λαός · " καὶ μετεστράφη ἡ καρδία Φαραὼ καὶ ἡ καρδία τῶν θεραπόντων αὐτοῦ ἐπὶ τὸν λαόν, καὶ εἶπαν " Τί τοῦτο ἐποιήσαμεν τοῦ ἐξαποστεῖλαι τοὺς υἱοὺς Ἰσραὴλ τοῦ μὴ δουλεύειν ἡμῖν ; " ⁶ἔζευξεν οὖν Φαραὼ τὰ ἅρματα αὐτοῦ, καὶ πάντα τὸν λαὸν αὐτοῦ συναπήγαγεν μεθ' ἑαυτοῦ, ⁷καὶ λαβὼν ἑξακόσια ἅρματα ἐκλεκτὰ καὶ πᾶσαν τὴν ἵππον τῶν Αἰγυπτίων καὶ τριστάτας ἐπὶ πάντων. ⁸καὶ ἐσκλήρυνεν Κύριος τὴν καρ-

2. τῆς ἐπαύλεως : 8¹¹ n. This is the LXX substitute for the Pi-hahiroth of the Hebrew text, which is supposed to be Egyptian. Presumably the Alexandrian translators knew its meaning. — Μαγδώλου : Migdol, a Hebrew word meaning 'fort.' — Βεελσεπφών : Baalzephon. Jos. Ant. II 15 § 1 Βελσεφών. — αὐτῶν : this can only refer to Baalzephon.

3. τῷ λαῷ αὐτοῦ : the Greek here differs slightly from the Hebrew. — πλανῶνται : R.V. 'are entangled in.'

5. ἀνηγγέλη : § 24. — τοῦ ἐξαποστεῖλαι : § 60. — τοῦ μὴ δουλεύειν ἡμῖν : § 60.

7. τὴν ἵππον : the cavalry. There is a tendency in Greek for words denoting collective ideas to be feminine. Thus ὁ ἅλς 'salt,' but ἡ ἅλς 'the sea' (the brine). The Hebrew has the same word for τὴν ἵππον as for τὰ ἅρματα. — τριστάτας : captains. Cp. 15⁴ ; iv K.

Exodus XIV 9

δίαν Φαραὼ βασιλέως Αἰγύπτου καὶ τῶν θεραπόντων αὐτοῦ, καὶ κατεδίωξεν ὀπίσω τῶν υἱῶν Ἰσραήλ· οἱ δὲ υἱοὶ Ἰσραὴλ ἐξεπορεύοντο ἐν χειρὶ ὑψηλῇ. ⁹καὶ κατεδίωξαν οἱ Αἰγύπτιοι ὀπίσω αὐτῶν, καὶ εὕροσαν αὐτοὺς παρεμβεβληκότας παρὰ τὴν θάλασσαν· καὶ πᾶσα ἡ ἵππος καὶ τὰ ἅρματα Φαραὼ καὶ οἱ ἱππεῖς καὶ ἡ στρατιὰ αὐτοῦ ἀπέναντι τῆς ἐπαύλεως, ἐξ ἐναντίας Βεελσεπφών. ¹⁰καὶ Φαραὼ προσῆγεν· καὶ ἀναβλέψαντες οἱ υἱοὶ Ἰσραὴλ τοῖς ὀφθαλμοῖς ὁρῶσιν, καὶ οἱ Αἰγύπτιοι ἐστρατοπέδευσαν ὀπίσω αὐτῶν, καὶ ἐφοβήθησαν σφόδρα. ἀνεβόησαν δὲ οἱ υἱοὶ Ἰσραὴλ πρὸς Κύριον· ¹¹καὶ εἶπαν πρὸς Μωυσῆν "Παρὰ τὸ μὴ ὑπάρχειν μνήματα ἐν γῇ Αἰγύπτῳ ἐξήγαγες ἡμᾶς θανατῶσαι ἐν τῇ ἐρήμῳ; τί τοῦτο ἐποίησας ἡμῖν, ἐξαγαγὼν ἐξ Αἰγύπτου; ¹²οὐ τοῦτο ἦν τὸ ῥῆμα ὃ ἐλαλήσαμεν πρὸς σὲ ἐν Αἰγύπτῳ λέγοντες 'Πάρες ἡμᾶς ὅπως δουλεύσωμεν τοῖς Αἰγυπτίοις'; κρεῖσσον γὰρ ἡμᾶς δουλεύειν τοῖς Αἰγυπτίοις ἢ ἀποθανεῖν ἐν τῇ ἐρήμῳ ταύτῃ." ¹³εἶπεν δὲ Μωυσῆς πρὸς τὸν λαόν "Θαρσεῖτε· στῆτε καὶ ὁρᾶτε τὴν σωτηρίαν τὴν παρὰ τοῦ θεοῦ, ἣν ποιήσει ἡμῖν σήμερον· ὃν τρόπον γὰρ ἑωράκατε τοὺς Αἰγυπτίους σήμερον, οὐ προσθήσεσθε ἔτι ἰδεῖν αὐτοὺς εἰς τὸν αἰῶνα χρόνον· ¹⁴Κύ-

---

6⁴, 7², ¹⁷·¹⁹, 9²⁵, 10²⁵, 15²⁵. The word is evidently chosen by the translators because it contains the number three, as the Hebrew original does also.

**8. ἐν χειρὶ ὑψηλῇ** : 6¹ n.

**9. εὕροσαν** : § 16. — **παρεμβεβληκότας** : encamped. A common word in late Greek. It is explained by L. & S. as being properly used of distributing auxiliaries among other troops, as in Polyb. I 33 § 7 τῶν δὲ μισθοφόρων τοὺς μὲν ἐπὶ τὸ δεξιὸν κέρας παρενέβαλε, τοὺς δὲ κτλ. Hence παρεμβολή 'a camp,'

as in v. 19 or 'army,' as in i K. 17⁴⁶. — **τῆς ἐπαύλεως** : v. 2 n.

**10. προσῆγεν** : led on (his forces). — **ἐστρατοπέδευσαν** : R.V. 'marched.' Στρατοπεδεύειν seems to have this meaning in Dt. 1⁴⁰ : ii Mac. 9²³ : iv Mac. 18⁶.

**11. παρὰ τὸ μὴ ὑπάρχειν** : owing to there not being. Cp. Nb. 14¹⁶. This use of παρά is classical. — **θανατῶσαι** : § 77.

**13. ὃν τρόπον γάρ** : the meaning is — "Ye have seen them to-day, but ye shall see them no more." — **εἰς τὸν αἰῶνα χρόνον** : for ever. Αἰῶνα is here

ριος πολεμήσει περὶ ὑμῶν, καὶ ὑμεῖς σιγήσετε." ¹⁵Εἶπεν
δὲ Κύριος πρὸς Μωυσῆν "Τί βοᾷς πρὸς μέ; λάλησον τοῖς
υἱοῖς Ἰσραὴλ καὶ ἀναζευξάτωσαν· ¹⁶καὶ σὺ ἔπαρον τῇ
ῥάβδῳ σου, καὶ ἔκτεινον τὴν χεῖρά σου ἐπὶ τὴν θάλασσαν
καὶ ῥῆξον αὐτήν, καὶ εἰσελθάτωσαν οἱ υἱοὶ Ἰσραὴλ εἰς
μέσον τῆς θαλάσσης κατὰ τὸ ξηρόν. ¹⁷καὶ ἰδοὺ ἐγὼ
σκληρυνῶ τὴν καρδίαν Φαραὼ καὶ τῶν Αἰγυπτίων πάντων,
καὶ εἰσελεύσονται ὀπίσω αὐτῶν· καὶ ἐνδοξασθήσομαι ἐν
Φαραὼ καὶ ἐν πάσῃ τῇ στρατιᾷ αὐτοῦ καὶ ἐν τοῖς ἅρμασιν
καὶ ἐν τοῖς ἵπποις αὐτοῦ. ¹⁸καὶ γνώσονται πάντες οἱ Αἰγύπτιοι ὅτι ἐγώ εἰμι Κύριος, ἐνδοξαζομένου μου ἐν Φαραὼ
καὶ ἐν τοῖς ἅρμασιν καὶ ἵπποις αὐτοῦ." ¹⁹ἐξῆρεν δὲ ὁ
ἄγγελος τοῦ θεοῦ ὁ προπορευόμενος τῆς παρεμβολῆς τῶν
υἱῶν Ἰσραήλ, καὶ ἐπορεύθη ἐκ τῶν ὄπισθεν· ἐξῆρεν δὲ καὶ
ὁ στύλος τῆς νεφέλης ἀπὸ προσώπου αὐτῶν, καὶ ἔστη ἐκ
τῶν ὀπίσω αὐτῶν. ²⁰καὶ εἰσῆλθεν ἀνὰ μέσον τῶν Αἰγυπτίων καὶ ἀνὰ μέσον τῆς παρεμβολῆς Ἰσραήλ, καὶ ἔστη·
καὶ ἐγένετο σκότος καὶ γνόφος, καὶ διῆλθεν ἡ νύξ, καὶ οὐ
συνέμιξαν ἀλλήλοις ὅλην τὴν νύκτα. ²¹ἐξέτεινεν δὲ Μωυσῆς τὴν χεῖρα ἐπὶ τὴν θάλασσαν· καὶ ὑπήγαγεν Κύριος

grammatically an adverb, εἰς τὸν ἀεὶ
χρόνον.
**14.** σιγήσετε: literally *shall say
nothing = do nothing.* This is the
characteristic attitude of Hebrew piety
in and after the age of the literary
prophets. *Cp.* Ps. 46¹⁰ ' Be still and
know that I am God' : Is. 30¹⁵ ' in
quietness and in confidence shall be
your strength.' The text 'their
strength is to sit still ' (Is. 30⁷) has
vanished from the Bible under the
hand of the Revisers.
**16.** ἔπαρον τῇ ῥάβδῳ σου: Ex.
7²⁰.

**18.** ἵπποις : Hebrew 'horsemen.'
**19.** ἐξῆρεν : Gen. 37¹⁷ n. — παρεμβολῆς: the context seems to show
that this word here means ' army
on the march ' (Lat. *agmen*), not
' camp.' *Cp.* v. 24. The Hebrew
original admits of either meaning.
— ἐκ τῶν ὄπισθεν . . . ἐκ τῶν ὀπίσω :
the Hebrew phrase is the same in
both cases.
**20.** διῆλθεν ἡ νύξ : Hebrew, 'gave
light during the night.' The Greek
ought to mean ' the night passed.'
Perhaps the Greek translator had a
different reading.

Exodus XIV 22

τὴν θάλασσαν ἐν ἀνέμῳ νότῳ βιαίῳ ὅλην τὴν νύκτα, καὶ
ἐποίησεν τὴν θάλασσαν ξηράν, καὶ ἐσχίσθη τὸ ὕδωρ.
²²καὶ εἰσῆλθον οἱ υἱοὶ Ἰσραὴλ εἰς μέσον τῆς θαλάσσης
κατὰ τὸ ξηρόν, καὶ τὸ ὕδωρ αὐτοῖς τεῖχος ἐκ δεξιῶν καὶ
τεῖχος ἐξ εὐωνύμων· ²³καὶ κατεδίωξαν οἱ Αἰγύπτιοι, καὶ
εἰσῆλθον ὀπίσω αὐτῶν καὶ πᾶς ἵππος Φαραὼ καὶ τὰ ἅρματα
καὶ οἱ ἀναβάται εἰς μέσον τῆς θαλάσσης. ²⁴ἐγενήθη δὲ
ἐν τῇ φυλακῇ τῇ ἑωθινῇ καὶ ἐπέβλεψεν Κύριος ἐπὶ τὴν
παρεμβολὴν τῶν Αἰγυπτίων ἐν στύλῳ πυρὸς καὶ νεφέλης,
καὶ συνετάραξεν τὴν παρεμβολὴν τῶν Αἰγυπτίων, ²⁵καὶ
συνέδησεν τοὺς ἄξονας τῶν ἁρμάτων αὐτῶν, καὶ ἤγαγεν
αὐτοὺς μετὰ βίας. καὶ εἶπαν οἱ Αἰγύπτιοι " Φύγωμεν ἀπὸ
προσώπου Ἰσραήλ· ὁ γὰρ κύριος πολεμεῖ περὶ αὐτῶν τοὺς
Αἰγυπτίους." ²⁶Εἶπεν δὲ Κύριος πρὸς Μωυσῆν "Ἔκτεινον τὴν χεῖρά σου ἐπὶ τὴν θάλασσαν, καὶ ἀποκαταστήτω
τὸ ὕδωρ καὶ ἐπικαλυψάτω τοὺς Αἰγυπτίους, ἐπί τε τὰ ἅρματα
καὶ τοὺς ἀναβάτας." ²⁷ἐξέτεινεν δὲ Μωυσῆς τὴν χεῖρα ἐπὶ
τὴν θάλασσαν, καὶ ἀπεκατέστη τὸ ὕδωρ πρὸς ἡμέραν ἐπὶ

---

**21.** ἐν ἀνέμῳ : § 91.— νότῳ : *south
wind.* Hebrew, 'east wind.'

**22.** τὸ ὕδωρ αὐτοῖς τεῖχος : imagination here calls up the picture of a
wall of water on either side of the
Israelites, but, as the cleaving of the
water has been ascribed to the wind in
v. 21, the meaning here may be only
that the water protected them from
attack on both flanks. In 15⁸ however it is clear that the other meaning
is intended.

**24.** τῇ φυλακῇ τῇ ἑωθινῇ : *cp.* i K.
11¹¹ : Judith 12⁵ ἀνέστη πρὸς τὴν ἑωθινὴν
φυλακήν : i Mac. 5³⁰ καὶ ἐγένετο ἑωθινή.
Prior to Roman times the Jews are
said to have divided the night into

three watches — 'The beginning of
the watches' (Lam. 2¹⁹), 'the middle
watch' (Jdg. 7¹⁹), and 'the morning
watch.'

**25.** συνέδησεν : *clogged.* This represents a better reading than that
accepted in our Hebrew text. See R.V.
margin. — ἤγαγεν : causative *made
them drive.* § 84.— πολεμεῖ . . . τοὺς
Αἰγυπτίους : this transitive use is not
uncommon in late authors. Instead
of περί we should here have ὑπέρ in
classical Greek.

**27.** ἀπεκατέστη : § 19.— ἐπὶ χώρας : genitive singular *towards its
(usual) place.* R.V. text 'to its
strength,' margin 'to its wonted flow.'

Exodus XV 2

χώρας. οἱ δὲ Αἰγύπτιοι ἔφυγον ὑπὸ τὸ ὕδωρ, καὶ ἐξετίναξεν Κύριος τοὺς Αἰγυπτίους μέσον τῆς θαλάσσης. ²⁸ καὶ ἐπανα-στραφὲν τὸ ὕδωρ ἐκάλυψεν τὰ ἅρματα καὶ τοὺς ἀναβά-τας καὶ πᾶσαν τὴν δύναμιν Φαραώ, τοὺς εἰσπεπορευμένους ὀπίσω αὐτῶν εἰς τὴν θάλασσαν· καὶ οὐ κατελείφθη ἐξ αὐτῶν οὐδὲ εἷς. ²⁹ οἱ δὲ υἱοὶ Ἰσραὴλ ἐπορεύθησαν διὰ ξηρᾶς ἐν μέσῳ τῆς θαλάσσης, τὸ δὲ ὕδωρ αὐτοῖς τεῖχος ἐκ δεξιῶν καὶ τεῖχος ἐξ εὐωνύμων. ³⁰ καὶ ἐρρύσατο Κύριος τὸν Ἰσραὴλ ἐν τῇ ἡμέρᾳ ἐκείνῃ ἐκ χειρὸς τῶν Αἰγυπτίων· καὶ ἴδεν Ἰσραὴλ τοὺς Αἰγυπτίους τεθνηκότας παρὰ τὸ χεῖλος τῆς θαλάσσης. ³¹ ἴδεν δὲ Ἰσραὴλ τὴν χεῖρα τὴν μεγάλην, ἃ ἐποίησεν Κύριος τοῖς Αἰγυπτίοις· ἐφοβήθη δὲ ὁ λαὸς τὸν κύριον, καὶ ἐπίστευσαν τῷ θεῷ καὶ Μωυσῇ τῷ θεράποντι αὐτοῦ.

¹ Τότε ᾖσεν Μωυσῆς καὶ οἱ υἱοὶ Ἰσραὴλ τὴν ᾠδὴν ταύτην τῷ θεῷ, καὶ εἶπαν λέγοντες

" Ἄσωμεν τῷ κυρίῳ, ἐνδόξως γὰρ δεδόξασται·
ἵππον καὶ ἀναβάτην ἔρριψεν εἰς θάλασσαν.
² βοηθὸς καὶ σκεπαστὴς ἐγένετό μοι εἰς σωτηρίαν·
οὗτός μου θεός, καὶ δοξάσω αὐτόν,
θεὸς τοῦ πατρός μου, καὶ ὑψώσω αὐτόν.

---

—ἔφυγον ὑπὸ τὸ ὕδωρ : Hebrew, 'were fleeing to meet it.' The Greek per-haps means the same. —μέσον τῆς θα-λάσσης : for this prepositional use of μέσον cp. Nb. 33⁸, 35⁵: i K. 5⁶, 11¹¹ : Phil. 2¹⁵.

**31.** τὴν χεῖρα : *work.* A Hebraism.
—ἃ ἐποίησεν Κύριος : *even the things which the LORD did,* explanatory of τὴν χεῖρα.

**1.** τὴν ᾠδὴν ταύτην : composed by Moses, says Josephus (*Ant.* II 16 § 4) ἐν ἑξαμέτρῳ τόνῳ. This is not however

a very exact description of the metre, which runs somewhat as follows —

I sing unto Jahveh, for his mÍght is grÉat :
hórse and rÍder he flúng to drówn.

—ἐνδόξως γὰρ δεδόξασται : § 82.

**2.** σκεπαστής : the vocative σκε-παστά occurs in iii Mac. 6⁹. The He-brew word here used means ' song,' *i.e.* subject of song. The Greek translators may have had another reading. The LXX also omits the subject of the sen-tence, which in the Hebrew is *Jah.* In

³Κύριος συντρίβων πολέμους,

Κύριος ὄνομα αὐτῷ.

⁴ἅρματα Φαραὼ καὶ τὴν δύναμιν αὐτοῦ ἔρριψεν εἰς θάλασσαν,

ἐπιλέκτους ἀναβάτας τριστάτας·

κατεπόθησαν ἐν ἐρυθρᾷ θαλάσσῃ.

⁵πόντῳ ἐκάλυψεν αὐτούς·

κατέδυσαν εἰς βυθὸν ὡσεὶ λίθος.

⁶ἡ δεξιά σου, Κύριε, δεδόξασται ἐν ἰσχύι·

ἡ δεξιά σου χείρ, Κύριε, ἔθραυσεν ἐχθρούς.

⁷καὶ τῷ πλήθει τῆς δόξης σου συνέτριψας τοὺς ὑπεναντίους·

ἀπέστειλας τὴν ὀργήν σου, καὶ κατέφαγεν αὐτοὺς ὡς
καλάμην.

⁸καὶ διὰ τοῦ πνεύματος τοῦ θυμοῦ σου διέστη τὸ ὕδωρ·

ἐπάγη ὡσεὶ τεῖχος τὰ ὕδατα,

ἐπάγη τὰ κύματα ἐν μέσῳ τῆς θαλάσσης.

⁹εἶπεν ὁ ἐχθρός 'Διώξας καταλήμψομαι·

μεριῶ σκῦλα, ἐμπλήσω ψυχήν μου,

Is. 12², where the same words are used just after an allusion to the Exodus (Is. 11¹⁶), the subject is 'Jah Jehovah.' The LXX has there simply Κύριος, which might go to show that Jehovah is a gloss on the rare word Jah. The same Hebrew which is here rendered βοηθὸς καὶ σκεπαστής appears there as ἡ δόξα μου καὶ ἡ αἴνεσις μου.

**3. Κύριος συντρίβων πολέμους** : Hebrew, 'Jehovah (is) a man of war.'

**4. ἐπιλέκτους ἀναβάτας τριστάτας** : asyndeton. *Cp.* 10²². The Hebrew here is simply 'the choice of his captains,' there being nothing to correspond to ἀναβάτας, and the expression is subject to the verb that follows, not object of that which went before.

**5. πόντῳ ἐκάλυψεν αὐτούς** : R.V. 'The deeps cover them.'

**8. διὰ τοῦ πνεύματος κτλ.** : *through the blast of thine anger* (Hb. 'nostrils') *the waters stood apart* (R.V. 'were piled up'). The metaphorical use of 'nostrils' in Hebrew seems to be derived from the behaviour of angry cattle. — **ἐπάγη ὡσεὶ τεῖχος κτλ.** : *the waters became solid as a wall.* R.V. 'The floods stood upright as an heap.' Ἐπάγη is inexact here, but quite corresponds to the different Hebrew word in the next clause rendered in R.V. 'were congealed.' Ὡσεί is post-classical.

Exodus XV 15

ἀνελῶ τῇ μαχαίρῃ μου, κυριεύσει ἡ χείρ μου.'

¹⁰ἀπέστειλας τὸ πνεῦμά σου, ἐκάλυψεν αὐτοὺς θάλασσα·
ἔδυσαν ὡσεὶ μόλιβος ἐν ὕδατι σφοδρῷ.

¹¹τίς ὅμοιός σοι ἐν θεοῖς, Κύριε; τίς ὅμοιός σοι;
δεδοξασμένος ἐν ἁγίοις, θαυμαστὸς ἐν δόξαις, ποιῶν
τέρατα.

¹² ἐξέτεινας τὴν δεξιάν σου·
κατέπιεν αὐτοὺς γῆ.

¹³ ὡδήγησας τῇ δικαιοσύνῃ σου τὸν λαόν σου τοῦτον ὃν
ἐλυτρώσω,
παρεκάλεσας τῇ ἰσχύι σου εἰς κατάλυμα ἅγιόν σου.

¹⁴ἤκουσαν ἔθνη καὶ ὠργίσθησαν·
ὠδῖνες ἔλαβον κατοικοῦντας Φυλιστιείμ.

¹⁵τότε ἔσπευσαν ἡγεμόνες Ἐδὼμ καὶ ἄρχοντες Μωαβειτῶν·

9. ἀνελῶ : future of ἀναιρεῖν. § 21.
R.V. 'I will draw my sword.' — μαχαίρῃ : § 3. — κυριεύσει ἡ χείρ μου :
R.V. 'my hand shall destroy them.'
The usual meaning of the word which
is rendered 'destroy' is 'make to
possess.' Here we get very close to
κυριεύσει.
10. μόλιβος : earlier and poetic
form of μόλυβδος. § 35.
11. τίς ὅμοιός σοι ἐν θεοῖς : this admission of the existence of other gods
might be used as an argument for the
early date of this poem. When the
Rabshakeh (ii Kings 18³⁵, 19⁴) represents the 'living God' as but one
among many, he is regarded as having spoken blasphemy. — ἐν ἁγίοις :
Hebrew, 'in holiness.' The Greek
ought rather to mean 'among holy
ones.'
12. κατέπιεν αὐτοὺς γῆ : a general
expression for destruction, since in

this instance it was the sea that swal-
lowed them.
13. τῇ δικαιοσύνῃ : R.V. 'mercy.'
Dr. Hatch (Essays in Biblical Greek,
p. 49) has shown how the meanings of
δικαιοσύνη and ἐλεημοσύνη run into one
another in the LXX. In the N.T.
there is one instance (Mt. 6¹) of the use
of δικαιοσύνη in the sense of ἐλεημοσύνη,
and the use of δίκαιος Mt. 1¹⁹ would
be explained, if we could render it
'a merciful man.' — παρεκάλεσας κτλ. :
Thou hast summoned (Hb. 'guided')
them by thy might to thy holy resting-
place. Cp. 17 ἁγίασμα, sanctuary.
These expressions look like references
to the Temple.
14. Φυλιστιείμ : the references to
the Philistines, Edomites, and Moabites argue a poet of later times acquainted with the subsequent history
of Israel.
15. ἔσπευσαν : R.V. 'were amazed.'

ἔλαβεν αὐτοὺς τρόμος,

ἐτάκησαν πάντες οἱ κατοικοῦντες Χανάαν.

¹⁶ ἐπιπέσοι ἐπ᾽ αὐτοὺς τρόμος καὶ φόβος,

μεγέθει βραχίονός σου ἀπολιθωθήτωσαν·

ἕως ἂν παρέλθῃ ὁ λαός σου, Κύριε,

ἕως ἂν παρέλθῃ ὁ λαός σου οὗτος ὃν ἐκτήσω.

¹⁷ εἰσαγαγὼν καταφύτευσον αὐτοὺς εἰς ὄρος κληρονομίας σου,

εἰς ἕτοιμον κατοικητήριόν σου ὃ κατηρτίσω, Κύριε,

ἁγίασμα, Κύριε, ὃ ἡτοίμασαν αἱ χεῖρές σου.

¹⁸ Κύριος βασιλεύων τὸν αἰῶνα καὶ ἐπ᾽ αἰῶνα καὶ ἔτι."

¹⁹ Ὅτι εἰσῆλθεν ἵππος Φαραὼ σὺν ἅρμασιν καὶ ἀναβάταις

εἰς θάλασσαν, καὶ ἐπήγαγεν ἐπ᾽ αὐτοὺς Κύριος τὸ ὕδωρ τῆς

15. καὶ ἄρχοντες Μωαβειτῶν : To make these words tally with the Hebrew verse-division, they should be taken with what follows, thus — καὶ ἄρχοντες Μωαβειτῶν, ἔλαβον αὐτοὺς τρόμος. For ἄρχοντες the R.V. has 'mighty men.' The Hebrew word really means 'rams.' Moab was specially a sheep-breeding country, and in ii K. 3⁴ Mesha, king of Moab, is described as a 'sheep-master.' The rams seem to be put by a poetic figure for their owners.

16. ἐπιπέσοι . . . ἀπολιθωθήτωσαν : the R.V. has the indicative in both cases. The difference is sufficiently accounted for by the ambiguity of the verbal form in Hebrew. — ἀπολιθωθήτωσαν : *let them be petrified.* The notion of being turned into stone by terror was current among the Greeks, as is shown by the story of the Gorgon's head. In the Hebrew phrase however it is the notion of quiescence that is uppermost.

17. εἰς ὄρος κληρονομίας σου : until

Solomon built the Temple no hill in Palestine was especially the abode of Jehovah ; and it was not until the time of Hezekiah and Isaiah, after the destruction of the Northern Kingdom, that Sion became the one recognised centre of the national religion. — ἁγίασμα, Κύριε : the Hebrew word here rendered Κύριε is *Adonai*, not, as in the preceding clause, *Jehovah.* The Greek translators are obliged to use the same word for both. In our version they are distinguished by the use of different type.

18. βασιλεύων : the participle is not due to the Hebrew. § 80. — τὸν αἰῶνα κτλ. : Hebrew, 'for ever and ever.' Possibly the addition of καὶ ἔτι in the Greek is due to a confusion between the latter part of the Hebrew expression and the very similar word for 'and still.'

19. Ὅτι εἰσῆλθεν : this explanatory note appended to the song seems to show that it was not originally intended for this place.

Exodus XV 21

θαλάσσης· οἱ δὲ υἱοὶ Ἰσραὴλ ἐπορεύθησαν διὰ ξηρᾶς ἐν μέσῳ τῆς θαλάσσης. ²⁰Λαβοῦσα δὲ Μαριὰμ ἡ προφῆτις ἡ ἀδελφὴ Ἀαρὼν τὸ τύμπανον ἐν τῇ χειρὶ αὐτῆς, καὶ ἐξήλθοσαν πᾶσαι αἱ γυναῖκες ὀπίσω αὐτῆς μετὰ τυμπάνων καὶ χορῶν. ²¹ἐξῆρχεν δὲ αὐτῶν Μαριὰμ λέγουσα

"Ἄσωμεν τῷ κυρίῳ, ἐνδόξως γὰρ δεδόξασται·
ἵππον καὶ ἀναβάτην ἔρριψεν εἰς θάλασσαν."

20. Μαριάμ: Hebrew *Miriam*. The name is the origin of our Mary. The mother of Jesus is called Μαριάμ in Mt. 1²⁰. In the 19th chapter of the Koran, Mohammed makes the people of Mary, the mother of Jesus, address her as 'O sister of Aaron!'—τύμπανον: Hebrew *tôph*, plural *tuppim*, from the verb *tapap* (probably onomatopoetic: *cp.* 'tap-tap'). The Greek word τύμπανον or τύπανον is doubtless from

stem τυπ-: but the thing was foreign to the Greeks and used chiefly in the worship of Asiatic or Egyptian goddesses. Our word 'timbrel' is, according to Skeat, a diminutive of Middle English *timbre*, which comes from Latin *tympanum* through the French.

21. ἐξῆρχεν δὲ αὐτῶν: R.V. 'answered them.'—Ἄσωμεν: as in 15¹, but the Hebrew there is 'I will sing' and here 'Sing ye.'

# INTRODUCTION TO THE STORY OF BALAAM
## AND BALAK

THE scene is now changed. Egypt is left behind, and the Israelites are hovering on the confines of Palestine. Moses is still their
leader, though he is nearing his end, and the bones of Joseph are
being carried with them for burial. Over the Israelites themselves
a great change has come. Instead of being slaves cowering under a
taskmaster, they are now an invading horde, spreading terror before
them and leaving destruction behind. Already mighty kings have
been slain for their sake, while others are quaking on their thrones.
Balak, the king of Moab, in his perplexity sends for Balaam, the
prophet of God, whose fame filled the land from Mesopotamia to the
Mediterranean, to curse these intruders from Egypt. Balaam, the son
of Beor, is represented in our story as being fetched all the way from
Pethor on the Euphrates (Nb. 22⁵, 23⁷ : cp. Dt. 23⁴), a place which
has been identified with the Pitru of the Assyrian monuments, near
Carchemish. He is made to speak of himself (Nb. 22¹⁸) as being the
servant of Jehovah, and is everywhere thus spoken of (22⁸, ³⁴, ³⁵,
23⁸, ¹⁷, 24¹¹, ¹³). This looks like an admission on the part of the
writer that the worship of the 'one true God' was to be found in
Mesopotamia, where Abraham came from, and was not confined to
the children of Israel. Balaam indeed figures as the foe of Israel,
having all the will to curse, but being allowed only the power to
bless (Dt. 23⁴, ⁵). He is credited with having counselled the Moabites and Midianites to entice the Israelites away from the worship
of Jehovah through the wiles of their women (Nb. 31¹⁶); and, when
the five kings of the Midianites are slain in revenge for this act, we
read 'Balaam also the son of Beor they slew with the sword'
(Nb. 31⁸). The passages which connect Balaam with Midian are referred to the priestly document (P), the association of the elders of
Midian with the elders of Moab (22⁴, ⁷) being set down to the har-
monizing hand of the editor. In our story, which is made up from

201

J and E, Balaam, having delivered himself of his prophecies, goes back to his home on the Euphrates (Nb. 24²⁵).

It is probably a mere coincidence that the first king who is recorded to have reigned in Edom is Bela the son of Beor (Gen. 36³²). The words in Micah 6⁵ look like an allusion to some account of conversation between Balak and Balaam which has not come down to us.

In the New Testament Balaam is the type of the covetous prophet, 'who loved the hire of wrong-doing' (ii Pet. 2¹⁵). This is in strong contrast with his own words in Nb. 22¹⁸ — 'If Balak would give me his house full of silver and gold, I cannot go beyond the word of Jehovah, my God.' In Rev. 2¹⁴ there is a reference to 'the teaching of Balaam' in connexion with idolatry and fornication.

Plato says of Minos that he was not a bad man, but had the misfortune to offend a literary nation. The same may have been the case with Balaam. The literature of the Jews, though so much scantier than that of the Athenians, has gone deeper into our hearts, and the character of Balaam seems to have suffered in proportion.

The great stumbling-block in the story before us is not the incident of 'the dumb ass speaking with man's mouth': for, if once we pass the limits of mundane reality, who shall pronounce judgement on degrees of credibility? As Charles Lamb truly remarked — 'We do not know the laws of that country.' It is rather the moral difficulty arising from the arbitrary and unreasonable conduct ascribed to Jehovah, in first commanding the prophet to go, and then being angry with him for going. From the time of Josephus (*Ant.* IV. 6 § 2), who says that God's command was given in deceit, various attempts have been made to get over this difficulty, but they cannot be considered successful. It ought therefore to be a relief to the mind and conscience of the devout, when the critics come forward with their supposition that there are again two stories mixed up here — that the bulk of the narrative in ch. 22 (vv. 2–21, 36–41) comes from E, while the incident of the ass (vv. 22–35) comes from J. If this be so, then in the story, as told in E, Balaam is perfectly obedient to the divine command, not going with the messengers until he has been told in a vision at night to do so; whereas in the J narrative Balaam's way is perverse before God, in that he went against the divine will. The vision at night and the spiritual perception of the ass are thus seen to be two different literary contrivances for leading up to the same end, namely, that Balaam was to go, but to speak only as God told him (cp. v. 20 with v. 35). In confirmation of the hypothesis of a double source it may be noticed that in 22²¹ (E) Balaam is accompanied by the princes of Moab, whereas in 22²² (J) he has only his own two servants with him.

That the future may be, and has been, foretold is an opinion which has been widely held in past times and may be widely held again, notwithstanding that the current of thought has been running of late the other way. The flourishing institution of oracles among the Greeks rested upon this persuasion. The prophecies of the Cumæan Sibyl were an engine of Roman state-management; but, as they were also a state-secret, they do not help us much. The Sibylline verses so abundantly quoted by Lactantius as evidences of Christianity would indeed be overpowering proofs of prophecy, if they had not been composed after the events. The same, it is now admitted, is the case with the remarkable mention (i K. 13²) of Josiah by name some three centuries before he was born; while the similar mention of Cyrus in the book of Isaiah (44²⁸), instead of being the stronghold of the defenders of prophecy, is now one of the chief arguments for the composite authorship of that work. But prophecy is likely to gain no fairer trial than the witches of old, if fulfilment is to be taken as proof of spuriousness. The last words of Balaam's prophecies appear to predict the destruction of the Persian Empire by Alexander the Great. Are we therefore to set them down to that period? To this it may be replied — Certainly not as a whole, but we must take account of the universal tendency to alter existing prophecies and even to compose new ones suited to fresh events as they occur. The former tendency is dwelt on by Thucydides (II 54) in his comments on the oracular verse

$$\text{ἥξει Δωριακὸς πόλεμος καὶ λοιμὸς ἅμ' αὐτῷ,}$$

which could be made to suit either a pestilence or a famine at will by the insertion or omission of a single letter. So again Strabo (XIII 1 § 53, p. 608), speaking of the well-known prophecy of Poseidon in the 20th book of the *Iliad* (ll. 307, 308) —

$$\text{νῦν δὲ δὴ Αἰνείαο βίη Τρώεσσιν ἀνάξει}$$
$$\text{καὶ παίδων παῖδες, τοί κεν μετόπισθε γένωνται,}$$

says that some people in his day read πάντεσσιν in place of Τρώεσσιν, and understood the lines as a prophecy of the Roman Empire.

The oracular verses which circulated among the Greeks in the sixth and fifth centuries, such as are recorded by Herodotus and Thucydides and jeered at by Aristophanes, afford a fairly close parallel to these prophecies of Balaam. These Greek prophecies are generally assigned to Bacis of Bœotia: but according to Ælian (*V.H.* XII 35) there were three Bacides; and, as Bacis merely means 'the speaker,' to ascribe them to Bacis may be no more than adding them to the numerous works of 'the author called Anon.'

## III. THE STORY OF BALAAM AND BALAK

Numbers XXII

¹καὶ ἀπάραντες οἱ υἱοὶ Ἰσραὴλ παρενέβαλον ἐπὶ δυσμῶν Μωὰβ παρὰ τὸν Ἰορδάνην κατὰ Ἱερειχώ.

²Καὶ ἰδὼν Βαλὰκ υἱὸς Σεπφὼρ πάντα ὅσα ἐποίησεν Ἰσραὴλ τῷ Ἀμορραίῳ, ³καὶ ἐφοβήθη Μωὰβ τὸν λαὸν σφόδρα, ὅτι πολλοὶ ἦσαν· καὶ προσώχθισεν Μωὰβ ἀπὸ προσώπου υἱῶν Ἰσραήλ. ⁴καὶ εἶπεν Μωὰβ τῇ γερουσίᾳ Μαδιάμ " Νῦν ἐκλίξει ἡ συναγωγὴ αὕτη πάντας τοὺς κύκλῳ ἡμῶν, ὡς ἐκλίξαι ὁ μόσχος τὰ χλωρὰ ἐκ τοῦ πεδίου." καὶ Βαλὰκ υἱὸς Σεπφὼρ βασιλεὺς Μωὰβ ἦν κατὰ τὸν καιρὸν ἐκεῖνον. ⁵καὶ ἀπέστειλεν πρέσβεις πρὸς Βαλαὰμ υἱὸν Βεὼρ Φαθούρα, ὅ ἐστιν ἐπὶ τοῦ ποταμοῦ γῆς υἱῶν λαοῦ αὐτοῦ, καλέσαι

1. **ἐπὶ δυσμῶν Μωάβ**: *in the west of Moab* or *to the west of Moab*. The reading however seems to arise out of a misunderstanding of the Hebrew. The word for 'plains' is like that for 'evening,' and 'evening' stands for 'west.' The *'Arābah, i.e.* the plain, was used as a proper name of the Jordan valley. — **παρὰ τὸν Ἰορδάνην**: Hebrew, 'beyond Jordan.' As the Israelites are now east of the Jordan, we may infer that the writer lived west. — **κατὰ Ἱερειχώ**: *over against Jericho*, which was west of the river.

2. **Καὶ ἰδὼν Βαλάκ**: § 80.

3. **προσώχθισεν...ἀπὸ προσώπου**: *shrank in loathing from, loathed the sight of.* § 98. It is only here that προσοχθίζειν is constructed with ἀπό.

Generally it takes a dative of the thing loathed.

4. **γερουσίᾳ**: γερουσία = γέροντες, as in Ex. 3¹⁶. — **ἐκλίξει**: = ἐκλείξει, future of ἐκλείχω, the stem of which is identical with our word 'lick.' *Cp.* iii K. 18³⁸ ἐξέλιξεν, 22³⁸ ἐξέλιξαν: Judith 7⁴ ἐκλίξουσιν: Ep. Jer. 19 ἐκλείχεσθαι. — **ἐκλίξαι**: this must be aorist optative, *as the ox might lick.*

5. **Βαλαάμ**: Hebrew *Bilʿâm.* — **Φαθούρα**: Hebrew, 'to Pᵉthor.' The final α represents a Hebrew suffix, which has the force of motion to. *Cp.* Σοκχώθα Ex. 12³⁷: Θαμνάθα Jdg. 14¹. — **ἐπὶ τοῦ ποταμοῦ κτλ.**: Hebrew, 'He sent . . . to Pᵉthor, which is on the river, to the land of the children of his people.' We ought therefore to put a

205

αὐτὸν λέγων " Ἰδοὺ λαὸς ἐξελήλυθεν ἐξ Αἰγύπτου, καὶ ἰδοὺ
κατεκάλυψεν τὴν ὄψιν τῆς γῆς· καὶ οὗτος ἐνκάθηται ἐχόμενός μου.   ⁶καὶ νῦν δεῦρο ἄρασαί μοι τὸν λαὸν τοῦτον,
ὅτι ἰσχύει οὗτος ἢ ἡμεῖς, ἐὰν δυνώμεθα πατάξαι ἐξ αὐτῶν,
καὶ ἐκβαλῶ αὐτοὺς ἐκ τῆς γῆς· ὅτι οἶδα οὓς ἐὰν εὐλογήσῃς
σύ, εὐλόγηνται, καὶ οὓς ἐὰν καταράσῃ σύ, κεκατήρανται."
⁷καὶ ἐπορεύθη ἡ γερουσία Μωὰβ καὶ ἡ γερουσία Μαδιάμ,
καὶ τὰ μαντεῖα ἐν ταῖς χερσὶν αὐτῶν· καὶ ἦλθον πρὸς
Βαλαὰμ καὶ εἶπαν αὐτῷ τὰ ῥήματα Βαλάκ.   ⁸καὶ εἶπεν
πρὸς αὐτούς " Καταλύσατε αὐτοῦ τὴν νύκτα, καὶ ἀποκριθή-
σομαι ὑμῖν πράγματα ἃ ἐὰν λαλήσῃ Κύριος πρὸς μέ."   καὶ
κατέμειναν οἱ ἄρχοντες Μωὰβ παρὰ Βαλαάμ.   ⁹καὶ ἦλθεν
ὁ θεὸς παρὰ Βαλαὰμ καὶ εἶπεν αὐτῷ " Τί οἱ ἄνθρωποι οὗτοι
παρὰ σοί;"   ¹⁰καὶ εἶπεν Βαλαὰμ πρὸς τὸν θεόν " Βαλὰκ υἱὸς
Σεπφὼρ βασιλεὺς Μωὰβ ἀπέστειλεν αὐτοὺς πρὸς μὲ λέγων
¹¹' Ἰδοὺ λαὸς ἐξελήλυθεν ἐξ Αἰγύπτου, καὶ ἰδοὺ κεκάλυφεν
τὴν ὄψιν τῆς γῆς, καὶ οὗτος ἐνκάθηται ἐχόμενός μου· καὶ
νῦν δεῦρο ἄρασαί μοι αὐτόν, εἰ ἄρα δυνήσομαι πατάξαι

comma at ποτάμου, and take γῆς as a
local genitive, *in the land.*  In 23⁷
Balaam's home is called Mesopotamia
(Hb. *Aram*).  In 24²⁵ we read that
Balaam immediately returned to his
place (*i.e.* to Pᵉthor on the Euphrates),
yet in 31⁸ he is slain among the Midianites.  The passages which connect him
with Midian are supposed to belong to
P and 22⁴, ⁷ to be the device of an editor
for harmonising two different stories.
— τὴν ὄψιν τῆς γῆς : Ex. 10⁵ n.

**6.** ἰσχύει οὗτος ἢ ἡμεῖς : § 65. — ἐὰν
δυνώμεθα : *if haply we may be able.*
Like si forte in Latin. — πατάξαι ἐξ
αὐτῶν : *to smite some of them.* — κεκατήρανται : § 20.  *Cp.* 24⁹.  One of
these passages has evidently suggested

the other.  Presumably the prophecy
is older than the narrative.

**7.** ἡ γερουσία : this must not be
pressed, as though the whole body
went, especially in view of 15. — τὰ
μαντεῖα : *the rewards of divination.*
In Prov. 16¹⁰ and Ezk. 21²² μαντεῖον is
used in its ordinary sense.

**9.** Τί οἱ ἄνθρωποι κτλ. : a repro-
duction of the vague Hebrew interrogative, and perhaps intended to mean
"Why are these men with thee?"
R.V. ' What men are these with
thee? '

**11.** Ἰδοὺ λαὸς ἐξελήλυθεν : Hebrew,
' Behold, the people that is come out.'
— εἰ ἄρα δυνήσομαι : cp. ἐὰν δυνώμεθα
in 6.

Numbers XXII 22

αὐτὸν καὶ ἐκβαλῶ αὐτὸν ἀπὸ τῆς γῆς.'" ¹²καὶ εἶπεν ὁ θεὸς πρὸς Βαλαάμ "Οὐ πορεύσῃ μετ' αὐτῶν οὐδὲ καταράσῃ τὸν λαόν· ἔστιν γὰρ εὐλογημένος." ¹³καὶ ἀναστὰς Βαλαὰμ τὸ πρωὶ εἶπεν τοῖς ἄρχουσιν Βαλάκ "'Αποτρέχετε πρὸς τὸν κύριον ὑμῶν· οὐκ ἀφίησίν με ὁ θεὸς πορεύεσθαι μεθ' ὑμῶν." ¹⁴καὶ ἀναστάντες οἱ ἄρχοντες Μωὰβ ἦλθον πρὸς Βαλὰκ καὶ εἶπαν "Οὐ θέλει Βαλαὰμ πορευθῆναι μεθ' ἡμῶν." ¹⁵καὶ προσέθετο Βαλὰκ ἔτι ἀποστεῖλαι ἄρχοντας πλείους καὶ ἐντιμοτέρους τούτων. ¹⁶καὶ ἦλθον πρὸς Βαλαὰμ καὶ λέγουσιν αὐτῷ "Τάδε λέγει Βαλὰκ ὁ τοῦ Σεπφώρ ''Αξιῶ σε, μὴ ὀκνήσῃς ἐλθεῖν πρὸς μέ· ¹⁷ἐντίμως γὰρ τιμήσω σε, καὶ ὅσα ἐὰν εἴπῃς ποιήσω σοι· καὶ δεῦρο ἐπικατάρασαί μοι τὸν λαὸν τοῦτον.'" ¹⁸καὶ ἀπεκρίθη Βαλαὰμ καὶ εἶπεν τοῖς ἄρχουσιν Βαλάκ "'Εὰν δῷ μοι Βαλὰκ πλήρη τὸν οἶκον αὐτοῦ ἀργυρίου καὶ χρυσίου, οὐ δυνήσομαι παραβῆναι τὸ ῥῆμα Κυρίου τοῦ θεοῦ, ποιῆσαι αὐτὸ μικρὸν ἢ μέγα ἐν τῇ διανοίᾳ μου. ¹⁹καὶ νῦν ὑπομείνατε αὐτοῦ καὶ ὑμεῖς τὴν νύκτα ταύτην, καὶ γνώσομαι τί προσθήσει Κύριος λαλῆσαι πρὸς μέ." ²⁰καὶ ἦλθεν ὁ θεὸς πρὸς Βαλαὰμ καὶ εἶπεν αὐτῷ "Εἰ καλέσαι σε πάρεισιν οἱ ἄνθρωποι οὗτοι, ἀναστὰς ἀκολούθησον αὐτοῖς· ἀλλὰ τὸ ῥῆμα ὃ ἂν λαλήσω πρὸς σέ, τοῦτο ποιήσεις." ²¹καὶ ἀναστὰς Βαλαὰμ τὸ πρωὶ ἐπέσαξεν τὴν ὄνον αὐτοῦ, καὶ ἐπορεύθη μετὰ τῶν ἀρχόντων Μωάβ. ²²καὶ ὠργίσθη θυμῷ ὁ θεὸς ὅτι ἐπορεύθη αὐτός, καὶ ἀνέστη ὁ

12. ἔστιν γὰρ εὐλογημένος : § 72.
13. 'Αποτρέχετε : a dignified word in late Greek. 24¹⁴ n. Frequent in the inscriptions of manumission at Delphi.
— πρὸς τὸν κύριον ὑμῶν : Hebrew, 'to your land.'
17. ἐντίμως . . . τιμήσω : § 82.
18. ποιῆσαι αὐτὸ μικρὸν κτλ. : to make it small or great, i.e. to take from

or add to it. Cp. 24¹³ ποιῆσαι αὐτὸ μικρὸν ἢ καλὸν παρ' ἐμαυτοῦ. The Greek translators seem to have had here also the word which there corresponds to παρ' ἐμαυτοῦ.
19. καὶ ὑμεῖς : like the former messengers.
20. καλέσαι : § 77.— ὃ ἄν : § 105.
22. αὐτός : § 13.— ἀνέστη : Hebrew,

ἄγγελος τοῦ θεοῦ ἐνδιαβαλεῖν αὐτόν· καὶ αὐτὸς ἐπιβεβήκει
ἐπὶ τῆς ὄνου αὐτοῦ, καὶ δύο παῖδες αὐτοῦ μετ᾽ αὐτοῦ. ²³καὶ
ἰδοῦσα ἡ ὄνος τὸν ἄγγελον τοῦ θεοῦ ἀνθεστηκότα ἐν τῇ ὁδῷ
καὶ τὴν ῥομφαίαν ἐσπασμένην ἐν τῇ χειρὶ αὐτοῦ, καὶ ἐξέκλινεν ἡ ὄνος ἐκ τῆς ὁδοῦ αὐτῆς καὶ ἐπορεύετο εἰς τὸ
πεδίον· καὶ ἐπάταξεν τὴν ὄνον τῇ ῥάβδῳ, τοῦ εὐθῦναι αὐτὴν
ἐν τῇ ὁδῷ. ²⁴καὶ ἔστη ὁ ἄγγελος τοῦ θεοῦ ἐν ταῖς αὔλαξιν
τῶν ἀμπέλων, φραγμὸς ἐντεῦθεν καὶ φραγμὸς ἐντεῦθεν·
²⁵καὶ ἰδοῦσα ἡ ὄνος τὸν ἄγγελον τοῦ θεοῦ προσέθλιψεν
αὐτὸν πρὸς τὸν τοῖχον, καὶ ἀπέθλιψεν τὸν πόδα Βαλαάμ,
καὶ προσέθετο ἔτι μαστίξαι αὐτήν. ²⁶καὶ προσέθετο ὁ
ἄγγελος τοῦ θεοῦ καὶ ἀπελθὼν ὑπέστη ἐν τόπῳ στενῷ, εἰς
ὃν οὐκ ἦν ἐκκλῖναι δεξιὰν οὐδὲ ἀριστεράν. ²⁷καὶ ἰδοῦσα
ἡ ὄνος τὸν ἄγγελον τοῦ θεοῦ συνεκάθισεν ὑποκάτω Βα-
λαάμ· καὶ ἐθυμώθη Βαλαὰμ καὶ ἔτυπτεν τὴν ὄνον τῇ
ῥάβδῳ. ²⁸καὶ ἤνοιξεν ὁ θεὸς τὸ στόμα τῆς ὄνου, καὶ
λέγει τῷ Βαλαάμ "Τί ἐποίησά σοι ὅτι πέπαικάς με τοῦτο

---

'placed himself in the way.' — ἐνδιαβαλεῖν αὐτόν : for an adversary against
him. Cp. 32 εἰς διαβολήν σου, where the
Hebrew is the same. Διάβολος = satan,
'adversary.' In such passages we have
the doctrine of the Devil in germ. —
ἐπιβεβήκει : § 19. An imperfect in
meaning = was riding on.
23. ἀνθεστηκότα : a present participle in meaning. Cp. 31 and 34
ἀνθέστηκας. — τῇ ῥάβδῳ : not in the
Hebrew, which has here the name
Balaam.
24. αὔλαξιν : furrows is the usual
meaning of this word. The R.V. has
here 'in a hollow way between the
vineyards.' — φραγμὸς κτλ. : § 51. Jos.
Ant. IV 6 § 2 κατά τι στενὸν χωρίον
περιειλημμένον αἱμασίαις διπλαῖς.

25. προσέθλιψεν . . . ἀπέθλιψεν :
the preposition in the former compound has its full force, but not in the
latter. Neither word is used again in
the LXX. The Hebrew is the same
for both. In the N.T. ἀποθλίβειν
occurs only in Lk. 8⁴⁵ in the sense of
'to crush.' — τοῖχον : Josephus here
uses the word θριγκός.
26. εἰς ὅν : in which. § 90. — δεξιὰν
οὐδὲ ἀριστεράν : cp. i Mac. 5⁴⁶ οὐκ ἦν
ἐκκλῖναι ἀπ᾽ αὐτῆς δεξιὰν ἢ ἀριστεράν :
Nb. 20¹⁷ καὶ οὐκ ἐκκλινοῦμεν δεξιὰ οὐδὲ
εὐώνυμα : Dt. 2²⁷, 17²⁰ : i K. 6¹² : ii Chr.
34² : Is. 30²¹ — in all which passages
the mere accusative is employed, as
here.
27. ἐθυμώθη . . . καὶ ἔτυπτεν : got
angry and began to strike.

Numbers XXII 36

τρίτον;" ²⁹καὶ εἶπεν Βαλαὰμ τῇ ὄνῳ "Ὅτι ἐμπέπαιχάς μοι· καὶ εἰ εἶχον μάχαιραν ἐν τῇ χειρί, ἤδη ἂν ἐξεκέντησά σε." ³⁰καὶ λέγει ἡ ὄνος τῷ Βαλαάμ " Οὐκ ἐγὼ ἡ ὄνος σου, ἐφ' ἧς ἐπέβαινες ἀπὸ νεότητός σου ἕως τῆς σήμερον ἡμέρας; μὴ ὑπεροράσει ὑπεριδοῦσα ἐποίησά σοι οὕτως;" ὁ δὲ εἶπεν "Οὐχί." ³¹ἀπεκάλυψεν δὲ ὁ θεὸς τοὺς ὀφθαλμοὺς Βαλαάμ, καὶ ὁρᾷ τὸν ἄγγελον Κυρίου ἀνθεστηκότα ἐν τῇ ὁδῷ καὶ τὴν μάχαιραν ἐσπασμένην ἐν τῇ χειρὶ αὐτοῦ, καὶ κύψας προσεκύνησεν τῷ προσώπῳ αὐτοῦ. ³²καὶ εἶπεν αὐτῷ ὁ ἄγγελος τοῦ θεοῦ "Διὰ τί ἐπάταξας τὴν ὄνον σου τοῦτο τρίτον; καὶ ἰδοὺ ἐγὼ ἐξῆλθον εἰς διαβολήν σου, ὅτι οὐκ ἀστεία ἡ ὁδός σου ἐναντίον μου. ³³καὶ ἰδοῦσά με ἡ ὄνος ἐξέκλινεν ἀπ' ἐμοῦ τρίτον τοῦτο· καὶ εἰ μὴ ἐξέκλινεν, νῦν οὖν σὲ μὲν ἀπέκτεινα, ἐκείνην δὲ περιεποιησάμην." ³⁴καὶ εἶπεν Βαλαὰμ τῷ ἀγγέλῳ Κυρίου "Ἡμάρτηκα, οὐ γὰρ ἠπιστάμην ὅτι σύ μοι ἀνθέστηκας ἐν τῇ ὁδῷ εἰς συνάντησιν· καὶ νῦν εἰ μή σοι ἀρέσκει, ἀποστραφήσομαι." ³⁵καὶ εἶπεν ὁ ἄγγελος τοῦ θεοῦ πρὸς Βαλαάμ " Συνπορεύθητι μετὰ τῶν ἀνθρώπων· πλὴν τὸ ῥῆμα ὃ ἐὰν εἴπω πρὸς σέ, τοῦτο φυλάξῃ λαλῆσαι." καὶ ἐπορεύθη Βαλαὰμ μετὰ τῶν ἀρχόντων Βαλάκ. ³⁶καὶ ἀκούσας Βαλὰκ ὅτι "ἥκει Βαλαάμ," ἐξ-

29. ἐμπέπαιχας : there is a perfect πέπαικα from παίζω as well as from παίω. The later form πέπαιχα, which treats the stem as a guttural, is here useful by way of distinction from πέπαικας in 28. Ex. 10² n. — ἂν ἐξεκέντησά σε : would have stabbed thee to death. Ἐκκεντεῖν occurs in seven other passages of the LXX.

30. τῆς σήμερον ἡμέρας : Ex. 5¹⁴ n. — μὴ ὑπεροράσει κτλ. : Did I out of contempt do so unto thee ? Hebrew, ' Was I with custom accustomed to do so ? '

32. εἰς διαβολήν : v. 22 n.—οὐκ ἀστεία : R.V. 'perverse.' On the moral sense which came to be attached to the word ἀστεῖος see Ex. 2² n.

33. σὲ μέν . . . ἐκείνην δέ : § 39. — ἀπέκτεινα . . . περιεποιησάμην : § 76.

34. ἀνθέστηκας : v. 23 n. — ἀποστραφήσομαι : passive in form, but middle in meaning. Cp. 23⁶, ¹⁶, ¹⁷, § 83. — φυλάξῃ λαλῆσαι : the Hebrew here is simply ' thou shalt speak.' — εἰς πόλιν Μωάβ : to a town of the Moabites. Vulg. in oppido Moabitarum.

ἦλθεν εἰς συνάντησιν αὐτῷ εἰς πόλιν Μωάβ, ἥτις ἐπὶ τῶν
ὁρίων Ἀρνῶν, ὅ ἐστιν ἐκ μέρους τῶν ὁρίων.   ³⁷ καὶ εἶπεν
Βαλὰκ πρὸς βαλαάμ " Οὐχὶ ἀπέστειλα πρὸς σὲ καλέσαι
σε; διὰ τί οὐκ ἤρχου πρὸς μέ; οὐ δυνήσομαι ὄντως
τιμῆσαί σε;"   ³⁸ καὶ εἶπεν Βαλαὰμ πρὸς Βαλάκ " Ἰδοὺ ἥκω
πρὸς σὲ νῦν· δυνατὸς ἔσομαι λαλῆσαί τι; τὸ ῥῆμα ὃ ἐὰν
βάλῃ ὁ θεὸς εἰς τὸ στόμα μου, τοῦτο λαλήσω."   ³⁹ καὶ ἐπορεύθη Βαλαὰμ μετὰ Βαλάκ, καὶ ἦλθον εἰς Πόλεις ἐπαύλεων.
⁴⁰ καὶ ἔθυσεν Βαλὰκ πρόβατα καὶ μόσχους, καὶ ἀπέστειλεν
τῷ Βαλαὰμ καὶ τοῖς ἄρχουσι τοῖς μετ᾽ αὐτοῦ.   ⁴¹ καὶ ἐγενήθη πρωί, καὶ παραλαβὼν Βαλὰκ τὸν Βαλαὰμ ἀνεβίβασεν
αὐτὸν ἐπὶ τὴν στήλην τοῦ Βάαλ, καὶ ἔδειξεν αὐτῷ ἐκεῖθεν
μέρος τι τοῦ λαοῦ.   ¹ Καὶ εἶπεν Βαλαὰμ τῷ Βαλάκ
" Οἰκοδόμησόν μοι ἐνταῦθα ἑπτὰ βωμούς, καὶ ἑτοίμασόν μοι
ἐνταῦθα ἑπτὰ μόσχους καὶ ἑπτὰ κριούς."   ² καὶ ἐποίησεν
Βαλὰκ ὃν τρόπον εἶπεν αὐτῷ Βαλαάμ, καὶ ἀνήνεγκεν μόσχον καὶ κριὸν ἐπὶ τὸν βωμόν.   ³ καὶ εἶπεν Βαλαὰμ πρὸς

36. Ἀρνών: an indeclinable proper
name. The Arnon was a river flowing
into the Dead Sea from the west, and
seems here to be regarded as forming
the northern boundary of the territory
of Moab ('the border of Arnon' =
the border made by the Arnon). As
rivers are masculine in Greek, we might
expect ὅς here instead of ὅ. — ἐκ μέρους
τῶν ὁρίων: in the direction of the
borders. Hebrew, 'on the extremity
of the border.'

37. Οὐχὶ ἀπέστειλα: the Hebrew
corresponding to this might have been
rendered ἀποστέλλων ἀπέστειλα, but
the Greek translator seems at this
point to be getting tired of the emphatic repetition. He fails to mark
it again in 38 where δυνάμει δυνατὸς

ἔσομαι would be justified by the
original.

39. Πόλεις ἐπαύλεων: this shows
the meaning which the translator put
upon the Hebrew proper name.

40. ἀπέστειλεν: perhaps sent some
of the meat, since a sacrifice among
the Jews, as among the Pagans, was
preliminary to a good dinner.

41. τὴν στήλην τοῦ Βάαλ: Hebrew Bamoth-Baal. Bamoth is the
word commonly rendered 'high places.'
The situation was chosen also as
affording a good view of the Israelite
encampment.

2. καὶ ἀνήνεγκεν: Hebrew, 'and
Balak and Balaam offered.' — ἐπὶ τὸν
βωμόν: more literal than the R.V. 'on
every altar.' So in v. 4.

Numbers XXIII 8

Βαλάκ "Παράστηθι ἐπὶ τῆς θυσίας σου, καὶ πορεύσομαι,
εἴ μοι φανεῖται ὁ θεὸς ἐν συναντήσει· καὶ ῥῆμα ὃ ἐάν μοι
δείξῃ ἀναγγελῶ σοι." καὶ παρέστη Βαλὰκ ἐπὶ τῆς θυσίας
αὐτοῦ· καὶ Βαλαὰμ ἐπορεύθη ἐπερωτῆσαι τὸν θεόν, καὶ
ἐπορεύθη εὐθεῖαν. ⁴καὶ ἐφάνη ὁ θεὸς τῷ Βαλαάμ, καὶ
εἶπεν πρὸς αὐτὸν Βαλαάμ "Τοὺς ἑπτὰ βωμοὺς ἡτοίμασα,
καὶ ἀνεβίβασα μόσχον καὶ κριὸν ἐπὶ τὸν βωμόν." ⁵καὶ
ἐνέβαλεν ὁ θεὸς ῥῆμα εἰς στόμα Βαλαὰμ καὶ εἶπεν "Ἐπιστραφεὶς πρὸς Βαλὰκ οὕτως λαλήσεις." ⁶καὶ ἐπεστράφη
πρὸς αὐτόν· καὶ ὅδε ἐφιστήκει ἐπὶ τῶν ὁλοκαυτωμάτων
αὐτοῦ, καὶ πάντες οἱ ἄρχοντες Μωὰβ μετ᾽ αὐτοῦ. καὶ ἐγενήθη πνεῦμα θεοῦ ἐπ᾽ αὐτῷ· ⁷καὶ ἀναλαβὼν τὴν παραβολὴν
αὐτοῦ εἶπεν

"Ἐκ Μεσοποταμίας μετεπέμψατό με Βαλάκ,
βασιλεὺς Μωὰβ ἐξ ὀρέων ἀπ᾽ ἀνατολῶν, λέγων
'Δεῦρο ἄρασαί μοι τὸν Ἰακώβ,
καὶ δεῦρο ἐπικατάρασαί μοι τὸν Ἰσραήλ.'
⁸τί ἀράσωμαι ὃν μὴ καταρᾶται Κύριος;

3. Παράστηθι ἐπί: *Stand by at.* A regard for Greek would make παραστῆναι to be constructed with a dative, but a preposition follows in the Hebrew, which is represented by ἐπί. — εἴ μοι φανεῖται κτλ.: *in case God shall appear unto me.* — ὁ θεός: Hebrew, 'Jehovah.' — καὶ παρέστη . . . τὸν θεόν: not in the Hebrew. — εὐθεῖαν: *sc.* ὁδόν. R.V. 'and he went to a bare height.' The Greek can only mean 'he went straight.'

6. ἐφιστήκει: = ἐφειστήκει *was standing. Cp.* v. 17. — ὁλοκαυτωμάτων: in this form of sacrifice the meat was wholly burnt, and not eaten. — καὶ ἐγενήθη πνεῦμα θεοῦ ἐπ᾽ αὐτῷ: not in the Hebrew.

7. παραβολήν: the word παραβολή

was not inaptly chosen by the Greek translator to represent the Hebrew original, which is often rendered 'proverb.' The Hebrew word originally meant 'setting beside,' and was applied to a species of composition like that which follows, consisting of couplets, in which each second line is a repetition under another form of its predecessor. The meaning of 'parable' in the N.T. is different. It is there 'comparison' in the sense of 'illustration' or 'analogy,' which was a recognised use of παραβολή in good Greek: *cp.* i K. 24¹⁴ ἡ παραβολὴ ἡ ἀρχαία. From παραβολή comes the French *parler* through the Latin *parabolare.*

8. τί ἀράσωμαι: *What curse am I*

Numbers XXIII 9

ἢ τί καταράσωμαι ὃν μὴ καταρᾶται ὁ θεός;
⁹ὅτι ἀπὸ κορυφῆς ὀρέων ὄψομαι αὐτόν,
καὶ ἀπὸ βουνῶν προσνοήσω αὐτόν.
ἰδοὺ λαὸς μόνος κατοικήσει,
καὶ ἐν ἔθνεσιν οὐ συλλογισθήσεται.
¹⁰τίς ἐξηκριβάσατο τὸ σπέρμα Ἰακώβ;
καὶ τίς ἐξαριθμήσεται δήμους Ἰσραήλ;
ἀποθάνοι ἡ ψυχή μου ἐν ψυχαῖς δικαίων,
καὶ γένοιτο τὸ σπέρμα μου ὡς τὸ σπέρμα τούτων."
¹¹καὶ εἶπεν Βαλὰκ πρὸς Βαλαάμ "Τί πεποίηκάς μοι; εἰς
κατάρασιν ἐχθρῶν μου κέκληκά σε, καὶ ἰδοὺ εὐλόγηκας
εὐλογίαν."    ¹²καὶ εἶπεν Βαλαὰμ πρὸς Βαλάκ "Οὐχὶ ὅσα
ἐὰν ἐμβάλῃ ὁ θεὸς εἰς τὸ στόμα μου, τοῦτο φυλάξω λαλῆσαι;"    ¹³καὶ εἶπεν πρὸς αὐτὸν Βαλάκ "Δεῦρο ἔτι μετ' ἐμοῦ
εἰς τόπον ἄλλον, ἐξ ὧν οὐκ ὄψῃ αὐτὸν ἐκεῖθεν, ἀλλ' ἢ μέρος

to pronounce upon him? τί is cognate accusative.

**9.** ὄψομαι, προσνοήσω: R.V. 'I see, I behold.' Προσνοεῖν occurs eight times in the LXX. In L. & S. it is recognised only as a false reading in Xenophon. — βουνῶν: iv K. 2¹⁶ n. — λαὸς μόνος κατοικήσει: this prophecy was amply fulfilled by the isolation of the Jews among the nations of the world, which was brought about by their religion. This, according to the High Priest Eleazar in the Letter of Aristeas, was the express object of the Mosaic system. — ἐν ἔθνεσιν: the Jews habitually spoke of τὰ ἔθνη (the Gentiles) in contradistinction to themselves. — ἐξηκριβάσατο: aorist middle of ἐξακριβάζειν. This verb occurs also in Job 28³, Dan. O' 7¹⁹.

**10.** τὸ σπέρμα: Hebrew, 'dust.' The translator has seized upon the

meaning. — δήμους: Hebrew, 'fourth part of.' The word for 'multitude' differs only by a letter from that for 'fourth part.' — ἀποθάνοι ἡ ψυχή κτλ.: Hebrew, 'Let my soul die the death of the righteous.' The meaning of this prayer in this particular context is not clear. In the Greek the last two lines do not correspond in meaning, which shows that something is wrong. But the Greek of the second line gives a more natural close to the prophecy, which relates to the prosperity of Israel, than the Hebrew as translated in our version. Perhaps the word rendered 'last end' ought to be taken to mean 'posterity.'

**11.** εὐλόγηκας εὐλογίαν: § 56.

**13.** ἐξ ὧν: there is another reading ἐξ οὗ, which grammar requires. — οὐκ ὄψῃ αὐτόν: the Hebrew here has no negative, but either reading makes good sense. — ἀλλ' ἤ: § 108. — ἐκεῖθεν: § 87.

Numbers XXIII 19

τι αὐτοῦ ὄψῃ, πάντας δὲ οὐ μὴ ἴδῃς· καὶ κατάρασαί μοι αὐτὸν ἐκεῖθεν." ¹⁴καὶ παρέλαβεν αὐτὸν εἰς ἀγροῦ σκοπιὰν ἐπὶ κορυφὴν Λελαξευμένου, καὶ ᾠκοδόμησεν ἐκεῖ ἑπτὰ βωμούς, καὶ ἀνεβίβασεν μόσχον καὶ κριὸν ἐπὶ τὸν βωμόν. ¹⁵καὶ εἶπεν Βαλαὰμ πρὸς Βαλάκ "Παράστηθι ἐπὶ τῆς θυσίας σου, ἐγὼ δὲ πορεύσομαι ἐπερωτῆσαι τὸν θεόν." ¹⁶καὶ συνήντησεν ὁ θεὸς τῷ Βαλαὰμ καὶ ἐνέβαλεν ῥῆμα εἰς τὸ στόμα αὐτοῦ καὶ εἶπεν "Ἀποστράφητι πρὸς Βαλάκ, καὶ τάδε λαλήσεις." ¹⁷καὶ ἀπεστράφη πρὸς αὐτόν· ὁ δὲ ἐφιστήκει ἐπὶ τῆς ὁλοκαυτώσεως αὐτοῦ, καὶ πάντες οἱ ἄρχοντες Μωὰβ μετ' αὐτοῦ. καὶ εἶπεν αὐτῷ Βαλάκ "Τί ἐλάλησεν Κύριος;" ¹⁸καὶ ἀναλαβὼν τὴν παραβολὴν αὐτοῦ εἶπεν

"Ἀνάστηθι Βαλάκ, καὶ ἄκουε·
ἐνώτισαι μάρτυς, υἱὸς Σεπφώρ.
¹⁹οὐχ ὡς ἄνθρωπος ὁ θεὸς διαρτηθῆναι,
οὐδὲ ὡς υἱὸς ἀνθρώπου ἀπειληθῆναι·
αὐτὸς εἶπας οὐχὶ ποιήσει;
λαλήσει, καὶ οὐχὶ ἐμμενεῖ;

**14. εἰς ἀγροῦ σκοπιὰν κτλ.** : *to the look-out place of the field, to the top of that which is hewn in stone.* R.V. 'into the field of Zophim, to the top of Pisgah.' Zophim is here a proper name, but means 'The Watchmen.' Pisgah is also the proper name of a well-known mountain overlooking the Jordan valley from the east. The translator is supposed to have arrived at Λελαξευμένου from an Aramaic sense of the root.

**15. ἐγὼ δὲ πορεύσομαι ἐπερωτῆσαι τὸν θεόν** : Hebrew, 'while I meet yonder.' Here, as in v. 3, the Hebrew omits the reference to 'questioning God' — possibly out of a feeling of reverence. Here the sense is incomplete without it.

**18. ἐνώτισαι μάρτυς** : *give ear to me as a witness.* Hebrew, 'hearken unto me.' The Greek rendering can here be traced to a different pointing of the Hebrew text. The same consonants which can be read 'unto me' may also be taken to mean 'my witness.' Ἐνωτίζεσθαι is a common word in the LXX, *e.g.* Gen. 4²³ : Jdg. 5³ : Jer. 23¹⁸. It occurs also in Acts 2¹⁴.

**19. διαρτηθῆναι** : *to be misled.* Hebrew, 'that he should lie.' Διαρτᾶν occurs only here in the LXX. In Judith 8¹⁶ we find οὐχ ὡς ἄνθρωπος ὁ θεὸς ἀπειληθῆναι, | οὐδὲ ὡς υἱὸς ἀνθρώπου διαρτηθῆναι. —ἀπειληθῆναι : *to be terrified with threats.* R.V. 'that he should repent.'

# 214    SELECTIONS FROM THE SEPTUAGINT

²⁰ἰδοὺ εὐλογεῖν παρείλημμαι·
εὐλογήσω, καὶ οὐ μὴ ἀποστρέψω.
²¹ οὐκ ἔσται μόχθος ἐν Ἰακώβ,
οὐδὲ ὀφθήσεται πόνος ἐν Ἰσραήλ·
Κύριος ὁ θεὸς αὐτοῦ μετ᾽ αὐτοῦ,
τὰ ἔνδοξα ἀρχόντων ἐν αὐτῷ.
²² θεὸς ὁ ἐξαγαγὼν αὐτοὺς ἐξ Αἰγύπτου·
ὡς δόξα μονοκέρωτος αὐτῷ.
²³ οὐ γάρ ἐστιν οἰωνισμὸς ἐν Ἰακώβ,
οὐδὲ μαντεία ἐν Ἰσραήλ.
κατὰ καιρὸν ῥηθήσεται Ἰακὼβ καὶ τῷ Ἰσραήλ
τί ἐπιτελέσει ὁ θεός.

**20. ἰδοὺ εὐλογεῖν κτλ.** : the Greek
here reproduces the Hebrew — ‘Behold, I have received to bless.’ The
R.V. supplies the word ‘command-
ment.’ — **εὐλογήσω κτλ.** : R.V. ‘and he
hath blessed, and I cannot reverse it.’
— **οὐ μὴ ἀποστρέψω** : intransitive, as
often — *I will not turn back*.
**21. οὐκ ἔσται μόχθος κτλ.** : R.V.
‘He hath not beheld iniquity in
Jacob, | Neither hath he seen per-
verseness in Israel.’  The Hebrew
nouns here used may mean either ‘sin’
or ‘sorrow.’  ‘Iniquity’ and ‘perverse-
ness’ decide the question in the one
way, μόχθος and πόνος in the other:
but the derivatives of these latter,
μοχθηρία and πονηρία, would coincide
with the English version. — **τὰ ἔνδοξα
ἀρχόντων κτλ.** : *the glories of chiefs
are in him*, i.e. “Israel has glorious
chiefs.”  R.V. ‘and the shout of a
king is among them.’  Perhaps the
Greek translators changed ‘king’ into
‘rulers’ to avoid the appearance of
anachronism.

**22. ὡς δόξα μονοκέρωτος** : the ‘uni-
corn’ figures all together in eight passages of the LXX — Nb. 23²², 24⁸ : Dt.
33¹⁷ : Job 39⁹ : Ps. 21²², 28⁶, 77⁶⁹, 91¹⁰.
In the R.V. it is everywhere reduced
to a ‘wild-ox,’ except where it is
absent altogether (Ps. 77⁶⁹).  From Dt.
33¹⁷ it appears plainly that the animal
had more than one horn.  The rendering of the Vulgate then — cuius for-
titudo similis est rhinocerotis
— is devoid of plausibility.  It should
be noticed that the parallelism in sense,
which is very close in most of these
couplets, is here absent altogether.
**23. οὐ γάρ ἐστιν οἰωνισμὸς κτλ.** :
this is a literal rendering of the Hebrew.
The R.V. margin puts a meaning into
the words thus : ‘Surely there is no en-
chantment *against* Jacob, | Neither is
there any divination *against* Israel,’
i.e. it is useless to call in diviners to
curse them. — **κατὰ καιρὸν κτλ.** : quite
correct as a rendering of the Hebrew,
except that ἐπιτελέσει ought to be perfect, but the meaning is not plain in

Numbers XXIV 1

²⁴ ἰδοὺ λαὸς ὡς σκύμνος ἀναστήσεται,

καὶ ὡς λέων γαυριωθήσεται·

οὐ κοιμηθήσεται ἕως φάγῃ θήραν,

καὶ αἷμα τραυματιῶν πίεται."

²⁵ καὶ εἶπεν Βαλὰκ πρὸς Βαλαάμ " Οὔτε κατάραις καταράσῃ μοι αὐτόν, οὔτε εὐλογῶν μὴ εὐλογήσῃς αὐτόν." ²⁶ καὶ ἀπο-κριθεὶς Βαλαὰμ εἶπεν τῷ Βαλάκ " Οὐκ ἐλάλησά σοι λέγων ' Τὸ ῥῆμα ὃ ἐὰν λαλήσῃ ὁ θεός, τοῦτο ποιήσω';" ²⁷ καὶ εἶπεν Βαλὰκ πρὸς Βαλαάμ " Δεῦρο παραλάβω σε εἰς τόπον ἄλλον, εἰ ἀρέσει τῷ θεῷ, καὶ κατάρασαί μοι αὐτὸν ἐκεῖ-θεν." ²⁸ καὶ παρέλαβεν Βαλὰκ τὸν Βαλαὰμ ἐπὶ κορυφὴν τοῦ Φογώρ, τὸ παρατεῖνον εἰς τὴν ἔρημον. ²⁹ καὶ εἶπεν Βαλαὰμ πρὸς Βαλάκ " Οἰκοδόμησόν μοι ὧδε ἑπτὰ βωμούς, καὶ ἑτοίμασόν μοι ὧδε ἑπτὰ μόσχους καὶ ἑπτὰ κριούς." ³⁰ καὶ ἐποίησεν Βαλὰκ καθάπερ εἶπεν αὐτῷ Βαλαάμ, καὶ ἀνήνεγκεν μόσχον καὶ κριὸν ἐπὶ τὸν βωμόν. ¹ Καὶ ἰδὼν Βαλαὰμ ὅτι καλόν ἐστιν ἔναντι Κυρίου εὐλογεῖν τὸν Ἰσραήλ, οὐκ ἐπορεύθη κατὰ τὸ εἰωθὸς εἰς συνάντησιν τοῖς οἰωνοῖς, καὶ ἀπέστρεψεν τὸ πρόσωπον εἰς τὴν ἔρημον.

either language. The parallelism of sense is here also absent, and it looks as though Israel had been originally meant to balance Jacob.

**24.** γαυριωθήσεται: this must come from γαυριοῦν, not from γαυριᾶν. There is also a form γαυροῦν Wisd. 6²: iii Mac. 3¹¹. Γαυριᾶν occurs in Judith 9⁷: Job 3¹⁴, 39²¹, ²³. On the voice see § 83. — τραυματιῶν: τραυματίας properly means a wounded man, as in Ar. Poet. 14 § 13 : Lucian V.H. II 38. In the LXX it is used for one who has met his death by wounding, e.g. Nb. 19¹⁶, 31⁸ : Jdg. 16²⁴ : i K. 17⁵². The word is very common.

**25.** οὔτε εὐλογῶν κτλ. : § 81.

**27.** Δεῦρο παραλάβω κτλ. : punctu-ate here εἰς τόπον ἄλλον· The words εἰ ἀρέσει τῷ θεῷ go with καὶ κατάρασαι — If it shall please God, do thou curse me him from there.

**28.** Φογώρ : = Peor. — τὸ παρατεῖ-νον εἰς τὴν ἔρημον : to the place which stretches along to the desert, in apposi-tion with κορυφήν. R.V. 'that looketh down upon the desert.'

**1.** εἰς συνάντησιν τοῖς οἰωνοῖς : to meet the omens, i.e. to observe signs from which he might infer the will of God. Cp. 23³, ¹⁵. R.V. 'to meet with enchantments.' The Hebrew

Numbers XXIV 2

²καὶ ἐξάρας Βαλαὰμ τοὺς ὀφθαλμοὺς αὐτοῦ καθορᾷ τὸν
Ἰσραὴλ ἐστρατοπεδευκότα κατὰ φυλάς· καὶ ἐγένετο πνεῦμα
θεοῦ ἐν αὐτῷ.     ³καὶ ἀναλαβὼν τὴν παραβολὴν αὐτοῦ εἶπεν
  " Φησὶν Βαλαὰμ υἱὸς Βεώρ,
    φησὶν ὁ ἄνθρωπος ὁ ἀληθινῶς ὁρῶν,
  ⁴φησὶν ἀκούων λόγια θεοῦ,
    ὅστις ὅρασιν θεοῦ εἶδεν,
    ἐν ὕπνῳ, ἀποκεκαλυμμένοι οἱ ὀφθαλμοὶ αὐτοῦ·
  ⁵ὡς καλοί σου οἱ οἶκοι, Ἰακώβ,
    αἱ σκηναί σου, Ἰσραήλ·
  ⁶ὡς νάπαι σκιάζουσαι,
    καὶ ὡσεὶ παράδεισος ἐπὶ ποταμῶν·
    καὶ ὡσεὶ σκηναὶ ἃς ἔπηξεν Κύριος,
    ὡσεὶ κέδροι παρ᾽ ὕδατα.

word is the plural of that which is
translated οἰωνισμός in 23²³.

3. ὁ ἀληθινῶς ὁρῶν: this seems to
point to a different reading from that
of the Hebrew as we have it. See
R.V.

4. λόγια θεοῦ: cp. v. 16 : Dt. 33⁹ :
and Psalms passim. St. Paul in Rom.
3² uses the expression τὰ λόγια τοῦ
Θεοῦ, which is there rendered 'the
oracles of God.' Cp. Acts 7³⁸ : i Pet.
4¹¹ : Hb. 5¹². — ἐν ὕπνῳ: R.V. 'falling
down.' — ἀποκεκαλυμμένοι κτλ. : § 51.
To sleep with the eyes open seems to
have been regarded as the sign of a
wizard. In φησίν . . . αὐτοῦ we have
a triplet instead of the usual couplets.
It would seem from v. 16 that a line
has dropped out.

5. ὡς καλοὶ κτλ. : the sight of the
Israelites encamped, which has made
a desert place seem populous, suggests
a vision of the people permanently set-

tled in a fruitful land, and flourishing
like a well-watered grove of trees.

6. ὡς νάπαι σκιάζουσαι : even as
shady dells. R.V. ' As valleys are they
spread forth.' — παράδεισος : a Persian
word meaning a 'park' or 'pleasure-
ground,' which is familiar to readers
of Xenophon. The Hebrew word is
here the same as that which is translated 'garden' in Gen. 2 and 3. In
Nehemiah, Ecclesiastes, Canticles, and
Sirach the Hebrew has pardês, which
is probably a loan-word from the Persian. — σκηναί: R.V. ' lign aloes.' Curious as this variation seems, it is not
an unnatural one. For the Hebrew
word in v. 5, which is rendered οἶκοι by
the Greek and 'tents' by the English
translators, differs only by a point
from the one which is here employed.
The word 'lign-aloes' stands for lig-
num aloēs, which is a Latin translation of the Greek ξυλαλόη. The bitter

<sup>7</sup> ἐξελεύσεται ἄνθρωπος ἐκ τοῦ σπέρματος αὐτοῦ,
  καὶ κυριεύσει ἐθνῶν πολλῶν·
  καὶ ὑψωθήσεται ἢ Γὼγ βασιλεία,
  καὶ αὐξηθήσεται ἡ βασιλεία αὐτοῦ.
<sup>8</sup> θεὸς ὡδήγησεν αὐτὸν ἐξ Αἰγύπτου,
  ὡς δόξα μονοκέρωτος αὐτῷ·
  ἔδεται ἔθνη ἐχθρῶν αὐτοῦ,
  καὶ τὰ πάχη αὐτῶν ἐκμυελιεῖ,
  καὶ ταῖς βολίσιν αὐτοῦ κατατοξεύσει ἐχθρόν.
<sup>9</sup> κατακλιθεὶς ἀνεπαύσατο ὡς λέων καὶ ὡς σκύμνος·
  τίς ἀναστήσει αὐτόν;
  οἱ εὐλογοῦντές σε εὐλόγηνται,
  καὶ οἱ καταρώμενοί σε κεκατήρανται."

aloe was also known as ἀγάλλοχον, which is perhaps the Semitic word borrowed and modified so as to give it something of a Greek air.

**7. ἐξελεύσεται ἄνθρωπος κτλ. : R.V.** ' Water shall flow from his buckets, | And his seed shall be in many waters.' —**ὑψωθήσεται ἢ Γὼγ βασιλεία**: his kingdom shall be higher than Gog. Hebrew, 'his king shall be higher than Agag.' Gog (Ezek. 38², 39¹) seems out of place here. Perhaps the true reading is Og (cp. 24²³), which has three consonants in Hebrew and might easily get changed into either Gog or Agag. Moreover Og is elsewhere mentioned as typical of a mighty king (Ps. 134¹¹, 136²⁰) and he had just been subdued by Israel (Nb. 21³³⁻³⁵). On this supposition the ' king ' will be Jehovah. With the reading ' Agag ' the king would naturally be Saul. But to take a person yet unborn as a standard of comparison for another person who is in the same predicament is too much of an

anachronism even for prophecy. For the form of the comparison, see § 65.

**8. θεὸς ὡδήγησεν κτλ. :** in 23²² with a slight variation. The difference in the original amounts only to that between singular and plural (αὐτὸν, αὐτούς).— **καὶ τὰ πάχη κτλ. :** and shall suck the marrow out of their fatness. R.V. ' And shall break their bones in pieces.' The two can hardly be renderings of the same original, though the one process is preliminary to the other. The metaphor is in either case from a beast of prey, but the Greek lends itself very well to the idea of the Jews absorbing the wealth of other nations. Ἐκμυελίζειν occurs only here. For πάχος cp. Eur. Cyclops 380 : οἱ σαρκὸς εἶχον εὐτραφέστατον πάχος. — **βολίσιν :** arrows. Cp. Ex. 19¹³ ἢ βολίδι κατατοξευθήσεται : Jer. 27⁹ ὡς βολὶς μαχητοῦ συνετοῦ. This line is out of keeping with the simile of the wild beast, which is resumed in the following couplet.

**9. κεκατήρανται : § 20.**

¹⁰καὶ ἐθυμώθη Βαλὰκ ἐπὶ Βαλαάμ, καὶ συνεκρότησεν ταῖς χερσὶν αὐτοῦ· καὶ εἶπεν Βαλὰκ πρὸς Βαλαάμ "Καταρᾶσθαι τὸν ἐχθρόν μου κέκληκά σε, καὶ ἰδοὺ εὐλογῶν εὐλόγησας τρίτον τοῦτο. ¹¹νῦν οὖν φεῦγε εἰς τὸν τόπον σου· εἶπα 'Τιμήσω σε,' καὶ νῦν ἐστέρεσέν σε Κύριος τῆς δόξης." ¹²καὶ εἶπεν Βαλαὰμ πρὸς Βαλάκ "Οὐχὶ καὶ τοῖς ἀγγέλοις σου οὓς ἀπέστειλας πρὸς μὲ ἐλάλησα λέγων ¹³'Ἐάν μοι δῷ Βαλὰκ πλήρη τὸν οἶκον αὐτοῦ ἀργυρίου καὶ χρυσίου, οὐ δυνήσομαι παραβῆναι τὸ ῥῆμα Κυρίου, ποιῆσαι αὐτὸ πονηρὸν ἢ καλὸν παρ᾽ ἐμαυτοῦ· ὅσα ἐὰν εἴπῃ ὁ θεός, ταῦτα ἐρῶ.' ¹⁴καὶ νῦν ἰδοὺ ἀποτρέχω εἰς τὸν τόπον μου· δεῦρο συμβουλεύσω σοι τί ποιήσει ὁ λαὸς οὗτος τὸν λαόν σου ἐπ᾽ ἐσχάτου τῶν ἡμερῶν." ¹⁵καὶ ἀναλαβὼν τὴν παρα-βολὴν αὐτοῦ εἶπεν

"Φησὶν Βαλαὰμ υἱὸς Βεώρ,

φησὶν ὁ ἄνθρωπος ὁ ἀληθινὸς ὁρῶν,

¹⁶ἀκούων λόγια θεοῦ,

ἐπιστάμενος ἐπιστήμην παρὰ Ὑψίστου,

καὶ ὅρασιν θεοῦ ἰδών,

ἐν ὕπνῳ, ἀποκεκαλυμμένοι οἱ ὀφθαλμοὶ αὐτοῦ·

---

10. **συνεκρότησεν ταῖς χερσίν**: cp. Lucian *Somn.* 14 ἠγανάκτει καὶ τῶ χεῖρε συνεκρότει, καὶ τοὺς ὀδόντας ἐνέπριε. 13. **ποιῆσαι αὐτὸ πονηρὸν κτλ.** : to make it bad or good (*i.e.* a curse or a blessing). 22¹⁸ n. 14. **ἀποτρέχω** : this appears to have been the regular word for 'go away' in Alexandrian Greek, and not to have been suggestive of anything undignified, being used on the most solemn occasions, as in Josh. 23¹⁴ : Tob. 14³ : Aristeas § 273 κἂν ἐκ τοῦ ζῆν ἀποτρέχωσιν. *Cp.* also Gen. 12¹⁹, 24⁵¹, 32⁹ :

Ex. 3²¹, 10²⁴, 21⁵,⁷ : i K. 8²². It seems to have supplanted ἀπέρχομαι. Jer. 44⁹ ἀποτρέχοντες ἀπελεύσονται. — **ἐπ᾽ ἐσχάτου τῶν ἡμερῶν** : Dan. O′ 10¹⁴. This is the phrase which is used at the beginning of Hebrews. *Cp.* ii Pet. 3³ ἐλεύσονται ἐπ᾽ ἐσχάτων τῶν ἡμερῶν . . . ἐμπαῖκται. 15. **ὁ ἀληθινὸς ὁρῶν**: ὁρῶν is here a substantive, not a participle, as in v. 3. 16. **ἐπιστάμενος κτλ.** : here we have the line which was wanting to complete the first couplet in v. 4.

Numbers XXIV 20

<sup>17</sup>δείξω αὐτῷ, καὶ οὐχὶ νῦν·

μακαρίζω, καὶ οὐκ ἐγγίζει·

ἀνατελεῖ ἄστρον ἐξ Ἰακώβ,

καὶ ἀναστήσεται ἄνθρωπος ἐξ Ἰσραήλ,

καὶ θραύσει τοὺς ἀρχηγοὺς Μωάβ,

καὶ προνομεύσει πάντας υἱοὺς Σήθ.

<sup>18</sup>καὶ ἔσται Ἐδὼμ κληρονομία,

καὶ ἔσται κληρονομία Ἠσαῦ ὁ ἐχθρὸς αὐτοῦ·

καὶ Ἰσραὴλ ἐποίησεν ἐν ἰσχύι.

<sup>19</sup>καὶ ἐξεγερθήσεται ἐξ Ἰακώβ,

καὶ ἀπολεῖ σωζόμενον ἐκ πόλεως."

<sup>20</sup>καὶ ἰδὼν τὸν Ἀμαλὴκ καὶ ἀναλαβὼν τὴν παραβολὴν αὐτοῦ εἶπεν

17. δείξω αὐτῷ: Hebrew, 'I see him.' The Greek has no sense, and is due to an error on the part of the translator. — μακαρίζω, καὶ οὐκ ἐγγίζει: *I pronounce him blessed, though he is not nigh.* R.V. 'I behold him, but not nigh.' The seer in vision sees the distant future, not the present. Cp. v. 14. — ἀνατελεῖ ἄστρον κτλ.: this must refer to David, the one Israelite king who is recorded to have conquered both Moab and Edom. — ἄνθρωπος: R.V. 'sceptre.'— τοὺς ἀρχηγούς: R.V. 'the corners.' — προνομεύσει: προνομεύειν is a late Greek word meaning 'ravage.' Both it and προνομή 'spoil' (Nb. 31<sup>11</sup>) are common in the LXX. — υἱοὺς Σήθ: R.V. 'sons of tumult.' The Greek translator either took 'sheth' to be a proper name or left it untranslated. His difficulty seems to have been occasioned by a mispointing of the initial consonant.

18. Ἠσαύ: Hebrew *Seir*. 'Esau' is an alternative for 'Edom'; Seir is a mountain in the land of Edom. — ἐποίησεν ἐν ἰσχύι: R.V. 'While Israel doeth valiantly.' On ἐν see § 91.

19. ἐξεγερθήσεται: sc. τις. R.V. 'shall one have dominion.' — καὶ ἀπολεῖ κτλ.: *and shall destroy one who is escaping out of a city.* R.V. 'And shall destroy the remnant from the city.' This seems to refer to some blow to Moab later than the time of David.

20. ἰδὼν τὸν Ἀμαλήκ: Balaam is supposed to catch sight of some encampment of the nomad Amalekites, which happened to be within the field of vision. He can only prophesy of a people when he has some portion of it before his eyes. So the modern clairvoyant requires to be somehow put *en rapport* with the person about whom he is questioned. — τὸ σπέρμα αὐτῶν: R.V. 'his latter end.' Both the Greek and the English translators are consistent with their rendering of the same Hebrew word at the close of the first

Numbers XXIV 21

" Ἀρχὴ ἐθνῶν Ἀμαλήκ,
καὶ τὸ σπέρμα αὐτῶν ἀπολεῖται."
²¹ καὶ ἰδὼν τὸν Κεναῖον καὶ ἀναλαβὼν τὴν παραβολὴν αὐτοῦ
εἶπεν

" Ἰσχυρὰ ἡ κατοικία σου·
καὶ ἐὰν θῆς ἐν πέτρᾳ τὴν νοσσιάν σου,
²² καὶ ἐὰν γένηται τῷ Βεὼρ νεοσσιὰ πανουργίας,
Ἀσσύριοί σε αἰχμαλωτεύσουσιν."

prophecy in 33¹⁰. But the Greek rendering has here the disadvantage of quite losing the verbal antithesis which exists in the original between 'beginning' and 'end.' In i Chron. 4⁴² we read that 500 men of the sons of Simeon went to Mount Seir and smote the remnant of the Amalekites. This appears from the context to have been in the days of Hezekiah.

**21.** τὸν Κεναῖον : in Jdg. 1¹⁶ (LXX) the Kenites are spoken of as the descendants of Jothor, the father-in-law of Moses (Ex. 2¹⁸ n.). In i Sam. 15⁶ Saul, when about to attack the Amalekites, warns the Kenites, as old friends of Israel, to withdraw from among them. — καὶ ἐὰν θῆς κτλ. : R.V. 'and thy nest is set in the rock.' The parallelism of the couplets requires this line to repeat the preceding one ; it is therefore a mistake to subordinate it to the sentence that follows. — νοσσιάν : = νεοσσιάν. Cp. v. 22. The Hebrew word thus rendered (qēn) contains an untranslatable pun on the name 'Kenites' (qēni).

**22.** καὶ ἐὰν γένηται κτλ. : *and if it become unto Beor a nest of wickedness.* R.V. 'Nevertheless Kain shall be wasted.' This extraordinary divergence may be partly accounted for

without supposing a difference of reading. The Greek translator took the proper name *Qain* here for the common term 'nest' (qēn) used in the preceding verse, and on the other hand treated as a proper name the word *ba'er*, which means 'wasting.' Gray even suggests an explanation of πανουργίας. — Ἀσσύριοί σε αἰχμαλω-τεύσουσιν : when did this take place ? It was in the time of Shalmaneser II (B.C. 860) that the Assyrians first came into direct contact with Israel. That monarch defeated the king of Damascus, and mentions Ahab among the allies of his opponent. But his campaigns were apparently confined to the region of Damascus, and would hardly affect a nomad tribe on the borders of Moab and Judah. The earliest possible date seems to be the reign of Rammannirari II (B.C. 811), who 'subjugated all the coast lands of the west, including Tyre, Sidon, Israel, Edom, and Philistia.' At that date however Assyrian action on the regions of Palestine was still exceptional. It was not till the time of Tiglath-Pileser III (B.C. 745) that the danger of Assyrian conquest became pressing and constant ; and it seems likely that the Kenites, who were so closely con-

Numbers XXIV 25

²³καὶ ἰδὼν τὸν *Ὢγ καὶ ἀναλαβὼν τὴν παραβολὴν αὐτοῦ εἶπεν

" *Ω ὦ, τίς ζήσεται ὅταν θῇ ταῦτα ὁ θεός ;

²⁴καὶ ἐξελεύσεται ἐκ χειρὸς Κιτιαίων,

καὶ κακώσουσιν Ἀσσούρ, καὶ κακώσουσιν Ἑβραίους,

καὶ αὐτοὶ ὁμοθυμαδὸν ἀπολοῦνται."

²⁵καὶ ἀναστὰς Βαλαὰμ ἀπῆλθεν, ἀποστραφεὶς εἰς τὸν τόπον

αὐτοῦ · καὶ Βαλὰκ ἀπῆλθεν πρὸς ἑαυτόν.

nected with Judah (Jdg. 1¹⁶), did not suffer seriously till the invasion of Sennacherib (B.C. 701).

**23. καὶ ἰδὼν τὸν "Ωγ**: there is nothing answering to these words in the Hebrew, though the analogy of vs. 20 and 21 requires it. The destruction of Og has already been recorded (Nb. 21³³⁻³⁵). —**ὅταν θῇ ταῦτα**: θεῖναι here seems to have the sense of *appoint*. As this is the beginning of a new παραβολή, it would appear that ταῦτα refers to what follows.

**24. καὶ ἐξελεύσεται κτλ.** : Hebrew, literally 'and ships from the hand of Kittim.' — **Κιτιαίων** : Hebrew *Kittim* = Κίτιον, a town in Cyprus. The name was extended from the town, which was originally a Phœnician settlement, to the island (Jos. *Ant.* I 6 § 1 Χέθεμος δὲ χεθεμὰ τὴν νῆσον ἔσχεν · Κύπρος αὔτη νῦν καλεῖται), and from that

to the Greeks generally. In i Mac. 1¹ Alexander the Great is spoken of as having come from the land of Χεττιείμ, and in 8⁵ of the same, Perses is called Κιτιέων βασιλεύς. Kittim is represented in Gen. 10⁴ as a son of Javan (= Ἰάϝονες, Ἰῶνες). The destruction of the Assyrian Empire took place about B.C. 606, but not in any way owing to the action of Greek ships. If the Hebrew text is sound and this last prophecy was fulfilled at all, it would seem to refer to the time of Alexander the Great, when Assyria shared the fate of the Persian Empire, of which it then formed a part. — Ἑβραίους : Hebrew *Eber*. In Gen. 10²¹ Shem is spoken of as 'the father of all the children of Eber.' — ὁμοθυμαδόν : properly *with one heart, with one accord*. Here perhaps = *all together*. Hebrew, 'also.'

# INTRODUCTION TO THE STORY OF SAMSON

SAMSON is the most frankly Pagan figure in the whole Bible — a
hero like Hercules, with a good appetite, ready to feast or ready
to fight, invincible against the foe, but helpless before women.

His name in the Hebrew is Shimshon. The form Samson comes
from the Vulgate, representing the Σάμψων of the Septuagint. This
last may be an error of the translators or it may represent an older
and truer tradition than that of the Massoretes with regard to the
pronunciation of Hebrew.

The name, according to Josephus (*Ant.* V 8 § 4), means 'strong.'
Modern scholars, however, connect it with *Shemesh*, the Hebrew
word for the sun ; and, as *Beth-shemesh*, or the 'House of the Sun,'
was near the hero's birthplace, some would have us resolve Samson
into a solar myth. For ourselves we prefer the more terrestrial
view which sees in the story of Samson a number of local legends
drawn from the annals of the tribe of Dan. There was doubtless
really a strong man in the district of Zorah and Eshtaol, who did
doughty deeds against the Philistines, which were afterwards related
with embroidery. We must remember that, though the legends of Samson are to all appearance very early, they were not put into writing
as we have them until after the Captivity (*cp.* Jdg. $15^{19}$ with $18^{30}$).

The story of Samson as a whole may be analysed into the following parts —

(1) The birth-story 13.
(2) The marriage-story 14.
(3) The story of the foxes $15^{1-8}$.
(4) The jawbone-story $15^{9-20}$.
(5) The story of the gates of Gaza $16^{1-3}$.
(6) The story of Delilah and the death of Samson $16^{4-31}$.

Of these the first and the last two have no organic connexion
either with one another or with the rest, while the second, third,
and fourth cohere closely together.

There is reason to consider that the first story is the latest of all ;

for the fact that an annunciation of birth should be thought appropriate shows that the person of whom it is told has already become celebrated. As in the case of Sarah (Gen. 16¹), of Hannah (i S. 1⁵), and in the New Testament of Elisabeth (Lk. 1⁷), the mother of the wonderful child had previously been barren.

The connexion of Samson with the institution of the Nazirate which is common to the first and the last story (Jdg. 13⁵, ⁷, 16¹⁷), looks like a priestly attempt to throw some cloak of pious purpose over the otherwise unsanctified proceedings of the hero. This institution is mentioned as early as Amos 2¹¹, ¹², side by side with prophecy. The law of the Nazirite may be read in Nb. 6¹⁻²¹ : but the regulations there given refer to a temporary vow made by the individual himself for some special purpose. The only parallels to the lifelong Nazirate of Samson are Samuel (i S. 1¹¹) in the Old Testament and John the Baptist (Lk. 1¹⁵) in the New. But the notion that Samson was a Nazirite in any sense is hard to reconcile with the general tenor of the story. In eating honey taken from the carcase of the lion Samson was breaking the law of the Nazirite (Nb. 6⁶) ; nor is it likely that he abstained from wine during the seven days' feast (Jdg. 14¹⁷) ; moreover men were peculiarly apt to 'die very suddenly beside him' (Nb. 6⁹) without his consecration appearing to have been in any way affected thereby. It is to be noticed also that in all but the first and last legends the secret of Samson's strength lies, not in his unshorn hair, but in the spirit of the Lord coming mightily upon him (14⁶, ¹⁹, 15¹⁴), a form of inspiration which reminds us of the Berserker rage of the old Norsemen.

In the days of Samson, as in those of Samuel and Saul, the Philistines were the oppressors of Israel. These were foreign invaders who succeeded in giving to the whole country of the Jews the name of Palestine, which it retains to this day. They established themselves in the fertile lowlands on the sea-coast of Canaan. It is an interesting question where they came from. Possibly it may have been from Crete during the Mycenæan period, when Crete was the centre of a naval dominion, the power and wealth of which is illustrated by the recently excavated ruins of Cnossus. If so, their culture and mode of life may have been similar to that of the early Greeks as depicted in the Homeric poems. The epithet 'uncircumcised' specially applied to the Philistines indicates the Jewish sense of the difference between themselves and these foreigners: for many of their other neighbours were of Semitic race and practised circumcision like themselves. These considerations might afford a reason for the name of the Philistines being translated 'foreigners' (ἀλλόφυλοι) in the LXX. On the other hand we may be looking too far back. In the books of Maccabees ἀλλόφυλοι is several times used as a name for Gentiles generally. Now the inhabitants of the maritime plain of Palestine were thoroughly Hellenized at the time when the translation of the LXX was made, and may for this reason be called ἀλλόφυλοι by the translator.

How far the rule of the Philistines over the Israelite tribes extended does not appear. The northern tribes do not come within the purview of the story. But the southern Danites and the adjacent tribe of Judah (Jdg. 15⁹⁻¹³) are represented as being completely subdued by the Philistines and living in unresisting subjection. Samson is no military leader, like Barak, Gideon, or Jephthah, and organizes no armed rebellion. He like his neighbours, lives at first on peaceful terms with the dominant race, and is ready even to take a wife from among them. His feats of arms are not acts of war, but outbreaks of fury provoked by personal wrongs.

In the peculiar relations of Samson with his Philistine wife, whom he goes to visit at her father's house, it has been thought that we have an instance of an old form of marriage, which is believed to have existed among certain peoples, in which the wife, instead of migrating to her husband's house, continued to reside with her own family, and was visited there by her husband. At the time of the Samson-story this usage may have prevailed in the case of intermarriage between Israelite and foreign races. Abimelech had similar relations with a Canaanite woman in Shechem. Similarly we find in the *Iliad* that the married daughters of Priam continued to reside in his palace; and traces of the same usage survived in the Spartan institutions.

To the story of the foxes and the firebrands there is a curious parallel in Roman folk-lore. At the Cerealia, on April 19, foxes with burning firebrands tied to them used to be let loose in the Circus. Ovid *Fasti* IV 681 —

Cur igitur missæ vinctis ardentia tædis
terga ferant vulpes, causa docenda mihi.

He goes on to tell the story, as it was told to him by an old inn-keeper at Carseoli, of how a boy of twelve, having caught a fox that had been robbing the fowl-yard, wrapped it in straw and set it on fire, and how the fox escaped and burnt the corn-fields.

> Factum abiit, monimenta manent; nam vivere captum
> nunc quoque lex vulpem Carseolana vetat.
> Utque luat pœnas gens hæc Cerealibus ardet,
> quoque modo segetes perdidit, ipsa perit.

The fox episode ended in dire disaster to Samson's wife and father-in-law. This however is passed lightly over as having happened to Philistines. Not so the tragedy of the closing scene, in which the hero, blind and captive, is brought out of the prison-house to make sport for his enemies. Milton has seen how the pathos of this situation lends itself to a drama after the Greek model. What can be finer than the dithyrambic lament of the chorus over the stricken hero —

> ' with languish'd head unprop
> As one past hope, abandon'd. . . .
> \* \* \* \* \* \* \* \*
> Or do my eyes misrepresent ? Can this be he
> That heroic, that renown'd,
> Irresistible Samson ? whom unarm'd
> No strength of man, or fiercest wild beast, could withstand ;
> Who tore the lion, as the lion tears the kid ;
> Ran on embattled armies clad in iron ;
> And, weaponless himself,
> Made arms ridiculous, useless the forgery
> Of brazen shield and spear . . .'

Samson slew at his death more than he slew in his life, yet he brought no deliverance to his countrymen. The moral of his story is the same as that of Ajax as depicted by Sophocles, and is thus drawn by Milton —

> ' But what is strength without a double share
> Of wisdom ? vast, unwieldy, burdensome,
> Proudly secure, yet liable to fall
> By weakest subtleties, not made to rule,
> But to subserve where wisdom bears command.'

# IV. THE STORY OF SAMSON

Judges XIII

¹Καὶ προσέθηκαν οἱ υἱοὶ Ἰσραὴλ ποιῆσαι τὸ πονηρὸν
ἐνώπιον Κυρίου, καὶ παρέδωκεν αὐτοὺς Κύριος ἐν χειρὶ
Φυλιστιεὶμ τεσσεράκοντα ἔτη. ²Καὶ ἦν ἀνὴρ εἷς ἀπὸ
Σαρὰλ ἀπὸ δήμου συγγενείας τοῦ Δανεὶ καὶ ὄνομα αὐτῷ
Μανῶε, καὶ γυνὴ αὐτῷ στεῖρα καὶ οὐκ ἔτεκεν. ³καὶ ὤφθη
ἄγγελος Κυρίου πρὸς τὴν γυναῖκα καὶ εἶπεν πρὸς αὐτήν
" Ἰδοὺ σὺ στεῖρα καὶ οὐ τέτοκας, καὶ συλλήμψῃ υἱόν. ⁴καὶ
νῦν φύλαξαι δὴ καὶ μὴ πίῃς οἶνον καὶ μέθυσμα, καὶ μὴ
φάγῃς πᾶν ἀκάθαρτον· ⁵ὅτι ἰδοὺ σὺ ἐν γαστρὶ ἔχεις καὶ
τέξῃ υἱόν, καὶ σίδηρος οὐκ ἀναβήσεται ἐπὶ τὴν κεφαλὴν
αὐτοῦ, ὅτι ναζεὶρ θεοῦ ἔσται τὸ παιδάριον ἀπὸ τῆς κοιλίας·
καὶ αὐτὸς ἄρξεται τοῦ σῶσαι τὸν Ἰσραὴλ ἐκ χειρὸς Φυλι-

1. ἐν χειρί: into the hand. § 91.
2. ἀνὴρ εἷς: § 2. — Σαράλ: R.V.
'Zorah.' A town lying near the edge
of the highlands, on the present rail-
way from Jaffa to Jerusalem. Josh.
15³³, 19⁴¹. — ἀπὸ δήμου: an accommo-
dation to Greek ideas, to which there
is nothing to answer in the Hebrew. —
τοῦ Δανεί: the translator has retained
the Hebrew termination of the tribe
name, which is here plural in sense —
of the Danites. For the termination
cp. 15⁶ τοῦ Θαμνεί. — Μανῶε: Hebrew
Manoah (= rest). In i Chr. 2⁵⁴ the
Zorites are called Manahathites, which
may be only a coincidence.
4. μέθυσμα: cp. vs. 7, 14: i K. 1¹¹, ¹⁵:
Hos. 4¹¹: Mic. 2¹¹: Jer. 13¹³. — μὴ . . .
πᾶν: § 88.

5. ναζείρ: a retention of the Hebrew
word for want of a Greek equivalent.
It is from root 'nazar,' 'to separate'
or 'consecrate.' On the law of the
Nazirite see Nb. 6¹⁻²¹. The Alexandrian Ms. has here ηγιασμενον Ναζι-
ραιον, which is perhaps referred to in
Mt. 2²³

ὅπως πληρωθῇ τὸ ῥηθὲν διὰ τῶν προφητῶν ὅτι

Ναζωραῖος κληθήσεται.

— ἄρξεται τοῦ σῶσαι: Samson did not,
like Barak, Gideon, or Jephthah, liberate his countrymen from a foreign
yoke: he only killed a large number of
individual Philistines. The work of
'delivering Israel' was, according to
the book of Samuel, begun by Samuel
and Saul and completed by David.

227

στιείμ." ⁶καὶ εἰσῆλθεν ἡ γυνὴ καὶ εἶπεν τῷ ἀνδρὶ αὐτῆς λέγουσα "Ἄνθρωπος θεοῦ ἦλθεν πρὸς μέ, καὶ εἶδος αὐτοῦ ὡς εἶδος ἀγγέλου θεοῦ φοβερὸν σφόδρα· καὶ οὐκ ἠρώτησα αὐτὸν πόθεν ἐστίν, καὶ τὸ ὄνομα αὐτοῦ οὐκ ἀπήγγειλέν μοι. ⁷καὶ εἶπέν μοι 'Ἰδοὺ σὺ ἐν γαστρὶ ἔχεις καὶ τέξῃ υἱόν· καὶ νῦν μὴ πίῃς οἶνον καὶ μέθυσμα, καὶ μὴ φάγῃς πᾶν ἀκάθαρτον, ὅτι ἅγιον θεοῦ ἔσται τὸ παιδάριον ἀπὸ γαστρὸς ἕως ἡμέρας θανάτου αὐτοῦ.' " ⁸καὶ προσηύξατο Μανῶε πρὸς Κύριον καὶ εἶπεν "Ἐν ἐμοί, Κύριε Ἀδωναῖε, τὸν ἄνθρωπον τοῦ θεοῦ ὃν ἀπέστειλας, ἐλθέτω δὴ ἔτι πρὸς ἡμᾶς, καὶ συνβιβασάτω ἡμᾶς τί ποιήσωμεν τῷ παιδίῳ τῷ τικτομένῳ." ⁹καὶ εἰσήκουσεν ὁ θεὸς τῆς φωνῆς Μανῶε, καὶ ἦλθεν ὁ ἄγγελος τοῦ θεοῦ ἔτι πρὸς τὴν γυναῖκα· καὶ αὐτη ἐκάθητο ἐν ἀγρῷ, καὶ Μανῶε ὁ ἀνὴρ αὐτῆς οὐκ ἦν μετ' αὐτῆς. ¹⁰καὶ ἐτάχυνεν ἡ γυνὴ καὶ ἔδραμεν καὶ ἀνήγγειλεν τῷ ἀνδρὶ αὐτῆς, καὶ εἶπεν πρὸς αὐτόν "Ἰδοὺ ὦπται πρὸς μὲ ὁ ἀνὴρ ὃς ἦλθεν ἐν ἡμέρᾳ πρὸς μέ." ¹¹καὶ ἀνέστη καὶ ἐπορεύθη Μανῶε ὀπίσω τῆς γυναικὸς αὐτοῦ, καὶ ἦλθεν πρὸς τὸν ἄνδρα καὶ εἶπεν αὐτῷ "Εἰ σὺ εἶ ὁ ἀνὴρ ὁ λαλήσας πρὸς τὴν γυναῖκα;"

---

**6.** Ἄνθρωπος θεοῦ : used as a title of Moses in Dt. 33¹ : Josh. 14⁶.

**8.** Ἐν ἐμοί : a literal rendering of a Hebrew formula of entreaty. *Cp.* Jdg. 6¹³,¹⁵ : i K. 1²³, 25²⁴. In Gen. 43²⁰ the same original is represented by δεόμεθα and in 44¹⁸ by δέομαι : so also in Ex. 4¹⁰, where it is reduced in the English to ' O.' — Κύριε Ἀδωναῖε : our Hebrew text has here only *Adonai* without Jehovah before it : but the translator's text evidently had both words, as ours has in 16²⁸. *Adonai*, when it occurs by itself, is regularly rendered by Κύριε, so also is *Jehovah* : when the two therefore come together, one has to

be transliterated, as in i K. 1¹¹, or else they are left indistinguishable, so that we get the combination Κύριος Κύριος, as in Amos 5⁸ : Ps. 140⁸. — τὸν ἄνθρωπον : inverse attraction. *Cp.* Verg. *Æn.* I 573 — Urbem quam statuo, vestra est. — ἐλθέτω δὴ ἔτι : Josephus ( *Ant.* V 8 § 3) represents the second appearance of the angel as being granted to the prayers of Samson's mother to allay the jealousy aroused in her husband's mind by her interview with a handsome stranger. — συνβιβασάτω : Ex. 4¹² n.

**10.** ἐν ἡμέρᾳ : *the other day.* A Hebraism.

**11.** Εἰ σὺ εἶ : § 100.

Judges XIII 16

καὶ εἶπεν ὁ ἄγγελος " Ἐγώ." ¹²καὶ εἶπεν̣ Μανῶε " Νῦν
ἐλεύσεται ὁ λόγος σου· τίς ἔσται κρίσις τοῦ παιδίου καὶ
τὰ ποιήματα αὐτοῦ;" ¹³καὶ εἶπεν ὁ ἄγγελος Κυρίου πρὸς
Μανῶε " Ἀπὸ πάντων ὧν εἴρηκα πρὸς τὴν γυναῖκα φυλά-
ξεται· ¹⁴ἀπὸ παντὸς ὃ ἐκπορεύεται ἐξ ἀμπέλου τοῦ οἴνου
οὐ φάγεται, καὶ οἶνον καὶ σίκερα μέθυσμα μὴ πιέτω, καὶ
πᾶν ἀκάθαρτον μὴ φαγέτω· πάντα ὅσα ἐνετειλάμην αὐτῷ
φυλάξεται." ¹⁵καὶ εἶπεν Μανῶε πρὸς τὸν ἄγγελον Κυρίου
" Κατάσχωμεν ὧδέ σε, καὶ ποιήσωμεν ἐνώπιόν σου ἔριφον
αἰγῶν." ¹⁶καὶ εἶπεν ὁ ἄγγελος Κυρίου πρὸς Μανῶε " Ἐὰν
κατάσχῃς με, οὐ φάγομαι ἀπὸ τῶν ἄρτων σου· καὶ ἐὰν
ποιήσῃς ὁλοκαύτωμα, τῷ κυρίῳ ἀνοίσεις αὐτό·" ὅτι οὐκ

12. Νῦν ἐλεύσεται κτλ. : the Alexandrian Ms. subordinates this clause to
the next in the manner suggested in the
margin of the R.V.— νῦν δὲ ἐλθόντος
τοῦ ῥήματός σου, τί ἔσται τὸ κρίμα τοῦ
παιδαρίου καὶ τὰ ἔργα αὐτοῦ; — κρίσις :
this word seems to be chosen because
of its etymological correspondence with
the Hebrew, without much regard to
the meaning in Greek. The original it
represents is derived from the same
root as shophet, 'a judge' (cp. the
Carthaginian sufet-). Κρίσις is used to
translate the same Hebrew in Dt. 18⁸
and iv K. 1⁷. In the former of these
passages it refers to the priests' 'dues';
in the latter the English runs thus —
'What manner of man was he?' The
latter is the meaning that suits this
passage: so that κρίσις may be taken
to mean distinctive marks (the Alexandrian Ms. has here το κριμα).

13. Ἀπὸ πάντων . . . φυλάξεται :
§ 98.

14. ἐξ ἀμπέλου τοῦ οἴνου : a literal
rendering of the Hebrew. — σίκερα μέ-

θυσμα : a doublet. In v. 4 the Alexandrian Ms. has σίκερα, which is a
transliteration of the Hebrew, in place
of μέθυσμα, which is a translation of
the same. Here both have somehow
been allowed to appear. Σίκερα was a
generic name for fermented liquor. It
is used 13 times in the LXX and once
in the N.T. (Lk. 1¹⁵). — πᾶν . . . μή :
= μηδέν. § 88.

15. ποιήσωμεν : dress, i.e. make
ready for food. Cp. i K. 25¹⁸, where
Abigail brings to David πέντε πρόβατα
πεποιημένα. See iii K. 18²³ n. — ἔριφον
αἰγῶν : Gen. 37³¹ n.

16. ἄρτων : bread, in the sense of
food generally. — καὶ ἐὰν ποιήσῃς κτλ. :
better sense would be got by putting
the comma after ποιήσῃς, instead of
after ὁλοκαύτωμα — and, if thou dost
prepare it, offer it as a whole burnt-
offering unto the Lord. The Hebrew
too seems to admit of being thus taken.
Manoah could not have thought of
making an offering to his visitor, whom
he still supposes to be a man.

Judges XIII 17

ἔγνω Μανῶε ὅτι ἄγγελος Κυρίου αὐτός. ¹⁷καὶ εἶπεν Μανῶε πρὸς τὸν ἄγγελον Κυρίου " Τί τὸ ὄνομά σοι ; ὅτι ἔλθοι τὸ ῥῆμά σου, καὶ δοξάσομέν σε." ¹⁸καὶ εἶπεν αὐτῷ ὁ ἄγγελος Κυρίου " Εἰς τί τοῦτο ἐρωτᾷς τὸ ὄνομά μου ; καὶ αὐτό ἐστιν θαυμαστόν." ¹⁹καὶ ἔλαβεν Μανῶε τὸν ἔριφον τῶν αἰγῶν καὶ τὴν θυσίαν καὶ ἀνήνεγκεν ἐπὶ τὴν πέτραν τῷ κυρίῳ, καὶ διεχώρισεν ποιῆσαι· καὶ Μανῶε καὶ ἡ γυνὴ αὐτοῦ βλέποντες. ²⁰καὶ ἐγένετο ἐν τῷ ἀναβῆναι τὴν φλόγα ἐπάνω τοῦ θυσιαστηρίου ἕως τοῦ οὐρανοῦ, καὶ ἀνέβη ὁ ἄγγελος Κυρίου ἐν τῇ φλογὶ τοῦ θυσιαστηρίου· καὶ Μανῶε καὶ ἡ γυνὴ αὐτοῦ βλέποντες, καὶ ἔπεσαν ἐπὶ πρόσωπον αὐτῶν ἐπὶ τὴν γῆν. ²¹καὶ οὐ προσέθηκεν ἔτι ὁ ἄγγελος Κυρίου ὀφθῆναι πρὸς Μανῶε καὶ πρὸς τὴν γυναῖκα αὐτοῦ· τότε ἔγνω Μανῶε ὅτι ἄγγελος Κυρίου οὗτος. ²²καὶ εἶπεν Μανῶε πρὸς τὴν γυναῖκα αὐτοῦ " Θανάτῳ ἀποθανούμεθα, ὅτι θεὸν εἴδομεν." ²³καὶ εἶπεν αὐτῷ ἡ γυνὴ αὐτοῦ " Εἰ ἤθελεν ὁ κύριος θανατῶσαι ἡμᾶς, οὐκ ἂν ἔλαβεν ἐκ χειρὸς ἡμῶν ὁλοκαύτωμα καὶ θυσίαν, καὶ οὐκ ἂν ἔδειξεν ἡμῖν ταῦτα πάντα· καὶ καθὼς καιρός, οὐκ ἂν ἠκούτισεν ἡμᾶς ταῦτα."

17. ὅτι ἔλθοι κτλ.: the clause with ἔλθοι is really subordinate to the one which follows. R.V. 'that when thy words come to pass we may do thee honour.' The Alexandrian Ms. has ἵνα, ὅταν ἔλθῃ το ῥῆμα σου, δοξασωμεν σε.

18. Εἰς τί: To what end? Cp. 15¹⁰.— τοῦτο ἐρωτᾷς κτλ.: τοῦτο may be regarded as a cognate accusative after ἐρωτᾷς with τὸ ὄνομά μου in apposition to it. But it really owes its position here merely to the Hebrew.

19. καὶ τὴν θυσίαν: R.V. 'with the meal-offering.' The θυσία is distinct from the kid, resembling the Greek οὐλοχύται. Cp. v. 23 ὁλοκαύτωμα

καὶ θυσίαν.— διεχώρισεν ποιῆσαι: the literal rendering of the Hebrew here is 'and (the angel was) acting-wonderfully for-doing.' This is not very intelligible in itself, and the Greek translation is less so. Apart from the original the latter might be taken to mean 'cut it up to dress it.' — βλέποντες: participle = finite verb: cp. v. 20. § 80.

20. ἔπεσαν: § 18.

22. θεόν: notice that 'the angel of the Lord' is here spoken of as God. Cp. Ex. 3².

23. καθὼς καιρός: a literal translation of the Hebrew, but meaningless

Judges XIV 8

²⁴Καὶ ἔτεκεν ἡ γυνὴ υἱόν, καὶ ἐκάλεσεν τὸ ὄνομα αὐτοῦ Σαμψών· καὶ ἡδρύνθη τὸ παιδάριον, καὶ εὐλόγησεν αὐτὸ Κύριος. ²⁵καὶ ἤρξατο πνεῦμα Κυρίου συνεκπορεύεσθαι αὐτῷ ἐν παρεμβολῇ Δὰν καὶ ἀνὰ μέσον Σαραὰ καὶ ἀνὰ μέσον Ἐσθαόλ. ¹Καὶ κατέβη Σαμψὼν εἰς Θαμνάθα, καὶ εἶδεν γυναῖκα εἰς Θαμνάθα ἀπὸ τῶν θυγατέρων τῶν ἀλλοφύλων. ²καὶ ἀνέβη καὶ ἀπήγγειλεν τῷ πατρὶ αὐτοῦ καὶ τῇ μητρὶ αὐτοῦ καὶ εἶπεν " Γυναῖκα ἑόρακα ἐν Θαμνάθα ἀπὸ τῶν θυγατέρων Φυλιστιείμ, καὶ νῦν λάβετε αὐτὴν ἐμοὶ εἰς γυναῖκα." ³καὶ εἶπεν αὐτῷ ὁ πατὴρ αὐτοῦ καὶ ἡ μήτηρ αὐτοῦ "Μὴ οὐκ εἰσὶν θυγατέρες τῶν ἀδελφῶν σου καὶ ἐκ παντὸς τοῦ λαοῦ μου γυνή, ὅτι σὺ πορεύῃ λαβεῖν γυναῖκα

in Greek. R.V. 'at this time,' i.e. at the very time when her husband supposed that they were incurring God's anger. — ἠκούτισεν : 'made us hear.' This word occurs eight times in the LXX, e.g. Ps. 50¹⁰, Jer. 30². 

**24.** Σαμψών : Jos. Ant. V 8 § 4 Καὶ γενόμενον τὸ˙ παιδίον Σαμψῶνα καλοῦσιν, ἰσχυρὸν δὲ ἀποσημαίνει τὸ ὄνομα. See Introduction to the story. — ἡδρύνθη : Ex. 2¹⁰ n. 

**25.** συνεκπορεύεσθαι αὐτῷ : to go forth with him, i.e. to aid him when he went forth. R.V. 'to move him.' The words seem to point to some legends of Samson which have not come down to us. — παρεμβολῇ : this word is said to be Macedonian, which probably only means that it is of military origin. See Ex. 14⁹ n. 'The camp of Dan' is the proper name of a place. Hence the R.V. here retains the Hebrew Mahaneh-dan. In our text of the Hebrew the situation of this place is given as between Zorah and Eshtaol, i.e. in the heart of the Danite

territory ; but in Jdg. 18¹², where an account of the origin of the name is given, the place is said to be 'behind Kirjath-Jearim' in Judah. It would seem therefore that the καί, which the LXX has after Δάν, but to which there is nothing to correspond in the Hebrew, represents the true reading. There are reasons for supposing that the expedition of the Danites recorded in chapter 18 took place before the time of Samson ; so that there is no inconsistency in its name being mentioned here, though the story of how it came by its name is told later. — ἀνὰ μέσον . . . καὶ ἀνὰ μέσον : cp. Ex. 8²⁸. 

**1.** εἰς Θαμνάθα : subducting the two last letters, which are due to Hebrew inflexion, we are left with Θαμνά = Timnah. Jos. Ant. V 8 § 4 εἰς Θαμνὰ πόλιν. See Ex. 12³⁷ n. — ἀλλοφύλων : a LXX variety for Φυλιστιείμ. Cp. Amos 1⁸ : i Mac. 5⁶⁸. See Introduction to story. 

**2.** ἑόρακα : § 33. 

**3.** Μὴ οὐκ : cp. 15² μὴ οὐχί. —

Judges XIV 4

ἀπὸ τῶν ἀλλοφύλων τῶν ἀπεριτμήτων ; " καὶ εἶπεν Σαμψὼν πρὸς τὸν πατέρα αὐτοῦ " Ταύτην λάβε μοι, ὅτι αὕτη εὐθεῖα ἐν ὀφθαλμοῖς μου." ⁴καὶ ὁ πατὴρ αὐτοῦ καὶ ἡ μήτηρ αὐτοῦ οὐκ ἔγνωσαν ὅτι παρὰ Κυρίου ἐστίν, ὅτι ἐκδίκησιν αὐτὸς ζητεῖ ἐκ τῶν ἀλλοφύλων. καὶ ἐν τῷ καιρῷ ἐκείνῳ οἱ ἀλλόφυλοι κυριεύοντες ἐν Ἰσραήλ. ⁵καὶ κατέβη Σαμ- ψὼν καὶ ὁ πατὴρ αὐτοῦ καὶ ἡ μήτηρ αὐτοῦ εἰς Θαμνάθα · καὶ ἦλθεν ἕως τοῦ ἀμπελῶνος Θαμνάθα, καὶ ἰδοὺ σκύμνος λέοντος ὠρυόμενος εἰς συνάντησιν αὐτοῦ. ⁶καὶ ἥλατο ἐπ' αὐτὸν πνεῦμα Κυρίου, καὶ συνέτριψεν αὐτὸν ὡσεὶ συντρίψει ἔριφον · καὶ οὐδὲν ἦν ἐν ταῖς χερσὶν αὐτοῦ. καὶ οὐκ ἀπήγγειλεν τῷ πατρὶ αὐτοῦ καὶ τῇ μητρὶ αὐτοῦ ὃ ἐποίησεν. ⁷καὶ κατέβησαν καὶ ἐλάλησαν τῇ γυναικί, καὶ ηὐθύνθη ἐν ὀφθαλμοῖς Σαμψών. ⁸καὶ ὑπέστρεψεν μεθ' ἡμέρας λαβεῖν αὐτήν · καὶ ἐξέκλινεν ἰδεῖν τὸ πτῶμα τοῦ λέοντος, καὶ ἰδοὺ συναγωγὴ μελισσῶν ἐν τῷ στόματι τοῦ λέοντος καὶ μέλι.

εὐθεῖα : cp. v. 7 ηὐθύνθη. 'She is right in my eyes.' The Hebrew word is the same as in Nb. 23¹⁰, 'Let me die the death of the *righteous*.'

**4. ἐκδίκησιν**: *revenge*, namely, for the wrongs done to the Israelites. — **αὐτός**: *i.e.* Jehovah. Samson was only seeking a wife. Jos. *Ant.* V 8 § 6 τοῦ θεοῦ κατὰ τὸ Ἑβραίοις συμφέρον ἐπι- νοοῦντος τὸν γάμον. — **κυριεύοντες**: § 80.

**5. ὠρυόμενος** : ὠρύεσθαι ( = Lat. *rugire*) occurs 11 times in LXX, *e.g.* Ps. 21¹⁴ ὡς λέων ὁ ἁρπάζων καὶ ὠρυόμενος : Ezk. 22²⁵ ὡς λέοντες ὠρυόμενοι.

**6. ἥλατο ἐπ' αὐτὸν κτλ.** : *i.e.* he had a sudden access of supernatural strength. For the phrase *cp.* i K. 10⁶ καὶ ἐφαλεῖται ἐπὶ σὲ πνεῦμα Κυρίου. The low view of inspiration in the Samson legend shows a primitive tone of thought and is an argument for its

early date.—**συνέτριψεν**: Hebrew, 'tore asunder.' The Alexandrian Ms. has διέσπασεν.—ὡσεὶ συντρίψει : R.V. 'as he would have rent.' Milton — 'Who tore the lion as the lion tears the kid.'

**7. κατέβησαν καὶ ἐλάλησαν**: singu- lar in the Hebrew.

**8. συναγωγὴ μελισσῶν** : A has here συστροφή. Polybius IV 7 has τὴν συνα- γωγὴν τῶν ὄχλων. As συναγωγή is the translator's habitual rendering of the Hebrew word which occurs in this passage, we cannot infer that συναγωγή μελισσῶν is Alexandrian Greek for a 'swarm of bees.' Jos. *Ant.* V 8 § 6 has ἐπιτυγχάνει σμήνει μελιττῶν ἐν τῷ στήθει τοῦ λέοντος ἐκείνου νενοσσευκότων. — **στόματι** : Hebrew, 'body.' Possibly στόματι is a mistake in the Greek for σώματι, but it recurs in 9.

⁹καὶ ἐξεῖλεν αὐτὸ εἰς χεῖρας, καὶ ἐπορεύετο πορευόμενος καὶ ἐσθίων· καὶ ἐπορεύθη πρὸς τὸν πατέρα αὐτοῦ καὶ τὴν μητέρα αὐτοῦ, καὶ ἔδωκεν αὐτοῖς καὶ ἔφαγον, καὶ οὐκ ἀπήγγειλεν αὐτοῖς ὅτι ἀπὸ τοῦ στόματος τοῦ λέοντος ἐξεῖλεν τὸ μέλι. ¹⁰καὶ κατέβη ὁ πατὴρ αὐτοῦ πρὸς τὴν γυναῖκα· καὶ ἐποίησεν ἐκεῖ Σαμψὼν πότον ζ´ ἡμέρας, ὅτι οὕτως ποιοῦσιν οἱ νεανίσκοι. ¹¹καὶ ἐγένετο ὅτε εἶδον αὐτόν, καὶ ἔλαβον τριάκοντα κλητούς, καὶ ἦσαν μετ᾽ αὐτοῦ. ¹²καὶ εἶπεν αὐτοῖς Σαμψών " Πρόβλημα ὑμῖν προβάλλομαι· ἐὰν ἀπαγγέλλοντες ἀπαγγείλητε αὐτὸ ἐν ταῖς ἑπτὰ ἡμέραις τοῦ πότου καὶ εὕρητε, δώσω ὑμῖν τριάκοντα σινδόνας καὶ τριάκοντα στολὰς ἱματίων· ¹³καὶ ἐὰν μὴ δύνησθε ἀπαγγεῖλαί μοι, δώσετε ὑμεῖς ἐμοὶ τριάκοντα ὀθόνια καὶ τριάκοντα ἀλλασσομένας στολὰς ἱματίων." καὶ εἶπαν αὐτῷ " Προβαλοῦ τὸ πρόβλημα καὶ ἀκουσόμεθα αὐτό." ¹⁴καὶ εἶπει αὐτοῖς

9. **ἔδωκεν αὐτοῖς** : Josephus in telling the story makes Samson bring the honeycomb as a present to his bride. Perhaps this is an attempt to make the conduct of Samson more consistent with the law of the Nazirite.

10. **ἐποίησεν . . . πότον** : for the phrase ποιεῖν πότον cp. Gen. 19³, 40²⁰. **— ζ´ ἡμέρας** : *for seven days.* Not in the Hebrew. **— ὅτι οὕτως ποιοῦσιν οἱ νεανίσκοι** : A has ἐποίουν and the R.V. 'used to do,' implying that the custom was obsolete.

11. **ἐγένετο . . . καί** : § 41. **— ὅτε εἶδον αὐτόν** : A ἐν τῷ φοβεῖσθαι αὐτοὺς αὐτον. The two verbs meaning 'to see' and 'to fear' are easily confused in Hebrew. **— κλητούς** : *invited guests.* R.V. ' companions.'

12. **Πρόβλημα** : apart from this context the word πρόβλημα appears only four times in the LXX — Ps. 48⁴, 77² : Hbk. 2⁶ : Dan. Θ 8²³. **— σινδόνας** : Hdt. I 200 ; II 86 (σινδόνος βυσσίνης), 95 ; VII 181. Σινδών here means a garment of cambric or muslin. *Cp.* Mk. 14⁵¹ περιβεβλημένος σινδόνα : Mt. 27⁵⁹. The name points to the introduction of the material from India.

13. **ὀθόνια** : another rendering of the same word which has just been translated by σινδόνας. *Cp.* Mt. 27⁵⁹ with Jn. 19⁴⁰ for the equivalence of the two words. Josephus (*Ant.* V 8 § 6) has ὀθόνας where the LXX in v. 12 has σινδόνας. **— ἀλλασσομένας στολὰς ἱματίων** : the Hebrew is the same as for στολὰς ἱματίων in v. 12. *Cp.* Gen. 45²² ἀλλασσούσας στολάς.

Judges XIV 15

" Τί βρωτὸν ἐξῆλθεν ἐκ βιβρώσκοντος

καὶ ἀπὸ ἰσχυροῦ γλυκύ ; "

καὶ οὐκ ἠδύναντο ἀπαγγεῖλαι τὸ πρόβλημα ἐπὶ τρεῖς ἡμέρας. ¹⁵ καὶ ἐγένετο ἐν τῇ ἡμέρᾳ τῇ τετάρτῃ καὶ εἶπαν τῇ
γυναικὶ Σαμψών " Ἀπάτησον δὴ τὸν ἄνδρα σου καὶ ἀπαγ-
γειλάτω σοι τὸ πρόβλημα, μή ποτε κατακαύσωμέν σε καὶ
τὸν οἶκον τοῦ πατρός σου ἐν πυρί· ἢ ἐκβιάσαι ἡμᾶς κε-
κλήκατε ; " ¹⁶ καὶ ἔκλαυσεν ἡ γυνὴ Σαμψὼν πρὸς αὐτὸν καὶ
εἶπεν " Πλὴν μεμίσηκάς με καὶ οὐκ ἠγάπησάς με, ὅτι τὸ
πρόβλημα ὃ προεβάλου τοῖς υἱοῖς τοῦ λαοῦ μου οὐκ ἀπήγγειλάς μοι." καὶ εἶπεν αὐτῇ Σαμψών " Εἰ τῷ πατρί μου καὶ
τῇ μητρί μου οὐκ ἀπήγγελκα, σοὶ ἀπαγγείλω ; " ¹⁷ καὶ
ἔκλαυσεν πρὸς αὐτὸν ἐπὶ τὰς ἑπτὰ ἡμέρας ἃς ἦν αὐτοῖς
ὁ πότος· καὶ ἐγένετο ἐν τῇ ἡμέρᾳ τῇ ἑβδόμῃ καὶ ἀπήγγειλεν αὐτῇ, ὅτι παρενώχλησεν αὐτῷ· καὶ αὐτὴ ἀπήγγειλεν
τοῖς υἱοῖς τοῦ λαοῦ αὐτῆς. ¹⁸ καὶ εἶπαν αὐτῷ οἱ ἄνδρες
τῆς πόλεως ἐν τῇ ἡμέρᾳ τῇ ἑβδόμῃ πρὸ τοῦ ἀνατεῖλαι τὸν
ἥλιον

" Τί γλυκύτερον μέλιτος,

καὶ τί ἰσχυρότερον λέοντος ; "

14. Τί βρωτὸν κτλ. : in the original
this forms a verse-couplet (3 + 3).
A has ἐκ του ἐσθοντος ἐξηλθεν βρωσις,
και ἐξ ἰσχυρου ἐξηλθεν γλυκυ. Josephus
(Ant. V 8 § 6) gives the riddle thus
— φησὶν ὅτι τὸ πάμβορον γεγεννήκει
βορὰν ἡδεῖαν ἐξ αὐτοῦ, καὶ πανὺ ἀηδοῦς
ὄντος.

15. τετάρτῃ : Hebrew, ' seventh.'
The Greek reading improves the sense,
though even it is not consistent with
v. 17. — ἐκβιάσαι : to dispossess us by
force. A πτωχευσαι : R.V. ' to impov-
erish us ' : R.V. Margin ' take that we

have.' There is a confusion here between two words that are similar in
the original.

16. πλήν: only. Cp. Gen. 41⁴⁰.

17. ἐπὶ τὰς ἑπτὰ ἡμέρας : strictly
from the fourth to the seventh day.
For the reinforcement of the accusative of duration of time by ἐπί cp. v. 14
ἐπὶ τρεῖς ἡμέρας.

18. ἀνατεῖλαι : A δυναι. R.V. ' before the sun went down.' — Τί γλυκύτερον κτλ. : the answer, like the riddle,
is expressed in a verse-couplet (again
3 + 3), as is also Samson's retort. —

Judges XV 8

καὶ εἶπεν αὐτοῖς Σαμψών

"Εἰ μὴ ἠροτριάσατε ἐν τῇ δαμάλει μου,

    οὐκ ἂν ἔγνωτε τὸ πρόβλημά μου."

[19] καὶ ἥλατο ἐπ' αὐτὸν πνεῦμα Κυρίου, καὶ κατέβη εἰς
'Ασκάλωνα καὶ ἐπάταξεν ἐξ αὐτῶν τριάκοντα ἄνδρας καὶ
ἔλαβεν τὰ ἱμάτια αὐτῶν, καὶ ἔδωκεν τὰς στολὰς τοῖς ἀπαγ-
γείλασιν τὸ πρόβλημα· καὶ ὠργίσθη θυμῷ Σαμψών, καὶ
ἀνέβη εἰς τὸν οἶκον τοῦ πατρὸς αὐτοῦ. [20] καὶ ἐγένετο ἡ
γυνὴ Σαμψὼν ἑνὶ τῶν φίλων αὐτοῦ ὧν ἐφιλίασεν. [1] Καὶ
ἐγένετο μεθ' ἡμέρας ἐν ἡμέραις θερισμοῦ πυρῶν καὶ ἐπεσκέψατο Σαμψὼν τὴν γυναῖκα αὐτοῦ ἐν ἐρίφῳ αἰγῶν, καὶ
εἶπεν "Εἰσελεύσομαι πρὸς τὴν γυναῖκά μου εἰς τὸ ταμεῖον·"
καὶ οὐκ ἔδωκεν αὐτὸν ὁ πατὴρ αὐτῆς εἰσελθεῖν. [2] καὶ εἶπεν
ὁ πατὴρ αὐτῆς "Λέγων εἶπα ὅτι μισῶν ἐμίσησας αὐτήν,
καὶ ἔδωκα αὐτὴν ἑνὶ τῶν ἐκ τῶν φίλων σου· μὴ οὐχὶ ἡ
ἀδελφὴ αὐτῆς ἡ νεωτέρα αὐτῆς ἀγαθωτέρα ὑπὲρ αὐτήν;
ἔστω δή σοι ἀντὶ αὐτῆς." [3] καὶ εἶπεν αὐτοῖς Σαμψών
"'Ηθῴωμαι καὶ τὸ ἅπαξ ἀπὸ ἀλλοφύλων, ὅτι ποιῶ ἐγὼ μετ'

---

**Εἰ μὴ κτλ.** : Josephus (*Ant.* V 8 § 6) transforms the reply thus — Καὶ ὁ Σαμψὼν εἶπεν οὐδὲ γυναικὸς εἶναί τι δολερώτερον, ἥτις ὑμῖν ἐκφέρει τὸν ἡμέτερον λόγον. — **ἠροτριάσατε** : *cp.* iii K. 19¹⁹. Ἀροτριᾶν for ἀροῦν occurs in some dozen passages in the LXX. *Cp.* Gen. 45⁶ n.

**19. εἰς Ἀσκάλωνα** : *i.e.* to a Philistine city at some distance. The thirty companions themselves were protected by the laws of hospitality.

**20. ἐγένετο . . . ἑνί** : *became the wife of one.* Α καὶ συνῴκησεν ἡ γυνὴ Σαμψων τῷ νυμφαγωγῷ αὐτοῦ, ὃς ἦν ἑταῖρος αὐτοῦ. Jos. *Ant.* V 8 § 6 καὶ ἡ παῖς . . . συνῆν τῷ αὐτοῦ φίλῳ νυμφοστόλῳ γεγονότι. — **ὧν ἐφιλίασεν** : ὧν is

attracted into the case of φίλων preceding. In the Hebrew the pronoun is in the singular. Φιλιάζειν in the LXX is constructed with a dative ; ii Chr. 19², 20³⁷ : i Esd. 3²¹ : Sir. 37¹.

**1. μεθ' ἡμέρας** : *after some time.* — **ἐν ἐρίφῳ αἰγῶν** : § 91. — **ταμεῖον** : Gen. 43³⁰ n. § 10. — **οὐκ ἔδωκεν αὐτόν** : R.V. ' would not suffer him.'

**2. Λέγων εἶπα** : § 81. Notice that λέγων and εἶπα are treated as parts of one verb. — **ἀγαθωτέρα ὑπέρ** : §§ 12, 94.

**3. Ἠθῴωμαι κτλ.** : *I am made guiltless once for all as regards the Philistines in doing mischief to them.* — **μετ' αὐτῶν** : not *along with them*, but *in dealing with them.* § 93. The construction is due to the Hebrew.

αὐτῶν πονηρίαν." ⁴καὶ ἐπορεύθη Σαμψὼν καὶ συνέλαβεν τριακοσίας ἀλώπηκας, καὶ ἔλαβεν λαμπάδας, καὶ ἐπέστρεψεν κέρκον πρὸς κέρκον, καὶ ἔθηκεν λαμπάδα μίαν ἀνὰ μέσον τῶν δύο κέρκων καὶ ἔδησεν. ⁵καὶ ἐξέκαυσεν πῦρ ἐν ταῖς λαμπάσιν, καὶ ἐξαπέστειλεν ἐν τοῖς στάχυσιν τῶν ἀλλο-φύλων· καὶ ἐκάησαν ἀπὸ ἅλωνος καὶ ἕως σταχύων ὀρθῶν, καὶ ἕως ἀμπελῶνος καὶ ἐλαίας. ⁶καὶ εἶπαν οἱ ἀλλόφυλοι "Τίς ἐποίησεν ταῦτα;" καὶ εἶπαν "Σαμψὼν ὁ νυμφίος τοῦ Θαμνεί, ὅτι ἔλαβεν τὴν γυναῖκα αὐτοῦ καὶ ἔδωκεν αὐτὴν τῷ ἐκ τῶν φίλων αὐτοῦ·" καὶ ἀνέβησαν οἱ ἀλλόφυλοι καὶ ἐνέπρησαν αὐτὴν καὶ τὸν πατέρα αὐτῆς ἐν πυρί. ⁷καὶ εἶπεν αὐτοῖς Σαμψών "Ἐὰν ποιήσητε οὕτως ταύτην, ὅτι εἰ μὴν ἐκδικήσω ἐν ὑμῖν, καὶ ἔσχατον κοπάσω." ⁸καὶ ἐπάτα-ξεν αὐτοὺς κνήμην ἐπὶ μηρόν, πληγὴν μεγάλην· καὶ κατέβη

---

**4. ἀλώπηκας:** = ἀλώπεκας. § 11. The Hebrew word may also mean 'jackals.' — **κέρκον πρὸς κέρκον:** a lit-eral following of the Hebrew, which happens to coincide with our idiom. — **καὶ ἔδησεν:** in place of the Hebrew 'in between,' which A represents here by ἐν τῷ μεσῷ.

**5. ἐν τοῖς στάχυσιν:** § 91. — ἀπό . . . καὶ ἕως . . . καὶ ἕως: both . . . and . . . and. § 92. — ἅλωνος: put by the Greek translator for the word ren-dered in the R.V. 'shocks,' which represents an earlier stage of harvest work. On the form of the word see § 8. — ἕως ἀμπελῶνος καὶ ἐλαίας: R.V. 'and also the oliveyards.' The differ-ence seems due to the fact that the word for *yards* is often used specially of *vineyards*.

**6. νυμφίος:** *son-in-law.* For this meaning cp. ii Esd. 23²⁸ (= Neh. 13²⁸). A has here γαμβρος. — **τοῦ Θαμνεί:** *of the man of Timnah.* 13² n. — τῷ ἐκ τῶν φίλων αὐτοῦ: R.V. 'to his com-panion.' Perhaps we should here read τῳ — *to one of his friends.*

**7. ταύτην:** feminine for neuter. § 47. Οὕτως looks like a gloss on ταύ-την, one of the two being redundant. R.V. 'after this manner.' — ὅτι εἰ μὴν ἐκδικήσω ἐν ὑμῖν: (*know*) *that of a truth I will have my vengeance on you.* § 107. On εἰ μήν see § 103. — ἔσχατον κοπάσω: *at the last I will cease.* Cp. Ruth 1¹⁸ ἐκόπασε τοῦ λαλῆσαι πρὸς αὐτὴν ἔτι. Samson is careful through-out to avoid aggressive action; he merely retaliates for wrongs done to him.

**8. κνήμην ἐπὶ μηρόν:** *leg on thigh,* a literal rendering of the Hebrew, but what it meant originally is hard to say. For the adverbial accusative cp. Dt. 5⁴ πρόσωπον κατὰ πρόσωπον. — πλη-γὴν μεγάλην: accusative in apposition

Judges XV 14

καὶ ἐκάθισεν ἐν τρυμαλιᾷ τῆς πέτρας Ἠτάμ. ⁹Καὶ ἀνέβησαν οἱ ἀλλόφυλοι καὶ παρενέβαλον ἐν Ἰούδᾳ, καὶ ἐξερίφησαν ἐν Λεύει. ¹⁰ καὶ εἶπαν ἀνὴρ Ἰούδα "Εἰς τί ἀνέβητε ἐφ' ἡμᾶς;" καὶ εἶπον οἱ ἀλλόφυλοι "Δῆσαι τὸν Σαμψὼν ἀνέβημεν, καὶ ποιῆσαι αὐτῷ ὃν τρόπον ἐποίησεν ἡμῖν." ¹¹ καὶ κατέβησαν τρισχίλιοι ἄνδρες ἀπὸ Ἰούδα εἰς τρυμαλιὰν πέτρας Ἠτάμ, καὶ εἶπαν τῷ Σαμψών "Οὐκ οἶδας ὅτι κυριεύσουσιν οἱ ἀλλόφυλοι ἡμῶν, καὶ τί τοῦτο ἐποίησας ἡμῖν;" καὶ εἶπεν αὐτοῖς Σαμψών "Ὃν τρόπον ἐποίησάν μοι, οὕτως ἐποίησα αὐτοῖς." ¹² καὶ εἶπαν αὐτῷ "Δῆσαί σε κατέβημεν, τοῦ δοῦναί σε ἐν χειρὶ ἀλλοφύλων." καὶ εἶπεν αὐτοῖς Σαμψών "Ὀμόσατέ μοι μή ποτε συναντήσητε ἐν ἐμοὶ ὑμεῖς." ¹³ καὶ εἶπον αὐτῷ λέγοντες "Οὐχί, ὅτι ἀλλ' ἢ δεσμῷ δήσομέν σε καὶ παραδώσομέν σε ἐν χειρὶ αὐτῶν, καὶ θανάτῳ οὐ θανατώσομέν σε·" καὶ ἔδησαν αὐτὸν ἐν δυσὶ καλωδίοις καινοῖς, καὶ ἀνήνεγκαν αὐτὸν ἀπὸ τῆς πέτρας ἐκείνης. ¹⁴ καὶ ἦλθον ἕως Σιαγόνος· καὶ οἱ ἀλλόφυλοι ἠλάλαξαν

to the sentence.—τρυμαλιᾷ : this word is used six times in the LXX and once in the N.T., in Mk. 10²⁵, where it signifies the *eye* of a needle.—Ἠτάμ : Jos. *Ant.* V 8 § 8 Αἰτὰν κατῴκει · πέτρα δ' ἐστὶν ὀχυρὰ τῆς Ἰούδα φυλῆς.

9. ἐξερίφησαν : R.V. 'spread themselves.' § 83. Veitch quotes *Anth.* 12, 234 for the poetical form ἐρίφη. But in the LXX the double or single ρ is a question of Ms. spelling.—Λεύει : Hebrew *Lĕchi.*

10. εἶπαν ἀνήρ : a too faithful rendering of the Hebrew, which employs the singular of *man* after a plural verb to denote the inhabitants of a country collectively. § 48.

11. κυριεύσουσιν : R.V. 'are rulers over us.' *Cp.* 14⁴.

12. δοῦναι . . . ἐν χειρί : § 91. The meaning is not quite the same as that of δοῦναι διὰ χειρός in Gen. 39⁴, ²². — μή ποτε συναντήσητε : a literal rendering of the Hebrew—*lest ye fall upon me yourselves.* *Cp.* 14 and Ex. 9¹⁴ n.

13. ὅτι ἀλλ' ἤ : § 109. — καλωδίοις : in LXX only here, in 14, and in 16¹¹, ¹². The word is classical.

14. ἦλθον : Hebrew, 'he came.' — ἕως Σιαγόνος : *i.e.* to the place which is reputed to have been so called after the exploit which is about to be related. See Jos. *Ant.* V 8 § 8. The Hebrew is *Lĕchi* and the place is the same as that which is intended by Λεύει in 9. — ἠλάλαξαν . . . αὐτοῦ : R.V. 'shouted as they met him.' The Hebrew word for *meet* here is different from that trans-

238     SELECTIONS FROM THE SEPTUAGINT

καὶ ἔδραμον εἰς συνάντησιν αὐτοῦ· καὶ ἥλατο ἐπ᾽ αὐτὸν πνεῦμα Κυρίου, καὶ ἐγενήθη τὰ καλώδια τὰ ἐπὶ βραχίοσιν αὐτοῦ ὡσεὶ στιππύον ὃ ἐξεκαύθη ἐν πυρί, καὶ ἐτάκησαν δεσμοὶ αὐτοῦ ἀπὸ χειρῶν αὐτοῦ. ¹⁵καὶ εὗρεν σιαγόνα ὄνου ἐκρεριμμένην, καὶ ἐξέτεινεν τὴν χεῖρα αὐτοῦ καὶ ἔλαβεν αὐτήν, καὶ ἐπάταξεν ἐν αὐτῇ χιλίους ἄνδρας. ¹⁶καὶ εἶπεν Σαμψών

" Ἐν σιαγόνι ὄνου ἐξαλείφων ἐξήλειψα αὐτούς,
    ὅτι ἐν τῇ σιαγόνι τοῦ ὄνου ἐπάταξα χιλίους ἄνδρας."

¹⁷καὶ ἐγένετο ὡς ἐπαύσατο λαλῶν, καὶ ἔρριψεν τὴν σιαγόνα ἐκ τῆς χειρὸς αὐτοῦ, καὶ ἐκάλεσεν τὸν τόπον ἐκεῖνον Ἀναίρεσις σιαγόνος. ¹⁸καὶ ἐδίψησεν σφόδρα, καὶ ἔκλαυσεν πρὸς Κύριον καὶ εἶπεν "Σὺ εὐδόκησας ἐν χειρὶ δούλου σου τὴν σωτηρίαν τὴν μεγάλην ταύτην, καὶ νῦν ἀποθανοῦμαι τῷ δίψει καὶ ἐμπεσοῦμαι ἐν χειρὶ τῶν ἀπεριτμήτων." ¹⁹καὶ ἔρρηξεν ὁ θεὸς τὸν λάκκον τὸν ἐν τῇ Σιαγόνι καὶ ἐξῆλθεν

lated by συναντᾶν in 12. — στιππύον: = στυππεῖον. Cp. 16⁹: Sir. 21⁹: Is. 1³¹: Dan. 3⁴⁶. — δεσμοὶ: Gen. 42²⁷ n.

15. ἐκρεριμμένην: the Hebrew here has new. On the form of the word see § 20.

16. ἐξαλείφων ἐξήλειψα: the Hebrew does not here contain the idiom which corresponds to this formula, but runs thus — 'With the jaw-bone of an ass a heap, two heaps (have I slain).' The Hebrew word for heap however is the same as that for ass, so that there is a play on words, as though one were to say — " With the jawbone of an ass have I ass-ass-inated them."

17. Ἀναίρεσις σιαγόνος: the nominative is right because we have here what is known as the suppositio materialis of the words. The genitive is subjective, " the destruction made by

a jawbone." Hebrew Ramath-Lĕchi = Jawbone Hill. Names have been known to give rise to legends as well as legends to names.

18. ἔκλαυσεν: cp. 16²⁸. Hebrew, 'called.' A has ἐβόησεν. Cp. the double meaning of the English cried. — εὐδόκησας: aorist without augment. Hebrew, 'thou hast given.' A ἔδωκας. Translate — Thou hast vouchsafed through the hand of thy servant. The force of the construction εὐδοκεῖν ἐν here is different from that in Mt. 3¹⁷: ii Cor. 12¹⁰, where it means acquiesce in, be pleased with.

19. ἔρρηξεν τὸν λάκκον: R.V. 'clave the hollow place.' Proleptic. — αὐτῆς: the feminine may be justified on the ground that it agrees with πηγή understood, but it is probably due merely to the presence of a feminine suffix in

Judges XVI 8

ἐξ αὐτοῦ ὕδωρ· καὶ ἔπιεν, καὶ ἐπέστρεψεν τὸ πνεῦμα αὐτοῦ καὶ ἔζησεν. διὰ τοῦτο ἐκλήθη τὸ ὄνομα αὐτῆς Πηγὴ τοῦ ἐπικαλουμένου, ἥ ἐστιν ἐν Σιαγόνι, ἕως τῆς ἡμέρας ταύτης. ²⁰καὶ ἔκρινεν τὸν Ἰσραὴλ ἐν ἡμέραις ἀλλοφύλων εἴκοσι ἔτη. ¹Καὶ ἐπορεύθη Σαμψὼν εἰς Γάζαν, καὶ εἶδεν ἐκεῖ γυναῖκα πόρνην καὶ εἰσῆλθεν πρὸς αὐτήν. ²καὶ ἀνηγγέλη τοῖς Γαζαίοις λέγοντες "Ἥκει Σαμψὼν ὧδε." καὶ ἐκύκλωσαν καὶ ἐνήδρευσαν ἐπ' αὐτὸν ὅλην τὴν νύκτα ἐν τῇ πύλῃ τῆς πόλεως, καὶ ἐκώφευσαν ὅλην τὴν νύκτα λέγοντες "Ἕως διαφαύσῃ ὁ ὄρθρος, καὶ φονεύσωμεν αὐτόν." ³καὶ ἐκοιμήθη Σαμψὼν ἕως μεσονυκτίου· καὶ ἀνέστη ἐν ἡμίσει τῆς νυκτός, καὶ ἐπελάβετο τῶν θυρῶν τῆς πύλης τῆς πόλεως σὺν τοῖς δυσὶ σταθμοῖς, καὶ ἀνεβάστασεν αὐτὰς σὺν τῷ μοχλῷ καὶ ἔθηκεν ἐπ' ὤμων αὐτοῦ, καὶ ἀνέβη ἐπὶ τὴν κορυφὴν τοῦ ὄρους τοῦ ἐπὶ προσώπου Χεβρών,

the Hebrew. — Πηγὴ τοῦ ἐπικαλουμένου: Hebrew, 'Spring of the Caller.' As the partridge is known in Hebrew as *the caller*, it has been suggested that the name may have originally meant *Partridge Spring* and have had its meaning adapted to the story of Samson. **20. καὶ ἔκρινεν κτλ.**: this is the remark which generally closes the account of a ruler. *Cp.* 12⁷, ⁹, ¹¹, ¹⁴. In the story itself Samson is not represented as a ruler, but rather as an insubordinate subject of the Philistines. The next chapter, which ends with the same remark, may have come from another source, especially as the story of Delilah is a duplicate of the story of Samson's Philistine wife. **1. Γάζαν**: one of the five chief cities of the Philistines. **2. ἀνηγγέλη ... λέγοντες**: the word

corresponding to ἀνηγγέλη has slipt out from the Hebrew. On the construction see § 112, and on the verbal form § 24. — ἐκώφευσαν: literally *were dumb*. *Cp.* 18¹⁹. The word occurs eleven times in the LXX. —Ἕως διαφαύσῃ κτλ.: (*Wait*) *until the morning dawns, and let us kill him*. Present διαφαύσκειν (Polyb.), διαφώσκειν (Hdt.). **3. μεσονυκτίου**: *cp.* Ruth 3⁸: Is. 59¹⁰. In Ps. 118⁶² the word is used adverbially. — ἐν ἡμίσει τῆς νυκτός: § 62. The Hebrew is the same as that which has just been represented by μεσονυκτίου.—τῶν θυρῶν τῆς πύλης τῆς πόλεως: *the doors of the city-gate*. — ἀνεβάστασεν . . . μοχλῷ: *lifted them up bar and all*. R.V. 'plucked them up.' — ἀνέβη: Hebrew, 'carried them up.' — τοῦ ἐπὶ προσώπου Χεβρών: *which faces Hebron*. It is not necessary to suppose that Samson carried the gates all

240     SELECTIONS FROM THE SEPTUAGINT

καὶ ἔθηκεν αὐτὰ ἐκεῖ.    ⁴Καὶ ἐγένετο μετὰ τοῦτο καὶ
ἠγάπησεν γυναῖκα ἐν Ἀλσωρήχ, καὶ ὄνομα αὐτῇ Δαλειδά.
⁵καὶ ἀνέβησαν πρὸς αὐτὴν οἱ ἄρχοντες τῶν ἀλλοφύλων καὶ
εἶπαν αὐτῇ " Ἀπάτησον αὐτόν, καὶ ἴδε ἐν τίνι ἡ ἰσχὺς αὐτοῦ
ἡ μεγάλη καὶ ἐν τίνι δυνησόμεθα αὐτῷ καὶ δήσομεν αὐτὸν
τοῦ ταπεινῶσαι αὐτόν· καὶ ἡμεῖς δώσομέν σοι ἀνὴρ χιλίους
καὶ ἑκατὸν ἀργυρίου."    ⁶καὶ εἶπεν Δαλειδὰ πρὸς Σαμψών
" Ἀπάγγειλον δή μοι ἐν τίνι ἡ ἰσχύς σου ἡ μεγάλη, καὶ ἐν
τίνι δεθήσῃ τοῦ ταπεινωθῆναί σε."    ⁷καὶ εἶπεν πρὸς αὐτὴν
Σαμψών " Ἐὰν δήσωσίν με ἐν ἑπτὰ νευρέαις ὑγραῖς μὴ
διεφθαρμέναις, καὶ ἀσθενήσω καὶ ἔσομαι ὡς εἷς τῶν ἀνθρώπων."    ⁸καὶ ἀνήνεγκαν αὐτῇ οἱ ἄρχοντες τῶν ἀλλοφύλων
ἑπτὰ νευρὰς ὑγρὰς μὴ διεφθαρμένας, καὶ ἔδησεν αὐτὸν ἐν

the forty miles from Gaza to Hebron :
still this may be what was intended.
Cp. Jos. Ant. V 8 § 10 εἰς τὸ ὑπὲρ Χεβρῶ-
νος ὄρος φέρων κατατίθησι. — καὶ ἔθηκεν
αὐτὰ ἐκεῖ : not in the Hebrew.

4. ἠγάπησεν : = ἐφίλησεν.  Cp. 15.
— ἐν Ἀλσωρήχ : A has here ἐπι του
χειμαρρου Σωρηχ.  The Hebrew is
nahal Sorek.  It seems plain that the
first syllable has somehow disappeared,
leaving the reading before us.  Nahal
= wady or torrent-valley. — Δαλειδά :
Hebrew Dᵉlilah.  Jos. Ant. V 8 § 11
Δαλίλης τὸ ὄνομα.  Josephus assumes,
perhaps hastily, that the woman was
a Philistine.  We may notice that the
lords of the Philistines came up to her,
i.e. from the maritime plain to the hills.

5. οἱ ἄρχοντες : the Hebrew for
this is Sᵉranim, which is used only for
the five princes of the Philistines, and
is therefore presumably Philistian.  It
has been conjectured that this is the
same word as τύραννος.  It recurs in
vs. 8, 18, 23, 27, 30, in all which pas-

sages B renders it, as here, by ἄρχοντες,
but A by σατραπαι.  In i K. 5⁸, ¹¹,
6⁴, ¹², ¹⁶, ¹⁸, 7⁷, 29², ⁶, ⁷ B also has σα-
τράπαι.  This rendering reproduces the
foreign effect, but is otherwise inappropriate. — δυνησόμεθα αὐτῷ : a result
of literal translation rather than any
recognised Greek construction. — δώσομέν σοι ἀνήρ : ἀνήρ here = each.  A
Hebraism.  § 70.  As there were five
lords of the Philistines, the bribe
amounts to 5500 shekels of silver, or
275 times the price paid for Joseph.

7. νευρέαις : = νευραῖς.  Cp. v. 9.
Properly ' bowstrings.'  R.V. ' withes.'
Jos. Ant. V 8 § 11 φάμενος, εἰ κλήμασιν
ἑπτὰ κτλ. — ὑγραῖς : literally moist and
so supple — a recognised classical use.
Ὑγρός is a rare word in the LXX.  It
recurs in 8 and is used in its literal
sense in Job 8¹⁶ : Sir. 39¹³. — διεφθαρμέναις : R.V. ' dried.' — ὡς εἷς τῶν ἀνθρώπων : cp. 17 ὡς πάντες οἱ ἄνθρωποι :
Ps. 81⁷ ὡς εἷς τῶν ἀρχόντων.

8. μὴ διεφθαρμένας : in v. 7 the

Judges XVI 13

αὐταῖς· ⁹καὶ τὸ ἔνεδρον αὐτῇ ἐκάθητο ἐν τῷ ταμείῳ, καὶ εἶπεν αὐτῷ " 'Αλλόφυλοι ἐπὶ σέ, Σαμψών·" καὶ διέσπασεν τὰς νευρέας ὡς εἴ τις ἀποσπάσοι στρέμμα στιππύου ἐν τῷ ὀσφρανθῆναι αὐτὸ πυρός, καὶ οὐκ ἐγνώσθη ἡ ἰσχὺς αὐτοῦ. ¹⁰καὶ εἶπεν Δαλειδὰ πρὸς Σαμψών " 'Ιδοὺ ἐπλάνησάς με καὶ ἐλάλησας πρὸς μὲ ψευδῆ· νῦν οὖν ἀνάγγειλόν μοι ἐν τίνι δεθήσῃ." ¹¹καὶ εἶπεν πρὸς αὐτήν " 'Εὰν δεσμεύοντες δήσωσίν με ἐν καλωδίοις καινοῖς οἷς οὐκ ἐγένετο ἐν αὐτοῖς ἔργον, καὶ ἀσθενήσω καὶ ἔσομαι ὡς εἷς τῶν ἀνθρώπων." ¹²καὶ ἔλαβεν Δαλειδὰ καλώδια καινὰ καὶ ἔδησεν αὐτὸν ἐν αὐτοῖς, καὶ τὰ ἔνεδρα ἐξῆλθεν ἐκ τοῦ ταμείου, καὶ εἶπεν " 'Αλλόφυλοι ἐπὶ σέ, Σαμψών·" καὶ διέσπασεν αὐτὰ ἀπὸ βραχιόνων αὐτοῦ ὡς σπαρτίον. ¹³καὶ εἶπεν Δαλειδὰ πρὸς Σαμψών " 'Ιδοὺ ἐπλάνησάς με καὶ ἐλάλησας πρὸς ἐμὲ ψευδῆ· ἀπάγγειλον δή μοι ἐν τίνι δεθήσῃ." καὶ εἶπεν πρὸς αὐτήν " 'Εὰν ὑφάνῃς τὰς ἑπτὰ σειρὰς τῆς κεφαλῆς μου σὺν τῷ διάσματι καὶ ἐνκρούσῃς τῷ πασσάλῳ

hypothetical nature of the sentence justifies μὴ διεφθαρμέναις: but here we ought certainly to have οὐ. For another clear case of μή for οὐ take Sus. Θ⁴³.

9. ἔνεδρον: this form is common in the LXX, whereas ἐνέδρα occurs only in Josh. 8⁷,⁹ : Ps. 9²⁹. — στρέμμα: in the literal sense only here in the LXX. Used in a metaphorical sense in iv K. 15³⁰ συνέστρεψεν στρέμμα = made a conspiracy. — ἐν τῷ ὀσφρανθῆναι αὐτὸ πυρός: when it smelleth the fire. A literal translation of the Hebrew.

12. καὶ τὰ ἔνεδρα . . . ταμείου: if our Hebrew text is correct, this clause in the Greek is both wrongly translated and comes in the wrong place. A here agrees with the Hebrew.

13. 'Ιδού: Hebrew, 'hitherto.' The latter part of the Hebrew word for hitherto is the same, apart from the pointing, as that for behold. — ὑφάνῃς: § 23. — σειράς: locks, literally chains, in which sense the word is used in Prov. 5²² σειραῖς δὲ τῶν ἑαυτοῦ ἁμαρτιῶν ἕκαστος σφίγγεται. Samson's long hair was plaited into seven tails. — διάσματι: = στήμονι, warp. The word occurs in Biblical Greek only in this context. Delilah was to weave Samson's hair into the web she has been weaving on her loom, and fix the web, with his hair in it, to the wall by means of a peg.

13, 14. καὶ ἐνκρούσῃς . . . ὕφανεν ἐν τῷ διάσματι: this passage is absent from our Hebrew, but it is needed to

εἰς τὸν τοῖχον, καὶ ἔσομαι ὡς εἷς τῶν ἀνθρώπων ἀσθενής."
¹⁴καὶ ἐγένετο ἐν τῷ κοιμᾶσθαι αὐτὸν καὶ ἔλαβεν Δαλειδὰ
τὰς ἑπτὰ σειρὰς τῆς κεφαλῆς αὐτοῦ καὶ ὕφανεν ἐν τῷ
διάσματι καὶ ἔπηξεν τῷ πασσάλῳ εἰς τὸν τοῖχον, καὶ εἶπεν
"Ἀλλόφυλοι ἐπὶ σέ, Σαμψών·" καὶ ἐξυπνίσθη ἐκ τοῦ ὕπνου
αὐτοῦ, καὶ ἐξῆρεν τὸν πάσσαλον τοῦ ὑφάσματος ἐκ τοῦ
τοίχου. ¹⁵καὶ εἶπεν Δαλειδὰ πρὸς Σαμψών· "Πῶς λέγεις
'Ἠγάπηκά σε,' καὶ οὐκ ἔστιν ἡ καρδία σου μετ' ἐμοῦ; τοῦτο
τρίτον ἐπλάνησάς με, καὶ οὐκ ἀπήγγειλάς μοι ἐν τίνι ἡ
ἰσχύς σου ἡ μεγάλη." ¹⁶καὶ ἐγένετο ὅτε ἐξέθλιψεν αὐτὸν
ἐν λόγοις αὐτῆς πάσας τὰς ἡμέρας καὶ ἐστενοχώρησεν
αὐτόν, καὶ ὠλιγοψύχησεν ἕως τοῦ ἀποθανεῖν. ¹⁷καὶ ἀνήγγειλεν αὐτῇ τὴν πᾶσαν καρδίαν αὐτοῦ καὶ εἶπεν αὐτῇ "Σίδηρος οὐκ ἀνέβη ἐπὶ τὴν κεφαλήν μου, ὅτι ἅγιος θεοῦ ἐγώ
εἰμι ἀπὸ κοιλίας μητρός μου· ἐὰν οὖν ξυρήσωμαι, ἀπο-
στήσεται ἀπ' ἐμοῦ ἡ ἰσχύς μου, καὶ ἀσθενήσω καὶ ἔσομαι ὡς πάντες οἱ ἄνθρωποι." ¹⁸καὶ εἶδεν Δαλειδὰ ὅτι
ἀπήγγειλεν αὐτῇ πᾶσαν τὴν καρδίαν αὐτοῦ, καὶ ἀπέστειλεν
καὶ ἐκάλεσεν τοὺς ἄρχοντας τῶν ἀλλοφύλων λέγουσα "Ἀνάβητε ἔτι τὸ ἅπαξ τοῦτο, ὅτι ἀπήγγειλέν μοι τὴν πᾶσαν
καρδίαν αὐτοῦ·" καὶ ἀνέβησαν πρὸς αὐτὴν οἱ ἄρχοντες τῶν
ἀλλοφύλων, καὶ ἀνήνεγκαν τὸ ἀργύριον ἐν χερσὶν αὐτῶν.

tell the story fully. It seems to have
dropped out owing to the occurrence
of the word corresponding to τῷ διάσματι both at the beginning and end
of it.

**14.** εἰς τὸν τοῖχον: not in the Hebrew. — ἐξῆρεν . . . τοίχου: *carried
away the peg of the web from the wall*.
R.V. 'plucked away the pin of the
beam, and the web.'

**16.** ἐστενοχώρησεν αὐτόν: Josh.
17¹⁵: Is. 28²⁰, 49¹⁹: iv Mac. 11¹¹ τὸ

πνεῦμα στενοχωρούμενος: ii Cor. 4⁸, 6¹².
— ὠλιγοψύχησεν: the subject here
changes to Samson. Ὀλιγοψυχεῖν occurs ten or eleven times in the LXX,
but corresponds to the same Hebrew as
here only in Nb. 21⁴: Jdg. 10¹⁶ (A).
It occurs in the Flinders Petrie Papyri
(Swete *Introd.* p. 292).

**17.** τὴν πᾶσαν καρδίαν: § 46. —
ἅγιος θεοῦ: a translation of Hebrew
*nazir*, which A here represents by
ναζειραιος. 13⁵ n.

Judges XVI 25

¹⁹καὶ ἐκοίμισεν Δαλειδὰ τὸν Σαμψὼν ἐπὶ τὰ γόνατα αὐτῆς, καὶ ἐκάλεσεν ἄνδρα καὶ ἐξύρησεν τὰς ἑπτὰ σειρὰς τῆς κεφαλῆς αὐτοῦ· καὶ ἤρξατο ταπεινῶσαι αὐτόν, καὶ ἀπέστη ἡ ἰσχὺς αὐτοῦ ἀπ' αὐτοῦ. ²⁰καὶ εἶπεν Δαλειδά " Ἀλλόφυλοι ἐπὶ σέ, Σαμψών." καὶ ἐξυπνίσθη ἐκ τοῦ ὕπνου αὐτοῦ καὶ εἶπεν " Ἐξελεύσομαι ὡς ἅπαξ καὶ ἅπαξ, καὶ ἐκτιναχθήσομαι·" καὶ αὐτὸς οὐκ ἔγνω ὅτι ἀπέστη ὁ κύριος ἀπάνωθεν αὐτοῦ. ²¹καὶ ἐκράτησαν αὐτὸν οἱ ἀλλόφυλοι καὶ ἐξέκοψαν τοὺς ὀφθαλμοὺς αὐτοῦ, καὶ κατήνεγκαν αὐτὸν εἰς Γάζαν καὶ ἐπέδησαν αὐτὸν ἐν πέδαις χαλκείαις· καὶ ἦν ἀλήθων ἐν οἴκῳ τοῦ δεσμωτηρίου. ²²καὶ ἤρξατο θρὶξ τῆς κεφαλῆς αὐτοῦ βλαστάνειν, καθὼς ἐξυρήσατο.

²³Καὶ οἱ ἄρχοντες τῶν ἀλλοφύλων συνήχθησαν θῦσαι θυσίασμα μέγα τῷ Δαγὼν θεῷ αὐτῶν καὶ εὐφρανθῆναι, καὶ εἶπαν " Ἔδωκεν ὁ θεὸς ἐν χειρὶ ἡμῶν τὸν Σαμψὼν τὸν ἐχθρὸν ἡμῶν." ²⁴καὶ εἶδαν αὐτὸν ὁ λαός, καὶ ὕμνησαν τὸν θεὸν αὐτῶν ὅτι " Παρέδωκεν ὁ θεὸς ἡμῶν τὸν ἐχθρὸν ἡμῶν ἐν χειρὶ ἡμῶν, τὸν ἐρημοῦντα τὴν γῆν ἡμῶν καὶ ὃς ἐπλήθυνεν τοὺς τραυματίας ἡμῶν." ²⁵καὶ ὅτε ἠγαθύνθη ἡ καρδία αὐτῶν, καὶ εἶπαν " Καλέσατε τὸν Σαμψὼν ἐξ οἴκου φυλακῆς, καὶ παιξάτω ἐνώπιον ἡμῶν." καὶ ἐκάλεσαν τὸν Σαμψὼν ἀπὸ οἴκου δεσμωτηρίου, καὶ ἔπαιζεν ἐνώπιον αὐτῶν· καὶ ἐρά-

---

**20.** ὡς ἅπαξ καὶ ἅπαξ : no Greek phrase, but due to literal translation. A has καθως αει. *Cp.* 20³⁰, ³¹ : i K. 3¹⁰, 20²⁵ : i Mac. 3³⁰ ὡς ἅπαξ καὶ δίς. — ἐκτιναχθήσομαι : passive in middle sense. § 83.

**21.** χαλκείαις : § 35. — ἦν ἀλήθων : to turn the hand-mill was the work of the lowest slaves.

**22.** καθὼς ἐξυρήσατο : R.V. 'after he was shaven.' § 83.

**23.** Δαγών : Dagon, who used to be considered a fish-god, is regarded by modern scholars as a corn-god. On him *cp.* i K. 5¹⁻⁵ : i Mac. 10⁸³, ⁸⁴. — ὁ θεός : *i.e.* Dagon. Hebrew, 'our god.'

**24.** εἶδαν : § 18.

**25.** ὅτε ἠγαθύνθη κτλ. : R.V. 'when their hearts were merry.' Ἀγαθύνειν is common in the LXX. For the meaning *to cheer*, *cp.* 18²⁰, 19⁶, ⁹, ²² : Ruth 3⁷ : ii K. 13²⁸ : Eccl. 11⁹. — παιξάτω : the more classical form of the aorist is ἔπαισα. — καὶ ἐράπιζον αὐτόν : not

Judges XVI 26

πιζον αὐτόν, καὶ ἔστησαν αὐτὸν ἀνὰ μέσον τῶν κιόνων. ²⁶καὶ εἶπεν Σαμψὼν πρὸς τὸν νεανίαν τὸν κρατοῦντα τὴν χεῖρα αὐτοῦ "᾿Αφες με καὶ ψηλαφήσω τοὺς κίονας ἐφ᾽ οἷς ὁ οἶκος στήκει ἐπ᾽ αὐτούς, καὶ ἐπιστηριχθήσομαι ἐπ᾽ αὐτούς." ²⁷καὶ ὁ οἶκος πλήρης τῶν ἀνδρῶν καὶ τῶν γυναικῶν, καὶ ἐκεῖ πάντες οἱ ἄρχοντες τῶν ἀλλοφύλων, καὶ ἐπὶ τὸ δῶμα ὡς ἑπτακόσιοι ἄνδρες καὶ γυναῖκες οἱ θεωροῦντες ἐν παιγνίαις Σαμψών. ²⁸καὶ ἔκλαυσεν Σαμψὼν πρὸς Κύριον καὶ εἶπεν "᾿Αδωναῖε Κύριε, μνήσθητι δή μου νῦν καὶ ἐνίσχυσόν με ἔτι τὸ ἅπαξ τοῦτο, θεέ· καὶ ἀνταποδώσω ἀνταπόδοσιν μίαν περὶ τῶν δύο ὀφθαλμῶν μου τοῖς ἀλλοφύλοις." ²⁹καὶ περιέλαβεν Σαμψὼν τοὺς δύο κίονας τοῦ οἴκου ἐφ᾽ οὓς ὁ οἶκος ἱστήκει, καὶ ἐπεστηρίχθη ἐπ᾽ αὐτούς, καὶ ἐκράτησεν ἕνα τῇ δεξιᾷ αὐτοῦ καὶ ἕνα τῇ ἀριστερᾷ αὐτοῦ. ³⁰καὶ εἶπεν Σαμψών "᾿Αποθανέτω ψυχή μου μετὰ ἀλλοφύλων·" καὶ ἐβάσταξεν ἐν ἰσχύι, καὶ ἔπεσεν ὁ οἶκος ἐπὶ τοὺς ἄρχοντας καὶ ἐπὶ πάντα τὸν λαὸν τὸν ἐν αὐτῷ· καὶ ἦσαν οἱ τεθνηκότες οὓς ἐθανάτωσεν Σαμψὼν ἐν τῷ θανάτῳ αὐτοῦ πλείους ἢ οὓς

in the Hebrew. On the spelling *cp.* 15⁹ n.

**26.** στήκει: § 27. — ἐπιστηριχθήσομαι: § 83.

**27.** ἐπὶ τὸ δῶμα: § 95. — θεωροῦντες ἐν: *looking on at.* § 98.

**28.** ἔκλαυσεν: 15¹⁸ n. — ᾿Αδωναῖε Κύριε: A has here Κύριε Κύριε; see 13⁸ n. Perhaps the second translator avoided the term ᾿Αδωναῖε as having misleading associations for Greek ears. The Syrian god Thammuz had ever since the fifth century B.C. been worshipped by the Greeks under the name ᾿Αδωνις, derived from the title Adon (Lord) by which his Semitic worshippers addressed him. Ausonius (*Epi-*

*gram* 49) mentions Adoneus as a nether-world title of Bacchus. The name got confused with the Greek ᾿Αϊδωνεύς. — θεέ: § 4. — τῶν δύο ὀφθαλμῶν: § 14.

**29.** τοὺς δύο κίονας: R.V. 'the two middle pillars.' A supplies the missing word — τοὺς δύο στύλους τοὺς μέσους. Josephus (*Ant.* V 8 § 12) says parenthetically — οἶκος δ᾽ ἦν δύο κιόνων στεγόντων αὐτοῦ τὸν ὄροφον. — ἱστήκει: § 37. — καὶ ἐκράτησεν: not in the Hebrew. — ἕνα . . . καὶ ἕνα: no one who was writing Greek as Greek could here avoid τὸν μέν . . . τὸν δέ. § 39.

**30.** ἐβάσταξεν: A εκλεινεν. R.V. 'bowed himself.'

ἐθανάτωσεν ἐν τῇ ζωῇ αὐτοῦ.    ³¹ καὶ κατέβησαν οἱ ἀδελφοὶ αὐτοῦ καὶ ὁ οἶκος τοῦ πατρὸς αὐτοῦ, καὶ ἔλαβον αὐτὸν
καὶ ἀνέβησαν· καὶ ἔθαψαν αὐτὸν ἀνὰ μέσον Σαραὰ καὶ ἀνὰ
μέσον Ἐσθαλαὸλ ἐν τῷ τάφῳ Μανῶε τοῦ πατρὸς αὐτοῦ.
καὶ αὐτὸς ἔκρινεν τὸν Ἰσραὴλ εἴκοσι ἔτη.

# INTRODUCTION TO THE STORY OF DAVID
# AND GOLIATH

WHILE the death of Samson has in it all the elements of a Greek tragedy, the combat between David and Goliath breathes the very spirit of Epic poetry. The resemblance of Goliath in all respects to a Homeric hero is striking. We might call him an Ajax depicted from the Trojan point of view.

The slaying of giants is the delight of the infancy both of the individual and of the race. In the nursery we are told of Jack the Giant-killer, while in the *Odyssey* we read the adventures of Ulysses among the Læstrygons and the Cyclopes, which have their manifest echo in the story of Sindbad the Sailor in the *Arabian Nights*. Older than all these is an Egyptian story of a fight with a giant, which dates from the XIIth Dynasty, and is therefore some 1300 years earlier than the time of David.[1]

But there are giants and giants. It was a Peripatetic doctrine that a difference in degree may constitute a difference in kind. Thus a ship, according to Aristotle, will not be really a ship, if it is either a span long or two stades. In the same way, though man is defined merely as a rational animal, yet inches have a good deal to do with our feeling of a common humanity. The giant that is to come home to us as a fellow-creature, whom we can either hate or love, must not go beyond all bounds. He must not be like the giant that met the children of Israel in the wilderness, of whom the Talmud has to tell — how Moses, being himself a strapping fellow thirty feet high, took a sword thirty feet long, and, making a leap of thirty feet into the air, just managed to nick that giant in the knee and bring him sprawling helpless to the ground. A giant like that we may dread, as we might some elemental force, but we cannot properly hate him, as we are expected to do in the case of a giant —

καὶ γὰρ θαῦμ᾽ ἐτέτυκτο πελώριον, οὐδὲ ἐῴκει
ἀνδρί γε σιτοφάγῳ, ἀλλὰ ῥίῳ ὑλήεντι (Hom. *Od*. IX 190, 191).

[1] Budge *History of Egypt* III, p. 8.

247

Now Goliath, especially as depicted in the Septuagint, is a giant within quite reasonable limits. In his braggart defiance of 'the armies of the living God' he reminds us of the huge Gaul who stood insulting the might of Rome, until Torquatus slipped under his targe and stabbed him with his short blade (Liv. VII 9, 10), or of that other champion of the same race, whom Valerius Corvinus despatched with the aid of the heaven-sent raven (Liv. VII 26).

The Hexateuch is full of references to races of extraordinary stature that inhabited Canaan before and at the time of the Israelitish invasion. It was the report which the spies brought of these giant forms that chiefly daunted the people and made them plot a return to Egypt (Nb. 14⁴) — 'And there we saw the giants, the sons of Anak, which come of the giants; and we were in our own sight as grasshoppers, and so we were in their sight' (Nb. 13³³). But their bulk does not seem to have helped these people to survive in the struggle for existence. The Emim, 'a people great and many and tall as the Anakim' (Dt. 2¹⁰) were driven out by the Moabites; and the Zamzummim, who are similarly described, were in like manner dispossessed by the Ammonites (Dt. 2²⁰,²¹: cp. Gen. 14⁵); Og, the king of Bashan, notwithstanding the dimensions of his bedstead, fell an easy prey to the Israelites under Moses; and the children of Anak themselves, who dwelt about Hebron (Nb. 12²²: Josh. 15¹³, 21¹¹), were utterly destroyed by Joshua out of the land of the children of Israel.[1] 'Only in Gaza, in Gath, and in Ashdod' we are told in this context 'did some remain' (Josh. 11²²). Of this stock evidently sprung Goliath and the others who 'were born to the giant in Gath' (ii S. 21²²).

In the account of the introduction of Saul to David it is more than usually manifest that two different narratives are mixed up. In the one David is known and loved of Saul before his combat with Goliath (i S. 16²¹), in the other Saul asks Abner who he is, when he sees him going forth against the Philistine (17⁵⁵); in the one David on his first introduction to Saul is already 'a mighty man of valour and a man of war and prudent in speech' (16¹⁸), in the other he is a mere stripling (17⁵⁶); in the one he is Saul's armour-bearer (16²¹) and presumably on the field in that capacity, in the other he comes up unexpectedly from the country (17²⁰). The additional touch of

---

[1] Josh. 11²¹. The feat is ascribed to Caleb in 15¹⁴.

romance imparted to the story by the extreme youth of the hero has made the latter version predominate, not only in our minds, but in that of the Biblical editor, who seems to have adapted his language to it. Josephus attempts to harmonise the two by saying that, when the war broke out with the Philistines, Saul sent David back to his father Jesse, being content with the three sons of the latter whom he had in his army (*Ant.* VI 9 § 3). This however does not help us over the difficulty of Saul being represented as not knowing David at the time of the combat, which has had to be accounted for as a consequence of mental derangement.

To us at present the matter is considerably simplified by the fact that the Seventy themselves (or, more properly, the translator of this book) seem to have made a bold essay at the work of higher criticism. The Vatican manuscript of the Septuagint contains the account of David being sent for to play on the harp to Saul, but it does not contain 16$^{12-31}$, in which David is introduced as a new character making his first entry on the scene, nor does it contain 17$^{54}$–18$^{5}$, which cohere with 16$^{12-31}$, but not with the story of the harp playing. Of course the reason why the Seventy give only one account may be that they had only one account to give : but there seems to be some reason to believe that they deliberately suppressed one version of the story with a view to consistency. But this question had better be left to the Higher Critics. This much however is evident to the least instructed intelligence, namely that the omission of 16$^{12-31}$ improves the sequence of the story as much as it impairs its picturesqueness. David was left in attendance on Saul in 16$^{23}$ and can be made to speak to him in 17$^{32}$ without further introduction. His words of encouragement follow suitably on the statement in 16$^{11}$ that Saul and all Israel were dismayed.

The omissions of the Vatican manuscript are supplied in the Alexandrian, but the translation presents the appearance of being by another hand from that of the rest of the book. Thus in v. 19 ἐν τῇ κοιλάδι τῆς δρυός is used for ἐν τῇ κοιλάδι 'Ηλά of 21$^{9}$; in v. 23 again the strange expression ἀνὴρ ὁ ἀμεσσαῖος takes the place of ἀνὴρ δυνατός in 17$^{4}$ (*cp.* ὁ δυνατὸς αὐτῶν 17$^{51}$); while Φιλιστιαῖος is employed, instead of ἀλλόφυλος as in 21$^{9}$.

The story of David and Goliath represents the battle of Ephes-Dammim as a mere rout of the Philistines after their champion had been slain. Yet there are passages in the Bible which have been thought to set the matter in a different light. The Pas-Dammim of i Chr. 11[13] can hardly be any other place than the Ephes-Dammim of i S. 17[1], with which the margin of the Revised Version identifies it. Now at Pas-Dammim 'the Philistines were gathered together to battle, where was a plot of ground full of barley; and the people fled from before the Philistines' (i Chr. 11[3]: cp. ii S. 23[11, 12]). But David and his three mighty men 'stood in the midst of the plot and defended it and slew the Philistines; and the Lord saved them by a great victory.' But, though the place of this incident is the same with that of the slaying of Goliath, the time seems altogether different, the battle of the barley-plot belonging to the period when David was 'in the hold.'[1] The account of David's mighty men given in ii S. 28[8-39] and in i Chr. 11[10-47] looks like a fragment of genuine history, perhaps drawn from the records of Jehosaphat the son of Ahilud, who was official chronicler to David and Solomon (ii S. 8[16], 20[24]: i K. 4[3]). A union of this with the story of David and Goliath seems illegitimate. The latter belongs to the realm of romance: its date is of all time and no time. David, the ruddy and comely youth, will remain for ever the slayer of Goliath, just as William Tell, in spite of the Reverend Baring-Gould, will always have shot the apple off his son's head. It is best to leave the matter so. Indeed, if we began to treat the story as sober history, we might be driven to the conclusion that David never slew Goliath at all. For in ii S. 12[19] we have the statement that 'Goliath the Gittite, the staff of whose spear was like a weaver's beam,' was slain by one El-hanan of Bethlehem. Professor Kirkpatrick in his commentary on this passage says — 'There is no difficulty in supposing that another giant, beside the one slain by David, bore the name of Goliath.' St. Jerome however found so much difficulty about this that he boldly identified El-hanan with David. The passage in which this disconcerting statement is contained (ii S. 21[15-22]) has no connexion with its context and looks like another fragment of the official chronicle, from which we have supposed the list of David's mighty men to have been drawn. There are four giants mentioned, of whom Goliath is one, and each of these has his own slayer. Then the fragment concludes with these words — ' These four were born to the giant in Gath; and

---

[1] i.e. the cave of Adullam. i S. 22[1, 4] : ii S. 23[13, 14].

they fell by the hand of David, and by the hand of his servants.' David then, as a matter of fact, would seem to have slain Goliath not directly and in his own person, but on the principle of — Qui facit per alium facit per se, just as Cæsar says that *he* cut to pieces the Tigurini on the banks of the Saône, whereas Plutarch and Appian let us know that it was his lieutenant Labienus who did so, or rather, if we are going to be exact, the soldiers under him.

# V. THE STORY OF DAVID AND GOLIATH

i Kings XVII

¹Καὶ συνάγουσιν ἀλλόφυλοι τὰς παρεμβολὰς αὐτῶν εἰς πόλεμον, καὶ συνάγονται εἰς Σοκχὼθ τῆς Ἰδουμαίας, καὶ παρεμβάλλουσιν ἀνὰ μέσον Σοκχὼθ καὶ ἀνὰ μέσον Ἀζηκὰ Ἐφερμέμ. ²καὶ Σαοὺλ καὶ οἱ ἄνδρες Ἰσραὴλ συνάγονται καὶ παρεμβάλλουσιν ἐν τῇ κοιλάδι· αὐτοὶ παρατάσσονται εἰς πόλεμον ἐξ ἐναντίας ἀλλοφύλων. ⁸καὶ ἀλλόφυλοι ἵστανται ἐπὶ τοῦ ὄρους ἐνταῦθα, καὶ Ἰσραὴλ ἵσταται ἐπὶ τοῦ ὄρους ἐνταῦθα, κύκλῳ ἀνὰ μέσον αὐτῶν. ⁴καὶ ἐξῆλθεν ἀνὴρ δυνατὸς ἐκ τῆς παρατάξεως τῶν ἀλλοφύλων, Γολιὰθ ὄνομα αὐτῷ, ἐκ Γέθ· ὕψος αὐτοῦ τεσσάρων πήχεων καὶ

1. ἀλλόφυλοι : = Φυλιστίειμ ; cp. Jdg. 14¹. Josephus calls them Παλαιστῖνοι. — παρεμβολάς: here *armies*. Jdg. 13²⁵ n. — Ἰδουμαίας: a mistake in the Greek text for Ἰουδαίας. R.V. 'which belongeth to Judah.' — Ἐφερμέμ: a corruption for 'in Ephes-Dammim.' A has εναφεσδομμειν. The meaning of the name is 'boundary of blood.'

2. αὐτοί: not a translation of a corresponding Hebrew pronoun, but due to a misreading of the word rendered in our version 'of Elah.' The Vale of the Terebinth was a pass running up from the Philistine plain into the highlands of Judah.

3. ἐνταῦθα . . . ἐνταῦθα: a classical writer would have balanced these clauses by μέν and δέ. Cp. Josh. 8²² οὗτοι ἐντεῦθεν καὶ οὗτοι ἐντεῦθεν. Jdg. 16²⁹ n. — κύκλῳ ἀνὰ μέσον αὐτῶν: He-

brew 'and the valley between them.' Α και ο αυλων ανα μεσον αυτων. We may surmise that κύκλῳ is a corruption for καὶ ὁ αὐλών.

4. ἀνὴρ δυνατός: R.V. 'a champion.' The word in the original seems to mean 'man of the space between the two lines' (μεταίχμιον). — παρατάξεως: παράταξις = Latin *acies* occurs in Attic authors, but came into more frequent use in Hellenistic Greek. — τεσσάρων πήχεων καὶ σπιθαμῆς: a cubit is roughly a foot and a half, and a span is half a cubit. According to this statement then Goliath would have been six feet nine inches high. Josephus (*Ant.* VI 9 § 1) agrees with the LXX — ἦν γὰρ πηχῶν τεσσάρων καὶ σπιθαμῆς. But the Hebrew text raises his stature to six cubits and a span, which would make him nine feet nine inches.

252

σπιθαμῆς. ⁵καὶ περικεφαλαία ἐπὶ τῆς κεφαλῆς αὐτοῦ,
καὶ θώρακα ἀλυσιδωτὸν αὐτὸς ἐνδεδυκώς, καὶ ὁ σταθμὸς
τοῦ θώρακος αὐτοῦ πέντε χιλιάδες σίκλων χαλκοῦ καὶ σιδή-
ρου· ⁶καὶ κνημῖδες χαλκαὶ ἐπάνω τῶν σκελῶν αὐτοῦ, καὶ
ἀσπὶς χαλκῆ ἀνὰ μέσον τῶν ὤμων αὐτοῦ· ⁷καὶ ὁ κοντὸς
τοῦ δόρατος αὐτοῦ ὡσεὶ μέσακλον ὑφαινόντων, καὶ ἡ λόγχη
αὐτοῦ ἑξακοσίων σίκλων σιδήρου· καὶ ὁ αἴρων τὰ ὅπλα
αὐτοῦ προεπορεύετο αὐτοῦ. ⁸καὶ ἀνέστη καὶ ἀνεβόησεν

---

**5. περικεφαλαία:** a Hellenistic word
used by Polybius and also by St. Paul
(i Th. 5⁸ : Eph. 6¹⁷). It occurs eleven
times in the LXX. The words ' of
brass ' do not appear in the Greek,
perhaps because they are implied by
the use of περικεφαλαία, just as *cassis*
in Latin implies that the helmet is of
metal ; but in verse 38 we have χαλκῆν added. — ἀλυσιδωτόν: Ex. 28²², ²⁴ :
i Mac. 6³⁵ τεθωρακισμένους ἐν ἀλυσιδω-
τοῖς. — αὐτός: not to be explained by
any niceties of Greek scholarship, but
due to the presence of the pronoun
'he' at this point in the Hebrew. —
πέντε χιλιάδες σίκλων : about 157
pounds avoirdupois. — σίκλων: *shekel*
is usually thus represented in the
LXX, though it is not uncommon to
find δίδραχμον used for it, as in Gen.
23¹⁵ : Dt. 22²⁹ : ii Esdr. 15¹⁵. Σίγλος is
used by Xenophon (*Anab.* I 5 § 6) for
a Persian coin of the value of 7½ Attic
obols. — καὶ σιδήρου: not in the Hebrew, according to which the champion's defensive armour is of bronze
and his spear-head only of iron. This
closely agrees with the use of the metals
as represented in the Iliad, where
bronze is the material in common use
for armour and weapons, while iron,
though not unknown, is (at least in the

earlier strata of the Homeric poetry)
rare and exceptional.

**6. ἀσπὶς χαλκῆ:** this is intrinsically more probable than the Hebrew
reading, which makes Goliath have a
'javelin' of brass between his shoul-
ders, but it leaves his armour-bearer
nothing to carry. What seems needed
here, to complete the account of his
equipment, is a mention of the sword
which is referred to in verses 45 and
51. This, if he were armed in Homeric
fashion, would be suspended by a strap
passing over one shoulder. *Cp. Il.* II
45 —

ἀμφὶ δ' ἄρ' ὤμοισιν βάλετο ξίφος ἀργυ-
ρόηλον.

**7. κοντός:** this word in classical
Greek means a punt-pole (called a
*quant* on the Norfolk Broads at this
day), as in Eur. *Alc.* 254. In later
Greek it means a spear-shaft. *Cp.* Ezk.
39⁹. Vegetius speaks of *conti mis-
sibiles* (p. 140 l. 4, ed. Lang) and
uses *contati* for horsemen armed with
lances. — μέσακλον: only here, at least
in this form. See L. & S. The Hebrew
is the same which is rendered elsewhere
ὡς ἀντίον ὑφαινόντων ii K. 21¹⁹ : i Chr.
11²³, 20⁵. — ἑξακοσίων σίκλων: about
nineteen pounds. — ὁ αἴρων: Gen.
45²³ n.

254    SELECTIONS FROM THE SEPTUAGINT

εἰς τὴν παράταξιν Ἰσραὴλ καὶ εἶπεν αὐτοῖς "Τί ἐκπορεύεσθε
παρατάξασθαι πολέμῳ ἐξ ἐναντίας ἡμῶν; οὐκ ἐγώ εἰμι
ἀλλόφυλος, καὶ ὑμεῖς Ἑβραῖοι καὶ Σαούλ; ἐκλέξασθε
ἑαυτοῖς ἄνδρα καὶ καταβήτω πρὸς μέ· ⁹ καὶ ἐὰν δυνηθῇ
πρὸς ἐμὲ πολεμῆσαι καὶ ἐὰν πατάξῃ με, καὶ ἐσόμεθα ὑμῖν
εἰς δούλους· ἐὰν δὲ ἐγὼ δυνηθῶ καὶ πατάξω αὐτόν, ἔσεσθε
ἡμῖν εἰς δούλους καὶ δουλεύσετε ἡμῖν." ¹⁰ καὶ εἶπεν ὁ ἀλλόφυλος "Ἰδοὺ ἐγὼ ὠνείδισα τὴν παράταξιν Ἰσραὴλ σήμερον
ἐν τῇ ἡμέρᾳ ταύτῃ· δότε μοι ἄνδρα καὶ μονομαχήσομεν
ἀμφότεροι." ¹¹ καὶ ἤκουσεν Σαοὺλ καὶ πᾶς Ἰσραὴλ τὰ
ῥήματα τοῦ ἀλλοφύλου ταῦτα, καὶ ἐξέστησαν καὶ ἐφοβήθησαν σφόδρα. ³² Καὶ εἶπεν Δαυεὶδ πρὸς Σαούλ " Μὴ
δὴ συνπεσέτω καρδία τοῦ κυρίου μου ἐπ᾽ αὐτόν· ὁ δοῦλός
σου πορεύσεται καὶ πολεμήσει μετὰ τοῦ ἀλλοφύλου τούτου."
³³ καὶ εἶπεν Σαοὺλ πρὸς Δαυείδ " Οὐ μὴ δύνῃ πορευθῆναι
πρὸς τὸν ἀλλόφυλον τοῦ πολεμεῖν μετ᾽ αὐτοῦ, ὅτι παιδάριον εἶ σύ, καὶ αὐτὸς ἀνὴρ πολεμιστὴς ἐκ νεότητος αὐτοῦ."
³⁴ καὶ εἶπεν Δαυεὶδ πρὸς Σαούλ " Ποιμαίνων ἦν ὁ δοῦλός σου
τῷ πατρὶ αὐτοῦ ἐν τῷ ποιμνίῳ· καὶ ὅταν ἤρχετο ὁ λέων

8. ἀλλόφυλος: Hebrew, 'the Philistine,' meaning that he stands for the
Philistines. — Ἑβραῖοι καὶ Σαούλ: Hebrew, 'servants to Saul.' Σαούλ may
here be meant for the genitive. Ἑβραῖοι
is the usual word for Israelites in the
mouth of a foreigner. Ex. 1¹⁶ n. —
ἑαυτοῖς: § 13. — καταβήτω: quite classical, like the Latin in certamen de-
scendere. — ἐσόμεθα ... εἰς δούλους:
§ 90.

10. σήμερον ἐν τῇ ἡμέρᾳ ταύτῃ: this
amplification is not due to imitation
of the Hebrew, which has simply 'this
day.' Ex. 5¹⁴ n. It is not necessary
to suppose that we have here a 'doublet.' — μονομαχήσομεν: in the LXX

μονομαχεῖν occurs only here and in the
title of Psalm 151, which has reference
to this incident.

32. συνπεσέτω: used here like
Latin concidere = collapse. — τοῦ κυρίου μου: this represents a better
Hebrew reading than that of the Massoretic text ' of a man.' ' My lord ' is
the usual form of address to a king
and corresponds to 'thy servant' in
the next sentence. — ἐπ᾽ αὐτόν: upon
him, a literal rendering of the Hebrew.

33. ἀνὴρ πολεμιστής: a poetical
expression common in the LXX.

34. Ποιμαίνων ἦν: § 72. — ὅταν
ἤρχετο: whenever there came. § 104.
— ὁ λέων καὶ ἡ ἄρκος: a lion or a bear.

i Kings XVII 89 :

καὶ ἡ ἄρκος καὶ ἐλάμβανεν πρόβατον ἐκ τῆς ἀγέλης, ³⁵ καὶ
ἐξεπορευόμην ὀπίσω αὐτοῦ καὶ ἐπάταξα αὐτόν, καὶ ἐξέ-
σπασα ἐκ τοῦ στόματος αὐτοῦ· καὶ εἰ ἐπανίστατο ἐπ' ἐμέ,
καὶ ἐκράτησα τοῦ φάρυγγος αὐτοῦ καὶ ἐπάταξα καὶ ἐθα-
νάτωσα αὐτόν. ³⁶ καὶ τὴν ἄρκον ἔτυπτεν ὁ δοῦλός σου καὶ
τὸν λέοντα, καὶ ἔσται ὁ ἀλλόφυλος ὁ ἀπερίτμητος ὡς ἓν
τούτων· οὐχὶ πορεύσομαι καὶ πατάξω αὐτόν, καὶ ἀφελῶ
σήμερον ὄνειδος ἐξ Ἰσραήλ; διότι τίς ὁ ἀπερίτμητος οὗτος
ὃς ὠνείδισεν παράταξιν θεοῦ ζῶντος; ³⁷ Κύριος ὃς ἐξεί-
λατό με ἐκ χειρὸς τοῦ λέοντος καὶ ἐκ χειρὸς τῆς ἄρκου,
αὐτὸς ἐξελεῖταί με ἐκ χειρὸς τοῦ ἀλλοφύλου τοῦ ἀπεριτμή-
του τούτου." καὶ εἶπεν Σαοὺλ πρὸς Δαυείδ "Πορεύου, καὶ
ἔσται Κύριος μετὰ σοῦ." ³⁸ καὶ ἐνέδυσεν Σαοὺλ τὸν Δαυεὶδ
μανδύαν καὶ περικεφαλαίαν χαλκῆν περὶ τὴν κεφαλὴν αὐτοῦ, ³⁹ καὶ ἔζωσεν τὸν Δαυεὶδ τὴν ῥομφαίαν αὐτοῦ ἐπάνω
τοῦ μανδύου αὐτοῦ· καὶ ἐκοπίασεν περιπατήσας ἅπαξ καὶ
δίς. καὶ εἶπεν Δαυεὶδ πρὸς Σαούλ "Οὐ μὴ δύνωμαι πορευ-

Generic use of the article, as in the Hebrew. § 44. — ἡ ἄρκος : later form of ἄρκτος and one of those epicene nouns which use the feminine for both sexes.

35. φάρυγγος : throat, Hebrew, 'beard.' Josephus (Ant. VI 9 § 3) makes David take up the lion by the tail and dash him against the ground.

36. οὐχὶ πορεύσομαι κτλ. : the Greek here is much fuller than the Hebrew, as may be seen by a comparison with the English version.

37. Κύριος κτλ. : before this the Hebrew has the words 'And David said,' which appear superfluous. On the other hand it may be maintained that they are in the Hebrew manner, giving the substance of what has been

already said, as in verse 10. — ἐξελεῖ-ται : § 21.

38. μανδύαν : according to L. & S. μανδύας is a Persian word meaning 'a woollen cloak,' but the word in the Hebrew text is very like the Greek, especially in the form used in ii K. 10⁴ : i Chr. 19⁴. Μανδύας is employed seven times all together in the LXX. — κεφα-λὴν αὐτοῦ : after these words the Hebrew has 'and he clad him in a coat of mail.'

39. καὶ ἔζωσεν . . . μανδύου αὐτοῦ : R.V. 'And David girded his sword upon his apparel.' — αὐτοῦ . . . αὐτοῦ: probably both meant by the translator to refer to Saul as the subject of ἔζω-σεν. — ἐκοπίασεν . . . δίς: 'he was wearied when he had walked once or

θῆναι ἐν τούτοις, ὅτι οὐ πεπείραμαι·" καὶ ἀφαιροῦσιν αὐτὰ ἀπ᾽ αὐτοῦ. ⁴⁰καὶ ἔλαβεν τὴν βακτηρίαν αὐτοῦ ἐν τῇ χειρὶ αὐτοῦ, καὶ ἐξελέξατο ἑαυτῷ πέντε λίθους τελείους ἐκ τοῦ χειμάρρου καὶ ἔθετο αὐτοὺς ἐν τῷ καδίῳ τῷ ποιμενικῷ τῷ ὄντι αὐτῷ εἰς συλλογήν, καὶ σφενδόνην αὐτοῦ ἐν τῇ χειρὶ αὐτοῦ· καὶ προσῆλθεν πρὸς τὸν ἄνδρα τὸν ἀλλόφυλον. ⁴²καὶ εἶδεν Γολιὰδ τὸν Δαυεὶδ καὶ ἠτίμασεν αὐτόν, ὅτι αὐτὸς ἦν παιδάριον καὶ αὐτὸς πυρράκης μετὰ κάλλους ὀφθαλμῶν. ⁴³καὶ εἶπεν ὁ ἀλλόφυλος πρὸς Δαυείδ "Ὡσεὶ κύων ἐγώ εἰμι, ὅτι σὺ ἔρχῃ ἐπ᾽ ἐμὲ ἐν ῥάβδῳ καὶ λίθοις;" καὶ εἶπεν Δαυεὶδ "Οὐχί, ἀλλ᾽ ἢ χείρω κυνός." καὶ κατηράσατο ὁ ἀλλόφυλος τὸν Δαυεὶδ ἐν τοῖς θεοῖς ἑαυτοῦ. ⁴⁴καὶ εἶπεν ὁ ἀλλόφυ- λος πρὸς Δαυείδ "Δεῦρο πρὸς μὲ καὶ δώσω τὰς σάρκας σου τοῖς πετεινοῖς τοῦ οὐρανοῦ καὶ τοῖς κτήνεσιν τῆς γῆς."

twice.' R.V. 'he essayed to go.' The Greek here seems to indicate a better Hebrew reading than that in our text. —ἀφαιροῦσιν κτλ.: the Hebrew has the verb in the singular, referring to David.

**40.** τελείους: Hebrew, 'smooth.' Lucian's recension has λείους, which is no doubt right. —χειμάρρου: χείμαρ- ρος is shortened from χειμάρροος, Attic χειμάρρους. It is the proper word for a river-bed which is dry in summer. iii K. 17⁷ n. —καδίῳ: diminutive of κάδος, Latin cadus. In the LXX only here and in 49. The Hebrew word which it represents is a very general one, like Greek σκεῦος or Latin vas. — τῷ ὄντι αὐτῷ εἰς συλλογήν: which he had for collecting things in. The word rendered 'scrip' in our version is de- rived from a verb meaning 'to collect.' —τὸν ἀλλόφυλον: after this comes verse 41 in the Hebrew, which is ab- sent from the Greek.

**42.** καὶ εἶδεν κτλ.: shorter than the Hebrew. Cp. R.V.—Γολιάδ: in verse 4 Γολιάθ. —πυρράκης: Gen. 25²⁵: i K. 16¹². The word is used by Arta- panus in his description of Moses (Eus. Pr. Ev. IX 27 ad fin.) and is found in Papyri of the latter half of the third century B.C.

**43.** ἐν ῥάβδῳ: § 91. For the par- ticular expression ἐν ῥάβδῳ cp. i Cor. 4²¹. — καὶ λίθοις: these words are not in the Hebrew, but they add point to the question of Goliath. — καὶ εἶπεν . . . κυνός: this repartee of David's appears only in the Greek, but it seems not without bearing on the cursing which follows. Josephus (Ant. VIII 9 § 4) has also preserved it — Μὴ αὐτὸν ἀντὶ ἀνθρώπου κύνα εἶναι δοκεῖ; Ὁ δ᾽ οὐχὶ τοιοῦτον ἀλλὰ καὶ χείρω κυνὸς αὐτὸν νομίζειν ἀπεκρίνατο.

**44.** κτήνεσιν: properly used of cattle which constituted wealth (κτᾶ- σθαι) in early times. Here put for

i Kings XVII 49

⁴⁵καὶ εἶπεν Δαυεὶδ πρὸς τὸν ἀλλόφυλον " Σὺ ἔρχῃ πρὸς μὲ ἐν ῥομφαίᾳ καὶ ἐν δόρατι καὶ ἐν ἀσπίδι, κἀγὼ πορεύομαι πρὸς σὲ ἐν ὀνόματι Κυρίου θεοῦ σαβαὼθ παρατάξεως Ἰσραὴλ ἦν ὠνείδισας ⁽⁴⁶⁾σήμερον· ⁴⁶καὶ ἀποκλείσει σε Κύριος σήμερον εἰς τὴν χεῖρά μου, καὶ ἀποκτενῶ σε καὶ ἀφελῶ τὴν κεφαλήν σου ἀπὸ σοῦ, καὶ δώσω τὰ κῶλά σου καὶ τὰ κῶλα παρεμβολῆς ἀλλοφύλων ἐν ταύτῃ τῇ ἡμέρᾳ τοῖς πετεινοῖς τοῦ οὐρανοῦ καὶ τοῖς θηρίοις τῆς γῆς· καὶ γνώσεται πᾶσα ἡ γῆ ὅτι ἔστιν θεὸς ἐν Ἰσραήλ. ⁴⁷καὶ γνώσεται πᾶσα ἡ ἐκκλησία αὕτη ὅτι οὐκ ἐν ῥομφαίᾳ καὶ δόρατι σώζει Κύριος· ὅτι τοῦ Κυρίου ὁ πόλεμος, καὶ παραδώσει Κύριος ὑμᾶς εἰς χεῖρας ἡμῶν." ⁴⁸καὶ ἀνέστη ὁ ἀλλόφυλος καὶ ἐπορεύθη εἰς συνάντησιν Δαυείδ. ⁴⁹καὶ ἐξέτεινεν Δαυεὶδ τὴν χεῖρα αὐτοῦ εἰς τὸ κάδιον καὶ ἔλαβεν ἐκεῖθεν λίθον ἕνα, καὶ ἐσφενδόνησεν καὶ ἐπάταξεν τὸν ἀλλόφυλον ἐπὶ τὸ μέτωπον αὐτοῦ, καὶ διέδυ ὁ λίθος διὰ τῆς περικεφαλαίας εἰς τὸ μέτωπον αὐτοῦ, καὶ ἔπεσεν

θηρίοις, which A has. The Hebrew word which it is used to translate originally meant 'dumb creatures,' and is used of beasts either tame or wild.

**45.** ἐν ἀσπίδι: Hebrew, 'with a javelin.'—Κυρίου θεοῦ κτλ. : taken as they stand these words ought to mean 'of the LORD God of the hosts of the army of Israel.' But θεοῦ and σαβαὼθ seem to have accidentally changed place. The passage should run—Κυρίου σαβαὼθ, θεοῦ παρατάξεως Ἰσραήλ. Σαβαὼθ is a transliteration from the Hebrew and means 'of hosts.' It is thought to have referred originally to the hosts of heaven, but this passage is enough to show that it was not so understood in the writer's time. For other instances of transliteration in

place of translation cp. Jdg. 13⁵ ναζείρ, iii K. 19⁴ ῥαθμέν, iv K. 2¹⁴ ἀφφώ, iv K. 19¹⁵ χερουβείν.

**46.** σήμερον: not in the Hebrew. —ἀφελῶ: § 21.—τὰ κῶλά σου καί: not in the Hebrew.—παρεμβολῆς: Ex. 14⁹ n.—θηρίοις: the Hebrew word here is different from that in verse 44 and means literally 'living creatures.'

**47.** ἐκκλησία: i.e. the assembled Israelites. Cp. 19²⁰ τὴν ἐκκλησίαν τῶν προφητῶν.

**48.** καὶ ἀνέστη κτλ. : the Greek in this verse is much shorter than the Hebrew ; cp. R.V.

**49.** λίθον ἕνα: § 2.—διὰ τῆς περικεφαλαίας: not in the Hebrew.—ἐπὶ τὴν γῆν: after this in the Hebrew comes verse 50, which is not in the Greek.

258    SELECTIONS FROM THE SEPTUAGINT

ἐπὶ πρόσωπον αὐτοῦ ἐπὶ τὴν γῆν.  ⁵¹καὶ ἔδραμεν Δαυεὶδ
καὶ ἐπέστη ἐπ᾽ αὐτόν, καὶ ἔλαβεν τὴν ῥομφαίαν αὐτοῦ καὶ
ἐθανάτωσεν αὐτὸν καὶ ἀφεῖλεν τὴν κεφαλὴν αὐτοῦ· καὶ
εἶδον οἱ ἀλλόφυλοι ὅτι τέθνηκεν ὁ δυνατὸς αὐτῶν, καὶ ἔφυγον.  ⁵²καὶ ἀνίστανται ἄνδρες Ἰσραὴλ καὶ Ἰούδα καὶ
ἠλάλαξαν, καὶ κατεδίωξαν ὀπίσω αὐτῶν ἕως εἰσόδου Γὲθ
καὶ ἕως τῆς πύλης Ἀσκάλωνος· καὶ ἔπεσαν τραυματίαι
τῶν ἀλλοφύλων ἐν τῇ ὁδῷ τῶν πυλῶν καὶ ἕως Γὲθ καὶ ἕως
Ἀκκαρών.  ⁵³καὶ ἀνέστρεψαν ἄνδρες Ἰσραὴλ ἐκκλίνοντες
ὀπίσω τῶν ἀλλοφύλων, καὶ κατεπάτουν τὰς παρεμβολὰς
αὐτῶν.  ⁵⁴καὶ ἔλαβεν Δαυεὶδ τὴν κεφαλὴν τοῦ ἀλλοφύλου
καὶ ἤνεγκεν αὐτὴν εἰς Ἰερουσαλήμ, καὶ τὰ σκεύη αὐτοῦ
ἔθηκεν ἐν τῷ σκηνώματι αὐτοῦ.

51.  τὴν ῥομφαίαν αὐτοῦ: after this
the Hebrew has 'and drew it out of
the sheath thereof.'

52.  Ἰσραὴλ καὶ Ἰούδα: from this
it may fairly be inferred that the
writer lived after the separation of
the two kingdoms. — Γὲθ: Gath. The
Hebrew here has Gai, the same word
which is translated valley in 3. Here
it is taken by the R.V. as a proper
name, but no such place is otherwise
known.  It seems likely therefore that
the LXX here has preserved the right
reading. If the Philistines fled down
the 'Vale of the Terebinth,' the pass
by which they had entered the highlands, Gath would lie straight before
them; while some of the fugitives

may have diverged to the right and
made for Ekron (Hb.) or continued
their course to the gate of Askelon
(LXX). — Ἀσκάλωνος: Hebrew Ekron, as in the LXX at the end of this
verse. — ἔπεσαν: § 18. — τῶν πυλῶν:
R.V. 'to Shaaraim,' which means 'the
two gates.'

53.  ἐκκλίνοντες ὀπίσω: turning
aside from after. — κατεπάτουν τὰς
παρεμβολὰς αὐτῶν: trod down their
armies.  R.V. 'spoiled their camp.'

54.  εἰς Ἰερουσαλήμ: Jerusalem
was still a Jebusite stronghold, and
was captured later by David himself.
According to 21¹⸴ ⁹ the sword of Goliath
was deposited in the sanctuary at Nob,
a few miles to the north of Jerusalem.

# INTRODUCTION TO THE STORY OF ELIJAH

ELIJAH the Tishbite bursts upon us with the suddenness of the whirlwind in which he disappears. From first to last he is a man of mystery. Who was his father? Who was his mother? These questions must remain unanswered. Perhaps, like Melchizedek, he had no parents at all. Where did he come from? From Gilead. That much seems certain. But that renders his designation of the Tishbite unintelligible. For no such place as Tishbeh is known of in Gilead, that is, in the mountainous district east of the Jordan. The only name resembling it is Thisbé in Naphtali, which is mentioned in Tobit 1². We have to suppose then that Elijah was born in Tishbeh, but brought up in Gilead, unless we follow those who have recourse to conjecture, and surmise that 'Tisbi' in the Hebrew text is a false reading for what would mean 'man of Jabesh,' Jabesh being one of the chief cities in Gilead. Gilead was just the wildest part of all Palestine, and so a 'meet nurse for a' prophetic 'child.' As the worship of Jehovah originated in the desert and amid the awful solitudes of Sinai, so its most zealous supporters were sons of the desert, whose walk was in lonely places, whereas the rival worship of Baal was the cult of populous cities like Tyre and Zidon.

The Hebrew name of the prophet, 'Yahweh is God,' is so appropriate to the cause he maintained that it looks as if it may have been assumed by himself, or assigned to him by the popular voice, as significant of his teaching, rather than borne by him originally. If it was so borne, it would seem to show that he came of a stock already devoted to the same cause. Perhaps it was given to him in the Schools of the Prophets.

Elijah's first appearance on the scene is in the capacity of a great rain-maker, claiming as the mouthpiece of Jehovah to have control over the weather — 'As the Lord, the God of Israel, liveth, before whom I stand, there shall not be dew nor rain these years, but according to my word.' It is implied, in accordance with the prophetic view of nature and history, that the rain is withheld on account of the sins of Ahab in following the Baalim (18¹⁸). But the narrative at the same time admits that the drought was not confined to Ahab's dominions, but affected also the neighbouring country of Zidon (17¹⁴). There is other evidence for this drought. Josephus (*Ant.* VIII 13 § 2) quotes Menander as saying in the *Acts of Ithobalus, King of Tyre* — ' And under him there took place a drought, from about the middle of September in one year until the same time the next: but, when he made supplication, there was a great thunderstorm.' Here we have the rare opportunity of hearing the other side. Ithobalus is no other than Ethbaal, the father of Jezebel and the father-in-law of Ahab (i K. 16³¹). But it should be noticed that, while the drought which Ethbaal is related to have removed by prayer, was exactly of one year's duration, that in our story continued at least into the third year (i K. 18¹), and, according to the tradition preserved in the New Testament (Lk. 4²⁵: James 5¹⁷) lasted for three years and six months.

Ethbaal was a priest of Astarte, who obtained the throne of Tyre by slaying Pheles, who himself had purchased by fratricide a reign of eight months.[1] He reigned for thirty-two years and was succeeded by his son and grandson, who between them only occupied fifteen years. To the latter succeeded Pygmalion, who, according to the historian of Tyre, lived fifty-six years and reigned forty-seven. It was in his seventh year, according to the same authority, that his sister founded Carthage. Thus it would appear from Menander that Ethbaal's daughter, whom Ahab married, was an elder contemporary of Dido, and presumably of the same family, since Pygmalion can hardly be supposed to have usurped the throne at the age of nine. If Pygmalion was the son of his predecessor Metten, then Jezebel must have been grand-aunt, and her daughter Athaliah first-cousin once removed, to Eliza, who is known to us as Dido.

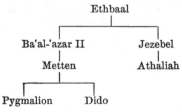

---

[1] Menander in Josephus *Against Apion* I § 18.

Isabel or Jezebel, the daughter of the priest of Astarte, was as zealous for her own religion as Elijah for his, and no less ruthless in her manner of supporting it. They were both ready to slay or to be slain. In their two persons the war of the faiths took visible shape — Jehovah on the one hand, on the other Baal and Ashteroth; on the one hand the austere son of the desert in his shaggy mantle, on the other the queen in her vestures of fine linen, with all the power of the state behind her. For Ahab ruled the state and Jezebel ruled Ahab. Ahab, had he been left alone, might have tolerated both creeds and have given the 'still, small voice' a chance of being heard: but that would have pleased neither the imperious and fanatical queen nor yet the champion of the 'jealous' God. It was literally war to the knife. Either Baal or Jehovah *was* God, and one only was to be worshipped. Of how much bloodshed has an incomplete alternative often been the cause!

Jezebel began the duel by cutting off the prophets of Jehovah on that occasion when Obadiah saved one hundred of them alive in a cave. When this event took place we are not told. It lies behind the narrative, like one of those dark and terrible deeds which are 'presupposed in the plot of a tragedy instead of being represented on the stage.'

There was good reason then for Elijah's going into hiding at the brook Cherith, where he was fed morning and evening by the ravens. Some commentators have tried to get rid of the ravens from the story by so pointing the consonants of the Hebrew word as to turn it into 'Arabs' or 'merchants.' But many pointless things may be done by a careful manipulation of points. This is only a mild piece of Euhemerism, a discredited tendency of thought, which, wherever it encounters a picturesque marvel, would substitute for it some prosaic possibility, less alluring, but equally imaginary.

The next episode in the story is the pleasing and pathetic one of the widow of Zarephath. After the brook Cherith had dried up, the prophet was sent to Zarephath, where he was supported by a poor widow, one of the countrywomen of the fierce queen from whom he was flying, and rewarded her hospitality with the miraculous replenishment of her barrel of meal and cruse of oil. To this incident we have a partial parallel in pagan legend, in the wonderful thing that happened at table, when Baucis and Philemon were entertaining angels unawares in the shape of Jupiter and Mercury, who had come down in human form to see what piety was to be found in Phrygia. The first hint that the guests gave of their divinity was in the supernatural increase of the wine —

> Interea,*quoties haustum cratera repleri
> sponte sua, per seque vident succrescere vina
> attoniti novitate pavent, manibusque supinis
> concipiunt Baucisque preces, timidusque Philemon.
> — Ovid *Met.* VIII 679-682.

The moral of the two stories is the same, though conveyed in very different language —

> Cura pii Dis sunt, et, qui coluere, coluntur.

This moral is brought home still more powerfully in the story of Elijah by the restoration to the widow of her son after the breath had left his body. So in Greek legend Heracles rewards the hospitality of Admetus by restoring to him his wife. But the poet's imagination there conjures up a struggle with Death on the brink of the grave. This we feel to be unreal. It is not the thews and sinews of the strong man that can avail to recall 'the fleeting breath.' But the Jewish story has nothing in it that repels belief. Who can measure the powers of the strong soul?

From this benigner aspect of Elijah we turn at once to the grim episode of the contest with the prophets of Baal, on the grandeur of which we need not dilate: it is generally felt that it is one of the finest stories in all literature. As the result of his victory Elijah slays the prophets of Baal with his own hands (i K. 18⁴⁰).

Ahab is represented as accepting this measure with indifference. He would no doubt regard it as the legitimate outcome of Elijah's challenge to a trial by fire. Not so however the zealot queen. 'So let the gods do to me, and more also, if I make not thy life like the life of one of them by to-morrow about this time' was her answer to the prophet.

This leads on to the next episode, in which Elijah retires to the sacred mount of Horeb, where the worship of Jehovah began. Here he may have taken up his abode in that very 'cleft of the rock' (Ex. 33²²) from which Moses is related to have seen the back of Jehovah. The story that follows of 'the still, small voice' seems to show that the teller of it himself misdoubted the whirlwind ways of the prophet. Or are we to say that he ' builded better than he knew ' and left the world a moral which was not of his own time or country ?

In the next episode, which is that of Naboth's vineyard, the prophet of Jehovah stands forth as the champion of civil justice, and denounces the tyranny of the weak ruler and his wicked wife. As the conscience-stricken king cowered beneath his curse, there stood one behind his chariot, who, years afterwards, took up the quarrel of Elijah against Jezebel and the house of Ahab, and destroyed Baal out of Israel (ii K. 9[25, 26]).

Athaliah, the daughter of Jezebel, whose methods were even more drastic than her mother's, did her best to establish Baal-worship in Judah, but Jehoiada the priest rallied the Levites, and the foreign cult was suppressed there also, and finally extirpated under Josiah. Racine, it will be remembered, availed himself of this subject for his grand tragedy of *Athalie*. His would be a daring genius that should attempt to dramatise the story of Elijah and Jezebel. While more sublime than the other, it does not lend itself so well to the unities of time and place.

So far in the story of Elijah there is no sign of any mixture of documents. But some critics think that the episode of the three captains (ii K. 1[2-17]) is from a different hand. The form of the prophet's name in ii K. 1[3, 8, 12] is in the Hebrew *Elijah*, as in Malachi 3[23], not *Elijahu*, as in the rest of the narrative; also ' the angel of the Lord ' speaks to Elijah in ii K. 1[3, 15] instead of ' the word of the Lord ' coming unto him. Whether these critics are right or not we will not attempt to decide. Professor Driver does not seem to endorse their opinion. But this much we seem entitled, or rather bound, to say — that the story, from whatever source derived, is one which shocks the moral sense; nor need the most pious Christian hesitate to condemn it, when he recalls the judgement pronounced upon it, at least by implication, by Jesus Christ himself (Lk. 9[55]).

The last episode, namely, that of the translation of Elijah, is treated with great reticence by Josephus. His words are as follows (*Ant.* IX 2 § 2) — ' At that time Elias disappeared from among men, and no one knows unto this day how he came by his end. But he left a disciple Elisha, as we have shown before. Concerning Elias however and Enoch, who lived before the Flood, it is recorded in the

Sacred Books that they disappeared, but of their death no one knows.'
Josephus evidently thought it indiscreet to submit to a Gentile
audience a story which, as internal evidence shows, could rest solely
on the report of the prophet's successor.

The proposition ' All men are mortal' is the type of universality
to the intellect, but the heart is ever seeking to evade its stringency.
' He cannot be dead' and ' He will come again' are the words that
rise to men's lips, when some grand personality is taken away.   The
Old Testament, as we arrange it, closes with the prediction — ' Behold I will send you Elijah the prophet before the great and terrible
day of the Lord come' — and the New Testament begins with his
coming in the person of John the Baptist (Mt. 17[12, 13]), while he came
again later, on the Mount of Transfiguration (Mk. 9[4]).   If a man did
signs and wonders, the natural question to ask him was ' Art thou
Elijah ? '   To the present day, it is said, some of the Jews set a seat
for Elijah at the circumcision of a child.   None of the ' famous men
of old' among the Jews, not even excepting Moses himself, left a
deeper impression than Elijah on the hearts of his countrymen.
Listen to the words of the son of Sirach (Ecclesiasticus 48[1-11]) —

Elijah arose as a flame, and his word like a lamp did burn :
Famine did walk in his train and the land to weakness turn.
In the word of the Lord he stayed the heavens that they sent not rain,
And he called down fire from above, yea twice, and once again.
How wert thou honoured, Elijah, in thy wondrous deeds of might !
Never again like thee shall another arise in our sight.
Thou didst raise up the dead from death, and his soul from Sheol didst call :
For the word of the Lord Most High in thy mouth could accomplish all.
Thou didst bring down kings to the dust and the mighty from their seat :
Yet in Sinai heardest rebuke and in Horeb judgement meet.
It was thine to anoint earth's kings, when the Lord would vengeance take ;
And the prophets that followed upon thee — them also thou didst make.
Thou wert rapt to heaven at the last in a whirl of blazing flame ;
The car and the steeds of fire from the skies to take thee came.
Is it not written of thee that thou shalt reprove at the end,
Lulling the wrath of God, that men their ways may mend,
So that the father's heart may be turned to the son once more,
And Israel's tribes again may stand as they stood before ?
Blessed are they that saw thee — the sight could blessing give —
But, as thou livest, Elijah, we too shall surely live.

# VI. THE STORY OF ELIJAH

iii Kings XVII

¹ Καὶ εἶπεν Ἡλειοὺ ὁ προφήτης ὁ Θεσβείτης ἐκ Θεσβὼν τῆς Γαλαὰδ πρὸς Ἀχαάβ " Ζῇ Κύριος ὁ θεὸς τῶν δυνάμεων, ὁ θεὸς Ἰσραὴλ ᾧ παρέστην ἐνώπιον αὐτοῦ, εἰ ἔσται τὰ ἔτη ταῦτα δρόσος καὶ ὑετός· ὅτι εἰ μὴ διὰ στόματος λόγου μου." ² Καὶ ἐγένετο ῥῆμα Κυρίου πρὸς Ἡλειού ³ " Πορεύου ἐντεῦθεν κατὰ ἀνατολάς, καὶ κρύβηθι ἐν τῷ χειμάρρῳ Χορρὰθ τοῦ ἐπὶ προσώπου τοῦ Ἰορδάνου. ⁴ καὶ ἔσται ἐκ τοῦ χειμάρρου πίεσαι ὕδωρ, καὶ τοῖς κόραξιν ἐντελοῦμαι διατρέφειν σε ἐκεῖ." ⁵ καὶ ἐποίησεν Ἡλειοὺ κατὰ τὸ ῥῆμα Κυρίου, καὶ ἐκάθισεν ἐν τῷ χειμάρρῳ Χορρὰθ ἐπὶ προσώ-

1. Ἡλειού: a transliteration from the Hebrew, instead of the Grecised form Ἡλίας, which is sometimes used. Mal. 4⁴ acc. Ἡλίαν: Lk. 1¹⁷, 4²⁵, 9⁵⁴ (A.S.M.) Ἡλίας. — ὁ προφήτης: not in the Hebrew. It serves to soften a little the abruptness of Elijah's appearance on the scene. — ἐκ Θεσβῶν: the word which in the R.V. is rendered ' of the sojourners' was taken by the Greek translator as the name of a town in Gilead. Josephus (Ant. VIII 13 § 2) was of the same opinion — ἐκ πόλεως Θεσβώνης τῆς Γαλααδίτιδος χώρας. — Ἀχαάβ: the name is taken to mean ' brother of his father,' i.e. probably ' like his father.' — Ζῇ Κύριος: a Hebrew mode of introducing a solemn asseveration. Cp. 18¹⁰, ¹⁵: iv K. 2². In addressing a superior ζῇ ἡ ψυχή σου may be added or substituted. i K. 1²⁶, 25²⁶: Judith 12⁴. — ὁ θεὸς τῶν δυνά-

μεων: not in the Hebrew. τῶν δυνάμεων represents the Hebrew word which in 18¹⁵ and elsewhere is rendered ' of hosts.' — ᾧ παρέστην ἐνώπιον αὐτοῦ: § 69. — εἰ ἔσται: there shall not be. § 101. — τὰ ἔτη ταῦτα: during the years that are to come. — ὅτι εἰ μή: § 110. — διὰ στόματος: a verbal rendering of the Hebrew idiom. R.V. ' according to.'

2. πρὸς Ἡλειού: Hebrew, 'unto him.' Ἡλειού here seems to have arisen out of a misreading of the Hebrew, and πρός to have been put in to make sense.

3. κρύβηθι: passive in middle sense. Cp. 18¹. § 83. — Χορρὰθ: Hebrew Cherith. The particular ravine is not known, but, as it appears to have been east of Jordan, it was presumably in Elijah's own country of Gilead.

4. πίεσαι: § 17.

που τοῦ Ἰορδάνου. ⁶καὶ οἱ κόρακες ἔφερον αὐτῷ ἄρτους τὸ πρωὶ καὶ κρέα τὸ δείλης, καὶ ἐκ τοῦ χειμάρρου ἔπινεν ὕδωρ. ⁷καὶ ἐγένετο μετὰ ἡμέρας καὶ ἐξηράνθη ὁ χειμάρρους, ὅτι οὐκ ἐγένετο ὑετὸς ἐπὶ τῆς γῆς. ⁸Καὶ ἐγένετο ῥῆμα Κυρίου πρὸς Ἠλειού ⁹"Ἀνάστηθι καὶ πορεύου εἰς Σάρεπτα τῆς Σειδωνίας· ἰδοὺ ἐντέταλμαι ἐκεῖ γυναικὶ χήρᾳ τοῦ διατρέφειν σε." ¹⁰καὶ ἀνέστη καὶ ἐπορεύθη εἰς Σάρεπτα, εἰς τὸν πυλῶνα τῆς πόλεως· καὶ ἰδοὺ ἐκεῖ γυνὴ χήρα συνέλεγεν ξύλα, καὶ ἐβόησεν ὀπίσω αὐτῆς Ἠλειοὺ καὶ εἶπεν αὐτῇ "Λάβε δὴ ὀλίγον ὕδωρ εἰς ἄγγος καὶ πίομαι." ¹¹καὶ ἐπορεύθη λαβεῖν, καὶ ἐβόησεν ὀπίσω αὐτῆς Ἠλειοὺ καὶ εἶπεν "Λήμψῃ δή μοι ψωμὸν ἄρτου τοῦ ἐν τῇ χειρί σου." ¹²καὶ εἶπεν ἡ γυνή "Ζῇ Κύριος ὁ θεός σου, εἰ ἔστιν μοι ἐνκρυφίας ἀλλ᾽ ἢ ὅσον δρὰξ ἀλεύρου ἐν τῇ ὑδρίᾳ, καὶ ὀλίγον ἔλαιον ἐν τῷ καψάκῃ· καὶ ἰδοὺ συλλέγω δύο ξυλάρια, καὶ εἰσελεύσομαι καὶ ποιήσω αὐτὸ ἐμαυτῇ καὶ τοῖς τέκνοις μου,

---

6. τὸ δείλης: Gen. 40⁶ n.

7. μετὰ ἡμέρας: § 86. — χειμάρρους: i K. 17⁴⁰ n. Here we have the Attic, instead of the later shortened form. So in 18⁴⁰, Nb. 34⁵, and other passages.

9. Σάρεπτα τῆς Σειδωνίας: Zarephath lay between Tyre and Sidon in the country from which Jezebel came. — τοῦ διατρέφειν σε: genitive infinitive for the latter of two verbs. We had the simple infinitive above in verse 4.

11. Λήμψῃ: jussive future. § 74. — ψωμόν: a word as old as Homer, which occurs a dozen times in the LXX. It means simply 'morsel.' Its dim. ψωμίον, which does not occur in the LXX, is the word rendered 'sop' in Jn. 13²⁶, ²⁷, ³⁰ (= bread in Mod. Greek).

12. Ζῇ Κύριος κτλ.: the woman,

though a Gentile, is made to swear by Elijah's God, not by her own. — ἐνκρυφίας: Ex. 12³⁹ n. — δρὰξ: handful. Cp. Gen. 37⁷ n. Josephus also uses δρὰξ in this context (Ant. VIII 13 § 2). The word occurs some eight or nine times in the LXX, and its proper meaning seems to be that of the hand regarded as a receptacle. Is. 40¹² Τίς ἐμέτρησεν . . . πᾶσαν τὴν γῆν δρακί; In iii Mac. 5² there is a dative plural δράκεσι, as though from δράκος. — καψάκῃ: cp. 17¹⁴, ¹⁶, 19⁶ καψάκης ὕδατος: Judith 10⁵ καψάκην ἐλαίου. The word is also spelt καμψάκης and is connected with κάμψα = Latin capsa. It was perhaps a bottle cased in wicker work. Josephus (Ant. VIII 13 § 2) here uses κεράμιον. — ξυλάρια: the diminutive of ξύλον firewood occurs only here in LXX. — τοῖς τέκνοις: so in

iii Kings XVII 19

καὶ φαγόμεθα, καὶ ἀποθανούμεθα." ¹⁸καὶ εἶπεν πρὸς αὐτὴν Ἡλειού " Θάρσει, εἴσελθε καὶ ποίησον κατὰ τὸ ῥῆμά σου. ἀλλὰ ποίησον ἐμοὶ ἐκεῖθεν ἐνκρυφίαν μικρὸν ἐν πρώτοις καὶ ἐξοίσεις μοι, σαυτῇ δὲ καὶ τοῖς τέκνοις σου ποιήσεις ἐπ᾽ ἐσχάτου, ¹⁴ὅτι τάδε λέγει Κύριος ᾽ Ἡ ὑδρία τοῦ ἀλεύρου οὐκ ἐκλείψει καὶ ὁ καψάκης τοῦ ἐλαίου οὐκ ἐλαττονήσει ἕως ἡμέρας τοῦ δοῦναι Κύριον τὸν ὑετὸν ἐπὶ τῆς γῆς.᾽ " ¹⁵καὶ ἐπορεύθη ἡ γυνὴ καὶ ἐποίησεν· καὶ ἤσθιεν αὐτὴ καὶ αὐτὸς καὶ τὰ τέκνα αὐτῆς. ¹⁶καὶ ἡ ὑδρία τοῦ ἀλεύρου οὐκ ἐξέλιπεν καὶ ὁ καψάκης τοῦ ἐλαίου οὐκ ἐλαττονώθη, κατὰ τὸ ῥῆμα Κυρίου ὃ ἐλάλησεν ἐν χειρὶ Ἡλειού. ¹⁷καὶ ἐγένετο μετὰ ταῦτα καὶ ἠρρώστησεν ὁ υἱὸς τῆς γυναικὸς τῆς κυρίας τοῦ οἴκου· καὶ ἦν ἡ ἀρρωστία αὐτοῦ κραταιὰ σφόδρα ἕως οὗ οὐχ ὑπελείφθη ἐν αὐτῷ πνεῦμα. ¹⁸καὶ εἶπεν πρὸς Ἡλειού " Τί ἐμοὶ καὶ σοί, ὁ ἄνθρωπος τοῦ θεοῦ; εἰσῆλθες πρὸς μὲ τοῦ ἀναμνῆσαι ἀδικίας μου καὶ θανατῶσαι τὸν υἱόν μου ; " ¹⁹καὶ εἶπεν Ἡλειού πρὸς τὴν γυναῖκα " Δός μοι τὸν υἱόν σου." καὶ ἔλαβεν αὐτὸν ἐκ τοῦ κόλπου αὐτῆς καὶ ἀνήνεγκεν αὐτὸν εἰς τὸ ὑπερῷον ἐν ᾧ αὐτὸς ἐκάθητο ἐκεῖ,

15 τὰ τέκνα, but in 17 ὁ υἱός, as though there were but one. The Hebrew has the singular throughout.

13. ἐν πρώτοις: like Latin *inprimis*. — ποίησον . . . καὶ ἐξοίσεις: § 74. — ἐπ᾽ ἐσχάτου: here merely *afterwards*. In Swete's text ἐπ᾽ ἐσχάτῳ is read in Dt. 4³⁰, 13⁹: ii K. 24²⁵: Sir. 12¹², 13⁷, 30¹⁰, 34²² ; ἐπ᾽ ἐσχάτου in Is. 41²³ : Jer. 23²⁰, 25¹⁹ : Ezk. 38⁸ : Dan. Oʹ 8²³, 10¹⁴.

14. ἡ ὑδρία τοῦ ἀλεύρου: cp. 12. From meaning a waterpot, as in 18³⁴, the meaning of this word has been generalised, so as to cover any kind of vessel. — ἐλαττονήσει: ἐλαττονεῖν = *be less*, ἐλαττονοῦν in 16 = *make less*.

15. καὶ ἐποίησεν: after this the Hebrew has 'according to the word of the Lord.'

16. ἐν χειρί: a Hebraism = *by means of*. Cp. 20²⁸ : iv K. 19²³.

17. ἠρρώστησεν: ἀρρωστεῖν in the LXX has dislodged νοσεῖν, which occurs only in Wisd. 17⁸, and is there used metaphorically. Cp. iv K. 1².

18. ὁ ἄνθρωπος τοῦ θεοῦ: nominative for vocative. § 50. — τοῦ ἀναμνῆσαι: genitive infinitive of purpose. § 59.

19. ἐν ᾧ . . . ἐκεῖ: § 87. — ἐκοίμισεν: here = *laid*. Cp. ii K. 8².

καὶ ἐκοίμισεν αὐτὸν ἐπὶ τῆς κλίνης.   ²⁰καὶ ἀνεβόησεν
Ἠλειοὺ καὶ εἶπεν " Οἴμοι Κύριε, ὁ μάρτυς τῆς χήρας μεθ'
ἧς ἐγὼ κατοικῶ μετ' αὐτῆς, σὺ κεκάκωκας τοῦ θανατῶσαι
τὸν υἱὸν αὐτῆς."   ²¹καὶ ἐνεφύσησεν τῷ παιδαρίῳ τρίς, καὶ
ἐπεκαλέσατο τὸν κύριον καὶ εἶπεν " Κύριε ὁ θεός μου, ἐπι-
στραφήτω δὴ ἡ ψυχὴ τοῦ παιδαρίου τούτου εἰς αὐτόν."
²²καὶ ἐγένετο οὕτως, καὶ ἀνεβόησεν τὸ παιδάριον.   ²³καὶ
κατήγαγεν αὐτὸν ἀπὸ τοῦ ὑπερῴου εἰς τὸν οἶκον καὶ ἔδωκεν
αὐτὸν τῇ μητρὶ αὐτοῦ· καὶ εἶπεν Ἠλειού " Βλέπε, ζῇ ὁ υἱός
σου."   ²⁴καὶ εἶπεν ἡ γυνὴ πρὸς Ἠλειού " Ἰδοὺ ἔγνωκα
ὅτι σὺ ἄνθρωπος θεοῦ, καὶ ῥῆμα Κυρίου ἐν στόματί σου
ἀληθινόν."

¹Καὶ ἐγένετο μεθ' ἡμέρας πολλὰς καὶ ῥῆμα Κυρίου ἐγένετο πρὸς Ἠλειοὺ ἐν τῷ ἐνιαυτῷ τῷ τρίτῳ λέγων " Πορεύθητι
καὶ ὄφθητι τῷ Ἀχαάβ, καὶ δώσω ὑετὸν ἐπὶ πρόσωπον τῆς
γῆς."   ²καὶ ἐπορεύθη Ἠλειοὺ τοῦ ὀφθῆναι τῷ Ἀχαάβ, καὶ
ἡ λιμὸς κραταιὰ ἐν Σαμαρείᾳ.   ³καὶ ἐκάλεσεν Ἀχαὰβ τὸν
Ἀβδειοὺ τὸν οἰκονόμον· καὶ Ἀβδειοὺ ἦν φοβούμενος τὸν
κύριον σφόδρα.   ⁴καὶ ἐγένετο ἐν τῷ τύπτειν τὴν Ἰεζάβελ

20. ἀνεβόησεν Ἠλειού: Hebrew,
'he cried unto the LORD.' The words
'unto the LORD' in Hebrew might
easily be taken for ' Elijah.' — ὁ μάρτυς
τῆς χήρας: here the Greek departs from
the Hebrew, and is not very intelligible. ὁ μάρτυς seems to be nominative
for vocative, in apposition with Κύριε,
like Κύριε ὁ θεός μου in 21. A agrees
with B here, which is surprising in
view of the general conformity of A
to the Massoretic text.
21. ἐνεφύσησεν τῷ παιδαρίῳ: he
breathed into the child. R.V. 'he
stretched himself upon the child.'
22. καὶ ἐγένετο κτλ.: this verse is

shorter in the Greek than in the Hebrew. Cp. R.V. — ἀνεβόησεν: this
word seems to have crept in here
from verse 20, in place of ἀνεβίωσεν,
which Josephus (Ant. VIII 13 § 2)
employs in this context. A has
εζησεν.
1. μεθ ἡμέρας πολλάς: § 86. Josephus (Ant. VIII 13 § 4) says χρόνου
δ' ὀλίγου διελθόντος. — ἐν τῷ ἐνιαυτῷ τῷ
τρίτῳ: presumably explanatory of μεθ'
ἡμέρας πολλάς, and so three years after
the miracle just recorded.
3. Ἀβδειού: Hebrew 'Obadyahu,
Vulgate Abdias, English Obadiah. —
ἦν φοβούμενος: analytic form of im-

τοὺς προφήτας Κυρίου καὶ ἔλαβεν 'Αβδειοὺ ἑκατὸν ἄνδρας προφήτας καὶ ἔκρυψεν αὐτοὺς κατὰ πεντήκοντα ἐν σπηλαίῳ, καὶ διέτρεφεν αὐτοὺς ἐν ἄρτῳ καὶ ὕδατι. ⁵καὶ εἶπεν 'Αχαὰβ πρὸς 'Αβδειού " Δεῦρο καὶ διέλθωμεν ἐπὶ τὴν γῆν ἐπὶ πηγὰς τῶν ὑδάτων καὶ ἐπὶ χειμάρρους, ἐάν πως εὔρωμεν βοτάνην καὶ περιποιησώμεθα ἵππους καὶ ἡμιόνους, καὶ οὐκ ἐξολοθρευθήσονται ἀπὸ τῶν σκηνῶν." ⁶καὶ ἐμέρισαν ἑαυτοῖς τὴν ὁδὸν τοῦ διελθεῖν αὐτήν· 'Αχαὰβ ἐπορεύθη ἐν ὁδῷ μιᾷ, καὶ 'Αβδειοὺ ἐπορεύθη ἐν ὁδῷ ἄλλῃ μόνος. ⁷Καὶ ἦν 'Αβδειοὺ ἐν τῇ ὁδῷ μόνος, καὶ ἦλθεν 'Ηλειοὺ εἰς συνάντησιν αὐτοῦ μόνος· καὶ 'Αβδειοὺ ἔσπευσεν καὶ ἔπεσεν ἐπὶ πρόσωπον αὐτοῦ καὶ εἶπεν " Εἰ σὺ εἶ αὐτός, κύριέ μου 'Ηλειού; " ⁸καὶ εἶπεν 'Ηλειοὺ αὐτῷ " 'Εγώ· πορεύου, λέγε τῷ κυρίῳ σου ' Ἰδοὺ 'Ηλειού.' " ⁹καὶ εἶπεν 'Αβδειού " Τί ἡμάρτηκα, ὅτι δίδως τὸν δοῦλόν σου εἰς χεῖρα 'Αχαὰβ τοῦ θανατῶσαί με; ¹⁰ζῇ Κύριος ὁ θεός σου, εἰ ἔστιν ἔθνος ἢ βασιλεία οὗ οὐκ ἀπέστειλεν ὁ κύριός μου ζητεῖν σε, καὶ εἰ εἶπον ' Οὐκ ἔστιν·' καὶ ἐνέπρησεν τὴν βασιλείαν καὶ τὰς χώρας αὐτῆς, ὅτι οὐχ εὕρηκέν σε. ¹¹καὶ νῦν σὺ λέγεις

perfect. Here due to imitation of the Hebrew.

**4.** ἐν ἄρτῳ: § 91.

**5.** Δεῦρο καὶ διέλθωμεν: this gives a better sense than the Hebrew, ' Go.' — ἐπὶ . . . ἐπὶ: over the land, to look for. — ἐξολοθρευθήσονται: Ex. 8²⁵ n.— ἀπὸ τῶν σκηνῶν: A has here κτηνων, for which σκηνῶν seems here to have been written by mistake.

**6.** τὴν ὁδόν: Hebrew, ' the land.' — μιᾷ . . . ἄλλῃ: for the classical ἄλλῃ μὲν . . . ἄλλῃ δέ. § 39. After μιᾷ the Hebrew adds ' alone.' On the other hand the Greek here inserts μόνος twice, where it is not in the Hebrew.

**7.** καὶ 'Αβδειοὺ ἔσπευσεν: Hebrew, ' and he knew him.' — Εἰ σὺ εἶ αὐτός: literally, Art thou he ? The εἰ represents the Hebrew interrogative prefix = Latin -ne. § 100.

**10.** ὁ θεός σου : Obadiah is not disowning the worship of Jehovah on his own part, but acknowledging the higher religious standing of the prophet. Cp. i K. 15³⁰: iv K. 19⁴.— οὗ: = οἷ. § 34. — καὶ ἐνέπρησεν κτλ.: here the Greek differs from the Hebrew. Cp. R.V. ' And when they said, " He is not here," he took an oath from the kingdom and nation, that they found thee not.'

iii Kings XVIII 12

' Πορεύου, ἀνάγγελλε τῷ κυρίῳ σου.' ¹²καὶ ἔσται ἐὰν ἐγὼ ἀπέλθω ἀπὸ σοῦ, καὶ πνεῦμα Κυρίου ἀρεῖ σε εἰς τὴν γῆν ἣν οὐκ οἶδα· καὶ εἰσελεύσομαι ἀπαγγεῖλαι τῷ Ἀχαάβ, καὶ ἀποκτενεῖ με· καὶ ὁ δοῦλός σού ἐστιν φοβούμενος τὸν κύριον ἐκ νεότητος αὐτοῦ. ¹³καὶ οὐκ ἀπηγγέλη σοι τῷ κυρίῳ μου οἷα πεποίηκα ἐν τῷ ἀποκτείνειν Ἰεζάβελ τοὺς προφήτας Κυρίου, καὶ ἔκρυψα ἀπὸ τῶν προφητῶν Κυρίου ἑκατὸν ἄνδρας ἀνὰ πεντήκοντα ἐν σπηλαίῳ καὶ ἔθρεψα ἐν ἄρτοις καὶ ὕδατι; ¹⁴καὶ νῦν σὺ λέγεις μοι ' Πορεύου, λέγε τῷ κυρίῳ σου " Ἰδοὺ Ἠλειού·"' καὶ ἀποκτενεῖ με." ¹⁵καὶ εἶπεν Ἠλειού "Ζῇ Κύριος τῶν δυνάμεων ᾧ παρέστην ἐνώπιον αὐτοῦ, ὅτι σήμερον ὀφθήσομαι αὐτῷ." ¹⁶καὶ ἐπορεύθη Ἀβδειοὺ εἰς συναντὴν τῷ Ἀχαὰβ καὶ ἀπήγγειλεν αὐτῷ· καὶ ἐξέδραμεν Ἀχαὰβ καὶ ἐπορεύθη εἰς συνάντησιν Ἠλειού. ¹⁷Καὶ ἐγένετο ὡς εἶδεν Ἀχαὰβ τὸν Ἠλειού, καὶ εἶπεν Ἀχαὰβ πρὸς Ἠλειού " Εἰ σὺ εἶ αὐτὸς ὁ διαστρέφων τὸν Ἰσραήλ;" ¹⁸καὶ εἶπεν Ἠλειού "Οὐ διαστρέφω τὸν Ἰσραήλ, ὅτι ἀλλ' ἢ σὺ καὶ ὁ οἶκος τοῦ πατρός σου ἐν τῷ καταλιμπάνειν ὑμᾶς τὸν κύριον θεὸν ὑμῶν, καὶ ἐπορεύθης

12. καὶ ἔσται κτλ.: § 41. — εἰς τὴν γῆν ἣν οὐκ οἶδα: Hebrew, 'to where I know not.' A omits τήν. — ἐστιν φοβούμενος: the Hebrew has simply the participle, to which the copulative verb is supplied by the translator.

13. σοι τῷ κυρίῳ μου: the σοι seems to be inserted by the translator for clearness, since otherwise ' my lord' might be supposed to refer to Ahab. — ἀπὸ τῶν προφητῶν: the ἀπό here represents a Hebrew preposition having a partitive meaning. § 92. — ἀνὰ πεντήκοντα: if the translator had been in his most literal mood, he would here have given us πεντήκοντα πεντήκοντα. § 85.

15. Ζῇ κύριος . . . ὅτι: § 101.

16. συναντήν: used again in iv K. 2¹⁵, 5²⁶. In all three places A has συναντησιν. Cp. iii K. 20¹⁸ ἀπαντήν. — ἐξέδραμεν Ἀχαὰβ καὶ ἐπορεύθη: Hebrew, ' Ahab went.'

17. ὁ διαστρέφων: R.V. ' thou troubler.' The reference is apparently to the drought, with which Ahab taxes Elijah.

18. ὅτι ἀλλ' ἤ: § 109. — καταλιμπάνειν: Gen. 39¹⁶ n. — καὶ ἐπορεύθης: for the irregularity of construction cp. ii Jn.² διὰ τὴν ἀλήθειαν τὴν μένουσαν ἐν ἡμῖν, καὶ μεθ' ἡμῶν ἔσται εἰς τὸν αἰῶνα. — τὸν κύριον θεὸν ὑμῶν: Hebrew, 'the commandments of Jehovah.' — Βαα-

iii Kings XVIII 23

ὀπίσω τῶν Βααλείμ. ¹⁹ καὶ νῦν ἀπόστειλον, συνάθροισον πρὸς μὲ πάντα Ἰσραὴλ εἰς ὅρος τὸ Καρμήλιον, καὶ τοὺς προφήτας τῆς αἰσχύνης τετρακοσίους καὶ πεντήκοντα καὶ τοὺς προφήτας τῶν ἀλσῶν τετρακοσίους, ἐσθίοντας τράπεζαν Ἰεζάβελ.ʼʼ ²⁰ καὶ ἀπέστειλεν Ἀχαὰβ εἰς πάντα Ἰσραήλ, καὶ ἐπισυνήγαγεν πάντας· τοὺς προφήτας εἰς ὅρος τὸ Καρμήλιον. ²¹ καὶ προσήγαγεν Ἠλειοὺ πρὸς πάντας· καὶ εἶπεν αὐτοῖς Ἠλειού "Ἕως πότε ὑμεῖς χωλανεῖτε ἐπʼ ἀμφοτέραις ταῖς ἰγνύαις; εἰ ἔστιν Κύριος ὁ θεός, πορεύεσθε ὀπίσω αὐτοῦ· εἰ δὲ Βάαλ, πορεύεσθε ὀπίσω αὐτοῦ.ʼʼ καὶ οὐκ ἀπεκρίθη ὁ λαὸς λόγον. ²² καὶ εἶπεν Ἠλειοὺ πρὸς τὸν λαόν "Ἐγὼ ὑπολέλειμμαι προφήτης τοῦ κυρίου μονώτατος, καὶ οἱ προφῆται τοῦ Βάαλ τετρακόσιοι καὶ πεντήκοντα ἄνδρες, καὶ οἱ προφῆται τοῦ ἄλσους τετρακόσιοι· ²³ δότωσαν

λείμ.: the Hebrew plural of Baal, which originally meant only *owner* or master. Each Canaanite community gave this name to the god of its own special worship, sometimes with a distinctive addition, as Baal-zebub at Ekron (iv K. 1²).

**19. ὅρος τὸ Καρμήλιον:** Jos. *Ant.* VIII 13 § 5 τὸ Καρμήλιον ὅρος. — **τῆς αἰσχύνης:** substituted for 'of Baal' here and in 25, but in 22 we have Βάαλ, as in the Hebrew throughout. — τῶν ἀλσῶν: Hebrew, 'of the Ashêrah.' Jos. *Ant.* VIII 13 § 5 τοὺς τῶν ἀλσέων προφήτας: Vulg. prophetasque lucorum. It is generally agreed now that an asherah was a sacred pole or treetrunk set up beside the altar in Canaanite places of worship (Jdg. 6²⁵). It seems certain however from Second Kings 21⁷ (*cp.* First Kings 15¹³) that there was also a goddess named Asherah. 'The Asherah' occurs in Jdg.

6²⁵ : i K. 16³³ : ii K. 13⁶, 23⁶, ⁷, ¹⁶. The plural occurs in two forms — *Asheroth,* Jdg. 3⁷ ; *Asherim,* Ex. 34¹³ : i K. 14¹⁵ : ii K. 23¹⁴. — **ἐσθίοντας τράπεζαν :** the use of the accusative here is a Hebraism. *Cp.* Dan. Θ 1¹³ τῶν ἐσθόντων τὴν τράπεζαν τοῦ βασιλέως, where Oʼ has τοὺς ἐσθίοντας ἀπὸ τοῦ βασιλικοῦ δείπνου.

**21. προσήγαγεν :** intransitive, *drew nigh.* This use occurs in Xenophon, and probably originated in military language. *Cp.* v. 30. — χωλανεῖτε ἐπʼ ἀμφοτέραις ταῖς ἰγνύαις: *will ye be lame on both legs.* R.V. 'halt ye between two opinions.' Ἰγνύα occurs only here in the LXX.

**22. μονώτατος:** for the superlative *cp.* Jdg. 3²) : ii K. 13³², ³³, 17² : iii K. 8³⁹, 19¹⁰, ¹⁴, 22⁸¹ : iv K. 10²³, 17¹⁸ : i Mac. 10⁷⁰. — καὶ οἱ προφῆται τοῦ ἄλσους τετρακόσιοι : not in the Hebrew.

ἡμῖν δύο βόας, καὶ ἐκλεξάσθωσαν ἑαυτοῖς τὸν ἕνα, καὶ μελισάτωσαν καὶ ἐπιθέτωσαν ἐπὶ τῶν ξύλων καὶ πῦρ μὴ ἐπιθέ-
τωσαν· καὶ ἐγὼ ποιήσω τὸν βοῦν τὸν ἄλλον, καὶ πῦρ οὐ
μὴ ἐπιθῶ. ²⁴καὶ βοᾶτε ἐν ὀνόματι θεῶν ὑμῶν, καὶ ἐγὼ ἐπι-
καλέσομαι ἐν ὀνόματι Κυρίου τοῦ θεοῦ μοῦ· καὶ ἔσται ὁ
θεὸς ὃς ἐὰν ἐπακούσῃ ἐν πυρί, οὗτος θεός." καὶ ἀπεκρίθησαν πᾶς ὁ λαὸς καὶ εἶπον "Καλὸν τὸ ῥῆμα ὃ ἐλάλησας."
²⁵καὶ εἶπεν Ἠλειοὺ τοῖς προφήταις τῆς αἰσχύνης "Ἐκλέξασθε ἑαυτοῖς τὸν μόσχον τὸν ἕνα καὶ ποιήσατε πρῶτοι, ὅτι
πολλοὶ ὑμεῖς, καὶ ἐπικαλέσασθε ἐν ὀνόματι θεοῦ ὑμῶν,
καὶ πῦρ μὴ ἐπιθῆτε." ²⁶καὶ ἔλαβον τὸν μόσχον καὶ ἐποίησαν, καὶ ἐπεκαλοῦντο ἐν ὀνόματι τοῦ Βάαλ ἐκ πρωίθεν
ἕως μεσημβρίας καὶ εἶπον "Ἐπάκουσον ἡμῶν, ὁ Βάαλ,
ἐπάκουσον ἡμῶν·" καὶ οὐκ ἦν φωνὴ καὶ οὐκ ἦν ἀκρόασις·
καὶ διέτρεχον ἐπὶ τοῦ θυσιαστηρίου οὗ ἐποίησαν. ²⁷καὶ
ἐγένετο μεσημβρία καὶ ἐμυκτήρισεν αὐτοὺς Ἠλειοὺ ὁ
Θεσβείτης καὶ εἶπεν "Ἐπικαλεῖσθε ἐν φωνῇ μεγάλῃ, ὅτι
θεός ἐστιν, ὅτι ἀδολεσχία αὐτῷ ἐστιν, καὶ ἅμα μή ποτε
χρηματίζει αὐτός, ἢ μή ποτε καθεύδει αὐτός, καὶ ἐξανα-

---

**23.** μελισάτωσαν: *dismember*. A
sacrificial term. *Cp.* 33, Lev. 1⁶ μελιοῦσιν
αὐτὸ κατὰ μέλη. It occurs also in Jdg.
19²⁹, 20⁶: i K. 11⁷: Mic. 3³.— ποιήσω:
*will dress*, *i.e.* make ready for burning.
*Cp.* 25²⁶, ²⁹: Jdg. 6¹⁹. See Jdg. 13¹⁵ n.
**24.** ἐν πυρί: § 91.
**25.** ἑαυτοῖς: § 13.
**26.** ἐκ πρωίθεν: § 34.— ὁ Βάαλ:
nominative for vocative. A transcript
from the Hebrew, and at the same
time in accordance with popular usage
in Greek. § 50.
**27.** ἐμυκτήρισεν: a rare word outside the LXX, but familiar to us
through its use in Gal. 6⁷. *Cp.* iv K.

19²¹.— ὁ Θεσβείτης: not in the Hebrew. — ἀδολεσχία: this word is used
in classical Greek, not only for ' idle
chatter,' but also for ' subtle reason-
ing.' The latter meaning appears to
have originated out of the former in
connexion with the discourses of Socrates, and we have the key to the transition in *Crat.* 401 B, where Plato
ironically takes up the term ἀδολέσχης,
which had been flung at Socrates (Ar.
*Nub.* 1485). Hence ἀδολεσχία αὐτῷ
ἐστιν becomes possible as a translation
of the same Hebrew, which is rendered
by the Revisers ' he is musing.' — μή
ποτε: *haply*. Gen. 43¹² n. — χρηματί-

iii Kings XVIII 32

στήσεται." ²⁸καὶ ἐπεκαλοῦντο ἐν φωνῇ μεγάλῃ, καὶ κα-
τετέμνοντο ἐν μαχαίρᾳ καὶ σειρομάσταις ἕως ἐκχύσεως
αἵματος ἐπ᾽ αὐτούς, ²⁹καὶ ἐπροφήτευσαν ἕως οὗ παρῆλθεν
τὸ δειλινόν. καὶ ἐγένετο ὡς ὁ καιρὸς τοῦ ἀναβῆναι τὴν
θυσίαν, καὶ ἐλάλησεν Ἠλειοῦ πρὸς τοὺς προφήτας τῶν
προσοχθισμάτων λέγων " Μετάστητε ἀπὸ τοῦ νῦν, καὶ ἐγὼ
ποιήσω τὸ ὁλοκαύτωμά μου · " καὶ μετέστησαν καὶ ἀπῆλθον.
³⁰καὶ εἶπεν Ἠλειοῦ πρὸς τὸν λαόν " Προσαγάγετε πρὸς μέ · "
καὶ προσήγαγεν πᾶς ὁ λαὸς πρὸς αὐτόν. ³¹καὶ ἔλαβεν
Ἠλειοῦ δώδεκα λίθους κατ᾽ ἀριθμὸν φυλῶν Ἰσραήλ, ὡς
ἐλάλησεν Κύριος πρὸς αὐτὸν λέγων " Ἰσραὴλ ἔσται τὸ
ὄνομά σου." ³²καὶ ᾠκοδόμησεν τοὺς λίθους ἐν ὀνόματι
Κυρίου, καὶ ἰάσατο τὸ θυσιαστήριον τὸ κατεσκαμμένον,

ζει: R.V. 'he is gone aside'; cp. German Abtritt. After this the Hebrew
has 'or he is on a journey,' which
Josephus (Ant. VIII 13 § 5) also read
—μεγάλῃ βοῇ καλεῖν αὐτοὺς ἐκέλευε τοὺς
θεούς, ἢ γὰρ ἀποδημεῖν αὐτοὺς ἢ καθεύδειν.
**28.** σειρομάσταις : σιρομάστης or
σειρομάστης is literally a pit-searcher,
and then used for a kind of lance;
see L. & S. The word occurs also in
Nb. 25⁷ : Jdg. 5⁸ (A) : iv K. 11¹⁰ : Joel
3¹⁰. Josephus also uses it in this
context.
**29.** ἐπροφήτευσαν: § 19. — ἕως οὗ
παρῆλθεν τὸ δειλινόν: until the afternoon was gone by. These words seem
to correspond to those rendered in the
R.V. 'when midday was past.' But
there is some difference in the order of
the words here between the text of the
Seventy and our Hebrew. Elsewhere in
the LXX τὸ δειλινόν, when used of time,
is adverbial — Gen. 3⁸ : Ex. 29³⁹,⁴¹ :
Lvt. 6²⁰ : Susannah O¹⁷. In i Esd. 5⁴⁹
we have ὁλοκαυτώματα Κυρίῳ τὸ πρωινὸν

καὶ τὸ δειλινόν. — ὡς ὁ καιρὸς κτλ. : cp.
i Esd. 8⁶⁹ ἐκαθήμην περίλυπος ἕως τῆς
δειλινῆς θυσίας. — καὶ ἐλάλησεν . . .
ἀπῆλθον: the Greek here departs altogether from the Hebrew, as may be
seen by a comparison with the R.V. —
προσοχθισμάτων: offences, a substitution for 'Baal,' like τῆς αἰσχύνης in 19.
So in 11³³, 16³² καὶ ἔστησεν θυσιαστήριον
τῷ Βάαλ ἐν οἴκῳ τῶν προσοχθισμάτων
αὐτοῦ (R.V. 'in the house of Baal').
Cp. iv K. 23¹³ τῇ Ἀστάρτῃ προσοχθί-
σματι Σιδωνίων καὶ τῷ Χαμὼς προσοχθί-
σματι Μωὰβ καὶ τῷ Μολχὸλ βδελύγματι
υἱῶν Ἀμμών. — ὁλοκαύτωμα: very common in the LXX, in which it does duty
for five different Hebrew words.
**30.** Προσαγάγετε: v. 21 n.
**31.** Ἰσραήλ: Hebrew, 'of the sons
of Jacob.'
**32.** ἰάσατο: for this use of ἰάσατο
we may compare Nehemiah 4² (=
ii Esd. 14²) in the Oxford text of the
Vatican Ms. καὶ σήμερον ἰάσονται τοὺς
λίθους, where the R.V. has 'will they

iii Kings XVIII 33

καὶ ἐποίησεν θάλασσαν χωροῦσαν δύο μετρητὰς σπέρμα-
τος κυκλόθεν τοῦ θυσιαστηρίου. ³³καὶ ἐστοίβασεν τὰς
σχίδακας ἐπὶ τὸ θυσιαστήριον ὃ ἐποίησεν, καὶ ἐμέλισεν
τὸ ὁλοκαύτωμα καὶ ἐπέθηκεν τὰς σχίδακας, καὶ ἐστοίβασεν
ἐπὶ τὸ θυσιαστήριον. ³⁴καὶ εἶπεν "Λάβετέ μοι τέσσαρας
ὑδρίας ὕδατος, καὶ ἐπιχέετε ἐπὶ τὸ ὁλοκαύτωμα καὶ ἐπὶ
τὰς σχίδακας·" καὶ ἐποίησαν οὕτως. καὶ εἶπεν "Δευτερώ-
σατε·" καὶ ἐδευτέρωσαν. καὶ εἶπεν "Τρισσώσατε·" καὶ
ἐτρίσσευσαν. ³⁵καὶ διεπορεύετο τὸ ὕδωρ κύκλῳ τοῦ θυσιαστηρίου, καὶ τὴν θάλασσαν ἔπλησαν ὕδατος. ³⁶καὶ
ἀνεβόησεν Ἠλειοὺ εἰς τὸν οὐρανὸν καὶ εἶπεν "Κύριε ὁ θεὸς
Ἀβραὰμ καὶ Ἰσαὰκ καὶ Ἰσραήλ, ἐπάκουσόν μου, Κύριε,
ἐπάκουσόν μου σήμερον ἐν πυρί, καὶ γνώτωσαν πᾶς ὁ λαὸς
οὗτος ὅτι σὺ Κύριος ὁ θεὸς Ἰσραήλ, κἀγὼ δοῦλός σου καὶ
διὰ σὲ πεποίηκα τὰ ἔργα ταῦτα. ³⁷ἐπάκουσόν μου, Κύριε,

revive the stones?' The words relating
to the repair of the altar come in the
Hebrew at the end of verse 30.— θάλασσαν: cp. verses 35, 38. Θάλασσα in
these passages means 'trench.' They
are the only ones in which it is employed to translate the particular word
here used in the Hebrew. Josephus
(Ant. VIII 13 § 5) uses δεξαμενή in this
connexion.— δύο μετρητάς: this represents a dual form in the Hebrew, which
the Revisers render in the margin 'a
two-seah measure.'— κυκλόθεν: this
and κύκλῳ in 35 are renderings of the
same Hebrew original. § 97.

**33.** ἐστοίβασεν: he piled. Cp.
Lvt. 1⁷ ἐπιστοιβάσουσιν ξύλα ἐπὶ τὸ
πῦρ: also Lvt. 6¹²: Josh. 2⁶: Cant. 2⁵.
— σχίδακας: σχίδαξ = σχίζα, Latin
scindula, a piece of cleft wood, occurs
in the LXX only here and in verse 38.
— ἐπὶ τὸ θυσιαστήριον ὃ ἐποίησεν: not

in the Hebrew.— ἐμέλισεν: verse 23 n.

**34.** Δευτερώσατε: a word confined
to Biblical Greek, and perhaps coined
to translate the particular Hebrew
word here used. See Gen. 41³² n. —
Τρισσώσατε: probably another coin-
age to suit this particular passage.
— ἐτρίσσευσαν: A has ἐτρισσωσαν.
Τρισσεύειν occurs without variant in
i K. 20¹⁹, ²⁰ in the sense of 'doing a
thing a second time.' Δευτερεύειν in
the four passages in which it occurs in
the LXX means 'to be second,' e.g.
Esther 4⁸ Ἀμὰν ὁ δευτερεύων τῷ βασιλεῖ.

**35.** κύκλῳ: verse 32 n.— ἔπλησαν:
Hebrew, 'he filled.'

**36.** καὶ ἀνεβόησεν Ἠλειοὺ εἰς τὸν
οὐρανόν: different from the Hebrew.
Cp. R.V.— ἐπάκουσόν μου . . . ἐν πυρί:
not in the Hebrew.— γνώτωσαν πᾶς ὁ
λαὸς οὗτος: R.V. 'let it be known this
day.'

iii Kings XVIII 44

ἐπάκουσόν μου, καὶ γνώτω ὁ λαὸς οὗτος ὅτι σὺ Κύριος ὁ θεός, καὶ σὺ ἔστρεψας τὴν καρδίαν τοῦ λαοῦ τούτου ὀπίσω." ³⁸ καὶ ἔπεσεν πῦρ παρὰ Κυρίου ἐκ τοῦ οὐρανοῦ, καὶ κατέφαγεν τὰ ὁλοκαυτώματα καὶ τὰς σχίδακας καὶ τὸ ὕδωρ τὸ ἐν τῇ θαλάσσῃ, καὶ τοὺς λίθους καὶ τὸν χοῦν ἐξέλιξεν τὸ πῦρ. ³⁹ καὶ ἔπεσεν πᾶς ὁ λαὸς ἐπὶ πρόσωπον αὐτῶν καὶ εἶπον " Ἀληθῶς Κύριος ὁ θεός· αὐτὸς ὁ θεός·" ⁴⁰ καὶ εἶπεν Ἠλειοὺ πρὸς τὸν λαόν " Συλλάβετε τοὺς προφήτας τοῦ Βάαλ, μηθεὶς σωθήτω ἐξ αὐτῶν·" καὶ συνέλαβον αὐτούς, καὶ κατάγει αὐτοὺς Ἠλειοὺ εἰς τὸν χειμάρρουν Κεισὼν καὶ ἔσφαξεν αὐτοὺς ἐκεῖ. ⁴¹ Καὶ εἶπεν Ἠλειοὺ τῷ Ἀχαάβ " Ἀνάβηθι καὶ φάγε καὶ πίε, ὅτι φωνὴ τῶν ποδῶν τοῦ ὑετοῦ." ⁴² καὶ ἀνέβη Ἀχαὰβ τοῦ φαγεῖν καὶ πιεῖν· καὶ Ἠλειοὺ ἀνέβη ἐπὶ τὸν Κάρμηλον, καὶ ἔκυψεν ἐπὶ τὴν γῆν καὶ ἔθηκεν τὸ πρόσωπον ἑαυτοῦ ἀνὰ μέσον τῶν γονάτων ἑαυτοῦ, ⁴³ καὶ εἶπεν τῷ παιδαρίῳ αὐτοῦ " Ἀνάβηθι καὶ ἐπίβλεψον ὁδὸν τῆς θαλάσσης." καὶ ἐπέβλεψεν τὸ παιδάριον καὶ εἶπεν " Οὐκ ἔστιν οὐθέν·" καὶ εἶπεν Ἠλειού " Καὶ σὺ ἐπίστρεψον ἑπτάκι, καὶ ἀπόστρεψον ἑπτάκι." ⁴⁴ καὶ ἀπέστρεψεν τὸ παιδάριον ἑπτάκι· καὶ ἐγένετο ἐν τῷ ἑβδόμῳ, καὶ ἰδοὺ νεφέλη μικρὰ ὡς ἴχνος ἀνδρὸς ἀνάγουσα ὕδωρ.

---

**37.** γνώτω: in 36 γνώτωσαν. The difference is not due to the Hebrew, which has the plural here.

**38.** καὶ τὸ ὕδωρ τὸ ἐν τῇ θαλάσσῃ: in the Hebrew this comes more naturally at the end of the verse. — χοῦν: dust, as generally in the LXX. Cp. Mk. 6¹¹ and see Ex. 8¹⁶ n. — ἐξέλιξεν: = ἐξέλειξεν. Nb. 22⁴ n.

**41.** τῶν ποδῶν: an unexpectedly poetical turn. Hebrew, 'of abundance.'

**43.** ὁδὸν τῆς θαλάσσης: towards the sea, a Hebraism. Cp. Dt. 1¹⁹ ὁδὸν ὄρους τοῦ Ἀμορραίου: Mt. 4¹⁵ ὁδὸν θαλάσσης. — ἐπίστρεψον ... ἀπόστρεψον: R.V. 'Go again seven times.' — ἑπτάκι: A has ἑπτάκις here and in verse 44.

**44.** ἴχνος: used in the LXX, not only for the sole of the foot, as in Josh. 1³ πᾶς ὁ τόπος ἐφ' ὃν ἂν ἐπιβῆτε τῷ ἴχνει τῶν ποδῶν ὑμῶν, but also for the palm of the hand. i K. 5⁴: iv K. 9³⁵ τὰ ἴχνη τῶν χειρῶν. Jos. Ant. VIII 13 § 16 οὐ πλέον ἴχνους ἀνθρωπίνου. — ἀνάγουσα ὕδωρ: not in the Hebrew.

καὶ εἶπεν "'Ανάβηθι καὶ εἰπὸν 'Αχαάβ 'Ζεῦξον τὸ ἅρμα
σου καὶ κατάβηθι, μὴ καταλάβῃ σε ὁ ὑετός.'" ⁴⁵καὶ ἐγένετο ἕως ὧδε καὶ ὧδε, καὶ ὁ οὐρανὸς συνεσκότασεν νεφέ-
λαις καὶ πνεύματι, καὶ ἐγένετο ὁ ὑετὸς μέγας· καὶ ἔκλαεν
καὶ ἐπορεύετο 'Αχαὰβ εἰς 'Ισραήλ. ⁴⁶καὶ χεὶρ Κυρίου
ἐπὶ τὸν 'Ηλειού· καὶ συνέσφιγξεν τὴν ὀσφὺν αὐτοῦ, καὶ
ἔτρεχεν ἔμπροσθεν 'Αχαὰβ εἰς 'Ισραήλ.

¹Καὶ ἀνήγγειλεν 'Αχαὰβ τῇ 'Ιεζάβελ γυναικὶ αὐτοῦ πάντα
ἃ ἐποίησεν 'Ηλειοὺ καὶ ὡς ἀπέκτεινεν τοὺς προφήτας ἐν
ῥομφαίᾳ. ²καὶ ἀπέστειλεν 'Ιεζάβελ πρὸς 'Ηλειοὺ καὶ εἶπεν
"Εἰ σὺ εἶ 'Ηλειοὺ καὶ ἐγὼ 'Ιεζάβελ, τάδε ποιήσαι μοι ὁ θεὸς
καὶ τάδε προσθείη, ὅτι ταύτην τὴν ὥραν αὔριον θήσομαι
τὴν ψυχήν σου καθὼς ψυχὴν ἑνὸς ἐξ αὐτῶν." ³καὶ ἐφοβήθη 'Ηλειού, καὶ ἀνέστη καὶ ἀπῆλθεν κατὰ τὴν ψυχὴν
ἑαυτοῦ, καὶ ἔρχεται εἰς Βηρσάβεε γῆν 'Ιούδα, καὶ ἀφῆκεν
τὸ παιδάριον αὐτοῦ ἐκεῖ. ⁴καὶ αὐτὸς ἐπορεύθη ἐν τῇ
ἐρήμῳ ὁδὸν ἡμέρας, καὶ ἦλθεν καὶ ἐκάθισεν ὑποκάτω
'Ραθμέν· καὶ ᾐτήσατο τὴν ψυχὴν αὐτοῦ ἀποθανεῖν καὶ

**45. ἕως ὧδε καὶ ὧδε**: a Hebraism, literally *until thus and thus*. Here the context gives the force of *meanwhile*. — **ἔκλαεν**: Hebrew, 'rode.' How ἔκλαεν comes here is not plain, and the usual LXX form is ἔκλαιεν, which A has. — **'Ισραήλ**: a mistake for 'Jezreel.' So also in the next verse and in chapter 20. Jos. *Ant.* VIII 13 § 6 καὶ ὁ μὲν εἰς 'Ιεσράηλαν πόλιν παραγίνεται.

**46. συνέσφιγξεν**: this compound, which is not to be found in L. & S., occurs also in Ex. 36²⁹ : Lvt. 8⁷ : Dt. 15⁷. — **εἰς 'Ισραήλ**: a distance of about sixteen miles.

**1. γυναικὶ αὐτοῦ**: not in the Hebrew.

**2. Εἰ σὺ . . . 'Ιεζάβελ**: not in the Hebrew. — **τάδε . . . καὶ τάδε προσθείη**: a Hebraism. *Cp.* Ruth 1¹⁷ : i K. 14⁴⁴, 20¹³, 25²² : ii K. 3⁹, ³⁵, 19¹³ : iii K. 2²³, 21¹⁰ : iv K. 6³¹. — **ὁ θεός**: the verb being plural, the R.V. has here 'the gods.' — **ὅτι**: (*know*) *that*, etc. § 107.

**3. κατὰ τὴν ψυχὴν ἑαυτοῦ**: R.V. 'for his life.' A Hebraism. — **γῆν 'Ιούδα**: in apposition to Βηρσάβεε, but the genitive would be more appropriate. The specification of Beer-Sheba as belonging to Judah has been thought to stamp the story of Elijah as emanating from the Northern Kingdom. If so, it must have been written before the capture of Samaria in B.C. 722.

**4. 'Ραθμέν**: here the translator has

iii Kings XIX 10

εἶπεν " Ἰκανούσθω νῦν, λάβε δὴ τὴν ψυχήν μου ἀπ᾽ ἐμοῦ, Κύριε, ὅτι οὐ κρείσσων ἐγώ εἰμι ὑπὲρ τοὺς πατέρας μου." ⁵καὶ ἐκοιμήθη καὶ ὕπνωσεν ἐκεῖ ὑπὸ φυτόν· καὶ ἰδού τις ἥψατο αὐτοῦ καὶ εἶπεν αὐτῷ " Ἀνάστηθι καὶ φάγε." ⁶καὶ ἐπέβλεψεν Ἠλειού, καὶ ἰδοὺ πρὸς κεφαλῆς αὐτοῦ ἐνκρυφίας ὀλυρείτης καὶ καψάκης ὕδατος· καὶ ἀνέστη καὶ ἔφαγεν καὶ ἔπιεν, καὶ ἐπιστρέψας ἐκοιμήθη. ⁷καὶ ἐπέστρεψεν ὁ ἄγγελος Κυρίου ἐκ δευτέρου, καὶ ἥψατο αὐτοῦ καὶ εἶπεν αὐτῷ " Ἀνάστα, φάγε· ὅτι πολλὴ ἀπὸ σοῦ ἡ ὁδός." ⁸καὶ ἀνέστη καὶ ἔφαγεν καὶ ἔπιεν· καὶ ἐπορεύθη ἐν τῇ ἰσχύι τῆς βρώσεως ἐκείνης τεσσεράκοντα ἡμέρας καὶ τεσσεράκοντα νύκτας ἕως ὄρους Χωρήβ. ⁹Καὶ εἰσῆλθεν ἐκεῖ εἰς τὸ σπήλαιον καὶ κατέλυσεν ἐκεῖ· καὶ ἰδοὺ ῥῆμα Κυρίου πρὸς αὐτὸν καὶ εἶπεν " Τί σὺ ἐνταῦθα, Ἠλειού; " ¹⁰καὶ εἶπεν Ἠλειού " Ζηλῶν ἐζήλωκα τῷ κυρίῳ Παντοκράτορι, ὅτι

found himself at a loss, and left the word before him untranslated, which gives it the appearance of being a proper name. There is something wrong, as the consonants do not correspond with the Hebrew. The R.V. gives 'juniper tree' with a marginal alternative 'broom.' — τὴν ψυχὴν αὐτοῦ: R.V. 'for himself.' A Hebraism. — Ἰκανούσθω: cp. Nb. 16⁷ : Dt. 1⁶, 2³, 3²⁶ : iii K. 12²⁸, 21¹¹ : i Chr. 21¹⁵ : Ezra 44⁶, 45⁹. — κρείσσων . . . ὑπέρ: § 94.

5. φυτόν: the Hebrew here is the same as that which was transliterated 'Ραθμὲν, so that the translator is aware that it means a plant of some kind. Josephus (Ant. VIII 13 § 7) has πρός τινι δένδρῳ. — τίς: Hebrew, 'an angel.'

6. Ἠλειού: not in the Hebrew. — ἐνκρυφίας : Ex. 12³⁹ n. — ὀλυρείτης : made of rye. Gen. 40¹⁶ n. For ἐνκρυφίας ὀλυρείτης the R.V. has 'a cake

baken on the coals.' — καψάκης: 17¹² n.

7. Ἀνάστα: § 32.

8. ὄρους Χωρήβ: Hebrew, ' Horeb, the mount of God.' Jos. Ant. VIII 13 § 7 εἰς τὸ Σιναῖον καλούμενον ὄρος. On Horeb see Ex. 3¹, 17⁶, 33⁶. The Jahvist is supposed to represent Sinai as the sacred mountain and the Elohist Horeb. The length of time assigned for the journey indicates geographical ignorance on the part of the writer.

9. τὸ σπήλαιον: so also in the Hebrew, though the English has here ' a cave.' The reference is evidently to some place known in the writer's time, haply the spot which had been identified with the ὀπὴ τῆς πέτρας of Ex. 33²². Josephus (Ant. VIII 13 § 7) has σπήλαιόν τι κοῖλον.

10. τῷ κυρίῳ Παντοκράτορι: for Jehovah the God of hosts. The word which is here rendered παντοκράτωρ

ἐνκατέλιπόν σε οἱ υἱοὶ Ἰσραήλ· τὰ θυσιαστήριά σου κατέσκαψαν καὶ τοὺς προφήτας σου ἀπέκτειναν ἐν ῥομφαίᾳ, καὶ ὑπολέλειμμαι ἐγὼ μονώτατος, καὶ ζητοῦσί μου τὴν ψυχὴν λαβεῖν αὐτήν." ¹¹καὶ εἶπεν " Ἐξελεύσῃ αὔριον καὶ στήσῃ ἐνώπιον Κυρίου ἐν τῷ ὄρει· ἰδοὺ παρελεύσεται Κύριος." καὶ πνεῦμα μέγα κραταιὸν διαλῦον ὄρη καὶ συντρῖβον πέτρας ἐνώπιον Κυρίου, ἐν τῷ πνεύματι Κυρίου· καὶ μετὰ τὸ πνεῦμα συνσεισμός, οὐκ ἐν τῷ συνσεισμῷ Κύριος· ¹²καὶ μετὰ τὸν συνσεισμὸν πῦρ, οὐκ ἐν τῷ πυρὶ Κύριος· καὶ μετὰ τὸ πῦρ φωνὴ αὔρας λεπτῆς. ¹³καὶ ἐγένετο ὡς ἤκουσεν Ἡλειού, καὶ ἐπεκάλυψεν τὸ πρόσωπον αὐτοῦ ἐν τῇ μηλωτῇ ἑαυτοῦ, καὶ ἐξῆλθεν καὶ ἔστη ὑπὸ σπήλαιον· καὶ ἰδοὺ πρὸς αὐτὸν φωνὴ καὶ εἶπεν " Τί σὺ ἐνταῦθα, Ἡλειού; " ¹⁴καὶ εἶπεν Ἡλειού " Ζηλῶν ἐζήλωκα τῷ κυρίῳ Παντοκράτορι, ὅτι ἐγκατέλιπόν σε οἱ υἱοὶ Ἰσραήλ, τὴν διαθήκην σου καὶ τὰ θυσιαστήριά σου καθεῖλαν καὶ τοὺς προφήτας σου ἀπέκτειναν ἐν ῥομφαίᾳ, καὶ ὑπολέλιμμαι ἐγὼ μονώτατος, καὶ ζητοῦσι τὴν ψυχήν μου λαβεῖν αὐτήν."· ¹⁵καὶ εἶπεν Κύριος πρὸς αὐτόν " Πορεύου, ἀνάστρεφε εἰς τὴν ὁδόν σου,

---

was in 18¹⁵ translated by τῶν δυνάμεων. παντοκράτωρ occurs first in the LXX in ii K. 5¹⁰, after which it becomes very common.—σέ: Hebrew, 'thy covenant.'

**11. αὔριον**: not in the Hebrew. — **ἐν τῷ πνεύματι Κυρίου**: the Oxford text here gives the reading required — οὐκ ἐν τῷ πνεύματι Κύριος. — **συνσεισμός**: there are ten occurrences of this word in the LXX, of which three are before us. Zech. 14⁵ is the only passage in which it corresponds to the same Hebrew original as here.

**12. φωνὴ αὔρας λεπτῆς**: R.V. margin 'a sound of gentle stillness.'

**13. μηλωτῇ**: *sheepskin*, a kind of

cloak. The word occurs in the LXX five times (iii K. 19¹³, ¹⁹: iv K. 2⁸, ¹³, ¹⁴), always as a transliteration of the same word, and always in connexion with Elijah. Hence we may infer that its use in Hb. 11³⁷ contains a tacit reference to him. Cp. Clem. i Cor. 17¹ Μιμηταὶ γενώμεθα κἀκείνων οἵτινες ἐν δέρμασιν αἰγείοις καὶ μηλωταῖς περιεπάτησαν. In Zech. 13⁴ the same Hebrew word is translated δέρρις τριχίνη.

**14. σέ**: this is not wanted here, as ἐγκατέλιπον ought to govern τὴν διαθήκην σου. In verse 10 it was substituted for it. — ὑπολέλιμμαι: = ὑπολέλειμμαι in verse 10. § 37.

iii Kings XIX 21

καὶ ἥξεις εἰς τὴν ὁδὸν ἐρήμου Δαμασκοῦ· καὶ ἥξεις καὶ
χρίσεις τὸν Ἀζαὴλ εἰς βασιλέα τῆς Συρίας· ¹⁶καὶ τὸν
υἱὸν Εἰοὺ υἱοῦ Ναμεσθεὶ χρίσεις εἰς βασιλέα ἐπὶ Ἰσραήλ·
καὶ τὸν Ἐλεισαῖε υἱὸν Σαφὰθ χρίσεις ἐξ Ἐβαλμαουλὰ
προφήτην ἀντὶ σοῦ. ¹⁷καὶ ἔσται τὸν σωζόμενον ἐκ
ῥομφαίας Ἀζαὴλ θανατώσει Εἰού, καὶ τὸν σωζόμενον
ἐκ ῥομφαίας Εἰοὺ θανατώσει Ἐλεισαῖε. ¹⁸καὶ καταλείψεις ἐν Ἰσραὴλ ἑπτὰ χιλιάδας ἀνδρῶν, πάντα γόνατα ἃ
οὐκ ὤκλασάν γόνυ τῷ Βάαλ, καὶ πᾶν στόμα ὃ οὐ προσεκύνησεν αὐτῷ." ¹⁹Καὶ ἀπῆλθεν ἐκεῖθεν, καὶ εὑρίσκει
τὸν Ἐλεισαῖε υἱὸν Σαφάτ, καὶ αὐτὸς ἠροτρία ἐν βουσίν·
δώδεκα ζεύγη ἐνώπιον αὐτοῦ, καὶ αὐτὸς ἐν τοῖς δώδεκα·
ἐπῆλθεν ἐπ' αὐτόν, καὶ ἐπέρριψε τὴν μηλωτὴν αὐτοῦ ἐπ'
αὐτόν. ²⁰καὶ κατέλιπεν Ἐλεισαῖε τὰς βόας, καὶ κατέδρα-
μεν ὀπίσω Ἠλειοὺ καὶ εἶπεν "Καταφιλήσω τὸν πατέρα
μου καὶ ἀκολουθήσω ὀπίσω σου·" καὶ εἶπεν Ἠλειού "Ἀνάστρεφε, ὅτι πεποίηκά σοι." ²¹καὶ ἀνέστρεψεν ἐξόπισθεν

15. **καὶ ἥξεις εἰς τὴν ὁδόν**: not in
the Hebrew.
16. **τὸν υἱὸν Εἰοὺ υἱοῦ Ναμεσθεί**:
Hebrew, 'Jehu the son of Nimshi.'
A comparison with iv K. 9² υἱὸν Ἰωσαφὰθ Εἰοῦ υἱοῦ Ναμεσσεί, *Jehu the son of
Jehoshaphat the son of Nimshi*, makes
it seem likely that Ἰωσαφάθ has
dropped out here before Jehu.
17. **καὶ τὸν σωζόμενον . . . Ἐλεισαῖε**: Josephus (*Ant.* VIII 13 § 7) has
suppressed this, or else did not find it
in his copy.
18. **καταλείψεις**: Hebrew, 'I will
leave.' — **ὤκλασαν γόνυ**: the repetition
of γόνυ is not due to the Hebrew, but
apparently to a feeling that the first
aorist must be transitive. In 8⁵⁴ the
perfect participle ὀκλακώς is used in-

transitively. The word is used only
in these two passages of the LXX,
but is quite classical.
19. **Ἐλεισαῖε**: Hebrew *Elisha'* =
'God is salvation.' — **ἠροτρία**: Jdg.
14¹⁸ n. — **δώδεκα ζεύγη κτλ.**: Josephus
(*Ant.* VIII 13 § 7) explains that there
were other persons ploughing with
Elisha. Twelve oxen yoked to one
plough have been seen within living
memory on Beachy Head, but δώδεκα
ζεύγη would be double this number.
20. **καταφιλήσω . . . ἀκολουθήσω**:
the former is aorist subjunctive, the
latter future indicative. — **ὅτι πεποίηκά
σοι**: R.V. 'for what have I done to
thee?' The Greek translator has neglected the interrogative, and so left the
words without a meaning, unless we

αὐτοῦ, καὶ ἔλαβεν τὰ ζεύγη τῶν βοῶν καὶ ἔθυσεν καὶ ἤψησεν αὐτὰ ἐν τοῖς σκεύεσι τῶν βοῶν, καὶ ἔδωκεν τῷ λαῷ καὶ ἔφαγον· καὶ ἀνέστη καὶ ἐπορεύθη ὀπίσω Ἠλειού, καὶ ἐλειτούργει αὐτῷ.

¹Καὶ ἀμπελὼν εἷς ἦν τῷ Ναβουθαὶ τῷ Ἰσραηλείτῃ παρὰ τῷ ἅλῳ Ἀχαὰβ βασιλέως Σαμαρείας. ²καὶ ἐλάλησεν Ἀχαὰβ πρὸς Ναβουθαὶ λέγων " Δός μοι τὸν ἀμπελῶνά σου καὶ ἔσται μοι εἰς κῆπον λαχάνων, ὅτι ἐγγίων οὗτος τῷ οἴκῳ μου, καὶ δώσω σοι ἀμπελῶνα ἄλλον ἀγαθὸν ὑπὲρ αὐτόν· εἰ δὲ ἀρέσκει ἐνώπιόν σου, δώσω σοι ἀργύριον ἄλλαγμα ἀμπελῶνός σου τούτου, καὶ ἔσται μοι εἰς κῆπον λαχάνων." ³καὶ εἶπεν Ναβουθαὶ πρὸς Ἀχαάβ " Μὴ γένοιτό μοι παρὰ θεοῦ μου δοῦναι κληρονομίαν πατέρων μου σοί." ⁴καὶ ἐγένετο τὸ πνεῦμα Ἀχαὰβ τεταραγμένον, καὶ ἐκοιμήθη ἐπὶ τῆς κλίνης αὐτοῦ καὶ συνεκάλυψεν τὸ πρόσωπον αὐτοῦ, καὶ οὐκ ἔφαγεν ἄρτον. ⁵καὶ εἰσῆλθεν Ἰεζάβελ ἡ γυνὴ αὐτοῦ πρὸς αὐτὸν καὶ ἐλάλησεν πρὸς αὐτόν " Τί τὸ πνεῦμά σου τεταραγμένον, καὶ οὐκ εἶ σὺ ἐσθίων ἄρτον; " ⁶καὶ εἶπεν πρὸς αὐτήν "'Ότι ἐλάλησα πρὸς Ναβουθαὶ τὸν Ἰσραηλείτην λέγων ' Δός μοι τὸν ἀμπελῶνά σου ἀργυρίου· εἰ δὲ βούλει, δώσω σοι ἀμπελῶνα ἄλλον ἀντ' αὐτοῦ·' καὶ εἶπεν ' Οὐ δώσω σοι κληρονομίαν πατέρων μου.'" ⁷καὶ εἶπεν

read ὅτι, and render *for anything I have done to thee.*

1. καὶ ἀμπελών: the connecting formula 'And it came to pass after these things' is absent from the LXX, which brings in the chapter about Ben-hadad after and not before this. — εἰς : § 2. — Ἰσραηλείτη : *Jezreelite.* 18⁴⁵ n. — τῷ ἅλῳ : Hebrew, 'the palace.' On ἅλως see § 8.

2. ἔσται μοι εἰς : § 90. — ἐγγίων :

§ 12. — ἀγαθὸν ὑπὲρ αὐτόν : § 94. — καὶ . . . λαχάνων : not in the Hebrew.

4. καὶ ἐγένετο κτλ. : the Greek in this verse is much shorter than the Hebrew. *Cp.* R.V. — συνεκάλυψεν : R.V. 'turned away.'

5. οὐκ εἶ σὺ ἐσθίων : analytical form of the present, as in English, *art thou not eating bread?* § 72.

6. κληρονομίαν πατέρων μου : Hebrew, 'my vineyard.'

πρὸς αὐτὸν Ἰεζάβελ ἡ γυνὴ αὐτοῦ "Σὺ νῦν οὕτως ποιεῖς βασιλέα ἐπὶ Ἰσραήλ; ἀνάστηθι, φάγε ἄρτον καὶ σαυτοῦ γενοῦ· ἐγὼ δώσω σοι τὸν ἀμπελῶνα Ναβουθαὶ τοῦ Ἰσραηλείτου." ⁸καὶ ἔγραψεν βιβλίον ἐπὶ τῷ ὀνόματι Ἀχαὰβ καὶ ἐσφραγίσατο τῇ σφραγῖδι αὐτοῦ, καὶ ἀπέστειλεν τὸ βιβλίον πρὸς τοὺς πρεσβυτέρους καὶ τοὺς ἐλευθέρους τοὺς κατοικοῦντας μετὰ Ναβουθαί. ⁹καὶ ἐγέγραπτο ἐν τοῖς βιβλίοις λέγων "Νηστεύσατε νηστείαν, καὶ καθίσατε τὸν Ναβουθαὶ ἐν ἀρχῇ τοῦ λαοῦ· ¹⁰καὶ ἐνκαθίσατε δύο ἄνδρας, υἱοὺς παρανόμων." ¹³καὶ ἐκάθισαν ἐξ ἐναντίας αὐτοῦ, καὶ κατεμαρτύρησαν αὐτοῦ λέγοντες "Ηὐλόγηκας θεὸν καὶ βασιλέα·" καὶ ἐξήγαγον αὐτὸν ἔξω τῆς πόλεως καὶ ἐλιθοβόλησαν αὐτὸν λίθοις, καὶ ἀπέθανεν. ¹⁴καὶ ἀπέστειλαν πρὸς Ἰεζάβελ λέγοντες "Λελιθοβόληται Ναβουθαὶ καὶ τέθνηκεν." ¹⁵καὶ ἐγένετο ὡς ἤκουσεν Ἰεζάβελ, καὶ εἶπεν πρὸς Ἀχαάβ "Ἀνάστα, κληρονόμει τὸν ἀμπελῶνα Ναβουθαὶ τοῦ Ἰσραηλείτου ὃς οὐκ ἔδωκέν σοι ἀργυρίου, ὅτι οὐκ ἔστιν Ναβουθαὶ

---

**7. ποιεῖς βασιλέα ἐπί**: play the king over. R.V. 'govern the kingdom of.' The Greek is a verbal translation of the Hebrew. — σαυτοῦ γενοῦ: regain thy self-possession. R.V. 'let thine heart be merry.'

**8. τοὺς ἐλευθέρους**: R.V. 'the nobles.'

**9. λέγων**: § 112. — ἐν ἀρχῇ τοῦ λαοῦ: Hebrew, 'at the head of the people.'

**10. υἱοὺς παρανόμων**: this is a LXX equivalent (cp. Jdg. 19²², 20¹³: ii Chr. 13⁷) for the phrase 'sons of Belial,' of which the commonly accepted explanation is 'sons of unprofitableness.' The personification of Belial, as in ii Cor. 6¹⁵, is later than the Old Testament. Another LXX

rendering of 'sons of Belial' is υἱοὶ λοιμοί, as in i K. 2¹². Josephus (Ant. VIII 13 § 8) has here τρεῖς τολμηρούς τινας.

**13. καὶ ἐκάθισαν**: the greater part of verse 10 and the whole of 11 and 12 are omitted in the LXX. This is perhaps a deliberate piece of compression on the part of the Greek translator. — ἐκάθισαν: intransitive. — Ηὐλόγηκας: the Hebrew word for this is neutral in sense, meaning originally to say good-by to. It is used both of blessing and cursing. Here the translator has chosen the wrong sense, as in Job 1¹¹. Jos. Ant. VIII 13 § 7 ὡς τὸν θεόν τε εἴη βλασφημήσας καὶ τὸν βασιλέα.

**15. ὅς**: here the translator has chosen the wrong case for the inde-

ζῶν, ὅτι τέθνηκεν." ¹⁶καὶ ἐγένετο ὡς ἤκουσεν ᾽Αχαὰβ ὅτι τέθνηκεν Ναβουθαὶ ὁ ᾽Ισραηλείτης, καὶ διέρρηξεν τὰ ἱμάτια ἑαυτοῦ καὶ περιεβάλετο σάκκον· καὶ ἐγένετο μετὰ ταῦτα καὶ ἀνέστη καὶ κατέβη ᾽Αχαὰβ εἰς τὸν ἀμπελῶνα Ναβουθαὶ τοῦ ᾽Ισραηλείτου κληρονομῆσαι αὐτόν. ¹⁷Καὶ εἶπεν Κύριος πρὸς ᾽Ηλειοὺ τὸν Θεσβείτην λέγων ¹⁸"᾽Ανάστηθι καὶ κατάβηθι εἰς ἀπαντὴν ᾽Αχαὰβ βασιλέως ᾽Ισραὴλ τοῦ ἐν Σαμαρείᾳ, ὅτι οὗτος ἐν ἀμπελῶνι Ναβουθαί, ὅτι καταβέβηκεν ἐκεῖ κληρονομῆσαι αὐτόν. ¹⁹καὶ λαλήσεις πρὸς αὐτὸν λέγων ᾽ Τάδε λέγει Κύριος " ῾Ως σὺ ἐφόνευσας καὶ ἐκληρονόμησας," διὰ τοῦτο τάδε λέγει Κύριος " ᾽Εν παντὶ τόπῳ ᾧ ἔλιξαν αἱ ὕες καὶ οἱ κύνες τὸ αἷμα Ναβουθαί, ἐκεῖ λίξουσιν οἱ κύνες τὸ αἷμά σου, καὶ αἱ πόρναι λούσονται ἐν τῷ αἵματί σου." ᾽ " ²⁰καὶ εἶπεν ᾽Αχαὰβ πρὸς ᾽Ηλειού " Εἰ εὕρηκάς με, ὁ ἐχθρός μου; " καὶ εἶπεν " Εὕρηκα, διότι μάτην πέπρασαι ποιῆσαι τὸ πονηρὸν ἐνώπιον Κυρίου, παροργίσαι αὐτόν. ²¹ἰδοὺ ἐγὼ ἐπάγω ἐπὶ σὲ κακά, καὶ

clinable Hebrew relative. The sense requires ὅν.

**16. καὶ ἐγένετο . . . σάκκον**: these words, which represent Ahab as feeling a temporary repentance, are not to be found in the Hebrew. Josephus (*Ant.* VIII 13 § 8) represents Ahab as bounding from his bed with joy.

**18. ἀπαντήν**: ἀπαντή = ἀπάντησις seems to be confined to the LXX, where it occurs frequently, but hardly ever without the other form as a variant. *Cp.* 18¹⁶ συναντήν.

**19. ῾Ως σὺ . . . διὰ τοῦτο**: the Greek here diverges slightly from the Hebrew. *Cp.* R.V. — ᾽Εν παντὶ τόπῳ: the παντὶ here has nothing to correspond to it in the Hebrew, nor is it easy to assign a meaning to it. — ᾧ:

not Greek at all, but the result of literal translation. — καὶ οἱ κύνες: not in the Hebrew. — καὶ αἱ πόρναι . . . αἵματί σου: not in the Hebrew at this point. Yet in 22³⁸, where the fulfilment of the prophecy is recorded, there are words corresponding to these, which have been enclosed in brackets by the Revisers. Their presence there seems to show that the Hebrew, and not the Greek, is at fault in this passage.

**20. Εἰ εὕρηκάς με**: § 100. — ὁ ἐχθρός μου: nominative for vocative. § 50. — μάτην: not in the Hebrew, but in keeping with its spirit. Μάτην has here the implication of folly and wickedness which so often attaches itself to μάταιος. — παροργίσαι αὐτόν: not in the Hebrew.

iii Kings XX 26

ἐκκαύσω ὀπίσω σου καὶ ἐξολεθρεύσω τοῦ Ἀχαὰβ οὐροῦντα πρὸς τοῖχον καὶ συνεχόμενον καὶ ἐνκαταλελειμμένον ἐν Ἰσραήλ· ²²καὶ δώσω τὸν οἶκόν σου ὡς τὸν οἶκον Ἱεροβοὰμ υἱοῦ Ναβὰθ καὶ ὡς τὸν οἶκον Βαασὰ υἱοῦ Ἀχειά, περὶ τῶν παροργισμάτων ὧν παρώργισας καὶ ἐξήμαρτες τὸν Ἰσραήλ." ²³καὶ τῇ Ἰεζάβελ ἐλάλησεν Κύριος λέγων "Οἱ κύνες καταφάγονται αὐτὴν ἐν τῷ προτειχίσματι τοῦ Ἰσραήλ. ²⁴τὸν τεθνηκότα τοῦ Ἀχαὰβ ἐν τῇ πόλει φάγονται οἱ κύνες, καὶ τὸν τεθνηκότα αὐτοῦ ἐν τῷ πεδίῳ φάγονται· τὰ πετεινὰ τοῦ οὐρανοῦ." ²⁵πλὴν ματαίως Ἀχαάβ, ὡς ἐπράθη ποιῆσαι τὸ πονηρὸν ἐνώπιον Κυρίου, ὡς μετέθηκεν αὐτὸν Ἰεζάβελ ἡ γυνὴ αὐτοῦ· ²⁶καὶ ἐβδελύχθη σφόδρα

21. ἐκκαύσω ὀπίσω σου: R.V. 'will utterly sweep thee away.' The Greek translator is here more faithful to his original than the English. — οὐροῦντα πρὸς τοῖχον: every male. A Hebraism. The omission of the article is due to following the Hebrew. Cp. i K. 25²², ³⁴: iii K. 14¹⁰: iv K. 9⁸. — καὶ συνεχόμενον κτλ. : R.V. 'him that is shut up and him that is left at large.' It is in the Hebrew manner to offer two categories under one or other of which everything is supposed to be included. So in Dt. 29¹⁹ 'the moist with the dry' is intended to be exhaustive. The same Hebrew phrase as here occurs at the end of Dt. 32³⁶, and in iv K. 14²⁶, in both which passages it is obscured by the Greek translation. In iii K. 14¹⁰ we have ἐχόμενον καὶ ἐγκαταλελιμμένον : in iv K. 9⁸ the rendering is exactly as here. Ἐνκαταλελειμμένον, however, does not give the required sense of 'left at large.'

22. δώσω: R.V. 'I will make.' A

Hebraism. — Ἱεροβοάμ : Hebrew Yarŏb'am. The form of the name in our Bible is due to the Vulgate through the LXX. — ὧν παρώργισας : ὧν must be taken as standing for οἷς, but attracted into agreement with its antecedent. The R.V. has 'provoked me,' but in the omission of any object after παρώργισας the Greek is following the Hebrew. — ἐξήμαρτες τὸν Ἰσραήλ : a Hebraism. § 84.

23. Ἰσραήλ: = Jezreel. 18⁴⁵ n.

25. πλὴν ματαίως κτλ. : this and the next verse manifestly interrupt the narrative. Hence they are enclosed in brackets by the Revisers. The Greek here departs slightly from the Hebrew, and may be rendered as follows: *But Ahab did foolishly in the way he let himself be sold to do evil before the LORD, according as Jezebel his wife disposed him.*

26. ἐβδελύχθη : behaved abominably. Cp. Ps. 13¹ διέφθειραν καὶ ἐβδελύχθησαν ἐν ἐπιτηδεύμασιν : cp. 52² ἐβδελύχθησαν ἐν ἀνομίαις.

iii Kings XX 27

πορεύεσθαι ὀπίσω τῶν βδελυγμάτων κατὰ πάντα ἃ ἐποίησεν
ὁ 'Αμορραῖος, ὃν ἐξωλέθρευσεν Κύριος ἀπὸ προσώπου υἱῶν
'Ισραήλ. ²⁷καὶ ὑπὲρ τοῦ λόγου ὡς κατενύγη 'Αχαὰβ ἀπὸ
προσώπου τοῦ κυρίου, καὶ ἐπορεύετο κλαίων καὶ διέρρηξεν
τὸν χιτῶνα αὐτοῦ καὶ ἐζώσατο σάκκον ἐπὶ τὸ σῶμα αὐτοῦ
καὶ ἐνήστευσεν· καὶ περιεβάλετο σάκκον ἐν τῇ ἡμέρᾳ
ᾗ ἐπάταξεν Ναβουθαὶ τὸν 'Ισραηλείτην, καὶ ἐπορεύθη.
²⁸καὶ ἐγένετο ῥῆμα Κυρίου ἐν χειρὶ δούλου αὐτοῦ 'Ηλειοὺ
περὶ 'Αχαάβ, καὶ εἶπεν Κύριος ²⁹" 'Εώρακας ὡς κατενύγη
'Αχαὰβ ἀπὸ προσώπου μου; οὐκ ἐπάξω τὴν κακίαν ἐν
ταῖς ἡμέραις αὐτοῦ· καὶ ἐν ταῖς ἡμέραις υἱοῦ αὐτοῦ ἐπάξω
τὴν κακίαν."

¹Καὶ ἠθέτησεν Μωὰβ ἐν 'Ισραὴλ μετὰ τὸ ἀποθανεῖν
'Αχαάβ. ²καὶ ἔπεσεν 'Οχοζείας διὰ τοῦ δικτυωτοῦ τοῦ ἐν

**27.** καὶ ὑπὲρ τοῦ λόγου : here again
the Greek diverges from our Hebrew.
It may be rendered thus : *And when
Ahab, owing to what was said, was
smitten with remorse before the face
of the LORD, he went weeping*, etc.—
κατενύγη : *cp.* Acts 2³⁷ ἀκούσαντες δὲ
κατενύγησαν τὴν καρδίαν. — ἐζώσατο
σάκκον : Jos. *Ant.* VIII 13 § 8 καὶ
σακκίον ἐνδυσάμενος γυμνοῖς τοῖς ποσὶ
διῆγεν.— καὶ περιεβάλετο σάκκον . . .
ἐπορεύθη : these words are not in the
Hebrew. They look like a marginal
note referring to verse 16. — ἐπορεύθη :
*went about in it.*
**28.** καὶ ἐγένετο : in this and the
following verse again the Hebrew
original of the Greek translators seems
to have differed somewhat from ours.
The Hebraism ἐν χειρί is hardly likely
to have been inserted gratuitously.
**29.** κατενύγη : R.V. ' humbleth
himself.'

**1.** ἠθέτησεν . . . ἐν : ἀθετεῖν is a
favourite word in the LXX, being used
for no less than seventeen Hebrew
originals. The primary meaning of
the word is *to set aside, disregard.* It
may be followed by a simple accusative, as in Is. 1² αὐτοὶ δέ με ἠθέτη-
σαν : Mk. 6²⁶ οὐκ ἠθέλησεν αὐτὴν ἀθετῆ-
σαι. For ἀθετεῖν ἔν τινι *cp.* iv K. 3⁵·⁷,
18²⁰ : ii Chr. 10¹⁹ καὶ ἠθέτησεν 'Ισραὴλ
ἐν τῷ οἴκῳ Δαυίδ.
**2.** 'Οχοζείας : = Ahaziah, the son
of Ahab, who succeeded his father
after the latter had been slain in battle
(iii K. 22⁴⁰). — ἠρρώστησεν : iii K.
17¹⁷ n. — δικτυωτοῦ : *lattice-window.*
*Cp.* Ezk. 41¹⁶ θυρίδες δικτυωταί. In
Jdg. 5²⁸ A has διὰ τῆς δικτυωτῆς (*sc.*
θυρίδος). The phrase ἔργον δικτυωτόν
is used in Ex. 27⁴, 38²⁴⁽⁴⁾ ; *cp.* Aristeas
§ 31 δικτυωτὴν ἔχουσα τὴν πρόσοψιν.
The Hebrew is nowhere else the same
as here. Josephus (*Ant.* IX 2 § 1) says

iv Kings I 6

τῷ ὑπερῴῳ αὐτοῦ τῷ ἐν Σαμαρείᾳ, καὶ ἠρρώστησεν· καὶ ἀπέστειλεν ἀγγέλους καὶ εἶπεν πρὸς αὐτούς " Δεῦτε καὶ ἐπιζητήσατε ἐν τῷ Βάαλ μυῖαν θεὸν 'Ακκαρών, εἰ ζήσομαι ἐκ τῆς ἀρρωστίας μου ταύτης·" καὶ ἐπορεύθησαν ἐπερωτῆσαι δι' αὐτοῦ. ³καὶ ἄγγελος Κυρίου ἐκάλεσεν 'Ηλειοὺ τὸν Θεσβείτην λέγων "'Αναστὰς δεῦρο εἰς συνάντησιν τῶν ἀγγέλων 'Οχοζείου βασιλέως Σαμαρείας καὶ λαλήσεις πρὸς αὐτούς 'Εἰ παρὰ τὸ μὴ εἶναι θεὸν ἐν 'Ισραὴλ ὑμεῖς πορεύεσθε ἐπιζητῆσαι ἐν τῷ Βάαλ μυῖαν θεὸν 'Ακκαρών ;' ⁽⁴⁾καὶ οὐχ οὕτως· ⁴ὅτι τάδε λέγει Κύριος 'Η κλίνη ἐφ' ἧς ἀνέβης ἐκεῖ οὐ καταβήσῃ ἀπ' αὐτῆς, ὅτι θανάτῳ ἀποθανῇ.'" καὶ ἐπορεύθη 'Ηλειοὺ καὶ εἶπεν πρὸς αὐτούς. ⁵καὶ ἐπεστράφησαν οἱ ἄγγελοι πρὸς αὐτόν, καὶ εἶπεν πρὸς αὐτούς " Τί ὅτι ἐπεστρέψατε ; " ⁶καὶ εἶπαν πρὸς αὐτόν "'Ανὴρ ἀνέβη εἰς συνάντησιν ἡμῶν καὶ εἶπεν πρὸς ἡμᾶς ' Δεῦτε ἐπιστράφητε πρὸς τὸν βασιλέα τὸν ἀποστείλαντα ὑμᾶς καὶ λαλήσατε πρὸς αὐτόν " Τάδε λέγει Κύριος 'Εἰ παρὰ τὸ μὴ εἶναι θεὸν ἐν 'Ισραὴλ σὺ πορεύῃ ζητῆσαι ἐν τῇ

that Ahaziah had a fall in descending from the roof of his house.— ἐπιζητήσατε ἐν: for ἐπιζητεῖν ἐν cp. 3 : Sir. 40²⁶ οὐκ ἔστιν ἐπιζητῆσαι ἐν αὐτῷ βοήθειαν.—Βάαλ μυῖαν:= Baal-zebub or 'Fly-lord.' Professor Cheyne suggests that this is only a contemptuous Jewish modification of the true name, Baal-zebul, 'lord of the high house.' Cp. Mk. 3²². — θεόν: a regard for grammar would require θεῷ. § 57.—'Ακκαρών: i K. 17⁵² n.—ἀρρωστίας: iii K. 17¹⁷.—καὶ ἐπορεύθησαν . . . δι' αὐτοῦ: not in the Hebrew.

3. ἐκάλεσεν . . . λέγων: Hebrew 'said to.'—καὶ οὐχ οὕτως: a misreading of the word meaning therefore at the beginning of the next verse. So

again in verses 6 and 16 and 19³² οὐχ οὕτως.

4. 'Η κλίνη κτλ.: the syntax is Hebrew, but intelligible in any language—As to the bed to which thou hast gone up thither, thou shalt not come down from it.—ἐφ' ἧς . . . ἐκεῖ: § 50.—θανάτῳ ἀποθανῇ: § 61.—καὶ εἶπεν πρὸς αὐτούς: not in the Hebrew.

6. τῇ Βάαλ: cp. verse 16 : i K. 7⁴ (τὰς Βααλείμ) : ii Chr. 24⁷ (ταῖς Βααλείμ, but in 33⁸ τοῖς B.) : Hos. 2⁸, 13¹: Zeph. 1⁴ : Jeremiah passim ; Tobit 1⁵ : Rom. 11⁴ (where τῇ Βάαλ is used notwithstanding the presence of the masculine article in the passage quoted, namely, iii K. 19⁸). Josephus (Ant. IX 2 § 1) expressly tells us that the

iv Kings I 7

Βάαλ μυῖαν θεὸν ᾿Ακκαρών; οὐχ οὕτως· ἡ κλίνη ἐφ᾿ ἧς
ἀνέβης ὅτι οὐ καταβήσῃ ἀπ᾿ αὐτῆς, ὅτι θανάτῳ ἀποθανῇ.᾿᾿᾿
⁷καὶ ἐλάλησεν πρὸς αὐτούς "Τίς ἡ κρίσις τοῦ ἀνδρὸς τοῦ
ἀναβάντος εἰς συνάντησιν ὑμῖν καὶ λαλήσαντος πρὸς ὑμᾶς
τοὺς λόγους τούτους;"     ⁸καὶ εἶπον πρὸς αὐτόν "᾿Ανὴρ
δασὺς καὶ ζώνην δερματίνην περιεζωσμένος τὴν ὀσφὺν
αὐτοῦ·" καὶ εἶπεν "῾Ηλειοὺ ὁ Θεσβείτης οὗτός ἐστιν."
⁹καὶ ἀπέστειλεν πρὸς αὐτὸν πεντηκόνταρχον καὶ τοὺς πεντήκοντα αὐτοῦ, καὶ ἀνέβη πρὸς αὐτόν· καὶ ἰδοὺ ῾Ηλειοὺ
ἐκάθητο ἐπὶ τῆς κορυφῆς τοῦ ὄρους. καὶ ἐλάλησεν ὁ
πεντηκόνταρχος πρὸς αὐτὸν καὶ εἶπεν "῎Ανθρωπε τοῦ θεοῦ,
ὁ βασιλεὺς ἐκάλεσέν σε, κατάβηθι."     ¹⁰καὶ ἀπεκρίθη
῾Ηλειοὺ καὶ εἶπεν πρὸς τὸν πεντηκόνταρχον "Καὶ εἰ ἄνθρωπος θεοῦ ἐγώ, καταβήσεται πῦρ ἐκ τοῦ οὐρανοῦ καὶ
καταφάγεται σὲ καὶ τοὺς πεντήκοντά σου·" καὶ κατέβη
πῦρ ἐκ τοῦ οὐρανοῦ καὶ κατέφαγεν αὐτὸν καὶ τοὺς πεντήκοντα αὐτοῦ.     ¹¹καὶ προσέθετο ὁ βασιλεὺς καὶ ἀπέστειλεν
πρὸς αὐτὸν ἄλλον πεντηκόνταρχον καὶ τοὺς πεντήκοντα

deity in this case was a female one —
καὶ νοσήσαντα πέμψαι πρὸς τὴν ᾿Ακκαρὼν
θεὸν Μυῖαν, τοῦτο γὰρ ἦν ὄνομα τῇ θεῷ.
He was apparently unaware of the
ingenious explanation which is now
offered of the variation of gender,
namely, that the feminine article does
not denote the sex of the deity, but
indicates that the word αἰσχύνη is to
be substituted for the name in reading.
Cp. iii K. 18¹⁹ n. — οὐχ οὕτως: 3 n.
— ὅτι οὐ καταβήσῃ: the insertion of
ὅτι seems to be due to the fact that the
words of Elijah are being repeated.
7. ἡ κρίσις: Jdg. 13¹² n.
8. δασύς: hairy, shaggy. Jos. Ant.
IX 2 § 1 ἄνθρωπον ἔλεγον δασὺν καὶ
ζώνην περιειλημμένον δερματίνην. The

Hebrew expression may mean 'owner
of a shaggy coat,' an interpretation
which is carried out by what is said of
John the Baptist, who was regarded
as a reincarnation of Elijah. Mk. 1⁶
ἦν δὲ ᾿Ιωάννης ἐνδεδυμένος τρίχας καμή-
λου καὶ ζώνην δερματίνην περὶ τὴν ὀσφὺν
αὐτοῦ.
9. πεντηκόνταρχον κτλ.: Josephus
has ταξίαρχον καὶ πεντήκοντα ὁπλίτας.
— ἐκάλεσέν σε, κατάβηθι: R.V. 'the
king hath said, Come down.'
11. προσέθετο . . . καὶ ἀπέστειλεν:
Hebrew, 'returned and sent' = sent
again. The use of προστιθέναι is very
common in the LXX, but this passage
and verse 13 differ from the others in
the Hebrew which underlies it.

αὐτοῦ· καὶ ἐλάλησεν ὁ πεντηκόνταρχος πρὸς αὐτὸν καὶ εἶπεν "Ἄνθρωπε τοῦ θεοῦ, τάδε λέγει ὁ βασιλεύς 'Ταχέως κατάβηθι.' " ¹²καὶ ἀπεκρίθη Ἠλειοὺ καὶ ἐλάλησεν πρὸς αὐτὸν καὶ εἶπεν " Εἰ ἄνθρωπος θεοῦ ἐγώ, καταβήσεται πῦρ ἐκ τοῦ οὐρανοῦ καὶ καταφάγεταί σε καὶ τοὺς πεντήκοντά σου· " καὶ κατέβη πῦρ ἐκ τοῦ οὐρανοῦ καὶ κατέφαγεν αὐτὸν καὶ τοὺς πεντήκοντα αὐτοῦ. ¹³καὶ προσέθετο ὁ βασιλεὺς ἔτι ἀποστεῖλαι ἡγούμενον καὶ τοὺς πεντήκοντα αὐτοῦ· καὶ ἦλθεν ὁ πεντηκόνταρχος ὁ τρίτος καὶ ἔκαμψεν ἐπὶ τὰ γόνατα αὐτοῦ κατέναντι Ἠλειού, καὶ ἐδεήθη αὐτοῦ καὶ ἐλάλησεν πρὸς αὐτὸν καὶ εἶπεν "Ἄνθρωπε τοῦ θεοῦ, ἐντιμωθήτω ἡ ψυχή μου καὶ ἡ ψυχὴ τῶν δούλων σου τούτων ἐν ὀφθαλμοῖς σου· ¹⁴ἰδοὺ κατέβη πῦρ ἐκ τοῦ οὐρανοῦ καὶ κατέφαγεν τοὺς δύο πεντηκοντάρχους τοὺς πρώτους· καὶ νῦν ἐντιμωθήτω δὴ ἡ ψυχή μου ἐν ὀφθαλμοῖς σου." ¹⁵καὶ ἐλάλησεν ἄγγελος Κυρίου πρὸς Ἠλειοὺ καὶ εἶπεν " Κατάβηθι μετ' αὐτοῦ, μὴ φοβηθῇς ἀπὸ προσώπου αὐτῶν· " καὶ ἀνέστη Ἠλειοὺ καὶ κατέβη μετ' αὐτοῦ πρὸς τὸν βασιλέα. ¹⁶καὶ ἐλάλησεν πρὸς αὐτὸν καὶ εἶπεν Ἠλειού " Τάδε λέγει Κύριος ' Τί ὅτι ἀπέστειλας ζητῆσαι ἐν τῇ Βάαλ μυῖαν θεὸν Ἀκκαρών; οὐχ οὕτως· ἡ κλίνη ἐφ' ἧς ἀνέβης ἐκεῖ οὐ καταβήσῃ ἀπ' αὐτῆς, ὅτι θανάτῳ ἀποθανῇ.' " ¹⁷καὶ ἀπέθανεν κατὰ τὸ ῥῆμα Κυρίου ὃ ἐλάλησεν Ἠλειού.

12. κατέβη πῦρ: instead of ' fire,' as before, the Hebrew here has ' fire of God.'

13. ἡγούμενον: Hebrew, 'prince of fifty ' = πεντηκόνταρχον. Ἡγούμενος is a generic term for a ruler. Cp. Hb. 13⁷, ¹⁷, ²⁴: Clem. i Cor. 1³ ὑποτασσόμενοι τοῖς ἡγουμένοις ὑμῶν. — ἐντιμωθήτω: a rare word occurring in the LXX only in this context.

15. ἀπὸ προσώπου αὐτῶν: Hebrew, ' before his face.'

16. καὶ ἐλάλησεν ... Ἠλειού: Hebrew, 'and he said unto him,' 17² n. — οὐχ οὕτως: before these words the Hebrew has the clause which is rendered in the R.V. — ' Is it because there is no God in Israel to inquire of his word ?' On οὐχ οὕτως see 3 n.

¹Καὶ ἐγένετο ἐν τῷ ἀνάγειν Κύριον τὸν Ἠλειοὺ ἐν συνσεισμῷ ὡς εἰς τὸν οὐρανόν, καὶ ἐπορεύθη Ἠλειοὺ καὶ
Ἐλεισαῖε ἐξ Ἰερειχώ. ²καὶ εἶπεν Ἠλειοὺ πρὸς Ἐλεισαῖε
" Ἰδοὺ δὴ ἐνταῦθα κάθου, ὅτι ὁ θεὸς ἀπέσταλκέν με ἕως
Βαιθήλ." καὶ εἶπεν Ἐλεισαῖε " Ζῇ Κύριος καὶ ζῇ ἡ ψυχή
σου, εἰ καταλείψω σε·" καὶ ἦλθεν εἰς Βαιθήλ. ³καὶ ἦλθον
οἱ υἱοὶ τῶν προφητῶν οἱ ἐν Βαιθὴλ πρὸς Ἐλεισαῖε καὶ εἶπον
πρὸς αὐτόν " Εἰ ἔγνως ὅτι Κύριος σήμερον λαμβάνει τὸν
κύριόν σου ἀπάνωθεν τῆς κεφαλῆς σου;" καὶ εἶπεν " Κἀγὼ
ἔγνωκα, σιωπᾶτε." ⁴καὶ εἶπεν Ἠλειοὺ πρὸς Ἐλεισαῖε " Κάθου δὴ ἐνταῦθα, ὅτι Κύριος ἀπέσταλκέν με εἰς Ἰερειχώ·"
καὶ εἶπεν " Ζῇ Κύριος καὶ ζῇ ἡ ψυχή σου, εἰ ἐνκαταλείψω
σε·" καὶ ἦλθον εἰς Ἰερειχώ. ⁵καὶ ἤγγισαν οἱ υἱοὶ τῶν
προφητῶν οἱ ἐν Ἰερειχὼ πρὸς Ἐλεισαῖε καὶ εἶπαν πρὸς
αὐτόν " Εἰ ἔγνως ὅτι σήμερον λαμβάνει Κύριος τὸν κύριόν
σου ἐπάνωθεν τῆς κεφαλῆς σου;" καὶ εἶπεν " Καί γε ἐγὼ
ἔγνων, σιωπᾶτε." ⁶καὶ εἶπεν αὐτῷ Ἠλειού " Κάθου δὴ
ὧδε, ὅτι Κύριος ἀπέσταλκέν με ἕως εἰς τὸν Ἰορδάνην·"
καὶ εἶπεν Ἐλεισαῖε " Ζῇ Κύριος καὶ ζῇ ἡ ψυχή σου, εἰ
ἐνκαταλείψω σε·" καὶ ἐπορεύθησαν ἀμφότεροι. ⁷καὶ

---

**1. συνσεισμῷ:** iii K. 19¹¹ n. R.V.
'whirlwind.' The Hebrew is the same
as in 11. — ὡς εἰς: so in verse 11, but
there is nothing in the Hebrew to justify our assigning a qualifying force to
ὡς, which may in both passages be
devoid of meaning. — Ἰερειχώ: Hebrew
*Gilgal*. Verse 4 shows that the LXX
is wrong. The Gilgal from which Elijah
started is supposed to have been the
place now called *Jiljîliyeh*, about seven
miles north of Bethel.
**2. Ἰδοὺ δή:** this represents a particle of entreaty in the Hebrew. —

κάθου: § 33. — Ζῇ Κύριος: § 101. —
ἦλθεν: Hebrew, 'they went down.'
**3. Εἰ ἔγνως:** § 100. — ἀπάνωθεν:
*from above.* Cp. Jdg. 16²⁰: ii K.
11²⁰, ²⁴, 20²¹: iii K. 1⁵³. § 98.
**5. ἐπάνωθεν:** the Hebrew is the
same as for ἀπάνωθεν in verse 3. R.V.
'from.' — Καί γε ἐγὼ ἔγνων: the Hebrew is the same as for Κἀγὼ ἔγνωκα
in verse 3. The translator is trying
to impart a little variety to his style,
whereas a set formula is in accordance with the genius of the Hebrew
language.

iv Kings II 13

πεντήκοντα ἄνδρες υἱοὶ τῶν προφητῶν καὶ ἔστησαν ἐξ ἐναντίας μακρόθεν· καὶ ἀμφότεροι ἔστησαν ἐπὶ τοῦ Ἰορδάνου. ⁸καὶ ἔλαβεν Ἡλειοὺ τὴν μηλωτὴν αὐτοῦ καὶ εἵλησεν καὶ ἐπάταξεν τὸ ὕδωρ, καὶ διῃρέθη τὸ ὕδωρ ἔνθα καὶ ἔνθα· καὶ διέβησαν ἀμφότεροι ἐν ἐρήμῳ. ⁹καὶ ἐγένετο ἐν τῷ διαβῆναι αὐτοὺς καὶ Ἡλειοὺ εἶπεν πρὸς Ἐλεισαῖε " Τί ποιήσω σοι πρὶν ἢ ἀναλημφθῆναί με ἀπὸ σοῦ;" καὶ εἶπεν Ἐλεισαῖε " Γενηθήτω δὴ διπλᾶ ἐν πνεύματί σου ἐπ᾽ ἐμέ." ¹⁰καὶ εἶπεν Ἡλειού " Ἐσκλήρυνας τοῦ αἰτήσασθαι· ἐὰν ἴδῃς με ἀναλαμβανόμενον ἀπὸ σοῦ, καὶ ἔσται οὕτως· καὶ ἐὰν μή, οὐ μὴ γένηται." ¹¹καὶ ἐγένετο αὐτῶν πορευομένων, ἐπορεύοντο καὶ ἐλάλουν· καὶ ἰδοὺ ἅρμα πυρὸς καὶ ἵππος πυρός, καὶ διέστειλεν ἀνὰ μέσον ἀμφοτέρων· καὶ ἀνελήμφθη Ἡλειοὺ ἐν συνσεισμῷ ὡς εἰς τὸν οὐρανόν. ¹²καὶ Ἐλεισαῖε ἑώρα, καὶ ἐβόα " Πάτερ πάτερ, ἅρμα Ἰσραὴλ καὶ ἱππεὺς αὐτοῦ·" καὶ οὐκ εἶδεν αὐτὸν ἔτι, καὶ ἐπελάβετο τῶν ἱματίων αὐτοῦ καὶ διέρρηξεν αὐτὰ εἰς δύο ῥήγματα. ¹³καὶ ὕψωσεν τὴν μηλωτὴν Ἡλειοὺ ἣ ἔπεσεν ἐπάνωθεν

---

7. **καὶ ἔστησαν** : Hebrew, ' went and stood.' It looks as though ἐπορεύθησαν had dropped out in the Greek owing to its presence in the preceding sentence.

8. **ἐν ἐρήμῳ**: R.V. ' on dry ground.' The Greek rendering would be possible in another context.

9. **διπλᾶ ἐν πνεύματί σου**: *a double share in thy spirit*. Elisha is not asking for twice as much prophetic power as Elijah, but for the inheritance of the first-born (Dt. 21¹⁷) in his spirit.

10. **Ἡλειού**: not in the Hebrew. —**Ἐσκλήρυνας τοῦ αἰτήσασθαι**: Hebrew literally *thou hast made hard to*

*ask.* R.V. ' Thou hast asked a hard thing.'

11. **ἵππος**: Hebrew, ' horses.'

12. **Πάτερ . . . ἱππεὺς αὐτοῦ**: in 13¹⁴ the same words are put into the mouth of King Joash on the occasion of the death of Elisha. The meaning in both places seems to be that the prophet had been a bulwark to his country. —**ἅρμα**: the singular in the Hebrew has a collective force, *chariotry*. —**ἱππεύς**: Hebrew, ' horsemen.' The translator seems to have put it into the singular to accompany ἅρμα. — **αὐτοῦ**: referring to Elisha. § 13.

13. **ἐπάνωθεν**: R.V. ' from him.'

iv Kings II 14

Ἐλεισαῖε· καὶ ἔστη ἐπὶ τοῦ χείλους τοῦ Ἰορδάνου. ¹⁴καὶ
ἔλαβεν τὴν μηλωτὴν Ἠλειού, ἣ ἔπεσεν ἐπάνωθεν αὐτοῦ, καὶ
ἐπάταξεν τὸ ὕδωρ καὶ εἶπεν " Ποῦ ὁ θεὸς Ἠλειού ἀφφώ; "
καὶ ἐπάταξεν τὰ ὕδατα, καὶ διερράγησαν ἔνθα καὶ ἔνθα·
καὶ διέβη Ἐλεισαῖε. ¹⁵καὶ εἶδον αὐτὸν οἱ υἱοὶ τῶν προφητῶν καὶ οἱ ἐν Ἱερειχὼ ἐξ ἐναντίας καὶ εἶπον " Ἐπανα-
πέπαυται τὸ πνεῦμα Ἠλειού ἐπὶ Ἐλεισαῖε·" καὶ ἦλθον εἰς
συναντὴν αὐτοῦ καὶ προσεκύνησαν αὐτῷ ἐπὶ τὴν γῆν.
¹⁶καὶ εἶπον πρὸς αὐτόν " Ἰδοὺ δὴ μετὰ τῶν παιδων σου
πεντήκοντα ἄνδρες υἱοὶ δυνάμεως· πορευθέντες δὴ ζητησά-
τωσαν τὸν κύριόν σου, μή ποτε εὗρεν αὐτὸν πνεῦμα Κυρίου
καὶ ἔρριψεν αὐτὸν ἐν τῷ Ἰορδάνῃ ἢ ἐφ᾽ ἓν τῶν ὀρέων ἢ ἐφ᾽
ἕνα τῶν βουνῶν·" καὶ εἶπεν Ἐλεισαῖε " Οὐκ ἀποστελεῖτε."
¹⁷καὶ παρεβιάσαντο αὐτὸν ἕως οὗ ᾐσχύνετο, καὶ εἶπεν
" Ἀποστείλατε." καὶ ἀπέστειλαν πεντήκοντα ἄνδρας, καὶ
ἐζήτησαν τρεῖς ἡμέρας, καὶ οὐχ εὗρον αὐτόν· ¹⁸καὶ αὐτὸς
ἐκάθητο ἐν Ἱερειχώ· καὶ εἶπεν Ἐλεισαῖε " Οὐκ εἶπον πρὸς
ὑμᾶς ' Μὴ πορευθῆτε '; "

—Ἐλεισαῖε: nominative to ὕψωσεν,
but not in the Hebrew. After this the
Hebrew has 'and went back.' —χείλους: the use of χεῖλος for a bank or
brink, besides corresponding to the
Hebrew, is also good Greek. *Cp.* Hdt.
II 70 ἐπὶ τοῦ χείλεος τοῦ ποτάμου.

**14.** ποῦ ὁ θεὸς Ἠλειού: Hebrew,
'Where is Jehovah the god of Elijah?'
—ἀφφώ: a transliteration from the
Hebrew. Translate *even he.*

**15.** καὶ οἱ: the omission of καί here
would bring the Greek into accordance

with the Hebrew. —συναντήν: iii K.
18¹⁶ n.

**16.** ἐν τῷ Ἰορδάνῃ ἤ: not in the
Hebrew.—ἕν . . . ἕνα: εἷς for τις is
due here to a literal following of the
Hebrew. § 2. —βουνῶν: from Hdt.
IV 199 it has been inferred that this
word is of Cyrenaic origin. It is con-
demned by Phrynichus as non-Attic
(Swete *Introd.* p. 296).

**18.** καὶ αὐτὸς ἐκάθητο: before this
the Hebrew has 'and they came back
to him.'

# INTRODUCTION TO THE STORY OF HEZEKIAH
## AND SENNACHERIB

'THE prayer of a righteous man availeth much' — such is the moral of the story of Hezekiah and Sennacherib. This story is a favourite one in the Old Testament, being told in Kings, in Isaiah, and in Chronicles. The account given by the Chronicler (ii Chr. 32$^{1-23}$) is obviously a late echo of the other two. But it might admit of argument whether the passage in Kings (ii K. 18$^{13}$–19$^{37}$) is borrowed from Isaiah or the passage in Isaiah (chs. 36 and 37) borrowed from Kings. The differences between the two are merely verbal, and are almost invariably in the direction of greater fulness on the part of Kings. Hence Professor Driver infers that the narrative belonged originally to the Book of Kings and was adopted in a slightly abridged form by the compiler of Isaiah. One thing seems certain, namely, that the account does not come from the prophet Isaiah himself. It was written at a time when the imagination could already give play to itself among the events of a past age. A contemporary, as Professor Driver points out, would not have attributed to Sennacherib the successes against Hamath, Arpad, and Samaria, which were, in fact, achieved by Tiglath-Pileser or Sargon. Moreover, it was only the foreshortening of the perspective caused by time that could enable the writer to regard the murder of Sennacherib in his own country as following close upon his invasion of Judæa, when the two events were actually separated by a space of twenty years (B.C. 701–681). Hezekiah's own death (B.C. 697) took place sixteen years before that of Sennacherib. In the Book of Tobit it is said that Sennacherib was slain by his two sons within fifty days from the time when he 'came flying from Judæa ' (Tob. 1$^{18, 21}$). This book indeed is pure romance, but it serves to show that the Jews read the story of Sennacherib as indicating that a speedy judgement overtook the king on his return to his own country.

More even than David, Hezekiah has been fixed upon by the

Jewish writers as the type of the pious king. 'He trusted in the Lord, the God of Israel; so that after him was none like him among all the kings of Judah, nor among them that were before him' (ii K. 18⁶). Such is the verdict of the writer of Kings, and the Chronicler (ii Chr. 31²⁰, ²¹) is equally enthusiastic. In Ecclesiasticus also (Sir. 48²¹, ²²) the smiting of the camp of the Assyrians is said to have been due to the fact that Hezekiah did that which was pleasing to the Lord. That piety meant prosperity was a rooted idea in the Jewish mind, so that, as Hezekiah was admittedly pious, it was a logical consequence that he should prosper. 'And the Lord was with him; whithersoever he went forth he prospered' (ii K. 18⁷: *cp.* ii Chr. 31²¹). These words stand in curious contrast with the Assyrian records. This is how Sennacherib tells the story —

'And Hezekiah of the land of Judah, who did not submit himself to my yoke — forty-six of his strongest towns, fortresses, and small towns without number in their territory were captured with battering-rams (?) and attacked with instruments of war, in the storming of the infantry, with mines, breeching-irons, and (— ?). I besieged and conquered them. 200,150 persons, young and old, male and female, horses, mules, asses, camels, oxen, and small cattle without number, I caused to come out from them and counted them as booty.[1] Hezekiah himself I shut up like a caged bird in Jerusalem, his royal city; I fortified entrenchments against him, and those who came out of the gate of his city I punished [or 'I turned back'] for his transgression. His towns, which I had plundered, I separated from his land, and gave them to the Mitinti, king of Ashdod, to Pade, king of Ekron, and Ṣilbel, king of Gaza, and I diminished his territory. To the earlier tribute, their yearly payment, I added the tribute which is suitable to my lordship, and imposed it on them. Hezekiah was overpowered by the fear of the splendour of my lordship; the Urbi[2] and his valiant warriors, whom he had brought thither for the defence of Jerusalem, his royal city, laid down their arms. Be-

---

[1] Rogers *History of Babylonia and Assyria* II, p. 199, says: ' These inhabitants were not carried away into captivity. They were marched out from their cities and compelled to give allegiance to Assyria. The usual Assyrian expression for taking away into captivity is not used here.'

[2] Perhaps mercenary soldiers.

sides 30 talents of gold and 800 talents of silver,[3] I caused to be brought after me to Nineveh, the royal city of my lordship, for payment of the tribute, precious stones, shining stones, great stones of lapis-lazuli, ivory couches, thrones of elephant-hide and ivory, ivory, precious woods, all manner of things, a vast treasure, and his daughters, his palace-women and musicians and singing-women; and he sent his envoys to do homage to me.' (Rosenberg *Assyrische Sprachlehre*.)

There is no mention here of any disaster or ignominious retreat; rather Sennacherib represents himself as returning laden with spoils; but then the historiographers royal of Assyria were doubtless not in the habit of dwelling upon untoward incidents. Let us therefore call in the evidence of a third party.

There was a priest of Hephæstus, named Sethon, who became king of Egypt, and who slighted the warrior-caste and deprived them of their lands. Therefore when Sanacharibos, king of the Arabians and Assyrians, marched a great army against Egypt, the warriors refused to fight. So the priest, being at his wits' end, went into the temple and bewailed before the image of the God the dangers that threatened him. As he wept, sleep stole over him; and the God, appearing to him in a dream, promised to send him helpers. So the king went out to Pelusium with such rabble as would follow him. There, as the army of the invaders lay encamped at night, a multitude of field-mice poured in upon them and devoured their quivers, their bow-strings, and the handles of their shields, so that next day they fled defenceless before their enemies. Thus was Egypt saved by the prayers of its priestly king, a stone image of whom still stood in the days of Herodotus in the temple, holding in its hand a mouse, and with an inscription conveying the moral of the tale — 'Whoso looketh upon me, let him be pious' (Hdt. II 141).

If either the Jewish or the Egyptian story stood alone, one might be inclined to set them down as the invention of national vanity: but their concurrence seems to favour the idea that Sennacherib did meet with some sudden reverse, which both Jews and Egyptians turned to the praise of their own God and king.

The account of the matter, as given by Josephus (*Ant.* X 1 § 1), contains nothing incredible. The Jewish historian tells us that

---

[3] ii K. 18[14] says 300 talents. 'Brandis has attempted to show that the 300 Hebrew talents = 800 Assyrian.' — Rogers *ibid.* p. 200.

Sennacherib left Rabshakeh and his associates to sack Jerusalem, but himself went off to make war on the Egyptians and Ethiopians. He was engaged for a long time on the siege of Pelusium, and was about to deliver the assault, when he heard that Thersikes (=Tirhakah, ii K. 19⁹) was coming with a large force to the aid of the Egyptians and meant to cross the desert and invade Assyria. Accordingly he suddenly abandoned the siege and rejoined the force under Rabshakeh at Jerusalem.   But on the first night of his siege of this city, God sent the plague upon his army, which expedited his return to Nineveh.   There, after a short time, he was murdered by his two eldest sons Adramelechos and Sarasaros.   Josephus quotes Herodotus and goes on to quote Berosus the Chaldæan historian, but unfortunately there is a lacuna at this point in his work. It is worth noticing that Megasthenes, according to Strabo (XV, pp. 686, 687), speaks of Tearkon the Ethiopian as a great warrior, like Sesostris, who reached the Pillars of Hercules.   The historical aspect of the story however must be left to others.   Suffice it to say, that those who have studied the question seem to be agreed that the chronology of the Bible is here at fault.

We are concerned with the story only as a piece of literature. Viewed from that aspect it is magnificent, being told with all the solemn dignity and splendour which mark the Hebrew genius.   In the indication of the catastrophe which overtook the monarch who had presumed to defy the Holy One of Israel there is the vagueness which is of the very essence of the sublime.   It takes a poet to interpret poetry.   So let us close with a quotation from Byron —

> 'Like the leaves of the forest when Summer is green,
> That host with their banners at sunset were seen ;
> Like the leaves of the forest when Autumn hath blown,
> That host on the morrow lay withered and strown.
>
> For the Angel of Death spread his wings on the blast,
> And breath'd on the face of the foe as he pass'd ;
> And the eyes of the sleepers wax'd deadly and chill,
> And their hearts but once heav'd, and for ever grew still ! '

# VII. THE STORY OF HEZEKIAH AND SENNACHERIB

iv Kings XVIII 13

¹³ Καὶ τῷ τεσσαρεσκαιδεκάτῳ ἔτει βασιλεῖ Ἐζεκιοῦ ἀνέβη Σενναχηρεὶμ βασιλεὺς Ἀσσυρίων ἐπὶ τὰς πόλεις Ἰούδα τὰς ὀχυρὰς καὶ συνέλαβεν αὐτάς. ¹⁴ καὶ ἀπέστειλεν Ἐζεκίας βασιλεὺς Ἰούδα ἀγγέλους πρὸς βασιλέα Ἀσσυρίων εἰς Λαχεὶς λέγων " Ἡμάρτηκα, ἀποστράφητι ἀπ᾽ ἐμοῦ· ὃ ἐὰν ἐπιθῇς ἐπ᾽ ἐμὲ βαστάσω." καὶ ἐπέθηκεν ὁ βασιλεὺς Ἀσσυρίων ἐπὶ Ἐζεκίαν βασιλέα Ἰούδα τριακόσια τάλαντα ἀργυρίου καὶ τριάκοντα τάλαντα χρυσίου. ¹⁵ καὶ ἔδωκεν Ἐζεκίας πᾶν τὸ ἀργύριον τὸ εὑρεθὲν ἐν οἴκῳ Κυρίου καὶ ἐν θησαυροῖς οἴκου τοῦ βασιλέως. ¹⁶ ἐν τῷ καιρῷ ἐκείνῳ συνέκοψεν Ἐζεκίας τὰς θύρας ναοῦ καὶ τὰ ἐστηριγμένα

**13.** Σενναχηρείμ: Hebrew *Ṣanḫē-rib*. The form *Sennacherib* comes from the Vulgate. Josephus (*Ant.* X 1 § 1) Σεναχήριβος: Hdt. II 141 Σαναχάριβος. — Ἰούδα : Is. 36¹ τῆς Ἰουδαίας.

**14.** Ἐζεκίας: Grecized form of the name. Hebrew *Ḥizqiyyah* here, but more commonly *Ḥizqiyyahu*, as in verse 13. This difference is one of the signs that verses 14–16, which are omitted in Is. 36, come from a different source from the rest of the narrative. Josephus founds on them a charge of perjury against Sennacherib. — ἀγγέλους: not in the Hebrew. — Λαχείς: Sennacherib was at this time besieging this stronghold with all his forces. It was in the lowlands near the country of the Philistines, and was strategetically a place of importance as lying on the high-road between Egypt and Syria. Recent investigations tend to show its identity with the mound of Tell-el-Ḥesy. One of the slabs discovered by Layard contains a record of its capture and a picture of the siege. The inscription has been deciphered as follows — ' Sennacherib, the mighty king, king of the country of Assyria, sitting on the throne of judgement before (*or* at the entrance of) the city of Lachish (*Lakhisha*). I give permission for its slaughter.' Smith's *Dict. of the Bible, s.v. Lachish.* — ὃ ἐάν: § 105.

**16.** τὰ ἐστηριγμένα: *posts.* Only here as a substantive.

295

iv Kings XVIII 17

ἃ ἐχρύσωσεν Ἐζεκίας βασιλεὺς Ἰούδα, καὶ ἔδωκεν αὐτὰ
βασιλεῖ Ἀσσυρίων. ¹⁷Καὶ ἀπέστειλεν βασιλεὺς Ἀσσυρίων τὸν Θανθὰν καὶ τὸν Ραφεὶς καὶ τὸν Ραψάκην ἐκ
Λαχεὶς πρὸς τὸν βασιλέα Ἐζεκίαν ἐν δυνάμει βαρείᾳ ἐπὶ
Ἰερουσαλήμ· καὶ ἀνέβησαν καὶ ἦλθον εἰς Ἰερουσαλήμ,
καὶ ἔστησαν ἐν τῷ ὑδραγωγῷ τῆς κολυμβήθρας τῆς ἄνω ἥ
ἐστιν ἐν τῇ ὁδῷ τοῦ ἀγροῦ τοῦ γναφέως. ¹⁸καὶ ἐβόησαν
πρὸς Ἐζεκίαν, καὶ ἦλθον πρὸς αὐτὸν Ἐλιακεὶμ υἱὸς Χελκίου ὁ οἰκονόμος καὶ Σόμνας ὁ γραμματεὺς καὶ Ἰωσαφὰτ
ὁ ἀναμιμνήσκων. ¹⁹καὶ εἶπεν πρὸς αὐτοὺς Ραψάκης

17. τὸν Θανθάν: Hebrew *Tartan*. In Is. 20¹ the Hebrew has *Thartan* and the Greek Ταναθάν. It is not a name, but a title for the commander-in-chief of the Assyrian army.— τὸν Ραφεὶς: Hebrew *Rab-ṣâriṣ, chief of the eunuchs.* Cp. Jer. 39⁸, where the LXX (Jer. 46³) has Ναβουσαρείς. Josephus (*Ant.* X 1 § 1) says of the two companions of the Rabshakeh — Τούτων δὲ τὰ ὀνόματα Θαρατὰ καὶ Ἀνάχαρις ἦν.— τὸν Ραψάκην: this also is a title. Hebrew *Rabshâqêh*, which is taken to mean ' chief cupbearer.' Professor Cheyne holds that it is really Assyrian and means ' chief of the high ones.'— ἐν δυνάμει βαρείᾳ: Is. 36² μετὰ δυνάμεως πολλῆς.— ὑδραγωγῷ: cp. 20²⁰: Sir. 24³⁰: Is. 36², 41¹⁸. In the last passage the Hebrew is different from that in the rest.— κολυμβήθρας: this is the first of ten occurrences of the word in the LXX. It is used by Plato (*Rep.* 453 D) and by Plutarch (*Moralia* 902 E, *Plac.* IV 19) ; in N.T. by John (5², 9⁷).

18. Ἐζεκίαν: Hebrew ' the king.' The words καὶ ἐβόησαν πρὸς Ἐζεκίαν do not appear in Is. 36⁸. Josephus (*Ant.*

X 1 § 2) gratuitously ascribes to cowardice the non-appearance of the king in person.— Ἐλιακείμ: Hebrew *Elyâkim*, Vulgate *Eliacim.* Jos. *Ant.* X 1 § 2 τὸν τῆς βασιλείας ἐπίτροπον Ἐλιάκιμον ὄνομα.— Χελκίου: Hebrew *Ḥilqiyyâhû*, Vulgate *Helciæ* (gen.). Instead of υἱὸς Χελκίου the translator of Isaiah (36³) has the more classical ὁ τοῦ Χελκίου.— Σόμνας: Is. 36³ Σόβνας, Josephus Σοβναῖος, Hebrew *Shebnâh.* See the denunciation of him in Is. 22¹⁵⁻²⁵. The evils there predicted seem to have been only in part accomplished. — Ἰωσαφάτ: Hebrew *Yoah ben-Asaph.* In 26 he is called Ἰώας and in 37 Ἰώας υἱὸς Σαφάν, which makes it look as if Ἰωσαφάτ were here a mistake for Ἰώας υἱὸς Σαφάν, helped out by the fact that there had been a previous recorder of the name of Ἰωσαφάθ (ii K. 20²⁴).— ὁ ἀναμιμνήσκων: *the recorder.* Cp. ii K. 20²⁴ Ἰωσαφάθ υἱὸς Ἀχειλοὺθ ἀναμιμνήσκων: iii K. 2⁴⁶ʰ Βασὰ υἱὸς Ἀχειθάλαμ ἀναμιμνήσκων: iv K. 18⁸⁷ Ἰώας υἱὸς Σαφὰν ὁ ἀναμιμνήσκων: Jos. *Ant.* X 1 § 2 Ἰώαχον τὸν ἐπὶ τῶν ὑπομνημάτων. In Is. 36³ we have Ἰωὰχ ὁ τοῦ Ἀσαφ ὁ ὑπομνηματογράφος. This is mentioned

iv Kings XVIII 22

" Εἴπατε δὴ πρὸς Ἐζεκίαν ' Τάδε λέγει ὁ βασιλεὺς ὁ μέγας
βασιλεὺς Ἀσσυρίων " Τί ἡ πεποίθησις αὕτη ἦν πέποιθας;
²⁰ εἶπας, πλὴν λόγοι χειλέων ' Βουλὴ καὶ δύναμις εἰς πόλεμον · ' νῦν οὖν τίνι πεποιθὼς ἠθέτησας ἐν ἐμοί; ²¹ νῦν
ἰδοὺ πέποιθας σαυτῷ ἐπὶ τὴν ῥάβδον τὴν καλαμίνην τὴν
τεθλασμένην ταύτην, ἐπ' Αἴγυπτον · ὃς ἂν στηριχθῇ ἀνὴρ
ἐπ' αὐτήν, καὶ εἰσελεύσεται εἰς τὴν χεῖρα αὐτοῦ, καὶ
τρήσει αὐτήν · οὕτως Φαραὼ βασιλεὺς Αἰγύπτου πᾶσιν
τοῖς πεποιθόσιν ἐπ' αὐτόν. ²² καὶ ὅτι εἶπας πρὸς μέ ' Ἐπὶ
Κύριον θεὸν πεποίθαμεν · ' οὐχὶ αὐτὸς οὗτος ἀπέστησεν
Ἐζεκίας τὰ ὑψηλὰ αὐτοῦ καὶ τὰ θυσιαστήρια αὐτοῦ, καὶ
εἶπεν τῷ Ἰούδᾳ καὶ τῇ Ἰερουσαλήμ ' Ἐνώπιον τοῦ θυσια-

by Strabo (XVII 1 § 12, p. 797) as
the title of one of the native officials
at Alexandria under Augustus and
under the Ptolemies before him.

**19.** πεποίθησις: only here in the
LXX. The word is used by Josephus
(*Ant.* X I § 4) and occurs six times
in the N.T., *e.g.* ii Cor. 1¹⁵. In Is. 36⁴,
instead of Τί ἡ πεποίθησις, the same
Hebrew is rendered by Τί πεποιθὼς εἶ;

**20.** λόγοι χειλέων: Hebrew, 'a word
of the lips,' *i.e.* without reason behind
it. The Greek here faithfully reflects
the Hebrew, but there may be something
amiss with the latter. In Is. 36⁵ the
R.V. runs — 'I say *thy* counsel and
strength for the war are but vain
words.' The Greek translator there
gives — Μὴ ἐν βουλῇ καὶ λόγοις χειλέων
παράταξις γίνεται — *Does the battle de-
pend upon counsel and words of the
lips ?* — ἠθέτησας ἐν ἐμοί: cp. 1¹ n.
In iv K. 18⁷ and 24¹,²⁰ the Hebrew
word is the same as in this passage.
The rendering in Is. 36⁵ is ἀπειθεῖς μοι.

**21.** πέποιθας σαυτῷ ἐπί : no recog-

nised Greek construction, but a mere
following of the Hebrew. Is. 35⁶
πεποιθὼς εἶ ἐπί. — ὃς ἂν στηριχθῇ ἀνήρ :
treating this as Greek we might be led
to suppose that here was a case of ἄν
for ἐάν, but really the ἀνήρ is superfluous, being put in merely because
the Hebrew has 'man' in the same
place. Is. 36⁵ ὃς ἂν ἐπιστηρισθῇ ἐπ'
αὐτήν.

**22.** καὶ ὅτι εἶπας : *and as for thy
saying.* The verb is plural in the
Hebrew. Is 36⁷ εἰ δὲ λέγετε. — οὐχὶ
αὐτὸς οὗτος : either οὐ has dropped out
after these words or else they are a
mistranslation, since αὐτὸς οὗτος ought
not to refer to Hezekiah, but to Jehovah. Hezekiah's removal of the high
places (18⁴) is construed polemically
as an attack upon Jehovah. It was in
pursuance of the principle that the
Temple at Jerusalem should be the
sole centre of the national worship.
It is interesting to notice that this
verse is omitted in the Greek of Is. 36,
but not in the Hebrew.

στηρίου τούτου προσκυνήσετε ἐν Ἰερουσαλήμ᾽;" ²³καὶ
νῦν μίχθητε δὴ τῷ κυρίῳ μου βασιλεῖ Ἀσσυρίων, καὶ
δώσω σοι δισχιλίους ἵππους, εἰ δυνήσῃ δοῦναι σεαυτῷ ἐπι-
βάτας ἐπ᾽ αὐτούς. ²⁴καὶ πῶς ἀποστρέψετε τὸ πρόσωπον
τοπάρχου ἑνὸς τῶν δούλων τοῦ κυρίου μου τῶν ἐλαχί-
στων; "καὶ ἤλπισας σαυτῷ ἐπ᾽ Αἴγυπτον εἰς ἅρματα καὶ
ἱππεῖς. ²⁵καὶ νῦν μὴ ἄνευ Κυρίου ἀνέβημεν ἐπὶ τὸν
τόπον τοῦτον τοῦ διαφθεῖραι αὐτόν; Κύριος εἶπεν πρὸς
μέ᾽ Ἀνάβηθι ἐπὶ τὴν γῆν ταύτην καὶ διάφθειρον αὐτήν.᾽ "
²⁶καὶ εἶπεν Ἐλιακεὶμ υἱὸς Χελκείου καὶ Σόμνας καὶ Ἰώας
πρὸς Ῥαψάκην "Λάλησον δὴ πρὸς τοὺς παῖδάς σου Συρι-
στί· ἀκούομεν ἡμεῖς, καὶ οὐ λαλήσεις μεθ᾽ ἡμῶν Ἰουδαιστί·
καὶ ἵνα τί λαλεῖς ἐν τοῖς ὠσὶν τοῦ λαοῦ τοῦ ἐπὶ τοῦ τείχους;" ²⁷καὶ εἶπεν πρὸς αὐτοὺς Ῥαψάκης "Μὴ ἐπὶ τὸν
κύριόν σου καὶ πρὸς σὲ ἀπέστειλέν με ὁ κύριός μου
λαλῆσαι τοὺς λόγους τούτους; οὐχὶ ἐπὶ τοὺς ἄνδρας τοὺς
καθημένους ἐπὶ τοῦ τείχους, τοῦ φαγεῖν τὴν κόπρον αὐτῶν

**23. μίχθητε**: the sense required
here is 'make a wager with,' but it is
not clear how μίχθητε comes by that
meaning. Μιγνύναι is quite a rare
word in the LXX, occurring only six
times. In Ps. 105³⁵ and Is. 36⁸ the
Hebrew is the same as here, the word
being that from which ἀρραβών (ii Cor.
1²², 5⁵: Eph. 1¹⁴) is derived. — **δισχιλίους ἵππους**: Is. 36⁸ δισχιλίαν ἵππον.
Plural in the Hebrew.

**24. καὶ πῶς κτλ.**: this passage,
though somewhat involved, corresponds very well to the original, except
that ἀποστρέψετε ought to be singular.
The translator of Is. 36⁹ has made
nonsense out of the same Hebrew. —
**τοπάρχου**: the word τοπάρχης is common in Esther and Daniel; in Gen. 41³⁴

it represents a different original from
what it does here; it is used also by
the translator of Isaiah (36⁹).    *Cp.*
Gen. 41³⁴ n. — **ἤλπισας σαυτῷ ἐπί**: syntax Hebrew, not Greek.    *Cp.* verse 21.

**26. εἶπεν**: for the singular verb
followed by more than one subject *cp.*
verse 37.    § 49. — **ἀκούομεν**: = understand.    A Hebraism. — **οὐ λαλήσεις**:
Is. 36¹¹ μὴ λάλει. — **Ἰουδαιστί**: so in
Isaiah.    Josephus (*Ant.* X 1 § 2) Ἐβ-
ραιστί. — **ἵνα τί**: Gen. 42¹ n. — **ἐν τοῖς
ὠσίν**: Is. 36¹¹ εἰς τὰ ὦτα.

**27. ἐπί . . . πρός.** Is. 36¹² πρὸς . . .
πρός.    There is a corresponding difference in the Hebrew. — **τοῦ φαγεῖν κτλ.**:
this coarse expression evidently contains a reference to the extremities of
famine which the Rabshakeh thought

iv Kings XVIII 33

καὶ πιεῖν τὸ οὖρον αὐτῶν μεθ' ὑμῶν ἅμα;" ²⁸καὶ ἔστη
'Ραψάκης καὶ ἐβόησεν μεγάλῃ 'Ιουδαιστί· καὶ ἐλάλησεν
καὶ εἶπεν "'Ακούσατε τοὺς λόγους τοῦ μεγάλου βασιλέως
'Ασσυρίων ²⁹' Τάδε λέγει ὁ βασιλεύς " Μὴ ἐπαιρέτω ὑμᾶς
'Εζεκίας λόγοις, ὅτι οὐ μὴ δύνηται ὑμᾶς ἐξελέσθαι ἐκ χειρὸς
αὐτοῦ. ³⁰καὶ μὴ ἐπελπιζέτω ὑμᾶς 'Εζεκίας πρὸς Κύριον
λέγων ' 'Εξαιρούμενος ἐξελεῖται Κύριος· οὐ μὴ παραδοθῇ
ἡ πόλις αὕτη ἐν χειρὶ βασιλέως 'Ασσυρίων.' ³¹μὴ ἀκούετε 'Εζεκίου, ὅτι τάδε λέγει ὁ βασιλεὺς 'Ασσυρίων ' Ποιήσατε μετ' ἐμοῦ εὐλογίαν καὶ ἐξέλθατε πρὸς μέ, καὶ πίεται
ἀνὴρ τὴν ἄμπελον αὐτοῦ, καὶ ἀνὴρ τὴν συκῆν αὐτοῦ φάγεται, καὶ πίεται ὕδωρ τοῦ λάκκου αὐτοῦ, ³²ἕως ἔλθω καὶ
λάβω ὑμᾶς εἰς γῆν ὡς γῆ ὑμῶν, σίτου καὶ οἴνου καὶ
ἄρτου καὶ ἀμπελώνων, γῆ ἐλαίας ἐλαίου καὶ μέλιτος·
καὶ ζήσετε καὶ οὐ μὴ ἀποθάνητε.' καὶ μὴ ἀκούετε 'Εζεκίου, ὅτι ἀπατᾷ ὑμᾶς. λέγων ' Κύριος ρύσεται ὑμᾶς.' ³³μὴ

the inhabitants of Jerusalem were
likely to undergo, if they did not listen
to him. *Cp.* what is said of the famine
in Samaria (6²⁵). For τοῦ φαγεῖν the
translator of Is. 36¹² has ἵνα φάγωσι.
He also omits αὐτῶν after κόπρον and
οὖρον.

**28.** μεγάλῃ: Is. 36¹³ φωνῇ μεγάλῃ.
The omission of φωνῇ here is due to
Greek idiom. § 46. — τοῦ μεγάλου
βασιλέως 'Ασσυρίων: Hebrew, 'of the
great king, king of Assyria,' a formula
which is closely followed in Is. 36¹³
τοῦ βασιλέως τοῦ μεγάλου, βασιλέως
'Ασσυρίων.

**29.** ἐπαιρέτω ... λόγοις: Is. 36¹⁴
ἀπατάτω ... λόγοις.

**30.** ἐπελπιζέτω: *make you hope.*
This use of the word is classical,
though not with πρός following. —
'Εξαιρούμενος ἐξελεῖται: § 81.

**31.** Ποιήσατε ... πρὸς μέ: Is. 36¹⁶
Εἰ βούλεσθε εὐλογηθῆναι, ἐκπορεύεσθε
πρὸς μέ. The translation here is more
faithful to the original. — πίεται ἀνὴρ
... φάγεται: Is. 36¹⁶ φάγεσθε ἕκαστος
τὴν ἄμπελον αὐτοῦ καὶ τὰς συκᾶς. In
the Hebrew πίεται and φάγεται are expressed by one verb. — πίεται ὕδωρ
... αὐτοῦ: Is. 36¹⁶ πίεσθε ὕδωρ τοῦ
χαλκοῦ ὑμῶν. On λάκκος see Gen.
37²⁰ n.—ἀνήρ: = ἕκαστος. A Hebraism.
§ 70.

**32.** ἕως ἔλθω: Is. 36¹⁷ ἕως ἂν ἔλθω. —
ὡς γῆ ὑμῶν: Is. 36¹⁷ ὡς ἡ γῆ ὑμῶν.
Understand ἐστί. The γῆ following is
attracted into agreement with this. —
γῆ ἐλαίας ... μέλιτος: not in Isaiah
either in the Hebrew or in the Greek.
— ἐλαίας ἐλαίου: this is the order of
the Hebrew also, but our translators
have inverted it for an obvious reason.

iv Kings XVIII 34

ρυόμενοι ἐρύσαντο οἱ θεοὶ τῶν ἐθνῶν ἕκαστος τὴν ἑαυτοῦ χώραν ἐκ χειρός βασιλέως Ἀσσυρίων; ³⁴ποῦ ἐστίν ὁ θεὸς Αἱμὰθ καὶ Ἀρφάλ; ποῦ ἐστιν ὁ θεὸς Σεπφαρουμάιν; καὶ ὅτι ἐξείλαντο Σαμάρειαν ἐκ χειρός μου; ³⁵τίς ἐν πᾶσιν τοῖς θεοῖς τῶν γαιῶν οἳ ἐξείλαντο τὰς γᾶς αὐτῶν ἐκ χειρός μου, ὅτι ἐξελεῖται Κύριος τὴν Ἰερουσαλὴμ ἐκ χειρός μου;" ' " ³⁶καὶ ἐκώφευσαν καὶ οὐκ ἀπεκρίθησαν αὐτῷ λόγον, ὅτι ἐντολὴ τοῦ βασιλέως λέγων " Οὐκ ἀποκριθήσεσθε αὐτῷ." ³⁷καὶ εἰσῆλθεν Ἐλιακεὶμ υἱὸς Χελκείου ὁ οἰκονόμος καὶ Σόμνας ὁ γραμματεὺς καὶ Ἰώας υἱὸς Σαφὰν ὁ ἀναμιμνήσκων πρὸς τὸν Ἑζεκίαν διερρηχότες τὰ ἱμάτια, καὶ ἀνήγγειλαν αὐτῷ τοὺς λόγους Ῥαψάκου. ¹Καὶ ἐγένετο ὡς ἤκουσεν βασιλεὺς Ἑζεκίας, καὶ διέρρηξεν τὰ ἱμάτια ἑαυτοῦ καὶ περιεβάλετο σάκκον, καὶ εἰσῆλθεν εἰς οἶκον Κυρίου. ²καὶ ἀπέστειλεν Ἐλιακεὶμ τὸν οἰκονόμον καὶ Σόμναν τὸν γραμματέα καὶ τοὺς πρεσβυτέρους τῶν

---

**33.** ῥυόμενοι ἐρύσαντο: Is. 36¹⁸ ἐρύσαντο.— ἕκαστος : the Hebrew here is the same as for ἀνήρ in 31, but ἀνήρ would hardly do after θεοί.

**34.** Αἱμὰθ καὶ Ἀρφάλ: Is. 36¹⁹ Ἐμὰθ καὶ Ἀρφάθ. — Σεπφαρουμάιν : Is. 36¹⁹ τῆς πόλεως Ἐπφαρουαίμ. After this the Hebrew here adds ' of Hena ' and 'Ivvah,' but not so in Isaiah. — καὶ ὅτι ἐξείλαντο : there is nothing in the Hebrew here to correspond to the καί, though there is in Is. 36¹⁹. Translate — *And (do you say) that they have delivered Samaria out of my hand?* In Is. 36¹⁹ the rendering is μὴ ἐδύναντο ῥύσασθαι κτλ.

**35.** γαιῶν . . . γᾶς : § 3.—Κύριος: Is. 36²⁰ ὁ θεός. Hebrew, 'Jehovah.'

**36.** ἐκώφευσαν : cp. Jdg. 16¹². The word occurs all together eleven times in the LXX.— ἐντολὴ . . . λέγων: § 112.

Is. 36²¹ διὰ τὸ προστάξαι τὸν βασιλέα μηδένα ἀποκριθῆναι.

**37.** ὁ γραμματεύς : Is. 36²² ὁ γραμματεὺς τῆς δυνάμεως, without difference in the Hebrew. We may infer the translator's belief that the office of the Recorder was specially connected with the army.— διερρηχότες τὰ ἱμάτια : Is. 36²² ἐσχισμένοι τοὺς χιτῶνας. In classical authors the strong perfect διέρρωγα is used intransitively. The weak perfect διέρρηχα is so employed in the LXX here and in ii K. 14³⁰, 15³² : i Mac. 5¹⁴, 13⁴⁵. It is only in the Epistle of Jeremiah (verse 30) that we find the classical form — ἔχοντες τοὺς χιτῶνας διερρωγότας.

**1.** ὡς ἤκουσεν βασιλεὺς Ἑζεκίας: Is. 37¹ ἐν τῷ ἀκοῦσαι τὸν βασιλέα Ἑζεκίαν. — σάκκον : Hebrew *saq*, Latin *saccus*, English *sack*. Gen. 42²⁷ n.

iv Kings XIX 7

ἱερέων περιβεβλημένους σάκκους πρὸς Ἡσαίαν τὸν προφήτην υἱὸν Ἀμώς, ³καὶ εἶπεν πρὸς αὐτόν " Τάδε λέγει Ἐζεκίας ' Ἡμέρα θλίψεως καὶ ἐλεγμοῦ καὶ παροργισμοῦ ἡ ἡμέρα αὕτη, ὅτι ἦλθον υἱοὶ ἕως ὠδίνων, καὶ ἰσχὺς οὐκ ἔστιν τῇ τικτούσῃ. ⁴εἴ πως εἰσακούσεται Κύριος ὁ θεός σου πάντας τοὺς λόγους Ῥαψάκου, ὃν ἀπέστειλεν αὐτὸν βασιλεὺς Ἀσσυρίων ὁ κύριος αὐτοῦ ὀνειδίζειν θεὸν ζῶντα καὶ βλασφημεῖν ἐν λόγοις οἷς ἤκουσεν Κύριος ὁ θεός σου, καὶ λήμψῃ προσευχὴν περὶ τοῦ λήμματος τοῦ εὑρισκομένου.' " ⁵καὶ ἦλθον οἱ παῖδες τοῦ βασιλέως Ἐζεκίου πρὸς Ἡσαίαν, ⁶καὶ εἶπεν αὐτοῖς Ἡσαίας " Τάδε ἐρεῖτε πρὸς τὸν κύριον ὑμῶν 'Τάδε λέγει Κύριος " Μὴ φοβηθῇς ἀπὸ τῶν λόγων ὧν ἤκουσας, ὧν ἐβλασφήμησαν τὰ παιδάρια βασιλέως Ἀσσυρίων. ⁷ἰδοὺ ἐγὼ δίδωμι ἐν αὐτῷ πνεῦμα, καὶ ἀκούσεται ἀγγελίαν καὶ ἀποστραφήσεται εἰς τὴν γῆν

2. Ἡσαίαν : Hebrew Yᵉshaʹyahu, Vulgate Isaias. From the opening words of the Book of Isaiah we learn that the visions of that prophet were seen ' in the days of Uzziah, Jotham, Ahaz, and Hezekiah, kings of Judah.'— Ἀμώς : not the same name as that of the prophet Amos, though coinciding with it in Greek.

3. Ἡμέρα . . . αὕτη : Is. 37³ Ἡμέρα θλίψεως καὶ ὀνειδισμοῦ καὶ ἐλεγμοῦ καὶ ὀργῆς ἡ σήμερον ἡμέρα, the Hebrew being the same. — παροργισμοῦ : provocation. Cp. ii Esdr. 19¹⁸, ²⁶ καὶ ἐποίησαν παροργισμοὺς μεγάλους, where the Hebrew is the same as here. The R.V. has there ' provocations,' here ' contumely.' — ἦλθον . . . τικτούσῃ : Is. 37³ ἥκει ἡ ὠδὶν τῇ τικτούσῃ, ἰσχὺν δὲ οὐχ ἔχει τοῦ τεκεῖν. The R.V. gives the exact rendering.

4. εἴ πως εἰσακούσεται : Is. 37⁴

εἰσακούσαι (opt.). — ὄν : Is. 37⁴ οὖς. The Hebrew relative may refer to the Rabshakeh himself or to his words. The translator of Fourth Kingdoms has taken one view and the translator of Isaiah the other. — βλασφημεῖν ἐν λόγοις : Is. 37⁴ ὀνειδίζειν λόγους (cogn. acc.) ; R.V. ' and will rebuke the words.' — λήμψῃ . . . εὑρισκομένου : Is. 37⁴ δεηθήσῃ πρὸς κύριον σου περὶ τῶν καταλελιμμένων τούτων. A's reading here of λιμματος ( = λείμματος) gives the right sense. Λεῖμμα occurs nowhere else in the LXX, but is found in Rom. 11⁵.

6. ὧν ἐβλασφήμησαν : Is. 37⁶ οὖς ὠνείδισάν με. — τὰ παιδάρια : Is. 37⁶ οἱ πρέσβεις. The diminutive here expresses the scornful force of the original. In classical Greek we might here have νεανίαι.

7. δίδωμι ἐν αὐτῷ : Is. 37⁷ ἐμβάλλω

αὐτοῦ· καὶ καταβαλῶ αὐτὸν ἐν ῥομφαίᾳ ἐν τῇ γῇ αὐτοῦ." '"    ⁸Καὶ ἐπέστρεψεν 'Ραψάκης, καὶ εὗρεν τὸν βασιλέα 'Ασσυρίων πολεμοῦντα ἐπὶ Λομνά, ὅτι ἤκουσεν ὅτι
ἀπῆρεν ἀπὸ Λαχείς.  ⁹καὶ ἤκουσεν περὶ Θαρὰ βασιλέως
Αἰθιόπων λέγων " 'Ιδοὺ ἐξῆλθεν πολεμεῖν μετὰ σοῦ·" καὶ
ἐπέστρεψεν καὶ ἀπέστειλεν ἀγγέλους πρὸς 'Εζεκίαν λέγων
¹⁰" Μὴ ἐπαιρέτω σε ὁ θεός σου, ἐφ' ᾧ σὺ πέποιθας ἐν αὐτῷ
λέγων ' Οὐ μὴ παραδοθῇ 'Ιερουσαλὴμ εἰς χεῖρας βασιλέως
'Ασσυρίων.'  ¹¹ἰδοὺ σὺ ἤκουσας πάντα ὅσα ἐποίησαν βα-
σιλεῖς 'Ασσυρίων πάσαις ταῖς γαῖς, τοῦ ἀναθεματίσαι
αὐτάς· καὶ σὺ ῥυσθήσῃ;  ¹²μὴ ἐξείλαντο αὐτοὺς οἱ θεοὶ
τῶν ἐθνῶν; οὐ διέφθειραν οἱ πατέρες μου τήν τε Γωζὰν

εἰς αὐτόν. § 91.— καταβαλῶ αὐτὸν ἐν
ῥομφαίᾳ : Is. 37⁷ πεσεῖται μαχαίρᾳ.
The former is the more correct, as the
Hebrew verb is causative. It is to be
noticed that Isaiah's message contains
no reference to the destruction of the
host.

8. ἐπέστρεψεν : Is. 37⁸ ἀπέστρεψεν.—
εὗρεν : Is. κατέλαβεν.— πολεμοῦντα ἐπὶ
Λομνά : Is. πολιορκοῦντα Λόβναν. The
name of the place in the Hebrew is
Libnah. — ὅτι ἤκουσεν : Is. καὶ ἤκουσεν.
The ὅτι reflects the Hebrew.

9. καὶ ἤκουσεν . . . πολεμεῖν μετὰ
σοῦ : the translator of Isaiah throws
this into the form of an historical
statement — καὶ ἐξῆλθεν Θαράκα βασιλεὺς Αἰθιόπων πολιορκῆσαι αὐτόν· καὶ
ἀκούσας ἀπέστρεψεν. — Θαρά : Is. 37⁹
Θαράκα, Hebrew Tirhaqah, Jos. Ant.
X 1 § 4 Θαρσικῆς.— βασιλέως Αἰθιόπων :
Hebrew, 'king of Cush.'— λέγων : § 112.
— πολεμεῖν μετὰ σοῦ : to fight against
thee. In Attic Greek the phrase
would mean to fight on thy side.
— ἐπέστρεψεν καὶ ἀπέστειλεν : he sent

again. A Hebraism. — πρὸς 'Εζεκίαν
λέγων : after this in the Hebrew come
the words, ' Thus shall ye speak to
Hezekiah king of Judah, saying.' They
are to be found also (all but the last)
in Is. 37¹⁰.

10. ἐφ' ᾧ . . . ἐν αὐτῷ : Is. 37¹⁰
ἐφ' ᾧ . . . ἐπ' αὐτῷ. — εἰς χεῖρας :
Is. 37¹⁰ ἐν χειρί. § 91.

11. ἰδοὺ σὺ ἤκουσας : Is. 37¹¹ σὺ
οὐκ ἤκουσας . . . ; — πάσαις ταῖς γαῖς :
Is. 37¹¹ πᾶσαν τὴν γῆν. — τοῦ ἀναθεματίσαι αὐτάς : Is. ὡς ἀπώλεσαν. The
construction in the Hebrew is what
might be called a dative gerund, so
that the choice of the genitive is
prompted by Greek as known to the
translator. § 60. To make a place a
' votive offering' to God implied its
utter destruction. 'Αναθεματίζειν occurs
fourteen times in the LXX.

12. μὴ . . . οὐ : μή = num, οὐ =
nonne. A comparison with the Hebrew however and with Isaiah makes
it seem certain that the right reading
is οὖς, with a comma after μου, but

iv Kings XIX 17

καὶ τὴν Χαρρὰν καὶ 'Ράφεις καὶ υἱοὺς Ἔδεμ τοὺς ἐν
Θαεσθέν; ¹⁸ποῦ ἐστιν ὁ βασιλεὺς Μὰθ καὶ ὁ βασιλεὺς
'Αρφάθ; καὶ ποῦ Σεφφαρουάιν, 'Ανὲς καὶ Οὐδού;"
¹⁴καὶ ἔλαβεν 'Εζεκίας τὰ βιβλία ἐκ χειρὸς τῶν ἀγγέλων
καὶ ἀνέγνω αὐτά· καὶ ἀνέβη εἰς οἶκον Κυρίου καὶ ἀνέπτυξεν αὐτὰ 'Εζεκίας ἐναντίον Κυρίου, ¹⁵καὶ εἶπεν "Κύριε ὁ
θεὸς 'Ισραὴλ ὁ καθήμενος ἐπὶ τῶν χερουβείν, σὺ εἶ ὁ θεὸς
μόνος ἐν πάσαις ταῖς βασιλείαις τῆς γῆς, σὺ ἐποίησας τὸν
οὐρανὸν καὶ τὴν γῆν. ¹⁶κλῖνον, Κύριε, τὸ οὖς σου καὶ
ἄκουσον· ἄνοιξον, Κύριε, τοὺς ὀφθαλμούς σου καὶ ἴδε,
καὶ ἄκουσον τοὺς λόγους Σενναχηρεὶμ οὓς ἀπέστειλεν ὀνειδίζειν θεὸν ζῶντα. ¹⁷ὅτι ἀληθείᾳ, Κύριε, ἠρήμωσαν βασι-

no question mark till the end of the sentence. — **Γωζάν**: the Assyrian province of Guzanu, which was on the river Habor (17¹¹), a tributary of the Euphrates. — **Χαρράν**: *Haran*, an ancient city in north Mesopotamia.— **'Ράφεις**: Is. 'Ράφεθ, R.V. *Rezeph*. This is supposed to be identical with the modern *Ruṣâfa*, three and one-half miles southwest of Sura on the Euphrates, on the road leading to Palmyra. (Cheyne, *Enc. Bib.*) — **υἱοὺς Ἔδεμ τοὺς ἐν Θαεσθέν**: Is. αἵ εἰσιν ἐν χώρᾳ Θεεμάθ. Hebrew in both places 'and the children of Eden, which were in Telassar.' The children of Eden seem to correspond to the Assyrian Bît-Adini (*cp.* ' house of Eden ' in Amos 1⁵) ; Telassar has been thought to be Til-basere, a city in their country. The ruling house of Adini was subdued by Assurnasirpal (885–860 B.C.) and finally set aside by Salmanassar II (859–825).

**13.** **Μάθ**: 18³⁴ Αἱμάθ, Is. 37¹³ 'Εμάθ, Hebrew *Hămath*. Hamath had been

recently conquered by Sargon (721–705 B.C.). — **'Αρφάθ**: 18³⁴ 'Αρφάλ, Hebrew *Arpad*. Subjugated by Tiglath-Pileser III in 740. Arpad is now Tell-Erfâd, thirteen miles from Aleppo to northwest (*Enc. Bib.*). — **Σεφφαρουάιν**: 18³⁴ Σεπφαρουάμιν. — **'Ανὲς καὶ Οὐδού**: Is. 37¹³ 'Ανάγ, Οὐγανά, Hebrew *Hena*' and '*Ivvah*.

**14.** **τὰ βιβλία**: Is. 37¹⁴ τὸ βιβλίον. Plural in the Hebrew. — **ἀνέπτυξεν**: Is. ἤνοιξεν. — **'Εζεκίας**: omitted in Isaiah, but occupying just this place in the Hebrew. — **ἐναντίον Κυρίου**: after this Is. 37¹⁵ has καὶ προσεύξατο 'Εζεκίας πρὸς Κύριον λέγων, words which have their equivalent in the Hebrew also at this point.

**15.** **Κύριε ὁ θεός**: *cp.* 19 and the oft-recurring formula in St. Augustine's Confessions — *Domine Deus meus*. Is. 37¹⁶ has Κύριος σαβαὼθ ὁ θεὸς 'Ισραήλ. — **χερουβείν**: i K. 17⁴⁵ n. — **ἐν πάσαις βασιλείαις τῆς γῆς** : Is. 37¹⁶ πάσης βασιλείας τῆς οἰκουμένης.

**17.** **ὅτι ἀληθείᾳ**: Is. 37¹⁸ ἐπ' ἀληθείας

iv Kings XIX 18

λεῖς Ἀσσυρίων τὰ ἔθνη, ¹⁸καὶ ἔδωκαν τοὺς θεοὺς αὐτῶν
εἰς τὸ πῦρ, ὅτι οὐ θεοί εἰσιν ἀλλ᾽ ἢ ἔργα χειρῶν ἀνθρώπων, ξύλα καὶ λίθος, καὶ ἀπώλεσαν αὐτούς. ¹⁹καὶ νῦν,
Κύριε ὁ θεὸς ἡμῶν, σῶσον ἡμᾶς ἐκ χειρὸς αὐτοῦ, καὶ
γνώσονται πᾶσαι αἱ βασιλεῖαι τῆς γῆς ὅτι σὺ Κύριος
ὁ θεὸς μόνος." ²⁰Καὶ ἀπέστειλεν Ἡσαίας υἱὸς Ἀμὼς
πρὸς Ἐζεκίαν λέγων "Τάδε λέγει Κύριος ὁ θεὸς τῶν δυνάμεων θεὸς Ἰσραήλ ''Α προσηύξω πρὸς μὲ περὶ Σενναχηρεὶμ βασιλέως Ἀσσυρίων ἤκουσα.' ²¹οὗτος ὁ λόγος ὃν
ἐλάλησεν Κύριος ἐπ᾽ αὐτόν

''Εξουδένησέν σε καὶ ἐμυκτήρισέν σε παρθένος θυγάτηρ
   Σειών ·
ἐπὶ σοὶ κεφαλὴν αὐτῆς ἐκίνησεν θυγάτηρ Ἰερουσαλήμ.
²²τίνα ὠνείδισας καὶ ἐβλασφήμησας ;
   καὶ ἐπὶ τίνα ὕψωσας φωνὴν καὶ ἦρας εἰς ὕψος τοὺς
      ὀφθαλμούς σου ;
   εἰς τὸν ἅγιον τοῦ Ἰσραήλ.

γάρ. — τὰ ἔθνη : Is. 37¹⁸ τὴν οἰκουμένην
ὅλην, the Hebrew also being different.
After this the Hebrew has 'and their
lands,' and Isaiah καὶ τὴν χώραν αὐτῶν,
which does not suit with the rendering
of the preceding words.
**18. ἔδωκαν** . . . **πῦρ** : Is. 37¹⁹ ἐνέ-
βαλον τὰ εἴδωλα αὐτῶν εἰς τὸ πῦρ. The
Hebrew is in both places 'gods.' —
**ἀλλ᾽ ἤ** : § 108. — **καὶ ἀπώλεσαν αὐτούς** :
Is. 37¹⁹ καὶ ἀπώσαντο αὐτούς. These
renderings are more literal, but less
faithful, than that of our version —
'therefore they have destroyed them.'
**19. σῶσον ἡμᾶς** : the Greek neg-
lects the particle of entreaty which is
rendered in the English 'I beseech
thee.' — **καὶ γνώσονται** . . . **γῆς** : Is. 37²⁰
ἵνα γνῷ πᾶσα βασιλεία τῆς γῆς. — **ὅτι σὺ**
**Κύριος ὁ θεὸς μόνος** : Is. 37²⁰ ὅτι σὺ εἶ ὁ

θεὸς μόνος. — In the latter place the exact rendering of the Hebrew would be
— ὅτι σὺ Κύριος μόνος.
**20. ἀπέστειλεν** . . . **λέγων** : Is. 37²¹
ἀπεστάλη . . . καὶ εἶπεν, incorrectly. —
**θεὸς τῶν δυνάμεων** : not in the Hebrew
here or in Isaiah.
**21. Κύριος** : Is. 37²² ὁ θεός, against
the Hebrew. — ἐπ᾽ αὐτόν : Is. περὶ
αὐτοῦ, R.V. 'concerning him.' —'Εξου-
δένησεν : Is. 37²² Ἐφαύλισεν. Both
ἐξουδενεῖν and ἐξουδενοῦν are common
in the LXX. — ἐμυκτήρισεν : a favourite word with the writers of the LXX,
being used to represent six different
Hebrew originals. It occurs seventeen
times in all. iii K. 18²⁷ n.
**22. ἐβλασφήμησας** : Is. 37²³ παρώ-
ξυνας. — **καὶ ἦρας κτλ.** : the translator
of Isaiah here inserts a negative, καὶ

iv Kings XIX 26

²³ ἐν χειρὶ ἀγγέλων σου ὠνείδισας κύριόν σου καὶ εἶπας
"Ἐν τῷ πλήθει τῶν ἁρμάτων μου ἐγὼ ἀναβήσομαι εἰς
    ὕψος ὀρέων, μηροὺς τοῦ Λιβάνου·
καὶ ἔκοψα τὸ μέγεθος τῆς κέδρου αὐτοῦ, τὰ ἐκλεκτὰ
    κυπαρίσσων αὐτοῦ·
καὶ ἦλθεν εἰς μέσον δρυμοῦ καὶ Καρμήλου.
²⁴ ἐγὼ ἔψυξα καὶ ἔπιον ὕδατα ἀλλότρια,
    καὶ ἐξηρήμωσα τῷ ἴχνει τοῦ ποδός μου πάντας ποταμοὺς
    περιοχῆς."
²⁵ ἔπλασα αὐτήν, συνήγαγον αὐτήν·
καὶ ἐγενήθη εἰς ἐπάρσεις ἀπὸ οἰκεσιῶν μαχίμων,
    πόλεις ὀχυράς.
²⁶ καὶ οἱ ἐνοικοῦντες ἐν αὐταῖς ἠσθένησαν τῇ χειρί,
    ἔπταισαν καὶ κατῃσχύνθησαν·

οὐκ ἦρας, apparently from misunderstanding his original, the 'lifting up of the eyes,' denoting pride, not worship.

**23. ἐν χειρὶ ἀγγέλων** : Is. 37²⁴ δι' ἀγγέλων. On ἐν χειρί see § 91. — Κύριόν σου: the σού has no equivalent in the Hebrew, and is not in Isaiah. — Ἐν τῷ πλήθει : Is. Τῷ πλήθει. There is another reading here in the Hebrew, meaning 'with the driving,' which has not been adopted either by the Greek or English translators. — μηροὺς : Is. 37²⁴ καὶ εἰς τὰ ἔσχατα, R.V. 'innermost parts.' — ἔκοψα : R.V. 'I will cut down.' — τὰ ἐκλεκτὰ κυπαρίσσων αὐτοῦ : Is. τὸ κάλλος τῆς κυπαρίσσου. — ἦλθεν : Is. εἰσῆλθον, R.V. 'I will enter.'

**24. ἔψυξα** : R.V. 'I have digged.' With ἔψυξα cp. Jer. 6⁷ ὡς ψύχει λάκκος ὕδωρ. The translator of Isaiah has here gone astray altogether. So again in his rendering of 26 (Is. 37²⁷). — περιοχῆς : the R.V. here has 'Egypt' with

'defence' as a marginal alternative. The Hebrew word which is thus ambiguous is rendered in the LXX ten times in all by the word περιοχή. But περιοχή itself is not univocal. In iv K. 24¹⁰, 25², Jer. 19⁹ it clearly means 'siege'; perhaps so also in Nahum 3¹⁴, Zech. 12², ii Chr. 32¹⁰ : in the two remaining passages, Ps. 30²¹, 59⁶⁰, it is taken to mean 'stronghold,' which is the prevailing meaning of the word in the LXX, e.g. in i K. 22⁴·⁵, i Chr. 11⁵. The passage most akin to this is Nahum 3¹⁴ ὕδωρ περιοχῆς ἐπίσπασαι σεαυτῇ (R.V. 'Draw thee water for the siege'), from which perhaps we may infer that it is here intended in the sense of 'siege.' If so, the Greek translator agrees with the A.V. — 'and with the sole of my feet have I dried up all the rivers of besieged places.'

**25. ἔπλασα κτλ.** : the translation of this verse is defective and unintelligible, whereas the corresponding pas-

ἐγένοντο χόρτος ἀγροῦ ἢ χλωρὰ βοτάνη,
χλόη δωμάτων καὶ πάτημα ἀπέναντι ἑστηκότος.
²⁷ καὶ τὴν καθέδραν σου καὶ τὴν ἔξοδόν σου καὶ τὴν εἴσοδόν
    σου ἔγνων,
    καὶ τὸν θυμόν σου ἐπ᾽ ἐμέ.
²⁸ διὰ τὸ ὀργισθῆναί σε ἐπ᾽ ἐμέ,
    καὶ τὸ στρῆνός σου ἀνέβη ἐν τοῖς ὠσίν μου·
    καὶ θήσω τὰ ἄγκιστρά μου ἐν τοῖς μυκτῆρσίν σου καὶ
    χαλινὸν ἐν τοῖς χείλεσίν σου,
    καὶ ἀποστρέψω σε ἐν τῇ ὁδῷ ᾗ ἦλθες ἐν αὐτῇ.
²⁹ καὶ τοῦτό σοι τὸ σημεῖον·
    φάγε τοῦτον τὸν ἐνιαυτὸν αὐτόματα,
    καὶ τῷ ἔτει τῷ δευτέρῳ τὰ ἀνατέλλοντα·
    καὶ ἔτει τρίτῳ σπορὰ καὶ ἄμητος καὶ φυτεία ἀμπελώνων,
    καὶ φάγεσθε τὸν καρπὸν αὐτῶν.
³⁰ καὶ προσθήσει τὸν διασεσωσμένον οἴκου Ἰούδα τὸ ὑπολει-
    φθὲν ῥίζαν κάτω,
    καὶ ποιήσει καρπὸν ἄνω.

sage in Isaiah is not far from the original. The word οἰκεσία is not known elsewhere.

**26.** πάτημα ἀπέναντι ἑστηκότος : R.V. 'as corn blasted before it be grown up.' The word rendered πάτημα (*a thing trodden*) means *blighted grain*, and that rendered ἑστηκότος means *standing corn*. The word represented by ἀπέναντι means 'before' either of place or time. The Greek translator has mischosen the local instead of the temporal meaning.

**27.** καθέδραν : Is. 37²⁸ ἀνάπαυσιν. —ἔγνων : Is. ἐγὼ ἐπίσταμαι.

**28.** τὸ στρῆνός σου : Is. 37²⁹ ἡ πικρία σου. Στρῆνος does not occur else-

where in the LXX, but is found in Rev. 18³. — θήσω . . . μυκτῆρσίν σου : Is. ἐμβαλῶ φιμὸν εἰς τὴν ῥῖνά σου. — ἐν τοῖς χείλεσίν σου : Is. εἰς τὰ χείλη σου.

**29.** αὐτόματα : Is. 37³⁰ ἃ ἔσπαρκας erroneously. — τὰ ἀνατέλλοντα : Is. τὸ κατάλιμμα, R.V. 'that which springeth of the same.' — σπορὰ . . . ἀμπελώνων : Is. σπείραντες ἀμήσατε καὶ φυτεύσατε ἀμπελῶνας.

**30.** τὸν διασεσωσμένον : here the subject has been turned into the object of the verb, which makes havoc of the sentence. Is. 37³¹ καὶ ἔσονται οἱ καταλελειμμένοι ἐν τῇ Ἰουδαίᾳ, φυήσουσιν ῥίζαν κτλ.

iv Kings XIX 35

³¹ ὅτι ἐξ Ἰερουσαλὴμ ἐξελεύσεται κατάλειμμα,
καὶ ἀνασωζόμενος ἐξ ὄρους Σειών·
ὁ ζῆλος Κυρίου τῶν δυνάμεων ποιήσει τοῦτο.'

³² οὐχ οὕτως· τάδε λέγει Κύριος πρὸς βασιλέα Ἀσσυρίων
' Οὐκ εἰσελεύσεται εἰς τὴν πόλιν ταύτην,
καὶ οὐ τοξεύσει ἐκεῖ βέλος,
καὶ οὐ προφθάσει αὐτὸν θυρεός, καὶ οὐ μὴ ἐκχέῃ πρὸς
αὐτὴν πρόσχωμα.

³³ τῇ ὁδῷ ᾗ ἦλθεν, ἐν αὐτῇ ἀποστραφήσεται·
καὶ εἰς τὴν πόλιν ταύτην οὐκ εἰσελεύσεται,' λέγει Κύριος.

³⁴ ' καὶ ὑπερασπιῶ ὑπὲρ τῆς πόλεως ταύτης
δι' ἐμὲ καὶ διὰ Δαυεὶδ τὸν δοῦλόν μου.'"

³⁵ Καὶ ἐγένετο νυκτὸς καὶ ἐξῆλθεν ἄγγελος Κυρίου καὶ
ἐπάταξεν ἐν τῇ παρεμβολῇ τῶν Ἀσσυρίων ἑκατὸν ὀγδοήκοντα πέντε χιλιάδας· καὶ ὤρθρισαν τὸ πρωί, καὶ ἰδοὺ

---

**31. ἐξελεύσεται κατάλειμμα :** Is. 37³² ἔσονται οἱ καταλελιμμένοι, incorrectly. — ἀνασωζόμενος : Is. οἱ σωζόμενοι. — τῶν δυνάμεων : Is. σαβαώθ. The Hebrew equivalent is found in Isaiah, but is missing from the text here.

**32. οὐχ οὕτως :** Is. 37³³ διὰ τοῦτο, correctly. The translator of Fourth Kingdoms has fallen into this mistake before. 1⁸ n. — πρὸς βασιλέα : Is. ἐπὶ βασιλέα. — Οὐκ εἰσελεύσεται : Is. Οὐ μὴ εἰσέλθῃ. — καὶ οὐ τοξεύσει ἐκεῖ βέλος : Is. οὐδὲ μὴ βάλῃ ἐπ' αὐτὴν βέλος. — οὐ προφθάσει αὐτὸν θυρεός : Is. οὐδὲ μὴ ἐπιβάλῃ ἐπ' αὐτὴν θυρεόν, R.V. 'neither shall he come before it with shield.' — οὐ μὴ ἐκχέῃ πρὸς αὐτὴν πρόσχωμα : Is. οὐδὲ μὴ κυκλώσῃ ἐπ' αὐτὴν χάρακα, which is the spirit rather than the letter. χάραξ = vallum, προσχῶμα = agger.

**33. οὐκ εἰσελεύσεται :** Is. 37³⁴ οὐ μὴ εἰσέλθῃ.

**34. ὑπερασπιῶ ὑπέρ :** ὑπερασπίζειν occurs twenty-two times in the LXX. It is followed by ὑπέρ again in 20⁶ : Zech. 12⁸ : Is. 31⁵, 37³⁵, 38⁶. — τῆς πόλεως ταύτης : the Hebrew adds ' to save it,' which is represented in Is. 37³⁵ by τοῦ σῶσαι αὐτήν. — δοῦλον : Is. παῖδα.

**35. Καὶ ἐγένετο νυκτός :** not in Isaiah. — ἐπάταξεν ἐν κτλ. : Is. 37³⁶ ἀνεῖλεν ἐκ τῆς παρεμβολῆς. Cp. i Mac. 7⁴¹ ἐξῆλθεν ἄγγελός σου καὶ ἐπάταξεν ἐν αὐτοῖς ἑκατὸν ὀγδοήκοντα πέντε χιλιάδας. — καὶ ὤρθρισαν κτλ. : R.V. ' and when men arose early in the morning,' thus avoiding the bull which exists in the A.V. — ' and when they arose early in the morning, behold, they were all dead corpses.' The Greek translator of Isaiah escapes it thus — καὶ ἀνάσταντες τὸ πρωὶ εὗρον πάντα τὰ σώματα νεκρά.

iv Kings XIX 36

πάντες σώματα νεκρά.  ³⁶ καὶ ἀπῆρεν καὶ ἐπορεύθη καὶ ἀπέστρεψεν Σενναχηρεὶμ βασιλεὺς Ἀσσυρίων, καὶ ᾤκησεν ἐν Νινευή.  ³⁷ καὶ ἐγένετο αὐτοῦ προσκυνοῦντος ἐν οἴκῳ Ἐσδρὰχ θεοῦ αὐτοῦ, καὶ Ἀδραμέλεχ καὶ Σαράσαρ οἱ υἱοὶ αὐτοῦ ἐπάταξαν αὐτὸν ἐν μαχαίρᾳ· καὶ αὐτοὶ ἐσώθησαν εἰς γῆν Ἀραράθ· καὶ ἐβασίλευσεν Ἀσορδὰν ὁ υἱὸς αὐτοῦ ἀντ' αὐτοῦ.

**36. καὶ ἀπῆρεν καὶ ἐπορεύθη καὶ ἀπέστρεψεν** : Is. 37³⁷ καὶ ἀπῆλθεν ἀποστραφείς, but the wealth of predicates faithfully reflects the original. — ᾤκησεν : this is consistent with any interval between the return of Sennacherib and his murder.

**37. καὶ ἐγένετο αὐτοῦ προσκυνοῦντος** : Is. 37³⁸ καὶ ἐν τῷ αὐτὸν προσκυνεῖν. — Ἐσδράχ : Is. Νασαράχ, Hebrew Nisrokh. No such god is otherwise known.  Josephus (Ant. X 1 § 5)

understands the proper name to be that of the temple — καὶ ἀνηρέθη τῷ ἰδίῳ ναῷ Ἀράσκῃ λεγομένῳ. — θεοῦ αὐτοῦ : Is. τὸν πάτραρχον αὐτοῦ. § 57. — οἱ υἱοὶ αὐτοῦ : omitted in the Hebrew text here, but appearing in Isaiah.  Jos. Ant. X 1 § 5 δολοφονηθεὶς ὑπὸ τῶν πρεσβυτέρων παίδων Ἀδραμελέχου καὶ Σαρασάρου τελευτᾷ τὸν βίον. — ἐν μαχαίρᾳ : Is. μαχαίραις. — εἰς γῆν Ἀραράθ : Is. εἰς Ἀρμενίαν. — Ἀσορδάν : Josephus Ἀσαραχόδδας, Hebrew Esarhaddon.

# Indexes and Vocabulary

C. Mack Roark
Ruth Dickinson Professor of Bible
Oklahoma Baptist University

# INDEX OF ANCIENT SOURCES

328     SELECTIONS FROM THE SEPTUAGINT

ii Corinthians
1:13  95
1:15  297
1:19  70
1:22  298
2:17  70
3:1  43
3:15  85
4:2  43
4:8  242
4:18  58
5:5  298
5:10  64
5:12  43
5:14  63
6:4  43
6:12  242
6:14  71
6:15  281
6:18  81
8:2  28
8:12  92
8:16  83
9:12  70
10:12  43, 45
10:18  43
12:2  31
12:10  238
12:17  64

Galatians
1:10  31
1:14  85
1:17  93
1:18  31
1:22  31, 71
1:23  71
1:8–9  28
2:1  31
2:4  93
2:10  67
2:16  80
3:1  41
3:10  59
3:19  48

4:2  48
4:19  48
4:24  68
5:1  42, 61
5:4  36
5:9  175
5:14  63
6:7  92, 272

Ephesians
1:4  87
1:7  28
1:14  298
1:17  45
2:3  32
2:7  28
2:21  63
3:8  28
3:16  28, 81
4:1  57
4:13  63
4:29  80
5:5  75, 80
5:13  64
5:14  46
6:1  35
6:2  82
6:8  92
6:17  253

Philippians
1:27  42
2:15  195
2:21  63
2:23  182
2:26  71
3:6  28
3:11  89
3:12  89
4:1  42
4:12  42
4:19  28

Colossians
1:6  70
1:18  71

1:22  87
1:27  28
2:2  28
2:23  70
3:2  70
3:5  68
3:18  55
3:20  55
3:23  92

i Thessalonians
1:5  115
3:8  42
5:5  28
5:6  43
5:8  253

ii Thessalonians
2:8  39
2:15  42
3:6  33
3:14  183
3:16  45

i Timothy
5:15  87
6:9  68
6:13  155

ii Timothy
1:16  27
1:16  45
1:18  27, 45
2:25  45
3:8  152
5:4  33

Titus
1:5  73
2:8  183
3:5  27
3:12  19
3:14  33

Philemon
12  67
20  73

Hebrews
1:4  86
1:9  86
1:13  47
2:13  71
3:3  86
3:8  174
3:11  90
3:13  48
4:2  70
4:3  90
4:12  85
4:16  27
5:7  84
5:12  216
6:14  91
7:21  70
7:23  70
9:23  86
10:10  70
11:4  86
11:5  59
11:8  48
11:30  36
11:37  278
12:4  48
12:24  86
13:7  287
13:17  287
13:24  287

James
1:1  16
2:3  47
3:4  48
5:7  183
5:12  32
5:16  70
5:17  59, 61, 260

i Peter
2:24  65
3:1  93
3:14  73
3:17  73

# VOCABULARY: PROPER NOUNS
## IN SELECTED READINGS

| | | | |
|---|---|---|---|
| Ἀαρών | Aaron | Βενιαμείν | Benjamin |
| Ἀβδειού | Obadiah | Βεώρ | Beor |
| Ἀβραάμ | Abraham | Βηρσάβεε | Beer-sheba |
| Ἀδοναῖε | Adonai | | |
| Ἀδραμέλεχ | Adrammelech | Γάζα | Gaza |
| Ἀζαήλ | Hazael | Γαζαῖος | Gazite |
| Ἀζηκά | Azekah | Γαλαάδ | Gilead |
| Αἰγύπτιος | Egyptian | Γέθ | Gath |
| Αἴγυπτος | Egypt | Γεργεσαῖος | Gergessite |
| Αἰθίοψ | Ethiopian | Γέσεμ | Goshen |
| Αἰμάθ | Hamath | Γηρσάμ | Gershom |
| Ἀκκαρών | Ekron | Γολιάδ | Goliath |
| Ἀλσωρήχ | Sorek | Γολιάθ | Goliath |
| Ἀμαλήκ | Amalek | Γώγ | Gog |
| Ἀμορραῖος | Amorite | Γωζάν | Gozan |
| Ἀμώς | Amoz | | |
| Ἀνές | Hena | Δαγών | Dagon |
| Ἀραβία | Arabia | Δαλειδά | Delilah |
| Ἀραράθ | Ararat | Δαμασκός | Damascus |
| Ἀρνών | Arnon | Δάν | Dan |
| Ἀρφάλ | Arphad | Δαυείδ | David |
| Ἀσεννέθ | Aseneth | Δωθάειμ | Dothan |
| Ἀσκάλων | Ashkelon | | |
| Ἀσορδάν | Esar-haddon | Ἐβαλμαουλά | Abel-meholah |
| Ἀσσούρ | Asshur | Ἐβραῖος | Hebrew |
| Ἀσσύριος | Assyrian | Ἐδέμ | Eden |
| Ἀχαάβ | Ahab | Ἐδώμ | Edom |
| Ἀχειά | Ahijah | Ἐζεκίας | Hezekiah |
| | | Εἰού | Jehu |
| Βαάλ | Baal | Ἐλεισαῖε | Elisha |
| Βαιθήλ | Bethel | Ἐλιακείμ | Eliakim |
| Βαλαάμ | Balaam | Ἐσδράχ | Nisroch |
| Βαλάκ | Balak | Ἐσθαλαόλ | Eshtaol |
| Βάλλα | Bilhah | Ἐσθαόλ | Eshtaol |
| Βαλλείμ | Baals | Εὐαῖνος | Hivite |
| Βασσά | Baasha | Ἐφερμέμ | Ephes-dammim |
| Βεελσεπφών | Baal-zephon | Ἐφράιμ | Ephraem |

| | | | |
|---|---|---|---|
| Ζέλφα | Zilpah | Μάγδωλος | Migdol |
| | | Μαδιάμ | Midian |
| Ἠλειού | Elijah | Μαδιηναῖος | Midianite |
| Ἠλίου Πόλις | Heliopolis | Μάθ | Hamath |
| Ἠσαίας | Isaiah | Μανασσή | Manasseh |
| Ἠσαύ | Esau | Μανῶε | Manoah |
| Ἠτάμ | Etam | Μαριάμ | Miriam |
| Θαεσθέν | Telassar | Μεσοποταμία | Mesopotamia |
| Θαμνάθα | Timnah | Μωάβ | Moab |
| Θανθάν | Tartan | Μωαβειτῆς | Moabite |
| Θεσβείτης | Tishbite | Μωϋσῆς | Moses |
| Θεσβῶν | Tishbe | Ναβάθ | Nebat |
| Ἰακώβ | Jacob | Ναβουθαί | Naboth |
| Ἰδουμαία | Idumea | Ναμεσθεί | Nimshi |
| Ἰεβουσαῖος | Jebusite | Νινευή | Nineveh |
| Ἰεζάβελ | Jezebel | Ὀθόμ | Etham |
| Ἰερειχώ | Jericho | Οὐδού | Ivvah |
| Ἱεροβοάμ | Jeroboam | Ὀχοζείας | Ahaziah |
| Ἱεροσόλυμα | Jerusalem | | |
| Ἱερουσαλήμ | Jerusalem | Παντοκράτωρ | Almighty; transla- |
| Ἰοθόρ | Jethro | | tion of Sabaoth |
| Ἰορδάνης | Jordan | Πειθώ | Pithom |
| Ἰουδά | Judah | Πετεφρῆς | Potiphar or |
| Ἰουδαιστί | Jewish | | Potiphera |
| Ἰούδας | Judah | Πετρεφῆς | Potiphar or |
| Ἰσαάκ | Isaac | | Potiphera |
| Ἰσμαήλ | Ishmael | Ῥαγουήλ | Raguel (Reuel) |
| Ἰσμαηλείτης | Ishmaelite | Ῥαμεσσή | Rameses |
| Ἰσραήλ | Israel | Ῥαφείς | Rab-saris |
| Ἰσραηλείτης | Israelite | Ῥάφεις | Rezeph |
| Ἰωάς | Joah | Ῥαψάκης | Rabshakeh |
| Ἰωσαφάτ | Jehoshaphat | Ῥουβήν | Reuben |
| Ἰωσήφ | Joseph | | |
| | | Σαμάρεια | Samaria |
| Καρμήλιος | Carmel | Σαμψών | Samson |
| Κάρμηλος | Carmel | Σαούλ | Saul |
| Κεναῖος | Kenite | Σαραά | Zorah |
| Κιτιαίοι | Kittim | Σαράλ | Zorah |
| | | Σαράσαρ | Sharezer |
| Λαχείς | Lachish | Σάρεπτα | Zarepheth |
| Λευεῖ | Levi | Σαφάθ | Shaphat |
| Λευείτης | Levite | Σαφάν | Asaph |
| Λίβανος | Lebanon | Σαφάτ | Shaphat |
| Λομνά | Libnah | Σειδωνία | Sidon |

| | | | |
|---|---|---|---|
| Σειών | Zion | Φιλισταῖος | Philistine |
| Σενναχηρείμ | Sennacherib | Φιλιστιείμ | Philistine |
| Σεπφαρουάιν | Sepharvaim | Φογώρ | Peor |
| Σεπφώρ | Zippor | Φουά | Puah |
| Σεπφωρά | Zipporah | | |
| Σεφφαρουάιν | Sepharvaim | Χανάαν | Canaan |
| Σεφώρα | Zipporah | Χαναναῖος | Canaanite |
| Σήθ | Seth | Χαρράν | Haran |
| Σοκχώθ | Succoth | Χεβρών | Hebron |
| Σοκχώθα | Succoth | Χελκίας | Hilkiah |
| Σόμνας | Shebnath | Χετταῖος | Hittite |
| Συμεών | Simeon | Χορράθ | Cherith |
| Συρία | Syria | Χωρήβ | Horeb |
| Συριστί | Syriac | | |
| Συχέμ | Shechem | Ψονθομφανήχ | Psonthomphanech |
| | | | (Zaphenath-panech) |
| Φαθούρα | Pethor | | |
| Φαραώ | Pharoah | Ὤγ | Og |
| Φερεζαῖος | Perizzite | Ὤν | On |

# INDEX OF SELECTED GREEK WORDS

342 SELECTIONS FROM THE SEPTUAGINT

ὁ πᾶς 141
ὁ ὤν 162
ὁδὸν τῆς θαλάσσης 275
ὀθονία 233
οἰωνός 215-16
ὀκλάζω 279
ὀλιγοψυχέω 242
ὁλοκαύτωμα 211, 273
ὀλύρα 120
ὁμοθυμαδόν 221
ὀργίζω 142
ὀρθρίζω 177
ὁρισμός 176
ὅτι εἰ μή 265
ὅτι, with direct oration 114
οὗ = οἷ 269
οὐχ οὕτως 307
ὀχύρωμα 117
ὄψιμος 133
ὄψιν τῆς γῆς 184

παιγνία 244
παιδάριον 301
παῖς = servant 121
πᾶν ... μή 229
παντοκράτωρ 277-78
παρά ᾧ owing to 192
παρά, of comparison 109
παραβολή 211
παράδεισος 216
παραδοξάζω 178
παράνομος 281
παράταξις 252
παρεμβάλλω 192
παρεμβολή 192, 231, 252
παρίστημι 182, 211
παροικέω 108
παροργισμός 301
πᾶς, without article 177
πάχος 217
πεποίθησις 297
περικεφαλαία 253
περιοχή 305
πηγή 238-39
πηλός = mortar 154-55

πλῆθος, adverbial 178
πληθύνω 156
πλήν = only 125
πλινθία 155, 168
πλινθουργία 168
ποιέω = dress 272
πολεμέω 194, 302
πολυπληθύνω 167
πόρια, neuter pl. 141
ποταμός 205-6
ποῦ ᾧ ποῖ 113
πρᾶσις 127
πρὸ τῆς ἐχθές 164
πρόβλημα 233
προνομεύω 219
προσάγω 271, 273
προσδέχομαι 185-86
προσέθεντο ἔτι μισεῖν 110
προσκυνέω 109-10
προσνοέω 212
προσόχθισμα 273
προστίθημι 23, 110, 138, 168, 188, 276, 286
προφήτης 172
πυρράκης 256

ῥάβδος 256
Ῥαγουήλ 159
ῥῆμα 116, 118, 123
ῥητόν 180
ῥιτίνη 112, 132
ῥομφαία 169

σαβαώθ 257
-σαι in second sg. 264
σάκκος 300
Σαμψών 223, 231
-σαν in third pl. 192
Σαράλ 227
σειρά 241
σειρομάστης 273
Σενναχηρείμ 295
Σεπφωρά 155
Σήθ 219
σημεῖα καὶ τέρατα 172

# VOCABULARY

## A

| | |
|---|---|
| ἄβρα, -ας, ἡ | favorite servant, maid |
| ἀγαθός, -ή, -όν | good |
| ἀγαθύνω | cheer, make merry |
| ἀγαπάω | love |
| ἀγγεῖον, -ου, τό | vessel, container |
| ἄγγελος, -ου, ὁ | messenger, angel |
| ἄγγος, -ους, τό | vessel, vat |
| ἀγέλη, -ης, ἡ | herd, flock |
| ἀγίασμα, -ατος, τό | sanctuary |
| ἅγιος, -α, -ον | sacred, holy |
| ἄγκιστρον, -ου, τό | hook |
| ἀγνόημα, -ατος, τό | oversight, mistake |
| ἀγοράζω | buy |
| ἀγορασμός, -οῦ, ὁ | purchasing, purchase |
| ἀγρός, -οῦ, ὁ | field, land |
| ἀδελφός, -οῦ, ὁ | brother, kinsman |
| ἀδικέω | do wrong, wrong, act unjustly |
| ἀδολεσχία, -ας, ἡ | idle talk, conversation; *perhaps* meditation |
| ἀδρύνομαι | come to maturity, grow |
| ἄζυμος, -ον | unleavened |
| ἀθετέω | set aside, disregard, reject |
| ἀθῳόω | leave unavenged; be guiltless |
| αἰθάλη, -ης, ἡ | soot, ash |
| αἷμα, -ατος, τό | blood |
| αἴξ, αἰγός, ὁ | goat |
| αἴρω | lift, take up, carry |
| αἰσχρός, -ά, -όν | ugly, shameful |
| αἰσχύνη, -ης, ἡ | shame, dishonor |
| αἰσχύνω | shame, dishonor |
| αἰτέω | ask for, demand |
| αἰχμαλωτεύω | take prisoner, capture |
| αἰχμαλωτίς, -ίδος, ἡ | captive, prisoner |
| αἰών, αἰῶνος, ὁ | age, generation |
| αἰώνιος, -ον | eternal, everlasting |

| | |
|---|---|
| ἀκάθαρτος, -ον | unclean, impure |
| ἀκολουθέω | follow, go with |
| ἀκουστός, -ή, -όν | heard, audible |
| ἀκουτίζω | cause to hear |
| ἀκούω | hear |
| ἀκρίς, -ίδος, ἡ | locust, swarm of locusts |
| ἀκρόασις, -εως, ἡ | hearing, listening |
| ἀλαλάζω | shout, cry aloud |
| ἄλευρον, -ου, τό | wheat meal |
| ἀληθεύω | tell the truth, be honest |
| ἀληθής, -ές | true, genuine |
| ἀληθινός, -ή, -όν | true, genuine |
| ἀληθινῶς | truly, really |
| ἀλλά | but, yet, rather, only |
| ἀλλάγμα, -ατος, τό | that which is given or taken in exchange; price |
| ἀλλάσσω | change |
| ἀλλήλους, -ας, -α | one another *(gen., dat., acc. only)* |
| ἄλλομαι | leap, spring |
| ἄλλος, -η, -ον | other, another |
| ἀλλοτριόομαι | estrange oneself from, be reserved |
| ἀλλότριος, -α, -ον | strange, foreign |
| ἀλλόφυλος, -ον | of another tribe, foreign; Philistine |
| ἄλογος, -ον | lacking in eloquence |
| ἄλσος, -ους, τό | grove, sacred grove |
| ἀλυσιδωτός, -η, -ον | made of chainwork |
| ἄλων, -ωνος, ἡ/ὁ | threshing-floor |
| ἀλώπηξ, -εκος, ἡ | fox |
| ἅμα | at the same time, together |
| ἅμαξα, -ης, ἡ | wagon |
| ἁμαρτάνω | do wrong, sin |
| ἁμαρτία, -ας, ἡ | sin, mistake |
| ἄμητος, -η, -ον | harvest |
| ἄμμος, -ου, ὁ | sand |
| ἄμπελος, -ου, ἡ | vine, vineyard |
| ἀμπελών, -ῶνος, ὁ | vineyard |
| ἀμφότεροι, -αι, -α | both |
| ἄν | *particle rendering a statement contingent; sometimes* -ever |
| ἀνά | up; ἀνά μέσον between |
| ἀναβαίνω | go up |
| ἀναβαστάζω | lift up |
| ἀναβάτης, -ου, ὁ | horseman, *pl.* cavalry |
| ἀναβιβάζω | bring up, guide up, lift up |
| ἀναβλέπω | look up, lift up the eyes |
| ἀναβοάω | shout, cry out |

| | |
|---|---|
| ἀναγγέλλω | report, recount, announce, declare |
| ἀναγινώσκω | read, read aloud |
| ἀναγνωρίζομαι | make oneself known |
| ἀνάγω | bring up, raise up; lead to |
| ἀναζεύγνυμι | break camp, prepare to march |
| ἀναζέω | break out (of sores), ooze forth |
| ἀναζωπυρέω | rekindle, revive |
| ἀναθεματίζω | devote to evil, curse |
| ἀναίρεσις, -εως, ἡ | destruction, slaughter |
| ἀναιρέω | take up; destroy, kill |
| ἀναλαμβάνω | take up, lift up, take with |
| ἀναλίσκω | consume, destroy |
| ἀναμιμνήσκω | remember |
| ἀναπαύω | rest |
| ἀναπληρόω | fill up, complete, finish |
| ἀναπτύσσω | spread out, unfold |
| ἀναστρέφω | turn back, return |
| ἀνασῴζω | rescue, escape |
| ἀνατέλλω | raise; rise |
| ἀνατολή, -ῆς, ἡ | east; morning |
| ἀναφέρω | bring forth, bring up |
| ἀναφύω | grow up, spring up |
| ἀναχωρέω | depart, withdraw, flee |
| ἀνάψυξις, -εως, ἡ | respite, relief, relaxation |
| ἀνελῶ | future of ἀναιρέω |
| ἄνεμος, -ου, ὁ | wind |
| ἀνεμόφθορος, -ον | blasted by the wind |
| ἀνενηνοχυῖα | perfect participle feminine of ἀναφέρω |
| ἄνευ | without |
| ἀνέχω | withhold, hold back, restrain |
| ἀνήρ, ἀνδρός, ὁ | man, husband |
| ἀνθίσταμαι | stand against, stand in opposition |
| ἄνθρωπος, -ου, ὁ | man, person; pl., humankind, people |
| ἀνίστημι | get up, arise; stand |
| ἀνοίγω | open |
| ἀνταποδίδωμι | give back, repay |
| ἀνταπόδοσις, -εως, ἡ | repayment, retribution |
| ἀντί | in place of, instead of, in the presence of |
| ἀντιλέγω | speak against, contradict |
| ἀντλέω | draw water |
| ἄνω | above, upper |
| ἀξιόω | deem worthy; entreat, beseech |
| ἄξων, -ονος, ὁ | axle |
| ἀπαγγέλλω | announce, report, tell |
| ἀπάγω | lead away, carry off |

| | |
|---|---|
| ἀπαίρω | remove; depart |
| ἀπάνωθεν | from upon, from |
| ἅπαξ | once, once for all |
| ἀπατάω | deceive; seduce |
| ἀπειλέω | threaten; *pass.*, be terrified by threats |
| ἀπέναντι | opposite, against |
| ἀπερίτμητος, -ον | uncircumcised |
| ἀπέρχομαι | go away, depart |
| ἀπέχω | be far from, be distant; receive in full |
| ἀπῆκτο | *pluperfect of* ἀπάγω |
| ἀπό | from, away from |
| ἀποβαίνω | go away, depart; happen |
| ἀποδίδωμι | give back, return, restore; hand over |
| ἀποθλίβω | crush, press against |
| ἀποθνήσκω | die |
| ἀποκαθίστημι | reestablish, restore, return |
| ἀποκαλύπτω | uncover, open, disclose, reveal |
| ἀποκλείω | shut up, close |
| ἀποκρίνομαι | answer |
| ἀποκτείνω | kill, slay, destroy |
| ἀπολείπω | leave behind, leave undone |
| ἀπολιθόομαι | become petrified |
| ἀπόλλυμι | destroy, kill |
| ἀποπεμπτόω | give a fifth part of |
| ἀποσκευή, -ῆς, ἡ | baggage, household |
| ἀποσπάω | break, detach |
| ἀποστέλλω | send, send off, send away |
| ἀποστρέφω | turn back, turn away |
| ἀποτρέχω | run off, run away |
| ἅπτομαι | grasp, touch, take hold |
| ἄρα | *inferential particle* then, therefore, indeed; εἰ ἄρα if indeed |
| ἆρα | *interrog. particle usually expecting a negative answer* |
| ἀράομαι | curse |
| ἀργύριον, -ου, τό | silver |
| ἀργυροῦς, -ᾶ, -οῦν | silver, made of silver |
| ἀρέσκω | please, satisfy |
| ἀριθμέω | number, count |
| ἀριθμός, -οῦ, ὁ | number, amount |
| ἀριστάω | dine, take the midday meal |
| ἀριστερός, -ά, -όν | left, on the left |
| ἄρκος, -ου, ὁ | bear |
| ἅρμα, -ατος, τό | chariot |
| ἀροτρίασις, -εως, ἡ | plowing |
| ἀροτριάω | plow |

| | |
|---|---|
| ἁρπάζω | snatch away, carry off; seize |
| ἀρρωστέω | be sick |
| ἀρρωστία, -ας, ἡ | sickness, disease |
| ἄρσην, -ενος, ὁ | male |
| ἄρτος, -ου, ὁ | bread, cake |
| ἀρχή, -ῆς, ἡ | beginning; power, authority, office |
| ἀρχηγός, -οῦ, ὁ | chief, head, ruler |
| ἀρχιδεσμοφύλαξ, -ακος, ὁ | chief jailer |
| ἀρχιμάγειρος, -ου, ὁ | chief cook; chief of royal guard |
| ἀρχιοινοχοία, -ας, ἡ | office of chief cup-bearer |
| ἀρχιοινοχόος, -ου, ὁ | chief cup-bearer |
| ἀρχισιτοποιός, -οῦ, ὁ | chief baker |
| ἄρχω | active, rule; middle, begin |
| ἄρχων, -οντος, ὁ | ruler, overseer, chief |
| ἀσεβής, -ές | wicked, ungodly, profane |
| ἀσθενέω | be weak, be sick |
| ἀσπίς, -ίδος, ἡ | shield |
| ἀστεῖος, -α, -ον | charming, handsome, pretty; seemly |
| ἀστήρ, -έρος, ὁ | star |
| ἄστρον, -ου, τό | star |
| ἀσφαλτόπισσα, -ης, ἡ | bitumen, pitch |
| ἀτεκνόω | be barren, make childless |
| ἀτιμάζω | despise, belittle, esteem lightly |
| αὖλαξ, -ακος, ἡ | row, furrow |
| αὖρα, -ας, ἡ | breeze |
| αὔριον | tomorrow |
| αὐτόματος, -η, -ον | spontaneous |
| αὐτός, αὐτή, αὐτό | personal pronoun, he, she, it; self |
| ἀφαιρέω | take away, remove |
| ἀφανίζω | remove, get rid of |
| ἀφελῶ | future of ἀφαιρέω |
| ἀφηγέομαι | lead |
| ἀφίημι | leave, let, permit; forgive |
| ἀφίστημι | remove, withdraw, depart |
| ἀφφώ | even he |
| ἄχει (ἄχι) | indeclinable, grass |
| ἄχυρον, -ου, τό | straw, chaff |
| ᾅδης, -ου, ὁ | Hades, grave; hell |
| ᾄδω | sing |

# B

| | |
|---|---|
| βαδίζω | go, proceed |
| βακτηρία, -ας, ἡ | staff |
| βαρέω | weigh down, oppress; be heavy, depress |

| | |
|---|---|
| βαρύνω | make heavy, harden |
| βαρύς, -εῖα, -ύ | heavy, great, powerful |
| βασιλεία, -ας, ἡ | kingdom, reign |
| βασιλεύς, -έως, ὁ | king |
| βασιλεύω | reign, rule |
| βαστάζω | bear |
| βάτος, -ου, ὁ | bush, bramble |
| βάτραχος, -ου, ὁ | frog |
| βδέλυγμα, -ατος, τό | abomination |
| βδελύσσω | make repulsive, make abominable |
| βέλος, -ους, τό | arrow, dart |
| βία, -ας, ἡ | force, violence |
| βίαιος, -α, -ον | violent |
| βιβλίον, -ου, τό | *diminutive of* βίβλος; paper, book |
| βιβρώσκω | eat |
| βλαστάνω | grow |
| βλαστός, -οῦ, ὁ | bud, sprout |
| βλασφημέω | profane, slander |
| βλέπω | see |
| βοάω | cry, cry out |
| βοή, -ῆς, ἡ | cry |
| βοηθός, -οῦ, ὁ | help, helper |
| βολίς, -ίδος, ἡ | javelin, arrow |
| βόσκω | feed, graze |
| βοτάνη, -ης, ἡ | herb, vegetation |
| βότρυς, -υος, ὁ | cluster, bunch of grapes |
| βουλή, -ῆς, ἡ | counsel, advice |
| βούλομαι | will, be willing |
| βουνός, -οῦ, ὁ | hill, high place |
| βοῦς, βοός, ὁ/ἡ | cow; *plural* cattle |
| βραδύγλωσσος, -ον | slow of tongue |
| βραδύνω | delay, loiter |
| βραχίων, -ονος, ὁ | arm, strong |
| βρέχω | rain |
| βρῶμα, -ατος, τό | food, meat |
| βρῶσις, -εως, ἡ | food, eating |
| βρωτόν, -οῦ, τό | meat, food |
| βυθός, -οῦ, ὁ | depth, bottom |
| βύσσινος, -η, -ον | *made of* fine linen |
| βωμός, -ου, ὁ | altar |

# Γ

| | |
|---|---|
| γαῖα, -ας, ἡ | land, country |
| γάλα, γάλακτος, τό | milk |

γαμβρός, -οῦ, ὁ            father-in-law
γάρ                       for, since, as
γαστήρ, -τρός, ἡ          belly, stomach, womb; ἐν γαστρὶ ἔχω, be pregnant
γαυριόομαι                exalt
γε                        indeed, really (often untranslatable)
γείτων, -ονος, ὁ/ἡ        neighbor
γεμίζω                    load, fill full of
γέμω                      be full of, be laden with
γενεά, -ᾶς, ἡ             generation, family, offspring
γένεσις, -εως, ἡ          generation, offspring; birth
γένημα, -ατος, τό         offspring, product, fruit
γένος, -ους, τό           kind, species
γερουσία, -ας, ἡ          council of elders, senate
γῆ, γῆς, ἡ                land, earth
γῆρας, -ως, τό            old age
γίνομαι                   become, be, happen
γινώσκω                   know
γλυκύς, -εῖα, -ύ          sweet
γλῶσσα, -ης, ἡ            tongue, language
γναφεύς, -έως, ὁ          fuller, cloth-dresser
γνόφος, -ου, ὁ            darkness
γνωρίζω                   make known
γόνυ, γόνατος, τό         knee
γραμματεύς, -έως, ὁ       scribe
γράφω                     write
γρύζω                     growl; murmur
γυνή, -αικός, ἡ           woman, wife


## Δ

δακτύλιος, -ου, ὁ         ring, signet
δάκτυλος, -ου, ὁ          finger
δάμαλις, -εως, ἡ          heifer
δασύς, -εῖα, ύ            hairy, bushy
δέ                        and, now, but, moreover
δείκνυμι                  show, make known
δείλη, -ης, ἡ             late afternoon, evening
δειλινός, -ή, -όν         of the afternoon, of the evening
δέκα                      ten
δεξαμενή, -ῆς, ἡ          receptacle, trough, cistern
δεξιός, -ά, -όν           right, right hand
δέομαι                    pray
δερμάτινος, -η, -ον       of skin, leathern
δεσμεύω                   bind, tie

| | |
|---|---|
| δεσμός, -οῦ, ὁ | band, bond; *plural* chains |
| δεσμωτήριον, -ου, τό | prison |
| δεσμώτης, -ου, ὁ | prisoner, captive |
| δεῦρο | Come! Go! |
| δεῦτε | Come! |
| δεύτερος, -α, -ον | second, next |
| δευτερόω | repeat, double, do a second time |
| δέω | bind |
| δή | *intensive particle*, now, indeed |
| δηλόω | make visible, show, reveal |
| δῆμος, -ου, ὁ | people, tribe, family |
| διά | *with gen.*, through; *with acc.*, on account of, by reason of |
| διαβοάω | proclaim, publish |
| διάβολος, -ου, ὁ | adversary; threat; the Devil |
| διαγγέλλω | proclaim, tell abroad |
| διάδηλος, -ος, -ον | distinguishable among others; become perceptible |
| διαδύομαι | penetrate, pierce |
| διαθήκη, -ης, ἡ | covenant, treaty, testament |
| διαιρέω | divide, separate |
| διαλύω | break up, rend; put an end to |
| διαμαρτυρέομαι | warn |
| διαμαρτυρία, -ας, ἡ | testimony |
| διάνοια, -ας, ἡ | thought, mind |
| διαπληκτίζομαι | fight, come to blows |
| διαρρήσσω (διαρρήγνυμι) | break through; rend, tear |
| διαρτάω | mislead, deceive |
| διασάφησις, -εως, ἡ | explanation, interpretation |
| δίασμα, -ατος, τό | warp, woof; *perhaps* braid |
| διασπάω | tear apart, break |
| διασπείρω | scatter, spread about |
| διαστολή, -ῆς, ἡ | distinction |
| διαστρέφω | divert from, turn from |
| διασῴζω | save, preserve, keep safe |
| διατηρέω | hold fast, take care of, preserve |
| διατρέφω | sustain, nourish, feed |
| διατρέχω | run across, run over |
| διαφαύσκω | shine through, dawn |
| διαφθείρω | destroy, kill; spoil, rot |
| διαχωρίζω | separate, go away, depart |
| δίδωμι | give, put, set |
| διέρχομαι | go through, pass through, pass |
| διηγέομαι | relate, describe, tell |
| διίστημι | stand apart, separate, open |
| δικαιοσύνη, -ης, ἡ | righteousness, justice |

| | |
|---|---|
| δικαίοω | justify, vindicate, acquit |
| δικαστής, -οῦ, ὁ | judge |
| δικτυωτός, -ή, -όν | lattice-window |
| διπλοῦς, -ῆ, -οῦν | double, two-fold |
| διπλόω | double |
| δίς | twice, doubly |
| δισσός, -ή, -όν | double |
| δισχίλιοι, -αι, -α | two thousand |
| διψάω | be thirsty, thirst |
| δίψος, -ους, τό | thirst |
| διῶρυξ, -υγος, ἡ | canal, channel, brook |
| δόξα, -ης, ἡ | glory, reputation |
| δοξάζω | magnify, extol, honor |
| δόρυ, δόρατος, τό | spear |
| δουλεία, -ας, ἡ | slavery, bondage |
| δοῦλος, -ου, ὁ | slave, servant |
| δράγμα, -ατος, τό | handful, sheaf |
| δράκων, -οντος, ὁ | dragon, serpent |
| δράξ, δρακός, ἡ | handful |
| δρόσος, -ου, ἡ | dew |
| δρυμός, -οῦ, ὁ | thicket, forest |
| δύναμαι | be able, can |
| δύναμις, -εως, ἡ | power, might, strength |
| δυναστεία, -ας, ἡ | lordship, domination |
| δυνατός, -ή, -όν | strong; able, capable |
| δύνω | sink, go down |
| δύο | two |
| δύσκωφος, -ον | very hard of hearing |
| δυσμαί, -ῶν, ἡ | setting *of the sun; thus* west |
| δώδεκα | twelve |
| δῶμα, -ατος, τό | housetop, roof |
| δῶρον, -ου, τό | gift |

# E

| | |
|---|---|
| ἐάν | if *(with subjunctive)* |
| ἑαυτοῦ, -ῆς, -οῦ | *reflexive pronoun; also dative and accusative,* oneself |
| ἕβδομος, -η, -ον | seventh |
| ἐγγίζω | draw near, approach, bring near |
| ἐγγίων, -ον | nearer |
| ἐγείρω | awaken, rouse; raise |
| ἐγκάθημαι | encamp, settle, dwell |
| ἐγκαθίζω | set |
| ἐγκαταλείπω | leave behind, desert, forsake |

| | |
|---|---|
| ἐγκρατέω | exercise control over |
| ἐγκρούω | hammer in, fasten |
| ἐγκρυφίας, -ου, ὁ | loaf *baked in the ashes* |
| ἐγώ (pl. ἡμεῖς) | personal pronoun, I |
| ἔδραμον | *aorist of* τρέχω |
| ἔθνος, -ους, τό | nation, people; Gentile |
| εἰ | if; *often to introduce question* |
| εἶδον | *see* ὁράω |
| εἶδος, -ους, τό | form, appearance |
| εἴκοσι | twenty |
| εἰμί | be, exist |
| εἶπον | *see* λέγω |
| εἰρηνικός, -ή, -όν | peaceful, peaceable |
| εἰς | into, to; in, at |
| εἷς, μία, ἕν | one |
| εἰσάγω | bring in, introduce |
| εἰσακούω | hear, hearken |
| εἰσέρχομαι | go into, enter |
| εἴσοδος, -ου, ἡ | entrance, vestibule |
| εἰσπορεύομαι | go into, enter |
| εἰσφέρω | bring in, carry in |
| εἴωθα | *pf. used as pres.*, κατὰ τὸ εἰωθός, according to custom |
| ἐκ | out of, out, from |
| ἕκαστος, -η, -ον | each, each one |
| ἑκάτερος, -α, -ον | each *(of two)* |
| ἑκατόν | hundred |
| ἐκβάλλω | cast out, throw out, drive out |
| ἐκβιάζω | do violence, injure |
| ἐκβολή, -ῆς, ἡ | throwing out |
| ἐκδέχομαι | receive; undertake; be surety for |
| ἐκδίδωμι | give up, deliver, give *(in marriage)* |
| ἐκδικέω | avenge, punish |
| ἐκδίκησις, -εως, ἡ | vengeance |
| ἐκδύω (ἐκδύνω) | take off, strip off; escape |
| ἐκεῖ | there, in that place |
| ἐκεῖνος, -η, -ον | *demonstrative pronoun,* that |
| ἐκζητέω | seek out |
| ἐκθλίβω | squeeze, press |
| ἐκκαίω | light, kindle, inflame |
| ἐκκεντέω | pierce, stab |
| ἐκκλησία, -ας, ἡ | assembly |
| ἐκκλίνω | turn away, turn aside |
| ἐκκόπτω | cut off, cut out |
| ἐκλέγω | choose, elect |
| ἐκλείπω | fail, cease; die |

| | |
|---|---|
| ἐκλείχω | lick up |
| ἐκλεκτός, -ή, -όν | select, choice |
| ἐκμυελίζω | suck the marrow out of; deprive of strength |
| ἐκπετάζω (or ἐκπετάννυμι) | spread out, stretch out |
| ἐκπολεμέω | war against, fight for |
| ἐκπορεύομαι | go out, go forth, proceed from |
| ἐκρεριμμένος, -η, -ον | *perfect participle of* ἐκρίπτω |
| ἐκρίπτω | cast out, spread throughout |
| ἐκσπάω | draw out, draw forth |
| ἐκτείνω | stretch out, stretch forth |
| ἐκτινάσσω | shake out, shake off |
| ἐκτρέφω | rear, nourish |
| ἐκτρέχω | run out, run forth |
| ἐκτρίβω | rub out, destroy |
| ἐκφέρω | carry out, bring out, carry off |
| ἐκχέω | pour out, shed; come forth |
| ἔκχυσις, -εως, ἡ | outflow, pouring out |
| ἐλαία, -ας, ἡ | olive, olive tree |
| ἔλαιον, -ου, τό | olive oil |
| ἐλαττονέω | be less, lessen, diminish |
| ἐλαττονόω | make less, diminish |
| ἐλάχιστος, -η, -ον | least, lowest |
| ἐλεγμός, -ου, ὁ | rebuke, reproof |
| ἐλεέω | have pity on, show mercy to |
| ἔλεος, -ους, τό | mercy, compassion |
| ἐλεύθερος, -α, -ον | free |
| ἕλκος, -ους, τό | sore, festering wound |
| ἕλος, -ου, τό | marsh, marshy ground |
| ἐλπίζω | hope, hope in; trust, rely on |
| ἐμαυτοῦ, -ῆς, -οῦ | of me, of myself, mine |
| ἐμβάλλω | cast *or* throw in(to), put in(to) |
| ἐμμένω | abide by, stand by, cleave to |
| ἐμός, ἐμή, ἐμόν | mine |
| ἐμπαίζω | mock |
| ἐμπίμπλημι | fill full |
| ἐμπίμπρημι | set on fire |
| ἐμπίπτω | fall in(to), fall on |
| ἐμποιέομαι | lay claim to |
| ἐμπορεύομαι | travel for business, trade |
| ἔμπορος, -ου, ὁ | merchant, trader |
| ἔμπροσθεν | before |
| ἐμφανής, -ές | manifest, visible |
| ἐμφυσάω | blow in, breath in(to) |
| ἐν | in, on, at, among; with, by |
| ἔναντι | before |

| | |
|---|---|
| ἐναντίον | in the presence of; opposite |
| ἐναντίος, -α, -ον | opposite, facing; contrary |
| ἐνδείκνυμαι | display, exhibit, show forth oneself |
| ἕνδεκα | eleven |
| ἐνδέω | bind in, bind on, bind to |
| ἐνδιαβάλλω | divert from a course, stand in the way as an adversary |
| ἐνδοξάζομαι | be glorified, be glorious |
| ἔνδοξος, -ον | notable, glorious; *neuter plural* glories |
| ἐνδόξως | gloriously, honorably |
| ἐνδύω | put on, clothe in |
| ἐνεδρεύω | lie in wait, set an ambush |
| ἔνεδρον, -ου, τό | ambush |
| ἕνεκα (or ἕνεκεν) | on account of, for, because |
| ἐνέπρησα | *aorist of* ἐμπίμπρημι |
| ἔνθα | there |
| ἐνιαυτός, -οῦ, ὁ | year |
| ἐνισχύω | strengthen, confirm, prevail |
| ἐνοικέω | live in, dwell in |
| ἐνταῦθα | here |
| ἐντέλλομαι | command, charge, give orders |
| ἔντερον, -ου, τό | gut, bowel |
| ἐντεῦθεν | hence, from this place |
| ἐντιμόομαι | be held in honor |
| ἔντιμος, -ον | honorable, dignified |
| ἐντίμως | honorably |
| ἐντολή, -ῆς, ἡ | commandment, law |
| ἐντρέπομαι | reverence, feel regard for |
| ἐνυπνιάζομαι | dream |
| ἐνυπνιαστής, -οῦ, ὁ | dreamer |
| ἐνύπνιον, -ου, τό | dream |
| ἐνώπιον | in the presence of, before |
| ἐνωτίζομαι | give ear to, hearken |
| ἐξάγω | lead out, lead away |
| ἐξαιρέω | take out, remove; rescue, deliver |
| ἐξαίρω | raise, lift up |
| ἑξακόσιοι, -αι, -α | six hundred |
| ἐξακριβάζομαι | examine accurately |
| ἐξαλείφω | wipe out, destroy |
| ἐξαμαρτάνω | err, do wrong, fail |
| ἐξανίστημι | raise up, arise |
| ἐξαπατάω | deceive |
| ἐξαποστέλλω | send forth, send away, release |
| ἐξαριθμέω | enumerate, count, number |
| ἐξεγείρω | raise up, lift up |
| ἐξειλάμην | *aorist middle of* ἐξαιρέω |

| | |
|---|---|
| ἐξελέσθαι | *aorist middle infinitive of* ἐξαιρέω |
| ἐξέλκω | draw out |
| ἐξερεύγομαι | vomit forth, overflow with |
| ἐξερημόω | devastate, make desolate |
| ἐξέρχομαι | go out of, come out of |
| ἐξηγητής, -οῦ, ὁ | interpreter |
| ἑξῆς | in succession, in order, one after another |
| ἐξίστημι | amaze, confound |
| ἔξοδος, -ου, ἡ | going out, exit, exodus |
| ἐξοίσω | *future of* ἐκφέρω |
| ἐξολεθρεύω | destroy utterly |
| ἐξολοθρεύω | *see* ἐξολεθρεύω |
| ἐξόπισθεν | behind |
| ἐξουδενέω (or ἐξουδενόω) | scorn, despise, disdain |
| ἐξουθενέω | *see* ἐξουδενέω |
| ἐξυπνίζομαι | wake up, awaken |
| ἔξω | out, outside |
| ἑορτάζω | keep a festival, celebrate |
| ἑορτή, -ῆς, ἡ | feast, festival |
| ἐπάγω | bring, bring upon |
| ἐπαίρω | lift up, raise; stir up |
| ἐπακούω | hear, listen |
| ἐπαναστρέφω | return, bring back again |
| ἐπανίστημι | rise up against |
| ἐπάνω | above, upon, upper |
| ἐπαοιδός, -οῦ, ὁ | enchanter, charmer |
| ἐπαποστέλλω | send after, send upon |
| ἔπαρσις, -εως, ἡ | rising, swelling; *here* heap of ruins |
| ἔπαυλις, -εως, ἡ | dwelling |
| ἐπαύριον | on the next day, tomorrow |
| ἐπεί | when, since, for, as |
| ἐπειδή | when, since |
| ἔπειμι | be upon |
| ἐπελπίζω | give hope, cause to trust |
| ἐπέρχομαι | come upon, come forward |
| ἐπερωτάω | ask; consult, enquire |
| ἐπήνεγκα | *aorist of* ἐπιφέρω |
| ἐπί | upon, on, over, to |
| ἐπιβαίνω | tread on; mount on |
| ἐπιβάλλω | throw upon, cast upon |
| ἐπιβάτης, -ου, ὁ | rider, horseman |
| ἐπιβλέπω | look upon, observe |
| ἐπιγινώσκω | recognize, observe, acknowledge |
| ἐπιδιώκω | pursue |
| ἐπιζητέω | seek after, inquire, consult |

| | |
|---|---|
| ἐπικαλύπτω | cover |
| ἐπικαταράομαι | call down a curse on |
| ἐπικρατέω | have power, rule over |
| ἐπιλαμβάνομαι | take hold of, lay hold of |
| ἐπιλανθάνομαι | forget, lose thought of |
| ἐπίλεκτος, -ον | chosen |
| ἐπιμελέομαι (or ἐπιμέλομαι) | take care of |
| ἐπιμένω | tarry, wait, stay on |
| ἐπίμικτος, -ον | mixed |
| ἐπιπίπτω | fall upon |
| ἐπιρρίπτω | throw upon |
| ἐπισάσσω | pile a load on, saddle |
| ἐπισιτισμός, -οῦ, ὁ | stock, store of provisions |
| ἐπισκέπτομαι | visit, observe, look upon |
| ἐπισκοπή, -ῆς, ἡ | visitation, watchfulness |
| ἐπισπάομαι | draw (on)to oneself |
| ἐπίσταμαι | know, be capable |
| ἐπιστάτης, -ου, ὁ | chief, overseer, clerk |
| ἐπιστηρίζω | lean on, rest on |
| ἐπιστρέφω | turn, return |
| ἐπισυνάγω | gather together |
| ἐπιτελέω | complete, finish, accomplish |
| ἐπιτίθημι | put on, place (up)on; impose |
| ἐπιτιμάω | rebuke, censure |
| ἐπιτυγχάνω | attain to, reach; be successful |
| ἐπιφέρω | give (to), bring, put, lay upon |
| ἐπιχέω | pour out, pour over |
| ἐπλήγη | *aorist of* πλήσσω |
| ἔπλησα | *aorist of* πίμπλημι |
| ἐπόζω | become stinking, putrefy |
| ἐπονομάζω | name, call |
| ἑπτά | seven |
| ἑπτάκις (or ἑπτάκι) | seven times |
| ἑπτακόσιοι, -αι, -α | seven hundred |
| ἐργοδιώκτης, -ου, ὁ | task-master |
| ἔργον, -ου, τό | work, occupation |
| ἐρευνάω | search |
| ἔρημος, -ου, ἡ | wilderness, desert, (*substantive of* ἔρημος, -ον) |
| ἐρημόω | desolate, lay waste, waste |
| ἔριφος, -ου, ὁ | kid |
| ἑρμηνευτής, -οῦ, ὁ | interpreter |
| ἐρυθρός, -ή, -όν | red |
| ἔρχομαι | come, go |
| ἐρῶ | *future of* λέγω |
| ἐρωτάω | ask, question, inquire |

| | |
|---|---|
| ἐσθίω | eat, consume |
| ἔσχατος, -η, -ον | last |
| ἔσω | within, inside |
| ἐτάκησα | aorist of τήκω |
| ἕτερος, -α, -ον | other, another (of a different kind) |
| ἔτι | yet, still |
| ἑτοιμάζω | prepare |
| ἕτοιμος, -η, -ον | prepared, ready |
| ἔτος, -ους, τό | year |
| εὖ | well, good |
| εὐαρεστέω | be well pleasing |
| εὐδοκιμέω | be genuine |
| εὐθηνία, -ας, ἡ | prosperity, plenty |
| εὐθύνω | guide straight, direct, put straight; please |
| εὐθύς, -εῖα, ύ | straight, direct, right |
| εὐλαβέομαι | be afraid |
| εὐλογέω | bless |
| εὐλογητός, -ή, -όν | blessed |
| εὐλογία, -ας, ἡ | blessing; gift |
| εὐνοῦχος, -ου, ὁ | eunuch |
| εὐοδόω | help on the way, cause to prosper |
| εὑρίσκω | find, find out, discover |
| εὐφραίνω | cheer; rejoice |
| εὔχομαι | pray; vow |
| εὐώνυμος, -ον | left, left hand |
| ἔφαγον | aorist of ἐσθίω |
| ἐφίστημι | set, place, place over; rest on, stand on |
| ἐφοράω | look upon |
| ἐχθές | yesterday |
| ἐχθρός, -ά, -όν | hostile; as a substantive, enemy |
| ἔχω | have, hold, possess |
| ἑωθινός, -ή, -όν | in the morning, early |
| ἕως | until |

# Z

| | |
|---|---|
| ζ | seven |
| ζάω | live |
| ζεύγνυμι (ζευγνύω) | yoke, harness |
| ζεῦγος, -ους, τό | yoke; pair |
| ζηλόω | be jealous of, envy; be zealous for |
| ζητέω | seek, search for, desire |
| ζυμόομαι | ferment, be leavened |
| ζώννυμι | gird, gird upon |
| ζῳογονέω | produce alive, preserve alive |

# H

| | |
|---|---|
| ἤ | than; as; or |
| ἡγεμών, -όνος, ὁ | leader, chief |
| ἡγέομαι | lead, direct |
| ἤδη | already, by this time, now |
| ἠθῴωμαι | *see* ἀθῳόω |
| ἥκω | come to, be present, reach |
| ἡλάμην | *aorist of* ἅλλομαι |
| ἥλιος, -ου, ὁ | sun |
| ἡμέρα, -ας, ἡ | day |
| ἡμίονος, -ου, ὁ | mule |
| ἥμισυς, -εια, -υ | half, half of, middle |
| ἡνίκα | when, whenever |
| ᾖσα | *aorist of* ᾄδω |

# Θ

| | |
|---|---|
| θάλασσα, -ης, ἡ | sea |
| θάλλω | sprout, grow |
| θάνατος, -ου, ὁ | death |
| θανατόω | destroy, kill, slay |
| θάπτω | bury |
| θαρρέω (θαρσέω) | be courageous, be bold |
| θαυμάσιος, -α, -ον | wonderful, marvelous; *as a substantive,* wonder, miracle |
| θαυμαστός, -ή, -όν | wonderful, marvelous |
| θέλω | will, be willing, wish |
| θεός, -οῦ, ὁ | God |
| θεραπεία, -ᾶς, ἡ | service, attendance; *thus* court |
| θεράπων, -οντος, ὁ | servant |
| θερισμός, -οῦ, ὁ | harvest, harvest time |
| θεωρέω | look at, behold, see |
| θηλάζω | suckle, nurse |
| θῆλυς, -εις, ἡ | female, woman |
| θήρα, -ας, ἡ | prey, game |
| θηριόβρωτος, -ον | eaten by wild beasts |
| θηρίον, -ου, τό | wild animal, beast |
| θησαυρός, -οῦ, ὁ | treasure |
| θῖβις, -εως, ἡ (or θίβις) | basket |
| θιμωνιά, -ᾶς, ἡ | heap |
| θλάω | crush, bruise |
| θλίβω | compress; oppress, afflict |
| θλιμμός, -οῦ, ὁ | oppression, affliction |
| θλῖψις, -εως, ἡ | oppression, affliction, anguish |

| | |
|---|---|
| θνῆσκω | die |
| θραύω | shatter, break |
| θρίξ, τριχός, ἡ | hair |
| θρόνος, -ου, ὁ | throne, seat |
| θυγάτηρ, -τρός, ἡ | daughter |
| θύελλα, -ης, ἡ | storm |
| θῦμα, -ατος, ἡ | sacrifice, offering |
| θυμίαμα, -ατος, τό | incense, perfume; spice |
| θυμός, -οῦ, ὁ | temper, spirit, indignation |
| θυμόω | be angry; provoke |
| θυρεός, -ου, ὁ | *oblong* shield |
| θυσία, -ας, ἡ | sacrifice |
| θυσίασμα, -ατος, τό | sacrifice, offering |
| θυσιαστήριον, -ου, τό | altar |
| θύω | sacrifice, slaughter |
| θώραξ, -ακος, ἡ | breastplate |

## I

| | |
|---|---|
| ἰάομαι | heal; restore, repair |
| ἰγνύα, -ης, ἡ | ham, the part behind thigh and knee |
| ἰδού | Behold! *imperative of* εἶδον |
| ἱερεύς, -εως, ὁ | priest |
| ἱκανόομαι | be sufficient, be enough, suffice |
| ἱκανός, -ή, -όν | sufficient, adequate, well suited |
| ἵλεως, -ων | gracious, merciful |
| ἱμάτιον, -ου, ὁ | garment *(outer)*, clothes |
| ἱματισμός, -οῦ, ὁ | clothing, apparel |
| ἵνα | that, in order that |
| ἱππεύς, -έως, ὁ | horseman |
| ἵππος, -ου, ὁ | horse; ἡ ἵππος, cavalry, horses |
| ἵστημι | set, stand; appoint |
| ἰσχνόφωνος, -ον | weak-voiced |
| ἰσχυρός, -ά, -όν | strong, powerful, mighty |
| ἰσχύς, -ύος, ἡ | strength, might, power |
| ἰσχύω | be strong, prevail over |
| ἰχθύς, ἰχθύος, ὁ | fish |
| ἴχνος, -ους, τό | track, footstep |

## K

| | |
|---|---|
| κάδιον, -ου, τό | vessel |
| καθά | as, just as |
| καθαιρέω | lower, let drop |
| καθάπερ | just as |

| | |
|---|---|
| καθαρός, -ά, όν | clean, pure |
| καθέδρα, -ας, ἡ | chair, seat |
| καθεύδω | sleep, be asleep |
| καθήκω | be proper, be fitting, be customary |
| κάθημαι | sit |
| καθίζω | sit *(down)*; set |
| καθίστημι (καθιστάνω) | appoint, ordain |
| καθοράω | notice, perceive |
| καθότι | as, to the degree that; because |
| καθώς | just as, as |
| καί | and, also, even |
| καιρός, -οῦ, ὁ | time, season, occasion, opportunity |
| καίω | burn |
| κακόω | mistreat, afflict, harm |
| κάκωσις, -εως, ἡ | mistreatment, affliction |
| καλάμη, -ης, ἡ | straw, stubble |
| καλάμινος, -η, -ον | reed |
| καλέω | call |
| κάλλος, -ους, τό | beauty; delight, pleasure |
| καλός, -ή, -όν | beautiful, good, |
| καλύπτω | cover |
| καλῴδιον, -ου, τό | small cord |
| κάμηλος, -ου, ὁ/ἡ | camel |
| καμιναία, -ας, ἡ | furnace |
| κάμπτω | bend, bow |
| καμψάκης, -ου, ὁ | flask, vessel |
| κανᾶ | *see* κάνεον |
| κάνεον, -οῦ, τό | basket of reed, *esp.* bread-basket *(contracted to* κανοῦν *in Attic)* |
| καρδία, -ας, ἡ | heart |
| καρπός, -οῦ, ὁ | fruit |
| κάρυον, -ου, τό | *any kind of* nut; almond, chestnut, walnut |
| καταβαίνω | go down |
| καταβιάζω | constrain, press forcefully |
| καταβοάω | cry out, complain |
| καταγίνομαι | abide, dwell |
| κατάγω | lead down, bring down |
| καταδέομαι | entreat earnestly |
| καταδιώκω | pursue, hunt down |
| καταδουλόω | enslave, reduce to slavery |
| καταδυναστεία, -ας, ἡ | oppression |
| καταδυναστεύω | oppress |
| καταισχύνω | dishonor, disgrace, humiliate |
| κατακαίω | burn down, consume |
| κατακαλύπτω | cover |

| | |
|---|---|
| κατακενόω | empty, empty out |
| κατακλίνω | sit down, recline |
| καταλαμβάνω | overtake, overcome |
| κατάλειμμα, -ατος, τό | remnant |
| καταλείπω | leave, leave behind, abandon |
| καταλιμπάνω | *a late form of* καταλείπω |
| κατάλυμα, -ατος, τό | lodging, inn, guest room |
| καταλύω | throw down, destroy; *intransitive* rest |
| καταμαρτυρέω | bear witness against |
| καταμένω | stay, tarry |
| κατανοέω | notice, observe, consider |
| κατανύσσω | stab, gouge, smite |
| καταπατέω | trample, tread on |
| καταπαύω | stop, bring to an end, rest |
| καταπίνω | swallow down, devour |
| καταράομαι | curse |
| καταρτίζω | prepare |
| κατασκάπτω | tear down, raze |
| κατασκοπεύω | spy out |
| κατάσκοπος, -ου, ὁ | spy |
| κατασοφίζομαι | outwit by trickery |
| κατασπεύδω | hasten, make haste; urge, press |
| καταστενάζω | groan, sigh |
| κατατέμνω | cut, cut in pieces |
| κατατοξεύω | shoot down, pierce through |
| κατατρέχω | run down, run after |
| καταφέρω | bring against, bring down |
| καταφιλέω | kiss |
| καταφυτεύω | plant |
| καταχέω | pour out, pour down |
| κατέδραμον | *aorist of* κατατρέχω |
| κατεῖδον | look down, look down upon |
| κατεμβλέπω | look at, look in the face, *a strengthened form of* ἐμβλέπω |
| κατέναντι | opposite; in the presence of |
| κατεσθίω | eat up, devour |
| κατέχω | hold back, hold down; keep, confine |
| κατοδυνάω | afflict grievously |
| κατοικέω | settle, dwell, live |
| κατοικητήριον, -ου, τό | dwelling-place |
| κατόπισθεν | behind, after |
| κάτω | below; down |
| καψάκης, -ου, ὁ | *see* καμψάκης |
| κέδρος, -ου, ἡ | cedar tree |
| κενός, -ή, -όν | empty, without content |

| | |
|---|---|
| κέρκος, -ου, ἡ | tail |
| κεφαλή, -ῆς, ἡ | head |
| κῆπος, -ου, ὁ | garden |
| κήρυξ, -υκος, ὁ | herald |
| κηρύσσω | announce, proclaim |
| κίων, -ονος, ἡ | pillar |
| κλαίω | weep, mourn |
| κλαυθμός, -οῦ, ὁ | weeping, crying |
| κλέπτω | steal, rob |
| κληρονομία, -ας, ἡ | inheritance, heritage |
| κλῆρος, -ου, ὁ | lot; *thus* portion, share |
| κλητός, -ή, -όν | called, invited |
| κλίβανος, -ου, ὁ | oven |
| κλίνη, -ης, ἡ | couch, bed |
| κλίνω | incline, bend |
| κλοιός, -οῦ, ὁ | collar, chain |
| κλοπή, -ῆς, ἡ | theft, stealing |
| κνήμη, -ης, ἡ | leg |
| κνημίς, -ῖδος, ἡ | legging |
| κοιλάς, -άδος, ἡ | deep valley |
| κοιλία, -ας, ἡ | belly, stomach |
| κοιμάω | sleep |
| κοιμίζω | put to sleep, lull to sleep |
| κοιτών, -ῶνος, ὁ | bedroom |
| κόλπος, -ου, ὁ | bosom, breast, chest |
| κολυμβήθρα, -ας, ἡ | pool |
| κόνδυ, -υος, τό | cup |
| κονιορτός, -οῦ, ὁ | dust |
| κόντος, -ου, ὁ | shaft |
| κοπάζω | cease, rest |
| κοπιάω | be tired, grow weary |
| κόπρος, -ου, ἡ | dung |
| κόπτω | cut, cut off |
| κόραξ, κόρακος, ὁ | raven |
| κορυφή, -ῆς, ἡ | top, highest spot |
| κράζω | cry out, cry, call out |
| κραταιός, -ά, -όν | powerful, mighty |
| κρατέω | seize, take hold of, take into custody |
| κραυγή, -ῆς, ἡ | cry, shout |
| κρέας, -έως, τό | flesh, meat |
| κρείσσων, -ον | better, superior |
| κρεμάννυμι | hang |
| κριθή, -ῆς, ἡ | barley |
| κρίνω | judge; distinguish; approve |
| κριός, -οῦ, ὁ | ram |

| κρίσις, -εως, ἡ | judging, judgment |
| κρύπτω | hide, conceal, cover |
| κρυφῇ | in secret |
| κτάομαι | acquire, get, purchase |
| κτῆνος, -ους, τό | animal, livestock; cattle |
| κτίζω | create |
| κυκλόθεν | from all around |
| κυκλόω | go round, surround, encircle |
| κύκλῳ | around, all around |
| κῦμα, -ατος, τό | wave |
| κυνόμυια, -ας, ἡ | dog-fly |
| κυπαρισσίας, -ου, ὁ | cypress |
| κύπτω | bend down |
| κυρία, -ας, ἡ | mistress, lady of the house |
| κυριεύω | be master, dominate, rule |
| κύριος, -ου, ὁ | lord |
| κύων, κυνός, ὁ | dog |
| κῶλον, -ου, τό | carcass, dead body |
| κωφεύω | hold one's peace |
| κωφός, -ή, -όν | mute; deaf |

## Λ

| λάκκος, -ου, ὁ | pit, cistern |
| λαλέω | talk, speak, say |
| λαμβάνω | receive, get; take |
| λαμπάς, -άδος, ἡ | torch, lamp |
| λαός, -οῦ, ὁ | people |
| λατρεύω | worship, serve |
| λάχανον, -ου, τό | herb, vegetable |
| λέγω | say, speak, tell |
| λειτουργέω | serve, minister |
| λεπτός, -ή, -όν | thin, small |
| λέων, -οντος, ὁ | lion |
| λῆμμα, -ατος, τό | *anything received,* credit, profit, gain |
| λιθοβολέω | throw stones, stone |
| λίθος, -ου, ὁ | stone |
| λιμός, -οῦ, ὁ/ἡ | hunger, famine |
| λίνον, -ου, τό | flax, linen |
| λόγιον, -ου, τό | oracle, saying |
| λόγχη, -ης, ἡ | lance, spear |
| λοιπός, -ή, -όν | remaining, rest |
| λούω | bathe, wash |
| λυπέω | pain, grieve, vex |

λύπη, -ης, ἡ              pain, sorrow
λυτρόω                   redeem, ransom, liberate, deliver
λύω                      loose, release, destroy

# M

μαῖα, -ας, ἡ             midwife
μαιέω                    do the work of a midwife
μακαρίζω                 consider blessed or fortunate
μακρόθεν                 from a distance, from afar, at a distance
μακρός, -ά, -όν          far
μαλακία, -ας, ἡ          harm, weakness, sickness
μαλακίζομαι              be weak, be sick, be harmed
μανδύας, -ου, ὁ          woolen cloak
μανθάνω                  learn
μαντεία, -ας, ἡ          divination
μαντεῖον, -ου, τό        oracle; plural reward of divination
μάρσιππος, -ου, ὁ        sack, pouch
μάρτυς, μάρτυρος, ὁ      witness
μαστιγόω                 whip, flog
ματαίως                  foolishly, vainly
μάτη, -ης, ἡ             folly
μάχαιρα, -ας, ἡ          sword
μάχιμος, -η, -ον         strong, fit
μεγαλύνω                 enlarge, increase
μέγας, μεγάλη, μέγα      large, great
μέγεθος, -ους, τό        greatness, size
μεθίστημι                change, remove
μεθύσκομαι               become drunk
μέθυσμα, -ατος, τό       intoxicating drink
μείγνυμι                 mix, mingle
μέλι, -ιτος, τό          honey
μελίζω                   cut in pieces, dismember
μέλισσα, -ης, ἡ          bee
μέλλω                    be about to, intend
μέν (μέν / δέ)           an untranslatable particle; μέν . . . δέ implies a
                         contrast
μένω                     stay, remain, abide
μερίζω                   divide, distribute
μεριμνάω                 be anxious, care, be concerned, worry
μερίς, -ίδος, ἡ          part, portion
μέσακλον, -ου, τό        weaver's beam
μεσημβρία, -ας, ἡ        midday; south
μεσονύκτιον, -ου, τό     midnight

| | |
|---|---|
| μέσος, -η, -ον | middle |
| μετά | *with genitive*, with; *with accusative*, after |
| μεταβάλλω | change *something* to *something*, alter |
| μεταμέλομαι | change my mind, regret, repent |
| μεταπέμπω | send for, summon |
| μετεστρέφω | turn, change |
| μετρητής, -ου, ὁ | measure |
| μέτωπον, -ου, τό | forehead |
| μή | not, *with moods other than indicative* |
| μηδέ | not, nor, not ever, *with moods other than indicative* |
| μηλωτή, -ῆς, ἡ | sheepskin, mantle |
| μήν | indeed; εἰ μήν, surely |
| μήν, -ός, ὁ | month |
| μηρός, -οῦ, ὁ | thigh |
| μήτηρ, μητρός, ἡ | mother |
| μίγνυμι | *see* μείγνυμι |
| μικρός, -ά, -όν | small |
| μικρότερος, -α, -ον | smaller |
| μιμνῄσκομαι | remember, think of, mention |
| μισέω | hate, detest |
| μισθός, -οῦ, ὁ | wages, reward |
| μνῆμα, -ατος, τό | tomb, monument, memorial |
| μόλιβος, -ου, ὁ | lead |
| μολύνω | soil, stain, pollute, smear |
| μονόκερως, -ωτος, ὁ | unicorn; wild ox |
| μονομαχέω | fight in single combat |
| μόνος, -η, -ον | alone |
| μόσχος, -ου, ὁ | ox |
| μοχθος, -ου, ὁ | labor, hardship; calamity |
| μοχλός, -οῦ, ὁ | bar, bolt |
| μυελός, -οῦ, ὁ | marrow |
| μυῖα, -ας, ἡ | fly |
| μυκτήρ, -ῆρος, ὁ | nostril |
| μυκτηρίζω | sneer at, mock |
| μύλος, -ου, ὁ | mill, grinding mill; millstone |

# N

| | |
|---|---|
| ναζείρ | Nazarite |
| ναί | yes, indeed, certainly |
| ναός, -οῦ, ὁ | temple |
| νάπη, -ης, ἡ | wooded valley, vale |
| νεᾶνις, -ιδος, ἡ | girl, maiden |
| νεανίσκος, -ου, ὁ | young man, youth |

| | |
|---|---|
| νέμομαι | graze, feed |
| νέος, -α, -ον | young, new, fresh |
| νεότης, -ητος, ἡ | youth |
| νευρά, -ᾶς, ἡ | bow string, thong |
| νεφέλη, -ης, ἡ | cloud |
| νεώτερος, -α, -ον | younger |
| νή | *particle of strong affirmation; by followed by acc.* |
| νηστεία, -ας, ἡ | fast |
| νηστεύω | fast |
| νίπτω | wash, bathe |
| νοσσιά, -ᾶς, ἡ | nest |
| νότος, -ου, ὁ | south, south wind |
| νοῦς, νοός, ὁ | mind |
| νυμφίος, -ου, ὁ | bridegroom |
| νῦν | now, at the present time |
| νύξ, νυκτός, ἡ | night |

## Ξ

| | |
|---|---|
| ξηραίνω | dry, dry up |
| ξηρός, -ά, -όν | dry |
| ξυλάριον, -ου, τό | small piece of wood, stick, twig |
| ξύλον, -ου, τό | tree, wood |
| ξυράω | shave |

## Ο

| | |
|---|---|
| ὁ, ἡ, τό | *definite article,* the |
| ὀγδοήκοντα | eighty |
| ὅδε, ἥδε, τόδε | this one *(here)* |
| ὁδηγέω | lead, guide |
| ὁδοιπόρος, -ου, ὁ | traveller, wayfarer; *pl.,* caravan |
| ὁδός, -οῦ, ἡ | road, way |
| ὀδύνη, -ης, ἡ | pain *(especially mental)* |
| ὅθεν | from where, whence |
| ὀθόνιον, -ου, τό | linen cloth |
| οἶδα | *perfect used as present,* know |
| οἰκεσία, -ας, ἡ | city |
| οἰκέτης, -ου, ὁ | household servant, slave |
| οἰκέω | dwell, inhabit |
| οἰκία, -ας, ἡ | house |
| οἰκοδομέω | build, erect |
| οἰκονομος, -ου, ὁ | steward, administrator |
| οἶκος, -ου, ὁ | house |

| | |
|---|---|
| οἶμαι (οἴομαι) | think, suppose |
| οἴμοι | *exclamation* Woe is me! |
| οἶνος, -ου, ὁ | wine |
| οἰνοχόος, -ον | pouring out wine; *as a substantive*, cupbearer |
| οἰωνίζομαι | take omens from the flight of birds; divine |
| οἰωνισμός, -οῦ, ὁ | omen, portent; divination |
| οἰωνός, -ου, ὁ | bird; *then* omen *drawn from a bird* |
| ὀκλάζω | crouch down, bend |
| ὀκνέω | hesitate, delay |
| ὀλιγοψυχέω | be faint-hearted, be discouraged, be weary |
| ὀλιγοψυχία, -ας, ἡ | faint-heartedness |
| ὁλοκαύτωμα, -ατος, τό | whole burnt offering |
| ὁλοκαύτωσις, -εως, ἡ | sacrifice of a burnt offering |
| ὅλος, -η, -ον | whole, entire |
| ὄλυρα, -ας, ἡ | rye |
| ὀλυρίτης, -ου, ὁ | *made of* rye |
| ὀμνύω (or ὄμνυμι) | swear, take an oath |
| ὁμοθυμαδόν | with one accord, all together |
| ὅμοιος, -α, -ον | like |
| ὁμομήτριος, -α, -ον | born of the same mother; brother, sister |
| ὀνειδίζω | reproach, revile, insult |
| ὄνειδος, -ους, τό | disgrace, reproach, insult |
| ὄνομα, -ατος, τό | name |
| ὄνος, -ου, ὁ/ἡ | donkey |
| ὄντως | really, truly |
| ὀπίσω | behind, after |
| ὁπλή, -ῆς, ἡ | hoof |
| ὅπως | so that, in order that, that |
| ὅραμα, -ατος, τό | thing seen, sight, vision |
| ὅρασις, -εως, ἡ | vision, appearance |
| ὁράω | see |
| ὀργή, -ῆς, ἡ | anger, wrath |
| ὀργίζω | be angry |
| ὀρθός, -ή, -όν | upright, straight up |
| ὀρθόω | set upright |
| ὀρθρίζω | rise early, get up early |
| ὄρθρος, -ου, ὁ | dawn, early morning |
| ὀρθῶς | rightly, correctly |
| ὅριον, -ου, τό | boundary, border |
| ὁρισμός, -οῦ, τό | limit, boundary |
| ὁρκίζω | adjure, bind by oath |
| ὅρκος, -ου, ὁ | oath |
| ὄρνεον, -ου, τό | bird |
| ὅρος, -ου, ὁ | boundary, *limit of time or space* |
| ὄρος, -ου, τό | mountain |

| | |
|---|---|
| ὀρύσσω | dig |
| ὅς, ἥ, ὅ | *relative pronoun,* who, which, what, that |
| ὀσμή, ῆς, ἡ | fragrance, odor |
| ὅσος, -η, -ον | *relative pronoun,* as great, as much; all |
| ὀστοῦν, -οῦ, τό | bone |
| ὀσφραίνομαι | smell, smell of |
| ὀσφύς, -ύος, ἡ | waist, loins |
| ὅταν | whenever, when |
| ὅτε | when |
| ὅτι | because; that |
| οὐ, οὐκ | not |
| οὐδέ | nor, not even |
| οὐδείς, οὐδεμία, οὐδέν | no, no one |
| οὐδέποτε | never |
| οὐδέπω | not yet |
| οὐθείς | *see* οὐδείς |
| οὐκέτι | no more, no longer |
| οὖν | therefore; then |
| οὐρανός, -οῦ, ὁ | heaven |
| οὐρέω | make water |
| οὖρον, -ου, τό | urine |
| οὖς, ὠτός, τό | ear; hearing |
| οὗτος, αὕτη, τοῦτο | this |
| οὕτως | thus, so |
| οὐχί | no, not; *begins a sentence expecting an affirmative answer* |
| ὀφθαλμός, -οῦ, ὁ | eye |
| ὄφις, -εως, ὁ | serpent, snake |
| ὀχυρός, -ά, -όν | strong, firm |
| ὀχύρωμα, -ατος, τό | stronghold, fortress |
| ὄψιμος, -ον | late, slow; *neuter plural* late crops |
| ὄψις, -εως, ἡ | sight, seeing; face |
| ὄψομαι | *future of* ὁράω |

# Π

| | |
|---|---|
| παιγνία, -ας, ἡ | sport, play |
| παιδάριον, -ου, τό | boy; servant |
| παίζω | play, amuse oneself, mock |
| παῖς, παιδός, ὁ | boy; servant |
| παίω | strike, hit |
| πάλιν | again, once more |
| πανουργία, -ας, ἡ | craftiness, trickery |

| | |
|---|---|
| παρά | *with acc.*, beside, more than; *with gen.*, from; *with dat.*, beside |
| παραβαίνω | go aside; transgress |
| παραβιάζομαι | force, use violence, constrain |
| παραβολή, -ῆς, ἡ | parable |
| παραγίνομαι | come, appear, present oneself |
| παράδεισος, -ου, ὁ | paradise |
| παραδοξάζω | make wonderful, distinguish |
| παρακαλέω | summon, invite; encourage |
| παραλαμβάνω | take with, take along |
| παράνομος, -ον | lawless, violent |
| παραπορεύομαι | go by, go past |
| παράταξις, -εως, ἡ | battle line; army |
| παρατάσσω | arrange side-by-side; draw up in battle order |
| παρατείνω | extend, prolong, stretch |
| παρατίθημι | set, serve; entrust |
| πάρειμι | be here, be present; *present as perfect* have come |
| παρεμβάλλω | encamp *(of an army)* |
| παρεμβολή, -ῆς, ἡ | camp; army |
| παρενοχλέω | trouble, annoy, vex |
| παρέρχομαι | go by, pass by |
| παρθένος, -ου, ἡ/ὁ | virgin |
| παρίημι | let alone, disregard |
| παρίστημι | stand by to serve, attend |
| παροικέω | sojourn, live as a stranger, inhabit |
| πάροικος, -ου, ὁ | sojourner, resident alien |
| παροργίζω | provoke to anger, make angry, anger |
| παρόργισμα, -ατος, τό | provocation |
| πᾶς, πάσα, πᾶν | every, all |
| πάσσαλος, -ου, ὁ | pin, peg |
| πατάσσω | strike *(as with a sword)*, hit; slay |
| πάτημα, -ατος, τό | refuse, that which is walked on |
| πατήρ, πατρός, ὁ | father, forefather, ancestor |
| παύω | stop, cease |
| πάχος, -ους, τό | fatness, thickness |
| πέδη, -ης, ἡ | fetter, shackle |
| πεδίον, -ου, τό | plain, field |
| πεζός, -ή, -όν | on foot, walking |
| πεινάω | hunger, be hungry |
| πειράω | try, attempt |
| πέμπος, -η, -ον | fifth |
| πενθέω | mourn |
| πενταπλασίως | five-fold |
| πέντε | five |
| πεντήκοντα | fifty |

| | |
|---|---|
| πεντηκόνταρχος, -ου, ὁ | captain of fifty men |
| πέπειρος, -ον | ripe |
| πεποίθησις, -εως, ἡ | trust, confidence |
| περί | around, about; concerning |
| περιαιρέω | take away, remove |
| περιβάλλω | throw around, put around |
| περιβλέπομαι | look around, survey |
| περιζώννυμι | gird about |
| περικεφαλαία, -ας, ἡ | helmet |
| περιοχή, -ῆς, ἡ | stronghold; siege |
| περιπατέω | walk, walk about |
| περιποιέω | save, preserve; *middle* get for oneself |
| περισσός, -ή, -όν | excessive, extra |
| περιστρέφω | turn around |
| περιτίθημι | place on or around |
| πέσσω (πέπτω) | cook, bake |
| πετεινόν, -οῦ, τό | bird; *neuter substantive of* πετεινός, -ή, -όν |
| πέτρα, -ας, ἡ | rock |
| πήγνυμι | make firm, *of liquids* make solid; fix; pitch *a tent* |
| πηλός, -οῦ, ὁ | mud, clay; mortar |
| πῆχυς, -εως, ὁ | cubit *(about 18 inches)* |
| πίνω | drink |
| πίμπλημι | fill, fulfill |
| πιπράσκω | sell |
| πιστεύω | believe, trust |
| πλανάω | lead away, cause to wander; *passive* wander, stray |
| πλάσσω | form, mold, make |
| πλεῖος, -η, -ον | full |
| πληγή, -ῆς, ἡ | blow, stroke; plague |
| πλῆθος, -ους, τό | multitude, crowd |
| πληθύνω | increase, multiply |
| πλήν | except, only, but |
| πλήρης, -ες | full, complete |
| πλήσατε | *see* πίμπλαμι |
| πλησίον | *adverb* near, close by; *substantive* neighbor |
| πλησμονή, -ῆς, ἡ | plenty, satisfaction |
| πλήσσω (πλήγνυμι) | smite |
| πλινθεία, -ας, ἡ | brick-making |
| πλινθουργία, -ας, ἡ | brick-making |
| πνεῦμα, -ατος, τό | spirit; breath |
| πόθεν | whence, from where |
| ποιέω | do, make |
| ποίημα, -ατος, τό | workmanship, product, deed, act |
| ποικίλος, η, ον | many colored |
| ποιμαίνω | tend a herd, shepherd |

| | |
|---|---|
| ποιμενικός, -ή, -όν | pertaining to a shepherd, shepherd's |
| ποιμήν, -ένος, ὁ | shepherd |
| ποίμνιον, -ου, τό | flock |
| πολεμέω | make war, fight |
| πολεμιστής, -οῦ, ὁ | warrior |
| πόλεμος, -ου, ὁ | battle, war |
| πόλις, -εως, ἡ | city, city-state |
| πολυπληθύνω | be numerous, become great |
| πολύς, πολλή, πολύ | much, many |
| πονηρία, -ας, ἡ | wickedness |
| πονηρός, -ά, -όν | bad, evil |
| πόνος, -ου, ὁ | toil; misery, affliction |
| πόντος, -ου, ὁ | sea |
| πορεία, -ας, ἡ | trip, means of transport |
| πορεύομαι | travel, journey, go |
| ποταμός, -οῦ, ὁ | river, stream |
| ποτέ | once, formerly |
| πότε | when? at what time? |
| ποτήριον, -ου, τό | cup |
| ποτίζω | cause to drink, give to drink, water |
| πότος, -ου, ὁ | drinking party |
| ποῦ | *interrogative*, where? to what place? |
| πούς, ποδός, ὁ | foot |
| πρᾶγμα, -ατος, τό | matter, deed |
| πρᾶσις, -εως, ἡ | market; sale |
| πρεσβεῖον, -ου, τό | old age |
| πρέσβυς, -εως, ὁ | elder |
| πρεσβύτερος, -α, -ον | older, elder |
| πρίαμαι | buy, purchase |
| πρίν (πρὶν ἤ) | before |
| πρό | before, in front of |
| προβάλλω | put forward, propound |
| πρόβατον, -ου, τό | sheep |
| πρόβλημα, -ατος, τό | riddle |
| προήσεται | *see* προΐημι |
| προΐημι | allow, let |
| προνομεύω | plunder, ravage |
| προοράω | see previously, see beforehand, foresee |
| πρόπαππος, -ου, ὁ | great-grandfather |
| προπορεύομαι | go before, go in front |
| πρός | to, toward, with |
| προσάγω | lead to, bring to, approach |
| προσδέχομαι | accept; forgive |
| προσέρχομαι | approach |
| προσεύχομαι | pray, offer prayer |

| | |
|---|---|
| προσέχω | pay attention to, heed |
| προσθλίβω | press against |
| προσκαλέω | summon, call *(to oneself)* |
| πρόσκειμαι | be involved in, be devoted to |
| προσκυνέω | kneel, do obeisance, worship |
| προσνοέω | observe |
| προσοχθίζω | loathe, be incensed, be angry, be provoked |
| προσόχθισμα, -ατος, τό | offense |
| προστίθημι | add to |
| πρόσχωμα, -ατος, τό | mound *raised for attacking a city* |
| πρόσωπον, -ου, τό | face, countenance |
| προτείχισμα, -ατος, τό | outer wall of protection |
| πρότερος, -α, -ον | former, earlier; *neuter acc. as adv.* in former times |
| προφήτης, -ου, ὁ | spokesman; prophet |
| προφῆτις, -ιδος, ἡ | prophetess |
| προφθάνω | come before, anticipate |
| προχειρίζω | provide, choose, elect |
| πρωΐ | early, early in the morning |
| πρωΐθεν | from morning |
| πρῶτος, -η, -ον | first |
| πρωτότοκος, -ον | firstborn |
| πταίω | stumble, trip |
| πτῶμα, -ατος, τό | corpse |
| πυθμήν, -ένος, ὁ | base, stock, root, stem |
| πύλη, -ης, ἡ | gate, door |
| πῦρ, πυρός, τό | fire |
| πυρός, -οῦ, ὁ | wheat |
| πυρράκης, -ου, ὁ | red, ruddy |
| πωλέω | sell |
| πῶς | how? in what manner? |

## P

| | |
|---|---|
| ῥάβδος, -ου, ὁ | staff, rod, stick |
| ῥαθυμέω | be unconcerned, be idle; relax |
| ῥαπίζω | strike, beat with a rod |
| ῥέω | flow |
| ῥῆγμα, -ατος, τό | breakage, tear, torn piece |
| ῥήγνυμι (ῥήσσω) | break up, rend, tear asunder |
| ῥῆμα, -ατος, τό | word, utterance; matter, fact |
| ῥητός, -ή, -όν | specified, spoken of, aforementioned |
| ῥίζα, -ης, ἡ | root |
| ῥίπτω | throw, cast |
| ῥιτίνη, -ης, ἡ | balm |

ῥομφαία, -ας, ἡ     sword
ῥύομαι     save, rescue, protect

## Σ

σαβαώθ     Sabaoth
σάκκος, -ου, ὁ     sackcloth, sacking
σάρξ, σαρκός, ἡ     flesh
σεαυτοῦ, ῆς     *reflexive pronoun; also dat. and acc.*, yourself
σειρά, -ᾶς, ἡ     cord, chain; lock *of hair*
σειρομάστης, -ου, ὁ     barbed lance, probe
σελήνη, -ης, ἡ     moon
σημεῖον, -ου, τό     sign, indication, token
σήμερον     today
σιαγών, -όνος, ἡ     jaw, jawbone, cheek
σιγάω     be silent
σίδηρος, -ου, ὁ     iron; razor
σίκερα, τό     *indeclinable*, strong drink, liquor
σίκλος, -ου, ὁ (or σίγλος)     shekel
σινδών, -όνος, ἡ     linen
σιτοβολῶν, -ῶνος, ὁ     granary, barn
σιτοδοσία, -ας, ἡ     gratuitous distribution of corn
σιτοποιός, -οῦ, ὁ     one who grinds corn; baker
σῖτος, -ου, ὁ     wheat; *then* grain *of any kind*
σιωπάω     be silent
σκέλος, -ους, τό     leg
σκεπάζω     cover, shelter, hide
σκεπαστής, -οῦ, ὁ     protector
σκέπτομαι     look carefully, spy
σκευή, -ῆς, ἡ     equipment *(household)*, furnishings
σκεῦος, -ους, τό     equipment; arms
σκηνή, -ῆς, ἡ     tent
σκήνωμα, -ατος, τό     tent, dwelling
σκιάζω     provide protective cover
σκληρός, -ά, -όν     hard, harsh
σκληρύνω     harden
σκνίψ, -σκνιφός, ὁ     stinging gnat, flea, louse
σκοπιά, -ᾶς, ἡ     look-out, watch tower
σκότος, -ου, τό     darkness
σκυθρωπός, -ή, -όν     sad, gloomy
σκυλεύω     despoil, strip, plunder
σκῦλον, -ου, τό     booty, spoils
σκύμνος, -ου, ὁ     young lion
σκῶλον, -ου, τό     stumbling-block, hindrance

| | |
|---|---|
| σοφιστής, -οῦ, ὁ | expert, wise man |
| σοφός, -ή, -όν | wise, learned |
| σπάδων, -οντος, ὁ | eunuch |
| σπαρτίον, -ου, τό | small cord, thread |
| σπάω | draw, pull |
| σπέρμα, -ατος, τό | seed; offspring |
| σπερματίζω | sow |
| σπεύδω | hurry, hasten, make haste |
| σπήλαιον, -ου, τό | cave |
| σπιθαμή, -ῆς, ἡ | span *(about 9 inches)* |
| σπορά, -ᾶς, ἡ | sowing |
| σπουδάζω | hurry, make haste |
| σπουδή, -ῆς, ἡ | haste, speed |
| σταθμός, -οῦ, ὁ | station; weight-bearing pillar; weight |
| σταῖς, σταιτός, τό | dough |
| στακτή, -ῆς, ἡ | myrrh, oil of myrrh |
| σταφυλή, -ῆς, ἡ | bunch of grapes |
| στάχυς, -υος, ὁ | head *(of wheat)*, ear *(of corn)* |
| στεῖρα, -ας, ἡ | barren |
| στεναγμός, -ου, ὁ | sigh, groaning |
| στενός, -ή, -όν | straight, narrow |
| στενοχωρέω | crowd, press, confine |
| στήλη, -ης, ἡ | pillar |
| στηρίζω | make fast, prop; lean |
| στιππύον, -ου, ὁ | *see* στυππεῖον |
| στοιβάζω | pile, heap up |
| στολή, -ῆς, ἡ | robe |
| στόμα, -ατος, τό | mouth |
| στρατιά, -ᾶς, ἡ | army |
| στρατοπεδεύω | encamp, bivouac |
| στρέμμα, -ατος, τό | thread |
| στρέφω | turn; change |
| στρῆνος, -ους, τό | haughtiness |
| στύλος, -ου, ὁ | pillar |
| στυππεῖον, -ου, τό | coarse flax or hemp fiber, tow |
| σύ (pl. ὑμεῖς) | personal pronoun you |
| συγγένεια, -ας, ἡ | kinship, *thus* kin, relative |
| συγγίγνομαι | meet; be sexually intimate with |
| συγκαλέω | convene, convoke |
| συγκαλύπτω | cover up, veil |
| συγκλείω | shut in on all sides, hem in, enclose |
| συγκόπτω | cut off, strip away |
| συγκρίνω | explain, interpret |
| σύγκρισις, -εως, ἡ | comparison; interpretation, explanation |
| συγκροτέω | clap, strike together |

| συκῆ, -ῆς, ἡ | fig tree |
|---|---|
| συκοφαντέω | accuse falsely, inform against |
| συλλαμβάνω | seize, apprehend; conceive |
| συλλέγω | collect, gather |
| συλλογή, -ῆς, ἡ | gathering, collecting |
| συλλογίζομαι | reckon |
| συμβαίνω | happen, come about |
| συμμίγνυμι | mix, mingle |
| συμπορεύομαι | go with |
| σύν | with |
| συνάγω | gather together, collect, assemble |
| συναγωγή, -ῆς, ἡ | gathering, congregation |
| συναθροίζω | gather together, assemble |
| συναναβαίνω | go up with |
| συναναφέρω | bring up together, carry up with |
| συναντάω | meet |
| συνάντημα, -ατος, τό | encounter, incident |
| συνάντησις, -εως, ἡ | meeting |
| συναπάγω | lead away with, take along with |
| συνδειπνέω | dine with |
| συνδέω | bind together, entangle, clog |
| συνεκπορεύομαι | go out with, go forth with |
| συνεσθίω | eat with |
| συνετός, -ή, -όν | intelligent, wise |
| συνίστημι | combine, unite; present, commend; commit |
| συνπίπτω | fall, collapse |
| σύνταξις, -εως, ἡ | putting together in order, arranging; system |
| συνταράσσω | confuse, disturb, trouble |
| συντάσσω | direct, instruct, command |
| συντελέω | bring to an end, complete, finish, accomplish |
| συντρίβω | shatter, break to pieces, smash |
| σύσκηνος, -ον | living in one tent; comrade |
| συσκοτάζω | make dark; grow dark |
| συσσεισμός, -οῦ, ὁ | earthquake |
| συστρέφω | gather together, collect; press together |
| συσφίγγω | bind together, gird |
| σφάζω | slaughter, kill; sacrifice |
| σφενδονέω | sling |
| σφενδόνη, -ης, ἡ | sling |
| σφόδρα | greatly, very much |
| σφοδρός, -ά, -όν | excessive, vehement, violent |
| σφραγίζω | seal |
| σφραγίς, -ῖδος, ἡ | signet, seal |
| σχίδαξ, -ακος, ὁ | split wood; pole |
| σχίζω | split, divide, separate |

σχολάζω                         have leisure time, be idle
σχολαστής, -οῦ, ὁ               man of leisure; idler
σωτήριος, -ον                   saving, delivering; *neuter as substantive*, deliverance
σῴζω                            save, preserve, rescue

# T

τάλαντον, -ου, τό               talent
ταμιεῖον, -ου, τό               private room, closet
ταπεινόω                        make low, humble, humiliate
ταπείνωσις, -εως, ἡ             humiliation, humility
ταράσσω                         stir, shake; disturb, trouble
τάσσω                           arrange, set, fix
τάφος, -ου, ὁ                   tomb, grave
ταχέως                          quickly, at once
ταχύνω                          hasten, hurry
τε                              *enclitic particle*, and (*weaker than* καί); τε καί,
                                both ... and
τεῖχος, -εος, τό                wall
τέλειος, -α, -ον                perfect
τελευτάω                        come to an end; die
τέρας, -ατος, τό                wonder, omen, portent
τεσσαρεσκαιδέκατος, -η, -ον fourteenth
τεσσεράκοντα                    forty
τέταρτος, -η, -ον               fourth
τετραίνω                        pierce
τετρακόσιοι, -αι, -α            four hundred
τετράπους, -οδος, ὁ            four-footed
τήκω                            melt, dissolve
τίθημι                          place, put
τίκτω                           bear, give birth
τιμάω                           value, honor, show honor to
τιμή, -ῆς, ἡ                    honor; price
τίς, τί                         *interrogative*, who? which?
τις, τι (enclitic)              someone, something
τοιοῦτος, -αυτη, -οῦτον         of such kind, such
τοῖχος, -ου, ὁ                  wall *of a house*
τοξεύω                          shoot *with a bow*
τοπάρχης, -ου, ὁ                prefect, governor
τόπος, -ου, ὁ                   place
τράπεζα, -ης, ἡ                 table
τραυματίας, -ου, ὁ              wounded man; *plural*, the slain, the wounded *of an
                                army*
τράχηλος, -ου, ὁ                neck, throat

| | |
|---|---|
| τρεῖς | three |
| τρέφω | nourish |
| τρέχω | run |
| τριάκοντα | thirty |
| τριακόσιος, -αι, -α | three hundred |
| τρίς | three times, thrice |
| τρισσεύω | triple, do a thing three times |
| τρισσόω | *see* τρισσεύω |
| τριστάτης, -ου, ὁ | captain, chief |
| τρισχίλιοι, -αι, -α | three thousand |
| τρίτος, -η, -ον | third |
| τρόμος, -ου, ὁ | trembling *with* fear |
| τρόπος, -ου, ὁ | manner, way; ὃν τρόπον, in the manner in which, just as |
| τροφεύω | *later form of* τρέφω; nourish, feed; train, rear |
| τρυμαλιά, -ᾶς, ἡ | hole, hollow |
| τύμπανον, -ου, τό | timbrel; drum |
| τύπτω | strike, beat |
| τυφλός, -ή, -όν | blind |

## Υ

| | |
|---|---|
| ὑγιαίνω | be healthy, be well |
| ὑγίεια, -ας, ἡ | health |
| ὑγρός, -ά, -όν | moist, pliant, supple |
| ὑδραγωγός, -όν | bringing water; *as substantive* conduit, aqueduct |
| ὑδρία, -ας, ἡ | water-pot, pitcher, jar |
| ὕδωρ, -ατος, τό | water |
| ὑετός, -οῦ, ὁ | rain |
| υἱός, υἱοῦ, ὁ | son |
| ὑμνέω | sing, sing praise to |
| ὑπακούω | hearken, obey |
| ὑπάρχω | exist, be (τὰ ὑπάρχοντα, one's possessions) |
| ὑπεναντίος, -α, -ον | opposing, hostile |
| ὑπεξαιρέω | remove; *thus,* reserve, exclude |
| ὑπέρ | *with gen.,* for, on behalf of; *with acc.,* over, beyond |
| ὑπερασπίζω | put a shield over; protect |
| ὑπερεῖδον | *aorist of* ὑπεροράω |
| ὑπερέχω | excel, be superior to, have power over |
| ὑπεροράω | disdain, despise; overlook, disregard |
| ὑπερῷον, -ου, τό | upper chamber, upper story |
| ὕπνος, -ου, ὁ | sleep |
| ὑπό | *with acc.,* under; *with gen.,* by |
| ὑπόδημα, -ατος, τό | sandal, shoe |

| | |
|---|---|
| ὑποζύγιον, -ου, τό | animal, beast of burden |
| ὑποκάτω | under, below |
| ὑπολείπω | leave behind, leave remaining |
| ὑπομένω | remain, stay; wait, tarry |
| ὑποστρέφω | return; withdraw, turn back |
| ὗς, ὑός, ὁ/ἡ | pig |
| ὑφαίνω | weave |
| ὕφασμα, -ατος, τό | web |
| ὑφίστημι | withstand, resist, stand one's ground |
| ὑψηλός, -ή, -όν | high, lofty; *thus*, mighty, strong |
| ὕψος, -ους, τό | height |
| ὑψόω | raise, lift up; exalt, extol |
| ὕω | rain |

## Φ

| | |
|---|---|
| φαίνω | give light; appear |
| φανερός, -ά, -όν | manifest, clear, visible |
| φαρμακία, -ας, ἡ | use of drugs or spells |
| φαρμακός, -οῦ, ὁ | sorcerer, magician |
| φάρυγξ, φάρυγγος, ὁ | throat |
| φείδομαι | spare *someone*, refrain |
| φεύγω | flee, escape |
| φθείρω | ruin, waste, destroy |
| φιλέω | love |
| φιλιάζω | make *or* be a friend |
| φίλος, -η, -ον | beloved, dear; *as substantive*, friend |
| φλογίζω | set on fire, inflame |
| φλόξ, φλογός, ἡ | flame |
| φλυκτίς, -ίδος, ἡ | boil, blister |
| φοβέομαι | fear, be afraid |
| φοβερός, -ά, -όν | fearful, awful |
| φονεύω | kill, murder |
| φόνος, -ου, ὁ | murder, killing |
| φραγμός, -οῦ, ὁ | hedge, wall, fence |
| φρέαρ, -ατος, τό | well |
| φρόνιμος, -ον | prudent, thoughtful, wise |
| φυλακή, -ῆς, ἡ | prison |
| φυλάσσω | guard, watch, keep |
| φυλή, -ῆς, ἡ | tribe |
| φύραμα, -ατος, τό | kneaded dough |
| φυτεία, -ας, ἡ | planting |
| φυτόν, -οῦ, τό | plant, bush |
| φύω | grow, grow up |
| φωνή, -ῆς, ἡ | sound, voice |

# Χ

| | |
|---|---|
| χαίρω | rejoice, be glad |
| χάλαζα, -ης, ἡ | hail |
| χαλινός, -οῦ, ὁ | bit, bridle |
| χάλκειος, -η, -ον | brazen, made of brass *or* copper |
| χαλκός, -οῦ, ὁ | brass, bronze, copper |
| χάρις, χάριτος, ἡ | grace, favor |
| χεῖλος, -ους, τό | lip; *thus,* shore, bank |
| χείμαρρος, -ον (or χειμάρρους) | flowing, rain or snow-melt swollen; *as subst.* wady, brook |
| χείρ, χειρός, ἡ | hand |
| χερουβείν | cherubim |
| χήρα, -ας, ἡ | widow |
| χιλιάς, -άδος, ἡ | one thousand |
| χιτών, -ῶνος, ὁ | robe, tunic |
| χιών, χιόνος, ἡ | snow |
| χλόη, -ης, ἡ | new green grass |
| χλωρός, -ά, -όν | green; *substantive* grass, plant |
| χονδρίτης, -ου, ὁ | bread *made of coarse meal* |
| χορός, -οῦ, ὁ | chorus, choir |
| χόρτασμα, -ατος, τό | food, sustenance |
| χοῦς, χοός, ὁ | soil, dust |
| χράω | furnish, supply |
| χρηματίζω | conduct business, negotiate |
| χρήσιμος, -η, -ον | useful, advantageous |
| χρίω | anoint, pour over |
| χρόα, -ης, ἡ | color |
| χρόνος, -ου, ὁ | time |
| χρύσιος, -ου, ὁ | gold |
| χρυσός, -οῦ, ὁ | gold |
| χρυσοῦς, -ῆ, -οῦν | golden, made of gold |
| χρυσόω | gild, make golden |
| χωλαίνω | be lame, limp |
| χῶμα, -ατος, τό | mound, dam, dike |
| χώρα, -ας, ἡ | country, land, region |

# Ψ

| | |
|---|---|
| ψευδής, -ές | false, lying; *substantive* lie |
| ψηλαφάω | feel, touch, handle |
| ψηλαφητός, -ή, -όν | palpable, tangible |
| ψόγος, -ου, ὁ | censure |
| ψυχή, -ῆς, ἡ | life, soul |

| | |
|---|---|
| ψύχω | breathe; cool, refresh |
| ψωμός, -οῦ, ὁ | morsel, bit |

## Ω

| | |
|---|---|
| ὧδε | here, in this place |
| ὠδίν, -ῖνος, ἡ | pain, birth pain |
| ὦμος, -ου, ὁ | shoulder |
| ὦπται | *perfect passive of* ὁράω |
| ὥρα, -ας, ἡ | hour, time |
| ὡραῖος, -α, -ον | beautiful |
| ὠρύομαι | roar |
| ὡς | *adverb and conjunction, as, like, how, that, when* |
| ὡσαύτως | similarly, likewise |
| ὡσεί | as, like |
| ὥσπερ | as if, even as, as |
| ὥστε | so, for this reason; so that, in order that |
| ᾠδή, -ῆς, ἡ | song, ode |